Red Hat® Linux® 7

Bill Ball, David Pitts, et al.

SAMS

Unleashed

Red Hat® Linux® 7 Unleashed

Copyright © 2001 by Sams Publishing

International Standard Book Number: 0-672-31985-3

Library of Congress Catalog Card Number: 00-103513

Printed in the United States of America

First Printing: October, 2000

03   02   01   4

Trademarks

Warning and Disclaimer

ASSOCIATE PUBLISHER
Michael Stephens

EXECUTIVE EDITOR
Rosemarie Graham

ACQUISITIONS EDITOR
Angela Kozlowski

DEVELOPMENT EDITORS
Heather Goodell
Robyn Thomas

MANAGING EDITOR
Matt Purcell

PROJECT EDITOR
Christina Smith

COPY EDITOR
Kim Cofer

INDEXER
Erika Millen

PROOFREADERS
Angela Boley
Candice Hightower
Brad Lenser
Matt Wynalda

TECHNICAL EDITORS
Jason Byars
Steve Epstein
John C. Kennedy
Paul Love
Jeffrey Pajor
Jason R. Wright

TEAM COORDINATOR
Pamalee Nelson

MEDIA DEVELOPER
Dan Scherf

INTERIOR DESIGNER
Gary Adair

COVER DESIGNER
Aren Howell

LAYOUT TECHNICIANS
Ayanna Lacey
Heather Hiatt Miller
Stacey Richwine-DeRome
Mark Walchle

Contents at a Glance

Contents

About the Lead Authors

Bill Ball is the author of five best-selling books about Linux: *Sams Teach Yourself Linux in 24 Hours, Red Hat Linux 6 Unleashed, How to Use Linux, Linux Unleashed, Fourth Edition,* and Que's *Using Linux*. He is a technical writer, editor, and magazine journalist and has been working with computers for the past 20 years. He first started working with Linux, beginning with kernel version .99, after moving from BSD4.3 Machten for the Apple Macintosh. He has published articles in magazines such as *Computer Shopper* and *MacTech Magazine* and first started editing books for Que in 1986. An avid fly fisherman, he builds bamboo fly rods and fishes on the nearby Potomac River when he's not driving his vintage MG sports car. Bill is a member of the Northern Virginia Linux Users Group (NOVALUG), and lives in the Shirlington area of Arlington County, Virginia.

David Pitts has been a part of the writing of more than a half dozen books covering Linux, UNIX, and CGI programming in Perl. He is an author, consultant, systems administrator, programmer, instructor, Web developer and Christian. David can be reached at dpitts@mk.net. His Web page, www.dpitts.com, contains more information about him. Currently, David lives in Sacramento, California, with his wife, Dana, her beautiful teen-aged cousin, Ashley, and their invisible cat, Spot. David's favorite quote comes from Saint Francis of Assisi, "Preach the Gospel, and, if necessary, use words."

About the Contributing Authors

Tim Bogart is a network engineer employed by MCI Worldcom. He is currently working with the Network Integrity group investigating break-in attempts, fraud, and other crimes against the company, on the company's network infrastructure, in and outside the firewall. He has been working in different tele/data communications–related jobs for the past 28 years. Among them was a project in which he installed and programmed many of the CDPD systems used by "Yahoo!" cabs and Ricochette modems. If you use a Ricochette modem, chances are very good that your data is passing through one of the systems he built and programmed. He resides in Sterling, Virginia with his lovely, intelligent wife Claudia who also writes, and Firulais, their trilingual border collie (English, Spanish, and of course, dogspeak). When he's not at work he enjoys cooking in their gourmet kitchen and using Linux. Tim was largely responsible for convincing the people who feature the FOSE trade show in Washington, DC to include the first Linux pavilion exhibited there in April of 2000.

Patrik Grip-Jansson (patrikj@gnulix.org) lives in Borlänge, Sweden, with his fiancée, her kids, and two cats—Herbert and Havarthi. He has been active within the field of computer science for almost two decades. The past five years he has specialized in Web, Internet, and intranet issues. He is a co-author of *Apache Server Unleashed* and the author of several articles about Apache and Web programming. He is currently working as a systems architect for the Swedish National Road Administration. He is also one of the founding fathers of the Gnulix Society and a major contributor to its efforts to increase knowledge about Open Source solutions.

David B. Horvath, CCP is a Senior Consultant in the Philadelphia, Pennsylvania area. He has been in the field for over fifteen years and is also a part-time Adjunct Professor at local colleges, teaching topics that include C++ Programming, UNIX, and Database Techniques. He completed his M.S. degree in Organizational Dynamics at the University of Pennsylvania in 1998 (and is taking more classes as this book is being published). He has provided seminars and workshops to professional societies and corporations on an international basis.

David is the author of *UNIX for the Mainframer* (Prentice-Hall/PTR), co-author of *SAMS Teach Yourself C++ for Linux in 21 Days*, and contributing author to *UNIX Unleashed, Second Edition* (with cover credit); *Red Hat Linux Unleashed, Second* and *Third Editions; Red Hat Linux 6 Unleashed; Using UNIX, Second Edition* (Que); *UNIX Unleashed, Third Edition; Learn Shell Programming in 24 Hours;* and *Linux Unleashed, Fourth Edition*. He has also written numerous magazine articles.

When not at the keyboard working or writing, he can be found working in the garden or soaking in the hot tub. He has been married for over thirteen years and has several dogs and cats (the number of which seems to keep going up).

David can be reached at rhlinux7@cobs.com. No Spam please!

Declan Houlihan is currently a 3rd year computer systems student at the University of Limerick, Ireland. He is a Linux system administrator for the computer society network in college. He also works as a UNIX system administrator for Analog Devices in Limerick.

Steve Litt is the author of *Samba Unleashed, Rapid Learning: Secret Weapon of the Successful Technologist,* and *Troubleshooting: Tools, Tips and Techniques.* He's a contributing author of *Linux Unleashed, Fourth Edition*, as well as Webmaster of the

Troubleshooters.Com Web site, and creator of the *Universal Troubleshooting Process* courseware. A software developer for over ten years, Steve switched to Open Source to escape the workarounds and Blue Screens of Death bestowed by popular Windows "development environments."

Steve is an executive committee director for Linux Enthusiasts and Professionals of Central Florida (LEAP-CF), where he frequently gives technical presentations. He lives in Central Florida with his wife Sylvia and their three children, Brett, Rena, and Valerie. He can be reached at the Troubleshooters.Com Web site.

Kevin Lyda was `fork()`ed at `37058400`. After spending many years processing `stdin` in various locations (Brooklyn, New York; Salina, Kansas; Huntington, New York; Buffalo, New York), he began spewing results to `stdout`, first in Buffalo, then in Boston, Massachusetts, and now in Dublin, Ireland. It is his hope that all his calls to `read(STDIN_FILENO,...)` will succeed for the lifetime of his process and that the data output is of use.

Hugh McGauran is a fourth year student in the University of Limerick, Ireland. He has been working with Linux for the past 5 years. He is currently working with Piercom Ltd. as a systems administrator in an NT/Solaris and Linux environment. He is also working on his final year project incorporating XML and Java. Hugh is also a systems administrator on the UL computer society's server, skynet (`http://www.skynet.ie`).

Jeffrey J. Pajor (`jeff@pajor.com`, `http://www.pajor.com`) is a Software Engineer at HiddenMind Technology, a pioneer of service-oriented architecture for the creation of wireless applications. Jeff has also served as an e-business consultant for IBM Global Services and is a 1997 graduate of Purdue University where he earned a BS in Computer Science. It was at Purdue where Jeff first started experimenting with Linux. He has also participated as a contributing author on several other books and is always interested in your comments and feedback.

Dedications

Fur Scott Price. Zu meinen Kameraden und Bruder. Wo ist das Bier?

—Billy Ball

To Nadia—habibti, Ahmed, and Mohammed.

—Patrik Grip-Jansson

Although it may seem a bit odd, I dedicate my part of this book to my first computer/book groupie, the woman who asked me to sign her Linux T-shirt after sitting through my "LINUX and UNIX" presentation at the Mensa Annual Gathering (AG2K). She knows who she is.... And for those of you with dirty minds: her fiancé was there.

—David B. Horvath

To Louise Regan Lyda

—Kevin Lyda

To my wife, Sylvia Litt, whose constant love and support makes life wonderful.

—Steve Litt

Acknowledgments

First, thanks to my lovely wife Cathy for her patience and understanding for the many nights spent writing at a terminal. Also, thanks are due to the following people at Macmillan: Theresa Ball, Lynette Quinn (good luck in your new job!), Don Roche, Rosemarie Graham, and the host of Sams support staff in editorial and production. Special thanks are also due to fellow members of the Northern Virginia Linux Users Group, including Don Groves for a last-minute hint at sendmail configuration. As always, thanks to Linus Torvalds and Alan Cox for the latest Linux kernels, Richard M. Stallman for the GNU GPL, and Eric S. Raymond (esr) for carrying forward the Open Source Software banner. Finally, thanks are also due to Bill Gates and Microsoft for helping to make Linux more popular than ever.

—*Billy Ball*

Thanks to: Mom and Dad (gene splicing experiments and everything else), Jessica Hekman (for letting me try my hand at hairdressing), RMS and hackers everywhere (for giving me things to write about and an environment that's a joy).

—*Kevin Lyda*

I wish to acknowledge and thank all those who deserve it, you know who you are... Thanks!

—*Patrik Grip-Jansson*

I want to acknowledge all the good folks at Sams (Macmillan Publishing) and the other authors. As with any in-addition-to-the-day-job project, someone has to make a sacrifice. In my case the one who suffers most while I'm having fun writing is my wife Mary. The amazing thing is that she doesn't even complain (or at least not too much).

—*David B. Horvath*

Thanks to Laura Mae Canupp for all her editing help.

—*Jeffrey J. Pajor*

Thanks to the Macmillan people whose help was immeasurable: Angela Kozlowski, Heather Goodell, Robyn Thomas, Steve Epstein, Kim Cofer, Rosemarie Graham, Christina Smith, Pamalee Nelson, and Katie Robinson. I also want to thank lead author Bill Ball. Also my LUG, LEAP-CF in Orlando, the ultimate Linux brain trust. Last but not least, my family, friends, and all those who have taught me throughout the years, thank you.

—*Steve Litt*

Tell Us What You Think!

As the reader of this book, *you* are our most important critic and commentator. We value your opinion and want to know what we're doing right, what we could do better, what areas you'd like to see us publish in, and any other words of wisdom you're willing to pass our way.

As an Associate Publisher for Sams Publishing, I welcome your comments. You can fax, email, or write me directly to let me know what you did or didn't like about this book—as well as what we can do to make our books stronger.

Please note that I cannot help you with technical problems related to the topic of this book, and that due to the high volume of mail I receive, I might not be able to reply to every message.

When you write, please be sure to include this book's title and authors as well as your name and phone or fax number. I will carefully review your comments and share them with the authors and editors who worked on the book.

Fax: 317-581-4770

Email: linux_sams@macmillanusa.com

Mail: Michael Stephens
         Associate Publisher
         Sams Publishing
         201 West 103rd Street
         Indianapolis, IN 46290 USA

Introduction

Welcome to Red Hat Linux!

If you're new to Linux, choosing a Linux distribution to install can be confusing. Relax! You've made the right choice in choosing Red Hat Linux. Nearly 60% of Linux installations either are Red Hat or based on Red Hat Linux. You also made the right choice in choosing *Red Hat Linux 7 Unleashed*! This is the latest edition of the best-selling book on Red Hat Linux. A whole new team of authors has been put together for this edition with the task of giving you all the details about installing, administering, and using the latest version of the newest and best alternative computer operating system for today's PCs. You'll find CD-ROMs in the back of this book that contain the latest version of Intel-based Red Hat Linux and all the software you'll need to get started.

If you're a fan of Linux, you know that Linux is growing in popularity by leaps and bounds. Even better, major improvements and updates to existing software have been made right along with the increase in the Linux user base—Linux is now even easier to install! You'll also be quite pleased to learn about the new features and improvements included with the latest Linux kernels, such as support for a number of USB devices. If you've read a previous edition of *Red Hat Linux Unleashed*, take note of the vast number of improvements we've made to this edition. I think you'll agree that *Red Hat Linux 7 Unleashed* is an indispensable companion for the advanced Linux user.

What Is Linux?

Linux is the core of the operating system, or the *kernel*, while the Linux operating system and its collection of software is properly known as a *distribution*. Many of the programs in a Linux distribution come from the Berkeley Software Distribution, or BSD UNIX, and the Free Software Foundation's GNU software suite. Linux melds SysV UNIX and BSD features with POSIX compliance, and has inherited much of the best from more than 25 years of UNIX experience. Linux has also helped provide the recent impetus for the Open Source Software movement.

First released on October 5, 1991, by its author and trademark holder, Linus Torvalds, then at the University of Helsinki (now at Transmeta in California), Linux has spawned an increasingly vocal legion of advocates, users, and contributors from around the world. Originally written as a hobby, Linux now supports nearly all the features of a modern multitasking, multiuser operating system.

Linux is a full-fledged operating system. It provides full multitasking in a multiuser environment. Linux offers high-quality software at a cost far lower than other commercial versions of UNIX, and Red Hat Linux takes Linux a step further.

Red Hat, Inc. is a computer software development company that sells products and services related to Linux. Since 1993, Red Hat has built a solid reputation and marketable trademark by providing one of the very best implementations of Linux. After an initial public offering in August 1999, Red Hat, Inc. has grown and expanded, with ventures into numerous new Open Software-related technologies and markets. Red Hat's mission is to provide professional tools to computing professionals. Red Hat provides these tools by doing the following:

- Building tools, which Red Hat releases as freely redistributable software available for unrestricted download off of thousands of sites on the Internet
- Publishing books and software applications
- Manufacturing shrink-wrapped software, versions of the Linux OS, making Linux accessible to the broadest possible range of computer users
- Offering professional training and certification
- Providing technical support

Red Hat has a customer-oriented business focus, and recognizes that the primary benefits of the Linux OS are the availability of complete source code and its "freely distributable" GNU General Public License (also known as the *GPL*; see the GNU GENERAL PUBLIC LICENSE in the back of this book). This gives any home, corporate, academic, or government user the ability to modify the technology to his or her needs and to contribute to the ongoing development of the technology to the benefit of all users.

Using Linux provides benefits such as security and reliability that commercially restricted, binary-only operating systems simply cannot match. Some of these benefits include

- *There are no royalty or licensing fees.* Linus Torvalds holds the Linux trademark, but the Linux kernel and nearly all of the accompanying software is distributed under the GNU GPL. This means that you get source code to nearly everything.
- *Linux runs on nearly any CPU.* Linux runs on more CPUs and different platforms than any other computer operating system. One of the reasons for this, beside the programming talents of its rabid followers, is that Linux comes with source code to the kernel and is quite portable. There are versions for the Compaq Alpha, Sun SPARC, and even Motorola's low-power DragonBall processor (used in the Palm Pilot and other embedded systems). Linux for Intel-based computers from the 386 on up is on this book's CD-ROMs.

- *Linux extends the life of legacy hardware.* Recent trends in the software and hardware industry are to push consumers to purchase faster computers with ever-increasing amounts of system memory and hard drive storage. Linux doesn't suffer the prevalent bloat of "creeping featurism," and works quite well, even on aging x486-based computers with limited amounts of RAM. This means you'll get more life out of your older computers.

- *Linux controls the software and you control Linux.* This means that, on the rare occasion a program crashes, Linux won't collapse like a house of cards. You can kill the program and continue working with confidence. Linux uses sophisticated, state-of-the-art memory management to control all system processes. You won't lose control, and won't have to suffer the indignities of rebooting the system.

- *Linux works very well as a personal computer UNIX for the desktop.* You'll find many popular applications available for Linux, such as Netscape Navigator and Corel's WordPerfect. Red Hat Linux includes 3,000 or more programs (such as word processors, and spreadsheet and graphics applications), and a graphical interface, the X Window system. The included Red Hat Linux 7.0 is one of the newest Linux distributions, and uses an up-to-date version of the latest stable Linux kernel with several features of the new 2.4-series of the Linux kernel, such as support for a number of Universal Serial Bus devices. You'll also find the very latest in X11 window managers and software libraries. Tasks such as installing, configuring, and managing Linux are becoming point-and-click operations.

- *Linux works well for server operations.* If you need a support platform for server operations, Linux has real advantages, especially when compared to the cost of other operating systems, such as Windows 2000. Linux just makes sense for many home budgets and business financial models. Why anyone would pay $3,500 or more for a 25-client license to use proprietary server software when you can get the same functionality and even more for the price of this book is beyond me.

Linux, like UNIX, is a very modular operating system. The skills required to select, compile, link, and install the various components that are needed for a complete Linux OS can be beyond the experience of most people who might want to use Linux. The various Linux distributions go a long way toward solving this for the average Linux user, but most don't address the problem of how to upgrade your Linux system once you get it successfully installed. Most users found it easier to delete their whole Linux system and reinstall from scratch when they needed to upgrade.

What makes Red Hat Linux different is that its distribution is easier to install and maintain. There are a number of good reasons why nearly 60% of Linux users choose Red Hat Linux and Red Hat–based Linux distributions. These reasons include advanced package management, graphical (point and click!) system installation and control, and custom system administration tools. Red Hat Linux also includes an advanced version of the `linuxconf` utility, which makes system administration a snap!

Probably the best feature of Linux, the GNU utilities in general, and Red Hat Linux in particular, is that they are distributed under the terms of the GNU Public License (GPL). This feature has allowed research institutions, universities, commercial enterprises, and hackers to develop and use Red Hat Linux and related technologies cooperatively without fear that their work would someday be controlled and restricted by a commercial vendor. Use of the GPL (and similar licensing) is a growing trend among enlightened programmers, and an important ingredient in preventing the spread of restrictive patents and proprietary software.

The huge development effort and wide distribution of the Linux OS will ensure its place as a real, viable, and significant alternative to commercially restricted operating systems. The open development model, availability of source, and lack of license restrictions are features that commercial operating system developers simply cannot offer. Software development groups that need this model include groups from government-affiliated research organizations, to academic research and teaching projects, to commercial software application developers.

The number of new applications becoming available for Linux and the rapidly growing user base of these technologies are causing even the largest computer industry organizations to take Linux seriously. And Red Hat, Inc. is a serious contender, with corporate customers such as Boeing, Burlington Coat Factory, Iomega Corporation, Cisco Systems, Deutsche Bank, GTE, Oracle, GTSI, Hewlett-Packard, Hughes, IKEA, Intel, New York Life, Nationwide Insurance, Southwestern Bell, and Suzuki. Red Hat, Inc. is also involved with academic institutions such as Carnegie Mellon University, CERN Laboratories, the University of North Carolina, and the University of Rochester. Red Hat Linux is even used by government entities such as NASA, the U.S. Postal Service, and the Internal Revenue Service!

Even Datapro (a McGraw-Hill Company), in its recent 1996 survey of the UNIX industry, concluded that programmers are taking a hard look at the viability of Linux on production platforms now that Linux costs less than Microsoft and has the added benefits of UNIX, such as great performance, inherent power tool sets, and communication capabilities. Two years later, International Data Corporation estimated that Linux's market share grew 212% in 1998, with the number of Linux shipments nearly tripling, from 236,000 to 748,000. Note that this does not take into account the number of users downloading Linux for free from the Internet. This explosive interest is even more evident today, as IBM, Compaq, Hewlett-Packard, and Sun Microsystems announced in August 2000 the creation of the GNOME Foundation to build consensus and software for the Linux desktop. The Silicon Valley Linux Users Group estimates there are now 32 million Linux users worldwide, with the number set to double every six months!

Recent studies now show that more than half of the Web servers used around the world are run on Open Source software such as Apache. This shows the quality, power, and success of open software in taking on the commercial operating systems and succeeding.

With the purchase of this book, you are taking the first step necessary to take back control of your computing system from a closed-source, monopolistic software industry. You'll find the experience of stepping off the commercial software treadmill exhilarating and rewarding. There is an exciting future for Red Hat Linux, and we are glad that you are now a part of it!

Who Is This Book's Intended Audience?

This book is aimed at the intermediate to advanced computer user. You should be familiar with Linux or another version of the UNIX operating system. However, if you're a new user, this book will help you install Red Hat Linux and configure the X Window System for your Intel-based computer.

What This Book Can Offer You

The Red Hat Linux distribution goes a long way toward solving administrative and management tasks for the average Linux user. This book aims to provide technical advice on advanced topics, such as setting up Domain Name Service, configuring Apache, and understanding how to control system services. You'll also find advice throughout the book regarding system security, a topic of ever-increasing importance as more and more computer systems join the Internet.

How This Book Is Organized

The book is divided into the following five parts:

- Part I: "Red Hat Linux—Installation and User Services" —You'll read detailed instructions and technical tips on getting Red Hat Linux installed and configured for your computer. You'll learn how to configure and get the most out of the X Window System, how to choose the best X window manager or graphical interface for Red Hat Linux, how to connect to the Internet, and how to choose various graphic and multimedia tools.

- Part II: "Configuring Services"—This part contains nine chapters aimed at helping you set up local and network services for your system—essential information required for Internet operations.

- Part III: "System Administration and Management"—All Red Hat Linux systems require administration and management. Whether you have 1 user or 1,000 users, these chapters contain critical advice and analysis of software tools and administrative procedures used every day with Linux, including backup and restoration and security.

- Part IV: "Red Hat Development and Productivity"—Red Hat Linux comes with a wealth of programming and productivity tools. This section gives an overview of programming for Linux in C, how to use shell scripting, automate computer tasks, rebuild the Linux kernel, and use emulators and other windowing clients.

- Part V: "Appendixes"—You'll learn more about the licensing used for Red Hat Linux and read about the most often used software tools; you'll also get a handy cross-reference listing of the software included with this book's CD-ROMs.

Conventions Used in This Book

The following typographic conventions are used in this book:

- Code lines, commands, statements, variables, and any text you type or see onscreen appear in a `computer` typeface. When lines of input and output are shown, **`bold computer`** typeface is often used to show the user's input.

- Placeholders in syntax description appear in an *`italic computer`* typeface. Replace the placeholder with the actual filename, parameter, or whatever element it represents.

- *Italics* highlight technical terms when they first appear in the text and are being defined.

- A special icon ➥ is used before a line of code that is really a continuation of the preceding line. Sometimes a line of code is too long to fit as a single line in the book, given the book's limited width. If you see ➥ before a line of code, remember that you should interpret that "line" as part of the line immediately before it.

Red Hat Linux— Installation and User Services

PART

I

IN THIS PART

Introduction to Red Hat Linux

CHAPTER 1

Welcome to Red Hat Linux! This chapter introduces you to some of the unique features of Red Hat, Inc.'s distribution of the Linux operating system. You'll find out why Linux is so popular, why Red Hat's distribution is so popular, and what you'll find under the hood in the latest Red Hat distribution included with this book.

UNIX is one of the most popular operating systems in the world and was originally developed in 1969 by Ken Thompson, Dennis Ritchie, and others at AT&T. Four years later, the UNIX kernel was rewritten in the C programming language. In 1974, UNIX was released for academic license. As UNIX (especially the University of California Berkeley's enhanced version) spread from university to university, it was ported to different mainframes and minicomputers, and quickly spawned legions of users and fans around the world. Designed from the ground up to support multiple users and multiple processes at the same time, UNIX was one of the first *multiuser* and *multitasking* operating systems.

UNIX, and its offshoot brethren such as BSD, AIX, and HP/UX, will run on just about every platform made. Over the years, various vendors purchased the source code and developed new versions. The vendors (such as Apollo, Digital Equipment Corp., IBM, Hewlett-Packard, and Sun) added special touches, such as changing directory structures, improving networking services, and modifying configuration schemes. When UNIX entered the commercial operating system market, each vendor touted its version of UNIX as superior, more reliable, faster, and so on.

As you can imagine, UNIX versions and development branched out, or *forked* following its wide-ranging distribution. People all over the globe began to develop enhancements, bug fixes, and software tools for UNIX. Unfortunately, there was no coordination to guide all the development, resulting in a lot of differentiation between the various versions of UNIX. In the early 1990s standards finally started to appear. For UNIX, early standards fell under the Institute of Electrical and Electronics Engineers (IEEE) Portable Operating System Interface, or POSIX.1 standard, which has to do with application programming interfaces (APIs) in the C programming language. Adherence to this standard helped maintain a high level of portability for programs to run on different versions of UNIX. Since then, many other standards, such as UNIX95 and UNIX98 from The Open Group, have helped nurture cross-platform compatibility.

The downside of commercial UNIX is that it is big. It is also expensive, especially for a PC version, although Sun Microsystems and SCO Corp. have released free-for-noncommercial-use versions of their products in the last year. However, this is where Linux comes in. Linux, as explained in more detail later in this chapter, was designed from the ground up to be small, fast, and inexpensive. So far, the design has succeeded.

Linux was originally created by Linus Torvalds during his graduate studies at the University of Helsinki in Finland. Linus wrote Linux as a small PC-based implementation of UNIX. During the summer of 1991 Linus made Linux public on the Internet. In September of that same year, version 0.01 was released. A month later, version 0.02 was released, with version 0.03 following several weeks later. In December, Linux was numbered at 0.10, and by the end of the month, virtual memory (disk paging) was added. Within a year, Linux had a thousand more features and was well on its way to becoming a self-compiling, usable operating system. Linus made the source code freely available and encouraged other programmers to develop it further. They did, and Linux continues to be developed today by a worldwide team, led by Linus, over the Internet.

Linux shares many of the same traits and characteristics of UNIX: Linux is written in C and is very portable; source code is available; and it has a good design. The current stable version of Linux is version 2.2.17, but you'll find special features, such as Universal Serial Bus (USB) support in Red Hat's 2.2.16 kernel included with this book.

Stable or Beta?

Linux is constantly evolving and improving. New versions of the kernel can appear weekly, or even daily during periods of intense development. Most users should stick with the latest stable version of Linux available. Intrepid users or users with special needs and hardware may want to try beta versions of the kernel. You can always check for the latest version of the Linux kernel at http://www.kernel.org/.

Linux uses no code from AT&T or any other proprietary source. Software for Linux comes from a variety of sources. Many packages were developed by the Free Software Foundation's GNU project, whereas others come from the Berkeley Software Distribution (BSD UNIX), The XFree86 Project, Inc., and professional and hobbyist programmers from around the world. Because of its licensing, Linux and Linux distributions are very inexpensive; as a matter of fact, most are free—including Red Hat Linux!

Advantages of Linux

Why would you choose Linux over UNIX? As already mentioned, Linux is free. Like UNIX, it is very powerful and is a real operating system. Also, it is fairly small compared to other UNIX operating systems, although to be honest, some versions of BSD UNIX, such as OpenBSD, can be shoehorned onto a 60MB filesystem. Many commercial UNIX operating systems require 500MB or more, whereas some versions of Linux, such as the embedded uCLinux, can be run on as little as 2MB of file space and 2MB of RAM. You can even run Linux from a floppy disk!

Realistically, you will want room for development tools, data, and so on, which can take up 500MB or more, and your RAM should be 32–64MB (although the more, the merrier!). See Chapter 2, "Installation of Your Red Hat System," for more specifics on space requirements and later this chapter for more information on system hardware requirements. Here's what you get in exchange for that valuable space:

- **Full multitasking**—Multiple tasks can be run in the background, and multiple devices, such as a modem, printer, and hard drive, can be accessed at the same time.

- **Virtual memory**—Linux safely uses a portion of your hard drive as virtual memory, which increases the efficiency of your system by keeping active processes in RAM and placing less frequently used or inactive portions of memory on disk. Virtual memory also utilizes all your system's memory and doesn't allow memory segmentation to occur.

- **Hardware support**—Linux, especially Intel-based versions, supports nearly all hardware architectures and devices, with the best support for legacy hardware. This is an advantage in that new versions of the operating system will not make your older hardware obsolete.

- **The X Window System**—The X Window System is a graphics system for UNIX machines. This powerful interface supports many applications and is the standard interface for the industry.

- **Built-in networking support**—Linux uses standard TCP/IP protocols, including Network File System (NFS), Network Information Service (NIS, formerly known as YP), Session Message Block (SMB), and others. You can access the Internet by connecting your system with an Ethernet card, or a parallel-port, serial cable, or over a modem to another system.

- **Shared libraries**—Because each command shares a common library of subroutines it can call at runtime, Linux helps saves memory and hard drive space.

- **Compatibility with the IEEE POSIX.1 standard**—Because of this compatibility, Linux supports many of the standards set forth for all UNIX systems.

- **Open Source code**—The Linux kernel uses no code from AT&T or any other proprietary source. This allows other organizations, the GNU project, hackers, and programmers from all over the world to develop and contribute software for Linux.

- **Documentation**—Nearly every Linux distribution comes with more than 12,000 pages of documentation in the form of manual pages, info documents, or guides. You'll also find extra technical documentation for software packages under the /usr/share/doc directory. Unlike operating systems offered by the monopolistic software industry, Linux is fully documented—one problem might be that there is too much information!

- **Lower cost than most other UNIX systems and UNIX clones**—If you have a fast Internet connection and a CDR drive, you can freely download Linux off the Internet. Many books also come with a free copy (this book includes the latest version of Intel-based Red Hat Linux on the CD ROMs).

- **GNU software support**—Linux can run a wide range of free software available through the GNU project. This software includes everything from programming tools, such as compilers, assemblers, linkers, and loaders, to system administration utilities, such as stream editors, the venerable emacs editor, and even games.

The Magic of Red Hat Linux

The magic of Red Hat Linux happens the moment you boot to your first install. Unlike early installations of Linux and some current installations of other Open Source operating systems, such as BSD UNIX, you'll be greeted with a graphical, point-and-click interface to speed you through the process. Although every Linux distribution using a specific Linux kernel is the same underneath, there are several good reasons to use Red Hat Linux:

- **Red Hat Linux is the most popular Linux distribution**—Red Hat Linux has consistently been one of the top sellers in its category for several years, and provides distributions for the Compaq Alpha and Sun SPARC CPUs. Red Hat Linux offers superior flexibility in installation, better hardware recognition, and a wealth of easy-to-use system administration tools.

- **Red Hat Linux incorporates some of the features based on the upcoming 2.4-series of the Linux kernel**—The current version of Red Hat (version 7) is based on the latest stable version of the Linux kernel and incorporates many improvements included with the newer kernel, such as Universal Serial Bus support for mice, keyboards, and selected scanners.

- **Red Hat Package Manager**—Red Hat's Package Manager (RPM) is the leading software management tool for Linux. This means that after you load Red Hat, you'll never have to load it again in order to update the system or its software. The rpm command is a sophisticated tool that includes intelligent file handling across package upgrades, shared file handling, documentation searching support, and package installation via FTP. You can install, uninstall, query, verify, and upgrade individual RPM packages.

- **"Pristine Sources"**—Red Hat's commitment to providing clean, untouched sources, as well as patches and a control file, define the state of the art in building and packaging software. This method easily, effectively, and clearly separates and documents changes made to the software author's source code used in a software package included with a Red Hat distribution. Benefits include proper credit for bug fixes and the ability to track software versions and modifications.

- **Graphic administration tools**—Tools such as `linuxconf`, Disk Druid, and others mark Red Hat Linux as the distribution of choice for easy-to-use administration tools. Red Hat Linux can be entirely managed from a graphical interface.

- **Security**—Red Hat leads the industry in providing the most up-to-date security features and fixes.

- **Community**—Red Hat, Inc. develops many software tools and improvements for its Linux distribution, then turns around and returns the source code to the world via the GPL. This shows that Red Hat, unlike many other companies still grappling with the Open Source paradigm, definitely "gets it," and is firmly committed to the Open Source ethics of the worldwide online community.

- **Documentation**—Red Hat provides a user and installation guide in several formats, available in electronic form on its official and free CD-ROMs, or for free download from `http://www.redhat.com/support/manuals/`. Online help is present throughout the Linux installation process or through help buttons when using graphic administration tools.

- **Standards**—Red Hat tracks both UNIX and Linux standards. Red Hat conforms to the Linux filesystem standard (FSSTND).

- **Support**—Red Hat, Inc. provides official product support for registered buyers of its official copies through `http://www.redhat.com/apps/support/`. Users of free versions (such as the one included with this book), although not eligible for registered support, can still get help with links to tips, FAQs, HOWTO documents, timely changes, errata, and other bug fixes. Updates are available to anyone through `http://www.redhat.com/apps/support/ updates.html`.

- **Testing**—Red Hat depends on the open development model Linus started with. Thousands of people working around the world are testing applications and providing solutions for today's business and personal needs.

As you can see, Red Hat, Inc. goes beyond the normal Linux distributor, and provides an up-to-date Linux system with tools, documentation, and standardization.

Red Hat Linux Compared to Other Linux Distributions

Underneath, all Linux distributions are the same because all distributions use the Linux kernel. Nearly all distributions include the same base subset of GNU free software, command-line programs, manual pages, and documentation. However, the similarity stops there, and Linux distributions will differ in a number of significant ways:

- **Installation**—Nearly every Linux distribution is different in the appearance, and perhaps sequence, of installation dialogs and prompts. You'll find Red Hat's Linux installation flexible and easy to use—you can choose a graphical, text-based, or automatic install.

- **Layout of the /etc directory**—Linux is a blend of the best features of BSD and SysV UNIX. This means that some distributions, such as Red Hat, use a SysV type of configuration directory, structure, and naming conventions for initialization scripts. Some distributions, such as Debian GNU/Linux, may tend toward BSD's minimalist, plain /etc directory and scripts, while others, such as SuSE Linux, may opt for nearly all system configuration information to be contained in a single file.

- **Naming conventions for root-only software**—Red Hat Linux, like nearly all Linux distributions, places root-only commands under the /sbin directory; however, some distributions may use different names for similar commands, and may even place system initialization scripts in the /sbin directory.

- **Breadth and wealth of graphic administration tools**—Red Hat Linux provides one of the largest collections of graphical administration tools for Linux. Other distributions may use a single, centralized tool, such as SuSE Linux's YaST command, or Caldera OpenLinux's lisa command.

- **Location and naming of documentation**—Nearly all Linux distributions include documentation under the /usr/doc, /usr/share/info, or /usr/share/doc directories, but you may find differences in naming of subdirectories.

- **Software management tools and package structure**—Red Hat and many other (but not all) distributions use the Red Hat Package Manager approach to software management, specifically using the rpm command. However, you may find different "front-ends" to the rpm command used in different distributions, and some distributions, such as Debian or Slackware, will use different package formats, such as .deb or .tgz.

- **Support**—Commercially marketed Linux distributions usually come with a specified period of technical support, either over the phone, by email, or through the Web. Some Linux distributions, such as Debian, don't come with any support (aside from mailing lists), and you must go to a third-party service provider. Note that you should not call Red Hat, Inc. for support for use of this book's CD-ROMs! See the back page by the CD-ROMs for details on where and how to get support.

- **Value-added software**—Finally, Linux distributions will differ in the amount, quality, or type of value-added software included with the distribution. Red Hat, Inc.'s commercial versions of Red Hat Linux sometimes include an extra CD-ROM of third-party software.

When you choose to use Red Hat Linux, you'll be in good company. You'll find many other Red Hat Linux users out in cyberspace or around the corner. Once you learn how to use Red Hat Linux, changing to a different distribution may not be that difficult.

What's New in Red Hat and the Linux Kernel?

This section details what's new with your version of Red Hat Linux. As a distribution, Red Hat Linux has evolved over the past six years to always include new and up-to-date features of the Linux kernel and software tools. If you're an experienced hand, you'll find that this Red Hat Linux distribution continues with this tradition of improvement, especially in the form of updated software libraries, updated and improved management tools, the latest XFree86 X11 distribution, version 4.0.1, and of course, the latest stable series of the Linux kernel, version 2.2.16.

Linux has gone through a number of major changes in the past six years. Fans from the early years using the then stable 1.2.13 version of the Linux kernel remember having to recompile the kernel each and every time hardware was added to a system. The next major leap forward for Linux was the addition of loadable kernel modules. This made the task of adding new hardware much easier. The next leap was the movement of Linux binaries from the old `a.out` binary format to newer Executable and Linking Format (ELF) format, and the incorporation of new shared libraries for the now classic 2.0.38 stable kernel. Following the 2.2-series of the Linux kernel with its new shared libraries, multiprocessor support, additional filesystem support, improved memory handling, and various networking improvements brought the current 2.2.16 stable kernel.

Interestingly, and despite the advances being made in development of the upcoming 2.4-series of the Linux kernel, there are many Linux users still happily using versions 1.2.13 or 2.0.38 (hopefully with updated security and bug fixes). The good news for users of the 2.2-series Linux is that upgrading to the new 2.4 Linux kernel will not be as painful or introduce major incompatibilities with current filesystems and precompiled software as long as you follow a proper upgrade path. However, the new kernel has much to offer and includes some major improvements.

The Linux kernel binds numerous processes together to schedule tasks, allocate resources, manage memory and talk to hardware. When the new 2.4-series of Linux kernel is released, expect improvements to disk caching, raises to the limit on the number of active processes, new features to make server operations more efficient, support for new filesystems, and much wider support for Universal Serial Bus (USB) devices. Other improvements, according to kernel observer Joseph Pranevich (who prepares the "Wonderful World of Linux 2.4" at http://www.linuxtoday.com), include

- Linux will be able to (theoretically) support 4.2 billion users.
- Kernel log (console) messages may be redirected to the printer port.
- Support for the IRIX efs filesystem and partition table format.
- Read and write support for the OS/2 filesystem.
- Kernel-level support for ISA "Plug-and-Pray" devices.
- PCMCIA services are now (at long last) part of the kernel distribution.
- Support for (of course) Transmeta's Crusoe CPU.
- Linux will be able to use more than 4GB of RAM on supporting hardware.
- More than 16 Ethernet cards may be used on a system.
- More than 10 IDE controllers may be used on a system.
- The Linux kernel will require the same or less memory.

Journaling Support?

Missing in the stock Linux kernel is support for a journaling filesystem or the new Macintosh HFS+ filesystem. Look for improvements shortly. Journaling, a unique method of storing files and filenames in the filesystem with certain advantages for file recovery and system failure, has been available for Linux since November 1999 through the Reiserfs filesystem. This filesystem purportedly offers speed and storage improvements when dealing with many small files on a filesystem, along with other features. Implementing the Reiserfs involves recompiling the kernel, using loadable kernel modules, and formatting new Linux partitions. You can learn more about Reiserfs by browsing to http://devlinux.com/projects/reiserfs.

Copyright and Warranty

Red Hat Linux is copyrighted under the GNU General Public License. This section doesn't include the entire license nor its variants, but it does highlight a few items. Basically, the license provides three things:

1. The original author retains the copyright.
2. Others can do with the software what they want, including modifying it, basing other programs on it, and redistributing or reselling it. The software can even be sold for a profit. The source code must accompany the program.

3. The copyright cannot be restricted down the line. This means that if you sell a product for one dollar, the person you sold it to can change it in any way (or not even change it at all) and sell it to a second person for $10—or give it away at no charge to a thousand people.

Why have such unique licensing? The original Linux software authors didn't intend to make money from the software. It was intended to be freely available to everyone, without warranty. That is correct; there is no warranty. Does this mean you are left out in the cold when you have problems? Of course it doesn't. Numerous resources, including this book, newsgroups, and the Web, are available to assist you. What the no-warranty provision does do is provide the programmers the ability to release software at no cost without the fear of liability. Granted, this lack of liability is a two-edged sword, but it is the simplest method for providing freely available software.

There are several variants of the GNU General Public License. The first is the GNU GPL, a free software license and a copyleft license recommended for most software. Another is the GNU Lesser Public License, a free software license that permits linking with non-free modules, but recommended by the FSF only under special circumstances. There is also the license of Guile, the GNU GPL with blanket permission to link with non-free software (and also recommended by the FSF only under special circumstances).

Open Source Software and Licensing

Open Source licenses are also numerous variants of software licensing that fall under the category of Open Source software. These include the software license for the X Window System, the original and modified BSD UNIX licenses, and the software license for the Apache Web browser. You'll find a copy of the GNU GPL listed in this book; you'll definitely find copies of others included on this book's CD-ROM! (Hint: Look under the /usr/share/doc directory in each package directory!)

For more information regarding software licensing, browse to http://www.gnu.org/philosophy/license-list.html. If you plan to develop software for Linux and would like to retain copyright but would like to share the source code with others, consider using the GNU GPL. You can also assign the rights to the software to the Free Software Foundation. For an interesting read about copyright and free software, browse to http://www.gnu.org/philosophy/why-free.html, and read Richard M. Stallman's treatise "Why software should not have owners."

Where to Get Red Hat Linux

Try looking on the CD-ROM that came with this book—Red Hat Linux is there. You can also get Red Hat from the Internet by pointing your browser to `http://www.redhat.com/apps/download`. By browsing to a Red Hat mirror site, you can find Red Hat for each of the three supported platforms (Intel, Alpha, and SPARC), along with individual `.rpm` packages, upgrades, and updates. Browse to Red Hat, Inc.'s home page, `http://www.redhat.com`, for answers to frequently asked questions, mailing lists, and much more. You can call Red Hat at 888-RED-HAT1 and order products, as well.

Because you already have a copy of Red Hat Linux (from the CD-ROMs in this book), you might just need to know where you can get updates, tips, HOW-TOs, and errata. The timeliest source for this information is the Web. Just point the old Netscape browser to `http://www.redhat.com/support/docs` and you'll find a plethora of information.

System Requirements

Red Hat keeps a listing of the system requirements and supported hardware for the three platforms—Intel, Alpha, and SPARC—on which Linux will run. These lists are presented in this section. As with anything, these lists change. If the particular hardware you have is not listed, check Red Hat's Hardware Compatibility Lists Web page at `http://www.redhat.com/support/hardware/` to see if it has been listed there.

For Alpha and SPARC hardware, your best bet is to stick with Tier 1-supported equipment. Red Hat defines three tiers of support for SPARC and Alpha hardware:

> **Tier 1**—The Red Hat distribution can detect and use the system, and works reliably.
>
> **Tier 2**—The Red Hat distribution should properly detect and work with the hardware, but some users have reported problems.
>
> **Tier 3**—The Red Hat distribution should work with the hardware using certain setups, but support is experimental, or the hardware may pose problems.

System Requirements—Intel

In general, Linux will run on nearly any modern Intel-based computer. If the computer can run DOS or Windows, it will run Linux. However, new users need to understand that there is a big difference between being able to just run Linux, and being able to install and configure the X Window System for a specific graphics card. Other concerns may focus on your system's handling of Advanced Power Management, or an attached modem, scanner, or printer. Remember, if you can partition your hard drive, copy Linux and its software to the new partition, and then reboot and log into the console, you're running Linux!

That said, according to Red Hat, these are the general system requirements for running Red Hat Linux on an Intel platform:

- Intel 386 through Pentium III.

- Spare hard drive space. 850MB for workstation installations and 1.7GB for a server installation. However, by choosing an expert mode, you can reduce these footprints considerably and install less software. A full installation will generally require at least 2.4GB, and perhaps more if you plan to install additional software, such as office suites or games.

- 32MB of memory or more is recommended, but if you don't use X11, you can use 16MB RAM; realistically expect 64MB to be the minimum if you plan to use X11 and run numerous clients at the same time.

- Most video cards are supported. Note that support is better for video cards at least one or more years old; the latest and greatest graphics card may not be fully supported.

- A CD-ROM drive. For the easiest install, although not essential, your computer's BIOS should be set to enable your computer to boot from CD-ROM. Many different CD-ROM and CDRW drives are supported.

- A 3.5-inch disk drive. A boot floppy will only be needed if you need to perform a special install, such as via PCMCIA, PLIP, FTP, NFS, or HTTPD.

- A SCSI or IDE drive. If you're configuring a dual-boot system (to be able to boot one or two operating systems), you'll need to create a separate partition or install a separate drive for Linux.

Another issue is sound. In general, there is much greater support for sound cards today than ever. The good news is that you can turn to at least two additional sources for drivers if the "stock" Open Sound System (OSS) drivers on the CD-ROM do not work with your computer's sound card. These are the Advanced Linux Sound Architecture (ALSA) project, at `http://www.alsa-project.org`, and the commercial OSS drivers from 4Front-Tech at `http://www.opensound.com`. Among all three sources, more than 400 different sound cards are supported!

More critical is proper support for your computer's video card, especially if you plan to use the X Window System. While Linux works quite well as a text-only, or *console* operating system, you'll most likely want to use X11 and its graphical interface to run word processors, spreadsheet programs, or to play games. Although the free X11 distribution from The XFree86 Project, Inc. works flawlessly with hundreds of different graphics cards and graphics chipsets in notebooks, you can run into trouble, especially if you have

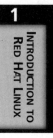

new and unsupported hardware. Fortunately, you can also turn to at least two commercial sources for specialized support. One source is Metro Link, Inc., which markets the low-cost Metro-X server (see `http://www.metrolink.com`). Another source is Xi Graphics, Inc., which markets specialized graphics drivers, including specialized accelerated drivers for 3D cards and notebooks (see `http://www.acceleratedx.com`).

The list of supported hardware is not a list set in stone—new device drivers are constantly being revised. To find the most up-to-date listing of supported hardware, check Red Hat's hardware URL: `http://www.redhat.com/support/hardware`. You can then click on the link for Intel hardware.

Red Hat also has an online database of supported peripherals, systems, and devices you can access with your Web browser. Go to

`http://hardware.redhat.com/redhatready/cgi-bin/us/genpage.cgi?pagename=hcl`

You'll see a Web-based form, as shown in Figure 1.1.

FIGURE 1.1

Use Red Hat, Inc.'s Web-based form to search for Linux-compatible peripherals and devices.

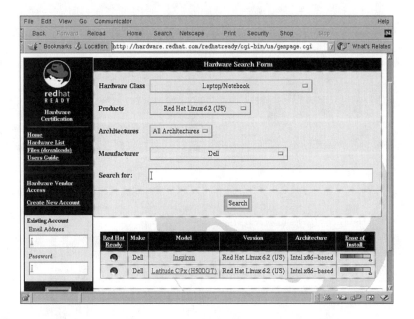

Click on the drop-down menus to select the hardware, Red Hat product, architecture, or manufacturer. You can also enter a search keyword. Click the Search button, and any matches will appear in list below the search dialog. You can then click on a link for additional information.

Summary

This chapter introduced you to Linux and Red Hat Linux. Coverage included a listing of differences among Linux distributions, various reasons why Red Hat Linux is the distribution of choice, and features of the new Linux kernel.

Finally, what higher praise could be bestowed upon Linux than the attention of the monopolistic software industry? Browse to `http://www.opensource.org/halloween` and read leaked internal corporate documents regarding the software industry, the Open Source movement, and Linux.

You can read Microsoft's response to the now infamous Halloween documents at `http://www.microsoft.com/NTServer/nts/news/mwarv/linuxresp.asp`.

Installation of Your Red Hat System

CHAPTER 2

One of the obvious differences between Red Hat Linux and other Linux versions is the ease with which Red Hat is installed. The process is quite straightforward and is automated by the Red Hat installation program. The installation program can handle many different system configurations and problems with ease and most of these things are taken care of for you.

Before looking at the methods used to install the operating system, you should understand the hardware on which the operating system will be installed. After examining the hardware, the rest of this chapter guides you, step by step, through the installation process, breaking it down to show some of the differences among the four basic methods of installation. This chapter briefly presents the installation of LILO (Linux Loader), but leaves many of those details to Chapter 3, "LILO and Other Boot Managers."

> **Caution**
>
> If you are not familiar with installing Linux then read this chapter at the very least twice, and make sure that you understand what you are doing before you start.

Preparing for Your Linux Installation

Before you start the install of your system, there are a few things you should do:

- Make sure your hardware is compatible with Linux. You can check the supported hardware list at `http://www.redhat.com/support/hardware`.
- Find all the manuals that came with your system—everything from the monitor manual to the sound card manual. These will come in very handy later on when you are configuring your system.
- Check to see if you have enough space on your hard drive to install Linux. It is preferable for this to be unpartitioned space. To give you an idea of how much space you will need, here is a list of the installation choices and how much space they take up:
  - GNOME Workstation—850MB
  - KDE Workstation—850MB
  - Server—1.7GB
  - Custom (Choosing Everything)—2.0GB

As Red Hat Linux has matured over the years, its installation and configuration have gotten simpler and simpler. Although there is an autoprobe program that the Linux community is continuously working on, it is often possible for things to still go wrong during an installation. The autoprobe might not pick up your hardware correctly or might have difficulty in detecting some hardware. Also, to our misfortune, not every piece of equipment ever produced is supported.

Because of this, it is important that you take a few minutes and, to the best of your ability, fill out the following sheet. Not only will it be helpful in configuring the system, but it also will help you in case something goes wrong.

Most of the following information can be found in your manuals for the particular equipment. Other pieces of information can be gathered by talking to your system administrator. The boldface items have been, historically speaking, problem areas. Obtaining the correct information on these areas may be critical if you are to have a successful installation.

Number of hard drives: _____

Size of each hard drive (MB): _____

Primary hard drive: _____

Amount of RAM (MB): _____

Type and number of CD-ROMs:
        IDE: _____

        SCSI: _____

Make and model of each CD-ROM: _____

Make and model of SCSI adapter(s): _____

Type of mouse: _____

Number of buttons on mouse: _____

If mouse is serial, COM port it is attached to: _____

Video card make, model, and amount of RAM: _____

Monitor's make and model: _____

Allowable horizontal refresh range: _____

Allowable vertical refresh range: _____

Networking:
  IP: _____

  Netmask: _____

  Gateway address: _____

  Domain name server's IP address: _____

  Domain name: _____

  Host name: _____

  Network card make and model: _____

Additional OSs either installed or to be installed on system: _____

Desired location for installation of LILO (if used): _____

Installed on master boot record (required if you want LILO to be your boot manager): _____

Installed on Linux partition (if you want to use a different bootloader, this would be where to install LILO): _____

> **Note**
>
> If you are running OS/2, you must create your disk partitions with the OS/2 partitioning software; otherwise, OS/2 might not recognize the disk partitions. Do not create any new partitions during the installation, but do use the Linux `fdisk` to set the proper partition types for your Linux partitions.

After you have answered these questions, the rest of the installation is fairly easy. The entire process is menu-driven, which means you don't have to remember all the configuration information you have to remember for other Linuxes you might want to install.

Choosing an Installation Method

There are a number of different ways in which you can install your system. They are all documented further later in the chapter. They are as follows:

- **CD-ROM**—This method needs a boot floppy, bootable CD, or a PCMCIA boot disk. This is the most common way to install your system.

- **Hard Drive**—This method requires you to have the Red Hat installation files on your hard drive. To install Red Hat Linux from a hard drive, you need the same startup and supplemental disks used by the FTP install. You must first create a Red Hat directory called RedHat at the top level of your directory tree. Everything you install should be placed in that directory. Copy the base subdirectory and then copy the packages you want to install to another subdirectory called RPMS (Red Hat Package Manager). Basically, these are your program installation files. You can use available space on an existing DOS partition or a Linux partition that is not required in the install procedure (for example, a partition that would be used for data storage on the installed system). With Red Hat 7 being a 3-CD install, there is going to be the overhead of having enough space free to store these files.

  If you are using a DOS filesystem, you might not be able to use the full Linux filenames for the RPM (Red Hat Package Manager) packages. The installation process does not care what the filesystem looks like, but it is a good idea to keep track of it so you will know what you are installing.

- **NFS (Network File System) Image**—You can install from an NFS server that has the install files exported. This requires a network or PCMCIA boot disk. You should either have nameservices configured or know the NFS server's IP address and the path to the exported CD-ROM. This method is only advisable if the NFS server is on a local network. It *will* take a long time to install using this, the FTP, and the HTTP install method. There is the possibility of the connection timing out.
- **FTP (File Transfer Protocol) and HTTP**—Comparable to an NFS image install. This also requires a network or PCMCIA boot disk. You must have a startup disk and a supplemental disk for an FTP install. You need to have a valid nameserver configured or the IP address of the FTP or HTTP server you will be using. You also need the root path of the Red Hat Linux directory on the site.
- **SMB Image**—Again comparable to NFS and FTP installs. This requires a network or PCMCIA boot disk. Select this option if you want to install over a network from a disk shared by a Windows system (or a Linux system running the Samba SMB connectivity suite). This is similar to installing from a hard drive except that in this case, the hard drive is on another system.

The rest of the installation procedures presented here are for a CD-ROM installation. As you can tell from the preceding descriptions, using other methods is not much different. As a matter of fact, the installation is the same; the difference is just a matter of the installation's origin. For example, if you are installing from a shared volume on a Windows 95/98/ME or Windows NT/2000 server, you have to supply the name of the server, the name of the shared volume, and the account name and password for the volume.

Because you have purchased this book, it is highly likely that you will be installing your system with the CDs provided in the back of this book. This is the simplest and generally the quickest method of installation.

GUI Versus Text-Based Installation

Red Hat gives you two choices for installation: GUI or text-based. If you have installed Linux before you can choose either. The graphical install is better for you if you are a new user because you are guided through every step with help in the side pane. The text-based install allows you more control over what is going on during the install. This, however, requires some experience with installing Linux. All choices will be the same in the GUI installation, but they may come in different order and you'll have mouse support and a more familiar interface. The only benefit, if you want to call it that, is the ability to click through options instead of having to tab through a list and press Enter. Pressing Enter at the wrong time could cause serious problems, so this can be awkward. You navigate through the installation dialogs using a simple set of keystrokes. To move the cursor, use the arrow keys. Use Tab and Alt+Tab to cycle forward or backward through each widget on the screen. A summary of available cursor positioning keys displays along the bottom of most screens.

To "press" a button, position the cursor over the button (using Tab, for instance) and press the spacebar (or Enter). To select an item from a list of items, move the cursor to the item you want to select and press Enter. To select an item with a check box, move the cursor to the check box and press the spacebar to select the item. To deselect, press the spacebar a second time.

Partitioning

Linux looks at hard drives differently than DOS/Windows. Instead of calling the first partition C:, the second one D:, and so on, it will usually be a combination of characters that signify the BUS and hard drive number. It works like this:

- hda—First IDE controller, Master
- hdb—First IDE controller, Slave
- hdc—Second IDE controller, Master
- hdd—Second IDE controller, Slave
- sda—First SCSI drive on the SCSI BUS

This is only the name of the devices as Linux sees them. The actual way Linux views your partitions is

- hda1—Primary partition on first hard drive.
- hda5—Extended partition on first hard drive. The extended partition will always have the number 5 as its partition number.
- hda6+—First logical partition inside the extended partition on the first hard drive.

This is the same for partitions on SCSI devices. Generally, your CD-ROM will be hdc because there are no partitions on a CD.

Two tools that come with Red Hat Linux can be used to set up Linux partitions: the old standby, fdisk, and a graphical partitioning tool, Disk Druid. Both are acceptable methods for configuring your partitions, but Disk Druid is easier. That is what is used here. There is another tool that can be used to resize and move around partitions. It is called fips.exe. It is in the dosutils directory on the CD. This is a DOS-based program, generally used to make room for Linux when crafting a dual-boot system. Extreme caution must be exercised when using this.

Automatic Partitioning

If you choose a workstation or server install, you'll have the opportunity to select Automatic Partitioning. However, automatic partitioning will remove any existing Linux partitions on all your computer's hard drivers, and will install the LILO boot loader into your primary volume's Master Boot Record (MBR). Do not choose automatic partitioning if you have data you'd like to preserve, or if you want to configure a custom partitioning scheme.

Partitioning Using fdisk

For you old-timers out there, here are some pointers for fdisk. Again, Disk Druid is the recommended (and safer) way of partitioning the disks. If you want to use the fdisk partitioning program during installation, start the install program in Expert mode.

Caution

This is the most volatile step of the entire procedure. If you mess up here, you could delete your entire hard drive. I highly recommend that you make a backup of your current system before proceeding with the disk partitioning.

Table 2.1 lists some commands and a walkthrough of fdisk.

TABLE 2.1   fdisk Key Commands

Key	What It Does
m	Provides a listing of the available commands
p	Provides a listing of the current partition information
n	Adds a new partition
t	Sets or changes the partition type
l	Provides a listing of the different partition types and their ID numbers
w	Saves your information and quits fdisk
q	Exits without saving any changes (handy when you make a mistake)

Use p to check the current partition information, but add your root partition beforehand. Use n to create a new partition and then select either e or p for extended or primary partition. Most likely you want to create a primary partition. You are asked what partition number should be assigned to it, at which cylinder the partition should start (you will be given a range—choose the lowest number), and the size of the partition. For example, for a 500MB partition, enter **+500M** for the size.

Using Disk Druid for Partitioning

Disk Druid is a tool that first shipped with Red Hat version 5. It is a graphical interface that enables you to configure your hard disk partitions.

There are three sections associated with Disk Druid. Each is explained in detail here.

The Partitions Section

Each line in the Partitions section represents a disk partition. Note the scrollbar in Figure 2.1.

FIGURE 2.1

Disk Druid partitioning during graphical installation of Red Hat Linux.

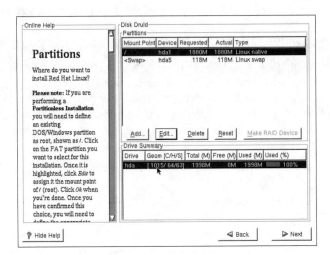

The scrollbar indicates additional items that cannot all be displayed at one time. Use the up and down arrow keys to look for any additional partitions. Each line (partition) has five fields, which are shown in Table 2.2.

TABLE 2.2   Current Partition Information

Field	Description
Mount Point	Indicates where the partitions will be mounted after the Red Hat Linux system is up and running. (At least one partition must have a mount point of / before you can move past the Disk Druid screen in the installation process.) Swap space does not get a mount point.
Device	Indicates the device name of the partition.

TABLE 2.2 continued

Field	Description
Requested	Indicates the minimum size requested when the partition was defined.
Actual	Indicates the actual amount of space allocated to that partition.
Type	Shows the partition's type.

Drive Summary

This section shows the *volumes*, or hard disk(s) on the system. Just like the Partitions section, this section will scroll in case more than a couple of drives are attached to this computer. Each line contains six fields, which are shown in Table 2.3.

TABLE 2.3   Drive Summary

Field	Description
Drive	Shows the device name of the volume.
Geom [C/H/S]	Shows drive's geometry. The three numbers represent the number of cylinders, heads, and sectors (reported by querying hard drive).
Total (M)	Shows how much space is on the entire hard drive.
Free (M)	Shows how much space is currently available on the hard drive. Indicates how much is unallocated.
Used (M)	Shows how much space is currently defined to a partition.
Used (%)	A graphical percentage indicator of how much space is used for partitioning the drive.

Disk Druid's Buttons

The third section of Disk Druid in a graphical install contains five buttons across the bottom of the screen. If you perform a text-based install you can also use corresponding F keys. The buttons and (text-based install F keys) are detailed in Table 2.4.

TABLE 2.4   Disk Druid Buttons

Button	Function
Add	Adds a new partition to the partition table. When pressed, a dialog box appears that contains fields that must be filled in. (F1)
Edit	Changes the attributes (such as size or type) of the highlighted partition in the Partitions section. If the Edit button is pressed, a dialog box appears with fields that can be edited. (F3)

TABLE 2.4 continued

Button	Function
Delete	Use this button to delete the selected partition in the Partitions section. Selecting Delete brings up a confirmation box. (F4)
OK	Active during a *text-based* install, and when selected, any changes made are written to disk. At this time, you can confirm that you want the changes written to disk. This information is also passed to the installation program for later filesystem creation. (F12)
Make RAID Device	This button is only active if you have created RAID partitions (of type fd if using fdisk); use the Add button to create a new partition, then select type RAID and the allowable drives (used for your RAID array).
Back	This is the abort button. If you select the Back button, Disk Druid exits without making changes and you are returned to the previous window, where you can select fdisk or Disk Druid to start over.
Function keys	As mentioned earlier, Disk Druid also has six handy function keys. Four of them map directly to the buttons just described (Add, Edit, Delete, and OK). Two are different and are explained next.
F2-Add NFS	The F2 function key opens a dialog box in which you can define a read-only NFS-served filesystem.
F5-Reset	This function does just what you think it does. (It does not reset your computer—that is Ctrl+Alt+Delete.) F5 resets the partitions to the way they were before you started editing them in this section.

Adding a Partition

To add a new partition, use the Add button (or select it, and press Enter during a text-based install). A dialog box opens and contains the fields shown in Table 2.5.

TABLE 2.5 Mounting Information

Field	Description
Mount Point	Highlight this field and enter the partition's mount point.
Size	Type a number (in megabytes) for the partition. The default of 1 can be removed with the Backspace key so you can enter a new number.
Growable?	Indicates whether the size you entered in the previous field is to be considered the partition's exact size or its minimum size. Press the spacebar to check and uncheck this box. When it's checked, the partition will grow to fill all available space on the hard disk.

TABLE 2.5 continued

Field	Description
Type	Contains a list of partition types. Select the appropriate type by using the up and down arrow keys.
Allowable Drives	Contains a list of the hard disks installed on your system, with a check box for each disk. If a box is checked, this partition can be created on that hard disk. If a box is not checked, the partition will never be created on that hard disk.
OK	Select this button and press the spacebar when you finish the settings for this particular partition and you're ready to create it.
Cancel	When you select this button, the partition you just defined will not be created.

2

INSTALLATION OF
YOUR RED HAT
SYSTEM

Note

You must define at least two filesystems; one for Linux native and one for Linux swap space. The recommendation, however, is six filesystems. One is swap space and the other five are /, /usr, /var, /home, and /usr/local.

Understanding Swap Space

A swap space is a space on a hard disk used as the virtual memory extension of a computer's real memory (RAM). Having a swap space allows your computer's operating system to pretend that you have more RAM than you actually do. The least recently used files in RAM can be "swapped out" to your hard disk until they are needed later so that new files can be "swapped in" to RAM.

When you create your swap partition, give some extra thought to the size of this partition (versus blindly picking a number or taking another person's recommendation). You should have at least 16MB total between your RAM and swap space. If you are running X, you should have at least 32MB between them. X is a hog on RAM and will generally use up to 50% of your RAM, so it makes sense to have a decent sized swap file.

The problem with using the generic formula to determine the swap space size is that it doesn't take into consideration what the user might be doing, even though a formula for determining the amount of swapping you need is given here. Note that if you run out of swap space, your system will thrash about, trying to move memory pages into and out of the swap space. This will bring your system to its knees.

A better way to estimate how much RAM you need is to figure out the size of all the programs you would run at one time. To this number, add 24MB to cover the OS. If the total is less than 64MB, use a 64MB swap space; otherwise, use the actual value. These days, with most machines coming with 64MB–128MB of RAM a swap space of 80MB–100MB is about right.

You should always configure some swap space, regardless of how much RAM you have. Even a small amount of swap space will have good results on a system with a lot of RAM. For example, I have 256MB of RAM on my system, which is more than enough for all of the programs I run. I have 127MB of swap space for programs I have running but am not actively using.

To create your swap partition using fdisk, you need to use **n** for a new partition. Choose either primary or extended; you most likely need primary. Give the partition a number and tell it where the first cylinder should be. Last, tell fdisk how big you want your swap partition. Now you need to change the partition type to Linux swap. Enter **t** to change the type and enter the partition number of your swap partition. Enter **82** for the hex code for the Linux swap partition.

You have created your Linux and Linux swap partitions, and it is time to add any partitions you might need (for example, Windows 95). Use **n** again to create a new partition and enter all the information just as before. However, after you enter the size of the partition, you need to change the partition type. Enter **l** to get a listing of the hex codes for the different partition types. Find the type of partition you need and use **t** to change the partition type. Repeat this procedure until all your partitions are created. You can create up to four primary partitions; then you must start putting extended partitions into each primary partition.

After your partitions are created, the installation program looks for Linux swap partitions and asks to initialize them. Choose the swap partitions you want to initialize, select the Check for Bad Blocks During Format box, and click OK. This formats the partition and makes it active so Linux can use it.

Formatting Partitions

After the swap space has been formatted, you are asked which partitions you would like formatted. I strongly suggest that you format all system partitions (/, /usr, and /var if they exist). You do not need to format /home or /usr/local if they have been configured during a previous install. Again, checking for bad blocks is a good thing.

The question that generally arises at this point is how big the partitions need to be. Table 2.6 gives a breakdown of the sizes of a typical installation. Of course, you can just have one great big partition called / if you decide not to have individual partitions for each major section.

TABLE 2.6 Suggested Partition Sizes

Partition Type	Minimal Size	Suggested Size
/	80MB	100MB–200MB
/usr	850MB	850+ applications and other documentation
/var	22MB	50MB
Paging space	0MB	Up to 2,047MB

Although minimal and suggested sizes are given, your system's particular needs may require that you go below or above these numbers. For example, /usr at 850MB assumes that you have both text and Web-based documentation loaded for at least one language. In addition, you see nothing here about a /home directory. Depending on the needs of your system and your users, you can elect to leave them in the / partition or put them in a separate partition. The recommendation is that they be put into a separate partition. This is so you will not lose your home data during a system upgrade.

Creating Boot Disks

Before you make the startup and supplemental disks, label the disks. The process for making the two disks differs in one way: When the program asks for the filename, you enter boot.img for the startup disk and supp.img for the supplemental disk. To create the floppy disks under MS-DOS, you need to use the following commands. This assumes your CD-ROM is drive D:

```
d:
cd \images
\dosutils\rawrite.exe
```

rawrite asks for the filename of the disk image. Enter **boot.img**. Insert a floppy disk into drive A. You are asked for a disk to write to. Enter **a:<return>** and label the disk **Red Hat boot disk**. Run **rawrite** again, enter **supp.img**, insert another disk, and type **a:**. Label this disk **Red Hat supplemental disk**. You will also have to create the drivers disk. Label the disk **Red Hat 7 drivers disk** and then insert it into the floppy drive. Run **rawrite** again and enter **drivers.img.** You are now ready to install your system using boot disks.

You can use the dd utility to create the disks under Linux or most UNIXes. Mount the first Red Hat Linux CD-ROM; insert a floppy disk in the drive (do not mount it), and change directories (**cd**) to the images directory on the CD-ROM. Use this command to create the startup disk:

```
dd if=boot.img of=/dev/fd0 bs=1440k
```

dd converts and copies `boot.img` to the floppy. `if` means input file; in our case this is `boot.img`. `of` means output file and in our case this is the first floppy device. Finally, `bs` means byte size and in our case this is 1.44MBs.

To make the supplemental disk, use the following command:

```
dd if=supp.img of=/dev/fd0 bs=1440k
```

Installing Without Using a Startup Disk

If you have MS-DOS on your computer, you can install without using a startup disk. The Red Hat installation program can be started by using these commands:

```
d:
cd \dosutils
autoboot.bat
```

If your computer can boot from CD-ROM you can also insert the Red Hat 7 CD and reboot your system.

Starting a Network Install

If you are performing an installation via FTP, HTTP, or NFS, you must create your own *network boot disk.* The network boot disk image file is `bootnet.img` and is located in the `images` directory on the first Red Hat Linux 7 CD or on the server that is exporting the install directories.

You must have the following information before you attempt to install over the network:

- The installation program will probe your system and attempt to identify your network card. Most of the time, the driver can locate the card automatically. If it is not able to identify your network card, you'll be asked to choose the driver that supports your network card and to specify any options necessary for the driver to locate and recognize it.
- A valid IP address for your machine.
- A valid netmask (generally 255.255.255.0).
- A valid gateway and nameserver IP.

Each type of network install starts off the same, booting from the `bootnet.img` boot disk. It will bring up the Welcome to Red Hat screen with a `boot:` prompt. Press Enter to start the installation. The installation will proceed much like the install outlined later in this chapter, but network installs take longer and risk being interrupted by dropped connections. You will see it load the boot kernel from the floppy drive. It then will bring up a screen asking you which language is to be used during install. Make your selection and press the OK button. Now you are asked to select which basic keyboard type you are using. After you make your selection, press the OK button again. A screen will now come up asking which type of install you would like to do. Make your selection and follow the directions for that choice as outlined in the following sections.

Starting an NFS Install

The first screen that will appear after selecting any of the network options is the TCP/IP Settings screen. It asks you for the IP, netmask, default gateway IP, and the primary nameserver of the computer you are setting up. If you have a BOOTP or DHCP server available on your network, you can also check the box above the form to have the system attempt to resolve these addresses for itself. After inputting this information, press the OK button to proceed to the next step. This next screen asks for your NFS server name and the path to the directory where the Red Hat installation files are. From this point on the install will be just like the standard install outlined in the section "Step-by-Step Installation" later in this chapter.

Starting an FTP Install

Starting an FTP install is almost exactly like starting an NFS install. You have to supply the same information regarding your network card and your network properties. Also, you must know the IP and point the installation program at the FTP site of your choice. Enter the name or IP address of the FTP site you are installing from and the name of the directory there that contains the Red Hat directory for your architecture. For example, if the FTP site contains the directory /pub/mirrors/redhat/i386/RedHat, enter /pub/mirrors/redhat/i386. If you are not using anonymous FTP, or if you need to use a proxy FTP server (if you're behind a firewall, for example), check the check box, and another dialog box will request the FTP account and proxy information.

Starting an HTTP Install

Again, follow exactly the same steps as you would for an NFS install except choose HTTP as the method of installation. Point the installation program at the HTTP site of your choice. Enter the name or IP address of the HTTP site you are installing from and the name of the directory there that contains the Red Hat directory for your architecture. For example, if the HTTP site contains the directory /pub/mirrors/redhat/i386/RedHat, enter /pub/mirrors/redhat/i386. If you are not using anonymous HTTP, or if you need to use a proxy HTTP server (if you're behind a firewall, for example), check the check box, and another dialog box will request the HTTP account and proxy information.

2

INSTALLATION OF YOUR RED HAT SYSTEM

Note

NFS, FTP, and HTTP methods of installation are vastly inferior to a CD or hard drive install, but sometimes necessary, especially if installing on hardware without a CD-ROM. While installing over a LAN is just as fast as a CD-ROM install, using the Internet can be slow and are prone to dropping the connection to the respective servers.

Addressing PCMCIA and External Issues

Most Intel-based laptop computers support PCMCIA (also known as PC Card). Computers that support PCMCIA devices contain a controller having one or more slots in which a PCMCIA device can be installed. These devices may be modems, LAN adapters, SCSI adapters, and so on.

When installing Red Hat Linux/Intel on a PCMCIA-capable computer, it is important to note if a PCMCIA device will be used during installation. For example, if you want to install Red Hat Linux 7 from CD-ROMs, and your CD-ROM drive is connected to a PCMCIA adapter, the installation program will require PCMCIA support. Likewise, if you are going to use one of the network-based installation methods, you will need PCMCIA support if your network adapter is PCMCIA-based.

Note

You don't need install-time PCMCIA support if you're installing Red Hat Linux on a laptop and using the laptop's built-in CD-ROM drive.

PCMCIA support is dependent on two things:

- The type of PCMCIA controller in your computer system.
- The type of PCMCIA device that you want to use during the installation.

While nearly every PCMCIA controller and most popular PCMCIA devices are supported, there are some exceptions. For more information, please consult the Red Hat Linux Hardware Compatibility List at `http://www.redhat.com/hardware` to see if your hardware is supported.

The main thing to remember is that if you require PCMCIA support to install Linux, you will need a support disk.

Here's a checklist that you can use to see if you'll need to create a PCMCIA support disk:

- Installing from a PCMCIA-Connected CD-ROM—If you'll be installing Red Hat Linux from a CD-ROM, and your CD-ROM drive is attached to your computer through a PCMCIA card, you'll need a support disk.

- Installing using a PCMCIA Network Card—If you will be using a PCMCIA network adapter during the installation, you'll need a support disk.

- If you have determined you will need a support disk, you will have to make one. The PCMCIA support disk image file is `pcmcia.img`, and is located in the `images` directory on the first Red Hat Linux CD.

Check out "Creating Boot Disks" earlier in this chapter. It will inform you on how best to create these disks and which kind is best for your system.

Step-by-Step Installation

This section takes a step-by-step look at the CD-ROM installation process. It will guide you through the install step by step and help you along the way. It will also inform you on the preferred options to select and why you should select them.

Starting the Installation

The best way to start your installation is to check and see if your BIOS supports booting from the CD drive. Most computers built after mid-1997 have this option. On boot you will see a line of text telling you to press either the F1 or the Delete key to enter the BIOS settings and change the boot order so that the computer can boot from the CD drive. Save these settings and reboot the machine. The computer will then boot from the CD drive. When the install is finished, change your settings back to the way they were. If your computer doesn't support this, create and boot off a boot disk.

Caution

If you change the BIOS setting regarding your hard drives, it can have adverse effects on your system.

Load the Red Hat Linux installation program by placing the first CD-ROM or the boot disk into your drive and restarting your computer. When your computer comes back up you will be greeted by the Welcome to Red Hat Linux 7.0! screen. Keep in mind that for the suggested and normal install (graphical mode) you will just have to press Enter at the boot: prompt to continue. You are also presented with a screen full of options, some which we will touch on briefly before proceeding to the standard install path starting in the section titled "The Installation Program" later in this chapter.

You can pass a number of parameters to the Linux kernel at startup. These do not include parameters for devices such as CD-ROM drives or Ethernet cards.

Certain hardware configurations sometimes have trouble with the automatic hardware detection during the installation. Although this is unusual, it does happen. If you experience problems during the installation, restart the installation using the Expert mode. To view problems during the install you can check what errors are being reported on the other virtual consoles.

Using Text Mode for Installation

You can still install Red Hat using the text mode install process by typing text at the boot: prompt. This will bring you down basically the same path as the default graphical installation. However, you will have to use the Tab, spacebar, arrow, and Enter keys to navigate the interface. Also, it is prone to unpredictable results if stray keys are pressed during the installation. It is recommended that you select the graphical install by just pressing Enter at the boot: prompt.

Using Expert Mode for Installation

The default method of installing Red Hat Linux uses autoprobing to automatically detect the hardware in your system. Although most systems can be autoprobed without difficulties, there can be problems in certain cases. You can overcome these problems by using Expert mode. Expert mode is only advisable if you know your system completely and are comfortable with Linux.

To start the installation using Expert mode, type **expert** and press Enter at the boot: prompt.

While in Expert mode, you have complete control over the installation process. You can also enter optional module parameters while in Expert mode.

Note

This chapter does not cover Expert mode installation in detail as it is assumed that if you are capable of performing one, you are experienced with installing Linux.

Using Rescue Mode for Installation

The Red Hat installation program has undergone changes that enable you to create a custom startup disk for your specific system. This new startup disk is customized according to your system's hardware configuration. This will ensure that you will always be able to start your system, even if LILO has been overwritten by another operating system.

You may also create a startup disk after the installation process completes. To do this, consult the `mkbootdisk` man page. Note that the `mkbootdisk` package must be installed to create a startup disk after the installation.

Your startup disk is the first disk in a two-part rescue disk set. The second disk required for Rescue mode must be created from the `rescue.img` image file, which is located in the Red Hat Linux CD-ROM's `images` directory (on the first disk). To create the second disk, insert a blank floppy in your system's floppy drive, and type the following:

```
dd if=rescue.img of=/dev/fd0 bs=72k
```

You can then start in Rescue mode by booting from your startup disk and typing **rescue** at the `boot:` prompt. Insert the disk created from `rescue.img` when you're prompted to do so.

Using Kernel Parameter Options

Some kernel parameters can be specified on the command line and thus passed to the running kernel. This does not include options to modules such as Ethernet cards or devices such as CD-ROM drives.

Use the following format to pass an option to the kernel:

```
linux options
```

If you want a different installation mode, enter it after the option(s). For example, to install on a system with 128MB of RAM, using Expert mode, type the following:

```
linux mem=128M expert
```

To pass options to modules, you need to use the Expert mode to disable PCI autoprobing. When the installation asks for the device type to which you need to pass an option or parameter, it gives you a place to type those at that time.

Watch the startup information to ensure that the kernel detects your hardware. If it doesn't properly detect your hardware, you might need to restart and add some options at the `boot:` prompt. The following is an example:

```
boot: linux hdX=cdrom
```

where X is a, b, c, or d depending on what IDE channel the CD drive is on. The meaning of a, b, c, or d is explained earlier in this chapter. If you need to enter any extra parameters here, write them down—you will need them later in the installation.

Using Virtual Consoles During Installation

Red Hat's installation goes beyond a simple sequence of dialog boxes. In fact, you can look at different diagnostic messages during the installation process. You can actually switch among five virtual consoles, which can be helpful if you encounter problems during installation. Table 2.7 shows the five consoles, the key sequence to switch to each console, and the purpose of that particular console.

TABLE 2.7 Virtual Console Information

Console	Keystroke	Purpose
1	Ctrl+Alt+F1	Installation dialog box
2	Ctrl+Alt+F2	Shell prompt
3	Ctrl+Alt+F3	Install log (messages from the install program)
4	Ctrl+Alt+F4	System log (messages from the kernel and other system programs)
5	Ctrl+Alt+F5	Other messages
7	Ctrl+Alt+F7	X Graphical Display

Most of the installation time will be spent in console 1, working through the dialog boxes if you are doing an expert or text install. If you are doing the default graphical mode install, you will be operating out of console 7.

The Installation Program

Welcome to Red Hat Linux 7.0! This is the screen that you should be seeing after you have booted from your CD-ROM or floppy. (See Figure 2.2.) This is where the real step-by-step install begins. For your install, I will assume that you have a mouse attached to your system (highly recommended) and you are installing off of CD-ROMs. Depending on if you booted to this point from the CD or the floppy, the first few screens may be slightly different. However, they will ask basically the same questions and will bring you to the same install screens outlined here. Differences will be noted throughout the process.

Pressing Enter now will start the loading of the boot kernel. It will autoprobe for some of your hardware as well. You may see it loading some SCSI drivers if you have any SCSI cards installed. It will also attempt to find your mouse so you can point and click your way through the interface.

FIGURE 2.2

The Welcome screen.

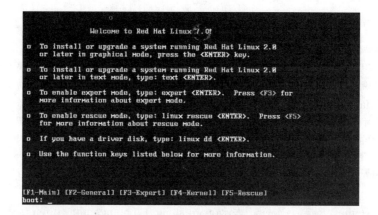

```
                     o
              Welcome to Red Hat Linux 7.0!

 o  To install or upgrade a system running Red Hat Linux 2.0
    or later in graphical mode, press the <ENTER> key.

 o  To install or upgrade a system running Red Hat Linux 2.0
    or later in text mode, type: text <ENTER>.

 o  To enable expert mode, type: expert <ENTER>.  Press <F3> for
    more information about expert mode.

 o  To enable rescue mode, type: linux rescue <ENTER>.  Press <F5>
    for more information about rescue mode.

 o  If you have a driver disk, type: linux dd <ENTER>.

 o  Use the function keys listed below for more information.



[F1-Main] [F2-General] [F3-Expert] [F4-Kernel] [F5-Rescue]
boot: _
```

The first screen you see is the Language Selection screen. It asked you which language you would like to use during the installation process. The default is English, but other options include Czech, Danish, Finnish, French, German, Italian, Norwegian, Romanian, Serbian, Slovak, Swedish, and Turkish. Click the Next button to continue. If you booted from a floppy, use the arrow keys to highlight your choice and press the Tab key to move to the OK button. Press Enter to continue using that selection.

The next screen is Keyboard Configuration. This step is a bit different depending on how you booted. The floppy disk boot asks you simply which keyboard layout you are using. Select which one you have and press OK to continue. If you booted directly from the CD, you will have three list boxes for Model, Layout, and Enable Dead Keys. Select the options that match your system and test it in the text box at the bottom of the screen. After your configuration is complete, press the Next button.

Most likely you will have chosen to boot from CD-ROM. If you have, you will see the Mouse Configuration screen next. If you booted from floppy you will be presented with a screen to select installation from the hard drive or CD-ROM. Select CD-ROM and press OK. You will be prompted to insert the CD-ROM into your drive if it is not already there. If you booted using another method such as a network install or floppy the system will scan for your mouse and load you into the graphical mode GUI at this point.

Unless you selected a full text install (or do not have a mouse) the Mouse Configuration screen is displayed. Select the type of mouse that you are using. You also have the option to check the Emulate 3 Buttons option if you have a two-button mouse. When you have made your selection, press Next.

You have now completed the Installation Program setup and are presented with the Welcome to Red Hat Linux system installer screen.

The System Installer

This part of the install is where you get to select what type of install (workstation, server, custom) you would like to do, the programs you would like to install, and system configuration.

New or Upgrade?

The installation program now asks whether you are installing a new system or upgrading a system that already contains Red Hat Linux 2.0 or greater. You are installing a new system, so highlight Install and press Enter.

There are three classes of installation: Workstation, Server, and Custom. By default the Workstation class is selected. As you go along, I'll point out the differences between the Workstation and Server classes. Select which installation you would like to do and press Next.

Partitioning

Because this is a new installation, the system installer assumes you do not have your Linux partitions set up. It does, however, give the following warning:

> You are about to erase any preexisting Linux installations on your system.
>
> If you don't want to do this, you can continue with this install by partitioning manually, or you can go back and perform a fully customized installation.

This warning should be heeded, because it will indeed write over any previously installed Linux partitions. You should only get this warning if the system sees Linux partitions already present on your system.

Caution

If you install as a Server class, all of your partitions will be overwritten. This means you lose whatever else is on the disks—including other operating systems.

If you do have a Linux partition and you did not choose Custom, the system assumes you want to use the same partitions for the new system and begins to overwrite what is already there.

Note

This means you can install more than one version of Linux on your system, but you must custom install any after the first.

If you are performing a new install (and you did not previously have a Linux partition), or if you chose Custom, you are next prompted to partition your disks. Depending on which install you selected you will be given the option to Automatically partition your drives (except in custom install) or Manually partition using Disk Druid or fdisk. It is recommended that if you are going to manually partition your drives that you use Disk Druid. You should only use fdisk if you are familiar with using it.

Make your partition selection. If you selected automatic partitioning, it will skip the next few screens and bring you to the Network Configuration screen (provided you have a network device installed). If you choose to manually partition your drives follow the information in the previous section on partitioning using the interface you select. After you partition your drives, you will be prompted to choose the partitions you wish to format. You also have the option to check for bad blocks while formatting. It is recommended that you do this, but it will increase the time it takes to format your drives. Next you are asked to configure the Linux Loader.

Configuring LILO

The next screen presents you with possible startup loader locations. A comment ensures that you do not overwrite the correct one. The choices are the Master Boot Record and the First Sector of Boot Partitions.

The Master Boot Record is the entire system's boot record. Replacing this causes LILO to start every time the system starts.

The First Sector of Boot Partitions can be used if you have another bootloader on your system. If these loaders are already in the primary drive's Master Boot Record, you probably do not want to replace them. (For more information refer to Chapter 3.)

If your system has SCSI drives, or you want to install LILO on a partition with more than 1023 cylinders, it may be necessary to enable the option to Use Linear Mode. If it is not, enabling this option shouldn't hurt anything, so it is probably a good idea to do so.

A few systems need to pass special options to the kernel at startup time in order for the system to function properly. If you need to pass startup options to the kernel, enter them at the next screen. The second part of bootloader states that it can start other operating systems that are on your system. If you have Windows 95 or 98, bootloader recognizes this and gives it a DOS startup label.

Press Next when you have made your selections. More often than not, you will just be able to accept the default selections.

Network Configuration

If you have one or more network interface cards (NIC) installed this next screen will allow you to enter configurations for each one. If you do not have a network card installed you may not see this screen at all.

Enter the IP address, netmask, network, and broadcast IPs for each NIC (or select the DHCP option if you have a DHCP server on your network). Also enter in the hostname for your system as well as its gateway and DNS addresses.

There is also an option for you to Activate on Boot. This will activate that NIC upon boot. You will have to manually start that interface once the system is booted if this is not selected. The install does probe your network cards but is not guaranteed to always be correct. If your card does not seem to be functioning after your install, you can go back in and change which driver your card is using, as well as all of these options.

Once you have filled this in, press Next to continue configuring your system.

If you do not want to configure your NIC at this moment, you can easily do it later after the install.

Setting the Time Zone

You are next asked to set up your system's time zone. You can simply mouse over the map, find your location, and click to select your time zone. Also, you may just select the correct time zone from the list box under the map. If you want to configure this by selecting your Universal Time Coordinated (UTC) offset, you can select that tab and find your offset in that list box. Press Next when you are ready to move to the Account Configuration portion of the setup.

Setting the root Password and the root Account

The root account has no limitations; therefore, the password for this account must be kept secure. You are asked to enter a password twice. The password must be at least six characters long. As you type in this new password, notice that the typing is hidden with "*". This is a security feature. You enter the password into the system twice to make sure you typed it correctly. The root password should be alphanumeric and a mixture of upper- and lowercase characters to make it harder for hackers to guess.

root is the all-powerful administrative account and is the most privileged account on a Linux system. This account gives you the ability to carry out all facets of system administration, including adding accounts, changing user passwords, examining log files, installing software, and so on. When using this account it is crucial to be as careful as possible. The root account has no security restrictions imposed upon it. This means it is easy to perform administrative duties without hassle. However, the system assumes you know what you are doing, and will do exactly what you request—no questions asked. Therefore, it is easy with a mistyped command to wipe out crucial system files. When you are logged in as or acting as root, the shell prompt displays # as the last character (if you are using bash). This is to serve as a warning to you of the absolute power of this account.

The rule of thumb is, never sign in as root unless absolutely necessary. While root, type commands carefully and double-check them before pressing Enter. Sign off from the root account as soon as you have accomplished the task you signed on for. During the install, you can create normal user accounts at the same dialog box that allows you to set the root password. It is advised that you set an account up here and use it all the time rather than the root account.

You may also set up other user accounts at this time as well. It is suggested that you set up at least one other user account at this time. Enter in the account name as well as the password. You may also include the full name of this person as well. Click Add to accept the user. If you want to edit a user you create, just highlight the account name and click Edit. You may also delete any users here.

Press Next to continue.

Authentication Configuration

Additional authentication configuration settings follow the setting of root's password. The first two choices have to do with added password security. It is recommended that you at least turn on shadow passwords, if not both shadow passwords and MD5 passwords. This is highly important—not using encrypted passwords means that hackers can have a field day if they gain access to your computer. In today's environment, with many people having a permanent connection to the Internet, it means that your computer is viewable to more or less the whole world, including hackers.

You are asked if you want to have NIS enabled. If you do, you also need to supply the NIS domain and server. (See Chapter 15, "NIS: Network Information Service," for more information on NIS.) You also get the option of choosing to have the system request services via a broadcast instead of providing a server name.

You may also enable Lightweight Directory Access Protocol (LDAP). If you do you will be asked to enter in the LDAP server and the LDAP base distinguished name (DN).

The last option you have is to enable Kerberos. You may enter the realm, Key Distribution Center (KDC), and admin server that apply.

Press Next to continue to select the package groups.

Packages to Install

The next screen asks which packages you want to install. Depending on which class of install you selected at the beginning, you will have a different amount of packages that you can choose to install. If you chose the workstation installation you will just have the GNOME, KDE, and Games packages to choose from. This does not mean that these are the only packages that will be installed, but the installer does limit your choices for extras you can add to the base installation.

The Server install gives you the options to install the news, NFS, Web, and DNS server packages. The other packages will be installed as defined by the base server install. If you want more control over which packages you want to install on your system, you should select the custom install, which gives you the full list of packages to choose from.

If you did choose the custom install option, you can select which packages you want to install from the full list. If you want to install everything, just go to the bottom of the list and select Everything. Red Hat Linux 7 now uses a three-CD-ROM install (you're asked to swap the CDs during the install)... an Everything install requires 1.9GB+! (Actually, /usr will require nearly 2GB (or 250MB more than indicated due to temporary installation files) for a full install.

No matter which one of these three you chose at the beginning, you can check the Select Individual Packages box at the bottom of the screen to customize the selections even further.

If you do decide to select individual packages, the next screen will let you select to install and not install items that were selected for that class of install.

After you have made your package selections or individual package selections, the installer will check the dependencies in the packages selected for installation. If some packages are lacking dependencies, the installer will prompt you to install them. It is a good idea to make sure that all the dependencies are installed.

If you have selected packages that install X you will next enter into the X Configuration. If you have selected a server install or have not included X in your installation you skip the X Configuration and will be ready to have the system format your partitions and load the packages you have selected.

X Configuration

If you selected to install X, you will be able to configure it now. The first screen attempts to detect your monitor. Select the monitor that you have and make sure that the horizontal and vertical sync match your monitor's specifications. If you do not select the correct monitor, you risk damaging your monitor.

> **Caution**
>
> Choosing the wrong monitor frequencies can—to use the vernacular—fry your monitor. Make sure you have the correct settings.

After you have selected the monitor that matches your system, click Next.

Now the system probes for your graphics card. If the settings found by the probe do not match your hardware, select the correct card from the list. Also specify the amount of RAM that you have on your video card. You can press the Test This Configuration button to test the settings you have selected.

Other options that you can choose now are to use the graphical login, your default desktop, and to customize X configuration. Customize X Configuration allows you to choose specific color and resolution settings. When you are finished selecting your video options, click Next.

About to Install

When you have finished all the configurations, you reach the About to Install screen. When you press the Next button on this screen, the system will format your partitions, load the packages you selected, and prepare the configurations you have selected in the previous screens. Also note that it leaves a complete log of your installation in `/tmp/install.log` after rebooting your system. Depending on the speed of your CD-ROM, your system, and how many packages you requested, this process may take 25 minutes or longer.

Installing Packages

The system now formats your partitions and starts installing the packages onto your system. The display tells you where it is currently in the install process and gives you an estimation on how long until the installation is complete. Sit back and relax and let the installer do the work! Keep an eye on the install though, because you will need to swap in disk two as the installation progresses.

When this process completes the system will ask you if you would like to create a boot disk.

Creating a Startup Disk

A custom startup disk provides a way of starting your Linux system without depending on the normal bootloader. This is useful if you don't want to install LILO on your system, another operating system removes LILO, or LILO doesn't work with your hardware configuration. A custom startup disk can also be used with the Red Hat Rescue image, making recovery from severe system failures much easier.

> **Note**
>
> Creating a startup disk is very much recommended at this stage in the game.

If you say Yes, you are asked to insert a blank floppy disk into the first diskette drive (`/dev/fd0`). The system creates a startup disk after you have inserted the blank disk.

Done

Installation is complete. You need to remove the disk and press Enter to restart. You are now ready to log in to your Red Hat Linux system!

Post-Installation and Configuration

Now that you have installed Linux and booted your system for the first time, here are a few useful things to know before using your system.

LILO lets you pass parameters to the Linux kernel, which overrides the default behavior. For example, you may have been experimenting with startup configuration files and done something to prevent the system from coming up properly. If so, you want to boot the system up to the point where it reads the configuration files and no further. The override for this is single. This boots the system in single user mode so you can take corrective action. This is also useful if your system doesn't boot all the way to the `login:` prompt for some reason.

The Red Hat Package Manager

If you want to add packages to your Linux system in the future or upgrade current packages, you can use the Red Hat Package Manager (RPM). RPM technology is a very easy way to manage package installs and uninstalls. It keeps track of what is installed and any dependencies that are not met and then notifies you of them. You can also access the graphical interface to RPM called `gnorpm` through the control panel while running X Window.

Installing and Removing Packages with RPM

The basic use of the `rpm` command to install a package is as follows:

```
rpm -i packagename.rpm
```

Use the following to uninstall a package:

```
rpm -e packagename.rpm
```

Many other options are available for RPM, but these two are the most common.

Packages for use with RPM are available at `ftp://ftp.redhat.com/pub/redhat/current/i386/RedHat/RPMS/` or any mirrors of this site.

Logging In and Shutting Down

Now that you are faced with the `login:` prompt for the first time, you may be wondering how to get into the system.

At this point on a newly installed system, there is generally only one account to log in to—the administrative account, `root`. This account is used to manage your system and do things like configure the system, add and remove users, software, and so on. To log in to the account, enter `root` at the `login:` prompt and press Enter. You are asked for the password you entered during installation. Enter that password at the `password:` prompt. The system prompt

```
[root@localhost] #
```

appears after you have successfully negotiated the login. The system prompt tells you two things: you are logged in as `root`, and in this case, your machine is called `localhost`. If you named your machine during the installation process, your host name will appear instead of `localhost`. If you decided to set up other users during the install process you can also log in with those usernames and passwords.

To shut down the system from a terminal session, sign in or `su` to the `root` account. Then type **/sbin/shutdown -r now**. It may take several moments for all processes to be terminated, and then Linux will shut down. The computer will reboot itself. If you are in front of the console, a faster alternative to this is to press Ctrl+Alt+Delete to shut down. Please be patient as it may take a couple of minutes for Linux to terminate.

The **su** command can be used to run `root` commands from a normal user account. For example, to run any `root` command as a normal user you would only have to type **su -c** *command* where *command* is any command. You can also use **su** to switch user. The format of this command would be **su - *user*** where user is any user that exists on the system. The hyphen logs you in to that user's home directory as the current working directory.

You can also shut down the system to a halt (that is, it will shut down and not reboot the system). The system will be unavailable until power-cycled or rebooted with Ctrl+Alt+Delete. This can be useful if you need to power down the system and move it to a different location, for example. To do this, type **/sbin/shutdown -h now** when signed into or su-ed to the `root` account. Linux will shut itself down then display the message "System halted". At this point you can power down the computer. It is important to note that you *cannot* just switch off a Linux system. The system must be allowed to unmount all partitions to provide for a clean startup. Just switching the system off can cause corruption of data on the hard drive.

It is probably a good idea to only shut down the system when you are at the console. Although you can shut it down remotely via a shell session, if anything goes wrong and the system does not restart properly, the system will be unavailable until action is taken at the system unit.

Upon system bootup, Linux will start automatically if it is the default OS defined in LILO, and load all necessary services including networking support and Internet services.

Summary

The Red Hat Linux installation is the simplest and most straightforward installation available. After going through this chapter and following the step-by-step installation, you should now have a running Linux system. Keeping your system updated with the latest versions of utilities and libraries will ensure compatibility with most new applications being developed for Linux and keep your system operating efficiently.

If you do have problems, you'll find HOWTOs and FAQs on the CD-ROMs that come with this book. Most of them are in HTML format, so you can view them straight from CD-ROM by using a Web browser. Also, the Red Hat Web site (`http://www.redhat.com`) contains installation documentation and errata sheets for Red Hat Linux.

LILO and Other Boot Managers

CHAPTER 3

There are many different ways to boot Linux. You can boot Linux from a floppy disk, directly from CD-ROM, via a network, or most commonly, from a specific partition on an installed hard drive. In each case, booting Linux requires an installed program to load the kernel into your computer's memory. This program is known as a *bootloader*, and you'll find at least two different free bootloaders included with this book's CD-ROMs.

Which bootloader you'll use depends on the version of Red Hat Linux and the computer you're using: LILO is for Intel-compatible PCs, MILO is for Compaq and other Alpha PCs, and SILO is used with SPARC-compatible workstations. Because the CD-ROMs included with this book contain Red Hat Intel/Linux, this chapter focuses on LILO, which—according to its author, Werner Almesberger—stands for *Linux Loader*, and Hans Lermen's LOADLIN.EXE loader. Instead of using LILO, you can start Linux from DOS with LOADLIN.EXE, which is included on the first CD-ROM under the dosutils directory. See the section "Using LOADLIN.EXE to Boot Linux" later in this chapter. You'll also learn about a commercial bootloader from PowerQuest, named BootMagic.

Alternative Loaders

There are even more commercial bootloaders you can use to boot Linux. Another alternative is V Communications, Incorporated's System Commander, which can come in handy if you need to boot 100 or more operating systems, such as OS/2, BeOS, Solaris, or Windows 2000, on your computer. This product also includes point-and-click partitioning. Browse to http://www.v-com.com for more details.

There are other free-software bootloaders you can try. These include GNU GRUB (GRand Unified Bootloader), found at http://www.gnu.org/software/grub/grub.html, and Tuomo Valkonen's Choose-OS bootloader, available through most popular Linux FTP sites, or at http://www.kac.poliod.hu/doc/chos/.

This chapter will help if you chose not to install LILO when you first installed Red Hat Linux, if you need help properly starting Linux with certain kernel options, or if you need help troubleshooting a problematic boot. You should already know how you want to start Linux on your computer, but the information here can show you alternative ways to install and start Linux.

You can also use your computer as a diskless workstation by booting Linux over a network. A discussion on this subject is beyond the scope of this chapter, but you'll find the details on how to do this in Robert Nemkin's Diskless-HOWTO, available through http://www.linuxdoc.org/HOWTO/HOWTO-INDEX/howtos.html. One newer Ethernet bootloader you can try is EtherBoot, available through http://etherboot.sourceforge.net/.

Note

Unlike previous editions, you won't find HOWTOs included on this book's Red Hat
CD-ROMs. Browse to http://www.linuxdoc.org to search for and read HOWTOs.

Choosing and Installing a Boot Manager

Simple boot managers, such at PowerQuest's BootMagic, offer a convenient menu or
graphical interface used to boot to different operating systems. Other boot managers,
such as LILO and LOADLIN, have more advanced features that may be critical to a successful boot and may be a necessary ingredient in your boot strategy. If your computer's
hardware requires pre-boot configuration, or if the Linux kernel needs to know critical
information about your computer's hardware before, during, or after the boot process,
you may need to use one of these bootloaders' special features in order to boot Linux.

For example, the LOADLIN command is used from the DOS command prompt to load
the Linux kernel. LOADLIN, like LILO, supports the passing of video, networking, and
disk geometry settings, known as kernel *arguments*, usually via a command line or boot
parameter. Some arguments need to be passed before Linux boots, while other arguments, such as memory settings, may be placed in a configuration file. LOADLIN, like
LILO, supports separate kernel arguments in the boot parameter or in a separate configuration file.

LOADLIN can be especially helpful if you need to boot directly to Linux with your
computer's hardware left in a specific state (usually to aid in recognition, configuration,
or use). LOADLIN may also be used in the Windows operating system config.sys
script to provide a boot menu, or as a desktop shortcut to a direct boot to Linux. LOAD-
LIN can be helpful if a particular subsystem of your computer's hardware, such as IBM
MWave adapter, requires DOS initialization before it can be used as a sound card for
Linux.

The good news is that as Linux has matured, there is now better hardware support during
or after the boot process. However, there may be situations where only a bootloader like
LOADLIN will work!

Installing and Configuring LILO

You should know where your Linux partition is before LILO is installed. You should also know if and where other operating systems are installed. For example (using the Linux df, or disk file usage command), partitions may appear as

```
$ df
```

```
Filesystem          1k-blocks      Used Available Use% Mounted on
/dev/hda5            6079464    2168440   3602200  38% /
/dev/hda1              21929       2421     18376  12% /boot
```

This simple example, typical of a single hard drive system, shows that the Linux /boot partition is installed on /dev/hda1, with the rest of the Linux filesystem resident on /dev/hda5 (there are other partitions present, such as swap and hibernation, but only those recognized are displayed). Here, LILO is installed in the Master Boot Record (MBR) of /dev/hda. Here is another example, using the output of the fdisk command's print partition table option:

```
Disk /dev/hda: 240 heads, 63 sectors, 1559 cylinders
Units = cylinders of 15120 * 512 bytes

    Device Boot    Start      End    Blocks   Id  System
/dev/hda1    *        1      218   1648048+    c  Win95 FAT32 (LBA)
/dev/hda2           219     1559  10137960     5  Extended
/dev/hda5           219      221     22648+   83  Linux
/dev/hda6           222      499   2101648+   83  Linux
/dev/hda7           500      534    264568+   82  Linux swap
/dev/hda8           535      881   2623288+   83  Linux
/dev/hda9           882     1559   5125648+   83  Linux
```

In this example, the Linux filesystem is installed across several partitions, such as /dev/hda5, /dev/hda6, /dev/hda8, and /dev/hda9. Although not obvious, these partitions correspond to /boot, root (/), and two additional volumes, with Windows installed on /dev/hda1. Again, LILO is installed in the MBR of /dev/hda, although it could also be installed in /dev/hda9.

If Linux is the only operating system on your computer or if you already have Windows installed, install LILO as the MBR of the boot drive. If you have OS/2 also, you will want to install LILO on the root partition of your hard drive and use OS/2's bootloader on the MBR to boot different operating systems.

> **Note**
>
> Some operating systems, such as Windows, will write over the MBR during installation. This means that if you are going to use your machine as a dual boot system, you need to either install the Microsoft product first and then overwrite the MBR with LILO, or use another type of software that performs the same type task, such as Partition Magic.

> **Note**
>
> Red Hat Linux installs LILO during an initial Linux installation or upgrade. You'll have the chance to create a bootdisk during the LILO installation process—do it! Even if you don't use the disk, you'll benefit from having a little insurance in case things ever go awry. If you don't install LILO, you'll definitely need the disk to boot Linux. If you forget to make a boot disk during the install, use Red Hat's `mkbootdisk` command to create one during your Linux session.

LILO is installed after you have partitioned your hard drives and after you have installed either Linux or other operating systems. LILO has capabilities that equal and, in some cases, exceed commercial solutions, and it's free. LILO is used to boot Linux in one of three traditional ways:

- From your hard drive's master boot record (MBR)
- From the superblock of your `root` Linux partition on your hard drive (either a primary or extended partition)
- From a floppy disk (or CD-ROM)

LILO has numerous configuration parameters and command-line arguments that demonstrate its special features.

Although LILO is easy to install by using the `lilo` command (located under the `/sbin` directory), you should first take the time to read its documentation, which you'll find under the `/usr/share/doc/lilo-21.4.4` directory. Along with the documentation, you'll find a shell script named `QuickInst`, which can be used for a first-time install. LILO's documentation contains details of its features and provides important tips and workarounds for special problems, such as installing bootloaders on very large capacity hard drives or booting from other operating systems.

Installing or Reconfiguring LILO

If you don't install LILO during your Red Hat install or decide not to use the QuickInst script, you can install LILO in two basic steps:

1. Create and then configure /etc/lilo.conf.
2. Run /sbin/lilo to install LILO and make it active.

This discussion describes modifying an existing lilo.conf file. Before making any changes, do yourself a favor and create a backup of the file either in the same directory or on a separate disk. Several files are important to LILO and are created during an initial install:

- /sbin/lilo—A map installer; see man lilo for more information.
- /boot/boot.b—A bootloader.
- /boot/map—A boot map that contains the location of the kernel.
- /etc/lilo.conf—LILO's configuration file.

Configuring LILO

Under Linux, your hard drives are abstracted to device files under the /dev directory. If you have one or more IDE drives, your first hard drive is referred to as /dev/hda and your second hard drive is /dev/hdb. SCSI drives are referred to as /dev/sda and /dev/sdb. When you installed Linux, you most likely partitioned your hard drive. The first partition on your first drive would be /dev/hda1 or /dev/sda1, your second partition would be /dev/hda2 or /dev/sda2, and so on.

Before configuring LILO, you should know which partitions have what operating system on them. You should also know where you want to install LILO. In almost all cases, you will want to put LILO on the MBR. You shouldn't do this, however, if you run OS/2, BootMagic, or the like. OS/2, BootMagic, and other similar software use the MBR. If you are using these types of software packages, LILO should be installed on the superblock of the root partition.

Armed with your information, you are now ready to edit LILO's configuration file, /etc/lilo.conf.

Editing `lilo.conf`

Editing lilo.conf is easy. Make sure you're logged in as root and load the file into your favorite editor, making sure to save your changes and to save the file as ASCII text. You'll edit lilo.conf for a number of reasons:

- You are testing a new kernel and want to be able to boot the same Linux partition with more than one kernel. You do this by using multiple entries of the `image =` section of `lilo.conf`. You may have multiple kernels installed on your Linux partition and can boot to a different kernel by typing its name (specified in the `label =` section).

- You want to add password protection to a partition.

- You have a hardware setup that requires you to specify special options, such as booting a remote filesystem.

- Your kernel is called something other than `/vmlinuz` or is in a nonstandard place, such as `/etc`.

Listing 3.1 shows a sample `lilo.conf` file.

> **Note**
>
> Need more information about configuring LILO? Although you'll find a lot of detailed technical information under the `/usr/share/doc/lilo*` directory, don't overlook Cameron Spitzer's LILO mini-HOWTO available at `http://www.linuxdoc.org` directory. You'll find additional troubleshooting tips on how to configure your `lilo.conf` file. Want to ask questions of other LILO users? Browse to `http://judi.greens.org/lilo/` and read the LILO FAQ. You'll find plenty of answers if you have special concerns.

LISTING 3.1   A Sample `lilo.conf`

```
boot=/dev/hda
map=/boot/map
install=/boot/boot.b
append="vga=791"
default=linux-up
keytable=/boot/us.klt
prompt
timeout=50
message=/boot/message
image=/boot/vmlinuz-2.2.15
        label=old-linux
        root=/dev/hda9
        append="vga=791"
        read-only
other=/dev/hda1
        label=dos
        table=/dev/hda
```

3

LILO AND OTHER BOOT MANAGERS

LISTING **3.1** continued

```
image=/boot/vmlinuz-secure
        label=linux-secure
        root=/dev/hda9
        append="vga=794"
        read-only
image=/boot/vmlinuz
        label=linux-up
        root=/dev/hda9
        append="vga=794"
        read-only
```

Listing 3.1 shows a dual-boot LILO configuration that offers the ability to boot DOS and three different versions of the Linux kernel. Each `lilo.conf` file consists of global, kernel, and non-Linux *parameters* with arguments. Global parameters detail the LILO's location, boot messages, prompts or delays, the default Linux kernel, kernel arguments, or password protection.

You can add the parameters listed in Table 3.1 to your `/etc/lilo.conf` file. They could also be given at the LILO boot prompt, but it is much simpler for them to reside in your `/etc/lilo.conf` file. Note that only the most common of LILO's 23 options are listed here. See LILO's documentation for details.

TABLE **3.1** `/etc/lilo.conf` Configuration Parameters

Parameter	Description
`boot=<boot_device>`	Tells the kernel the name of the device that contains the boot sector. If `boot` is omitted, the boot sector is read from the device currently mounted as `root`.
`linear`	Generates linear sector addresses instead of sector/head/cylinder addresses, which can be troublesome, especially when used with the compact option. See LILO's documentation for details.
`install=<boot_sector>`	Installs the specified file as the new boot sector. If `install` is omitted, `/boot/boot.b` is used as the default.
`message=<message_file>`	You can use this to display the file's text and customize the boot prompt, with a maximum message of up to 65,535 bytes. Rerun `/sbin/lilo` if you change this file.
`verbose=<level>`	Turns on progress reporting. Higher numbers give more verbose output, and the numbers can range from 1 to 5. This also has `-v` and `-q` options; see LILO's documentation for details.
`backup=<backup_file>`	Copies the original boot sector to `<backup_file>` (which can also be a device, such as `/dev/null`) instead of to `/etc/lilo/boot.<number>`.

TABLE 3.1 continued

Parameter	*Description*
force-backup<*backup_file*>	Similar to backup, this option overwrites the current backup copy, but backup is ignored if force-backup is used.
prompt	Requires you to type a boot prompt entry.
timeout=<*tsecs*>	Sets a timeout (in tenths of a second) for keyboard input, which is handy if you want to boot right away or wait for longer than the default five seconds. To make LILO wait indefinitely for your keystrokes, use a value of -1.
serial=<*parameters*>	Allows input from the designated serial line and the PC's keyboard to LILO. A break on the serial line mimics a Shift-key press from the console. For security, password-protect all your boot images when using this option. The parameter string has the syntax <*port*>,<*bps*><*parity*><*bits*>, as in /dev/ttyS1,8N1. The components <*bps*>, <*parity*>, and <*bits*> can be omitted. If one of these components is omitted, all of the following components have to be omitted as well. Additionally, the comma has to be omitted if only the port number is specified. See LILO's documentation for details.
ignore-table	Ignore corrupt partition tables.
password=<*password*>	Use this to password-protect your boot images. If you use this option but do not have lilo.conf set to root read-only permission (-rw------), LILO issues a warning—the password is not encrypted!
unsafe	This keyword is placed after a definition for a partition. The keyword tells LILO not to attempt to read the MBR or that disk's partition table entry.

3
LILO AND OTHER BOOT MANAGERS

After making your changes to lilo.conf, make sure to run /sbin/lilo. You should also always run /sbin/lilo after installing a new kernel; otherwise, the changes will not take effect. Experienced Red Hat Linux users will use a favorite text editor, such as vi, pico, or emacs, to edit the lilo.conf file. Hand-tuning your lilo.conf file is probably the best way to customize LILO's boot menu and add features, such as the splash screen used by Red Hat Linux. You'll find this file (which uses ASCII color graphics), named message, under the /boot directory.

LILO Boot Prompt Options

The following sample list of options can be passed to LILO at the boot prompt to enable special features of your system or to pass options to the Linux kernel to enable a proper boot. Knowing any needed options for your system is especially handy during the Red Hat Linux installation process because you'll be asked for any special options if you choose to install LILO at that time. Kernel arguments can be especially handy if you need to pass hard-drive geometry settings, the device names of designated boot volumes, or want to boot Linux to a particular user mode or *runlevel*, such as single or 0, with networking, multiple users and X11 disabled.

Although you'll normally type **linux** or **dos** at the LILO: prompt, you can also try one or two of the following options. (For a more up-to-date list of kernel messages or options, read Paul Gortmaker's BootPrompt-HOWTO available at http://www.linuxdoc.org.)

- rescue—Boots Linux into single-user mode to allow system fixes.
- single—Similar to rescue, but attempts to boot from your hard drive.
- root=<*device*>—Similar to the /etc/lilo.conf entry, this option allows you to boot from a CD-ROM or other storage device.
- vga=<*mode*>—Enables you to change the resolution of your console; try the ask mode.

> **Note**
>
> If you can't remember the exact labels you've specified in lilo.conf for the LILO: prompt, press the Tab key to have LILO print a list of available kernels. If this doesn't work, you can also try pressing the Alt or Shift keys before the LILO boot: prompt appears.

How to Uninstall LILO

You can uninstall LILO (as root) by using the lilo -u command, or, if LILO is not installed on the MBR, you can disable it by using fdisk under either Linux or MS-DOS to make another partition active. If LILO has been installed as the MBR, you can restore the original MBR by booting under MS-DOS and using the command fdisk /mbr.

Troubleshooting LILO

You shouldn't have any problems with LILO, but if you do, you'll get one of 70 different warnings or error messages. They're not all listed here, but Table 3.2 lists six of the most probable LILO: prompt or initial errors.

TABLE 3.2 LILO: Prompt Errors

Prompt	Description
L<nn>	nn represents one of 16 disk-error codes.
LI	The second-stage bootloader loaded, but could not run.
LIL	The descriptor table could not be read.
LIL?	The second-stage bootloader loaded at an incorrect address.
LIL	LILO found a corrupt descriptor table.
LILO	LILO ran successfully.

Disk error codes can indicate problems such as an open floppy door, a drive timeout, a controller error, a media problem, a BIOS error, or even transient read problems (which can be overcome by rebooting). Overall, some common problems with LILO include

- Not rerunning /sbin/lilo following a kernel change
- Incorrect use of /sbin/lilo in creating a new boot map
- Installing and booting Linux from a very large (2GB+) partition
- Installing another operating system (such as Windows 95, which overwrites the MBR) after installing Linux and LILO
- Errors in /etc/lilo.conf after manual edits
- A corrupted MBR
- Installation of LILO in a Linux swap partition (which should be impossible)
- A missing Linux kernel image (error in /etc/lilo.conf)
- Installing Linux on and booting from a DOS partition and then defragmenting the DOS partition
- Passing incorrect kernel messages at the LILO: prompt

If you run into trouble, definitely peruse Almesberger's readme file, found under the /usr/share/doc/lilo directory. Take his advice: Don't panic! With a little forethought, detection, and perseverance, you should be able to avoid or overcome problems.

Using LOADLIN.EXE to Boot Linux

LOADLIN.EXE is a program that uses the DOS MBR to boot Linux. This handy program by Hans Lermen also passes along kernel options. LOADLIN.EXE is very helpful when you must boot from DOS to properly initialize modems or sound cards to make them work under Linux.

You need to do two things before using `LOADLIN.EXE`:

1. Copy `LOADLIN.EXE` to a DOS partition (for example, `C:\LOADLIN`).
2. Put a copy of your kernel image (`/vmlinuz`) on your DOS partition.

For example, type the following from the DOS command line to boot Linux:

```
loadlin c:\vmlinuz root=/dev/hda3 ro
```

Make sure you insert your `root` partition in the command line. The `ro` stands for read-only. When you are first booting a Linux partition, it should be mounted as read-only to prevent data loss.

If you have a UMSDOS filesystem, you can type this:

```
loadlin c:\vmlinuz root=/dev/hda1 rw
```

The `rw` stands for read/write. Starting a UMSDOS filesystem this way is safe. Again, make sure you substitute your own partition. `LOADLIN.EXE` accepts a number of options; see its documentation in the `LOADLIN.TGZ` file under the `dosutils` directory on the first CD-ROM.

Jump-starting a Red Hat Install with LOADLIN

Another great use for LOADLIN is to jump-start a Linux install from the DOS command line. This method can be a lifesaver for notebook users without access to a boot floppy and CD-ROM drive! You'll need to partition your hard drive for Linux first. To use LOADLIN to start an install, use a remote computer on your LAN to copy the Red Hat directory from CD-ROM onto a DOS partition (usually at `C:\RedHat`). Next, copy the directory autoboot from the CD-ROM's `dosutils` directory to `C:\`. You can then use LOADLIN to boot to an install with `C:\loadlin C:\autoboot\vmlinuz initrd=C:\autoboot\initrd.img`. You'll then use a "Hard Drive" install to install Red Hat Linux!

Installing and Using BootMagic

BootMagic is a commercial bootloader included with PowerQuest's PartitionMagic program. This bootloader must be installed using Windows, and may be installed and configured after you have installed Linux in a separate partition. If your computer does not have a CD-ROM drive, you'll have to use another computer to copy the `BTMAGIC` directory from the PartitionMagic CD-ROM onto a floppy and then onto your Windows desktop. You can then click the `Setup.exe` program to install BootMagic. You'll see a dialog, as shown in Figure 3.1.

FIGURE 3.1

PowerQuest's BootMagic boot-loader features a graphical installa-tion and setup.

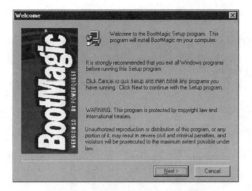

Click the Next button to install the BootMagic bootloader while running Windows.

Keep a Bootdisk Handy!

Always create a bootdisk for Linux if asked during your Linux install! Having a boot disk can save lots of grief if things go awry during installation or configuration of alternative bootloaders. BootMagic will write over the MBR of your main bootable hard drive, and will wipe out any previous LILO installation! If you want to use BootMagic and LILO, make sure to install LILO into the root native Linux partition first!

Follow through the next seven dialogs, filling out your user information, directory locations, and so on. You'll then be asked if you want to create a bootable BootMagic diskette. This is a good idea, and the diskette can come in handy later on if you have trouble booting either Windows or Linux on your computer. After creating the diskette, you'll see a BootMagic configuration dialog used to add other bootable partitions to BootMagic's initial boot menu. Click the Add button to begin.

In order to show your Linux partition(s), click the Advanced box and then click the root Linux partition. When finished, click OK to add Linux to BootMagic's boot menu. You'll then be asked (in a new dialog) to give your Linux partition a name and icon. Click OK when finished, and you'll see BootMagic's main dialog (as shown in Figure 3.2).

The main dialog is used to set the default operating system to boot. Click your new Linux entry, and then click the Up arrow Reorder button to move Linux to the top of the list. Click the Set as Default button while your Linux entry is highlighted to make sure your computer boots to Linux by default. Note that you can set a startup delay, delete or rename entries, and enable or disable BootMagic. When finished, click the Save/Exit button and BootMagic will be installed.

FIGURE 3.2

Use the BootMagic Configuration dialog's buttons to reorder the list of operating systems and to select a default operating system to boot.

When you reboot your computer, you'll be presented a graphic menu of operating systems to boot. You can click with your mouse, or wait the preset time delay, and Linux will boot.

Summary

This chapter covered the basics of configuring, installing, and using LILO, introduced you to the LOADLIN.EXE boot utility, and showed installation and configuration of one commercial boot utility, BootMagic, from PowerQuest. Hopefully, you've seen that using LILO can give you additional flexibility in the number of operating systems installed on your PC and that Linux can be used along with these other systems. Don't forget to read LILO's documentation, because you'll not only learn about how operating systems boot from your hard drive, but also how you can customize the Linux boot prompt.

Configuring the X Window System, Version 11

What Is X11?

The X Window System is a networking windowing system that provides a base set of communications protocols and functions for building graphical interface clients for computers with bitmapped displays. You should never refer to the X Window System as X Windows; the proper terms of reference are X, X11, X Version 11, or the X Window System, version 11.

X was first developed at the Massachusetts Institute of Technology in the early 1980s. The first commercial release of X was X10 in the mid-80s, with the first X11R1 release in 1987. Though the original MIT consortium has since disbanded, and X now falls under ownership of non-profit X.Org, a consortium whose executive membership includes Compaq, Hewlett Packard, Hummingbird, IBM, SGI, and Sun Microsystems, X11's general client/server model of operation has remained unchanged.

X was designed from the ground up to support networking graphics. Programs or applications under X are known as *clients*. X clients do not directly draw or manipulate graphics on your display, but instead communicate with your X server, which in turn controls your display. Although many home users will run clients and an X server on a single computer, it is also possible to run multiple X servers (and X sessions) on a single computer and to launch clients from remote computers—and to then have them displayed locally by a local server. This also means that it is possible to run X over various types of networks or even through a serial dial-up line!

XFree86 or Another X11?

The X Window System used with most Linux distributions, including Red Hat's, is the collection of programs from The XFree86 Project, Inc.. The version of X11 included with Red Hat Linux is XFree86 4.0.19, and is based on X11R6.4, or X11, revision 6.4.

Note

You can verify the version of XFree86 in use, even during an X session, by using the -version command-line option with the XFree86 command like this:

```
# XFree86 -version
XFree86 Version 4.0.1 / X Window System
(protocol Version 11, revision 0, vendor release 6400)
Release Date: 2 August 2000
        If the server is older than 6-12 months, or if your card is newer
        than the above date, look for a newer version before reporting
        problems.  (see http://www.XFree86.Org/FAQ)
Operating System: Linux 2.2.5-22smp i686 [ELF]
Module Loader present
```

The current version of XFree86 is the result of a lot of hard work and nearly three years' effort by Open Source programmers and XFree86 developers around the world. One of the advantages of using XFree86 is that currently most, if not all, of the source code to the servers, modules, libraries, clients, and related software is available. However, XFree86 is not distributed under the GNU General Public License. Instead, the distribution is covered by a BSD-style copyright and license, along with licenses from the X Consortium, NVIDIA Corp., GLX Public License (SGI), Bigelow and Holmes, Inc., and Y&Y, Inc. This means that not all the source to the software has to be provided, and vendors may be free to make improvements and distribute binary-only versions.

XFree86 works with an amazingly wide array of video chipsets, graphics cards, and notebook graphics systems, including non-Intel hardware. However, if you have special needs, one of the latest graphics cards, or find that XFree86 will not work with your computer's graphics system, you can turn to alternative sources.

Commercial versions of the X Window System are available from vendors such as Xi Graphics, Inc. (`http://www.xig.com`) or Metro Link, Incorporated (`http://www.metrolink.com`). These distributions range in price from $39 to $315.

However, the XFree86 distribution is free, and is included on this book's accompanying CD-ROM. This chapter focuses on configuring and using XFree86's version of X.

New Features of XFree86 4.0.1

The previous (now legacy) version of XFree86 for Intel-based PCs, 3.3.6, supported 550 graphics cards and chipsets using 14 different X11 servers. The new version, 4.0.1, supports nearly as many cards and more than 30 families of graphics chipsets using only one server! XFree86 has been redesigned to use loadable modules and drivers to provide support for specific cards, rather than use a monolithic, single server for a family or type of graphics chipset. This reduces maintenance, the distribution size, allows programmers to focus on module development, and provides a mechanism for rapid support of new graphics chipsets by manufacturers with the release of binary-only modules.

Along with the new architecture, XFree86 is now based on X11R6.4, the latest version of X11 from X.Org. Some of the improvements include multi-head displays (XINERAMA), simpler resource configuration, Display Power Management Signal (DPMS) for energy-saving monitors, reduced memory requirements, and additional Application Programming Interfaces (APIs, or functions).

This new release of XFree86 also provides new configuration utilities, such as the `xf86cfg` client, and also offers built-in configuration facilities in the main server, the `XFree86` client! Newer graphics cards are now supported, and although most older cards are still supported, not all legacy drivers have been ported to the new system. Also new with this release is code to enable Direct Rendering Infrastructure, or DRI support for 3D graphics.

Font support has also been improved. The new server architecture now supports Internationalization (ISO fonts), along with TrueType and Type 1 fonts, through the use of the loadable modules `freetype` and `xtt` (see the description of the "Modules" section of XF86Config later in this chapter).

XFree86 is normally installed on your system during installation, although this is optional, depending on the type of install selected for your computer. After installation, you'll find the majority of components under the `/usr/X11R6/` directory. Listing, 4.1 shows an abbreviated directory tree of the new software (not all the directories are shown).

LISTING 4.1   XFree86 4.0.1 Directory Tree

```
X11R6
|-- bin
|-- doc
|-- include
|-- lib
|    |-- X11
|    |    |-- doc
|    |    |-- fonts
|    |-- modules
|    |    |-- codeconv
|    |    |-- dri
|    |    |-- drivers
|    |    |    `-- linux
|    |    |-- extensions
|    |    |-- fonts
|    |    |-- input
|    |    `-- linux
|-- man
|    |-- man1
|    |-- man3
|    |-- man4
|    |-- man5
|    |-- man6
|    `-- man7
`-- share
```

Note the `/usr/X11R6/lib/modules/drivers` directory in Listing 4.1. This is the location for the new loadable modules used with XFree86. You'll also find various modules under the `input` directory to support devices such as touchpads and drawing tablets. Other directories under the `/usr/X11R6` tree include

`/usr/X11R6/bin`	Where most (but not all) X11 clients are stored
`/usr/X11R6/include`	Programming header files and directories of bitmaps and pixmaps

/usr/X11R6/include/doc	Documentation and release notes
/usr/X11R6/lib	X11 software libraries needed by X clients and programmers
/usr/X11R6/man	X manual pages

If you installed and configured X11 when you first installed Red Hat Linux, you'll find that most of the X Window System resides under the /usr/X11R6 directory (although a number of GNOME and KDE clients will be found under /usr/bin).

If you have an older version of X11 installed, you can use Red Hat's rpm command to upgrade X. First, you'll need to remove your existing XFree86 installation. You should first find all your XFree86 package names. You can do this easily by using rpm command's query option and the fgrep command like this (your output may look different):

```
# rpm -qa | fgrep XFree

XFree86-libs-4.0.1-1
XFree86-devel-4.0.1-1
XFree86-ISO8859-2-75dpi-fonts-4.0.1-1
XFree86-ISO8859-7-75dpi-fonts-1.0-7
XFree86-ISO8859-9-75dpi-fonts-2.1.2-13
XFree86-75dpi-fonts-4.0.1-1
XFree86-tools-4.0.1-1
XFree86-xdm-4.0.1-1
XFree86-100dpi-fonts-4.0.1-1
XFree86-ISO8859-2-1.0-12
XFree86-ISO8859-2-Type1-fonts-1.0-12
XFree86-ISO8859-7-1.0-7
XFree86-ISO8859-7-Type1-fonts-1.0-7
XFree86-ISO8859-9-2.1.2-13
XFree86-VGA16-3.3.6-33
XFree86-doc-4.0.1-1
XFree86-xfs-4.0.1-1
XFree86-4.0.1-1
XFree86-twm-4.0.1-1
XFree86-ISO8859-2-100dpi-fonts-1.0-12
XFree86-ISO8859-7-100dpi-fonts-1.0-7
XFree86-ISO8859-9-100dpi-fonts-2.1.2-13
XFree86-cyrillic-fonts-4.0.1-1
```

You can then erase various packages at a time by using the rpm command and its -e or erase option, along with a wildcard .rpm package name, like this:

```
# rpm -e XFree*ISO*
```

Next, insert the first Red Hat CD-ROM and make it available on your system using the mount command (it may also be mounted automatically):

```
# mount /mnt/cdrom
```

Since Red Hat Linux provides an entry in the filesystem table /etc/fstab, you could also mount the CD-ROM under the /mnt/cdrom directory by specifying your system's CD-ROM device, /dev/cdrom (a symbolic link to your CD-ROM's device), like this:

```
# mount /dev/cdrom
```

From the command line, use rpm like this:

```
# rpm -Uvh /mnt/cdrom/RedHat/RPMS/XFree86*rpm
```

If you did not install X, you can use Red Hat's rpm command to install the software. However, you should know that the process will involve solving many .rpm package dependencies!

Note

You can also try using the gnorpm command to install the software. Select Preferences and then set the interface preference RPM path to the RPMS directory on your mounted Red Hat CD-ROM. KDE also includes a similar package manager client named kpackage.

Depending on the software installed, these directories can take up 40–400MB of hard drive space, and even more if you install a lot of X window managers, programming libraries, or other software. (A typical full installation of XFree86 is about 80-123MB, depending on the number of extra clients.)

Choosing a Configuration Tool

The largest hurdle most new X users face after installing XFree86 is coming up with a working XF86Config file. This file can be initially generated during your install, but if you have a problematic graphics chipset, you may need to "tweak" your configuration after booting, or may even want to postpone configuring X11 until after you first log in.

This is sometimes the safest approach; trying to log in to a Linux system configured to boot directly to X11 without a properly configured system can be confounding. Fortunately, if you run into this problem, you can simply press Ctrl+Alt+Delete, reboot, then either press Ctrl+X at the Red Hat LILO login, or pass the kernel argument linux single at the LILO boot prompt like this:

```
boot: linux single
```

If you already have a working setup, chances are your old XFree86 3.3.6 XF86Config may work, as there is some compatibility built into the new server. However, the new version of XFree86 uses a new layout and structure for the XF86Config file!

If you're starting from scratch, one of the first things you should do after installing X and before configuration is to read as much of the documentation as possible. Although the daring and brave will launch right into configuring X11, even experienced users will benefit from reading about the latest XFree86 developments and checking the XFree86 documentation for tips about their specific hardware.

Documentation at the time of this writing was still a bit sparse, but you will find information under the /usr/X11R6/lib/X11/doc directory. Table 4.1 contains the details of this directory for XFree86 4.0.1. Note that documentation for the release is still somewhat sparse; just because you don't see a README file for your graphics chipset does not mean that it is not supported! This is true for Cirrus Logic, NeoMagic, Tseng, and Trident chipsets. You'll find detailed information regarding protocols, libraries, clients, and other services under the /usr/share/doc/XFree86-doc-4.0.1 directory.

TABLE 4.1 XFree86 Documentation

File	Description
DESIGN	Extensive server design information
LICENSE	Licensing and copyright statement
README	General information about the current XFree86 release
README.DECtga	Information for DEC 21030 users
README.DGA	How to program for the XFree86 DGA interface
README.DRI	Information about DRI support
README.DRIcomp	Compilation information about DRI
README.S3	Notes for S3 chipset users
README.s3virge	Notes for S3 ViRGE, ViRGE/DX, ViRGE/GX, ViRGE/MX, and ViRGE/VX users
README.SiS	Notes for SiS chipset users
README.apm	Notes about the Alliance Promotion chipset
README.ati	Information about XFree86's ATI Adapters video drivers
README.chips	Notes about Chips and Technologies chipsets
README.cyrix	Info for Cyrix MeidaGX users
README.fonts	Using fonts with XFree86
README.i740	Info for Intel 740-based graphics cards
README.i810	Info regarding Intel 810 motherboards
README.mouse	Details about XFree86's X11 mouse support
README.r128	ATI Rage 128 information

TABLE 4.1   continued

File	Description
README.rendition	Details about Rendition chipset users
RELNOTES	The definitive release notes for XFree86
ServersOnly	How your directories should look when building XFree86 X servers
Status	Driver status in the release
VideoBoard98	Info on the PC98 XFree86 server

If you're new to X11, first read the man pages for X and XFree86 for an overview of X. Before you begin configuring X, you need to know some technical details about your computer and your computer's video card and monitor. Here is some of the information that will help:

- The type, make, name, or model of video card installed in your computer
- How much video RAM (not system RAM) is installed for your card
- The type of clockchip used by your video card chipset
- The type of mouse you use (PS/2, serial, or USB, for example)
- The type, make, name, or model of monitor attached to your computer
- The vertical and horizontal refresh rates for your monitor (such as 55–100 vertical, 30–60 horizontal)
- The type of keyboard you use

Armed with this information, you then have to choose the method or tool for configuring XFree86 and generate a correct XF86Config file for your system. There are a number of ways to do this:

- XFree86   The main X11 server's built-in configuration facility
- Xconfigurator   Red Hat's graphical X11 setup tool
- xf86config   XFree86's traditional text-only tool
- xf86cfg   XFree86's graphical configuration client
- Manual   Create your own XF86Config with a favorite text editor

All these methods may be done from your console's command line or from a terminal window's command line.

Xconfigurator and xf86cfg have the advantage of providing a graphical interface; xf86config asks a series of questions in a text-mode screen; and XFree86 performs the configuration automagically. If you're lucky, your computer's hardware will exactly match the configuration generated by these programs. Problems can arise if the settings don't work, if you've entered incorrect information, or if your video chipset is not fully supported by the required module used by the XFree86 server.

In general, video hardware a couple years old will fare much better than "bleeding-edge" video cards because software contributors have had a chance to work with the video chipsets. Laptop users can also run into special problems, and it can be disheartening to buy the latest laptop, only to find that the embedded video system will not work with X—it pays to research!

Desktop users have the option of installing a new, supported video card. Laptop users should definitely check the Linux laptop user site at `http://www.cs.utexas.edu/users/kharker/linux-laptop`.

If you find you cannot get correct settings, or if your chipset is not supported, you can also buy a commercial X distribution from one of the vendors mentioned in the introduction. Finally, your last resort is to whine at, plead with, cajole, or bribe a knowledgeable programmer to build a module for you from the XFree86 sources (but this rarely works).

Remember: The aim is to generate the best possible working `XF86Config` file for your needs!

The `XF86Config` File

Without a doubt, the most important configuration file for XFree86 is the `XF86Config` file. This file is used to properly feed font, keyboard, mouse, video chipset module, monitor capabilities, and color-depth setting information to the XFree86 server. When you start an X session, your X server will search for this file. `XF86Config`, although normally located under the `/etc/X11` directory, may also be located under the `/usr/X11R6/lib/X11` directory, the `/etc` directory, the `/usr/X11R6/etc/X11` directory, or a directory pointed to by the environment variable `$XF86CONFIG` or `$HOME`.

`XF86Config` is a single text file, consisting of several sections:

- ServerLayout—Defines the configuration files, the screen, or display used, along with the two major input devices—the keyboard and mouse. You may have multiple ServerLayout sections (which can be specified through the servers `-layout` command-line option).

- Files—Tells the X server where fonts, colors, or modules are located; required for font use. Note that Red Hat Linux also uses the `xfs` font server, and that its configuration file, `config`, is found under the `/etc/X11/fs` directory.

- Module—Tells the X server what special modules should be loaded and options to be used. Not required, but useful.

- ServerFlags—You can use nearly 20 different on/off flags that allow or deny special actions, such as core dumps; specify power-management settings; control video-mode switching and video tuning; or use of a mouse. Not required, but a good idea.

- InputDevice—There may be one or more InputDevice sections to tell the X server what keyboard, mouse, or other pointing/drawing device to expect and what settings to use. Required, although the `AllowMouseOpenFail ServerFlags` option will allow the server to start without a mouse.

- Monitor—Specific details and settings for your monitor, such as name, horizontal sync, and vertical sync ranges. Note that modelines for different video resolutions, such as 640×480, 800×600, and 1024×768 are no longer required and will be calculated automagically (although you can specify a modeline if required). This section is required.

- Modes—Multiple Modes sections are allowed, and may be used to define alternate, independent video modes. Not required.

- Device—Details about your video chipset, such as clockchips, RAM, memory locations, and other options, along with the proper driver to use. There may be multiple Device sections; at least one is required.

- Videoadaptor—Undocumented (as yet). Not required.

- Screen—Tells what display and monitor to use, the color depth (such as 8-, 16-, 24-, or 32-bits per pixel), screen size (such as 640×480, 800×600, or 1024×768), and the size of the virtual screen. Required, and you may have multiple definitions and sections.

- Vendor—Provides vendor-specific information with an identifier and multiple options.

- DRI—Direct Rendering Infrastructure; if the `glx` and `dri` modules are loaded under the Module section, you can create a DRI section to contain specifics regarding use of the libraries.

- Keyboard or Pointer—Obviated, but still allowed for compatibility. Not required.

To learn more about the `XF86Config` file, read the `XF86Config` man page.

Using the XFree86 Server

One of the new features of XFree86 4.0.1 is that you can try using the `XFree86` to configure X11 automatically and create a working `XF86Config` file. Although this approach will not work for all graphics cards, you may find it a convenient way to configure and test your settings, especially if you've just installed a new graphics card in your system.

The XFree86 server has many different command-line options, but to create a test XF86Config file, first make sure that X11 is not running, and log in as the root operator. Next, make a backup of any working XF86Config file. Then use the server, along with its -configure option, like this:

```
# XFree86 -configure 2>test.txt
```

The server will create a report in the file test.txt that details the probe of your computer's graphics card and input hardware. For example, the file will contain results of loading various modules, a list of installed video drivers, results of loading each of the various drivers, file paths, probes of input hardware, and the result of the probe:

```
XFree86 Version 4.0.1 / X Window System
(protocol Version 11, revision 0, vendor release 6400)
...
(--) Chipset neo2200 found
...
```

During the configure operation, the server also creates a file named XF86Config.new under the /root directory. You can then test your new configuration by again using the server with its -xf86config command-line option, like this:

```
# XFree86 -xf86config /root/XF86Config.new
```

If the new XF86Config works, you can then copy it to the /etc/X11 directory, and hand-edit the file.

Using Xconfigurator

Red Hat's Xconfigurator generates an XF86Config file after it probes your system and asks several questions. This program may be used from the console (without X11) when you need to generate a new configuration file, such as after you change your computer's graphics card. You must run this program as the root operator. Start Xconfigurator from the command line of your console or from an X11 terminal window, like this:

```
# Xconfigurator
```

The screen clears and a dialog box appears, as shown in Figure 4.1.

Use the Tab key to navigate to different buttons on the screen, and then press Enter when the OK button is highlighted. Xconfigurator first probes to find your computer's graphics card, as shown in Figure 4.2.

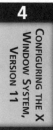

4

CONFIGURING THE X
WINDOW SYSTEM,
VERSION 11

FIGURE 4.1

Red Hat's Xconfigurator generates the required XF86Config *file for XFree86.*

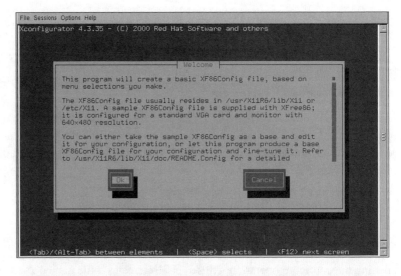

FIGURE 4.2

Xconfigurator reports on your video card with a small dialog box.

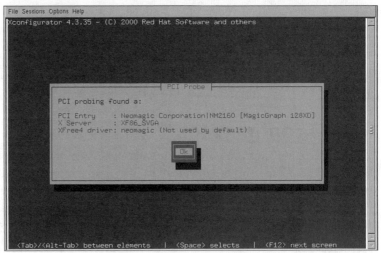

After you click OK, you are presented with a dialog box that asks for the type of monitor attached to your computer (see Figure 4.3). Nearly 1,800 monitors are listed in the Xconfigurator's database (found in the MonitorsDB file under the /usr/X11R6/share/ Xconfigurator directory). Desktop users will probably find their model listed. Scroll down the list until your model is highlighted and then click OK. Laptop users can try to select the different LCD Panel monitors from the list. If you have a desktop computer and your monitor is not listed, try to select a model that is close, or better yet, select the Custom monitor and enter the horizontal and vertical frequency specifications for your model (the information should be in your monitor's manual; if not, check with the manufacturer).

4

CONFIGURING THE X
WINDOW SYSTEM,
VERSION 11

FIGURE 4.3

Xconfigurator has nearly 1,800 monitors in its model database.

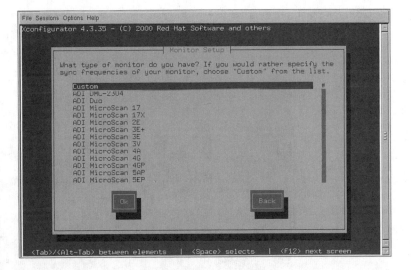

Don't panic if you don't find your monitor listed or are using a laptop. Select the Custom monitor and click OK. Xconfigurator presents an introductory dialog box. When you click OK, you're presented a list of monitor resolutions and frequencies, as shown in Figure 4.4.

FIGURE 4.4

Xconfigurator allows pre-selected or custom monitor settings.

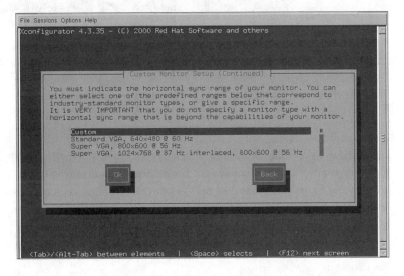

At this point, using Xconfigurator might be somewhat confusing. Although the program says a horizontal frequency is being selected, you are asked to select a video resolution and monitor frequency. The best bet is to pick a resolution you know is supported by your monitor and click OK, otherwise select the Custom item. If you're not sure the correct information for your monitor will be inserted into your XF86Config file (which

Xconfigurator will create after you've finished entering all the information), make sure to edit and change the inserted horizontal frequency settings before starting your first X session.

The next dialog box, shown in Figure 4.5, asks for the horizontal and vertical frequency ranges of your monitor. Click OK when finished.

FIGURE 4.5

Xconfigurator offers custom frequency monitor settings.

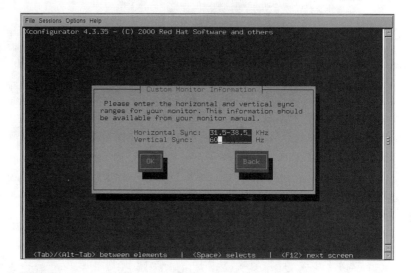

The next dialog box (shown in Figure 4.6) asks how much video memory your graphics card has. In general, the more video memory you have, the higher resolution or color depth supported by your computer. If you have upgradable video memory, you may benefit by adding memory (depending on your monitor and support by the XFree86 server for your video chipset).

Interestingly, no matter what memory value you select, the XFree86 server should automatically recognize the amount of installed memory. In some cases—especially where the correct video RAM values are not correctly probed at startup by the server, or if you want to reserve parts of video memory—you can edit XF86Config manually to use your selected memory setting. Select the currently installed amount of memory and click OK.

Xconfigurator next asks for the type of clockchip in your video subsystem (see Figure 4.7). If you're not sure whether your video card uses clockchip settings, select No Clockchip Setting.

If you're sure about the type of clockchip used (by checking your video card or computer documentation), select one of the 12 clockchips listed and click OK.

FIGURE 4.6

Xconfigurator offers eight video memory configurations.

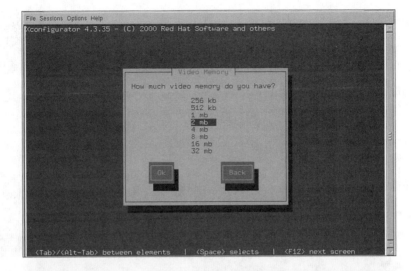

FIGURE 4.7

Xconfigurator lists 12 clockchips.

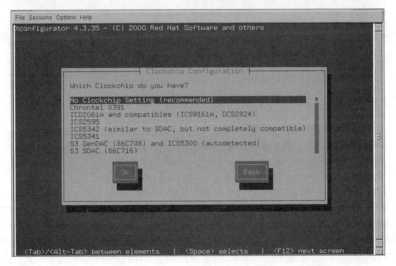

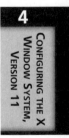

After probing your video, Xconfigurator will ask (as shown in Figure 4.8) for the desired video resolutions (such as 800×600) and color depths (such as 8 bit, or 256 colors, or 16 bit for thousands of colors). Select different settings by navigating with your Tab and cursor keys and pressing the spacebar. You can also choose to select what you think is the best setting possible. If you choose multiple resolutions at different color depths, you may be able to use the XFree86 "Zoom" feature to change resolutions on-the-fly during you X11 sessions (by using Ctrl+Alt+ the Keypad's plus (+) or minus (–) keys). Do not select video resolutions greater than allowed by your monitor unless you want to use *virtual resolutions* (in which your display becomes a movable window on a large display).

When you're finished, click OK.

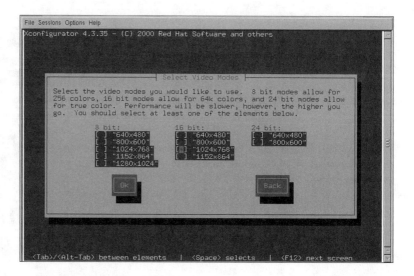

In the next step, Xconfigurator attempts to start X in order to test your settings (as shown in Figure 4.9). You can skip the test or press OK to start the X server. If you skip the test, Xconfigurator then creates and saves your XF86Config file, saving it under the /etc/X11 directory.

After you start the test (which uses the Xtest client found under the /usr/X11R6/bin directory), the screen clears and you may see a small dialog box. The dialog box asks if you can see this message. If you click Yes, you are then asked if you want to automatically start X upon booting. If you choose Yes, your Red Hat Linux system initialization table (the file inittab under the /etc directory) is modified to boot Linux directly to runlevel 5 (see Chapter 9, "System Startup and Shutdown" for details). You then need to log in through the gdm or GNOME display manager (discussed in Chapter 5, "Window Managers"). If you click No, you have to use the startx command to begin your X sessions.

After clicking Yes or No, Xconfigurator then creates and saves your XF86Config file under the /etc/X11 directory before quitting.

Using the `xf86cfg` Command

The `xf86cfg` command is a new client included with the XFree86 X11 distribution that you can use to configure X11. The command will launch an X11 session using the `twm` window manager, and offers a graphical interface to setting up your `XF86Config` file. You can launch the client by using the command line like this:

`# xf86cfg`

After you press Enter, the screen will clear, and you may (or may not) see a dialog you can use to configure various components. Note that this client is a "work-in-progress"; if it works on your computer, great! If not, try using a different method to configure your `XF86Config`. The `xf86cfg` command, like the XFree86 server, will create a file named `XF86Config.new` under the `/root` directory.

Using the `xf86config` Command

XFree86 also comes with an improved version of its legacy configuration command, `xf86config`, found under the `/usr/X11R6/bin` directory. This command works from the command line of your console or an X11 terminal window. Start the command like this:

`# xf86config`

After you press Enter, you'll see:

```
This program will create a basic XF86Config file, based on menu selections you
make.

The XF86Config file usually resides in /usr/X11R6/etc/X11 or /etc/X11. A sample
XF86Config file is supplied with XFree86; it is configured for a standard
VGA card and monitor with 640x480 resolution. This program will ask for a
pathname when it is ready to write the file.

You can either take the sample XF86Config as a base and edit it for your
configuration, or let this program produce a base XF86Config file for your
configuration and fine-tune it.

Before continuing with this program, make sure you know what video card
you have, and preferably also the chipset it uses and the amount of video
memory on your video card. SuperProbe may be able to help with this.

Press enter to continue, or ctrl-c to abort.
```

Press Enter again. You'll then get the mouse configuration screen, which contains this text:

```
First specify a mouse protocol type. Choose one from the following list:

1.  Microsoft compatible (2-button protocol)
2.  Mouse Systems (3-button protocol)
```

4

CONFIGURING THE X
WINDOW SYSTEM,
VERSION 11

```
3.  Bus Mouse
4.  PS/2 Mouse
5.  Logitech Mouse (serial, old type, Logitech protocol)
6.  Logitech MouseMan (Microsoft compatible)
7.  MM Series
8.  MM HitTablet
9.  Microsoft IntelliMouse

If you have a two-button mouse, it is most likely of type 1, and if you have
a three-button mouse, it can probably support both protocol 1 and 2. There are
two main varieties of the latter type: mice with a switch to select the
protocol, and mice that default to 1 and require a button to be held at
boot-time to select protocol 2. Some mice can be convinced to do 2 by sending
a special sequence to the serial port (see the ClearDTR/ClearRTS options).

Enter a protocol number: 4
```

As you can see, you have a choice of nine different pointers. If you use a USB mouse, don't worry! You can still configure X11 to use your pointer. For now, enter a number corresponding with your pointer and press Enter. You're asked whether you want three-button emulation:

```
If your mouse has only two buttons, it is recommended that you enable
Emulate3Buttons.

Please answer the following question with either 'y' or 'n'.
Do you want to enable Emulate3Buttons? y
```

Press the y key if desired, followed by the Enter key. Next you're asked for the Linux device corresponding with your pointer. For Red Hat users, this is /dev/mouse.

```
Now give the full device name that the mouse is connected to, for example
/dev/tty00. Just pressing enter will use the default, /dev/mouse.

Mouse device:
```

If you have a different pointer, enter its device name from the /dev directory and press Enter. The xf86config command follows up and asks about your choice of keyboards:

```
Please select one of the following keyboard types that is the better
description of your keyboard. If nothing really matches,
choose 1 (Generic 101-key PC)

  1  Generic 101-key PC
  2  Generic 102-key (Intl) PC
  3  Generic 104-key PC
  4  Generic 105-key (Intl) PC
  5  Dell 101-key PC
  6  Everex STEPnote
  7  Keytronic FlexPro
  8  Microsoft Natural
  9  Northgate OmniKey 101
```

```
10   Winbook Model XP5
11   Japanese 106-key
12   PC-98xx Series

Enter a number to choose the keyboard. 1
```

After you choose a keyboard, `xf86config` then asks you to choose a country (or language) for the keyboard:

```
 1   U.S. English
 2   U.S. English w/ISO9995-3
 3   Belgian
 4   Bulgarian
 5   Canadian
 6   Czech
 7   German
 8   Swiss German
 9   Danish
10   Spanish
11   Finnish
12   French
13   Swiss French
14   United Kingdom
15   Hungarian
16   Italian
17   Japanese
18   Norwegian

Enter a number to choose the country.
Press enter for the next page
```

If you do not see your country listed, press Enter again:

```
19   Polish
20   Portugese
21   Russian
22   Slovak
23   Swedish
24   Thai
25   PC-98xx Series

Enter a number to choose the country.
Press enter for the next page
1
```

After choosing your language, you'll then be presented with a short introductory screen before being asked for your monitor's specifics.

```
Now we want to set the specifications of the monitor. The two critical
parameters are the vertical refresh rate, which is the rate at which
the whole screen is refreshed, and most importantly the horizontal sync rate,
which is the rate at which scanlines are displayed.
```

The valid range for horizontal sync and vertical sync should be documented
in the manual of your monitor. If in doubt, check the monitor database
/usr/X11R6/lib/X11/doc/Monitors to see if your monitor is there.

Press enter to continue, or ctrl-c to abort.

Press the Enter key, and you'll see the following text:

You must indicate the horizontal sync range of your monitor. You can either
select one of the predefined ranges below that correspond to industry-
standard monitor types, or give a specific range.

It is VERY IMPORTANT that you do not specify a monitor type with a horizontal
sync range that is beyond the capabilities of your monitor. If in doubt,
choose a conservative setting.

```
    hsync in kHz; monitor type with characteristic modes
1   31.5; Standard VGA, 640x480 @ 60 Hz
2   31.5 - 35.1; Super VGA, 800x600 @ 56 Hz
3   31.5, 35.5; 8514 Compatible, 1024x768 @ 87 Hz interlaced (no 800x600)
4   31.5, 35.15, 35.5; Super VGA, 1024x768 @ 87 Hz interlaced, 800x600 @ 56 Hz
5   31.5 - 37.9; Extended Super VGA, 800x600 @ 60 Hz, 640x480 @ 72 Hz
6   31.5 - 48.5; Non-Interlaced SVGA, 1024x768 @ 60 Hz, 800x600 @ 72 Hz
7   31.5 - 57.0; High Frequency SVGA, 1024x768 @ 70 Hz
8   31.5 - 64.3; Monitor that can do 1280x1024 @ 60 Hz
9   31.5 - 79.0; Monitor that can do 1280x1024 @ 74 Hz
10  31.5 - 82.0; Monitor that can do 1280x1024 @ 76 Hz
11  Enter your own horizontal sync range

Enter your choice (1-11): 11
```

Enter a number corresponding to your monitor's characteristics. If you prefer, enter the
number 11 to give a specific horizontal sync range. You then see this text:

Please enter the horizontal sync range of your monitor, in the format used
in the table of monitor types above. You can either specify one or more
continuous ranges (e.g. 15-25, 30-50), or one or more fixed sync frequencies.

Horizontal sync range: 31.5-37.9

Press the Enter key. You are then asked to enter the vertical range.

You must indicate the vertical sync range of your monitor. You can either
select one of the predefined ranges below that correspond to industry-
standard monitor types, or give a specific range. For interlaced modes,
the number that counts is the high one (e.g. 87 Hz rather than 43 Hz).

```
1   50-70
2   50-90
3   50-100
4   40-150
5   Enter your own vertical sync range

Enter your choice: 5
```

If you prefer to enter your own range, choose 5 and press the Enter key. Now you'll see this text:

```
Vertical sync range: 50-70
```

Enter your monitor's vertical range, such as 50-70, and press the Enter key. You are asked to enter three lines of description for your monitor. Enter a description, as well as your monitor's manufacturer and model. You can also just press the Enter key; this information is not critical.

```
You must now enter a few identification/description strings, namely an
identifier, a vendor name, and a model name. Just pressing enter will fill
in default names.

The strings are free-form, spaces are allowed.
Enter an identifier for your monitor definition:
Enter the vendor name of your monitor:
Enter the model name of your monitor:
```

After you enter the model name and press the Enter key, xf86config presents an introduction dialog box to video card selection and asks if you want to look at the card database:

```
Now we must configure video card specific settings. At this point you can
choose to make a selection out of a database of video card definitions.
Because there can be variation in Ramdacs and clock generators even
between cards of the same model, it is not sensible to blindly copy
the settings (e.g. a Device section). For this reason, after you make a
selection, you will still be asked about the components of the card, with
the settings from the chosen database entry presented as a strong hint.

The database entries include information about the chipset, what server to
run, the Ramdac and ClockChip, and comments that will be included in the
Device section. However, a lot of definitions only hint about what server
to run (based on the chipset the card uses) and are untested.

If you can't find your card in the database, there's nothing to worry about.
You should only choose a database entry that is exactly the same model as
your card; choosing one that looks similar is just a bad idea (e.g. a
GemStone Snail 64 may be as different from a GemStone Snail 64+ in terms of
hardware as can be).

Do you want to look at the card database?  y
```

You'll see the following list of the first 18 video cards in XFree86's card database of more than 700 cards(!) (located in the file Cards, under the /usr/X11R6/lib/X11 directory):

```
0   2 the Max MAXColor S3 Trio64V+              S3 Trio64V+
1   3DLabs Oxygen GMX                           PERMEDIA 2
2   3DVision-i740 AGP                           Intel 740
3   3Dlabs Permedia2 (generic)                  PERMEDIA 2
```

```
 4   928Movie                              S3 928
 5   ABIT G740 8MB SDRAM                    Intel 740
 6   AGP 2D/3D V. 1N, AGP-740D              Intel 740
 7   AGX (generic)                         AGX-014/15/16
 8   ALG-5434(E)                           CL-GD5434
 9   AOpen AGP 2X 3D Navigator PA740        Intel 740
10   AOpen PA2010                          Voodoo Banshee
11   AOpen PA45                            SiS6326
12   AOpen PA50D                           SiS6326
13   AOpen PA50E                           SiS6326
14   AOpen PA50V                           SiS6326
15   AOpen PA80/DVD                        SiS6326
16   AOpen PG128                           S3 Trio3D
17   AOpen PG975                           3dimage975

Enter a number to choose the corresponding card definition.
Press enter for the next page, q to continue configuration.
```

Your choices are to enter a number corresponding to your card (or a card recommended as a close choice by the README file for your card under the /usr/X11R6/lib/X11/doc directory), to press the Enter key to page to the next screen, or to press q to continue the configuration. Note that if you press q, xf86config uses Unknown for your graphics device. On the other hand, if you pick a specific card, xf86config reports with an identifier, chipset, and selected driver appropriate for your chipset.

```
Your selected card definition:

Identifier: NeoMagic 256 (laptop/notebook)
Chipset:    MagicMedia 256 series
Driver:     neomagic

Press enter to continue, or ctrl-c to abort.
```

Next, you're asked to enter the amount of video memory installed in your graphics card:

```
Now you must give information about your video card. This will be used for
the "Device" section of your video card in XF86Config.

You must indicate how much video memory you have. It is probably a good
idea to use the same approximate amount as that detected by the server you
intend to use. If you encounter problems that are due to the used server
not supporting the amount of memory you have (e.g. ATI Mach64 is limited to
1024K with the SVGA server), specify the maximum amount supported by the
server.

How much video memory do you have on your video card:

1   256K
2   512K
3   1024K
```

```
4  2048K
5  4096K
6  Other
```

`Enter your choice:`

Either enter a number corresponding to the amount of memory or enter **6**, press Enter, and then enter the amount of memory, in kilobytes, supported by your card. Note that your video RAM value should be probed correctly by the X server.

You're asked to enter information as you did for your monitor, but now about your video card:

```
You must now enter a few identification/description strings, namely an
identifier, a vendor name, and a model name. Just pressing enter will fill
in default names (possibly from a card definition).

Your card definition is NeoMagic 256 (laptop/notebook).

The strings are free-form, spaces are allowed.
Enter an identifier for your video card definition:
You can simply press enter here if you have a generic card, or want to
describe your card with one string.
Enter the vendor name of your video card:
Enter the model (board) name of your video card:
```

Again, it's not necessary to fill out this information. After pressing the Enter key, you're asked if you want to change the resolutions for each color depth supported by your computer's video card:

```
For each depth, a list of modes (resolutions) is defined. The default
resolution that the server will start-up with will be the first listed
mode that can be supported by the monitor and card.
Currently it is set to:

"640x480" "800x600" "1024x768" "1280x1024" for 8-bit
"640x480" "800x600" "1024x768" for 16-bit
"640x480" "800x600" for 24-bit

Modes that cannot be supported due to monitor or clock constraints will
be automatically skipped by the server.

1  Change the modes for 8-bit (256 colors)
2  Change the modes for 16-bit (32K/64K colors)
3  Change the modes for 24-bit (24-bit color)
4  The modes are OK, continue.
```

`Enter your choice:`

If you choose to change some of the settings, you're asked to choose specific resolutions for each color depth and whether you'd like a virtual screen size larger than your display (such as an 800×600 virtual screen when using a 640×480 display). Change the settings for each mode by pressing a key (1 through 4; press 5 to accept the defaults) and then press Enter to continue.

You'll then be asked for a default color depth to use:

```
Please specify which color depth you want to use by default:

    1   1 bit (monochrome)
    2   4 bits (16 colors)
    3   8 bits (256 colors)
    4   16 bits (65536 colors)
    5   24 bits (16 million colors)

Enter a number to choose the default depth.
4
```

The `xf86config` command asks if you want to save the generated `XF86Config` file. Enter a **y** and press Enter—you're done.

```
I am going to write the XF86Config file now. Make sure you don't accidentally
overwrite a previously configured one.

Shall I write it to /etc/X11/XF86Config? y
```

Finally, if you don't want to use Xconfigurator, `xf86cfg`, or `xf86config` to generate an `XF86Config` file, you can create your own. You'll find a template file, `XF86Config.eg`, under the `/usr/X11R6/lib/X11` directory. Copy this file to your directory and edit it in your favorite text editor, inserting specifications for your system and X server.

Examining the XF86Config File

Before you try to start an X11 session using your new `XF86Config` settings, open the file in your favorite text editor, making sure to disable line wrapping, and check the settings. Doing this is essential, especially for laptop users, in order to check the created settings, enable or disable some X server graphics chipset-specific options, enter the correct amount of video memory, and fine-tune monitor or display settings. For example, you can open the file (as the root operator) with the `pico` text editor like this:

```
# pico -w /etc/X11/XF86Config
```

This section highlights some additional information and options you can use in your `XF86Config`, and found in the example `XF86Config.eg` file under the `/usr/X11R6/lib/X11` directory. For a detailed overview, and the latest format and options you can use in your `XF86Config` file, see the `XF86Config` man page.

Handy Command-Line Diagnostics

A handy way to diagnose your XF86Config settings before you start your first X session is to use a tip detailed by Eric S. Raymond in his *XFree86-HOWTO*. This method saves the output of the X server while it starts up and reads your XF86Config. You can save the output to a file such as myX11.txt with a command line like this: **X > myX11.txt 2>&1**. If you jump into your X session, kill the session by holding down the Alt+Ctrl keys and pressing the Backspace key. You can then read the X server's output with the more-or-less command less myX11.txt to ensure that everything is okay. This command is handy because the output normally scrolls too fast to be read.

XF86Config ServerLayout Section

The ServerLayout section is useful for describing one or more instances of an X session, and can be essential if you want to use one or more input devices or displays for your session. This section's use coincides with the new server's -layout command-line option (using the "Identifier" definition). This section is in the form:

```
# ServerLayout
Section "ServerLayout"
        Identifier              "Main Layout"
        Screen  0        "Screen0" 0 0
        InputDevice      "Mouse0" "CorePointer"
        InputDevice      "Keyboard0" "CoreKeyboard"
EndSection
```

If you want to define a layout with multiple displays, include two or more Screen definitions, then specify the screens in order from top, bottom, left, and right. To use more than one input device, use multiple InputDevice definitions, and specify "SendCoreEvents" as an option for the second device.

XF86Config Files Section

The Files section tells the X server the location of the color name database, system fonts, and location of modules.

```
" Files
Section "Files"
    RgbPath        "/usr/X11R6/lib/X11/rgb"

    FontPath       "unix/:-1"
    FontPath       "/usr/X11R6/lib/X11/fonts/local/"
    FontPath       "/usr/X11R6/lib/X11/fonts/misc/"
    FontPath       "/usr/X11R6/lib/X11/fonts/75dpi/:unscaled"
```

```
    FontPath      "/usr/X11R6/lib/X11/fonts/100dpi/:unscaled"
    FontPath      "/usr/X11R6/lib/X11/fonts/Type1/"
    FontPath      "/usr/X11R6/lib/X11/fonts/CID/"
    FontPath      "/usr/X11R6/lib/X11/fonts/Speedo/"
    FontPath      "/usr/X11R6/lib/X11/fonts/75dpi/"
    FontPath      "/usr/X11R6/lib/X11/fonts/100dpi/"
EndSection
```

Note that multiple font paths may be included. XFree86 now includes support for Type 1 and TrueType fonts. To enable this support, you'll need to have the following entries under the Module section:

```
    Load          "type1"
    Load          "freetype"
```

This will enable applications to take advantage of the font-rendering capabilities of the server. You should also use the xfs font server to provide fonts to the X server. Details about the design and operation of the xfs font server are found in the design.PS.gz file under the /usr/share/doc/XFree86-doc-4.0.1/xfs directory. The xfs configuration file is found under the /etc/X11/fs directory and is named config. This file includes a list of font directories under a catalogue entry, like this:

```
catalogue = /usr/X11R6/lib/X11/fonts/misc:unscaled,
        /usr/X11R6/lib/X11/fonts/75dpi:unscaled,
        /usr/X11R6/lib/X11/fonts/100dpi:unscaled,
        /usr/X11R6/lib/X11/fonts/misc,
        /usr/X11R6/lib/X11/fonts/Type1,
        /usr/X11R6/lib/X11/fonts/Speedo,
        /usr/X11R6/lib/X11/fonts/cyrillic,
        /usr/X11R6/lib/X11/fonts/TrueType,
        /usr/X11R6/lib/X11/fonts/75dpi,
        /usr/share/fonts/default/TrueType,
        /usr/share/fonts/default/Type1,
        /usr/X11R6/lib/X11/fonts/latin2/75dpi:unscaled,
        /usr/X11R6/lib/X11/fonts/latin2/100dpi:unscaled,
        /usr/X11R6/lib/X11/fonts/latin2/75dpi,
        /usr/X11R6/lib/X11/fonts/latin2/100dpi,
        /usr/X11R6/lib/X11/fonts/100dpi,
        /usr/share/fonts/ISO8859-9/misc:unscaled,
        /usr/share/fonts/ISO8859-9/75dpi:unscaled,
        /usr/share/fonts/ISO8859-9/100dpi:unscaled,
        /usr/share/fonts/ISO8859-9/misc,
        /usr/share/fonts/ISO8859-9/75dpi,
        /usr/share/fonts/ISO8859-9/100dpi,
        /usr/share/fonts/ISO8859-2/misc:unscaled,
        /usr/share/fonts/ISO8859-2/misc,
        /usr/share/fonts/ISO8859-2/Type1,
        /usr/share/fonts/ISO8859-7/misc:unscaled,
        /usr/share/fonts/ISO8859-7/75dpi:unscaled,
```

```
/usr/share/fonts/ISO8859-7/100dpi:unscaled,
/usr/share/fonts/ISO8859-7/misc,
/usr/share/fonts/ISO8859-7/Type1,
/usr/share/fonts/ISO8859-7/75dpi,
/usr/share/fonts/ISO8859-7/100dpi
```

As you can see, you'll find additional fonts for X11 installed under the /usr/share/fonts directory. The ISO8859-2 fonts are part of a collection of nearly 400 central European (or Latin 2) fonts, and provide support for encoding characters in nearly a dozen Slavic and Central European languages.

You can verify the inclusion and availability of these fonts with the xfontsel client. Use xfontsel like this at the command line of a terminal window:

 # xfontsel

You'll see a window (as shown in Figure 4.10) from which you can select different foundry and families of fonts (by clicking fmly).

FIGURE 4.10

Use the xfontsel *client's dialog buttons to view one of the 4,891 variations of X11 fonts included with Red Hat Linux.*

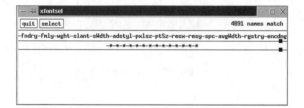

XF86Config Module Section

The Module section is used to load server and rendering support, and specifies the names of modules to load from the /usr/X11R6/lib/modules directory:

```
# Module
Section "Module"
        Load    "GLcore"
        Load    "dbe"
        Load    "dri"
        Load    "extmod"
        Load    "glx"
        Load    "pex5"
        Load    "record"
        Load    "xie"
        Load    "type1"
        Load    "freetype"
EndSection
```

In this example, nearly all rendering and drawing support libraries are loaded, along with support for Type1 and TrueType fonts. The software libraries reside under the `/usr/X11R6/lib/modules/extensions` directory, and not all are required for proper windowing support for your X11 window manager. For example, don't load the `dri` module if you do not use an accelerated 3D graphics card.

This new approach to providing support for new graphics hardware in the form of loadable modules is already being used by some manufacturers. For example, 3dfx Interactive, Inc., manufacturer of the Voodoo and Banshee line of graphics cards, provides numerous links and modules to support its new hardware under XFree86 4.0.1. Browse to `http://linux.3dfx.com` for more details.

XF86Config ServerFlags Section

The ServerFlags section can be used to configure special actions allowed by your XFree86 X server. Enable a particular action by including the `Option` keyword, followed by the desired option. Some options should generally not be enabled, such as disabling the ability to kill the server session (`"DontZap"`):

```
Section "ServerFlags"
#    Option      "DontZap"
#    Option      "DontZoom"
     Option      "blank time"    "10"    # 10 minutes
     Option      "standby time"  "20"
     Option      "suspend time"  "30"
     Option      "off time"      "60"
#    Option      "NoPM"
     Option      "AllowMouseOpenFail"
EndSection
```

Not all the available options are shown. The `"DontZoom"` feature may be disabled if you use X in only one video resolution, such as 800×600 pixels. However, you should note the new options to control screensaving (`"blank time"`) and DPMS. You can use these settings to control your display for power saving. The `"NoPM"` option disables DPMS. The `"AllowMouseOpenFail"` option allows the server to start without a pointer device.

XF86Config InputDevice Section

The InputDevice sections tell the X server to expect a keyboard and type of mouse. The XFree86 3.3.6-format Keyboard and Pointer sections are still recognized for compatibility, but the new InputDevice sections should be used in your `XF86Config` instead.

```
# InputDevice (keyboard)
Section "InputDevice"
        Identifier  "Keyboard0"
```

```
        Driver      "keyboard"
        Option      "XkbLayout"      "us"
EndSection

# InputDevice (PS/2 rodentiometer)
Section "InputDevice"
        Identifier  "Mouse0"
        Driver      "mouse"
#       Option      "auto"
        Option      "Device" "/dev/mouse"
        Option      "Protocol" "PS/2"
EndSection
```

In this example, a single keyboard, using US layout, and a single mouse, using PS/2 protocol, are defined for use during the X session. You may have multiple devices defined for use. The `"auto"` protocol option may be used if your system has Plug-and-Pray mouse detection.

To define a USB mouse, use the IMPS/2 device option (because Linux supports PS/2 mouse initialization), along with a pointer to the USB mouse device like this:

```
Section "InputDevice"
        Identifier  "Mouse0"
        Driver      "mouse"
        Option      "Protocol" "IMPS/2"
        Option      "Device" "/dev/input/mice"
EndSection
```

Note that you'll also want to run the gpm daemon with the proper settings before starting X:

```
# gpm -t ps2 -m /dev/input/mice
```

Of course, the best solution to install a USB mouse is to use the mouseconfig command. Two-button mouse users will definitely want to enable three-button emulation, in which a simultaneous pressing of both buttons simulates the middle (or Button 2) press. One common use of Button 2 is to paste text or graphics. For more information about configuring a mouse, see the file README.mouse under the /usr/X11R6/lib/X11/doc directory. Information regarding USB input devices will be found in the file input.txt under the /usr/share/doc/kernel-doc-2.2.16/usb directory.

XF86Config Monitor Section

The Monitor section contains details such as your monitor's identifier, vendor's name, model name, and horizontal and vertical sync ranges. Note that the legacy modelines (one for each video resolution) are no longer required! The XFree86 server should automatically calculate the correct timings and frequencies!

```
# Monitor
Section "Monitor"
        Identifier "LCD Panel 1024x768"
        VendorName "Unknown"
        ModelName  "Unknown"
        HorizSync 31.5-48.5
        VertRefresh 60
EndSection
```

However, if you need to include a modeline in the Monitor section, you can. This is especially helpful if you need to support an off-brand monitor or fine-tune your settings. The basic parts of a mode are different values representing (from left to right):

- A label of the screen resolution, such as 800×600
- A video frequency (DotClock) in MHz
- The number of visible dots per line on your display
- The Start Horizontal Retrace value (number of pulses before video sync pulse starts)
- The End Horizontal Retrace value (end of sync pulse)
- The total number of visible and invisible dots on your display
- The Vertical Display End value (number of visible lines of dots on your display)
- The Start Vertical Retrace value (number of lines before the sync pulse starts)
- The End Vertical Retrace value (number of lines at the end of the sync pulse)
- The Vertical Total value (total number of visible and invisible lines on your display):

```
Mode        "1024x768"
        DotClock   45
        HTimings   1024 1048 1208 1264
        VTimings    768  776  784  817
EndMode
```

This example defines a modeline for use with a 1024×768 display (perhaps a laptop or LCD panel monitor). Problems can arise when you're faced with crafting a custom modeline for a monitor or display that falls outside the range of normal displays. For example, what if your display is 1024×480 (such as for a Sony C1XS laptop)? In this case, you can try using Andreas Bohne's Web-based Modeline Calculator at http://www.dkfz-heidelberg.de/spec/linux/modeline/. Another, perhaps more flexible tool is Anders Ostrem's modeline command, found at http://home.kvalito.no/~bragthor/files/files.shtml.

XF86Config Device Section

The Device section details your video chipset, the proper driver to load for chipset support, the graphics card memory, frequency settings for a clockchip, and other options. This section of your XF86Config file is critical—the device definition is used to tell the X server exactly what type of video chipset and options to support. Note that your computer's Device section and Driver entry will certainly be different from this (for a NeoMagic laptop):

```
# Device
    Identifier  "NeoMagic Corporation|[MagicMedia 256AV]"
    Driver      "neomagic"
#   VideoRam    2048
#   Option      "intern_disp"
#   Option      "extern_disp"
#   Option      "lcd_center"
#   Option      "no_stretch"
EndSection
```

You may also have multiple Device sections defined in your XF86Config. This approach is used when you have more than one graphics card installed on your system, and want to use one or more displays. Also note that various Option entries may be included in the Device section.

Depending on the specified driver and your graphics chipset, you may find a number of options available for use. In the example, the "extern_disp" option may be used to enable the X session to be displayed on an external monitor (most likely by enabling a signal to the monitor port). You should always check your driver's documentation, in a README file under the /usr/X11R6/lib/X11/doc directory, man page, or through http://www.xfree86.org.

Some of the drivers included with XFree86 4.0.1 are listed in Table 4.2 (which was derived from the file named Status under the /usr/X11R6/lib/X11/doc directory. Note that the table reflects card support for the 4.0.1 release. Support for many more cards will be forthcoming in subsequent releases.

TABLE 4.2   XFree86 4.0.1 Drivers and Supported Cards

Driver	Card
apm	Alliance AT24, 25, 3D
ati	ATI Mach64 cards, others
chips	C&T 65520, 65525 65530, 65535, 65540, 65545, 65546, 65548, 65550, 65554, 69000, 64200, 64300
cirrus	Cirrus Logic Alpine and Laguna chipset

TABLE 4.2   continued

Driver	Card
glide	3dfx Voodoo 1, 2 graphics cards
glint	Permedia 2, 2v, GLINT 500TX, MX, Gamma, Delta
i740	Intel i740
i810	Intel i810 (requires agpgart kernel module)
mga	Matrox Millenium I, II, Mystique, G100, G200, G400
neomagic	NeoMagic NM-series (including 256AV)
nv	NVIDIAqRiva 238, 128ZX, TNT, TNT2, GeForce and Quadro
r128	ATI Rage 128
rendition	Redition/Micron Verite 1000, 2100, 2200
s3virge	S3 ViRGE, ViRGE/VX, DX, GX, GX2, MX, MX+, Trio3D, 2X
sis	SiS 530, 620, 6326 (partial support for 630, 300, 540)
tdfx	3dfx Voodoo 3, Banshee graphics cards
tga	DEC 21030 TGA
trident	Trident TVGA8900D, TGUI9420DGI, TGUI9440AGi, TGUI9660, TGUI9680, Providia 9685, Cyber9320, 9382, 9385, 9388, 9397, 9520, 9397/DVD, 9525/DVD, 3DImage975, 875, Blade3D, CyberBlade/i7, DSTN/i7 and i1
tseng	Tseng Labs ET4000AX, W32, W32i, W32p, ET6000, 6100
vga	IBM VGA and compatibles

XF86Config Screen Section

The XF86Config Screen section tells the X server the desired screen, device, monitor, and color settings to use, such as the color depth (such as 8-, 16-, 24- or 32-bits per pixel), the screen size (such as 640×480, 800×600, or 1024×768), and (possibly) the size of a virtual screen:

```
Section "Screen"
        Identifier "Screen0"
        Device "Neomagic Corporation|[MagicMedia 256AV]"
        Monitor "LCD Panel 1024x768"
#        DefaultColorDepth 16
        Subsection "Display"
                Depth 8
                Modes "640x480" "800x600" "1024x768"
                Virtual 1024 768
        EndSubSection
        Subsection "Display"
```

```
            Depth 16
            Modes "640x480" "800x600" "1024x768"
            Virtual 1024 768
        EndSubSection
EndSection
```

This example shows a Screen section with two Display subsections that define a 256-color (Depth 8) and a thousands of colors session (Depth 16). These two definitions allow flexibility in specifying the number of colors to use for an X session. If enabled, the DefaultColorDepth keyword will force the X session to thousands of colors.

The Screen section also contains directions for the X server on what resolutions and virtual screen size to try to support. The example configuration provides the choice of a 1024×768, 800×600, or 640×480 display, with 640×480 being the default. According to the example, if you use a resolution of say, 800×600, you'll also use a virtual display of 1024×768, which offers the ability to "pan" the display, or shift the display when your pointer reaches an edge of the screen. To disable the virtual display, comment out the Virtual line, or use a virtual setting equal to a desired resolution (such as 800×600 for the 800×600 mode).

You can toggle resolutions during your X session by holding down the Ctrl+Alt keys and pressing the plus (+) or minus (–) key on your keypad. Laptop users may need to also use an Fn key or the NumLock key before switching resolutions.

Note that you can reorder the different resolutions on the Modes line. You may also find that even though Xconfigurator, xf86config, or another tool automatically configured different modes, not all modes may work properly. In this case, simply remove the mode to avoid problem displays when toggling through the resolutions.

Starting X11 with the `startx` Command

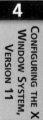

The startx command is an easy way to start an X session if you're working on a single computer or boot Linux to runlevel 3 mode (X11, multiuser and networking enabled). There are other ways to start X (see the section "Using xdm" later in this chapter). The startx command is a handy shell script that will pass on command-line options to the X server for your X sessions.

The startx command is typically used to pass starting color-depth information to the X server, as well as to find client commands or options to run for the session (usually your .xinitrc file in your home directory; see the section "The .xinitrc File").

If you use a similar Screen definition as in the previous section, the default X session will use 256 colors when you start your X session like this:

```
# startx
```

If your video card and monitor support a greater color depth, you can start a 16 *bitplanes*-per-pixel (thousands of colors represented by 16 bits per pixel) X session using the `-depth` command-line option like this:

```
# startx -- -depth 16
```

Unless you've used the `DefaultColordepth` option in your system's `XF86Config` file to set a specific color depth, using `startx` by itself will usually start an X session using 8-color bitplanes or 256 colors. Color values typically passed with the `-depth` option also include 24 and 32 for millions of colors.

Options, Options, Options!

The `XFree86` X server understands nearly 100 command-line options. However, you'll rarely need to use more than a few options. Some common options include:

- `-probeonly`—Useful when `stdout` is redirected to a file (such as `XFree86 2>report.txt`) to only probe and report on your graphics chipset
- `vtN`—Use virtual console *N* for the X session
- `-depth NN`—Use color depth *NN*, such as 8, 16, or 24
- `-allowMouseOpenFail`—Start a session without a pointer
- `-showconfig`—Display an internal report
- `-version`—Useful to display the version
- `-xf86config path`—Use specified file instead of `XF86Config`
- `-dpi NNN`—Use specified dots-per-inch
- `-screen name`—Use specified Screen section
- `-layout name`—Use specified Layout section

To see a complete list of options, read the `XFree86` man page or use `XFree86`'s `-help` command-line option.

Using the Console and Multiple X Sessions

You can also use `startx` to start multiple X11 sessions on the same computer, possibly using different window managers, and then navigate between the sessions using *virtual consoles.* Red Hat Linux supports up to six different login screens or consoles, accessed by pressing Alt+F*X*, where *X* is F1 through F6.

For example, if you log into Linux using a text-only console, you'll be at the first virtual console. After you log in, press Alt+F2; you'll then see another login prompt at the second console. To get back to your first login, press Alt+F1.

When you log into Linux and start an X11 session with `startx`, X uses a seventh virtual screen. Since you've started X from the first virtual console, this console will be unavailable for use. However, you can get to another virtual console, such as the second, by pressing Ctrl+Alt+F2 while in X11. You'll then see the Red Hat Linux login prompt. To go back to your X session, press Alt+F7. Using this approach, you can jump back and forth between your X session and different text consoles.

To use multiple X11 sessions at different color depths on different virtual consoles, first start a session with the `startx` command. After the X desktop appears, press Ctrl+Alt+F2 and log in to Linux again. If your graphics card supports thousands of colors again, use the `startx` command to start an X session. This time, however, include the `:1`, `-fbbpp 16`, and `vt8` command-line options:

```
# startx -- :1 -depth 16 vt8
```

The screen clears and you'll be running an X session with a different color depth! To jump to your other X11 session, press Ctrl+Alt+F7. To jump to another virtual console, press Ctrl+Alt+F3 (since the first and second consoles are in use). To jump back to your original X session, press Ctrl+Alt+F8.

The .xinitrc File

When you use the `startx` command to initiate an X session on your computer, details about which window manager to use or other X clients to start can be found in a file called `.xinitrc` in your home directory. A sample or template file called `xinitrc` is installed in the `/etc/X11/xinit` directory. You can copy this file to your home directory with the filename `.xinitrc` and modify it.

Although the default `.xinitrc` file contains shell script logic to load system resources or set different environment variables, you can define a simpler version from scratch, such as the one in Listing 4.2, which can be used to start 12 different X window managers. (For more information about several X window managers included on this book's CD-ROMs, see Chapter 5.)

LISTING 4.2   Sample `.xinitrc` File

```
# Sample .xinitrc file
#
# This .xinitrc file has configuration support for the following X11
# window managers: AnotherLevel, fvwm, fvmw2, KDE, twm, mlvwm, AfterStep
#                   WindowMaker, wm2, wmx, mwm, GNOME
#
# Use AnotherLevel's configuration of the fvwm2 window manager
# fvwm2 -cmd 'FvwmM4 -debug /etc/X11/AnotherLevel/fvwm2rc.m4'
#
# Use fvwm2
# fvwm2
#
# Use fvwm
# fvwm
#
# Use the K Desktop Environment
startkde
#
# Use twm - note: no longer needs an X terminal started!
# twm
#
# Use the mlvwm (Macintosh-like) window manager
# mlvwm
#
# Use AfterStep
# afterstep
#
# Use WindowMaker
# exec wmaker
#
# Use the wm2 window manager
# wm2
#
# Use the wmx window manager
# wmx
#
# Use Motif's or LessTif's mwm
# mwm
#
# Use GNOME
# exec gnome-session
```

Note that the sample `.xinitrc` file in Listing 4.2 is currently set to use the K Desktop Environment. To use a different window manager (if installed on your system), add or remove the appropriate pound sign in the file; then use the `startx` command to start a new session:

```
# startx
```

Using xdm

The xdm, X display manager, is an X client and one of three display managers included with Red Hat Linux that you can use to provide a small level of security by requiring a username and password before starting your X session. Note that if you need the security, you should enable the DontZap option in your XF86Config file. You can also disable the ability to use Ctrl+Alt+Del in order to foil rebooting the computer, and limit the number of virtual consoles available for Linux by editing /etc/inittab. You can use xdm to log in to Linux and directly to an X session, either locally or using a remote computer. However, if you choose to not use a display manager or boot directly to X, you can try xdm from the command line as the root operator by using the -nodaemon option:

```
# xdm -nodaemon
```

The display clears and you'll see an xdm login display. You can then log in to X or use Ctrl+Alt+F1.

Red Hat Linux uses the xsri client to display the Red Hat logo in the gdm, kdm, and xdm login screens. To customize your login display, edit the file Xsetup_0 under the /usr/X11R6/lib/X11/xdm directory and edit these lines:

```
/usr/bin/xsri -geometry +5+5 -avoid 300x250 -keep-aspect \
        /usr/share/pixmaps/redhat/redhat-transparent.png
```

Any small graphic named XFree86.xpm in the /etc/X11/xdm/pixmaps directory will be used inside your xdm login dialog.

> **Note**
>
> To learn more about the GNOME display manager, kdm, see Chapter 5. You'll find out how to set up Red Hat Linux to use different display managers and login screens.

After you have a working XF86Config, you may want to start Linux directly to X. To do this, change the default init entry in your system's initialization table file (/etc/inittab). Look for this line:

```
id:3:initdefault
```

Change it to this line:

```
id:5:initdefault
```

> **Caution**
>
> Be careful—editing `inittab` is dangerous, and any errors could render your system unbootable. Make sure you have an emergency boot disk on hand, and make a backup copy of the `inittab` file first. Also note that this might not work with other distributions of Linux. You have been warned!

> **Note**
>
> You can also boot directly to runlevel 5 through the LILO boot prompt. Turn on your computer, and type the following at the LILO boot prompt:
>
> `linux 5`

After you make this change, restart your system by using this shutdown command:

```
# shutdown -r now
```

Troubleshooting XFree86

One of the best sources for troubleshooting installation or other problems when using XFree86's X11 is the XFree86 FAQ, which is found at `http://www.xfree86.org`. The FAQ contains seven sections and covers difficulties such as

- Configuration problems
- Keyboard and mouse problems
- Display problems
- Problems using fonts
- Problems using configurations using symbolic links
- Chipset support fixes
- Other known problems

Note

If you cannot find the answer you need in the X manual pages, the FAQ, or other documentation, try lurking for a while on the `comp.os.linux.x` Usenet newsgroup. You can post a question, clearly stating your distribution and version of Linux, along with the version of XFree86 you've installed.

If your Internet service provider (ISP) doesn't have `comp.os.linux.x`, or if you don't feel like using a Usenet newsreader to look for answers about Linux and X11, point your favorite Web browser to `http://www.deja.com`.

Summary

This chapter covered the new features and basic installation and configuration of the XFree86 X11 distribution for Red Hat Linux. If you're a new user, you found out how to correctly configure and install X with fewer problems; if you're an experienced user, you hopefully discovered some new features that will make your X sessions more productive and enjoyable. The new XFree86 X11 distribution and new architecture of its server, supporting loadable and specific module support for new graphics hardware, provides the promise of even better support for X under Linux in the future. If your graphics card is not currently supported, don't worry—new versions of the distribution will soon follow, and many graphics card manufacturers are now supplying Linux drivers. New advances in font rendering technology, larger displays, and ever-faster graphics cards will mean that Linux users can look forward to enjoying X11 support on a par with commercial software and the very latest display and windowing systems available on the market.

Window Managers

CHAPTER 5

This chapter covers a variety of window managers for the X Window System. As you learned in Chapter 4, "Configuring the X Window System, Version 11," X11 provides the basic networking protocols and drawing primitives used to build the platform for various graphical interfaces, or window managers, you can use with Linux. You'll find a wealth of different *clients*, or programs, for X included on this book's CD-ROM, including the window managers discussed in this chapter. A number of these clients (because a window manager is just like any other X client), such as twm, are from the XFree86 distribution. Others, such as sawfish, the GNOME-enabled window manager, use additional clients developed with support from Red Hat Software, Inc. to provide a complete *desktop environment*. Also included is the K Desktop Environment (KDE), a similar and slightly more mature desktop distribution with features and a following that rivals the commercial Common Desktop Environment (CDE) used on non-Intel UNIX workstations (but also available for Linux from Xi Graphics at http://www.xig.com).

What Is a Window Manager?

Using Linux and the XFree86 distribution of X11 means freedom of choice—the choice of an operating system and the choice of how you'd like your computer's desktop or root window in X to look and act. Although a window manager is nothing more than an X11 client, you'll find that using a window manager is virtually necessary if you want to run different programs, drag windows around the display, click buttons, drag slider controls, use icons, create virtual desktops, resize windows, or customize how your X sessions work. Of course, you can run X without a window manager, but you'll lose a lot of functionality.

Note

Want to try X without a window manager? If you've configured Red Hat Linux to use a *display manager*, such as the GNOME display manager, gdm, select the Failsafe session. When X starts, you'll get an xterm window, as shown in Figure 5.1—but you won't be able to move or resize it. To quit your X session, either type the word **exit** at the command line of the xterm terminal window or use the Ctrl+Alt+Backspace key combination to kill your X session (as long as your XF86Config file doesn't use the DontZap option). Without a window manager to provide support for movable windows, you're pretty much stuck with a static xterm screen. Now do you see why window managers are so much fun (and necessary)?

FIGURE 5.1
*You can run X11
without a window
manager, but is it
worth it?*

Only one of the window managers included with Red Hat Linux is part of the XFree86 X11 distribution; the others are supported by Red Hat for your use. This chapter starts by discussing the GNOME software libraries for X11, then concentrates on the default window manager, `sawfish`, introduces you to KDE, and wraps up with `fvwm2` and `twm`, the XFree86 window manager.

The GNOME X Environment

This section covers GNOME, the GNU Network Object Model Environment, which is supported by and is being developed by programmers from Red Hat Software, Inc. and other developers around the world. GNOME has received increasing interest because it is distributed under the GNU GPL; in August 2000, IBM, Compaq, Hewlett-Packard, Sun Microsystems, and other corporate developers banded together to create the GNOME Foundation, aimed at grooming GNOME and incorporating technologies into a standard desktop for UNIX and Linux.

GNOME is an important part of the future of the graphical X desktop for Linux for a number of reasons:

- The software is fully Open Source and vendor neutral; commercial software may be built upon the software without purchasing a software license.

- Contributions, changes, and modifications may be made without control by a central source, and there are no licensing restrictions on making and distributing changes.

- The software supports multiple operating systems and external programming languages.
- The software works with any GNOME-aware X11 window manager, such as sawfish or Enlightenment.

What Is GNOME?

GNOME is a set of software libraries and X11 clients built to support an X11 desktop environment. GNOME can be used with any GNOME-aware window manager or any window manager that will support its panel component and client features, such as drag-and-drop desktop actions. GNOME is initialized and runs before you start your window manager. Like KDE, GNOME provides a rich user environment with application frameworks, a file manager, a panel, a suite of applications with consistent look and feel, and *session management*, so that a working desktop is restored between X11 sessions.

GNOME Installation Components

GNOME consists of a number of software components and, for Red Hat Linux, is distributed in a series of RPM files. You can install GNOME using the gnorpm X11 client, KDE's kpackage client, or through the rpm command. Most of the GNOME packages included with Red Hat Linux at the time of this writing are shown in Table 5.1. You'll probably find additional clients included with Red Hat Linux, and many more are available every day at http://www.gnome.org.

TABLE 5.1   GNOME Components

RPM File	Description
enlightenment-0.16.4-6	E window manager
glms-1.03-4	GNOME system temperature monitor applet
gmc-4.5.51-8	GNOME Midnight Commander
gnome-applets-1.2.1-5	Utilities for GNOME panel
gnome-audio-1.0.0-12	Sounds for GNOME
gnome-audio-extra-1.0.0-12	Extra sounds for GNOME
gnome-core-1.2.1-33	Core GNOME clients and libraries
gnome-core-devel-1.2.1-33	GNOME development libraries
gnome-games-1.2.0-9	GNOME games
gnome-games-devel-1.2.0-9	GNOME games development libraries
gnome-kerberos-0.2.1-1	GNOME gui Kerberos tools

TABLE 5.1 continued

RPM File	Description
gnome-libs-1.2.4-11	GNOME libraries
gnome-libs-devel-1.2.4-11	GNOME development libraries
gnome-linuxconf-0.33-7	GNOME gui for linuxconf
gnome-lokkit-0.41-5	GNOME firewall configuration client
gnome-media-1.2.0-7	GNOME multimedia support
gnome-objc-1.0.2-9	Objective C libraries for GNOME
gnome-objc-devel-1.0.2-9	Objective C GNOME development libraries and tools
gnome-pim-1.2.0-5	GNOME Personal Information Management clients (gnomecal, gnomecard)
gnome-pim-devel-1.2.0-5	PIM development files
gnome-print-0.20-8	GNOME printing libraries and fonts
gnome-print-devel-0.20-8	GNOME printing development libraries
gnome-users-guide-1.2-2	GNOME users guide (HTML)
gnome-utils-1.2.0-7	GNOME utilities (such as gcalc)
gnorpm-0.9.27	GNOME RPM client
gnotepad+-1.3.1-3	GNOME notepad client
gnumeric-0.54-4	GNOME spreadsheet client
gphoto-0.4.3-8	GNOME digital camera editor
gtop-1.0.9-4	A GNOME-enabled system monitor
pygnome-1.0.53-4	Python access to GNOME libs
pygnome-applet-1.0.53-4	GNOME applet development in Python
pygnome-capplet-1.0.53-4	GNOME capplet development in Python
pygnome-libglade-0.6.6-4	GNOME libglade Python support
rep-gtk-gnome-0.13-3	GNOME libraries for librep Lisp interpreter
sawfish-0.30.3-10	sawfish window manager
sawfish-themer-0.30.3-10	sawfish theme builder
switchdesk-gnome-3.6-1	GNOME desktop switcher
xmms-gnome-1.2.2-4	GNOME panel applet for xmms

5

WINDOW
MANAGERS

The majority of the GNOME-specific clients for X11 are installed under the /usr/bin directory when you install Red Hat Linux. System-wide configuration and support files will be installed under the /usr/share/gnome directory, but you may also find other GNOME client directories (such as those for gedit, gnibbles, or gnotepad+) under /usr/share.

Helix Code and GNOME

If you like using GNOME, but want to try a supercharged version that installs easily over the Internet, browse to `http://www.helixcode.com/`. By clicking a few links and running a single command line, you can download and install the Helix GNOME package, containing the latest applications, technology, and improvements available for GNOME. The Massachusetts-based Helix Code, Inc. also offers advanced versions of its Evolution groupware package, and the Gnumeric spreadsheet.

Configuring X11 to Use the GNOME or Other Display Managers

The GNOME distribution of X11 clients and software libraries does not include a window manager. GNOME libraries and clients, such as the panel application, are designed to work with your favorite X11 window manager.

If you install Red Hat Linux, configure an XFree86 X11 server to work with your computer's graphics card, and choose to boot directly to X, you'll end up using the `sawfish` window manager with the GNOME libraries by default. Your login will be through the GNOME display manager, `gdm` (shown in Figure 5.2). However, Red Hat Linux comes with other display managers, such as the K display manager (`kdm`), and the X display manager (`xdm`).

FIGURE 5.2

The GNOME gdm *display manager is the default graphical login for Red Hat Linux when booting directly to X11.*

The default display manager launched at startup is determined by a shell script named `prefdm` under the `/etc/X11` directory. When you examine the `prefdm` file, the shell script logic determines the default display manager according to the contents of the file named `desktop` under the `/etc/sysconfig` directory. The type of display manager used is then determined by turning the keywords GNOME, KDE, or AnotherLevel (another window manager) into shell environment variables, which will start gdm, kdm, or xdm, respectively.

The pertinent portion of the `prefdm` script looks like this:

```
preferred=
if [ -f /etc/sysconfig/desktop ]; then
        source /etc/sysconfig/desktop >/dev/null 2>&1
        if [ "$DESKTOP" = GNOME ]; then
                preferred=gdm
        elif [ "$DESKTOP" = KDE -o "$DESKTOP" = KDE1 ]; then
                preferred=/usr/bin/kdm
        elif [ "$DESKTOP" = KDE2 ]; then
                preferred=/usr/lib/kde2/bin/kdm
        elif [ "$DESKTOP" = AnotherLevel ] ; then
                preferred=/usr/X11R6/bin/xdm
        fi
fi
```

The runlevel entry for runlevel 5 in your Red Hat system initialization table, the file `/etc/inittab`, shows this:

```
x:5:respawn:/etc/X11/prefdm -nodaemon
```

As you can see, `prefdm` first looks for a filename `desktop` under the `/etc/sysconfig` directory. To set the default display manager, create the `desktop` file under `/etc/sysconfig`, then enter a keyword such as GNOME, KDE, or AnotherLevel.

The default *Session*, or type of window manager launched by the gdm display manager, is defined in the `/etc/X11/gdm/Sessions` directory. If you examine the `Sessions` directory, you'll see this:

```
Default Failsafe Gnome KDE default
```

These files are short shell scripts and show up under the Sessions drop-down menu in the gdm dialog box. The scripts use the Xsession command, found under the `/etc/X11/xdm` directory, to start a particular X session. For example, the Gnome session script contains

```
#!/bin/bash
/etc/X11/xdm/Xsession gnome
```

If you examine the `Xsession` script, you'll find this section:

```
case $# in
1)
    case $1 in
    failsafe)
        exec xterm -geometry 80x24-0-0
        ;;
    gnome)
        exec gnome-session
        ;;
    kde|kde1)
        exec /usr/share/apps/switchdesk/Xclients.kde
        ;;
    kde2)
        exec /usr/share/apps/switchdesk/Xclients.kde2
        ;;
    anotherlevel)
         # we assume that switchdesk is installed.
        exec /usr/share/apps/switchdesk/Xclients.anotherlevel
        ;;
    esac
esac
```

This shows the different commands used to start your X session after selection through a display manager. Note that the `Failsafe` session only launches the `xterm` client.

> **Note**
>
> For more information about shell scripts and shell programming, see Chapter 25, "Shell Scripting."

If you do not use a display manager to log in to Red Hat Linux and, for example, want to use GNOME for your X session, your `.xinitrc` should contain the following entry:

```
exec gnome-session
```

You would then use the `startx` command to start your X session:

```
# startx
```

The session will start the major GNOME components, such as the panel (a taskbar client from which to access `root` menus, configure your desktop, or launch X11 clients), along with desktop, keyboard, and mouse control software. Finally, the `sawfish` window manager is launched. Figure 5.3 shows what your X11 desktop might look like with several clients running.

FIGURE 5.3

The X11 desktop using the GNOME environment uses a panel, and nearly all clients provide common features, such as menus and tool-bars.

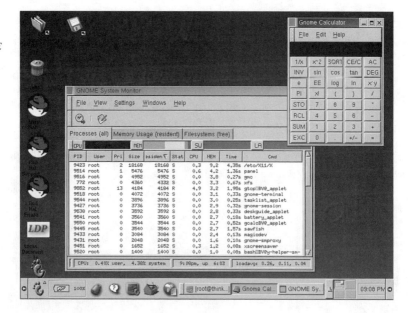

Using GNOME Clients and Tools

The most obvious and first GNOME client you'll see is the panel client, which offers a taskbar at the bottom of your X desktop. From the `root` menu of the taskbar (displayed by pressing the left mouse button, or mouse button 1 on the GNOME button), you can launch a variety of other GNOME clients:

- **Programs**—Menus for all GNOME clients
- **Favorites**—User-customized panel menu
- **Applets**—Menu of panel-specific clients
- **KDE Menus**—A submenu system providing access to KDE's panel menu
- **Run program**—A command-line dialog box
- **Panel**—The panel's configuration and control menu
- **Lock screen**—To lock (password protect) the desktop
- **Log out**—To end your X11 session

The Favorites panel menu may be customized with favorite clients by scrolling through the panel menus, then right-clicking a select menu item. From the pop-up menu, click the Add This to Favorites Menu menu item, and the client will appear under the Favorites menu. *Applets* are panel-specific GNOME clients that "dock" onto or into the panel to provide controls, information, status displays, even swimming fish!

5

WINDOW
MANAGERS

Because many of the GNOME clients are installed in the Linux file system in the normal places (such as the `/bin`, `/usr/bin`, or `/usr/X11R6/bin` directories), you can also start them from the command line of an X11 terminal window. You'll quickly recognize a GNOME client because most clients follow the GNOME style guide. This guide stipulates that each program should have supporting documentation and each client should have a File and Help menu, with an Exit menu item on the File menu and an About menu item on the Help menu (see Figure 5.4).

FIGURE 5.4

GNOME clients, such as the gedit editor, generally have a consistent interface with a standard menu and toolbar.

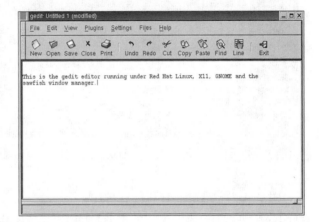

Other features common among many GNOME clients include tear-off menus and tool-bars. To tear off a menu bar, click and drag the mottled, vertical rectangle on the left end of the menu bar. The bar will drag with your mouse pointer. You can use this approach to rearrange the order of the controls of a GNOME client (such as placing the menu bar of a terminal at the bottom of the terminal window), or placing controls as floating tool windows beside a client's window. Each client will remember the toolbar or menu bar settings between launches.

Configuring Your Desktop with the GNOME Control Center

The GNOME Control Center, shown in Figure 5.5, configures your system and desktop. The Control Center can be started by clicking the GNOME Configuration tool button on the desktop panel, or by clicking the Panel menu, selecting Settings, and then clicking the GNOME Control Center menu item.

For example, to configure your desktop's background, launch the Control Center and then click the Background item, or *capplet*, under the Desktop group in the left side of the Control Center's window. The right side of the Control Center will clear, and you'll have access to a dialog box (shown in Figure 5.5) to configure your desktop's background color or wallpaper.

FIGURE 5.5

Use the GNOME Control Center to configure your system and session's desktop.

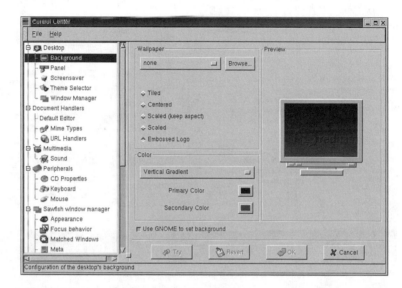

You can radically change your desktop's appearance by selecting other controls, such as the Theme Selector. The GNOME configuration included with Red Hat Linux offers 16 different *themes*, or color and decoration schemes you can use with the currently running window manager. Another way to alter your desktop is to change the current window manager on-the-fly through the Window Manager capplet.

By default (at the time of this writing), only Enlightenment, sawfish, WindowMaker, and twm are included as stable, alternative window managers. However, you can add others, such as fvwm2. Start the Control Center, then click the Window Manager capplet. In the Window Manager dialog box (shown in Figure 5.6), click the Add button and then type in the name of the window manager in the Name field. Next, type in the complete pathname and command line used to run the window manager in the Command field. If the window manager has a configuration tool, enter the complete pathname and necessary command-line options in the Configuration Command field. Do not click the Window Manager Is Session Managed button unless you are absolutely sure that the window manager is GNOME-aware. When finished, click OK.

You can then try your new choice by highlighting the name of the new window manager and clicking the Try button in the Window Manager dialog box.

5

WINDOW
MANAGERS

Figure 5.6

The Window Manager capplet in the GNOME Control Center may be used to switch window managers on-the-fly, or even add new window manager choices.

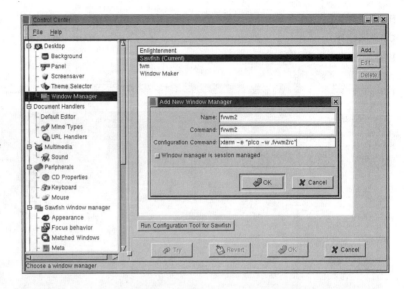

> **Note**
>
> The GNOME Control Center houses many types of desktop settings in one convenient dialog box, but you should know that you can also launch the individual settings capplets from the Settings menu on the GNOME desktop. These capplets (and other clients) cover desktop, sound, keyboard, and mouse settings, along with menu editing of the GNOME panel.

GNOME Panel Configuration

The GNOME Panel is an application and menu launcher for the GNOME desktop. By default, the panel is home for a number of important desktop elements, such as

- System menus for a dozen categories of clients, including menus for the AnotherLevel window manager and KDE desktop
- GNOME help
- GNOME configuration
- Virtual desktop navigation through the GNOME pager
- A taskbar container for currently running applications
- The date and time

The panel is configured by clicking the Panel menu item on the panel's pop-up menu, or by right-clicking a blank area of the panel. The pop-up Panel menu, shown in Figure 5.7, offers a choice of different configuration settings. You can create new panels on the top, bottom, left, or right edges of the display, and add or remove menus, drawers (to contain launcher applets), icons, or other applications. If you need a bit more screen real estate, click the Hide Panel button on either end of the panel to minimize or maximize the panel.

FIGURE 5.7

The Panel menu configures the appearance, contents, and location of your GNOME desktop's panel.

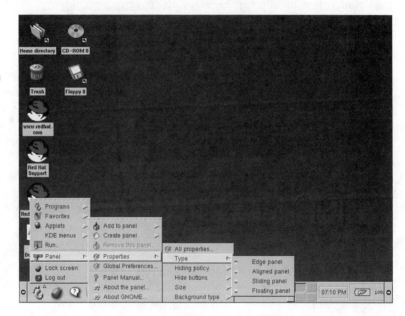

Launcher applets may be added to the panel in at least two ways. One way is to use GNOME's drag-and-drop. Use the GNOME file manager, GNU Midnight Commander, to navigate to a directory containing various commands, such as /usr/bin. Next, drag an icon of a command, such as gphoto, from the icon view window and drop the command directly on your desktop's panel. The Create Launcher applet appears, as shown in Figure 5.8.

FIGURE 5.8

The Create Launcher applet dialog box is a handy way to create customized applications (with icons) for your GNOME desktop's panel.

Type in a name for the command as well as a short comment. If the command usually runs inside a terminal window or from the console, click the Run in Terminal button. You can also assign an icon if you click the Icon button; a visual directory of the /usr/share/pixmaps directory will appear. If you click the Advanced tab, you can add translation strings in different languages for your comment.

When finished, click OK. A new icon will appear on your panel.

Panel elements such as icons can be changed, moved, or removed directly on the panel. Right-click an element and a small pop-up menu appears with several selections.

Features of the `sawfish` Window Manager

The `sawfish` window manager, formerly known as `sawmill`, is the default GNOME-aware window manager used by Red Hat Linux for X11 sessions. This is one of the newest window managers available for X11, and has been specifically configured to work well with the GNOME libraries.

The system-wide `sawfish` configuration files are stored under the /usr/share/sawfish directory, but you'll find a `sawfish` directory installed in your home directory the first time you use this window manager. This directory is used to store the custom settings, the past session, and window-management and decoration settings.

To launch `sawfish`'s configuration tool, use the `sawfish-ui` client (shown in Figure 5.9). Another way is through the Configuration Tool button in the GNOME Control Center's Window Manager capplet. To start the `sawfish-ui` client, use the command line of a terminal window like this:

```
# sawfish-ui &
```

After you press Enter, you'll see the `sawfish` configuration tool shown in Figure 5.9.

Just because `sawfish` is the default window manager for GNOME, does this mean you can't use `sawfish` by itself as a window manager? Certainly not! If you're tight on memory or computer resources or you don't need all the whiz-bang features such as desktop icons or drag-and-drop and a faster X11 session, simply create an .xinitrc file in your home directory with the following two entries:

```
exec xterm &
sawfish
```

Save the file, then use the `startx` command to start your X11 session. See "The .xinitrc File" in Chapter 4 for entries for other window managers. For more information about `sawfish`, see its FAQ under the /usr/share/doc/sawfish-0.30.2/ directory.

FIGURE 5.9

The sawfish *configuration tool is a nearly complete window management editor for configuring window decorations and other settings.*

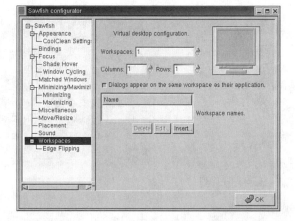

Features of the Enlightenment Window Manager

The Enlightenment window manager, also known as E, is one of the original GNOME-aware window managers used by Red Hat Linux for X11 sessions. This window manager also works well with the GNOME libraries.

The system-wide E configuration files are stored under the /usr/share/enlightenment directory. However, you'll find an .enlightenment directory installed in your home directory the first time you use this window manager. This directory is used to store the currently used E *theme*, or window management and decoration settings. Theme settings are only one of nine different settings categories used by E. Others include

- Basic options, such as window movement, resizing, and focus
- Virtual screen settings, such as the number and separation
- Window, pointer, and ToolTip behavior
- Sound effects for window operations
- Special effects for window, desktop, and menu animation
- Distinct background settings for desktops
- Extensive ToolTips and pop-up help
- Keyboard shortcuts for nearly 80 actions, such as window handling, desktop navigation, or cursor movement.

There are at least three ways to launch the Enlightenment Configuration Editor. One way is through the Configuration Tool button in the GNOME Control Center's Window Manager capplet. As shown in Figure 5.10, another way is to right-click in a blank area of the desktop, and then choose one of 15 different configuration menu items from the pop-up menu.

5

WINDOW
MANAGERS

Figure 5.10

*The
Enlightenment
Configuration
menus offer many
different settings
and configurations
of the E window
manager.*

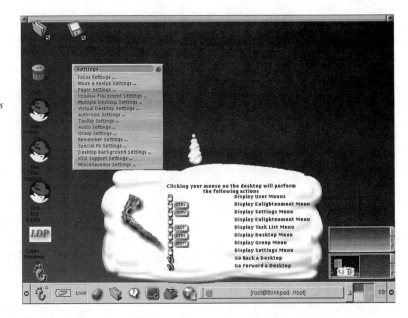

For more information about Enlightenment, see its man page, which contains detailed pointers and tips in an FAQ format. You can also browse to http://www. enlightenment.org for additional documentation or to obtain the latest copy.

Features of the K Desktop Environment

One of the most popular X11 window managers for Linux is the K Desktop Environment (KDE), which is used by many other Linux distributions, and which is also available with Red Hat Linux. KDE is much more than an X11 window manager—it is a complete desktop environment with more than 150 clients and a consistent interface, much like the one provided by GNOME.

KDE supports many of the features you'd expect in a modern desktop environment, including those commonly found in commercial software libraries such as Motif and in the Common Desktop Environment (CDE). These features include

- A suite of personal productivity tools, such as disk and network utilities, designed to use the desktop interface and the capability to import and export data to other tools

- Session management, so open applications and window positions are remembered between sessions

- "Sticky Buttons" to put an application or window on every desktop
- Network Transparent Access, or NTA, so you can click or drag and drop a graphic document's icon in an FTP window to display or transfer the graphic
- Pop-up menus and built-in help for nearly any desktop action and KDE client
- A desktop trash can for safe file deletions
- Graphic configuration of your system's desktop, keyboard, mouse, and sound
- Programs and other data represented as icons on the desktop or in windows with folder icons
- Drag-and-drop actions (such as copy, link, move, and delete) for files and devices

KDE Installation Components

Although KDE can be downloaded in source form from `http://www.kde.org`, you'll find one of the latest stable distributions included with Red Hat Linux. KDE and other KDE clients are installed from precompiled binaries in RPM files, listed in Table 5.2. Note that you can also install newer (but non-stable) versions of KDE RPMs included on the CD-ROMs.

TABLE 5.2   KDE `.rpm` Packages

Package Name	Description
`autologin-kde-1.0.0-2`	`kcontrol` login plugin
`kdeadmin-1.1.2*`	KDE system administration tools
`kdebase-1.1.2*`	KDE's window manager and other base clients, such as `kdehelp`
`kdegames-1.1.2*`	More than a dozen KDE games, such as `ksame`
`kdegraphics-1.1.2*`	KDE graphics clients, such as `kghostview`
`kdelibs-1.1.2*`	Shared software libraries
`kdelibs-devel-1.1.2*`	Development software libraries
`kdemultimedia-1.1.2*`	KDE media and sound clients, such as the `kscd` audio CD player
`kdenetwork-1.1.2*`	KDE network clients and utilities

5

WINDOW MANAGERS

TABLE 5.2 continued

Package Name	Description
kdesupport-1.1.2*	Software support libraries
kdesupport-devel-1.1.2*	Software support development libraries
kdetoys-1.1.2*	kworldwatch client and others
kdeutils-1.1.2*	Various KDE utilities, such as the kvt or konsole emulators
kdoc-2.0-1	KDE documentation files
kpackage-1.1.2*	KDE RPM utility client
kpilot-2.2.1	KDE Palm connectivity client
kpppload-1.04-16	PPP load monitor client

KDE clients under Red Hat Linux are installed in the /usr/bin directory. Support and configuration files will be found in a directory named .kde in your home directory. KDE may be installed during your initial Red Hat Linux installation, or afterward using the gnorpm or rpm commands.

KDE, like GNOME, is under rapid development, and new releases appear with some regularity. As of this writing the next release of KDE will be version 2.0. According the KDE developers at http://www.kde.org, you can expect a number of new features, including

- Diagnostic feedback via an information dialog during startup
- New window controls
- Enhanced toolbars
- New desktop pager and clock on the panel
- Browser bookmarks available via drop-down menu on the taskbar
- Major improvements to elements of the KOffice office suite

Logging In with kdm

The kdm, or K display manager (shown in Figure 5.11), is KDE's replacement of xdm or gdm. Using kdm is one way to boot directly to X and KDE after you start your computer.

To log in, enter your username and type in your password. Like gdm, kdm offers a choice of session types. Click the drop-down menu by the kdm Session Type field and then click the Go! button to log in to your favorite desktop environment. To shut down, reboot your computer, or restart your X server, click the Shutdown button on the kdm dialog box, and select the desired action.

FIGURE 5.11
The K display manager manages logins and desktop sessions when you boot directly to X11.

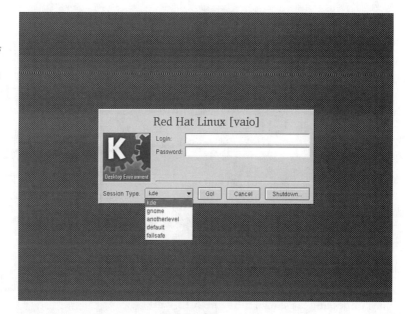

Features of the KDE Desktop

The KDE desktop is an alternative X11 session offered through the `gdm` client's Options, Sessions menu or the `kdm` client's Session Type menu. If you do not use a display manager to boot directly to X after starting Red Hat Linux, you can start KDE manually from the command line of your console. Insert the command `startkde` in the `.xinitrc` file in your home directory, and then start X11 with the `startx` command:

```
# startx
```

You'll see an initial diagnostic splash screen; the screen will clear and you'll see a desktop similar to that shown in Figure 5.12. When KDE first starts, a `Desktop` and `.kde` directory will be created in your home directory (according to the skeleton file system configuration under the `/etc/skel` directory). Changes, configurations, or modifications to your desktop or KDE clients will be saved under your `.kde` directory. The KDE desktop is a directory named `Desktop` in your home directory, and represents your KDE home folder.

The KDE desktop may be customized using a variety of techniques. You can run KDE's configuration wizard from the KDE welcome screen (shown in Figure 5.12), or by using various system and panel menus and dialogs.

5

WINDOW MANAGERS

FIGURE 5.12

The KDE is one of the most popular of the newer desktop environments for the X Window System and Linux.

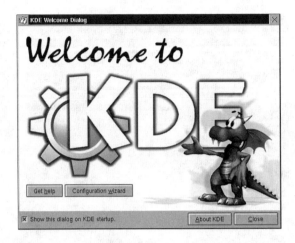

Performing Basic Desktop Actions

When you first start KDE, you see the kfm, or K file manager window, and a root display, or desktop, as shown in Figure 5.12.

The KDE desktop consists of several elements: a *taskbar menu* across the top of the display, the root background (or *root display*), and the *desktop panel* along the bottom of your screen. In the panel, starting from the left, is the *Application Starter* button (the large K), followed by several icons representing different applications, folders, devices (floppy, printer, or CD-ROM drive) and directories. There are four buttons on the panel representing the default four *virtual desktops*, or displays, along with application icons.

Using the Desktop Panel

The KDE panel, like the GNOME panel, is used to hold the Application Starter menu (accessed when you click the Application Starter menu), other application icons, the screen lock or logout button, virtual desktop buttons, and other program icons. KDE also uses a separate taskbar menu, unlike the GNOME panel, to store buttons of currently running clients or to quickly access client menus.

To change the panel's size or orientation, click the Application Starter button and click Control Center. Next, select Look and Feel from the Control Center's Modules menu, then click the Panel menu item. You can also right-click a blank area of the Panel to access the Configuration dialog box. A dialog box will appear, as shown in Figure 5.13, from which you can select different settings. When you're finished, click Apply and OK.

If you want to change how icons are placed or arranged on the panel, right-click a desired icon, and then select Remove (to delete the item) or Move from the small pop-up menu. If you click Move, you can drag the icon across the panel to a different place.

If the panel is getting in the way during your KDE session, click the small button to the far left or right of the panel to temporarily hide the panel from your screen. To restore the panel, click the small button again.

FIGURE 5.13

The KDE Control Center's Panel Configuration dialog box is used to change the panel and taskbar appearance and location.

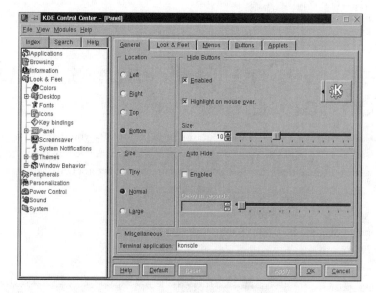

Using KDE's konqueror or the K File Manager

The newest K file manager, known as konqueror, is near the center of the magic of new versions of KDE. This file manager (included with the newer, but not stable version of KDE on your CD-ROMs) will eventually replace KDE's current kfm client, and provides a usable desktop where you can drag, drop, multiple-select, copy, move, or delete icons of data files or programs. Many of the desktop actions supported by konqueror become apparent when you drag or right-click a file's icon.

The konqueror client is launched like the kfm client when you ask for help or click on your KDE panel's home directory icon. After installation, this client may also be launched as a Web browser from the panel's Internet menu. Like kfm, if you have an active Internet connection, you can browse to remote Web sites and FTP files directly from remote computers by dragging icons of files from the konqueror window to your desktop.

The root display, which includes your home directory and your root display, is represented by the directory named Desktop in your home directory. If you drag files to this folder, the files' icons appear on your root display. Similarly, if you drag a file from another folder or directory to the desktop, it appears in your Desktop directory.

> **Note**
>
> The konqueror client is installed along with the newer KDE base files, support libraries, and other RPMs. You'll find the newer KDE distribution under the /preview directory of your second Red Hat Linux CD-ROM.

Configuring KDE with the KDE Control Center

The KDE Control Center is the main dialog box through which you can change numerous settings of your desktop, get system information (such as the currently mounted devices and capacities), or (if logged in as the root operator) configure and control KDE's appearance, background, fonts, and sessions for all users.

Click the Application Starter button on your desktop's panel, and then click KDE Control Center to display the Control Center dialog box. The main dialog box appears, as shown in Figure 5.14.

FIGURE 5.14

The KDE Control Center dialog box provides access to many different controls of your system's KDE sessions.

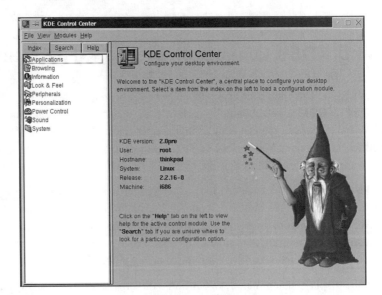

Using Display Manager Options

Use the Modules menu's Applications group login menu item in the Control Center to change the appearance or contents of the kdm login dialog box. You must be logged in as the root operator to access this portion of the Control Center, but you can get around this limitation without logging out of the current KDE session. Open a terminal window and type the su command, followed by the kcontrol client, on the command line:

```
# su -c kcontrol &
```

The Login Manager dialog box, shown in Figure 5.15, enables you to change how the kdm login dialog box appears when you set Linux to boot directly to X. You can change the greeting strings, the type of logo used, and even the language used for your KDE sessions. By clicking different tabs at the top of the dialog box, you can change the fonts, background, icons for users (perhaps using a scanned image of a person's face), and sessions using other window managers. After you make your changes, click Apply.

FIGURE 5.15

Use the Login Manager tab to change the appearance of kdm's login screen.

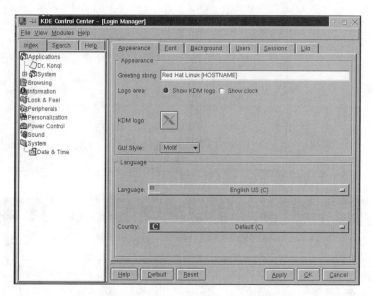

You can also control which users are permitted to log in. Click the Users tab in the Login Manager dialog box. The Users dialog box appears, as shown in Figure 5.16. To selectively control user logins, click the Show Only Selected Users button and then click and add users to the Selected Users section of the dialog box using the >> button.

To control reboot or shutdown through the kdm login screen, click the Sessions tab of the Login Manager dialog box and then click the Allow to Shutdown drop-down menu. Select None, All, Root Only, or Console Only. When finished, click the Apply button.

Changing Your Desktop's Wallpaper

KDE comes with nearly 150 different wallpapers to fill the root display or to fill your desktop's background. To configure the current desktop's wallpaper, again use the Control Center, then choose Look & Feel, Desktop, then Background from the Modules menus. You can also click a blank area of the desktop and select the Configure Background menu item. Additionally, you can click the Application Starter button on the desktop panel and select Preferences, Look & Feel, Desktop, then Background.

FIGURE 5.16

The Users tab can control who is permitted to log in to Linux through kdm.

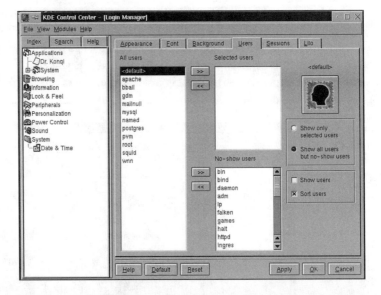

Note

KDE wallpapers are in JPEG format and are stored under the /usr/share/ wallpapers directory. Many of these wallpapers look best when used with a display using thousands of colors. Although the default KDE wallpapers are in JPEG format, other graphics formats may be used. Look under the /usr/share/ pixmaps/backgrounds/tiles directory for nearly two dozen images suitable in tiled format as a background. You'll find six directories of 230 swirling, colorful images under the /usr/share/pixmaps/backgrounds/Propaganda directory. You'll also find an excellent selection of stunning NASA photos under the /usr/share/pixmaps/backgrounds/space directory.

The Background dialog box, shown in Figure 5.17, enables you to set the name of each desktop, each desktop's colors, and whether the desktop uses a wallpaper. To set a different wallpaper, click the Wallpaper pop-up menu in the Wallpaper section of the dialog box and then click Apply. A random setting may be used to show wallpapers on the desktop from different directories in different order and at specified intervals.

FIGURE 5.17

Use the Background dialog box to set your desktop's name, colors, and wallpaper.

Changing Your Screensaver

KDE comes with 20 different screensavers. To configure a screensaver for your KDE desktop, click Preferences, Look & Feel, then the Screensaver menu item on the Panel menu. You can also use KDE's Control Center.

The Screensaver dialog box, shown in Figure 5.18, has a number of settings, such as the type of screensaver, the time delay before activating the screensaver, a random setting to cycle through installed screensavers, and whether you want to require a password to go back to work. After you make your changes, click Apply; click OK to close the dialog box.

FIGURE 5.18

The Screensaver dialog box has different settings you can use to test a screensaver, set a time delay, or require a password.

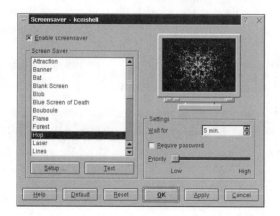

Changing Keyboard and Mouse Settings

Click Keyboard from the Peripherals menu in the Control Center's Modules menu to toggle keyboard character repeat (repeated printing of a character when a key is held down), and whether each key-press generates a key-click sound. Click Apply (shown in Figure 5.19) when you finish with your selection.

FIGURE 5.19

The Keyboard dialog box toggles Keyboard repeat and key-click sounds.

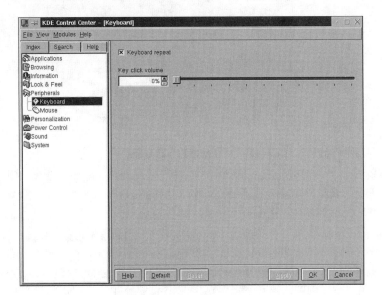

You can also access keyboard and mouse settings through the panel's Preferences menu or KDE's Control Center. The Mouse dialog's Advanced tab lets you change how fast your mouse cursor moves across the screen. To change the sequence of mouse buttons for right- or left-handed users, use the General tab (shown in Figure 5.20). These functions are similar to using the xset and xmodmap commands from the command line.

Note

Mouse behavior when clicking on windows may also be configured by using the Look & Feel, Windows Behavior, Mouse Behavior menu item in the Control Center.

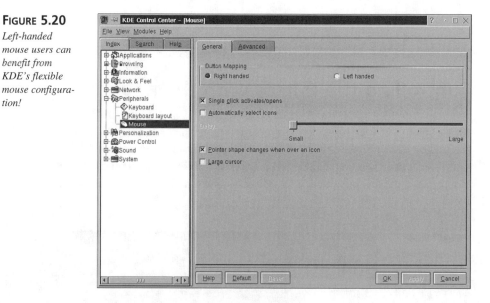

Changing Windows Actions

Click the Look & Feel, Windows Behavior, Actions menu item under the Control Center's Modules menu. The dialog (shown in Figure 5.21) is used to set how windows are placed and to determine focus policy.

FIGURE 5.21

Use the Windows dialog box to change how windows act during your KDE sessions.

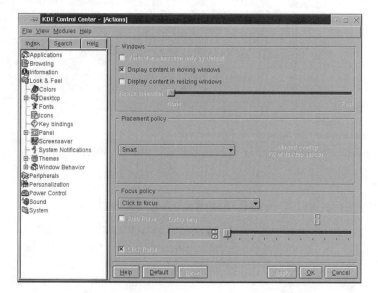

5

WINDOW MANAGERS

The Focus Policy section tells KDE how to make a window active. The default action is that you must click a window to activate it or enable it to receive keyboard input; other policies make a window active when your mouse pointer is over the window.

Controlling the Cursor with the Keyboard

A new feature for KDE is the Accessibility dialog (shown in Figure 5.22). This feature allows you to use your computer's keyboard to move the mouse using the numeric keypad (laptop users may find this a trifle inconvenient, but it works). Select the Module menu's Personalization menu, then click the Accessibility menu item. Next, click the Mouse tab in the dialog and click the Move Mouse with Keyboard (Using the Num Pad) check box.

FIGURE 5.22

KDE now features accessibility using the keyboard to move the mouse during your KDE sessions.

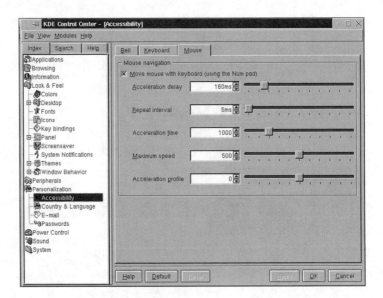

Other accessibility options include a visual bell, and sticky, slow, and bounce keys (useful to help people enter keys one-handed when two or more keys are required simultaneously).

Controlling KDE Desktop Borders

The Borders dialog box, accessed through the Control Center's Modules menu, then Look & Feel, Desktop and Borders menu item, is used to control cursor movement between virtual desktops. By default, you'll have to click a virtual desktop button on your desktop's panel to move between desktops. If you click the Enable Active Desktop

Borders item in the Borders dialog box (shown in Figure 5.23) and then click the Apply button, you can move to a different desktop by moving your mouse cursor to the edge of the current desktop.

Note

Don't want to click the panel's desktop buttons or drag your mouse to move between desktops? Use the keyboard instead! Press Ctrl+Tab to walk through the desktops (a pop-up window will appear). Press Alt+Tab to walk through (activate) windows in the current desktop.

You can also drag the different sliders to set the time delay for desktop switching and the width of the sensitive edge of each desktop.

FIGURE 5.23

The Borders dialog box is used to tell KDE whether to use the mouse to move between desktops, how fast to make the switch, and when to make the change.

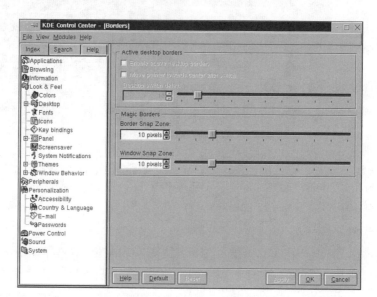

The `fvwm2` Window Manager

The `fvwm2` window manager (shown in Figure 5.24) has a configurable taskbar, 3D window frames, buttons, scrollbars, and the capability for extensive customization. Customized configurations of this window manager have been the basis of several complex and popular X desktops provided with Red Hat Linux in the earlier Red Hat distributions (such as `TheNextStep` and `AnotherLevel`).

5

WINDOW
MANAGERS

This window manager's default startup file is found under the /etc/X11/fvwm2 directory as system.fvwm2rc. Copy this file to your home directory as .fvwm2rc and make changes to customize your X sessions. To use fvwm2, insert its name in your .xinitrc file and use the startx command to start your X session.

FIGURE 5.24

The fvwm2 *window manager has basic window manager features, such as a pager for its virtual desktops.*

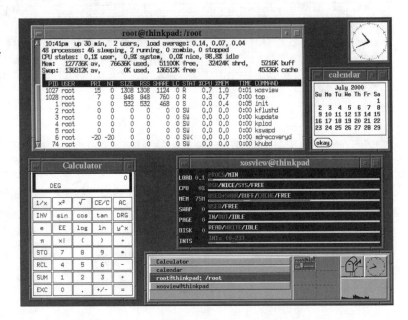

fvwm2's startup file contains sections for customizing window colors and styles, menus, keyboard actions, and the number of virtual desktops. Look for the desktop section, which looks like this:

```
DeskTopSize 2x2
```

fvwm2's default startup file defines four different virtual desktops. By changing the DeskTopSize value, you can either reduce or increase the number of virtual desktops. For example, use a setting like this to add another two desktops:

```
DeskTopSize 2x3
```

When you restart fvwm2, you'll see that an additional two desktops have been added to the fvwm2 pager window. You can move to a different desktop by pressing your left mouse button on the appropriate square in the desktop pager's window. However, another modification you can make that can be a lifesaver, especially if your computer's mouse is broken or you want to use just the keyboard for moving the pointer, is to insert definitions to enable your cursor keys to shift to different desktops or to move the pointer!

Scroll through your .fvwm2rc file until you find the default Key definitions:

```
# some simple default key bindings:
Key Next        A       SCM     Next [*] Focus
Key Prior       A       SCM     Prev [*] Focus
```

Add the following cursor key definitions:

```
# Shift + Ctrl moves 1 page in direction
Key Left        A       CS      Scroll -100 +0
Key Right       A       CS      Scroll +100 +0
Key Up          A       CS      Scroll +0 -100
Key Down        A       CS      Scroll +0 +100
```

These definitions define Shift+Ctrl+Cursor*X*, which will shift your desktop to the next available desktop in *X* direction. This means that you can move between desktops without using a mouse! Next, insert the following definitions:

```
# Alt + Shift move 1/10 page in direction
Key Left        A       MS      Scroll -10 +0
Key Right       A       MS      Scroll +10 +0
Key Up          A       MS      Scroll +0 -10
Key Down        A       MS      Scroll +0 +10
```

These definitions define Alt+Shift+Cursor*X*, which will shift the current desktop in the designation *X* direction. This means that you can work using clients whose windows exceed the current desktop borders by shifting the screen! Finally, add what is perhaps the most useful definition:

```
# Alt + Ctrl move cursor 1/100 page in direction
Key Left        A       CM      CursorMove   -1 +0
Key Right       A       CM      CursorMove   +1 +0
Key Up          A       CM      CursorMove   +0 -1
Key Down        A       CM      CursorMove   +0 +1
```

These definitions define Alt+Ctrl+Cursor*X*, which will move your mouse pointer 1/100 the width of the current page in the designated direction. This is fine enough resolution to handle nearly every desktop. After making the changes, use fvwm2's root menu (by clicking the left mouse button in a blank area of the desktop) to restart the window manager. This will put your changes into effect right away.

You'll probably also want to define additional keys (such as FKeys) in conjunction with Alt or Ctrl, to mimic mouse button presses or root menu operations. This is a handy way to create a pointerless X11 environment! "Pointers" on creating your own definitions can be found in the fvwm2 man page.

The `twm` Window Manager

The `twm`, or Tab window manager (shown in Figure 5.25), comes with the XFree86 X Window distribution. Installed under the `/usr/X11R6/bin` directory, this window manager provides the basics of window management for X:

- Custom keyboard commands
- Custom mouse commands
- Icon dock
- Icons
- Resizable windows
- Window titles

FIGURE 5.25

The `twm` provides basic window operations for your X sessions.

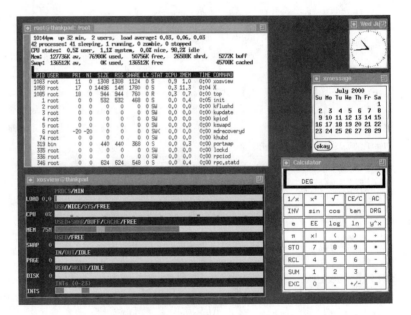

You'll find `twm`'s system-wide configuration file, `system.twmrc`, under the `/etc/X11/twm` directory. This file contains default definitions you can change and use for yourself. Copy `system.twmrc` to your home directory as `.twmrc` to make your changes. You can use `twm` by inserting the `twm` command in your `.xinitrc` file.

`twm`'s default startup file, which defines `twm`'s `root` menu (accessed by pressing the left mouse button in a blank area of the desktop) now includes a menu item definition for a terminal. You'll certainly want to customize this menu to add other clients. Before using twm, open your copy of .twmrc in your favorite text editor, such as pico (the -w option disables line wrapping):

 # pico -w .twmrc

Look for the section defining the root menu:

```
menu "defops"
{
"Twm"    f.title
"Iconify"        f.iconify
"Resize"         f.resize
"Move"           f.move
"Raise"          f.raise
"Lower"          f.lower
"-----------"  f.nop
"Focus"          f.focus
"Unfocus"        f.unfocus
"Show Iconmgr"  f.showiconmgr
"Hide Iconmgr"  f.hideiconmgr
"-----------"  f.nop
"Xterm"          f.exec "exec xterm &"
"-----------"  f.nop
"Kill"           f.destroy
"Delete"         f.delete
"-----------"  f.nop
"Restart"        f.restart
"Exit"           f.quit
}
```

This section of .twmrc contains root menu labels, followed by an appropriate command for the twm window manager. For example, to "kill" a window, you press your left mouse button on the desktop, drag down to select the Kill menu item, and then press your mouse button over the top of a desired window—twm then removes the selected window. Now insert a menu definition to create and display a calendar of the current month, like this:

```
menu "defops"
{
"Twm"    f.title
"Iconify"        f.iconify
"Resize"         f.resize
"Move"           f.move
"Raise"          f.raise
"Lower"          f.lower
"-----------"  f.nop
"Focus"          f.focus
"Unfocus"        f.unfocus
"Show Iconmgr"  f.showiconmgr
"Hide Iconmgr"  f.hideiconmgr
```

```
"------------"   f.nop
"Xterm"          f.exec "exec xterm &"
"Calendar"       f.exec "cal | xmessage -file - &"
"------------"   f.nop
"Kill"           f.destroy
"Delete"         f.delete
"------------"   f.nop
"Restart"        f.restart
"Exit"           f.quit
}
```

The example menu item uses the `cal` command to pipe its output into the `xmessage` client for display, resulting in a small floating-window calendar for the desktop. After making your changes, save the new `.twmrc` file. If you're running `twm`, press your left mouse button and drag down to select the Restart menu item (which restarts `twm`) using the newly defined menu. This is how you can customize not only `twm`, but also the `fvwm2` window manager discussed in this chapter.

Summary

This chapter presented an overview of various window managers for X11, including `sawfish`, Enlightenment, and the upcoming version of KDE's `konqueror`, along with a discussion of the current method of configuring a Red Hat system for different display managers. You also read about how other window managers, such as `fvwm2` and `twm` may be configured for use. Choosing a window manager or X11 environment can be a matter of personal preference or need. Some window managers require lots of disk space and memory, whereas others are minimalist in design and do not require large computing resources. Some restrictions may be memory, display resolution, hard drive space, or CPU speed. Red Hat Linux has always tried to provide the best and most flexible window managers available, and now includes two of the most powerful environments available for X11: GNOME and KDE. But you should know that there are literally hundreds of other window managers you can try with your system. For links to the source for many other window managers, or for pointers to the latest version of your favorite window manager, see `http://www.PLiG.org/xwinman`. You'll find lots of links to additional window themes, icons, and graphics you can use with your X11 desktop. You can make your Linux X11 desktop look like (or unlike) any computer operating system you want!

Connecting to the Internet

CHAPTER 6

Connections from a Red Hat Linux system to an ISP are usually made through a modem using the now common PPP (Point-to-Point Protocol), which provides TCP/IP via ethernet or serial (telephone) interfaces. A less frequently used protocol is SLIP (Serial Line Interface Protocol), which was created before PPP as a minimal way to link a network via telephone using TCP/IP. Both PPP and SLIP allow you to transfer mail, surf the World Wide Web, use FTP, and access all the other features of the Internet. Both PPP and SLIP use the TCP/IP network protocol, and because TCP/IP and UNIX evolved together, Linux is particularly adept at handling PPP and SLIP.

In this chapter you learn how to easily set up your Linux system to use PPP using manual scripts and graphical interface PPP clients, such as Red Hat's new Connection tool and KDE's kppp client. You will also learn one way to set up your Linux system for dial-in PPP, and see how to use the new Roaring Penguin utilities included with Red Hat Linux to set up a Digital Subscriber Line (DSL) connection. You probably will not want to set up both PPP and SLIP because most ISPs use PPP only, and SLIP seems to be "slipping" into obscurity. PPP is the faster of the two protocols, but you may sometimes need to use SLIP with older systems or legacy software.

Before setting up either PPP or SLIP, you need to create a *dummy interface* so that your machine knows about itself in a networking sense and because most protocols require this dummy interface to work properly.

Setting Up the Dummy Interface

A dummy interface is used by TCP/IP to assign an IP address to your machine, which is required for both SLIP and PPP. The reason for a dummy interface is simple: When you connect to an ISP, your IP address is often assigned dynamically, and you never know what the IP address will be in advance. This can cause problems for TCP/IP routines in your kernel that need to know an IP address to function properly. TCP/IP is happy when you assign an IP address—the dummy interface IP address—to your machine. The need for an IP address internally is most important when you are not connected to your ISP because many network-aware applications (such as email, newsreaders, and so on) need to have some IP address to connect to, even if it doesn't lead anywhere. This dummy interface IP address does not conflict with the one assigned by your ISP.

Fortunately, setting up a dummy interface is simple. All that is required are a couple of commands to create the interface and a couple more commands to test that the interface is working, and you're done. The file that Linux uses to store all network IP address information is called /etc/hosts, and every system should have one (even if it is empty).

The /etc/hosts file is an ASCII file that provides two pieces of information to the TCP/IP drivers and applications: an IP address and the names associated with that IP address. Usually, you will find the /etc/hosts file has a single line in it when you install Linux without network support:

```
127.0.0.1       localhost       localhost.localdomain
```

This line essentially tells TCP/IP that a special interface called localhost is assigned the IP address 127.0.0.1. The localhost interface is called the dummy interface because it is not a real address. This interface is also called the *loopback interface* because it leads back to the same machine.

> **Note**
>
> The terms *localhost*, *loopback*, and *dummy interface* all refer to the use of the IP address 127.0.0.1 to refer to the local machine. The term *loopback interface* indicates that to the networking drivers, it looks as though the machine is talking to a network that consists of only one machine. In internal terms, the kernel sends network traffic out one port and back in to another on the same machine. *Dummy interface* indicates that the interface doesn't really exist to the outside world, only to the local machine.

127.0.0.1 is a special IP address reserved for the local machines on all networks. Every networked Linux machine has this IP address for its localhost. If you display the contents of your /etc/hosts file and this line already exists, then the dummy interface is set up for you and you can skip this section. If the /etc/hosts file doesn't exist or this line is not in the file, you have to set up the interface yourself. If your machine has an IP address other than 127.0.0.1 in your /etc/hosts file, and the interface 127.0.0.1 is not there, you do not have the localhost interface set up.

> **Note**
>
> When you installed Red Hat Linux, you may have chosen to install and support networking. If you did, the dummy interface was probably set up automatically. If you chose a non-networking boot image, you may have to manually add the dummy interface.

To create the dummy interface, your Linux system needs the networking software installed. The installation happens automatically with most root and boot images, even if the network interfaces are not configured.

Begin the dummy interface setup by editing (or creating, if it doesn't exist) the
/etc/hosts file, and add the following line:

```
127.0.0.1        localhost        localhost.localdomain
```

The number of spaces between the IP address and the name localhost does not matter,
as long as there is at least one. Make sure you enter the IP address exactly as shown—
with no spaces between the parts of the dotted-quad notation. If you already had an IP
address in the /etc/hosts file for your local machine but no localhost entry with this
IP address, you still need to add this line. The localhost line is usually the very first
line in the /etc/hosts file.

After updating the /etc/hosts file, you need to tell TCP/IP about the new interface. To
set up the dummy interface, issue the following commands when you are logged in as
root:

```
# ifconfig lo 127.0.0.1
# route add 127.0.0.1
```

The first command tells the system to add an interface called the localhost (lo is the
short form for localhost) with an IP address of 127.0.0.1. The second command adds
the IP address 127.0.0.1 to an internal table that keeps track of routes to different
addresses.

After you have issued these two commands, the dummy interface should be created and
ready to use. A machine reboot usually helps ensure that the proper configurations are
read. To test the dummy interface, use the ifconfig command again with the name of
the interface (lo for localhost) to tell you statistics about the interface (or just use
ifconfig to see all interfaces). The command and a sample output look like this:

```
# ifconfig lo
lo        Link encap:Local Loopback
          inet addr:127.0.0.1  Mask:255.0.0.0
          UP LOOPBACK RUNNING  MTU:3924  Metric:1
          RX packets:60 errors:0 dropped:0 overruns:0 frame:0
          TX packets:60 errors:0 dropped:0 overruns:0 carrier:0
          collisions:0 txqueuelen:0
```

This output shows that the loopback interface is active and running, that it has been
assigned the IP address 127.0.0.1, that the broadcast mask of 255.0.0.0 is used, and
that the interface hasn't had much traffic. Don't worry about the errors in the last couple
of lines: You haven't used the interface yet so there are no meaningful statistics available.

As a check that your kernel knows about the interface and that your machine responds to
the IP address 127.0.0.1 and the name localhost (defined in your system's /etc/hosts
file), you can use the ping command to check that the interface is responding properly:

```
# ping localhost
PING localhost (127.0.0.1): 56 data bytes
64 bytes from 127.0.0.1: icmp_seq=0 ttl=255 time=0.3 ms
64 bytes from 127.0.0.1: icmp_seq=1 ttl=255 time=0.2 ms
64 bytes from 127.0.0.1: icmp_seq=2 ttl=255 time=0.1 ms
64 bytes from 127.0.0.1: icmp_seq=3 ttl=255 time=0.1 ms
64 bytes from 127.0.0.1: icmp_seq=4 ttl=255 time=0.2 ms
64 bytes from 127.0.0.1: icmp_seq=5 ttl=255 time=0.1 ms

--- localhost ping statistics ---
6 packets transmitted, 6 packets received, 0% packet loss
round-trip min/avg/max = 0.1/0.1/0.3 ms
```

To stop the output press Ctrl+C. You should get similar results using either the name localhost or the IP address 127.0.0.1 (because they both refer to exactly the same interface according to the /etc/hosts file).

If you get the following message, then the interface is not set up properly and you should check the /etc/hosts file and the ifconfig command to make sure you installed the interface properly:

```
# ping localhost
unknown host
```

Repeating the installation steps should correct the problem. After you complete those simple steps and tests, the dummy interface is ready to be used by your system, its applications, and both PPP and SLIP.

Setting Up PPP

Most dial-up ISPs today use PPP instead of SLIP. This is good for you because PPP is a faster and more efficient protocol. PPP and SLIP are both designed for two-way networking; in other words, your machine talking to one other machine—usually your ISP—and no other machines at the time (although it is possible to communicate with other computers on your internal network). PPP is not a replacement for a LAN protocol such as TCP/IP, but PPP can coexist with TCP/IP (which provides a transport protocol for data).

One of the major hurdles new Linux users face is setting up PPP and connecting to the Internet. If you're new to Linux, relax! You don't have to understand the intricacies of the protocol in order to use PPP, and setting up PPP on your system is not as scary as you might suspect (although if you want to examine the gritty details, look at the file ppp.c under the /usr/src/linux/drivers/net directory). You can do it manually from the command line, or by using one of several graphical interface clients. Both approaches produce the same results. However, using the command line offers the advantage that you get to understand what is going on and can use connection commands in shell scripts or crontab entries. See the section "Setting up PPP Using the PPP Scripts" for details on using shell scripts instead of the command line.

PPP uses two components on your system. The first is a daemon called pppd, which controls the use of PPP. The second is a driver called the high-level data link control (HDLC), which controls the flow of information between two machines. A third component of PPP is a routine called chat that dials the other end of the connection for you when you want it to.

> **Note**
>
> PPP is a complex protocol with many tunable parameters. Fortunately, most of these parameters concern things you will never care about, so you can ignore all those underlying details in the vast majority of installations. Unless you plan to use PPP to connect to the Internet all day (and there are better choices for that), you will do fine using the default settings PPP employs.

Installing PPP

PPP was most likely installed for you when you installed Red Hat Linux. If it wasn't, you need to load the package before you can continue to configure the system for PPP use. The PPP library and files are included with practically every CD-ROM distribution of Linux, and you can obtain the most recent versions from the usual Linux Web and FTP sites.

You can quickly check to see if PPP is installed on your system by using the rpm command's -q option, like this:

```
# rpm -q ppp
ppp-2.3.11-7
```

This example shows that PPP is installed. If for some reason PPP is not installed on your system, use Red Hat's rpm command to install the PPP package from your Red Hat Linux CD-ROM. Red Hat Linux includes version 2.3.11 of PPP. You can easily install the .rpm package (after downloading or copying from CD-ROM) like this:

```
# rpm -ivh ppp-2.3.11-7.i386.rpm
```

Setting Up a PPP User Account

To help protect your system from hackers and break-in attempts from your ISP (remember that if your machine can communicate to the Internet, users on the Internet can communicate with your machine), it is advisable to set up a special user login for PPP. This step is optional but highly recommended.

You can add the new user account for PPP (usually called ppp for convenience) using any of the user administration scripts you want, or you can simply edit the /etc/passwd file and add the user yourself (only if you do not use password shadowing). Because the PPP login does not have a home directory per se, you don't need to create mail boxes and other paraphernalia that is normally created by a user administration script. The line you want to add to the /etc/passwd file looks like this:

```
ppp:*:301:51:PPP account:/tmp:/etc/ppp/pppscript
```

This creates a user called ppp with no password. (The asterisk in the second field can't be matched.) The user ID is 301 in this example, but you can substitute any unused user ID. The group ID is best set to a new group called ppp, although this is not necessary. The fourth field is a comment that describes the account's purpose. The home directory is set to /tmp in this case because you don't want to keep files in the ppp account home directory. The last field in the /etc/passwd entry is used for a startup script. In this case, I've created a new script called /etc/ppp/pppscript, which takes care of starting PPP properly. You will have to create this script yourself. The contents of pppscript should look like this:

```
#!/bin/sh
mesg n
stty -echo
exec pppd -detach silent modem crtscts
```

The first line invokes the Bourne shell to run the script. The second line suppresses messages for this login. The third line stops the remote from echoing everything back. The fourth line invokes the pppd daemon with some options that control its behavior. (You'll look at the pppd daemon in more detail in a few moments.) Make sure the file pppscript is executable.

Setting Up chat

Because you are going to use a modem to connect to your ISP, you need to tell PPP about the modem and how to use it. PPP uses a program called chat to handle all these details. (You can use utilities other than chat, but experience has shown that chat is the most foolproof of the options as well as one of the easiest to set up quickly.) The chat utility takes a lot of its features from the UUCP program, which makes it familiar for many veteran system administrators.

The chat utility requires a command line that tells it what number to call to connect to your ISP and what types of login responses are required. All of this information is placed on a single-line chat script. These lines are often stored in files to prevent you from having to type the commands every time you want to access the Internet.

Here's a typical `chat` script for a connection to an ISP:

```
"" ATZ OK ATDT2370400 CONNECT "" ogin: ppp word: guessme
```

In this example, the ISP's phone number is 237-0400, while the username and password to login are `ppp` and `guessme`. `chat` scripts are always set up as a conversation between the `chat` utility and the modem. The script parts are separated by spaces, with the `chat` instruction and the expected reply one after another. This `chat` script tells `chat` the following: Expect nothing from the modem to start (the two quotation marks), then send the string `ATZ` and wait for the reply `OK`. After `OK` is received, `chat` sends the string `ATDT2370400` to dial out to the ISP's number. When a `CONNECT` string is received from the modem, send nothing and wait for the string `ogin:` from the ISP. (This covers all the case types such as `login` and `Login`.) After getting `ogin:`, send the login `ppp` and wait for `word:` (the end of `password`) and send the password `guessme`. After that, `chat` terminates and hands control over to PPP.

You can see in the script how the conversation goes through with each end (the modem and `chat`) taking turns communicating. You will need to set up a `chat` script like this in a file with your ISP's number and the proper login and password. Place it in an ASCII file. Use the `chat` command to call the file:

```
chat -f filename
```

`filename` is the name of the `chat` script file. The `chat` command has a lot of options for handling error conditions from your modem and the ISP, but these all complicate the script quite a bit. The easiest modifications are to build in handling for both a busy signal from the modem (the ISP's line was busy) or a no-carrier message from the modem (when it couldn't connect properly). To handle both these error conditions in the script and have `chat` terminate when these conditions occur, modify the script to look like this:

```
ABORT BUSY ABORT 'NO CARRIER' "" ATZ OK ATDT2370400
\ CONNECT "" ogin: ppp word: guessme
```

The two `ABORT` sequences in front of the older script tell `chat` to terminate if either the `BUSY` or `NO CARRIER` messages are sent by the modem. Make sure you use single quotation marks around the two words in `NO CARRIER`; otherwise, `chat` thinks these are two different parts of the script.

Configuring `pppd`

As mentioned earlier, most of the functions of PPP are controlled by a daemon called `pppd`. When `chat` has connected to a remote system and `chat` terminates cleanly, it hands control of the connection over to `pppd`. It is the `pppd` daemon that handles all the communications from this point forward.

The pppd daemon is usually started with arguments for the modem device and the speed of the connection. If you want to start pppd manually from the command line, your command looks like this:

```
pppd /dev/ttyS0 38400 crtscts defaultroute
```

This line tells pppd to use the serial port /dev/ttyS0 (COM1) to connect at 38,400bps. The crtscts option tells pppd to use hardware handshaking on the connection, and defaultroute tells pppd to use the local IP address for the connection.

Because most ISPs assign you a dynamic IP address when you connect, you can't hard-code the address into the pppd command line. The pppd daemon can accept any IP address the remote connection wants if you modify the command line like this:

```
pppd /dev/cua0 38400 crtscts IP_address:
```

You substitute whatever IP address your machine has (even 127.0.0.1) before the colon. The colon with nothing after it tells pppd to accept whatever IP address the remote sends as the other end of the connection.

The pppd daemon accepts options from configuration files if they exist. The most common configuration file for PPP is stored as /etc/ppp/options, although you may use any path and filename you want. The default settings in the /etc/ppp/options file look like this:

```
# /etc/ppp/options: global definitions

lock                    # use file locking UUCP-style
```

The single entry tells pppd to use UUCP-like file locking, which works well to prevent device problems. You can add any other valid pppd options to this file, but this suffices for most setups.

Combining chat and pppd

The way I've described setting up chat and pppd, you have to take two steps to connect to an ISP: Use chat to establish the connection and then launch pppd to use PPP over the connection. There is a way to take both steps with one command line, which can be added to the pppscript talked about earlier in this section. By calling chat from the pppd command line, you can simplify the entire process. Here's a modification of the pppd command line that accomplishes this (assuming your modem is attached to /dev/ttyS0):

```
# /usr/sbin/pppd connect "/usr/sbin/chat -v -f chatfile" /dev/ttyS0
\115200 -detach crtscts modem defaultroute
Serial connection established.
Using interface ppp0
Connect: ppp0 <--> /dev/ttyS1
local  IP address 207.172.52.61
remote IP address 10.11.64.57
```

With this command, pppd calls chat with the filename chatfile (or whatever you called your chat script file), creates the link, and then finishes establishing pppd. You must have the path to your chat file easily found by chat or specify the full pathname in the command line. The -v chat option outputs information as the connection is established. As mentioned, you can substitute this line for the pppd line in the pppscript file, and then the connection will be established in one step.

After these few steps, your system is ready to use PPP to dial out to your ISP. As long as the chat script has all the instructions for connecting to the ISP's modem bank, PPP will start properly once a connection is established.

Setting Up PPP Using the PPP Scripts

Manually creating PPP scripts is one way to set up a PPP user account; however, you'll find a dialer, chat script, and PPP on and off scripts under the /usr/share/doc/ppp-2.3.11/scripts directory when you install Red Hat Linux and PPP. Using these scripts is a lot easier; by performing a few simple edits, you'll be connected in a few minutes!

The important script files are

- ppp-on—Contains your ISP's phone number, your username and password, and modem options (such the baudrate)

- ppp-off—A utility script that kills the interface and PPP connection

- ppp-on-dialer—A PPP chat script

To set up these scripts, log in as the root operator and copy the scripts to the /etc/ppp directory:

```
# cp /usr/share/doc/ppp*/scripts/ppp-o* /etc/ppp
```

Open the ppp-on script with your favorite text editor. Look first for the entries for your ISP's phone number and your username and password, like this:

```
TELEPHONE=555-1212     # The telephone number for the connection
ACCOUNT=george         # The account name for logon (as in 'George Burns')
PASSWORD=gracie        # The password for this account (and 'Gracie Allen')
LOCAL_IP=0.0.0.0       # Local IP address if known. Dynamic = 0.0.0.0
REMOTE_IP=0.0.0.0      # Remote IP address if desired. Normally 0.0.0.0
```

Change the values for TELEPHONE, ACCOUNT, and PASSWORD, substituting your ISP's phone number and your username and password. Next, scroll through the script until you find this:

```
exec /usr/sbin/pppd debug lock modem crtscts /dev/ttyS0 38400 \
        asyncmap 20A0000 escape FF kdebug 0 $LOCAL_IP:$REMOTE_IP \
        noipdefault netmask $NETMASK defaultroute connect $DIALER_SCRIPT
```

This line of the script contains modem options for the chat script in the ppp-on-dialer script and starts the pppd daemon on your computer following a connection to your ISP's computer. Change the modem device (/dev/ttyS0 in this example) and the baud rate (38,400 in this case) to match your system and desired connection speed. When finished, save the script.

Next, use the chmod command to make these scripts executable like this:

```
# chmod +x /etc/ppp/ppp-o*
```

To debug or check the progress of your modem connection, dialing, and connection to your ISP, use the tail command with its -f "loop forever" option like this:

```
# tail -f /var/log/messages
```

Then, to connect to your ISP, execute the ppp-on script (as root):

```
# /etc/ppp/ppp-on
```

To stop your PPP connection, use the ppp-off script (as root):

```
# /etc/ppp/ppp-off
```

You can also move the ppp-on and ppp-off scripts to a recognized $PATH, such as /usr/local/bin.

On the Horizon

On the verge of release of the newer Linux 2.4-series of kernels, the authors of the current pppd daemon have developed new versions of the PPP driver. Written by Paul Mackerras, this driver (in addition to consisting of three separate kernel modules) will require the following entries in your /etc/modules.conf file:

```
alias tty-ldisc-3       ppp_async
alias tty-ldisc-14      ppp_synctty
alias char-major-108    ppp_generic
```

These entries will ensure that the correct modules are loaded or unloaded automatically during your PPP sessions. See the file README.linux under the /usr/share/doc/ppp-2.3.11 directory for more details.

Setting Up PPP with Red Hat's Dialup Configuration Tool

Using a manual PPP chat script or the PPP connection scripts is an easy way to start and stop a PPP connection. These manual scripts have the advantage of working with or without a graphical interface, such as the X Window System. The disadvantage of using these scripts becomes apparent when you must use or maintain multiple ISP accounts, have security issues for passwords, or want the point-and-click convenience of a graphical interface to PPP setup and connections.

Fortunately, Red Hat Linux comes with an easy-to-use dialup configuration tool. You must run an X session in order to use this tool, which is named `rp3-config`. For example, to start the client using the GNOME desktop panel, click the Programs, Internet menu then click the Dialup Configuration Tool menu item. The tool's window will then appear (as shown in Figure 6.1). Note that you can also start the tool by using the `rp3-config` command like this from the command line of a terminal window:

```
# rp3-config
```

FIGURE 6.1

Red Hat's dialup configuration tool is one way to set up a PPP connection when using Linux.

Click the Next button to start the configuration. If the symbolic link `/dev/modem` does not exist, you'll see a dialog box as shown in Figure 6.2. Click the Next button to continue.

FIGURE 6.2

The `rp3-config` tool can also help you set up your system's modem.

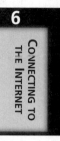

If a modem is found, the tool will display a dialog box, as shown in Figure 6.3. Click the
Keep This Modem button, then click Next to continue.

FIGURE 6.3

*Configuring a
modem is a snap
using Red Hat's
new dialup config-
uration tool.*

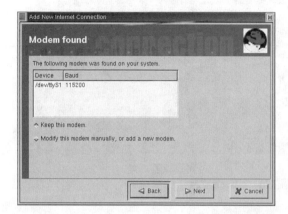

Next, enter a name for the dialup account (such as name of your ISP), along with the
ISP's dialup number, as shown in Figure 6.4.

FIGURE 6.4

*Enter a name and
phone number for
your PPP connec-
tion.*

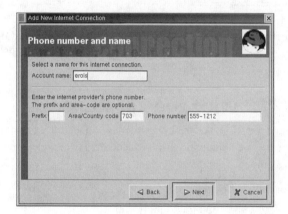

Click the Next button, then enter (in the dialog box shown in Figure 6.5) your assigned
username and password (given to you by your ISP).

After you click the Next button, you'll be asked to select your ISP. Click your ISP, click
Next, then click Finish to save your account. (Note that you may also have to close any
remaining dialogs.) To start your PPP connection from the GNOME's desktop panel,
select Programs, Internet, then click the RH PPP Dialer menu item .You can also access
this menu from KDE's desktop panel menu. You'll see a small dialog, as shown in Figure
6.6, that lists the ISP accounts you've created.

FIGURE 6.5
Enter your user-name and password for your PPP connection.

FIGURE 6.6
Click your ISP, then click OK to start your connection.

To start a PPP connection, first click a desired (defined) ISP, then click OK. Note that in order to successfully connect, you may need to have entries for your ISP's DNS servers in your system's /etc/resolv.conf file.

Setting Up PPP with the kppp Client

Red Hat Linux includes the K Desktop Environment and its suite of graphical clients for X. One of these clients is the kppp tool, a state-of-the-art PPP and Internet connection utility. This client has among its features

- Built-in terminal and script generator
- Connection statistics and pppd load monitoring
- Docking of modem send/receive lights in the K desktop panel
- Graphical front-end to the pppd daemon
- Multiple account maintenance for different users and ISPs
- Online time tracking and phone-cost accounting

To launch the kppp client if you're using a newer version of KDE, click the Application Starter button on the K desktop's panel, select Internet, and click the Internet Dialer menu item (or the kppp menu item if you are using the current stable version of KDE). You can also launch kppp from the command line of a terminal window:

```
# kppp &
```

The client's main dialog box will appear, as shown in Figure 6.7.

FIGURE 6.7
Click the Setup button to define new PPP accounts.

A Configuration dialog box appears when you click the Setup button. The dialog box is shown in Figure 6.8.

FIGURE 6.8
Click the New button to start configuring a PPP account.

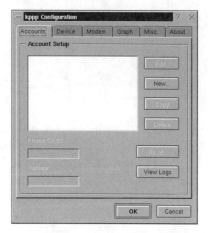

If you click the New button, you'll be asked if you want to use KDE's new PPP wizard, or to go through the standard, dialog-based setup, as shown in Figure 6.9.

FIGURE 6.9
KDE's kppp *now offers a wizard-based setup for PPP connections for seven different countries.*

If you live in Austria, Denmark, Germany, New Zealand, Norway, Portugal, or the United Kingdom and you're using the latest version of kppp, click the Wizard button, and you'll then be asked a series of questions regarding your account and ISP. U.S. users should select the Dialog setup button. A New Account dialog box then appears, as shown in Figure 6.10.

FIGURE 6.10

Enter a name and phone number for your PPP connection, then select the type of Authentication.

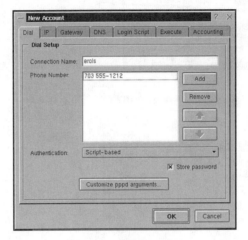

Enter the name of your ISP, along with your ISP's phone number. Most users will then want to select an Authentication, such as Script-based. When finished, click the IP tab at the top of the New Account dialog box. You'll see the IP dialog box like that shown in Figure 6.11 in which you select the type of IP address assigned to your computer after establishing a PPP connection with your ISP. If your account provides a *static*, or permanent IP address, enter that information in the IP dialog box.

FIGURE 6.11

Select dynamic addressing or enter a static IP address if assigned from your ISP.

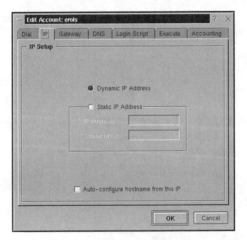

When finished, click the DNS tab in the New Account dialog box. The DNS, or Domain Name Services, dialog box shown in Figure 6.12 is used to specify the domain name and IP address(es) of your ISP's DNS servers. These servers provide translation service of active hostnames to IP numbers and back again.

FIGURE 6.12

Enter your ISP's domain name and DNS IP addresses in the dialog box.

To enter a DNS IP address, type in each IP number (provided by your ISP) and then click the Add button. When finished, click the Login Script tab (if you use the common script-based log in procedure). The Login Script dialog box appears, as shown in Figure 6.13.

FIGURE 6.13

Login scripts for usernames and passwords are entered in the Login Script dialog box.

The script used here is in the form `expect prompt`, `send prompt`, and is similar to the `chat` script discussed earlier in this chapter. Select the `Expect` keyword and then type in a portion of the prompt (such as `ogin:`) and click the Add button. Since your ISP will next expect a username, select the Send keyword and then type in your username and click the Add button. Repeat this step for your password. When finished, click OK. You'll see the Accounts dialog box as shown in Figure 6.14.

FIGURE 6.14

When you finish defining your PPP account, make sure to check the device, modem, and PPP settings for kppp.

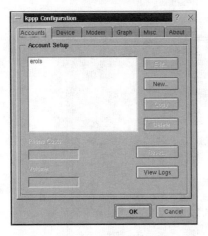

Click the Device tab to configure your modem (as shown in Figure 6.15).

FIGURE 6.15

The Device tab in the kppp Configuration dialog box is used for modem settings.

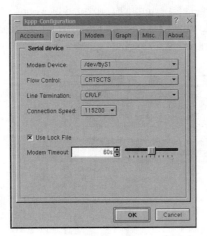

Select the correct device and connection speed for your modem. When finished, click the Modem tab. A dialog box appears, as shown in Figure 6.16.

FIGURE 6.16

The Modem tab in the kppp Configuration dialog box is used to set default modem commands and to query or test your modem.

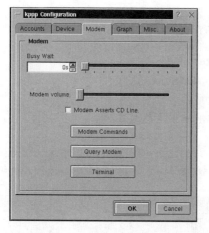

Use the buttons in the dialog box to change the default modem AT commands, to query your modem, or to test your modem by using kppp's built-in terminal program. You can also change your modem's volume by using the slider control in the dialog box. When finished, click the Misc. tab at the top of the dialog box. The options dialog box will appear, as shown in Figure 6.17.

FIGURE 6.17

Use the Misc. tab in the kppp Configuration dialog box to set how kppp uses its interface.

Select or unselect the various options in this dialog box according to your taste. If you click Dock into Panel on Connect, kppp will display a tiny modem icon with blinking send and receive lights! When finished, click OK. You'll see the main kppp window that is shown in Figure 6.18.

FIGURE **6.18**

To start your PPP connection, click the Connect button in the KPPP window.

If you click Show Log Window (see Figure 6.18) and then click the Connect button to start your PPP connection, you'll see a login script window (see Figure 6.19).

FIGURE **6.19**

The kppp *login script window shows dialing and connection progress of your connection.*

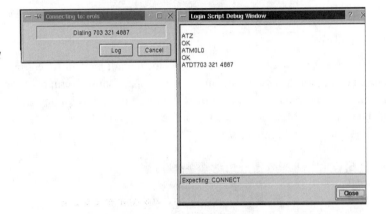

If you've set kppp to dock in your KDE panel, you can then right-click the resulting tiny modem icon in panel and select Details from the pop-up menu. A kppp Statistics dialog box appears, as shown in Figure 6.20. The dialog box shows your PPP connection's IP addresses, modem status lights, various packet information (similar to information returned by the pppstats command), and a scrolling load indicator of your PPP activity for the session.

FIGURE **6.20**

The kppp *Statistics window shows detailed PPP connection information, along with a load progress of your connection.*

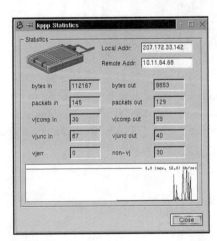

To close your connection, right-click the `kppp` indicator in your panel and then click the Disconnection menu item.

> **Note**
>
> `kppp` also comes with a PPP log utility (KPPP - `Logview`) and another standalone load viewer (KPPPLoad). To launch either tool, click the K desktop panel's Application Starter button and then select Internet.

> **Watch the Modem Lights!**
>
> If you don't use `kppp`, but like `kppp`'s modem light feature, use John Ellis' and Martin Baulig's Modem Lights Applet 1.2.1. You'll find the applet under your GNOME panel's Applets, Network menu as the Modem Lights menu item. You can also launch the applet by its name, `modemlights_applet`.

Setting Up PPP Using the `wvdial` Command

The `wvdial` command is yet another connection tool you'll find in your Red Hat Linux distribution. This command-line tool uses a single configuration file named `wvdial.conf`, located under the `/etc` directory. You can quickly create a bare-bones configuration file using the `wvdialconf` command like this:

```
# wvdialconf /etc/wvdial.conf
Scanning your serial ports for a modem.
ttyS1<*1>: ATQ0 V1 E1 -- OK
ttyS1<*1>: ATQ0 V1 E1 Z -- OK
ttyS1<*1>: ATQ0 V1 E1 S0=0 -- OK
ttyS1<*1>: ATQ0 V1 E1 S0=0 &C1 -- OK
ttyS1<*1>: ATQ0 V1 E1 S0=0 &C1 &D2 -- OK
ttyS1<*1>: ATQ0 V1 E1 S0=0 &C1 &D2 S11=55 -- OK
ttyS1<*1>: ATQ0 V1 E1 S0=0 &C1 &D2 S11=55 +FCLASS=0 -- OK
...
```

The command will scan your computer's serial ports, test any found modem, and then create your `wvdial.conf` file. You should then open the file with your favorite text editor and edit the Dialer Defaults section. The default will look like this:

```
[Dialer Defaults]
Modem = /dev/ttyS1
Baud = 115200
Init1 = ATZ
Init2 = ATQ0 V1 E1 S0=0 &C1 &D2 S11=55 +FCLASS=0
```

```
; Phone = <Target Phone Number>
; Username = <Your Login Name>
; Password = <Your Password>
```

Remove the leading semicolon (;) in the last three lines, then replace the information between brackets with your ISP's phone number, and your username and password. The change may look something like this:

```
[Dialer Defaults]
Modem = /dev/ttyS1
Baud = 115200
Init1 = ATZ
Init2 = ATQ0 V1 E1 S0=0 &C1 &D2 S11=55 +FCLASS=0
Phone = 703 321 4887
Username = bball
Password = mypassword
```

Save the file, then start your connection from the command line using the `wvdial` command, like this:

```
# wvdial
--> WvDial: Internet dialer version 1.41
--> Initializing modem.
--> Sending: ATZ
ATZ
OK
--> Sending: ATQ0 V1 E1 S0=0 &C1 &D2 S11=55 +FCLASS=0
ATQ0 V1 E1 S0=0 &C1 &D2 S11=55 +FCLASS=0
OK
--> Modem initialized.
--> Sending: ATDT 703 321 4887
--> Waiting for carrier.
ATDT 703 321 4887
CONNECT 115200 V42bis
--> Carrier detected.  Waiting for prompt.
** Ascend TNT8.BRD Terminal Server **
Login:
--> Looks like a login prompt.
--> Sending: bball
bball
Password:
--> Looks like a password prompt.
--> Sending: (password)
    Entering PPP Session.
    IP address is 207.172.33.49
    MTU is 1006.
--> Looks like a welcome message.
--> Starting pppd at Wed Jul 12 20:21:30 2000
```

The wvdial command will output diagnostic information during the connection, and will even reconnect if the connection is dropped! To end your session, press Ctrl+C.

Setting Up a DSL PPPOE Connection

There are many different ways to connect to the Internet, and there are many different commercial solutions offered by ISPs, giant network corporations, and the regional or governmental telephone companies. One of the newest and increasingly popular packages being snapped up by consumers (at least in the U.S.) is the Digital Subscriber Line, or DSL service.

DSL service is offered in a variety of packages, ranging from 256Kbps–640Kbps to 4.5Mbps–7.1Mbps. The service, which presently uses copper telephone lines from a central office to the home, is often cheaper than dedicated Internet connections or Integrated Services Digital Network, or ISDN lines. Like ISDN, a DSL connection offers voice and digital transmissions over the same phone line. Unlike ISDN, DSL does not break voice and data into different channels over a single line, but instead uses a different frequency for data transmission. This necessitates the use of digital filters for all phone lines in the home, and the use of a special modem between the phone line and your Ethernet LAN.

DSL service is an "always on" type of Internet service, although you can turn the connection on or off under Linux through software utilities. Using DSL will require the use of a network interface card in your computer or notebook. In order to share the connection with other computers on your LAN, you'll need to have a gateway, firewall, or other computer with at least two network interface cards.

Establishing a DSL connection with an ISP providing a static IP address is fairly easy. Unfortunately, most DSL providers now use a perverse form of the PPP protocol named PPPOE, or Point-to-Point Protocol over Ethernet, which provides dynamic IP address assignment and authentication by encapsulating PPP information inside Ethernet frames. Fortunately, you'll find a solution included with your Red Hat Linux distribution—Roaring Penguin's rp-pppoe clients!

Setting Up a PPPOE Connection

The basic steps involved in setting up a DSL connection using Red Hat Linux involve connecting the proper hardware, then running a simple configuration script. You'll find the necessary steps to establish a basic connection quite easy, and perhaps even easier than setting up a dial-up PPP connection.

First, connect your DSL modem to your phone line. Plug in your Ethernet cable from the modem to your computer's network interface card. If you plan to share your DSL connection with the rest of your LAN, you'll need at least two network cards, designated eth0 (for your LAN) and eth1 (for the DSL connection).

You'll also need your username and password, along with the IP addresses of your provider's DNS servers. The following example assumes that you have more than one computer and will share your DSL connection on a LAN. First, log in as `root`, and ensure your first eth0 device is enabled and up. You can use the `ifconfig` command to do this by typing the interface name and hostname like this:

```
# ifconfig eth0 stinky up
```

Next, bring up the other interface, but assign a null address like this:

```
# ifconfig eth1 0.0.0.0 up
```

Now use the `adsl-setup` command to set up your system. Type the command like this:

```
# adsl-setup
Welcome to the Roaring Penguin ADSL client setup.  First, I will run
some checks on your system to make sure the PPPoE client is installed
properly...

Looks good!  Now, please enter some information:

USER NAME

Enter your PPPoE user name (default bxxxnxnx@sympatico.ca): bball
```

At the first prompt, enter the username you received from your service provider, and then press Enter. You'll see:

```
INTERFACE

Enter the Ethernet interface connected to the ADSL modem
(default eth1): eth1
```

Enter the name of the interface connected to your DSL modem and press Enter. You'll then be asked about your connection:

```
Do you want the link to come up on demand, or stay up continuously?
If you want it to come up on demand, enter the idle time in seconds
after which the link should be dropped.  If you want the link to
stay up permanently, enter 'no'.
NOTE: Demand-activated links do not interact well with dynamic IP
addresses.  You may have some problems with demand-activated links.
Demand value (default no): no
```

After you type your answer and press Enter, you'll be asked about your ISP's DNS servers:

```
DNS

Please enter the IP address of your ISP's primary DNS server.
If you just press enter, I will assume you know what you are
doing and not modify your DNS setup.
```

```
Enter the address here: 199.45.32.38
Please enter the IP address of your ISP's secondary DNS server.
If you just press enter, I will assume there is only one DNS server.
Enter the address here: 199.45.32.43
```

Enter the IP addresses of your ISP's DNS servers and press Enter at each prompt. The
next section will query for your password:

```
PASSWORD
```

```
Please enter your PPPoE password:
Please re-enter your PPPoE password:
```

After you enter your password (twice), you'll be asked to choose the firewall and IP
masquerading rules. It is essential that you review your Red Hat Linux system to ensure
that all unneeded services are disabled and that you have installed all errata-, bug-, and
security-related fixes for your system!

```
FIREWALLING
```

```
Please choose the firewall rules to use.  Note that these rules are
very basic.  You are strongly encouraged to use a more sophisticated
firewall setup; however, these will provide basic security.  If you
are running any servers on your machine, you must choose 'NONE' and
set up firewalling yourself.  Otherwise, the firewall rules will deny
access to all standard servers like Web, e-mail, ftp, etc.

The firewall choices are:
0 - NONE: This script will not set any firewall rules.  You are responsible
          for ensuring the security of your machine.  You are STRONGLY
          recommended to use some kind of firewall rules.
1 - STANDALONE: Appropriate for a basic stand-alone web-surfing
                workstation
2 - MASQUERADE: Appropriate for a machine acting as an Internet gateway
                for a LAN
Your choice? 2
```

Enter a 0, 1, or 2 to choose the type of system you'll have connected to the Internet.
After you press Enter, you'll see:

```
** Summary of what you entered **

Ethernet Interface: eth1
User name:          bball99
Activate-on-demand: No
Primary DNS:        199.45.32.38
Secondary DNS:      199.45.32.43
Firewalling:        MASQUERADE

Accept these settings and adjust configuration files (y/n)? y
```

Accept the settings by typing a y and pressing Enter. The setup script will then report:

```
Adjusting /etc/ppp/pppoe.conf
Adjusting /etc/resolv.conf
  (But first backing it up to /etc/resolv.conf-bak)
Adjusting /etc/ppp/pap-secrets and /etc/ppp/chap-secrets
  (But first backing it up to /etc/ppp/pap-secrets-bak)
  (But first backing it up to /etc/ppp/chap-secrets-bak)

Congratulations, it should be all set up!

Type 'adsl-start' to bring up your ADSL link and 'adsl-stop' to bring
it down.
```

To start your connection, use the `adsl-start` command like this:

```
# adsl-start
```

Note that unlike a dial-up connection, the DSL connection should be nearly instantaneous. If you do not connect, ensure that your DSL modem is synched with the phone company's central office, that all cables are properly attached, that your interfaces are properly configured, and that you have entered the correct information to the setup script. There is very little troubleshooting to do on your end if you have a working setup that fails to start up. More likely than not, if a working connection becomes inactive, the problem is on the ISP side, not with your setup. This can happen if the ISP's DNS or authentication servers go down. When establishing a connection for the first time, you should follow your ISP's initial directions explicitly to establish a working connection. After you have a working connection, you can then experiment with different settings, such as the size of the Maximum Transfer Unit used by your Ethernet interface. To share ideas, ask questions, or learn more about ISPs in your area, check out the `comp.dcom.xdsl` Usenet newsgroup.

In this example, IP masquerading is enabled. This means that you can share your DSL connection with other computers on your LAN that use the same subnet address. For example, if the host computer with the DSL connection is named stinky, and has an IP address of 192.168.2.30, other computers on your LAN in the 192.168.2.XXX range can quickly access the Internet service by using the `route` command, along with the default and gateway options like this:

```
# route add default gw stinky
```

To stop your connection, use the `adsl-stop` command like this:

```
# adsl-stop
```

Besides man pages for the `adsl-setup`, `adsl-start`, and `adsl-stop` commands, you'll find additional information regarding DSL connections and the Roaring Penguin software under the `/usr/share/doc/rp-pppoe-2.2` directory.

Setting Up SLIP

SLIP is used by some ISPs who don't support PPP (a rarity these days). You may also find SLIP supported by some online services that don't use the Internet, such as bank access programs and stock trading. In the past, SLIP was usually compiled into the Linux kernel, as was a modification of SLIP called CSLIP (Compressed SLIP). With Red Hat Linux, however, SLIP support is supplied as a loadable kernel module.

To use SLIP, you need to dedicate a port to it. This means that the port cannot be used by other applications. This is necessary because of the way SLIP handles ports, which causes conflicts if shared with other programs.

> **Note**
>
> If you want SLIP installed in your kernel, you need to rebuild the kernel. See Chapter 27, "Configuring and Building Kernels," for more information.

Configuring SLIP

The fastest way to configure SLIP is to use the `slattach` program. This requires the name of the port that SLIP will use (which has a modem attached for the connection, usually). The command that sets up `slattach` is as follows:

```
# slattach /dev/ttyS0 &
```

In this case, I've configured `/dev/ttyS0` port (COM1) as the SLIP port. You can use any other port attached to your system. The ampersand at the end of the line puts the `slattach` program in the background so you can get your shell prompt back.

When you run `slattach`, the port is renamed to `/dev/sl0`, which indicates it is the first SLIP device. It doesn't matter what device name you used for the serial port; the first SLIP device is always called `/dev/sl0`. This can lead to some confusion if you are using `/dev/ttyS2`, for example, which becomes `/dev/sl0`. If more than one SLIP port is created, they are numbered increasingly as `/dev/sl1`, `/dev/sl2`, and so on. Linux usually supports up to eight SLIP lines, but it is unlikely you will need this many. To check if the SLIP device has been created, you can search the file named `dev` under the `/proc/net` directory using `fgrep` like this:

```
# fgrep sl0 /proc/net/dev
sl0:     0     0  0  0  0   0   0   0
...
```

Linux uses CSLIP by default for most SLIP lines because it packs more information in the same space as SLIP. If your ISP or whomever you are connecting to does not support CSLIP, you need to force Linux to use only SLIP. You can do this on the `slattach` line:

```
# slattach -p slip /dev/ttyS0 &
```

This tells `slattach` to use only the SLIP protocol. Other valid arguments after the `-p` option are `cslip` (for CSLIP), `adaptive` (which adjusts to whatever is at the other end of the connection), `ppp`, and `kiss` (for packet radio).

Now that the SLIP device has been created, you need to tell the Linux kernel about it, using the `ifconfig` program for setting up the dummy interface. The `ifconfig` line that establishes the interface requires the name of the remote system:

```
ifconfig sl0 mymachine-slip pointopoint remotemachine
```

`sl0` is the name of the interface (`/dev/sl0` in this case); *mymachine*-slip is the local name of the SLIP interface (you should substitute your machine's name, such as `merlin-slip` or `darkstar-slip`); `pointopoint` tells `ifconfig` the interface is a point-to-point connection (not to be confused with PPP); and *remotemachine* is the name of the machine at the other end of the connection. For example, if the remote machine's name is `darkstar` and your machine's name is `dogbert`, the `ifconfig` command looks like this:

```
ifconfig sl0 dogbert-slip pointopoint darkstar
```

The next step is to issue the `route` command to add the route to the remote machine to the system databases. The syntax is the same as when you set up the dummy interface:

```
route add darkstar
```

In this case, you are adding a route to the remote machine called `darkstar`. You should substitute whatever the remote machine is called.

> **Note**
>
> Many ISPs don't tell you their remote machine's names. That's fine because these machine names are only placeholders; the important information needed is the IP addresses. Although not recommended, you can substitute any name you want that identifies the other end of the connection, as long as the name is defined in your `/etc/hosts` file. However, the associated IP address must be correct.

Setting Up a Dial-In PPP Server

You can also set up a simple service on your Linux system to provide PPP for dial-in
users. Although commercial ventures such as ISPs must necessarily invest in leased lines,
switching service, modem pools, and routers, you can easily configure a standalone
Linux box to answer a modem and start PPP. The general steps may include

- Selecting a phone line, modem, and serial port

- Properly configuring the modem to answer incoming calls (using AT commands
  and saving the modem profile with AT&W)

- Installing a line-monitoring application (such as agetty, getty, or mgetty) to
  watch a serial port (in /etc/inittab)

- Possibly configuring a DNS server (see Chapter 14, "Domain Name Service and
  Dynamic Host Configuration Protocol," for more information)

- Configuring Linux to automatically start the pppd daemon after a user logs in

In general, and for many modems, the ATE1Q0V1&C1&S0S0=1&W modem string will set up
a modem to autoanswer calls using different terminal monitors. (Some, such as uugetty,
have configuration files to automatically set up the modem for a particular serial port.)
The next step is to make an appropriate entry in the /etc/inittab file:

```
3:2345:respawn:/sbin/uugetty ttyS1 38400 vt100
```

This entry assumes you have a modem attached to /dev/ttyS1. If you use the uugetty
command to monitor your modem's serial port, you'll also need to copy the file
uugetty.autoanswer from the /usr/doc/getty_ps-2.0.7j/Examples/default directory to the /etc/default directory. You should then edit this file and look for the
ALTLOCK entry:

```
# alternate lockfile to check... if this lockfile exists, then uugetty is
# restarted so that the modem is re-initialized
ALTLOCK=cua2
```

Change the ALTLOCK entry to match your modem's serial port. Using the previous
/etc/inittab entry, the string cua2 would be changed to ttyS1. The file should then be
saved in the /etc/default directory with the name uugetty and a suffix to match the
serial port (such as uugetty.ttyS0). You should then dial in from a remote computer to
check the login process.

The next step is to create a user to test PPP service. Use the adduser command to create
a user named **ppp** and then assign a password. Although users can log in to your system
and then start pppd from the command line (assuming you've set pppd to SUID), you can

have the `pppd` daemon started automatically by creating a short shell script and then assigning the shell script in the user's `/etc/passwd` entry like this:

```
ppp:x:501:501::/home/ppp:/usr/local/bin/doppp
```

In this instance, the script `doppp` (made executable with `chmod +x`) would contain the following:

```
exec /usr/sbin/pppd -detach
```

Using this approach, `pppd` will start automatically after the ppp dial-in user connects and logs in (using the `ppp-on` scripts or other clients, such as `netcfg` or `kppp`).

You should also edit the file `options` under the `/etc/ppp` directory to include general dial-in options for PPP service on your system, and create specific options files (such as `options.ttyS1` for this example) for each enabled dial-in port. For example, `/etc/ppp/options` could contain

```
asyncmap 0
netmask 255.255.255.0
proxyarp
lock
crtscts
modem
```

There are many approaches to providing PPP service. You may want to assign IP addresses dynamically, or assign static IP addresses for your users. You should probably have DNS enabled, although you will still be sharing hostnames via `/etc/hosts` and providing static address assignment by using `options.ttyX` files (where `X` is the serial port). For example, `/etc/ppp/options.ttyS1` could contain

```
IPofPPPserver:assignedIPofdialinuser
```

After you set up your `/etc/ppp/options` and `/etc/ppp/options.ttyS` files, dial in from a remote computer (perhaps using `netcfg`, `kppp`, or the `ppp-on` script). If your chat script uses `pppd`'s debug option, you can watch the progress of your connection by using the `tail` command on `/var/log/messages`:

```
...
May 21 17:05:55 aptiva pppd[7761]: Serial connection established.
May 21 17:05:56 aptiva pppd[7761]: Using interface ppp0
May 21 17:05:56 aptiva pppd[7761]: Connect: ppp0 <--> /dev/modem
May 21 17:06:02 aptiva pppd[7761]: local  IP address 198.168.2.36
May 21 17:06:02 aptiva pppd[7761]: remote IP address 198.168.2.34
```

6

PPP Service Setup and Security Tips

See the file `README.linux` under the `/usr/share/doc/ppp-2.3.11` directory for a detailed discussion about connecting two computers, a single computer to a network, or linking two networks using Linux PPP. You'll find loads of tips, and a special list of security concerns (such as permissions, relevant files, and electronic mail).

For more information about using PPP, see Robert Hart's PPP-HOWTO, available through `http://www.linuxdoc.org`.

Summary

In this chapter you learned a variety of ways to set up Internet connections using software included with your Red Hat Linux distribution. You found that there are numerous utilities and software packages you can use to establish connections over dial-up phone lines or over a network, even a simple network between two computers. PPP, PPPOE, and SLIP are mostly transparent to you once the interfaces are properly set up. The Linux user base (and most Internet users) will move toward broadband Internet access over the next several years. Even so, modem dialup for establishing remote connections will remain important. This is especially so when considering the growth of wireless Internet connections and current implementations of network access by cellular companies. You can be sure, however, that Linux will keep pace with any new change in technology, and that you'll find the tools you need to work efficiently with tomorrow's or next year's technology.

IRC, ICQ, and Chat Clients

CHAPTER 7

The Internet has become popular because it makes communication so easy and accessible. It is now one of the world's largest distribution channels for all types of communication. There are many different ways to communicate via the Internet. The World Wide Web serves as a great way to simultaneously distribute information to a large group of people, whereas email is an excellent channel for both personal communication as well as group communication. However, neither the Web nor mail are very well suited for interpersonal, real-time communication. For that reason, several protocols and programs have been created to suit this purpose.

There are many programs available that enable people to host group discussions about various topics. These programs are often referred to as chat programs. One of the most widely used systems for group chatting is Internet Relay Chat, or IRC. On UNIX systems you can often use the `talk` command for person-to-person conversations. Today's average Internet user is probably used to other, more modern instant messaging protocols and programs such as ICQ and AIM, which currently are the most widely used clients/protocols for real-time, personal discussions on the Internet.

The Talk Client and Server

This survey of different chat programs begins by looking at talk. This is arguably the grandfather of all network-aware chat programs. It is certainly the program that served as an inspiration for IRC—much the same way as both IRC and talk have provided the fundamental ideas used in newer chat and instant messaging protocols, such as ICQ and AIM.

`talk` is a very simple, basic chat program. All the client does is establish a link between the terminals of two computer users. The users can either reside on the same computer or on different, networked computers. Everything that one user types into his terminal will instantly be shown on the other user's terminal and vice versa.

There are several versions of the `talk` command and the underlying protocols. Unfortunately, not all of them are compatible with each other. The initial version of the talk protocol used machine-dependent byte ordering. Therefore, you could only use `talk` to communicate with people who used computers with the same processor architecture as your computer's processor. In order to overcome this problem, `ntalk` was created. This new talk client always uses network byte order. The first version of `ntalk` was not compatible with the old `talk` command. However, the version that is included with this release of Linux tries to fix talk packets with the wrong byte order, such as those that originate from legacy `talk` clients. To be able to differentiate between the talk and ntalk protocols, they are assigned to different TCP ports. If you look in your `/etc/services`, you will see that port 517 is used for `talk` and 518 for `ntalk`.

Setting Up and Configuring Talk

Naturally you need to have the talk client package installed to be able to use the `talk` command. Furthermore, to be able to receive talk requests you will also need to have the `talkd` daemon installed. This daemon is launched by `xinetd` whenever a talk request arrives at one of the TCP ports that have been defined for talk. If you have installed your computer as a workstation, `xinetd` will not have been installed automatically. In that case, you will have to install `xinetd` yourself.

The following example shows how you can determine whether the needed packages are installed on your computer (the version numbers in the query output may vary from system to system):

```
$ rpm -q xinetd talk talk-server
xinetd-2.1.8.9pre9-6
talk-0.17-7.i386
talk-server-0.17-7
```

If any of the packages are not installed, the output from `rpm` will inform you which packages are missing. You will need to obtain the missing RPM packages and install them. See the summary at the end of this chapter for places where you can obtain those RPMs.

Once you have obtained the RPM packages, it is time to install them on your computer. In order to do this you have to be logged in as the `root` user. You must be sure to install the RPMs in the correct order, because they depend and build upon functionality available in the other packages. You should first install the `talk` package, then the `xinetd` package, and finally the `talk-server` package. Of course, the last two packages are only needed if you want to be able to receive talk invitations. As an example, to install the talk client package you would issue the following command (once again, the version number may differ):

```
rpm -Uvh talk-0.17-7.i386.rpm.
```

If you have chosen to include a fully functional talk service, you should proceed to install the `talk-server` package as well as the `xinetd` RPM. When you have installed `xinetd`, be sure to start the `xinetd` daemon. You do this by typing

```
/etc/rc.d/init.d/xinetd start
```

Manually starting the service is only necessary directly after the installation. The installation process will have added an entry in your run-level files that will automatically start the daemon every time the system is restarted in the future.

After you have installed the necessary RPMs, try to run the talk command like this:

```
talk <your own user name>
```

7

IRC, ICQ, AND
CHAT CLIENTS

Something akin to the following message should appear on your terminal:

```
[Waiting for your party to respond]
Message from Talk_Daemon@test.gnulix.org at 21:31
talk: connection requested by wsb@test.gnulix.org.
Talk: respond with: talk wsb@test.gnulix.org
```

If either `talkd` or `xinetd` are not installed and enabled, you will receive the following message:

```
[No connection yet]
[ Error on read from talk daemon : Connection refused ]
```

Connecting with Talk

Basically, there are two ways to use talk. Either you try to initiate a chat with another user or someone tries to chat with you. You can either talk to a user that is logged on locally or to a user that is reachable via the network.

To connect to a user on the local machine you will only need to know his login name. You can check to see who is logged in for the moment with the `who` command. For example:

```
$ who
patrikj  tty1     Jul  6 21:51
wsb      pts/1    Jul 18 06:56
```

Assume that you would like to try to talk to another user who has `wsb` as his user id. You would need to send an invitation to him by issuing `talk wsb`. The other user will then get a message on his terminal informing him that you would like to chat.

When you want to talk to a user on another computer you need to know both his login id as well as the name of the computer that he logged onto. For example, assuming that you want to talk to the user from the previous example, who is now logged onto a computer named `test.gnulix.org`, you would type `talk wsb@test.gnulix.org`.

Assume that the `wsb` user from the previous example tries to contact you from his system, `test.gnulix.org`. You would receive something like this on your terminal:

```
Message from TalkDaemon@test.gnulix.org
talk: connection requested by wsb@test.gnulix.org.
talk: respond with: talk wsb@test.gnulix.org
```

As the message indicates, you would initiate a connection to `wsb` by typing `talk wsb@test.gnulix.org`. After the connection has been established you can chat with him via talk's rudimentary user interface.

When you try to establish a talk link, you can also define to which terminal, or tty as they are often referred to in UNIX lingo, your request should be directed. To do this you simply add the name of the tty after the username. This can be useful if the user to whom you wish to chat is logged in with several terminal sessions.

Chatting via Talk

After the talk session has been established your terminal screen will split into two parts. The upper part is where you will type text. Whatever you type will show up immediately on the recipient's side. The lower part of the terminal window will show whatever the person to whom you are chatting is writing.

Typing certain control sequences serve as commands to the talk client. Table 7.1 shows the command sequences that are available while chatting. The scroll commands will only affect your side of the talk session.

The Meta key is usually assigned to your Alt key. You may also use the Escape key as a substitute for the Meta key. To do this, press the Escape key and then press the key that you want to combine it with. Please note that this will not auto repeat—so you will need to perform the escape combination repeatedly to scroll more than one line at a time.

TABLE 7.1   Control Commands Used in Talk Sessions

Command	*Description*
Ctrl+c	Ends the talk session.
Ctrl+l	Redraws the screen.
Ctrl+n	Scrolls the upper text buffer down.
Ctrl+p	Scrolls the upper text buffer up.
Ctrl+u	Deletes the current row.
Ctrl+w	Deletes the current row.
Meta+n	Scrolls the lower text buffer down.
Meta+p	Scrolls the lower text buffer up.

Controlling Access to Your Terminal

Sometimes you might not want people to be able to interrupt you by requesting to talk to you. To avoid this you can use the mesg command to turn off external access to your terminal. There are two possible parameters for mesg: y or n. A y indicates that access is allowed, whereas an n is used to disallow access. Running mesg without any parameter will show the current state of your terminal. The default behavior of a new terminal is to have external access turned on.

If a user tries to talk to you while you have turned off access to your terminal, he will receive a similar error message:

```
[Your party is refusing messages]
```

> **Note**
>
> Certain programs will turn off access to your terminal automatically. They do this so that their outputs will not be disturbed by a talk request. Some examples of programs that might temporarily turn off access to your terminal are pine, pr, and nroff.

Turning off access to your terminal will affect all commands that try to write to your terminal. Examples of such commands are wall and write.

> **Note**
>
> The root user is treated differently than ordinary users when she tries to access your terminal. She will not be able to override your settings when it comes to the talk command. However, it is different for commands such as wall and write. These kinds of messages from root will always be displayed, no matter what your terminal settings are. This is because information from the system administrator is potentially very important. For example, it might be a warning that the system is about to be rebooted.

Talking with Multiple Users with ytalk

The regular talk client can only be used for chats involving two persons. To alleviate this restriction, a new talk client called ytalk has been created. Using this you can chat with multiple users at the same time. The functionality of ytalk is more or less the same as talk.

The ytalk command is not very common, even though it is becoming increasingly popular. Thankfully, it is compatible with the ordinary talk client. So there is nothing to stop you from using it to chat with other users who have access only to the talk command.

One nice feature of ytalk is that if you run it under the X Window System you will get a GUI version of the command; this behavior can be inhibited by specifying the -x switch. The GUI interface is pretty basic and consists of two windows. One window will be your input window, and anything you type there will be sent to all other users' talk clients. There will be a separate window for each user you are talking to.

If you run the client without the X Window interface, the screen will look more or less as it does in an ordinary talk session. The screen will be split once for each user who is taking part in the conversation and the output from them will be shown there.

Another feature of `ytalk` is that you can redirect the output of other commands to it. This can be very useful if you need to send a file listing or something similar to other users.

Because `ytalk` is not that common, I will not go into it much further. If you want more information about it please refer to its man page.

IRC—Internet Relay Chat

Internet Relay Chat, or as it is more commonly known, IRC, is one of the most popular ways to chat with other groups of people from around the world. From the beginning it was designed as an enhanced replacement for the talk program. Its main purpose is to enable users to participate in real-time, simultaneous discussions with many other users. However, during its lifetime of more than a decade, IRC has evolved into much more.

Much like Linux, IRC has its roots in Finland. It was created by Jarkko Oikarinen in 1988. At that time he was working at the Department of Information Processing Science at the University of Oulu. It was there, on `tolsun.oulu.fi`, that the world's first IRC server was set up in August 1988. IRC did not really take off with ordinary Internet users until early in 1991, when the Gulf War began. People in the west were desperate for timely, inside information about the war and Operation Desert Storm, whereas Kuwaitis and Saudi Arabians wanted to inform the world about what was happening to them. Several IRC channels specializing in war news and discussions sprang up on the IRC networks. People flocked to these IRC channels for live, uncensored, first-hand information and eyewitness accounts. Remember, this was before the proliferation of the World Wide Web!

The IRC protocol was originally documented in RFC 1459. This RFC was written in 1993 by Jarkko Oikarinen. The IRC specifications were recently updated in a number of RFCs. The updates were all written by Christophe Kalt. A list of the new RFCs can be found in Table 7.2. These new RFCs describe all of the important changes and addenda that have been done to the IRC protocol over the years. Most likely, these documents will only be of interest to you if you plan to implement your own IRC client or server. But it could also be of interest if you want a fuller understanding of the inner workings of IRC.

TABLE 7.2 RFC Specifications for the IRC Protocol

RFC	Title
2813	Internet Relay Chat: Server Protocol
2812	Internet Relay Chat: Client Protocol
2811	Internet Relay Chat: Channel Management
2810	Internet Relay Chat: Architecture

Today there are several different IRC nets, with servers located all over the world. The IRC nets are a collection of servers that share information. All user and channel data are propagated between all servers within the net. Every message that is sent in a conversation is mirrored to all other servers within the net. Depending on the size of the net, a server may be connected to dozens of other servers as well as being connected to several hundreds of clients. Some of the nets have tens of thousands of users. All of these servers are very busy and often under quite a heavy load.

There are thousands of different channels on the IRC nets. These channels cover very diverse subjects, from the extremely obscure to the utterly mundane. You will probably be able to find a channel covering just about every topic you can imagine—and probably several that you cannot imagine. If you can't find what you are looking for, there is no reason you can't start your own channel.

Basically, IRC is a multiuser chat system. People gather to chat in discussion forums called channels. Channels are usually created for a special-interest group and their names are mostly self-explanatory. Apart from a name, each channel can also be assigned a topic. This can be used to describe the purpose of the channel or it can be set to describe the current topic of conversation. There is practically no limit to the number of channels that may exist on any given IRC net.

Discussions are either held privately between two users or, more commonly, shared between all users in the channel. It can be quite bewildering the first few times you come into a busy channel with many users sending messages all at the same time. It might look quite chaotic, but you are likely to get used to it in no time. When you join a new channel, it might be a good idea to sit around for a while and observe how others behave on the channel. Sitting around doing nothing but reading the conversations is often referred to as lurking. Try to be polite and do not do anything to irritate other users. But most of all, try to enjoy yourself.

You need a client in order to access IRC. It is up to the client to interpret incoming information from the server and present it to the user in a workable fashion. The client will also need to interpret the user's actions and respond to them in some way, usually by sending them to the IRC server.

The first IRC clients were text-only. They were most often written with the use of the curses library, which is used to program terminal-independent, text-only user interfaces. The most popular of these text-based IRC clients is probably the `ircII` client, especially if you count the numerous spin-offs and clones of it that are available.

Later on several IRC clients with graphical user interfaces appeared on the Internet scene. The introduction of these clients has certainly helped to increase the popularity of IRC among less computer literate users. One of the most popular GUI clients is undoubtedly `mIRC`, which is only available for the Windows operating system. There are several very good GUI IRC clients available for Linux.

This chapter will look at both a GUI and a non-GUI IRC client that are included with the Red Hat 7 distribution. It will examine the non-GUI IRC client first because many of the commands that are used with it can also be used in the GUI client. You will get a much better understanding of how IRC works by seeing what commands are available and how they are used.

Using a Non-GUI IRC Client—`ircII`

The `ircII` client sprang from the original `irc` client created by Jarkko Oikarinen. It is widely used and most likely one of the most popular non-GUI IRC clients ever. There are several IRC clients that are either based on the `ircII` source or that clone the behavior of `ircII`. The command setup used in `ircII` has become so popular that the same, or very similar, commands are now widely used in several other UNIX programs, especially in other IRC clients. However, this might not be so strange since the commands are very similar to the actual commands used within the IRC protocol, which is used for the communication between the client and the server.

> **Tip**
>
> Another very popular IRC client is `bitchx`. This is not included with the Red Hat 7 distribution. However, if you like to use IRC via a non-GUI client, you will probably want to get your hands on `bitchx`. It has many enhancements and improvements over `ircII`. For example, it handles uploading and downloading of files via dcc and it also has support for ANSI graphics and mIRC colors. The `bitchx` client is available as an RPM package and you can find it at `http://www.bitchx.org/`.

GUI clients try to shield the user from having to use the sometimes obscure commands of text-only clients. Even so, most GUI clients also support the use of /-like commands. Since IRC to a large extent is about constantly typing, it can be much faster to actually type the IRC commands as well, rather than fumble for the mouse and find a button or a menu each time you want to do something. So, even if you use a GUI IRC Client, it can be useful to know the text versions of the basic commands because you will be able to use most of them even though you are running a GUI client.

Installing `ircII`

First check to see whether `ircII` is already installed on your system by typing

`rpm -q ircii`

If `ircII` is installed, the system will print the full package name of the `ircII` package.

If the RPM is not installed, you will need to get a copy of it and install it. Look at the resource list at the end of the chapter for places where you might find the RPM. To install `ircII` from an RPM you will need to type the following (the version number might be different from the one in this example):

`rpm -Uvh ircii-4.4M-4.i386.rpm`

You should now be able to use `ircII` on your system.

Starting `ircII`

The easiest way to start `ircII` is by issuing the following command:

`irc`

This will start the client, which will then try to connect to one of the predefined IRC servers. It will try to log in to that IRC server, using the name of your UNIX account as your nickname. See the section on using `ircII` for more about nicknames. The IRC client will not join any channels for you. Finally, the client will be waiting for you to type some commands.

There are several switches available for the `irc` command. The built-in help will display the following information:

```
$ irc --help
Usage: irc [switches] [nickname] [server list]
   The [nickname] can be at most 9 characters long on some server
   The [server list] is a whitespace separated list of server names
   The [switches] may be any or all of the following
    -c <channel> joins <channel> o startup
    -p <port>    default IRC server connection port (usually 6667)
    -P <port>    default ICB server connection port (usually 7326)
    -f           your terminal uses flow controls (^S/^Q), so IRCII shouldn't
    -F           your terminal doesn't use flow control (default)
    -s           don't use separate server processes (ircio)
    -S           use separate server processes (ircio)
```

```
-h <host>     source host, for multihomed machines
-d            runs IRCII in "dumb" terminal mode
-q            does not load .ircrc and not .ircquick
-a            adds default servers and command line servers to server list
-b            load .ircrc before connecting to a server
-l <file>     loads <file> in place of your .ircrc
-I <file>     loads <file> in place of your .ircquick
-icb          use ICB connections by default
-irc          use IRC connections by default
              icb [same switches]  (default to -icb)
```

The most important option to the client is the one that allows you to supply an IRC nickname at startup. Also, the -c switch is useful if you want to join a channel straight away. However, the best way to provide these options is to make your own ircII configuration file, which is covered in the section "Customizing ircII with a .ircrc File," later in the chapter.

Using ircII

There is not enough room to cover all commands that are available in ircII, especially not in any great depth. There are scores of commands and options available. However, the ones that are covered in this section should be more than enough to get you started on your way to becoming an IRC wizard.

All commands have a leading / character. This tells the client that it is a command and as such needs further processing before taking any action with it. Anything else will be sent straight away to the channel you are currently in.

All ircII commands can be abbreviated to their shortest possible unique and unambiguous forms. For example, the /connect command can be abbreviated as /con, but not as /co since that would be ambiguous, because there is also a /comment command. Do note that it is also possible to abbreviate the name of options and control switches.

There is an excellent, built-in help command. This can be accessed by typing /help, followed by the name of the command you want further help with. There you will find all the possible options and switches that can be specified for a command, as well as brief but explanatory text describing the usage of the command.

The following sections are an alphabetized list of some of the most common commands. For those commands that have them, there is a list of options and switches that you may use to change their behavior. For some commands there are more options available than the ones described here. Those options that are included are the most common and most useful ones and they should provide a good basis for your IRC usage.

alias

Syntax:

```
/alias name commands
```

This allows you to create an alias, or a macro, for commonly used commands. This is most useful in your ircII startup and configuration file. However, it can also be used within the client at runtime.

The *commands* part can consist of just about any ircII command. If you want to string together several commands, you separate them with a semicolon (;).

You can also insert special character sequences, such as ircII variables in the *commands* part. Such sequences are prefixed with a $. To see the built-in variables that are available in ircII you can use the /help alias special command. There are also special variables for macros that you can use to let the user specify options when running your macros. These option variables are called $0, $1, and so on. Each occurrence of one of these numbered variables will be expanded into the corresponding option that the user supplied with the macro. In some situations you will want the last variable to be set to all the remaining parts of the user input. This can, for example, be useful for a macro where the last part is a message. To accomplish this you will need to add a hyphen (-) after the variable name.

Note

Commands used in an alias statement should *not* be prefixed with a /!

Here is a short example of how to define an alias:

```
/alias reply msg $, $0-
```

The special variable $ expands to the nickname of the user who last sent a message to you. You would then use the alias like this:

```
/reply Hi there!
```

This would then be expanded, internally, into the following by ircII (if WSB was the user who last sent a message to you):

```
/msg WSB Hi there!
```

Finally, if you want to remove an alias, you can prefix the *name* parameter with a hyphen (-).

away

Syntax:

`/away message`

This will mark your status as being "away." If someone sends you a message or does a `/whois` on you, he will receive your *message* in reply.

To remove your away status, simply use the `/away` command once again, this time without supplying a *message*.

bye, exit, signoff, and quit

Syntax:

`/bye reason`

`/exit reason`

`/signoff reason`

`/quit reason`

All of these commands will terminate your current IRC session. There is no difference between the commands; they are different aliases for the same command. It is possible to supply a sign off *reason* as a parameter to the commands. For example:

`/bye Time to rejoin my real life...`

The previous example would result in the following output to the channel you where in (assuming your nickname on the server was set to `WSB`):

`*** Signoff: WSB (Time to rejoin my real life...)`

channel and join

Syntax:

`/channel channels`

`/join channels`

The `/channel` command is used to join channels on the IRC net you are currently connected to. This command can either be specified as `/channel` or as `/join`. If no *channels* are specified you will get a list of those channels that you are currently in.

Channel names can begin with a # or a &. The former are channels that are available on all servers within the IRC net to which you are currently connected. The latter type of channel is only available locally on the server you are connected to. Local channels are not very common. The channel name can consist of any character except space, carriage return, null, and line feed.

If you specify a channel that does not exist, it will be created and you will become the operator for that channel. Being an operator goes outside the scope of this section. However, you can refer to /help to find out more about the commands that are available for a channel operator.

disconnect

Syntax:

```
/disconnect
```

This command will disconnect you from the server specified. If you don't specify a server, the command will default to the current server.

dmsg and msg

Syntax:

```
/dmsg nickname message
```

```
/msg nickname message
```

This command is used to send a private message to the user with the specified *nickname*. Only the user with the specified nickname will be shown the message. If you specify . as the *nickname*, the message will be sent to the user to whom you last sent a message.

help

Syntax:

```
/help command
```

This will show a help section about the given *command*. The *command* should be specified without prefixing it with a /. At any given moment when using the help command you can issue a ? to be given a list of available topics and sub-topics.

leave or part

Syntax:

```
/leave channel
```

```
/part channel
```

Use this to leave a channel. If you do not specify a channel name, the client will assume that you want to leave the currently active channel.

list

Syntax:

```
/list expression
```

The /list command will present you with a list containing various information about the specified channels. In this list you will find channel name, how many users there are in the channel at the moment, and the topic of the channel (if one is set).

If you are in a channel and set the *expression* to a * character, you will only be shown information about the channel you are currently in. If you are not in a channel when you use a * character as an expression, then all available channels will be listed.

There are several options available for the /list command. These options are enabled by specifying one or several of the various switches together with the command. See Table 7.3 for a summary of the control switches that are available. Using the /list command without any *expression* or switches can produce quite a lot of output.

If the server you are connected to is under a high load you may not be allowed to run the /list command. If this occurs, you can usually retry the /list command again after a little while.

TABLE 7.3 Control Switches for the /list Command

Switch	Description
-ALL	Overrides previous -PUBLIC and -PRIVATE control switches.
-MAX *n*	Lists only those channels that currently have more than *n* users.
-MIN *n*	Lists only those channels that currently have fewer than *n* users.
-PRIVATE	Lists only channels that are marked as private.
-PUBLIC	Lists only channels that are open for everyone.
-TOPIC	Lists only channels that have a topic set.
-WIDE	Lists channel information in as little space as possible. This switch may take the following argument to change the sorting order of the list:
-NAME	Orders the list by the name of the channels.
-USERS	Orders the list by the number of users in each channel.

names

Syntax:

/names *switches channel*

This command will list the nicknames of all the users in the specified channel. If you do not specify a channel, information for all channels will be listed. To get information only about the channel you currently are in, use a * for channel name. See Table 7.4 for a list of available switches.

TABLE 7.4 Control Switches for the /names Command

Switch	Description
-ALL	Overrides any previous -PUBLIC and/or -PRIVATE switches.
-MAX *n*	Channels with more than *n* users will not be shown.
-MIN *n*	Channels with fewer than *n* users will not be shown.
-PRIVATE	Only shows channels marked as private.
-PUBLIC	Only shows channels that are public.

nick

Syntax:

/nick *nickname*

This command is used to set your nickname, or *nick* as it is often abbreviated. If some-one else is using the nick you requested, you will be prompted for a new nickname. When you start the ircII client it will use your Linux login name as the default nick-name. You can modify this behavior by creating an .ircrc configuration file for ircII.

On some IRC nets it is possible to register and reserve your nickname. Doing this makes sure that you are the only one that can use that nick on that net. This might be a good idea if you are going to use that IRC net a lot. Furthermore, your chat buddies can be reasonably sure that it is really you with whom they are chatting if you have a regis-tered nick.

The behavior of nick registration can be different on different IRC nets. The most com-mon method goes something like this: If you try to set your nickname to one that is already registered by someone else then you will be given 60 seconds to specify another nickname. If you do not change the name within the allotted 60 seconds, the server will change your nickname for you. It will set a nick patterned along the lines of guest<number>. Many IRC channels will not allow people with such a nickname to join them. Therefore, it is always best to change to a proper nickname as quickly as possible.

server

Syntax:

/server *servername:port*

/server *number*

This command allows you to connect to an IRC server. If you already are connected to a server, you will be disconnected from that one and the newly specified server will become your primary server. As long as you remain on the same IRC net, you should retain your nickname and stay within the channels. However, sometimes a server change is not performed fast enough. In such a case the new server will think that someone else is already using your nickname and that this user is logged in on the previous server. You will therefore be refused to use the same nick again. When this happens you will either need to wait a short while before setting your nick again and rejoining the channels you want, or you can specify a new nickname instead.

At the same time that you supply a server name you can also specify which port number the IRC server is to be contacted on. If you do not specify a port number, the default IRC port number will be used. The default port number for IRC traffic is 6667.

The `ircII` client has a built-in list of servers that you have visited. If you enter the `/server` command without any parameters, you will be shown a list of these servers. If you start the `ircII` client without naming a specific server, one will be picked from the built-in list.

version

Syntax:

`/version server`

This shows version information about your IRC client. You will also be shown information about the server you specified. If you do not supply a *server* parameter, the command defaults to the server you are currently connected to. If you are not connected to a server, there will be no output about any server.

who

Syntax:

`/who expression`

This will produce a list of users on the IRC server you are on. If you specify an * as the expression, only users on the current channel will be listed. If you specify a 0 as an expression, all users on the whole IRC net will be shown. Apart from these two special cases you can supply any valid string containing regular expressions and the command will try to list only those users who match this expression. See Table 7.5 for more information of switches that are available for the `/who` command.

TABLE 7.5 Control Switches for the /who Command

Switch	Description
-away	Lists only users who are marked away.
-chops	Lists only channel operators.
-file *filename*	Lists only people who are listed in the file.
-here	Lists only users who are marked as here.
-host	Lists only users from the specified host.
-lusers	Lists only non-operators.
-name *username*	Lists only the users who have user ids that match the *username* argument.
-nick	Lists only users with matching nicknames.
-operators	Lists only operators.
-server	Lists only users from the specified server.

whois

Syntax:

/whois *nicknames*

This is used to get detailed information about users with the specified nicknames. You will get the following information about each user: user name, host, server, real name, and their away message. The real name has to be taken with a grain of salt because the user can set this to whatever he wants.

For example, you might get the following output if you try the following command: /whois wsb.

```
*** wsb is wsb@test.gnulix.org (William B.)
*** on channels: @#gnulix
*** on irc via server irc-2.mit.edu (Massachusetts Institute of Technology)
*** wsb has been idle 27 seconds
```

whowas

Syntax:

/whowas *nickname*

This shows detailed information about the user who last used the specified nickname. This will be shown even if the user is not logged in. You will be shown the same information as the /whois command outputs.

Customizing `ircII` with a `.ircrc` File

When `ircII` starts up it will try to access its local configuration file. This file is named `.ircrc` and simply contains ordinary `ircII` commands, just as those you use during your `ircII` sessions. By putting the commands you often use, especially during start up, in a file you can save a lot of typing and start up IRC sessions much faster.

Listing 7.1 is a sample `.ircrc` script that is distributed in the `ircII` package. You can find this sample file at `/usr/share/irc/script/ircprimer`. Notice that it defines many powerful macros and aliases. This could probably serve as a good basis for your own `.ircrc` file.

> **Note**
>
> Commands used in your `.ircrc` files should *not* be prefixed with a `/`!

LISTING 7.1   A Sample `.ircrc` File

```
# Sample .ircrc script, from the IRCprimer v1.1
# ------------------------------------------------------------------
#    IRCII sample configuration file  (~/.ircrc)  (Nicolas Pioch)
# ------------------------------------------------------------------
# The aim of this file is to shorten all useful commands to 1 letter.

^set DISPLAY off
set NOVICE off
set INPUT_ALIASES off
set AUTO_WHOWAS on
set SHOW_CHANNEL_NAMES on
set SHOW_AWAY_ONCE on

# Speeds up ircII display 2 times
set SCROLL_LINES 2

# Put Hack notices down under
# Get rid of stupid 2.6 server messages "*** Nick: Channel not found"
on ^SERVER_NOTICE "% \*\*\* Notice -- Hack: *" set status_user Hack: $5-
on ^403 *

# Modified killpath script from YeggMan
ALIAS kpath ECHO ### Last received KILL for $nkp.path
ASSIGN nkp.path <empty>
ALIAS nkp.msg ECHO ### $Z -- KILL by $1 for $0 $2-
ALIAS nkp.idx ^ASSIGN FUNCTION_RETURN $({[$RINDEX(! $0)] + 1})
ALIAS nkp.srv ^ASSIGN FUNCTION_RETURN $INDEX(. $MID($nkp.idx($0) 512 $0))
```

LISTING 7.1   continued

```
ON ^SERVER_NOTICE "% \*\*\* Notice -- Received KILL*" {
        IF ( nkp.srv($12) > -1 )
            { nkp.msg $8 $10 }
            { nkp.msg $8 $10 $13- }
        ^ASSIGN nkp.path $8-
}

# Function to strip the less significant part of an internet hostname
alias userdomain {
   @ function_return = LEFT($INDEX(@ $0) $0)##[@]##MID(${1+INDEX(. $0)} 99 $0)
}

# Who is that ?
on ^msg * echo *$0!$userdomain($userhost())* $1-

# /w [<nickname>]                       get info on someone
# /q [<nickname>]                       query someone
# /m   <nickname> <text>                send a message
# /n   <nickname> <text>                send a notice
# /r <text>                             reply to last message I got
# /a <text>                             followup on my last message


alias w whois
alias q query
alias m msg
alias n notice
alias r msg $,
alias a msg $.

# /j <channel>                          join a channel
# /l <channel>                          list people in a channel
# /ll                                   list in the current channel
# /i <nickname> [<channel>]             invite someone
# /hop                                  leave the current channel


alias j join
alias l who
alias ll who *
alias i invite
alias hop part $C

# /o <nickname> [<nickname> <nickname>] give channel op status
# /d <nickname> [<nickname> <nickname>] remove channel op status
# /k <nickname>                         kick someone
# /mo [+|-]<modechars>                  change current channel mode


alias o mode $C +ooo
alias d mode $C -ooo
alias k kick $C
alias mo mode $C
```

LISTING 7.1   continued

```
# the "wrong person" alias! /oops <nickname> to resend message to
alias oops {
        ^assign _whoops $B
        msg $. Whooops ! Please ignore, that wasn't meant for you.
        msg $0 $_whoops
}

alias unset set -$*
alias unalias alias -$*
alias NickServ msg NickServ@Service.de
alias NoteServ msg NoteServ@Service.de

^set DISPLAY on

# --------------------------------------------------------------------
```

xchat

One of the most polished and feature-filled GUI IRC clients for Linux is xchat. It uses the GTK+ toolkit for its GUI and has a couple of extra features available if you run it with the Gnome Desktop. However, you can run it with any desktop or window manager and still have an excellent IRC client. The xchat client supports scripting in both Perl and Python, it supports dcc download/uploads of files, it has mIRC resumes for file transfers, and it also supports mIRC style color. It has all the features you can expect from a modern IRC client, and then some.

> **Caution**
>
> When you start xchat for the first time it will be configured to use your home directory as the target directory for downloads. This is potentially very dangerous, because someone might send you files that overwrite some of your script files with ones filled with malicious code. For example, someone might send you a new .login file, so the next time you start a command shell this would get executed. So be sure to set another download directory before you begin accepting downloads!

Starting xchat

Upon starting xchat you will be presented with a server list dialog, as shown in Figure 7.1.

194 Red Hat Linux—Installation and User Services

PART I

FIGURE 7.1

The server list dialog of xchat.

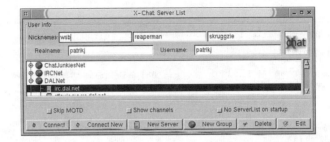

In this dialog you can specify your nickname and a couple of fallback nicknames in case your first choice is taken. You can also set a real name and username to be presented instead of those that are set in your Linux account. All of these options are preset to names taken from the information available in your Linux account. You will probably want to set these to something better.

You can also toggle some options in the dialog. For example, you can tell the client to skip the Message of The Day, or MOTD, when logging in to a server. You can also tell the server dialog not to pop up each time you start xchat.

The most important use for this dialog is of course to maintain groups and lists of IRC servers. This is where you maintain your list of servers. From here you can add, edit, and delete servers. You can then use the list widget to connect to the servers that you have defined. To get a better overview of the servers it is possible to arrange them into groups. For example, you might want to collect all servers from a specific IRC net into a group named after the net. The xchat client comes with a large collection of predefined servers. These servers should probably last you quite a while.

Using xchat

Once you have connected to a server you will be presented with the main window of xchat. See Figure 7.2 for a typical IRC session using xchat. This is the screen where you will be spending most of your time when you are using xchat.

FIGURE 7.2

A typical xchat *session.*

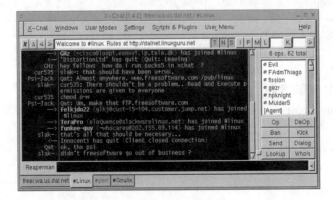

The tab buttons at the bottom of xchat's screen show you which servers you are connected to and which channels you have currently joined. Clicking on one of the tabs will change the view to the chosen channel or server so that you can see what is going on. Above the tab buttons is a text input field where you can type messages or IRC commands. The majority of the screen is taken up by the chat traffic from the current IRC channel. On the left part of this you will see the nickname of the person chatting and on the right you will see what he is writing. The look and feel of this widget can be configured in many ways.

On the right-hand side of the screen is a list box that displays all the users who are currently online in the channel. By performing a right-clicking on one of the users you will be presented with a menu filled with options. The top option will show information about the chosen user. You will also be able to initiate private conversations with the user and so on. Most of the options on this menu are pretty self-explanatory. However, should you feel inclined to experiment with the various user commands on the menu, be sure to choose a user who will not be offended if you happen to do something stupid...

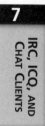

Finally, at the top of the screen, just below the menus, are various informational widgets. At the left are buttons that will allow you to rearrange the window and the tab buttons. In the middle is a string widget that shows the topic of the current channel. Toggle buttons that show which flags are in effect for the channel takes up the rest of this row. If you are the operator of the channel you can use these buttons to change the flags of the channel.

Joining Channels with xchat

Connecting to a channel is easy with xchat. Simply choose the Channel List Window menu option from the Windows menu and you will be presented with the dialog seen in Figure 7.3. There are a couple of options that let you customize the channel listings to some extent. You can specify a wildcard expression to list only channels that match this pattern. It is also possible to specify that only channels with a minimum number of users should be shown. When you are satisfied with your choices, click the Refresh button to get a channel list from the IRC server. Once the list is finished, you only have to double-click on a channel to join it. Of course, should you choose to, you can always use the /join command to join a channel.

FIGURE 7.3

The Channel List Window from xchat.

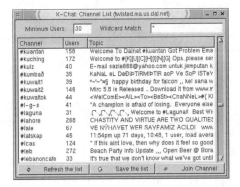

Configuring xchat

Using the setup option from the Settings menu will present you with a dialog with a score of options. These can be used to configure xchat to suit your personal preferences. As already noted it is very important that you change the download directory to something other than the default setting. See Figure 7.4 for an example of how the File Transfer Settings dialog might look.

FIGURE 7.4

The File Transfer Settings dialog of xchat.

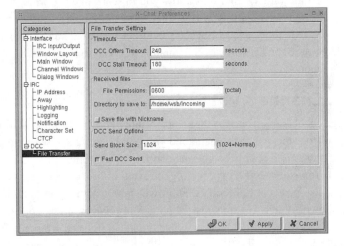

The most important option here is the Directory To Save To setting. Be sure to change this to a directory where you have nothing important and can be reasonably sure that an unsuspected download cannot cause any harm. Make sure that the directory you specify actually exists.

Apart from this setting there are multitudes of others. However, there are far too many settings with too many options to cover in detail here. The default options are very good and should suit almost anyone's needs. It is probably better to keep them as they are while you get to know both IRC and the xchat client better. Be sure to take a look at `http://xchat.org/docs.html`, where you will find the online user documentation for xchat.

Running an IRC Server

Finally, it is possible to run your own IRC server. However, if you want to join one of the major IRC nets, you should be aware that this requires a *huge* amount of bandwidth and *major* computer power! Also you will need to tweak your system quite a lot to get the needed performance from your system. You may even need to compile a special version of the Linux kernel to be able to cope with the resource drains imposed by an IRC server. Because each connection to the IRC server will consume file handles, you will need to increase the number of file handles that each process can use. You can do this dynamically by changing the value in `/proc/sys/fs/file-max`. You will also need to increase the number of file handles available for the whole system. In the Linux 2.2 kernel series this can only be changed at compile time.

There is no IRC server included with the Red Hat 7 distribution even though there are several available in RPM format. Running an IRC server is not something the casual user would want to do, and to run one that is to have lots of traffic is something that is best left up to power users and gurus.

Instant Messaging

Instant messaging, or IM as it is often referred to, provides you with several nice features, the first of which is an easy way to see when your friends and chat buddies are online and available for communication. Instant messaging also allows you to send messages directly to your friends to which your friends may reply immediately or when they feel like it. Different instant message protocols offer different features, but in the end they all supply more or less the same basic functionality.

There are Linux clients available for most of the instant message protocols. Included with your Red Hat system are clients for the two most widely used: the ICQ and the AIM protocols. There are also Linux versions of several other instant messaging protocols. For example, there are clients for Yahoo IM. However, these are not included with Red Hat 7. If you need to get a hold of such a client, you might want to check out `http://freshmeat.net/` and use their search engine do a search with Yahoo as the keyword.

ICQ

The concept of instant messaging, as it is known today, was more or less pioneered by Mirabilis, Ltd. The founders of the company had noticed that while more and more people connected to Web sites, they did not interconnect with each other to the extent that the Internet would allow. They thought that this was because of a shortage of components to enable interpersonal communication on the Internet. To remedy this situation, they formed their company in 1996 and began developing their own chat program. At the end of 1996, only four months after the company was founded, they released the first version of their chat system—ICQ (pronounced "I seek you"). It instantly became very popular and the number of users soon snowballed into hundreds of thousands. In June 1998, AOL acquired Mirabilis and it was restructured into the current company, which is called ICQ, Inc.

If you are totally new to the concepts and features of ICQ you might want to visit ICQ, Inc.'s Web site at `http://www.icq.com/`. There you will find plenty of beginner's guides that will explain ICQ in detail. It is a bit slanted toward their own client and Windows, however the concepts are the same in the Linux counterparts and most of the available options can be found in the ICQ client discussed in this section. ICQ, Inc. does not have a version of its client available for Linux, however there is a Java version, which you might want to use if you feel that you have to use the original client rather than a clone. Do note that the Java version is quite slow and uses lots of your computer's resources.

`licq`

The ICQ client included with Red Hat 7 is called `licq`. It is a very good, fully featured clone of the ICQ client. Apart from allowing you to chat, it allows you to send messages, URLs, files, contact lists, and so on. All this comes packaged within a nice GTK+ interface. See Figure 7.5 for a screenshot from a typical ICQ session.

FIGURE 7.5

A typical ICQ session with `licq`*.*

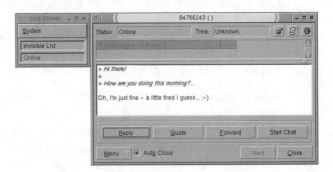

Creating a New ICQ User with `licq`

When you launch `licq` for the first time it will present you with a registration wizard. Here you can either register a new account on the ICQ server or connect to an old, existing account. Accounts are assigned numbers. Once you have logged on to an old account, or created a new one, you will be able to update your personal information, which will be stored on the ICQ server and can be seen by anyone. See Figure 7.6 for an overview of some of the information that may be supplied.

> **Caution**
>
> Do note that spam is quite usual on ICQ these days. Within less than five minutes after registering a new test account for this chapter, I received my first spam! Since ICQ has become infested with these sort of unscrupulous individuals, you should probably not make too much information about yourself public.

FIGURE 7.6

The personal information dialog of `licq`.

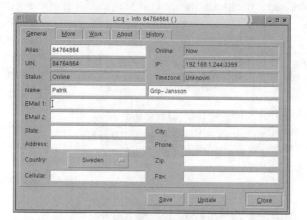

Sending and Receiving Messages with `licq`

After you acquire an ICQ number you will want to start chatting with someone. To do this you need to have the ICQ number of someone else who is online. When you have this, you will want to use the Add User option from the User Functions menu. This will pop up a dialog that asks you for the ICQ number of the user you wish to add. As soon as you have added some users they will show up in the user list of `licq`'s main window. If you want to you can include chat contacts into different groups. To send a message you only have to double-click on the ICQ number that corresponds to the user you are trying to contact. A new dialog window will open up. See Figure 7.7 for an example of how this might look. Type your message into the text box and then click Send to send it. If it's not possible to send the message directly to the recipient, the client will ask you if it should be sent via the server. This can be useful when your chat buddies are located behind a firewall that does not allow direct access.

FIGURE 7.7

The Message dialog window from licq.

The licq client will notify you when you receive an incoming message. Depending upon how you have configured the client, this can come in the form of the system playing a sound, a change in color on the username from whom the message comes, or else a window containing the new message can instantly pop up. When you received a message and are looking at it, you will see something like Figure 7.8. Using the command buttons in this dialog you can reply to the message or initiate a chat session with the user.

FIGURE 7.8

The incoming message dialog window from licq.

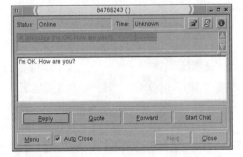

Configuring licq

The licq client is very configurable, as you can see in Figure 7.9. You can configure everything from how the client should behave when an incoming message arrives to how to treat URLs and similar material. You will probably find that the default settings are a very good starting place. There will be plenty of opportunities for you to modify the client to suit your needs once you are comfortable with ICQ.

FIGURE 7.9

The configuration dialog window for licq.

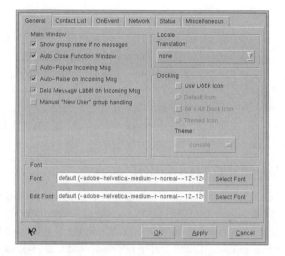

Other Features of licq

There are several more features of the licq client. Using the selections available on the status menu, you can change your status to being everything from Free for Chat to Offline. You can also search for an ICQ user based on many different criteria.

You can also choose to join chat groups on the ICQ. These are a little more primitive than their IRC counterparts. However, sometimes there are quite a few people in these groups and you might very well find a nice group of peers to communicate with within one of these chat groups.

AIM

AIM is an acronym for AOL Instant Messaging—yes, it is an acronym within an acronym. This instant messaging protocol was created by AOL before it acquired ICQ and AOL is now maintaining and supporting both protocols—unfortunately the protocols are not compatible with each other. AIM is one of the fastest growing IM standards today and there are well over 90 million registered AIM users. Because AOL owns both AIM and ICQ, you can probably guess that it is the largest company in the instant message business.

As of this writing, AOL has a Linux AIM client in beta testing. However, it is not yet finished and it is not included with the Red Hat 7 distribution. There are, however, several clones of AOL AIM client available, one of which we will examine in this section.

kit

The AIM client that comes included with Red Hat 7 is part of the KDE desktop environment. It is called `kit`, which stands for KDE Instant Messenger, and it aims to become a fully featured AIM client. At the moment it is not quite there because the KDE team began developing it quite recently, however they are quickly adding features to it. You can run this client even if you are running the Gnome Desktop; that is, as long as you have installed KDE as well, or at least the necessary components from KDE. See Chapter 5, "Window Managers," for more information on this.

Creating a New AIM User with kit

It is possible to maintain several different profiles in `kit`, each connected to a specific AIM user. Each profile can, apart from an AIM username, have totally different settings, user lists, and so on. If you choose to add a new profile in the Profile dialog, you will be asked if you want to connect to AOL and create a new account. If you choose to do so, a new Web browser window will be open directed to the AIM user registration site. (See Figure 7.10.)

FIGURE 7.10

Creating a new AIM user.

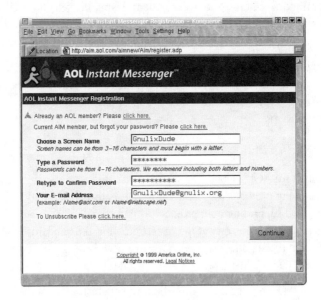

After being prompted for a name for the new profile, you will be presented with the configuration dialog in which you can supply personal information about yourself (see Figure 7.11). There are also several other options that you can use to configure `kit` to your personal liking, such as the appearance of `kit` and how you are connected to the Internet. You can also add buddy groups and insert the AIM nicks of your friends.

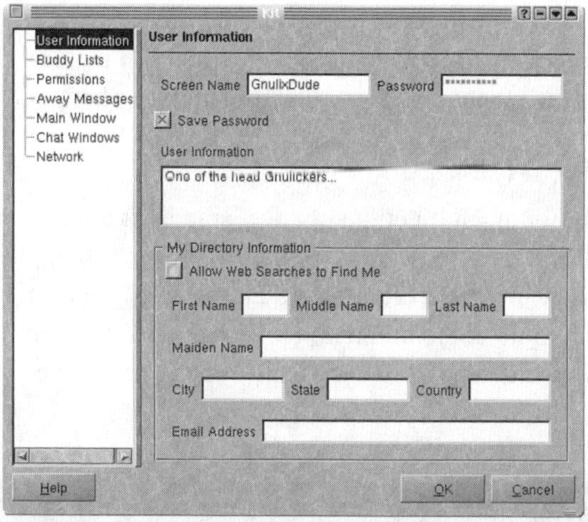

FIGURE 7.11

The configuration dialog of kit.

Caution

As with ICQ, you should probably be careful about what sort of personal information you release to the public. For example, if you include your mail address, and let it be published in the AOL directory, there is always the chance that you will become swamped by spam.

Sending and Receiving Messages with kit

It is easy to send a message using kit. You just need to double click on the nickname of the user to whom you want to send a message. You are then presented with a new chat window. See Figure 7.12 for an example of an ongoing discussion. It is possible to change the appearance of your message using the button widgets; for example, you can change the text color and the background color. There are also tool buttons in the dialog that will, for example, show information on the user you are chatting with, toggle the sound off or on, and toggle logging of the conversation on or off.

FIGURE 7.12

An ongoing chat using kit.

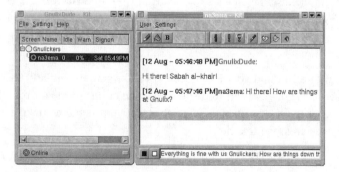

You receive messages in the same manner as you send them. When an incoming message arrives, the same chat window as in Figure 7.12 pops up with the new message and you can then reply in the same manner as if you had initiated the chat yourself.

Other Features of `kit`

At the moment there is not much functionality available in `kit`. You can toggle your status between online, offline, and away, and you can also search through the AIM directory for users using quite a few different criteria (see Figure 7.13). Apart from these features there really is not much more at the moment. However, the basic chatting capabilities are all available in the client and they work excellently. `kit` is sure to become much more improved as time goes by.

FIGURE 7.13

Searching for a user in the AIM directory.

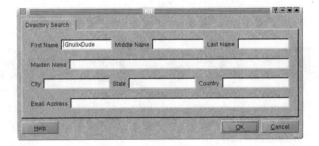

Summary

You will find a high level of support for various kinds of chatting in Linux. There are clients for almost every imaginable chat method. Many of the clients are available both in GUI and non-GUI versions to suit all tastes and requirements. In fact, it can be quite a bewildering experience to get hold of the client that suits you the best. But those that were covered in this chapter are quite good, and should serve as an excellent starting point for anyone who wants to chat.

There are many places where you can find the RPMs mentioned in this chapter. You can get them from the installation CDs for Red Hat, from Red Hat's FTP site, or from one of the many FTP sites that mirror Red Hat's distribution. See `http://www.redhat.com/download/mirror.html` for a list of FTP sites that carry Red Hat's distribution.

No matter where you find your RPMs, always make sure to regularly check for new versions in the update directory of Red Hat's FTP site or one of the mirrors. There might be important security fixes available! Remember that you should not take any chances when you are connected to the Internet.

The RFCs that were mentioned in the chapter can be found at `http://www.faqs.org/`.

Using Multimedia and Graphics Clients

This chapter provides an overview of the graphics commands, multimedia clients and other utilities you can use with Red Hat Linux. This topic could easily span 1,000 or more pages in a comprehensive book, but hopefully you'll find the information presented here to be helpful if you need to create, convert, edit, display, or play images and sound using Linux.

Linux Graphic Utilities

Red Hat Linux comes with a rich assortment of graphics clients. You'll also find more than 20,000 2D graphics images and icons included on this book's CD-ROMs. These images include

- 15,000 Portable Network Graphics (PNG) files
- 2,000 Graphics Interchange Format (GIF) files
- 2,000 X11 pixmap (XPM) graphics
- 700 X11 bitmap (XBM) graphics
- 500 Joint Photographic Experts Group (JPEG) images
- 200 Portable Bitmap (PBM) graphics

If you're familiar with Linux, you'll recognize many of these graphics formats and probably work with them every day. If you're new to Linux, you may or may not have worked with image formats commonly used in the Linux environment (such as XBM and XPM).

Common Graphics Formats

Computer graphics are used for Web page design and report documents, and they are also used by engineers, by computer artists (designers or photographers), and even by medical researchers and practitioners. Some graphics development tasks have only modest hardware and software requirements, whereas others, such as floating-point–intensive 3D renderings and raytracings, may require specialized equipment, such as graphics cards with 64MB or more video RAM, large (19" or larger) monitors, enormous amounts (512MB or more) of RAM, and fast CPUs. This section covers simpler graphics formats for home desktop and small business users.

Table 8.1 lists most of the types of graphics included with Red Hat Linux. You may find some new terms and acronyms, but in general, under Linux as well as other operating systems, graphics files are defined according to format, resolution, and color depth. Whereas black-and-white images are represented by resolution, or the number of pixels (dots) wide and high, and a simple "on" or "off" two-color scheme, color images may vary according to not only resolution, but the number of colors used by the graphics file. Typically, early graphics files used 16, 32, 64, or 256 colors. However, today many graphics images are stored in thousands and millions of colors (although the human eye is said to be able to distinguish only 160,000 distinct colors, many graphics monitors will only display thousands of colors, and most humans can only distinguish 30 levels of gray). Some pixel formats use three bytes of storage to represent red, green, and blue values to represent the color of each pixel of an image.

Note that not all graphics formats in Table 8.1 are pixel-oriented. Some, like PostScript, are based on page description and line drawing, creating vector-based graphics. If you view PostScript graphics in a text editor, such as emacs, you can read the "language" that describes the document. On the other hand, most pixel-based formats are binary only and unreadable.

What does this mean to the user? In general, 2D pixel-based graphics files will require ever-larger amounts of memory and hard drive storage as the resolution and color depth increase. To help stave off these requirements, many formats, such as JPEG and PNG, incorporate compression, or the removal of redundant and unneeded information in the file.

TABLE 8.1 Common 2D Graphics Formats

Name	Description
BMP	Windows bitmap
CGM	Computer Graphics Metafile
EPS, EPSF	Encapsulated PostScript File
GIF	Graphics Interchange Format
JPEG	Joint Photographic Experts Group
MIFF	Magick Image File Format
PBM	Portable bitmap
PCX	PC Paintbrush
PGM	Portable graymap
PNG	Portable Network Graphics
PNM	Portable anymap
PPM	Portable pixmap
RLE	Run Length Encoded
TGA	Targa File Format
TIFF	Tag(ged) Image File Format
XBM	X11 bitmap
XPM	X11 pixmap
XWD	X11 Windows Dump

There are also many types of 3D graphics formats. In the recent past, creating, editing, rendering, or displaying pictures using 3D software required high-end computational resources. Today, you'll find a number of Open Source 3D engines, applications, editors, games, software libraries, modeling clients, and visualization systems available for Linux. However, you'll still need a compliant graphics card and proper X11 driver support for your card in order to use this class of software. One of the best places to look for an index of 3D hardware and software for Linux is `http://www.linux3d.org/`.

The ability to use advanced modeling and rendering software and hardware is a relatively new development for Linux, but developers and manufacturers are picking up the pace as new software is ported to the Linux platform and new graphics cards are brought to market. Some of these software packages can have enormous resource requirements, so expect only modest performance, even on 450MHz Pentium-class computers, even if you have a capable graphics card! Few, if any, laptop users will be able to take advantage of this class of software and graphics until further advances are made in graphics chipset design, CPU speed, hard drive storage, and memory.

Use Portable Network Graphics!

The PNG format was crafted to replace the Graphics Interchange Format (GIF), along with the Tagged Image File Format (TIFF), commonly used on other computer platforms. The PNG format has a number of advantages, one of the most important of which is that it is patent-free. Other advantages include better response to compression, fully lossless characteristics when used as an intermediary format during graphics editing (that is, no loss of image quality on repeated or subsequent saves to disc), and greater portability across computer platforms and applications. For more detailed information about PNG, see the PNG home page at `http://www.libpng.org/pub/png`.

Converting Graphics

Fortunately, most desktop PC users don't need high-end graphics cards, monitors, CPUs, and software to work with graphics. Linux comes with hundreds of simple graphics applications that may be used to create, edit, and translate graphics without the need for loading a large application and windowing client. Many of the graphics commands discussed in this section don't even require a running X11 session!

Table 8.2 lists commands that may be used to read, convert, or save graphics files. Most commands will work from the command line, while others, such as the GIMP (see

"Using the GIMP" later in this chapter) must be run during an X11 session. Most of the commands belong to several distinct "families" from one or more developers:

- Portable anymap commands (bitmaps, graymaps, pixmaps), developed by Jeff Poskanzer, are used from the command line or in shell scripts to convert files from one graphic format to another. There are nearly 100 commands included in this software package.

- The `convert` command, by John Cristy, is part of the ImageMagick software package (included with Red Hat Linux, and which has a graphical X11 client named `display`), and can be used to "convert" graphics; this capable command has the ability to deal with nearly 70 graphics formats!

- The GIMP, by Spencer Kimball and Peter Mattis, is a comprehensive, sophisticated, and complex graphics editing client for X11, but does not convert graphics using the command line.

- The `xv` client by John Bradley is a free-for-personal-use graphics client that may be used from the command line or as a graphical client during an X11 session. However, this client has more than 100 command-line options with a formidable syntax. Although no longer included on Red Hat's CD-ROMs, `xv` is available for download at `ftp://ftp.redhat.com/pub/redhat/powertools/`.

- The GNOME `ee` client, which requires X11, will read and save graphics files in a variety of formats. This is also true of the `pixie` client, developed for the K Desktop Environment.

The `convert` command is one of the most flexible and useful graphics conversion commands included with Red Hat Linux. This command may be use to translate graphics formats on-the-fly using filename extensions. For example, to convert the graphic `kitty.gif` from GIF format to PCX format, use the `convert` command like this:

```
# convert kitty.gif kitty.pcx
```

After you press Enter, the `convert` command will create a new file in the desired format with name `kitty.pcx`, leaving the original untouched.

TABLE 8.2 Linux Graphics Formats and Conversion Programs

Extension	Description	Conversion Program
.10x	Gemini 10X	pbmto10x
.3d	Red/Blue 3D pixmap	ppm3d
.asc	ASCII text	pbmtoascii
.atk	Andrew Toolkit raster	atktopbm
		pbmtoatk

TABLE 8.2   continued

Extension	Description	Conversion Program
.avs	AVS X image	convert
.bie	Bi-level image expert	convert
.bg	BBN BitGraph graphics	pbmtobbnbg
.bmp	Windows, OS/2 bitmap	bmptoppm
		cjpeg
		convert
		gimp
		ppmtobmp
		xv
.bmp24	Windows 24-bit bitmap	convert
		xv
.brush	Xerox doodle brush	brushtopbm
.cgm	Computer graphics metafile	convert
.cmu	CMU window manager bitmap	cmuwmtopbm
		pbmtocmuwm
.dcx	ZSoft Paintbrush	convert
.ddif	DDIF image	pnmtoddif
.dib	Windows bitmap image	convert
.dxb	AutoCAD database file	ppmtoacad
		sldtoppm
.dvi	TeX printer file	dvips
		dvilj4
		dvilj4l
		dvilj2p
		dvilj
.eps2	Encapsulated PostScript Level II	convert
.epsf	Encapsulated PostScript	convert
		pixie
.epsi	PostScript preview bitmap	pbmtoepsi
		convert
.ept	Encapsulated PostScript	convert
.epson	Epson printer graphics	pbmtoepson
.fax	Group 3 fax	convert
.fig	TransFig image	convert

TABLE 8.2   continued

Extension	Description	Conversion Program
.fits	Flexible Image Transport	fitstopnm pnmtofits convert gimp xv
.fpx	FlashPix	convert
.g3	Group 3 fax file	g3topbm g32pbm g3cat pbm2g3 pbmtog3
.gif	Graphics Interchange	giftopnm gif2tiff gimp xpaint ppmtogif convert xv
.gif87	Graphics Interchange	convert xv
.go	Compressed GraphOn	pbmtogo
.gould	Gould scanner file	gouldtoppm
.icn	Sun icon	icontopbm pbmtoicon
.ico	Microsoft icon	convert
.ilbm	IFF ILBM file	ilbmtoppm ppmtoilbm
.img	GEM image file	gemtopbm pbmtogem imgtoppm
.icr	NCSA ICR raster	ppmtoicr
.jbig	Joint Bi-level Image Group	convert

TABLE 8.2 continued

Extension	Description	Conversion Program
.jpeg	Joint Photographic Experts Group	cjpeg
		djpeg
		jpegtran
		xpaint
		convert
		gimp
		pixie
		xv
.lj	HP LaserJet data	pbmtolj
.ln03	DEC LN03+ Sixel output	pbmtoln03
.mgr	MGR bitmap	mgrtopbm
		pbmtomgr
.miff	MNG multiple-image network	convert
.mitsu	Mitsubishi S340-10 file	ppmtomitsu
.mpeg	Motion Picture Group	convert
.mtv	MTV ray tracer	mtvtoppm
		convert
.pbm	Portable bitmap	pbm*
		convert
		xv
		pdftopbm
.pcd	Photo CD	convert
.pcl	HP PaintJet PCL	ppmtopjxl
		convert
.pcx	PCX graphics	pcxtoppm
		ppmtopcx
		convert
		gimp
		xv
.pdf	Portable Document Format	convert
		xpdf
		pdftops
		pdftotext
		pdftopbm

TABLE 8.2 continued

Extension	Description	Conversion Program
.pgm	Portable graymap	pbmtopgm
		pgmtoppm
		ppmtopgm
		convert
		cjpeg
		xv
		ee
.pi1	Atari Degas file	pi1toppm
		ppmtopi1
.pi3	Atari Degas file	pbmtopi3
		pi3topbm
.pict	Macintosh PICT file	picttoppm
		ppmtopict
		convert
.pj	HP PaintJet file	pjtoppm
		ppmtopj
.pk	PK format font	pbmtopk
		pktopbm
.plasma	Plasma fractal	convert
.plot	UNIX plot file	pbmtoplot
.png	Portable Network Graphic	pngtopnm
		pnmtopng
		convert
		gimp
		pixie
		xpaint
		xv
.pnm	Portable anymap	pnm*
		convert
		gimp
		ee
		pixie
.pnt	MacPaint file	macptopbm
		pbmtomacp
.ppa	HP Printing Architecture	pnm2ppa
		pbm2ppa

8

USING
MULTIMEDIA AND
GRAPHICS CLIENTS

TABLE 8.2   continued

Extension	Description	Conversion Program
.ppm	Portable pixmap	ppm*
		cjpeg
		convert
		xpaint
		xv
		ee
.ps	PostScript (lines)	pbmtolps
		pnmtops
		convert
		xv
		gimp
		gv
		ee
.psd	Abode PhotoShop bitmap	convert
.ptx	Printronix printer graphics	pbmtoptx
.qrt	QRT ray tracer	qrttoppm
.rad	Radiance image	convert
.ras	Sun rasterfile	pnmtorast
		rasttopnm
		gimp
		xv
.rla	Alias/Wavefront image	convert (read-only)
.rle	Utah run-length encoded	convert (read-only)
		xv
.sgi	Silicon Graphics image	pnmtosgi
		sgitopnm
		convert
		gimp
.sir	Solitaire graphics	pnmtosir
		sirtopnm
.sixel	DEC sixel format	ppmtosixel
.spc	Atari Spectrum file	spctoppm
.spu	Atari Spectrum file	sputoppm
.sun	Sun rasterfile	convert
		gimp

TABLE 8.2 continued

Extension	Description	Conversion Program
`.tga`	TrueVision Targa file	`ppmtotga`
		`tgatoppm`
		`convert`
		`gimp`
		`xv`
`.tiff`	Tagged Image File Format	`pnmtotiff`
		`tifftopnm`
		`tiff2ps`
		`convert`
		`gimp`
		`pixie`
		`xv`
		`xpaint`
		`ee`
`.tiff24`	Tagged Image File Format (24-bit)	`convert`
		`xv`
`.tim`	PSX TIM	`convert`
`.ttf`	TrueType font file	`convert`
`.txt`	text file bitmap	`pbmtext`
		`convert` (read-only)
`.uil`	Motif UIL icon	`ppmtouil`
		`convert`
`.upc`	Universal Product Code	`pbmupc`
`.uyvy`	16-bit YUV format	`convert`
`.vicar`		`convert` (read-only)
		`xv`
`.viff`	Khoros Visualization image	`convert`
`.x10bm`	X10 bitmap	`pbmtox10bm`
`.xbm`	X11 bitmap	`pbmtoxbm`
		`xbmtopbm`
		`convert`
		`pixie`
		`xpaint`
		`xv`
`.xim`	Xim file	`ximtoppm`

TABLE 8.2   continued

Extension	Description	Conversion Program
.xpm	X11 pixmap	ppmtoxpm
		xpmtoppm
		convert
		gimp
		pixie
		xpaint
		xv
.xv	xv thumbnail	xvminitoppm (xv)
.xvpic	xv thumbnail file	xvpictoppm (xv)
.xwd	X11 Window Dump	pnmtoxwd
		xwdtopnm
		convert
		gimp
		xpaint
		xv
.ybm	Bennet Yee face file	pbmtoybm
		ybmtopbm
.yuv	Abekas YUV file	ppmtoyuv
		yuvtoppm
		convert
.zeiss	Zeiss confocal file	zeisstopnm
.zinc	Zinc bitmap	pbmtozinc

Many of the programs listed in Table 8.2 that work with the command line may also use input-output redirection, along with pipes on the command line. For example, if you have a file named foo.pcx in PCX format, but would also like a copy in GIF and TIFF formats, you can combine the output of various commands, such as pcxtoppm, ppmtogif, giftopnm, and pnmtotiff like this:

```
# pcxtoppm foo.pcx | ppmtogif | tee foo.gif | giftopnm | pnmtotiff >foo.tif
```

This command line, which also uses the tee command to siphon off output from the ppmtogif command, creates two copies of the original file, one named foo.gif in GIF format and the other named foo.tif in TIFF format.

Linux also comes with a number of command-line programs that may be used to perform other manipulation tasks, such as cropping, resizing, and flipping horizontally or vertically. See the man pages for the pnmcrop, pnmcut, pnmenlarge, pnmflip, pnminvert, pnmrotate, or pnmscale commands.

Basic Graphic Editing Clients

This section introduces and lists some of the common graphics clients included with X11, GNOME, and the K Desktop Environment (KDE). You'll find a wealth of clients to use for simple graphics functions and editing. Although none of the these clients are as capable or comprehensive as the GNU Image Manipulation Program (GIMP; see "Using the GIMP" later in this chapter), you may discover practical uses in specific situations that will save time and effort when working with graphics.

X11 Graphics Clients

The X Window System has always included a number of graphics programs. Although most were developed to do one thing and to do that one thing well (like all good UNIX commands), some of the larger applications may seem a bit primitive to most Linux X11 desktop users today. Many provide just a bare minimum of functionality to get the job done, without all the frills of window decorations, buttons, or an overabundance of features.

Table 8.3 lists some common X11 graphics applications you'll find available for X and Red Hat Linux. One of the advantages of using these clients is that you'll rarely need to have specific, additional software libraries installed in order to make the client work—all the functionality is built into the client, and the client depends solely on the X11 software libraries.

8

USING MULTIMEDIA AND GRAPHICS CLIENTS

TABLE 8.3   X11 Graphics Clients

Client Name	Description
xdvi	Displays .dvi documents
xfig	Technical drawing application
xgc	X11 graphics demo client
xpaint	Bitmap graphics editor
xpdf	Displays PDF documents
xmag	Desktop display magnifier client
xpmroot	Saves current root display to graphics file
xsetroot	Sets color of current desktop
xsetbg	Replaces root display with an image
xwd	Saves designated display or window as a graphics file
xwud	Displays designated X11 Window Dump graphic

Half of the clients listed in Table 8.3 may be used from the command line of an X11 terminal window, or in the case of the xwd client, from the text-only console command line. The xwd client is used to take a snapshot of a running client or the root display of an X11 session. The output of the xwd command is sent directly to the standard output, so you'll need to use file redirection or the -out command-line option, along with a filename to save your graphic.

For example, if you're running X, you can press Ctrl+Alt+F2 to jump to the second virtual console, then use the xwd client to take a snapshot of your current X session like this:

```
# xwd -out shot1.xwd -root -display :0
```

> **Note**
>
> Note that you may have to enable access to your X11 session before taking screenshots from the console. You can do this by using the xhost command, followed by an allowed hostname (such as *stinky.home.org*), or a plus sign (+) to allow any host. Note that for security, afterwards you should rescind access by using the xhost and its minus option (-).

You can also use xwd from the command line of an X11 terminal window like this:

```
# xwd >out.xwd
```

After you press Enter, your cursor will turn into a cross-hair, and you can then click on another window or the root desktop to take a picture. To display your screenshot, you can use the xwud client like this:

```
# xwud <out.xwd
```

After you press Enter, the image will be displayed in a window. Click on the window to end the program.

Taking Screenshots with the `import` Command

Another capable client you can use to take pictures of the root display or selected windows is the import command, part of John Cristy's ImageMagick software package. This command, like xwd, is used from the command line, but features on-the-fly sizing, cropping, and rotation operations, along with graphics conversion. You can also use this command to take screenshots of other computers on your network (as long as you're properly authorized, perhaps with the xhost command). And, like xwd, you can use the import command from the text-only console while an X11 session is running to take pictures of a root display.

For example, to take a picture of the desktop from the command line of an X11 terminal window, use the `import` command, along with its `-window` option and the `root` keyword, like this:

```
# import -window root test.gif
```

This example will take a snapshot of the entire display and save it in GIF format in the file named `test.gif`. If you want to take a rotated snapshot of an X11 session on another computer in your LAN, you can use the `import` command's `-display` option with the hostname and display number and the `-rotate` option, like this:

```
# import -window root -display vaio.home.org:0.0 -rotate -90 display.pcx
```

This example will take a portrait-oriented (90-degree) snapshot of the computer vaio.home.org's X11 session and save it in a PCX graphics file named `display.pcx`. The `import` command has more than 30 different command-line options you can use for varied effects!

GNOME-Enabled Graphics Clients

The advent of The Gnu Image Manipulation Program (GIMP) with its GTK+ Toolkit and GDK Drawing Kit libraries ushered in the growing popularity of the GNOME software libraries and GNOME-aware window managers for X11. This interest on the part of software developers and users has spurred further development of GNOME clients, including various graphic software utilities for the GNOME distribution. You'll find a number of graphics utilities included with GNOME on your Red Hat Linux system.

Some of the graphics utilities (listed in Table 8.4) are aimed at a specific purpose, such as viewing a particular graphics document (such as a fax), creating and editing icons, viewing various images (such as PostScript), converting graphics, or perhaps taking pictures of the desktop or windows during an X11 session.

TABLE 8.4   GNOME Graphics Clients

Client Name	Description
dia	Diagram editor
ee	Displays graphics files
gcolorsel	X11 color browser
gimp	The Gnu Image Manipulation Program
GQview	Image browser, graphics editor launcher
gphoto	Digital camera photo editor

For example, the gphoto client will handily download images from a variety of digital cameras, then offer them for display in thumbnail views for editing. Connect your camera to your computer's serial port, then start the gphoto client from your GNOME desktop panel or the command line of a terminal window like this:

```
# gphoto &
```

After you press Enter, you'll see the main gphoto dialog, as shown in Figure 8.1.

FIGURE 8.1

The gphoto *client works with many different types of digital cameras.*

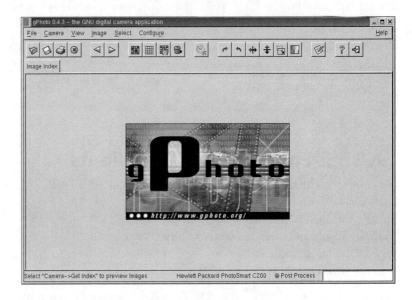

Click the Configure menu, then click the Select Port-Camera Model menu item. You'll see a dialog, as shown in Figure 8.2.

FIGURE 8.2

The gphoto *client must be configured for your camera before getting to work.*

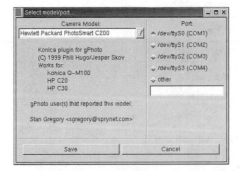

Click the drop-down menu to select your camera model, then click to select the proper serial port. When finished, click the Save button. To begin, click the thumbnail index icon on the toolbar, and gphoto will issue the proper instructions via the serial port to download images. You can also press Ctrl+I, or use the Camera menu to accomplish the same thing. When finished, you should see something like Figure 8.3.

FIGURE 8.3

To pick an image to edit with gphoto, first select a thumbnail image.

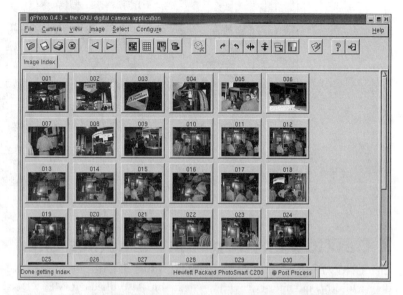

Digital Camera Support

The gphoto client directly supports 112 different digital cameras, but don't be disappointed if your camera's exact model is not listed in the gphoto configuration dialog. Pick the first camera, then scroll through the list. As each camera is selected, information about compatible cameras will appear in the dialog. For example, if you select the Toshiba PDR-M1 camera, you'll see that the Toshiba configuration will also support the Fuji DS-7, DX-5, 7, 10 and MX-500, as well as Samsung's Kenox SSC-350N, and others. For the latest version of gphoto, go to http://www.gphoto.org. You'll find that gphoto now also supports at least seven Canon, Kodak, and Mustek USB cameras.

Using thumbnails is a faster way to view the contents of your camera's memory and to pick and choose an image. To download one or more images, click to select the desired thumbnails, then click the Download Selected Images button. When finished, gphoto will display the images in tabbed windows behind its main window, as shown in Figure 8.4. You can then use the various toolbar buttons to rotate, flip, resize, and adjust color balance, brightness, and contrast.

FIGURE 8.4

The gphoto *client is a mini-photo editor, and can be used to organize, edit, and color-balance digital images!*

K Desktop Environment Graphics Clients

Like GNOME, KDE depends on special software libraries for its special features, such as drag-and-drop and inter-client communication. Also like GNOME, KDE developers have created and fine-tuned numerous graphics applications for use with KDE.

Red Hat Linux includes the latest stable version of KDE, along with its host of clients; however, newer (but unstable) versions of KDE include many new graphics productivity clients. You'll find a number of these included on your Red Hat CD-ROM's /preview directory. Again, many of the graphics utilities (listed in Table 8.5) have a specific purpose, such as viewing graphics files or creating and editing icons.

TABLE 8.5   KDE Graphics Clients

Client Name	Description
katalog	Image cataloging client
kchart	Charts graphic creation client
kpaint	Creates, edits graphic images
kghostview	Displays PostScript documents
kgrapher	KDE port of gnuplot client
kiconedit	Icon editor
killustrator	Vector-based drawing client
klipper	KDE clipboard client
kpresenter	Presentation editor

TABLE 8.5   continued

Client Name	Description
ksnapshot	KDE window capture client
kview	Displays various graphics documents
kviewshell	Versatile document viewer
pixie	Image viewer and editor

Each KDE client listed in Table 8.5 features similar menus, toolbars, buttons, and dialogs. This is also the case for each of the GNOME clients listed in Table 8.4—the use of supporting software libraries provides a consistent interface across each environment's suite of tools.

As an example, the kchart client may be used to quickly plot numerical data and create 3D line, bar, or pie charts. Start the client by clicking its name from the desktop's panel, or by typing the command on the command line of a terminal window like this:

```
# kchart &
```

After you press Enter, you'll see the initial window. Note that like other clients, kchart features a menu bar and a toolbar of graphic icons, along with a default chart graphic. (See Figure 8.5.)

FIGURE 8.5

The kchart client draws and saves graphs of data.

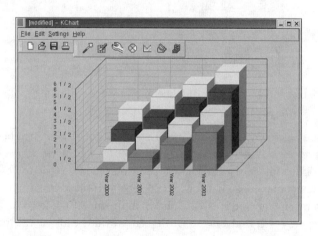

If you click on the graphic, a toolbar will appear. You can then change the default numerical data (using a mini-spreadsheet) and chart type.

Using the GIMP

The GIMP client is a sophisticated image editor on par with many expensive commercial graphics software clients. Fortunately for Linux users, the GIMP is distributed under the GNU General Public License, and will remain a highly regarded testament to the power of Open Source software and the prowess of Open Source programmers. When you use the GIMP, you'll have a powerful image editor at your beck and call!

The client, which requires a running X session, is started by clicking a KDE or GNOME desktop menu item, or by typing the command name on the command line of a terminal window like this:

```
# gimp &
```

When you run the GIMP for the first time, after you press Enter, you'll see a series of dialogs asking you to confirm creation of a .gimp-1.1 directory in your home directory, along with installation of necessary initialization, preference, configuration, and software tools. You'll then see a floating toolbox and Tip of the Day, as shown in Figure 8.6.

FIGURE 8.6

*The GIMP pro-
vides a tip when it
first starts.*

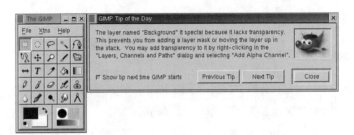

To open an existing image, click the File menu on the main floating toolbox, or press Ctrl+O. A dialog will appear, as shown in Figure 8.7.

If you click an image name, then click the Preview button, a thumbnail of the image will appear in the preview window (as shown in Figure 8.7). Select the desired image, then click OK to load the image. The image will be displayed in a separate floating window. If you right-click on the image window, you'll see a pop-up series of hierarchical menus you can use to manipulate the image (as shown in Figure 8.8). Used in combination with the GIMP toolbox, you'll find that the GIMP can provide nearly all the tools, effects, and techniques required of a modern computer image editor!

The GIMP features 86 types of brushes, 168 different patterns, nearly 40 color palettes, nearly 100 scripts, and more than 200 plug-ins that can be used to manipulate or create images. This client is, without a doubt, one of the most sophisticated and capable image clients available for Linux. Although Red Hat strives to include the very latest stable version of the GIMP with each distribution, you can find out more about this program and download additional patterns, palettes, brushes, gradients, scripts, and fonts by browsing to http://www.gimp.org.

FIGURE 8.7

Use the GIMP's file dialog to open an existing image.

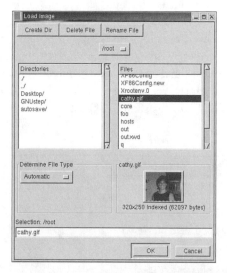

FIGURE 8.8

The GIMP has many menus of tools, effects, and editing actions you can use during image sessions.

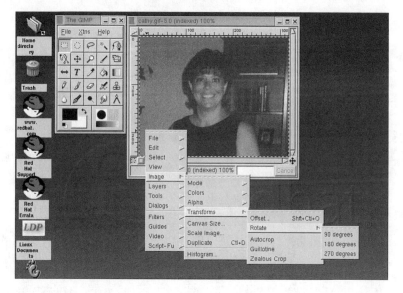

Displaying and Printing Graphics

PostScript is the most common graphics and document format when preparing documents and graphics under UNIX and Linux. Although many editors can prepare documents in ASCII text, HTML, LaTeX, or other markup languages, most applications, including graphics editors, will convert output to PostScript for printing. This is an advantage, because PostScript provides a common platform and document standard for handling by a number of Linux clients, and documents saved to a file may be previewed instead of being sent directly to a printer. You'll find a number of PostScript previewers and utilities included with Red Hat Linux, as shown in Table 8.6.

TABLE 8.6 Linux PostScript Utilities

Name	Description
enscript	Translates text to PostScript
gs	PostScript interpreter
gv	PostScript and PDF previewer
mpage	Creates multi-page PostScript documents
pbmtoepsi	Translates bitmap to EPSF
pbmtolps	Translates portable bitmap to PostScript
pdf2dsc	Creates PostScript page list of a PDF document
pdf2ps	Translates PDF to PostScript
pdftops	Translates PDF to PostScript
pnmtops	Translates portable anymap to PostScript
ps2ascii	Translates PostScript or PDF to text
ps2pdf	Translates PostScript to PDF
psidtopgm	Translates PostScript image data to portable graymap
pstopnm	Translates PostScript to portable anymap
sgml2latex	Creates LaTeX, DVI, or PostScript from SGML

Does this mean that you must use PostScript for printing? Of course not! But using PostScript may help ensure consistent handling and output quality of your documents. To view a PostScript graphic or document, use an associated client, such as the gv PostScript previewer. You'll find example PostScript graphics under the /usr/share/ghostscript/5.50/examples/ directory, or you can create a PostScript document for previewing from an existing text document using the mpage command.

For example, to view the graphic `tiger.ps`, use the `gv` command from the command line of a terminal window like this:

```
# gv /usr/share/ghostscript/5.50/examples/tiger.ps
```

After you press Enter, you'll see the graphic in gv's main window, as shown in Figure 8.9.

Note

See Chapter 19, "Printing with Linux," for details on setting up your printer to work with Red Hat Linux. You'll learn about how Red Hat Linux uses software filters and the `gs` PostScript interpreter to translate PostScript documents into a format or language understood by your printer.

FIGURE 8.9

The gv client previews, rotates, scales, and prints PostScript documents, or selected pages of PostScript documents.

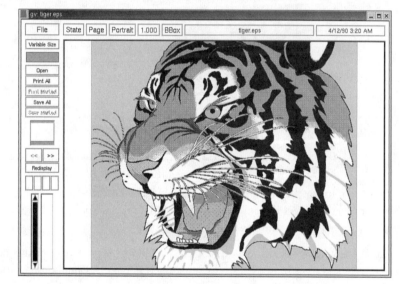

8

USING
MULTIMEDIA AND
GRAPHICS CLIENTS

You can use gv's various menus to rotate the image, reduce or enlarge the display, page through, or print selected pages of multi-page PostScript documents. Another client included with Red Hat Linux to support previewing PostScript is KDE's `kghostview` previewer.

If you'd like to display other types of graphics, use the `display` command, part of the ImageMagick software package. This command may be used to display one or more images, or a visual directory of images, and has many different features. For example, to display a single visual directory of all PCX files in a directory, use the display command like this:

```
# display 'vid:*pcx'
```

After you press Enter, a single window with a series of thumbnail images will be displayed, as shown in Figure 8.10.

FIGURE 8.10

The display command features a handy thumbnail visual directory.

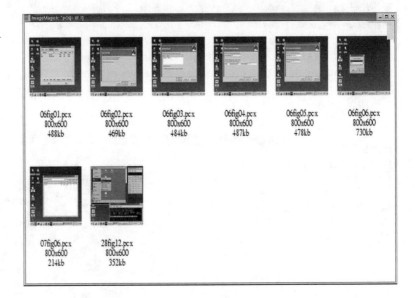

To load an image for display, editing, conversion, transformation, or printing, move your cursor to a thumbnail image, then right-click the image. You'll see a pop-up menu that allows you to load the image.

Each of the previewers discussed here has the ability to print documents, but you can also print a graphic directly from the command line. For example, to print the tiger.ps graphic, use the lpr to spool the file for printing, like this:

```
# lpr /usr/share/ghostscript/5.50/examples/tiger.ps
```

This will send the graphic to the default printer. Red Hat Linux uses intelligent print filters that will automatically translate a file with the proper extension (such as .ps) into the proper printer control language. The printing system recognizes and prints the following types of graphics:

- .bmp—Windows bitmap
- .dvi—Device-independent image

- .fig—Vector-based document
- .gif—GIF graphic
- .jpg—JPEG graphic
- .pbm—Portable bitmap
- .pgm—Portable graymap
- .ppm—Portable pixmap
- .ps—PostScript
- .tif—TIFF graphic

Configuring Sound

The sndconfig command is the Red Hat configuration tool to use to get Linux to work with your computer's sound system. This command, which may be launched without running X11, can automatically probe your computer's audio hardware, configure the card to work with Linux, then save the settings so that sound is enabled every time you boot Linux.

Start the sndconfig command from the command line of the console or an X11 terminal window by typing this:

 # sndconfig

After you press Enter, you should see a dialog, as shown in Figure 8.11.

FIGURE 8.11

Red Hat's sndconfig *command will probe your sound card.*

8

USING MULTIMEDIA AND GRAPHICS CLIENTS

If the probe is successful, sndconfig will then test your card. If the probe is not successful, you may have to proceed with a manual configuration. If you'd prefer to start with a manual configuration (no probe), use sndconfig's --noprobe command-line option. And if you don't want sndconfig to configure Linux to use the sound card (perhaps if you're testing a new sound card), use the --noautoconfig option.

If you manually configure your sound card, you'll see a dialog, as shown in Figure 8.12, that you can use to scroll and select your sound card.

FIGURE 8.12

Red Hat's sndconfig *command also offers manual configuration.*

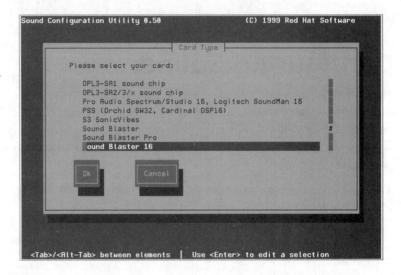

Scroll through the list of sound cards to highlight your card (or a compatible card), then use the Tab key to highlight the OK button and press Enter. You'll then have to use the next dialog, shown in Figure 8.13, to specify the correct I/O port addresses, IRQ settings, and DMA settings.

Use the Tab and spacebar to enable the specific settings, then tab to the OK button and press Enter. The command will update your /etc/modules.conf file (and back up an existing one). The command will then (after you click OK) play a sound sample. You'll then be asked if you were able to hear the sound sample, as shown in Figure 8.14.

Click Yes if sound was heard (Linus pronouncing "Linux" from the file sample.au under the /usr/share/sndconfig directory). If you click No, you can again attempt to configure your sound card. Upon success, the sndconfig will then try to play a MIDI sound, and you can again verify success. The program will then exit.

Sound support under Linux is generally in the form of loadable kernel modules, found under the /lib/modules/2.*X.X*/misc directory, where *XX* is the version of your kernel. Sound settings will be saved in the file soundcard under the /etc/sysconfig directory.

FIGURE 8.13

Manual sound card configuration may require specific hardware settings.

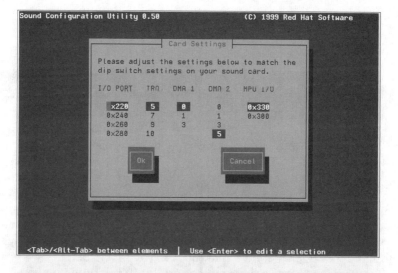

FIGURE 8.14

The sndconfig *command will play a sound sample and ask about its success.*

8

USING
MULTIMEDIA AND
GRAPHICS CLIENTS

You may also find that sndconfig has altered settings in your system's /etc/modules.conf file (these settings will cause the Linux kernel to load the proper sound modules upon startup).

For the examples shown in Figures 8.11 through 8.14, sndconfig created the following entry in /etc/sysconfig/soundcard:

```
# THIS FILE IS WRITTEN BY SNDCONFIG
# PLEASE USE SNDCONFIG TO MODIFY
# TO CHANGE THIS FILE!
```

```
# There should be no spaces at the start of a line
# or around the '=' sign
CARDTYPE=SB16
```

Note

If you find that you cannot get Red Hat Linux to work with your sound card, take heart! First, try to find someone who has the same sound card and has met with success. Linux laptop users should definitely browse to the Linux Laptop pages at http://www.cs.utexas.edu/users/kharker/linux-laptop/. You can also turn to the free Advanced Linux Sound Architecture sound drivers available from the ALSA project at http://www.alsa-project.org. If the ALSA drivers do not work, you can then browse to 4Front Technologies' Open Sound System at http://www.opensound.com and download a demo set of commercial drivers. The OSS drivers are relatively inexpensive, and the system currently supports more than 350 different sound cards, so you should be in luck. Users with new, cutting-edge hardware are most at risk for lack of sound support.

The corresponding entry in /etc/modules.conf looks like this:

```
alias sound-slot-0 sb
options sound dmabuf=1
alias midi opl3
options opl3 io=0x388
options sb io=0x220 irq=5 dma=0 dma16=5 mpu_io=0x330
```

These examples are for a SoundBlaster 16–compatible card, and the kernel module options create the settings for proper initialization of the card when Linux boots. After configuring your sound card and ensuring that it works with Linux, you should then launch an audio mixer to choose proper settings for different audio devices offered by your sound system. This may include volume, bass, treble, synthesizer, MIDI, line in, line out, microphone, and audio CD settings. Red Hat Linux comes with a number of audio mixers:

- aumix—A console audio mixer
- gmix—A GNOME X11 mixer
- kmix—A KDE mixer client
- xmixer—An X11 mixer client

All mixers provide the same functions, but you'll most likely use the one available in your desktop's panel. If you do not use X11, the aumix command can be used from the console. Interestingly, if you've properly configured the gpm or mouse daemon so that you can use your mouse for copying and pasting under the console, you can use your mouse to control the aumix slider controls (otherwise you'll need to use the cursor keys).

Playing Audio CDs

Playing audio CD-ROMs or music CDs requires a properly configured sound card, along with a Linux CD-ROM device pointing to your computer's CD drive. The default entry in your Red Hat Linux filesystem table, `/etc/fstab`, will show an entry that looks like this:

```
/dev/cdrom          /mnt/cdrom          iso9660 noauto,owner,ro 0 0
```

This entry shows (from left to right) that the device `/dev/cdrom` (which will be a symbolic link to the proper device, such as `/dev/hdc` for an ATAPI IDE CD-ROM drive), will be mounted under the `/mnt/cdrom` directory. The parts of the table entry designate the default filesystem to use, along with mounting and filesystem-checking options. You may also need to set correct permissions on the device (such as 0600) to allow users to play music.

You'll need a device entry for your CD-ROM in order to play audio CDs. Laptop users with an external CD-ROM will need to use an audio patch cable running from the external CD's audio-out jack to external speakers or the laptop's audio-in jack in order to hear the music.

The next step is to choose a music player. Red Hat Linux comes with several music CD players you can use with or without X11:

- `xplaycd`—A simple X11 CD player client
- `tcd`—A CD player for the text console
- `gtcd`—A GNOME CD player client with Internet features
- `kscd`—A KDE CD player client with Internet features

For example, to play an audio CD, insert the CD in your computer, then start a player such as `gtcd`, like this:

```
# gtcd &
```

Note that the player only has one slider control for volume. If you need more control, use a graphical mixer such as the `gmix` client. If you have an active Internet connection, `gtcd` will use its default settings, go out to a remote CD database server, and retrieve the name of your album, along with the name of each track. You can then click the Track Editor button to see your disc's information, as shown in Figure 8.15.

If your CD's information is not available, you can use the track editor (in Figure 8.15) to submit information back to the remote server. If you use KDE's `kscd` client, audio database information can be stored locally under the `/usr/share/apps/kscd/cddb` directory in one of 10 categories: blues, classical, country, folk, jazz, misc, newage, reggae, rock, or soundtrack.

FIGURE **8.15**

Track information retrieved over the Internet can be displayed, or if not present, submitted back to a remote server.

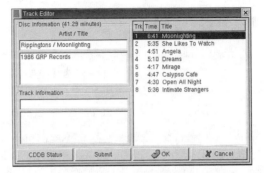

Playing .mp3s

Red Hat Linux also comes with several .mp3 audio players. The best player is the xmms client, which features a sophisticated interface and a plethora of features. You can launch this client from a desktop panel menu or from the command line of an X11 terminal window, like this:

```
# xmms &
```

Click the Open Tray button (upward-pointing arrow button), and you'll see a select file dialog, as shown in Figure 8.16.

FIGURE **8.16**

Load files for playing with xmms file dialog.

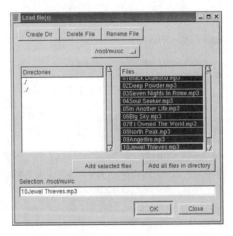

Scroll down with the Shift key held down to select multiple files, or click the Add All Files in Directory button to grab all files for playing. Click OK when finished. If you click the EQ button, you'll see a drop-down equalizer you can use to fine-tune the output sound, as shown in Figure 8.17.

FIGURE 8.17

The xmms *client also features an equalizer function to fine-tune your sound.*

To enable the equalizer, click the On button. You can then drag the vertical slider controls to set your sound. If you press Ctrl+P, you'll also see a custom control panel for loading, enabling, or configuring plug-in sound and light effects modules, as shown in Figure 8.18.

FIGURE 8.18

Playing .mp3 files may be extended and customized using various plug-in modules.

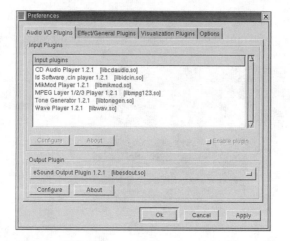

8

USING
MULTIMEDIA AND
GRAPHICS CLIENTS

There are many more features to this player. To see additional menus, right-click on the player, then use the various menus that will appear.

Playing Video

There are many different digital video formats produced for today's computer platforms, and it seems like there are different standards for different operating systems. Fortunately, Linux comes with several players that can handle different forms of video successfully. Some of the digital video formats include

- Amiga—Amiga MovieSetter animations
- AVI—Microsoft's Audio Video Interleave format
- FLI/FLC—Autodesk's Flic Animation format
- GIF87/89a—Animated GIF files

- MPEG—Moving Picture Expert Group
- QuickTime—Apple's QuickTime
- RealPlayer—RealPlayer streaming audio and video
- SGI—SGI Movie Format Files
- Utah Raster Toolkit—Run Length Encoded images

One of most common (and versatile) video players for Linux and X11 is Marc Podlipec's `xanim` client. You can find the latest version at `http://xanim.va.pubnix.com/home.html`. This player generally works from the command line of an X11 terminal window, along with the name of the video like this:

```
# xanim ibm_linux-02.avi
```

After you press Enter, the video will start playing in a small window, while the `xanim` controls are nearby in a floating window, such as that shown in Figure 8.19.

FIGURE 8.19

The `xanim` *client will play a variety of video clips under X11.*

Another popular player, automatically launched from the Netscape Navigator Web browser during Web sessions, or usable as a standalone streaming video player (as shown in Figure 8.20) is Real's RealPlayer. This client, which can be installed in a directory in your home directory, replays streaming audio and video over a network.

FIGURE 8.20

The `RealPlayer` *client plays audio and video over a network.*

The xanim client (at the time of this writing) plays clips from mounted filesystems, so performance is quite good. On the other hand, RealPlayer generally plays streaming audio or video via a network; performance can depend on your type of Internet connection, or the network traffic on your LAN.

Where is DVD Support for Linux?

As you know, digital video disc (DVD) drives work fine as normal CD-ROM drives under Linux. Red Hat Linux can also read the contents of DVD discs. In fact, SuSE, Inc. distributes a version of its six-CD-ROM Linux distribution on a single DVD! However, playing movies from DVD discs under Linux and X11 is another matter. On March 20, 2000, a Fremont, California-based company, InterVideo, Inc., announced that it would develop and release a software DVD player and decoder for Linux named LinDVD. Unfortunately, the product has not been released for consumers at the time of this writing. You can explore other methods to play DVDs under Linux, such as the one described in Nathan Rowlan's DVD Playing HOWTO, found at http://www.linuxdoc.org. Other sources of information, workarounds, and software include OpenDVD.org at http://www.opendvd.org, and the LiViD Project at http://linuxvideo.org.

Using a Web Cam

Web cams have been around for a while, and are supported under Linux. Some models use the parallel port for transmission of video data, usually at a reduced resolution, such as 320×240 pixels and 256 colors. Web cams will vary in quality, capability, and support (one problem being that some manufacturers have refused to release specifications so that drivers may be developed).

Newer models now use Universal Serial Bus (USB) for transmission of video data. Although a number of USB Web cams are supported under Linux, you'll generally need to track down, download, install, and configure software drivers for Red Hat Linux to support your Web cam.

One older type of parallel port-based Web cam that is supported is the Zora Web cam (part of White Pine's CuSeeMe software package for Windows, or available separately). You can find its standalone Linux driver, the mcam client, at http://www.panteltje.demon.nl/mcan/.

Installing mcam is as simple as downloading the source tarball, decompressing the source code, then typing

```
# ./make_x
```

Running the client is even easier. First, properly attach the camera to your computer, then type

```
# ./mcam
```

After you press Enter, type 4,5,9 to cycle the camera from low to high power, and then to display continuous frame-grabbing (as shown in Figure 8.21).

FIGURE 8.21

The mcam *client works with X11 and Linux to display continuous frames from a Web cam—even of penguins.*

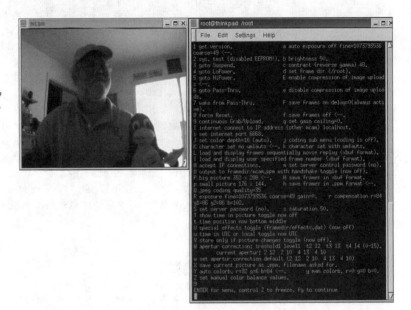

You'll also find that Red Hat Linux directly supports the IBM C-It USB video camera. Read the file `ibmcam.txt` under the `/usr/share/doc/kernel-doc-2.2.16/usb` directory for more details. If you browse to `http://webcam.sourceforge.net`, you'll see a list of at least a dozen other supported USB Web cams that work by using special Video4Linux drivers. And if you'd prefer a standalone Web cam that works independently via Ethernet, consider Axis Communications' 2100 Network Camera (which uses embedded Linux). Browse to `http://www.axis.com` for details.

Summary

This chapter presented an introduction to the wealth of graphics and multimedia commands, utilities, and clients that come with Red Hat Linux or that you can download over the Internet. Desktop users, marketing reps, graphic artists, and nearly any user will find a selection of tools that can be used to get graphics projects off the ground. Explore your system and experiment with different software packages to find the ones you enjoy the most. You'll soon find that Linux offers an almost overwhelming array of great software tools!

Configuring Services

PART
II

System Startup
and Shutdown

CHAPTER 9

This chapter explains how to start your Red Hat Linux system, what happens when it starts, and how to properly shut it down. It also covers system crashes and what to do if your system won't boot.

This chapter also presents some tips on how to customize your system and how to avoid problems with system crashes.

The Boot Process

In Chapter 2, "Installation of Your Red Hat System," you learned how to install Linux, and in Chapter 3, "LILO and Other Boot Managers," you found out how to install and use different loaders for different computers. A number of ways exist to start Linux with different computers, and there are different ways to load the Linux kernel. Intel Linux users will most likely use LILO, LOADLIN, SYSLINUX, BOOTLIN, or commercial alternatives such as System Commander or BootMagic. SPARC users will use SILO, and Alpha users will probably use MILO. You'll find the basic steps outlined in your *Red Hat Linux Users Guide* (if you purchased the "Official" distribution) or through Red Hat at http://www.redhat.com/support/manuals.

I'm assuming most readers will install Red Hat Linux/Intel, so here's a little background on how the Red Hat Linux startup process is different from that of other UNIX operating systems, such as BSD.

PCs start by looking at the first sector of the first cylinder of the boot drive and then trying to load and execute code found there (which is one way LILO can work, as explained in Chapter 3). This is also the case with other (but not all) hardware systems and versions of UNIX. You should be able to set the order in which your PC looks for the boot drive, usually through a BIOS change in a setup menu that you can invoke when you first turn on your machine (usually accomplished by pressing a Function key, such as F1 or F2, or a combination of keys, such as Fn and Esc on various laptops). Setting the boot order can be handy if you never use a boot floppy disk. For example, laptop users with an external floppy drive can speed up the boot process by directing the computer to look first at the internal hard drive or CD-ROM.

You can also start Linux over a network and run a diskless Linux box. For more information on how to do this, see Robert Nemkin's *Diskless Linux Mini HOWTO*, available at http://www.linuxdoc.org. Although Linux shares many similar traits with both System V and BSD UNIX, in the case of booting and starting the system, Linux is closer to the former. This means Linux uses the `init` command and a similar directory structure of associated scripts to start running the system and loading processes.

According to the Red Hat folks, this approach is becoming the standard in the Linux world because it is "easier to use and more powerful and flexible." Latest estimates, based on distribution sales, point to nearly 60% of Linux users using a Red Hat or Red Hat-based Linux system. Indeed, other distributions, such as Caldera's OpenLinux, use a similar initialization scheme (albeit with different naming conventions for scripts).

You'll also see why boot configuration is even easier for Red Hat Linux users when you learn about the linuxconf client later in this chapter in the section "linuxconf and Managing Your Services."

The Initialization Process and Startup Scripts

This section describes how Linux starts and details the functions of the startup scripts used to prepare your system for use. An important concept to note is the use of various runlevels or Linux system states.

System states grew from the need to separate how the system ran according to the forms of maintenance being performed on a system. This is similar to performing a software or hardware upgrade on older PCs, which generally requires a reboot or shutdown and restart of the computer. These days, however, this practice is partially obviated through new software and hardware technologies. *Hot-swappable* hardware and software indicates that you can change hard drives, PC cards, or associated software on-the-fly— while the system is running (such as loading or unloading Linux kernel modules with the insmod and rmmod commands).

You'll find a description of various runlevels in the /etc/inittab file or system initialization table. Although Linux differs from other versions of UNIX in several of the levels, Red Hat Intel/Linux mainly uses the following (as listed in /etc/inittab):

```
#    The runlevels used by RHS are:
#    0 - halt (Do NOT set initdefault to this)
#    1 - Single user mode
#    2 - Multiuser, without NFS (The same as 3, if you do not have networking)
#    3 - Full multiuser mode
#    4 - unused
#    5 - X11
#    6 - reboot (Do NOT set initdefault to this)
```

On older versions of Red Hat Linux, you would have found a line just below this listing that looked like this:

```
id:3:initdefault:
```

This line, which specifies runlevel 3 and uses the `initdefault` keyword, tells Linux to go to runlevel 3 (the Full multiuser mode) after loading the kernel (see the `inittab` man page for other keywords). However, newer versions of Red Hat Linux, where X11 is configured during installation, will most likely now boot to runlevel 5 with an `/etc/inittab` entry like this:

```
id:5:initdefault:
```

This means that Red Hat Linux, if you configure X11, will now boot directly to the X Window System if you choose to boot to a graphical login (using the `gdm` client, known as the GNOME display manager). See Chapter 5, "Window Managers," for details.

The next section describes these runlevels, including the first startup script in the initialization table, `/etc/rc.d/rc.sysinit`, or the system initialization script, which is run once at boot time by the `init` command. It also covers the `/etc/rc.d` directory structure and what some of these scripts do.

`init` and `/etc/inittab`

The `init` man page states, "init is the father of all processes." Its primary role is to create processes from a script stored in `/etc/inittab`. Much of how Linux starts its processes after loading the kernel comes from another UNIX, System V. In fact, the Linux `init` command is compatible with the System V `init` command, and the startup scripts model that approach. Although `init` starts as "the last step of the kernel booting," it is the first command that initializes and configures your system for use.

You can see evidence of this process by using the `pstree` command from the command line of your console or an X11 terminal window. At the command line, type

```
# pstree
```

After you press Enter, you'll see a tree listing of processes somewhat like this (especially if you use a laptop because of the Advanced Power Management and cardmgr PCMCIA manager daemons):

```
init-+-apmd
     |-atd
     |-2*[automount]
     |-battery_applet
     |-cardmgr
     |-crond
     |-deskguide_apple
     |-gdm-+-X
     |     `-gdm---gnome-session
     |-gmc
     |-gnome-name-serv
     |-gnome-smproxy
  ...
```

Although the entire output of `pstree` is not shown here, you can see that `init` has spawned the start of the system as the first process, and the parent of all subsequent processes. `init` works by parsing `/etc/inittab` and running scripts in `/etc/rc.d` according to either a default or desired runlevel. Each script can start or stop a service, such as a networking, mail, news, or Web service.

Here's a listing of the `/etc/rc.d` directory:

```
init.d/
rc*
rc.local*
rc.sysinit*
rc0.d/
rc1.d/
rc2.d/
rc3.d/
rc4.d/
rc5.d/
rc6.d/
```

Under the `init.d` directory, you'll find a number of scripts used to start and stop services. The details about each are not given here, but you should be able to guess at the function of some of them by their names and a short description, as shown in Table 9.1 Note that you may have more or less scripts than shown, because some scripts are part of a service package and will be installed when you install the software.

TABLE 9.1   Red Hat Linux System Initialization Scripts

Name	Description
amd	Controls the `automount` daemon
anacron	Scheduling control
apmd	Directory contains `apmd.init` for control of power management and logging
arpwatch	Tracks ethernet and Internet protocol address pairings
atd	Controls the `at` (personal scheduling) daemon
autofs	Controls the automount filesystem daemon
bootparamd	May be used to network boot older Sun workstations
crond	Controls the `cron` system scheduling daemon
dhcpd	Controls the Dynamic Host Control Protocol daemon
functions	Shell script functions used by `init` scripts
gated	Controls the routing gateway daemon
gpm	Controls the console mouse server (console cut-and-paste utility)
halt	Controls how shutdowns and reboots are handled

9

SYSTEM STARTUP AND SHUTDOWN

TABLE 9.1 continued

Name	Description
httpd	Controls the Apache Web server and HTTP service
identd	Controls the user identification server
innd	Controls InterNet News System
irda	Starts/stops IrDA daemon
isdn	Controls ISDN services
kdcrotate	Kerberos configuration script
keytable	Controls keyboard map loading
killall	Utility script used by amd, crond, inet, kerneld, mars-nwe, and the nfs init scripts to kill processes
krb5server	Starts/stops Kerberos server
kudzu	Hardware probe/config control
ldap	Control Directory Access Protocol daemons
linuxconf	Utility script for Red Hat's linuxconf tool
lpd	Controls print spooling services
mars-nwe	Controls Netware-compatible system services
mcserv	Controls Midnight Commander remote services
named	Controls start and stop of Domain Name Service
netfs	Control NFS, SMB, NCP mounts
network	Controls starting and stopping system networking
nfs	Controls Network Filesystem services
nfslock	Controls NFS file-locking
nfsfs	Controls mounting of NFS filesystems
nscd	Controls the Name Switch Cache daemon
pcmcia	Controls Card services for laptops
phhttpd	Controls HTTP accelerator
portmap	Controls Remote Procedure Call services
postgresql	Controls PostgreSQL database daemon
pppoe	Starts or stops an ADSL session
pulse	Controls clustering monitor
pxe	Controls remote-boot server
random	Controls random number generation
rarpd	Controls RARP daemon

TABLE 9.1 continued

Name	Description
reconfig	Manages anaconda's reconfig operation
routed	Controls network routing table daemon
rstatd	Controls the `rpc.statd` network kernel statistics daemon
rusersd	Controls the `rpc.rusersd` Network services
rwalld	Controls the `rpc.rwalld` Network Wall services
rwhod	Controls the `rwhod` daemon network `rwho` services
sendmail	Controls mail transport services
single	Used by `init` when Linux is booted to runlevel 1 or single-user administrative mode
smb	Controls the Samba `smbd` and `nmbd` daemons
snmpd	Controls the Simple Network Management Protocol daemon
sound	Saves and restores mixer information and levels
squid	Controls `httpd` object caching service
sshd	Controls the OpenSSH server
syslog	Starts and stops System Logging services
xdm	Controls whether to start or stop the X display manager, K display manager, or GNOME display manager for runlevel 5
xfs	Starts and stops the X11 `font` server
xinetd	Starts and stops `xinetd` daemon
xntpd	Starts and stops the Network Time Protocol (`NTPv3`) daemon for time synchronization
ypbind	Controls NIS binding services
yppasswdd	Controls the `YP password` server
ypserv	Controls Network Information services

9

SYSTEM STARTUP AND SHUTDOWN

In general, each script listed in Table 9.1 is designed to respond to commands of the following form:

```
script {start|stop|status|restart}
```

This means that a particular service may be controlled from other programs, depending on the syntax used.

Note

Not all scripts will respond to a restart or a status call.

You should also understand that each script in turn may control dozens of other processes or daemons. This is particularly true of the inet and xinetd scripts, used to control various networking services. The xinetd daemon, a new feature of Red Hat Linux, may be used to control nearly two dozen services, such as telnet, wu-ftpd, or POP3 mail server daemons.

/etc/inittab and System States

One of the most important scripts in /etc/inittab is rc.sysinit, the system initialization script. When init parses /etc/inittab, rc.sysinit is the first script found and executed. This differs slightly from other versions of UNIX, which might include the system initialization commands directly in the /etc/inittab file.

However, much like other versions of UNIX, the Red Hat Linux sysinit script performs some or all of the following functions:

- Sets some initial $PATH variables
- Configures networking
- Sets the system clock
- Loads keyboard configuration, system font
- Starts swapping for virtual memory
- Initializes USB controller and support
- Checks root filesystems for possible repairs
- Remounts the root filesystem read/write
- Checks filesystems for possible repairs
- Sets up Plug-and-Play devices
- Clears the mounted filesystems table /etc/mtab
- Enters the root filesystem into mtab
- Turns on hard drive optimizations
- Turns on user and group quotas for root filesystems
- Checks root filesystem quotas
- Sets the system hostname
- Readies the system for loading modules
- Finds module dependencies
- Loads sound modules
- Adds RAID devices, mounts all other filesystems

- Cleans out several /etc files: /etc/mtab, /etc/fastboot, and /etc/nologin
- Deletes UUCP lock files
- Deletes stale subsystem files
- Deletes stale pid files
- Initializes the serial ports
- Sets up SCSI tape (if present)

That's a lot of work just for the first startup script, but it's only the first step in a number of steps needed to start your system. You've seen that the init command is run after the Linux kernel is loaded. After the rc.sysinit is run by init, init runs rc.local. If you look at the Red Hat Linux rc.local script, you'll see that it gets the operating system name and architecture of your computer and puts it into a file called /etc/issue, which is later used for display at the login prompt.

Note

The purpose of rc.local is not to provide a place to put system-specific initializations, although some people do. In BSD UNIX, rc.local is generally used for controlling network services. Linux has not always used the same initialization scripts or approach to starting. You might find differences between distributions, such as Red Hat Linux, Caldera, Slackware, SuSe, or others. For Red Hat Linux, use one of the graphical interface tools such as tksysv, ntsysv, or linuxconf to control your system's services. Although you can do it manually by copying a skeleton script from the init.d directory and setting up the proper symbolic links, you'll find most of your needs met by the proper Red Hat tool.

The next init task is to run the scripts for each runlevel. If you look at the listing of the rc.d directory, you'll see the various rcX.d directories, where X is a number from 0 through 6. If you look at the files under one of these directories, you'll find that each is merely a link to a script under init.d, with an associated name for a particular service. For example, you may find the following under the rc3.d directory:

```
K01pppoe -> ../init.d/pppoe
K20nfs -> ../init.d/nfs
K20rstatd -> ../init.d/rstatd
K20rusersd -> ../init.d/rusersd
K20rwalld -> ../init.d/rwalld
K20rwhod -> ../init.d/rwhod
K34yppasswdd -> ../init.d/yppasswdd
K45arpwatch -> ../init.d/arpwatch
```

```
K84ypserv -> ../init.d/ypserv
K96irda -> ../init.d/irda
S05kudzu -> ../init.d/kudzu
S08ipchains -> ../init.d/ipchains
S10network -> ../init.d/network
S12syslog -> ../init.d/syslog
S13portmap -> ../init.d/portmap
S14nfslock -> ../init.d/nfslock
S20random -> ../init.d/random
S25netfs -> ../init.d/netfs
S35identd -> ../init.d/identd
S40atd -> ../init.d/atd
S45pcmcia -> ../init.d/pcmcia
S50xinetd -> ../init.d/xinetd
S55sshd -> ../init.d/sshd
S56rawdevices -> ../init.d/rawdevices
S60lpd -> ../init.d/lpd
S75keytable -> ../init.d/keytable
S80isdn -> ../init.d/isdn
S80sendmail -> ../init.d/sendmail
S85gpm -> ../init.d/gpm
S90crond -> ../init.d/crond
S90xfs -> ../init.d/xfs
S95anacron -> ../init.d/anacron
S97rhnsd -> ../init.d/rhnsd
S99linuxconf -> ../init.d/linuxconf
S99local -> ../rc.local
```

Note the *S* in the front of each name, meaning to start a process or service. Now, if you look at the files under `rc0.d`, you'll see this:

```
K00linuxconf -> ../init.d/linuxconf
K01pppoe -> ../init.d/pppoe
K03rhnsd -> ../init.d/rhnsd
K05keytable -> ../init.d/keytable
K10xfs -> ../init.d/xfs
K15gpm -> ../init.d/gpm
K20isdn -> ../init.d/isdn
K20nfs -> ../init.d/nfs
K20rstatd -> ../init.d/rstatd
K20rusersd -> ../init.d/rusersd
K20rwalld -> ../init.d/rwalld
K20rwhod -> ../init.d/rwhod
K25sshd -> ../init.d/sshd
K30sendmail -> ../init.d/sendmail
K34yppasswdd -> ../init.d/yppasswdd
K44rawdevices -> ../init.d/rawdevices
K45arpwatch -> ../init.d/arpwatch
K50xinetd -> ../init.d/xinetd
K60atd -> ../init.d/atd
```

```
K60crond -> ../init.d/crond
K60lpd -> ../init.d/lpd
K65identd -> ../init.d/identd
K75netfs -> ../init.d/netfs
K80random -> ../init.d/random
K84ypserv -> ../init.d/ypserv
K86nfslock -> ../init.d/nfslock
K87portmap -> ../init.d/portmap
K88syslog -> ../init.d/syslog
K90network -> ../init.d/network
K92anacron -> ../init.d/anacron
K92ipchains -> ../init.d/ipchains
K95kudzu -> ../init.d/kudzu
K96irda -> ../init.d/irda
K96pcmcia -> ../init.d/pcmcia
K99syslog -> ../init.d/syslog
S00killall -> ../init.d/killall
S01halt -> ../init.d/halt
```

Notice the *K* in front of each name, meaning to kill a process or service. If you look under each of the rcX.d directories, you'll see what services or processes are started or stopped in each runlevel. The symbolic links are numbered to run in the proper order and to start or stop services that might be interdependent. (For example, it wouldn't make sense to unmount your filesystem before stopping network file-sharing.) Later in this chapter you'll come back to some of the rc.sysinit tasks because some of the error-checking done when starting up can help pinpoint problems with your system. For now, however, the following section explains the runlevels and what basically happens in each.

Runlevel 0: /etc/rc.d/rc0.d

As you can see from the previous directory listing, this runlevel starts the shutdown sequence. Each script is run in the order listed. Some of the tasks run include

- Killing all processes
- Turning off virtual memory file swapping
- Unmounting swap and mounted filesystems

As shown in this section and discussed later in this chapter, some important things are done during a shutdown that involve your computer, its services, and its filesystems. Although Linux is a robust operating system with system-checking safeguards, executing a proper shutdown is essential to maintaining the integrity of your computer's hard drive as well as any Linux volumes or partitions.

9

SYSTEM STARTUP AND SHUTDOWN

Runlevel 1: `/etc/rc.d/rc1.d`

Runlevel 1 is the single-user mode, or administrative state, traditionally used by sysadmins while performing software maintenance. No one else can log in during this mode, and networking is turned off, although necessary filesystems are mounted. (Others can be mounted manually at the command-line prompt but then must be specifically unmounted before rebooting.)

If you use the LILO or LOADLIN bootloaders, you can boot Linux directly to this runlevel by passing a kernel *argument* or option on the LOADLIN command line or at the LILO `boot:` prompt. For LILO users, the argument generally takes the form

`boot:` **`linux single`**

After pressing Enter, Linux will boot to runlevel 1. You could also use the option 0 (numeral 0) instead of the single keyword like this:

`boot:` **`linux 0`**

Runlevel 2: `/etc/rc.d/rc2.d`

Runlevel 2 is the multiuser state. Networking is enabled, although NFS is disabled. This may be a good choice if you only use Red Hat Linux as a standalone desktop operating system for your PC.

Runlevel 3: `/etc/rc.d/rc3.d`

Runlevel 3 used to be the default runlevel specified as the first line in `/etc/inittab`; however, you may find that newer Red Hat Linux distributions use runlevel 5 as the default to boot directly to X and a display manager for logins. If you choose to use runlevel 3, you'll find that remote file-sharing is enabled, along with most other desired services.

Runlevel 4: `/etc/rc.d/rc4.d`

The runlevel 4 directory is set up so that you can define your own runlevel (and is, in fact, an exact copy of the settings for runlevel 5, enabling multiuser mode, networking, and X11). Note that in `/etc/inittab`, runlevel 4 is flagged as "unused." As in other versions of UNIX, if you want to define your own runlevel, here's where you can add the appropriate links, with directions to selectively start or stop processes.

Runlevel 5: `/etc/rc.d/rc5.d`

Runlevel 5 is used as the default runlevel when booting Linux with an X11 display manager. Many networking services are enabled by default.

Runlevel 6: `/etc/rc.d/rc6.d`

Runlevel 6 is the reboot runlevel. The contents of this directory contain links similar to those in runlevel 0, but logic in the halt script under `init.d` determines whether the system is being shut down or rebooted.

Keeping track of which process is started or stopped in which runlevel can be difficult. In the next section you'll see one more reason why using Red Hat Linux can make your system administration tasks easier.

`linuxconf` and Managing Your Services

One of the great things about Red Hat Linux is the number of tools included in the distribution to help you manage your system. One important tool is Jacque Gelinas's `linuxconf`, which can be called from a command line in a terminal window while you're running X, from the command line of your console screen, or through your favorite Web browser. You should use `linuxconf` for a number of reasons:

- `linuxconf` provides a comprehensive graphic interface for administering your Red Hat system.
- You can save different system configurations, allowing you, for example, to set up your computer as a desktop machine or Internet server at different times with a single command line.
- `linuxconf` replaces and maintains a number of user, file, and network utilities (such as the old `usercfg`, `fstool`, and `cabaret`); the program is used as a configuration tool and service activation tool.
- `linuxconf` has the capability to use modules to add new features or capabilities.
- The program features built-in help for many services or actions.
- `linuxconf` allows system maintenance over a network, enabling more efficient management of in-house or remote computers and networks.

`linuxconf` is found under the `/bin` directory and weighs in at nearly 950,000 bytes. The program, written with more than 80,000 lines of C++ code, also comes with a support directory, `/usr/lib/linuxconf`, containing nearly 32MB of data, help files in several languages, and code modules.

After you log in as the `root` operator, start the `linuxconf` program from the command line with the following and press the Enter key:

```
# linuxconf &
```

When you first run `linuxconf` you'll see a dialog of help text. If you're running X, have installed the GNOME software libraries, and run `linuxconf` a second time, the program's main window will appear as shown in Figure 9.1. Note that you can also use `linuxconf` without running X.

When used without GNOME libraries or from the console, the program (which started life as a configuration tool for the XFree86 X11 distribution) responds to keyboard commands just like Red Hat's Linux installation tool. Navigate around the program's dialog box by pressing the Tab key and then use the Enter key when the cursor is on a desired button or item in a list.

FIGURE 9.1

The `linuxconf` *client features a new generation of graphical Linux administration tools.*

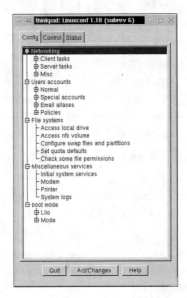

`linuxconf` can be used not only interactively, but also from the command line. The following related commands (and perhaps others by the time you read this) will be found in your filesystem after you install `linuxconf` (part of Red Hat Linux since version 5.1):

- `dnsconf`—A utility that can be used to configure a domain name server
- `fixperm`—A utility that checks system file permissions
- `fsconf`—A utility that manipulates the filesystem table, `/etc/fstab`, as shown in Figure 9.2.

FIGURE 9.2

The fsconf *command manipulates your system's filesystem table and can be used to configure various mounting options.*

- mailconf—A utility that configures the sendmail daemon
- netconf—A TCP/IP services configuration utility, as shown in Figure 9.3

FIGURE 9.3

The netconf *command is a graphical network configuration tool.*

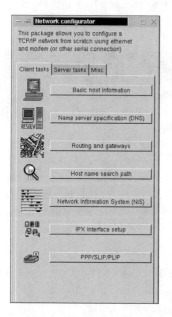

- userconf—User and group configuration (to add or delete users and groups)

Each program is a symbolic link to linuxconf. For example, to delete the user cloobie from the command line, use linuxconf's symbolic link userconf:

```
# userconf --deluser cloobie
```

You can get help for each utility by using the --help command-line option, or if using X11, by clicking the Help button in the utility's main dialog box.

The `linuxconf` command will also help you properly start and stop services under Linux while the system is running. Although you can selectively "kill" processes with the following code, where `pid` is the number of the running process, this is a crude, ineffective, and potentially harmful way to stop processes and system services.

```
# kill -9 pid
```

However, based on the information you have learned so far about the `init` scripts, you can use the following approach to stop the `httpd` Web server (as an example):

```
# /etc/rc.d/init.d/httpd.init stop
```

Both of these are manual approaches, but the Red Hat folks have taken great pains to make system administration easier, so why not take advantage of menu convenience? When you use `linuxconf`, you can see at one glance which processes are going to be enabled or disabled.

> **Note**
>
> Other tools included with Red Hat Linux include `ntsysv` and `tksysv`, which may be used to control what services are started automatically during boot up, or to reassign services to different runlevels.

If you manually configure your system's services by hand editing configuration files, be careful—making changes to default runlevels in `/etc/inittab` or indiscriminately using administration tools to change services or runlevels can put your system into an unusable state. If you run into trouble, reset your computer and enter runlevel 1.

Booting into single-user mode might allow you to fix any problems (a similar approach to another operating system's "safe mode"). When you boot into single-user mode, you go directly into a `root` operator command line, which is handy for enabling a quick fix or performing other system administration tasks.

You should also know that `linuxconf` is a work in progress; not every item in the program is documented or has an associated Help menu or complete help text. For some additional details about `linuxconf`, tips on using modules, or other errata, see `linuxconf`'s home page at `http://www.solucorp.qc.ca/linuxconf/`.

You can also subscribe to the `linuxconf` mailing list, `linuxconf@hub.xc.org`, or read archives of discussions about `linuxconf` through this site.

Shutting Down the Linux System

By now you've learned not only how Linux starts, but also a little bit about how it shuts down. If you look at the scripts in runlevel 0, you'll find a number of services being shut down, followed by the killing of all active processes, and finally, the `halt` script in `/etc/rc.d/init.d` directory executing the shutdown.

The halt script is used to either halt or reboot your system, depending on how it is called. What happens during a shutdown? If you're familiar with other operating systems (such as DOS), you remember that all you had to do was close any active application and then turn off the computer. Although Linux is easy to use, shutting down your computer is not as simple as turning it off. (You can try this, but you do so at your own risk.) A number of processes must take place before you or Linux turns off your computer. The following sections take a look at some of the commands involved.

shutdown

Although many people use Linux as single users on a single computer, many of us use computers on either a distributed or shared network. If you've ever been working under a tight deadline in a networked environment, you know the dreadful experience of seeing a `System is going down in 5 minutes!` message from the system administrator. You might also know the frustration of working on a system on which the system administrator is trying to perform maintenance, suffering seemingly random downtimes or frozen tasks.

Luckily for most users, maintenance jobs are performed during off hours, when most people are home with their loved ones or fast asleep in bed. Unluckily for sysadmins, this is the perfect time for system administration or backups, and one of the top reasons for the `alt.sysadmin.recovery` newsgroup.

The primary command to stop Linux is the `shutdown` command. Like most UNIX commands, `shutdown` has a number of options. A man page for the `shutdown` command is included with Red Hat Linux, but you can quickly read its command-line syntax if you use an illegal option, such as `-z`. Thanks to the programmer, here it is:

```
Usage:     shutdown [-akrhfnc] [-t secs] time [warning message]
                 -a:      use /etc/shutdown.allow
                 -k:      don't really shutdown, only warn.
                 -r:      reboot after shutdown.
                 -h:      halt after shutdown.
                 -f:      do a 'fast' reboot (skip fsck).
                 -F:      Force fsck on reboot.
                 -n:      do not go through "init" but go down real fast.
                 -c:      cancel a running shutdown.
                 -t secs: delay between warning and kill signal.
                 ** the "time" argument is mandatory! (try "now") **
```

To properly shut down your system immediately, use the `-h` option, followed by the word now or the numeral `0`:

```
# shutdown -h now
```

or

```
# shutdown -h 0
```

If you want to wait for a while, use the `-t` option, followed by a number (in seconds) before shutdown or reboot. If you want to restart your computer, use the `-r` option, along with the word now or the numeral `0`:

```
# shutdown -r now
```

or

```
# shutdown      -r 0
```

> **Note**
>
> You'll find two curious text strings embedded in the shutdown program:
> ```
> "You don't exist. Go away."
> "Oh hello Mr. Tyler - going DOWN?"
> ```
> Both are found by executing this:
> ```
> # strings /sbin/shutdown
> ```
> To find out about `"You don't exist. Go away"`, see Robert Kiesling's *Linux Frequently Asked Questions with Answers*. You should be able to find a copy at `http://www.linuxdoc.org/FAQ`.

You can also use `linuxconf` to shut down your computer. If you're logged in as the `root` operator, enter the following from the command line of your console or an X11 terminal window:

```
# linuxconf --shutdown
```

`linuxconf` presents a shutdown dialog box, as shown in Figure 9.4. To restart your system, press the Tab key until you highlight the Accept button, and then press the Enter key. You can also enter a time delay or halt your system immediately, and specify a message to broadcast to all your users when you execute the shutdown.

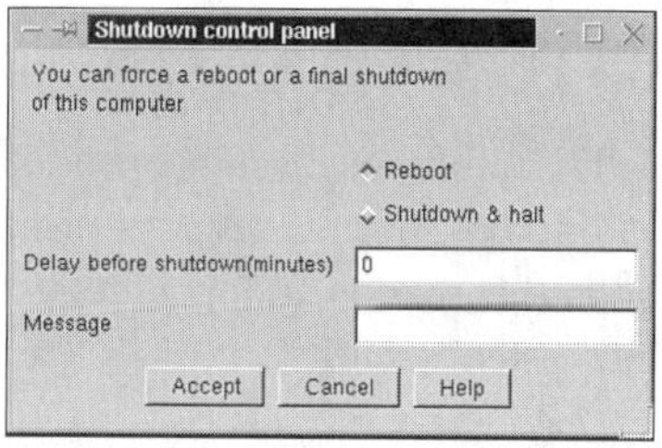

FIGURE 9.4

The linuxconf *command will perform a system reboot or shutdown.*

halt and reboot

Two other commands also stop or restart your system: halt and reboot. reboot is a symbolic link to halt, which notifies the kernel of a shutdown or reboot. Although you should always use shutdown to restart your system, you can use the "Vulcan neck pinch": Ctrl+Alt+Del.

If you use the keyboard form of this command, you'll find that Linux uses the following command:

```
# shutdown -t3 -r now
```

> **Note**
>
> This command is defined in your system's initialization table, /etc/inittab.

Restarting your computer with the shutdown command calls the sync command, which updates the *inodes* (structure representations)of each of your files. If you exit Linux without updating this information, Linux could lose track of your files on disk, and that spells disaster!

> **Note**
>
> The only time you'll want to risk shutting down Linux through a hard reset or the power-off switch on your computer is if you can't quickly kill a destructive process, such as an accidental rm -fr /*. Yet another reason to never run Linux as the root operator all the time!

By now you should know that exiting Linux properly can help you avoid problems with your system. What happens if something goes wrong? In the next section you learn preventive measures, how to maintain your filesystem, and how to recover and overcome problems.

When the System Crashes

The best time to deal with a system crash is before the crash happens. This means being prepared with a good backup plan, good backups, emergency boot disks, and copies of important files. These issues are covered in this section, along with tips and hints for maintaining your filesystem integrity and system security.

Here are some Do's to help you avoid problems:

- Do make a backup after a clean install and setup.
- Do create a set of emergency boot disks with your current kernel.
- Do use the `shutdown` command.
- Do consider using an uninterruptible power supply (UPS).
- Do use `fsck`, `mbadblocks`, or `badblocks` to check floppy disks.
- Do make backups of important files on floppy disks or other removable media.
- Do use your filesystem tools.
- Do consider using flash RAM if you use a laptop.
- Do read Lars Wirzenius's *Linux System Administrators' Guide 0.6.2* (available from `http://www.linuxdoc.org/LDP/sag/index.html`).

Here are some Don'ts that will help you avoid errors:

- Don't use Linux as the `root` user.
- Don't just turn off your computer when you finish.
- Don't disable `e2fsck` in `/etc/rc.d/rc.sysinit`.
- Don't run `fsck` on mounted filesystems.
- Don't worry about fragmentation of your Linux partitions.
- Don't fill your hard drive with unnecessary programs.

Running as `root`

Don't use Linux as `root` all of the time. Although you might be tempted, some very good reasons exist for not doing this. First, even though you might have aliased the `rm` command to `rm -i` in your `.bashrc` file, a simple `rm -fr /*` will wipe out not only your Linux system but also any DOS or Windows partitions mounted under `/mnt`. Instead, create a user for yourself and use the `su` command when you need to do things as the `root` operator.

> **Note**
>
> If you'd like to install a more flexible superuser command than su, try the sudo command. This program can be used to selectively extend superstatus to designated users for certain commands. For more information, navigate to http://www.courtesan.com/sudo.

Creating a Boot Disk

One of the most important things to do during your Red Hat Linux install is to make a boot disk. You should always have a working copy on hand.

If you skipped creating a boot disk, don't worry! Because you're a Red Hat Linux user, you'll find Erik Troan's handy mkbootdisk command installed on your system. Use mkbootdisk to create an emergency boot disk you can use to boot Linux in case LILO or your boot manager gets wiped out.

First, log in as the root operator. Next, use the uname command with the -r, or release number, option on the command line of your console or X11 terminal window like this:

```
# uname -r
2.2.16-22
```

As you can see, the uname has returned 2.2.16-22 as the release number of the currently running Linux kernel. Next, use mkbootdisk with its --device option, followed by the device name of your floppy drive and the release number of your Linux kernel returned by the uname command:

```
# mkbootdisk --device /dev/fd0 2.2.16-22
```

Insert a blank floppy disk and press the Enter key. You then see this:

```
Insert a disk in /dev/fd0. Any information on the disk will be lost.
Press <Enter> to continue or ^C to abort:
```

Press Enter to make your boot disk. When the command finishes, remove the floppy, label it, and place it in a safe place.

Another method of safeguarding your system is to make a secondary backup set of two emergency disks that use a minimal filesystem. These disks can help get you started on the road to recovery if you run into problems. Some excellent guides, scripts, and software are available to help you create your own diskette set (see "For More Information," at the end of this chapter). Generally, the approach is to create two disks, one containing a kernel and the other containing a compressed filesystem with a minimal directory of files, including file utilities.

The first disk is used to boot a kernel Linux, while the second is used as a "root" diskette with a minimal filesystem and a set of utilities (such as any required kernel modules, a text editor, tape restore commands, and the `mount` command). The approach is to then try to mount your existing Linux filesystem to make a repair.

Ackpht! Argggh! I've Deleted My Document!

If you accidentally delete a text file, don't panic. Here's a handy tip, called "Desperate person's text file undelete," from Paul Anderson's *The Linux Tips HOWTO*, courtesy of Michael Hamilton.

Assuming you remember some of the text, know which partition the file was on, and have a spare partition with some room, you should be able to recover a good portion of the file. Hamilton's approach uses the `egrep` and `strings` commands. For example, if you lose a 100-line file with the phrase `Xena`, followed by `Lawless`, and have room on your DOS partition, use this code:

```
# egrep -100 'Xena.+Lawless' /dev/hda3 > /mnt/dos/lucy
```

Then you can look for the text with this included:

```
# strings /mnt/dos/lucy | less
```

This approach to file recovery uses the `egrep` command to search for a string of text directly on your Linux partition. (Remember that everything under Linux is a file.) Each 100 lines of text before and after any match are saved into the designated file. Note, however, that this technique won't help you recover or undelete a binary file.

> **Note**
>
> If you need to recover binary files or want to explore other methods of file recovery, read Aaron Crane's *Linux Ext2fs-Undeletion mini-HOWTO*, found at `http://www.linuxdoc.org`. You'll read about several interesting techniques, including how to create a temporary Linux filesystem in your computer's memory to help provide recovery storage.

Your File Toolbox

You should also learn about and know how to use some of the file tools included with Red Hat Linux. Some of these tools, such as the `e2fsck` command, will be run automatically during booting as a diagnostic or if there is structural damage to any filesystem being mounted. Other commands, such as `dumpe2fs` and `debugfs`, can be used to provide detailed technical information concerning your Linux filesystem, while still others, such as badblocks, can be helpful if you have a non-IDE hard drive.

The following sections describe just some of the programs available.

e2fsck

Most Linux users choose to use ext2, the second extended filesystem, and with good reason: ext2 is robust, efficient, speedy, and relatively impervious to fragmentation. The staple companion utility, e2fsck, has nearly 20 command-line options that can help you check and repair a problem filesystem.

> **Caution**
>
> As mentioned, e2fsck is automatically run each time you boot Linux to check native filesystems before mounting. Although you can disable this check by altering the last field of a device's entry in your system's filesystem table, /etc/fstab, this is a bad idea and can cause problems.

For safety's sake, unmount the problem partition first. To diagnose and repair a device such as /dev/hda3, try this:

```
# e2fsck -p /dev/hda3
```

badblocks

The badblocks command searches a device for bad blocks and also has a number of options. Beware of the -w option; it is a "write-mode" test and will destroy data on a partition.

fsck

The fsck command, a front-end program for other filesystem commands such as e2fsck, checks and repairs Linux filesystems. Be sure to read its man page, because the -P option can be harmful.

dump and restore

The dump command can be used for filesystem backup because it can search for files that need to be backed up. dump can also do remote backups. The companion program is restore, which also works across networks. These commands may be used as preventive measure to guard against data loss.

dumpe2fs

The `dumpe2fs` command dumps your filesystem information. You'll get the inode count, block count, block size, last mount, and write time. Running `dumpe2fs` on a 450MB partition generates a 26,000-character report. An interesting part of the report is the mount and maximum `mount` count, which determines when `e2fsck` is run on a partition when Linux starts.

tune2fs

If you just have to mess with your system's performance, you can use the `tune2fs` command to adjust its tunable parameters—but only if you have an `ext2` filesystem. Use this command, along with its `-c` option, followed by a number, to adjust when `e2fsck` is run on a particular `ext2` partition, but don't do it when the partition is mounted.

mke2fs

Linux hackers will be familiar with the `mke2fs` program, which creates a Linux second-extended filesystem on a partition. You might need it, too, if you want to create compressed filesystems on emergency disks or if you install a new hard drive.

debugfs

`debugfs` is an `ext2` filesystem debugger, with 35 built-in commands. If you call it with the following you can examine your filesystem in read-only mode:

```
# debugfs /dev/hda3
```

Each of these utilities can help you maintain, diagnose, and repair a filesystem. What if you can't boot? Read on.

Red Hat to the Rescue! When the System Won't Boot

A Linux system might not boot for any of a number of reasons. The `rdev` command sets the `root` device following a kernel rebuild. If you use this command incorrectly after a rebuild, trying to use LILO or LOADLIN to load the new kernel won't work, and you could have problems booting. You'll also have problems if you've rebuilt the kernel and hard-coded in the wrong `root` device in your `/etc/lilo.conf` file.

I told you earlier that you'll appreciate being a Red Hat user. Here's another good reason: You get a set of emergency boot disks with your Red Hat distribution. If your system won't boot, here's how you might be able to recover your system:

First, always make a couple of emergency boot disks. Use the `mkbootdisk` command to create a boot disk with your Linux kernel. Then use the `dd` command to create a second disk containing the `rescue.img` file from the Red Hat Linux CD-ROM. Use the `mount` command to mount the CD-ROM:

```
# mount /mnt/cdrom
```

Log in as the `root` operator, insert a blank floppy disk in your computer (label it **rescue**), and then create the rescue disk, using `dd` to copy the `rescue.img` file:

```
# dd if=/mnt/cdrom/images/rescue.img of=/dev/fd0 bs=1440k
```

Boot Linux from your Red Hat Linux boot disk. Next, at the `boot:` prompt, type **rescue**, which loads a kernel from the disk. Follow the prompts and, when asked, eject the boot disk and insert the second rescue disk. You'll end up with a # bash shell prompt.

Under the `/bin` directory, you'll find a minimal set of programs to help you recover your files. Remember, the idea is to at least get you where you can try to check your existing partitions and possibly mount your drive. For example, if you have a Linux partition on `/dev/hda5`, you can try to first create a mount point by using the `mkdir` command, and then use `mnt` to mount your partition:

```
# mkdir /mnt/linux
# mount -t ext2 /dev/hda5 /mnt/linux
```

Your Linux partition will be found under `/mnt/linux`, and you can then attempt a fix or copy important files.

If you've installed Red Hat Linux and for some reason your system won't boot—and you don't have your Red Hat boot disks—you can also try booting directly from the first Red Hat Linux CD-ROM. (You might have to change your BIOS settings to alter the boot device sequence from your hard drive or floppy drive.)

You can also try to reboot your computer to DOS, change the directory to the CD-ROM and then DOSUTILS, and then type **AUTOBOOT**, which will execute the AUTOBOOT.BAT batch file and put you into the Red Hat installation process.

For More Information

For more information about the `linuxconf` tool, navigate to `http://www.solucorp.qc.ca/linuxconf`.

To subscribe to the `linuxconf` mailing list, put the following text into the body of an email message addressed to `linuxconf-request@solucorp.qc.ca`:

```
subscribe linuxconf
```

9

SYSTEM STARTUP AND SHUTDOWN

For information regarding the Linux boot process, a host of handy tips on building boot disks, pointers to bootdisk packages, and a number of helpful scripts, see Tom Fawcett and Graham Chapman's *Bootdisk HOWTO* at `http://www.linuxdoc.org`.

You should also look for the following rescue packages and other helpful utilities at `http://metalab.unc.edu/pub/Linux/system/recovery`:

- Scott Burkett's *Bootkit*
- Oleg Kibirev's *CatRescue*
- Thomas Heiling's *Rescue Shell Scripts*
- Karel Kubat's *SAR—Search and Rescue*
- Tom Fawcett's *YARD*

Read the man pages for the following commands on your Red Hat Linux system:

• `badblocks`	• `fstab`	• `mount`
• `debugfs`	• `halt`	• `rdev`
• `dump`	• `hdparm`	• `restore`
• `dumpe2fs`	• `init`	• `shutdown`
• `e2fsck`	• `inittab`	• `swapon`
• `fsck`	• `mke2fs`	• `tune2fs`

If you ever lose or destroy your copies of the Red Hat Linux boot disks, you can get replacements at `http://www.redhat.com/download/mirrors.html`.

For details on how 4.4BSD boots, see Tabbed Section 1 of the *4.4BSD System Manager's Manual*. For details about other UNIX boot processes, see *UNIX Unleashed: System Administrator's Edition*.

For loads of tips on maintaining your system and background information about various Linux filesystems, see Lars Wirzenius's *Linux System Administrators' Guide 0.6.2*. You'll find a copy through `http://www.linuxdoc.org`.

If you're interested in a Linux filesystem defragmenter, check out Stephen Tweedie and Alexei Vovenko's defragmenter, which you'll find at `http://metalab.unc.edu/pub/Linux/system/filesystems/defrag-0.70.tar.gz`.

Summary

Understanding how Linux boots and starts software services can be essential when tracking down problems or trying to troubleshoot filesystem or service problems. Hopefully, you've learned about Linux runlevels and how to start and stop processes properly using Red Hat Linux. Understanding the software tools available for the system administrator's toolbox and arming yourself with emergency bootdisks ahead of time can make the difference between failure and success when disaster (such as a hardware failure or system security breach) strikes. This chapter also covered a number of topics related to starting and shutting down Linux, including the following:

- How to use `linuxconf`
- How to properly shut down your Linux system
- How to properly restart your Linux system
- The do's and don'ts of maintaining your system
- How to possibly undelete a file
- How to possibly recover and remount a Linux partition

SMTP and Protocols

IN THIS CHAPTER

This chapter begins with some brief background on Internet email, including a discussion about the SMTP protocol. Other topics include setting up `sendmail` on Linux, including some basic configuration options; the Washington University IMAP/POP package, which implements POP3 and IMAP4 support for Linux; and methods to retrieve your mail messages using the POP3 and IMAP protocols.

A Brief History of Internet Email Standards

Electronic mail or email is arguably the most useful application of the Internet. (Yes, even more so than the relatively young World Wide Web.) Since the Internet's inception, there have been many public open standards published, which are called Requests for Comments (RFCs). Many of these RFCs were (and still are) related to email standards. The SMTP specification originally started with the Mail Transfer Protocol in 1980, evolved into Simple Mail Transfer Protocol (SMTP) in 1981, and since has been enhanced into the protocol we know today. (See `http://www.ietf.org/rfc.html`.)

Introduction to `sendmail`

During this time of rapid change in email protocols, one package emerged as a standard for mail transfer. `sendmail`, written by Eric Allman at U.C. Berkeley, was an unusual program for its time because it saw the email problem in a different light. Instead of rejecting email from different networks using so-called incorrect protocols, `sendmail` massaged the message and fixed it so it could be passed on to its destination. The trade-off for this level of flexibility has been complexity. Several books have been written on the subject (the authoritative texts have reached over 1,000 pages). However, for most administrators, this is overkill. `sendmail` was and still is written using the *open source* method of development. This means that all the source code is freely available and can be freely distributed. Eric has now established a company, Sendmail, Inc. (`http://www.sendmail.com`), that provides commercial products and add-ons for `sendmail`. However, the core `sendmail` product (now at version 8) will always remain free and open source.

One of the key features of `sendmail` that differentiated it from other mail transfer agents (MTAs) during the 1980s was the separation of mail routing, mail delivery, and mail readers. `sendmail` performed mail routing functions only, leaving delivery to local agents that the administrator could select. This also meant that users could select their preferred mail readers as long as the readers could read the format of the messages written by the delivery software.

The Post Office Protocol (POP)

With the advent of larger, heterogeneous networks, the need for mail readers that worked on network clients and connected to designated mail servers to send and receive mail gave way to the Post Office Protocol (POP). The POP RFC has undergone many revisions since its inception. The latest revision of the protocol is POP3, which has been updated a number of times since 1988. POP mail readers have since flourished: client software is available for every imaginable platform, and there is server software for not only various implementations of UNIX (including Linux), but for other operating systems as well.

POP3 does have its fair share of limitations, the main one being that it can access messages in only one mailbox (generally the user's incoming mailbox on the server). When you're reading email with a client program on Linux, such as Pine or Elm, you can create folders to manage your messages. When you're using a POP3 client, you can also create folders to organize your messages, but those folders will only exist on the machine that the POP3 client is running on. For example, if you run the Eudora email client on a Windows machine and access your mail via POP3 on a Linux server, you can save messages to Eudora folders, but these folders generally will be located on the Windows hard drive. If you use another PC to access your email with a POP3-compatible client, you will not be able to access those folders you created on the first Windows machine.

The Internet Mail Access Protocol (IMAP)

A protocol called Internet Message Access Protocol (IMAP) was developed to be an improvement on POP3. Its first RFC was based on version 4 of IMAP, so it is generally referred to as IMAP4. IMAP4 overcomes some of the limitations of POP3. The major feature is that a user can have multiple folders on the server to save their read mail. So wherever you access your email using IMAP, you have full access to all your previously read and saved messages.

Another limitation of the POP3 protocol is that it does not keep the state of messages in your mailboxes—different messages can have different states, such as read, unread, or marked for deletion. So most POP3 clients download all the messages in the user's mailbox. IMAP4 overcomes this problem by only downloading the headers of all mail items and, depending on which message is selected, downloading only that particular message. Again, there are implementations of IMAP4 servers for most major network operating systems in use today.

SMTP and `sendmail`

The Simple Mail Transfer Protocol (SMTP) is the established standard for transferring mail over the Internet. The `sendmail` program provides the services needed to support SMTP connections for Linux.

This section covers the details you need in order to understand, install, and configure the `sendmail` package. Before getting into the details, however, let's take a moment to discuss the SMTP protocol in better detail and how the Domain Name Service (DNS) interacts with email across the Internet. (See Chapter 14, "Domain Name Service and Dynamic Host Configuration Protocol," for more details on DNS configuration.)

Armed with a better understanding of the protocols, you can take on trying to understand `sendmail` itself, beginning with the various tasks that `sendmail` performs, such as mail routing and header rewriting, as well as its corresponding configuration files.

> **Caution**
>
> As with any large software package, `sendmail` has its share of bugs. Although the bugs that cause `sendmail` to fail or crash the system have been almost completely eliminated, security holes that provide `root` access are still found from time to time.
>
> When you're using any software that provides network connectivity, you *must* keep track of security announcements from the Computer Emergency Response Team (CERT) by either visiting its Web page at `http://www.cert.org/`, joining its mailing list, or reading its moderated newsgroup, `comp.security.announce`.
>
> In addition, Red Hat provides security updates and announcements on its site. The URL is `http://www.redhat.com/errata/` and the newsgroup is `redhat.security.general`.

Internet Mail Protocols

To understand the jobs that `sendmail` performs, you need to know a little about Internet protocols. Protocols are simply agreed-upon standards that software and hardware use to communicate.

Protocols are usually layered, with higher levels using the lower ones as building blocks. For example, the Internet Protocol (IP) sends packets of data back and forth without building an end-to-end connection such as that used by SMTP and other higher-level protocols. The Transmission Control Protocol (TCP), which is built on top of IP, provides for connection-oriented services such as those used by telnet and the Simple Mail

Transfer Protocol (SMTP). The TCP/IP protocols provide the basic network services for the Internet. Higher-level protocols such as the File Transfer Protocol (FTP) and SMTP are built on top of TCP/IP. The advantage of such layering is that programs that implement the SMTP or FTP protocols don't have to know anything about transporting packets on the network and making connections to other hosts. They can use the services provided by TCP/IP for that job.

SMTP defines how programs exchange email on the Internet. It doesn't matter whether the program exchanging the email is sendmail running on a Sun workstation or an SMTP client written for an Apple Macintosh. As long as both programs implement the SMTP protocol correctly, they can exchange mail.

The following example of the SMTP protocol in action might help demystify it a little. The user betty at gonzo.gov is sending mail to joe at whizzer.com:

```
$ /usr/sbin/sendmail -v joe@whizzer.com < letter
joe@whizzer.com... Connecting to whizzer.com via tcp...
Trying 123.45.67.1... connected.
220-whizzer.com SMTP ready at Mon, 6 Jun 1997 18:56:22 -0500
220 ESMTP spoken here
>>> HELLO gonzo.gov
250 whizzer.com Hello gonzo.gov [123.45.67.2], pleased to meet you
>>> MAIL From:<betty@gonzo.gov>
250 <betty@gonzo.gov>... Sender ok
>>> RCPT To:<joe@whizzer.com>
250 <joe@whizzer.com>... Recipient ok
>>> DATA
354 Enter mail, end with "." on a line by itself
>>> .
250 SAA08680 Message accepted for delivery
>>> QUIT
221 whizzer.com closing connection
joe@whizzer.com... Sent
$
```

The first line shows one way to invoke sendmail directly rather than letting your favorite Mail User Agent (MUA), such as Elm, Pine, or Mutt, do it for you. The -v option tells sendmail to be verbose and shows you the SMTP dialog. The other lines show an SMTP client and server carrying on a conversation. Lines prefaced with >>> indicate the client (or sender) on gonzo.gov, and the lines that immediately follow are the replies of the server (or receiver) on whizzer.com. The first line beginning with 220 is the SMTP server announcing itself after the initial connection, giving its hostname and the date and time, and the second line informs the client that this server understands the Extended SMTP protocol (ESMTP) in case the client wants to use it. Numbers such as 220 are reply codes that the SMTP client uses to communicate with the SMTP server. The text following the reply codes is only for human consumption.

Although this dialog still might look a little mysterious, it will soon be very familiar if you take the time to read RFCs 821 and 1869. Running `sendmail` with its `-v` option also will help you understand how an SMTP dialog works.

The Domain Name System and Email

Names like `whizzer.com` are convenient for humans, but computers insist on using numerical IP addresses like `123.45.67.1`. The Domain Name Service (DNS) provides this hostname-to-IP-address translation and other important information.

In the old days, only a few thousand hosts were on the Internet. All hosts were registered with the Network Information Center (NIC), which distributed a host table listing the hostnames and IP addresses of all the hosts on the Internet. Those simple times are gone forever. No one really knows how many hosts are connected to the Internet now, but they number in the millions. It is physically impossible for an administrative entity such as the NIC to keep track of every Internet address. Thus was born the DNS.

The DNS distributes the authority for naming and numbering hosts to autonomous administrative domains. For example, a company called `whizzer.com` can maintain all the information about the hosts in its own domain. When the host `a.whizzer.com` wants to send mail or telnet to the host `b.whizzer.com`, it sends an inquiry over the network to the `whizzer.com` nameserver, which might run on a host named `ns.whizzer.com`. The `ns.whizzer.com` nameserver replies to `a.whizzer.com` with the IP address of `b.whizzer.com` (and possibly other information), and the mail is sent or the telnet connection made. Because `ns.whizzer.com` is authoritative for the `whizzer.com` domain, it can answer any inquiries about `whizzer.com` hosts regardless of where they originate. The authority for naming hosts in this domain has been delegated.

Now, what if someone on `a.whizzer.com` wants to send mail to `joe@gonzo.gov`? `ns.whizzer.com` has no information about hosts in the `gonzo.gov` domain, but it knows how to find this information. When a nameserver receives a request for a host in a domain for which it has no information, it asks the `root` nameservers for the names and IP addresses of servers that are authoritative for that domain—in this case, `gonzo.gov`. The `root` nameserver gives the `ns.whizzer.com` nameserver the names and IP addresses of hosts running nameservers with authority for `gonzo.gov`. The `ns.whizzer.com` nameserver inquires of them and forwards the reply to `a.whizzer.com`.

From the preceding description, you can see that the DNS is a large, distributed database containing mappings between hostnames and IP addresses, but it contains other information as well. When a program such as `sendmail` delivers mail, it must translate the recipient's hostname into an IP address. This bit of DNS data is known as an A (Address) record, and it is the most fundamental data about a host. A second piece of host data is the Mail eXchanger (MX) record. An MX record for a host such as a.whizzer.com lists one or more hosts willing to receive mail for it.

What's the point? Why shouldn't a.whizzer.com simply receive its own mail and be done with the process? Isn't a postmaster's life complicated enough without having to worry about mail exchangers? Well, although it's true that the postmaster's life is often overly complicated, MX records serve some useful purposes:

- Hosts not on the Internet (for example, UUCP-only hosts) can designate an Internet host to receive their mail and so appear to have Internet addresses. This use of MX records allows non-Internet hosts to appear to be on the Internet (but only to receive email).

- Hosts can be off the Internet for extended times for unpredictable reasons. Thanks to MX records, even if your host is off the Internet, its mail can queue on other hosts until your host returns. The other hosts can be onsite (that is, in your domain), off-site, or both.

- MX records hide information and allow you more flexibility to reconfigure your local network. If all your correspondents know that your email address is joe@whizzer.com, it doesn't matter whether the host that receives mail for whizzer.com is named zippy.whizzer.com or pinhead.whizzer.com. It also doesn't matter if you decide to change the name to white-whale.whizzer.com; your correspondents will never know the difference.

Mail Delivery and MX Records

When an SMTP client delivers mail to a host, it must do more than translate the hostname into an IP address. First, the client asks for MX records. If any exist, it sorts them according to the priority given in the record. For example, whizzer.com might have MX records listing the hosts mailhub.whizzer.com, walrus.whizzer.com, and mailer.gonzo.gov as the hosts willing to receive mail for it (and the "host" whizzer.com might not exist except as an MX record, meaning that there might be no IP address available for it). Although any of these hosts will accept mail for whizzer.com, the MX priorities specify which host the SMTP client should try first, and properly behaved SMTP clients will do so. In this case, the system administrator has set up a primary mail relay mailhub.whizzer.com and an onsite backup walrus.whizzer.com, and has arranged with the system administrator at mailer.gonzo.gov for an offsite backup. The administrators have set the MX priorities so SMTP clients will try the primary mail relay first, the onsite backup second, and the off-site backup third. This setup takes care of problems with the vendor who doesn't ship your parts on time and the wayward backhoe operator who severs the fiber-optic cable that provides your site's Internet connection.

After collecting and sorting the MX records, the SMTP client gathers the IP addresses for the MX hosts and attempts delivery to them in order of MX preference. You should keep this fact in mind when you're debugging mail problems. Just because a letter is addressed to joe@whizzer.com doesn't necessarily mean a host named whizzer.com exists. Even if such a host does exist, it might not be the host that is supposed to receive the mail. You can easily check this using the nslookup command to check if any MX records are being used for a given domain name. For example:

```
# nslookup -querytype=mx linux.org
Server:  dns1.whizzer.com
Address:  192.168.1.2

Non-authoritative answer:
linux.org        preference = 30, mail exchanger = border-ai.invlogic.com
linux.org        preference = 10, mail exchanger = mail.linux.org
linux.org        preference = 20, mail exchanger = router.invlogic.com

Authoritative answers can be found from:
linux.org        nameserver = NS.invlogic.com
linux.org        nameserver = NS0.AITCOM.NET
border-ai.invlogic.com  internet address = 205.134.175.254
mail.linux.org  internet address = 198.182.196.60
router.invlogic.com     internet address = 198.182.196.1
NS.invlogic.com internet address = 205.134.175.254
NS0.AITCOM.NET  internet address = 208.234.1.34
```

The non-authoritative answer means that you didn't get the answer from one of the DNS servers authoritative for the domain linux.org. A list of these authoritative servers is the last part of the response. The MX records that you requested are listed with their preference value. A lower preference means that these servers are tried first followed by higher preferences until the mail is delivered successfully. For the full details on configuring DNS for Linux, see Chapter 20, "TCP/IP Network Management."

Header and Envelope Addresses

The distinction between header and envelope addresses is important because mail routers can process them differently. An example will help explain the difference between the two.

Suppose you have a paper memo you want to send to your colleagues Mary and Bill at the Gonzo Corporation and Ted and Ben at the Whizzer company. You give a copy of the memo to your trusty mail clerk Alphonse, who notes the multiple recipients. Because he's a clever fellow who wants to save your company 66 cents, Alphonse makes two copies of the memo and puts each in an envelope addressed to the respective companies instead of sending a copy to each recipient. On the cover of the Gonzo envelope, he writes "Mary and Bill," and on the cover of the Whizzer envelope, he writes "Ted and

Ben." When Alphonse's counterparts at Gonzo and Whizzer receive the envelopes, they make copies of the memo and send them to Mary, Bill, Ted, and Ben without inspecting the addresses in the memo itself. As far as the Gonzo and Whizzer mail clerks are concerned, the memo itself might be addressed to the Pope. They care only about the envelope addresses.

SMTP clients and servers work in much the same way. Suppose `joe@gonzo.gov` sends mail to his colleagues `betty@zippy.gov` and `fred@whizzer.com`. The recipient list in the letter's headers might look like this:

```
To: betty@zippy.gov, fred@whizzer.com
```

The SMTP client at `gonzo.gov` connects to the `whizzer.com` mailer to deliver Fred's copy. When it's ready to list the recipients (the envelope address), what should it say? If it gives both recipients as they are listed in the preceding `To:` line (the header address), Betty will get two copies of the letter because the `whizzer.com` mailer will forward a copy to `zippy.gov`. The same problem occurs if the `gonzo.gov` SMTP client connects to `zippy.gov` and lists both Betty and Fred as recipients. The `zippy.gov` mailer will forward a second copy of Fred's letter.

The solution is the same one that Alphonse and the other mail clerks used. The `gonzo.gov` SMTP client puts the letter in an envelope containing only the names of the recipients on each host. The complete recipient list is still in the letter's headers, but they are inside the envelope and the SMTP servers at `gonzo.gov` and `whizzer.com` don't look at them. In this example, the envelope for the `whizzer.com` mailer lists only `fred`, and the envelope for `zippy.gov` lists only `betty`.

Aliases illustrate another reason that header and envelope addresses differ. Suppose you send mail to the alias `homeboys`, which includes the names `alphonse`, `joe`, `betty`, and `george`. In your letter, you write **To: homeboys**. However, `sendmail` expands the alias and constructs an envelope that includes all the recipients. Depending on whether the names are also aliases, perhaps on other hosts, the original message might be put into as many as four different envelopes and delivered to four different hosts. In each case, the envelope contains only the names of the recipients, but the original message contains the alias `homeboys` (expanded to `homeboys@your.host.domain` so replies will work).

A final example shows another way in which envelope addresses might differ from header addresses. With `sendmail`, you can specify recipients on the command line. Suppose you have a file named `letter` that looks like this:

```
$ cat letter
To: null recipient <>
Subject: header and envelope addresses

testing
```

You send this letter with the following command, substituting your own login name for *yourlogin*:

```
$ /usr/sbin/sendmail yourlogin < letter
```

Because your address was on the envelope, you will receive the letter even though your login name doesn't appear in the letter's headers. Unless it's told otherwise (with the `-t` flag), `sendmail` constructs envelope addresses from the recipients you specify on the command line, and a correspondence doesn't necessarily exist between the header addresses and the envelope addresses.

sendmail's Jobs

To better understand how to set up `sendmail`, you need to know what jobs it does and how these jobs fit into the scheme of MUAs, MTAs, mail routers, final delivery agents, and SMTP clients and servers. `sendmail` can act as a mail router, an SMTP client, and an SMTP server. However, it does not do final delivery of mail.

sendmail as Mail Router

`sendmail` is primarily a mail router, meaning that it takes a letter, inspects the recipient addresses, and decides the best way to send it. How does `sendmail` perform this task?

`sendmail` determines some of the information it needs on its own, such as the current time and the name of the host on which it's running, but most of its brains are supplied by you, the postmaster, in the form of a configuration file, `sendmail.cf` (described in more detail later). This somewhat cryptic file tells `sendmail` exactly how you want various kinds of mail handled. `sendmail.cf` is extremely flexible and powerful, and seemingly inscrutable at first glance. However, one of the strengths of V.8 `sendmail` is its set of modular configuration file building blocks. Most sites can easily construct their configuration files from these modules, and many examples are included. Writing a configuration file from scratch is a daunting task, so you should avoid it if at all possible!

sendmail as MTA: Client (Sender) and Server (Receiver) SMTP

As mentioned before, `sendmail` can function as an MTA because it understands the SMTP protocol (V.8 `sendmail` also understands ESMTP). SMTP is a connection-oriented protocol, so a client and a server (also known as a sender and a receiver) always exist. The SMTP client delivers a letter to an SMTP server, which listens continuously on its computer's SMTP port. `sendmail` can be an SMTP client or an SMTP server. When run by an MUA, it becomes an SMTP client and speaks client-side SMTP to an SMTP server (not necessarily another `sendmail` program). When your `sendmail` starts in daemon mode, it runs as a server. When in this server mode it does two main tasks. The first is to continuously listen on the SMTP port for incoming mail. The second is to manage the queue of mail that has not been delivered yet and to periodically retry delivery until the message is finally delivered successfully or the retry limit is exceeded.

sendmail Is Not a Final Delivery Agent

One thing that sendmail doesn't do is final delivery. sendmail's author wisely chose to leave this task to other programs. sendmail is a big, complicated program that runs with superuser privileges. That's an almost guaranteed recipe for security problems, and quite a few have occurred in sendmail's past. The additional complexity of final mail delivery is the last thing sendmail needs. By default on Red Hat systems, procmail is used as the local delivery agent.

sendmail's Auxiliary Files

sendmail depends on a number of auxiliary files to do its job. Most important are the aliases file and the configuration file, sendmail.cf. The statistics file, sendmail.st, can be created or not, depending on whether you want statistics on how many messages are sent to and received from your host. This includes the total amount of email traffic in kilobytes as well. sendmail.hf, which is the SMTP help file, should be installed if you intend to run sendmail as an SMTP server (most sites do).

The other file that might be required on your host is sendmail.cw, which contains all of the alternate hostnames for your email server. For example, if your main email server is mail.whizzer.com, which is specified as an MX for whizzer.com, you would need to put whizzer.com in this file to tell sendmail to deliver whizzer.com email on mail.whizzer.com.

That's all that needs to be said about sendmail.st, sendmail.hf, and sendmail.cw. Other auxiliary files are covered in the *Sendmail Installation and Operating Guide*, or *SIOG* for short. The SIOG is usually found in /usr/share/doc/sendmail/doc/op/ op.ps, which comes from the sendmail-doc RPM or in the source distribution of sendmail. The aliases and sendmail.cf files, on the other hand, are important enough to be covered in their own sections.

The Aliases File

sendmail always checks recipient addresses for aliases, which are alternative names for recipients. For example, each Internet site is required to have a valid address postmaster to whom mail problems can be reported. Most sites don't have an actual account of that name but divert the postmaster's mail to the person or persons responsible for email administration. For example, at the fictional site `gonzo.gov`, the users `joe` and `betty` are jointly responsible for email administration, and the aliases file has the following entry:

```
postmaster: joe, betty
```

This line tells `sendmail` that mail to `postmaster` should instead be delivered to the login names `joe` and `betty`. In fact, these names could also be aliases:

```
postmaster: firstshiftops, secondshiftops, thirdshiftops
firstshiftops: joe, betty
secondshiftops: lou, emma
thirdshiftops: ben, mark, clara
```

In all these examples, the alias names are on the left side of the colon and the aliases for those names are on the right side. `sendmail` repeatedly evaluates aliases until they resolve to a real user or a remote address. To resolve the alias `postmaster` in the preceding example, `sendmail` first expands it into the list of recipients—`firstshiftops`, `secondshiftops`, and `thirdshiftops`—and then expands each of these aliases into the final list—`joe`, `betty`, `lou`, `emma`, `ben`, `mark`, and `clara`.

Although the right side of an alias can refer to a remote host, the left side cannot. The alias `joe: joe@whizzer.com` is legal, but `joe@gonzo.gov: joe@whizzer.com` is not.

Whenever you modify the alias file, you must run the command `newaliases`. Otherwise, `sendmail` will not know about the changes.

Reading Aliases from a File: The `:include:` Directive

Aliases can be used to create mailing lists. (In the example shown in the preceding section, the alias `postmaster` is, in effect, a mailing list for the local postmasters.) For big or frequently changing lists, you can use the `:include:` alias form to direct `sendmail` to read the list members from a file. Assume the aliases file contains this line:

```
homeboys: :include:/home/alphonse/homeboys.aliases
```

Assume also that the file `/home/alphonse/homeboys.aliases` contains this:

```
alphonse
joe
betty
george
```

The effect is the same as this alias:

```
homeboys: alphonse, joe, betty, george
```

This directive is handy for mailing lists that are automatically generated, change frequently, or are managed by users other than the postmaster. If you find that a user is asking for frequent changes to a mail alias, you might want to put it under her control. You must be careful; the latest versions of `sendmail` are very picky with permissions of files that they reference. If any of these files or parent directories have group or world writable permissions, the files will most likely be ignored, which might cause `sendmail` to cease working or not even start at all. These sorts of problems are usually logged to your system messages file (`/var/log/messages` or `/var/log/maillog`, depending on how your syslog is configured).

Mail to Programs

The aliases file can also be used to send the contents of email to a program. For example, many mailing lists are set up so you can get information about the list or subscribe to it by sending a letter to a special address, *list*-`request`. The letter usually contains a single word in its body, such as `help` or `subscribe`, which causes a program to mail an information file to the sender. Suppose the `gonzo` mailing list has such an address, called `gonzo-request`:

```
gonzo-request: |/usr/local/lib/auto-gonzo-reply
```

In this form of alias, the pipe symbol (`|`) tells `sendmail` to use the program mailer, which is usually defined as `/bin/sh` (see "The M Operator: Mailer Definitions" later in this chapter). `sendmail` feeds the message to the standard input of `/usr/local/lib/auto-gonzo-reply`, and if it exits normally, `sendmail` considers the letter to be delivered.

Mail to Files

You can also create an alias that causes `sendmail` to send mail to files. This sort of alias begins with a forward slash (`/`), which will be a full pathname to the file you want to append to. An example is the alias `nobody`, which is common on systems running the Network File System (NFS):

```
nobody: /dev/null
```

Aliases that specify files cause `sendmail` to append its message to the named file. Because the special file `/dev/null` is the UNIX bit-bucket, this alias simply throws mail away.

Setting Up `sendmail`

The easiest way to show you how to set up `sendmail` is to use a concrete example.

To summarize, first, you must install the included `sendmail` RPM package as well as the `sendmail-cf` package that installs all the files required to build your own configuration file. Next, choose a `sendmail.mc` file that closely models your site's requirements and tinker with it as necessary. The `.mc` files use a series of m4 macros, which will be covered later, to simplify the creation of the rather dense `sendmail.cf` file. To make the `sendmail.cf` from the `.mc` file you've modified, use the `make` utility. Then test `sendmail` and its configuration file. Finally, install `sendmail.cf` and other auxiliary files.

The preceding are the basic steps, but you might also have to make sure that sendmail is configured to start correctly when your system reboots. The easiest way to do this is to run the control-panel program as root. Then select the icon that looks like two traffic light symbols. This is the Runlevel editor and is shown in Figure 10.1.

Figure 10.1

The Red Hat control-panel.

After you click the Runlevel editor, you will see a number of runlevels as displayed in Figure 10.2. Make sure sendmail is located in all runlevels that you require it in. By default it should be in all of those displayed. If it isn't, just put it in Runlevel 3 for now by clicking in the leftmost window, scrolling down to sendmail, selecting it, and then clicking Add and selecting Runlevel 3.

Figure 10.2

The Runlevel editor.

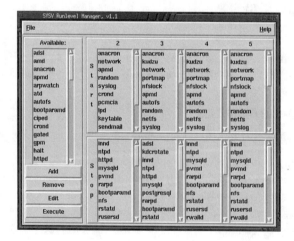

In addition, you must create an aliases file if your system doesn't already have one. In a Red Hat system it will be /etc/aliases, but some systems might locate it in /usr/lib/ aliases depending on your version of UNIX. The location of the aliases file is given in sendmail.cf, so you can put it wherever you want. You might also have to make changes to your system's DNS database, but that information is not covered here (see Chapter 20). Future versions of sendmail will place all ancillary sendmail files into the /etc/mail directory.

Obtaining the Source

Red Hat Linux ships with sendmail 8.10.1. Fortunately, this is the latest version at the time of this writing. If you are concerned with security (and you should be), you will want to keep track of any new versions by checking the comp.security.announce news-group regularly. The latest version of sendmail is always found at http://www. sendmail.org. New versions or patches are quickly brought out when a security flaw is found, and you should upgrade your own system as soon as possible after a new version is released. It would be wise to wait for a Red Hat RPM to be released with the new patches already applied; otherwise you need to get the patches and apply them to the source as well as the other Red Hat configuration changes. This process is not trivial. Check ftp://updates.redhat.com/7.0/i386 or the various Red Hat mirror sites around the world for any Red Hat RPM updates.

Note that the exact names of the files to download differ depending on the most current version of sendmail. In the case of the sendmail included in Red Hat 7 the sendmail RPM is called sendmail-8.11.0-8.i386.rpm. Also, because the files are compressed, you must give FTP the binary command before transferring them. Note too that you should include your complete email address as the FTP password—for example, mylogin@gonzo.gov.

Unpacking the Source and Compiling sendmail

You need to read this section only if there is a new version of sendmail that hasn't been released as an RPM yet and you need new features or bug fixes in place immediately. I assume you have downloaded the source from ftp://ftp.sendmail.org.

Now that you have the source, you need to unpack it. Because it's a compressed tar image, you must first decompress it and then extract the individual files from the tar archive. An example command to do this is

```
[root@gonzo src]# tar zxvf sendmail-8.10.1.tar.gz
```

Now you're almost ready to compile `sendmail`. But first read the following files, which contain the latest news about the specific release of `sendmail` you've downloaded:

```
RELEASE_NOTES

KNOWNBUGS

README
```

You might also want to check the Sendmail Frequently Asked Questions (FAQ) located at `http://www.sendmail.org/faq`. This is a useful source of information on common configuration mistakes or questions on how to set up a particular configuration.

Also take note that the *Sendmail Installation and Operation Guide (SIOG)* is in the `doc/op` subdirectory.

Now run `cd` and `ls` to see what files are in the source directory:

```
[root@gonzo src]# cd sendmail-8.11.0/src
[root@gonzo src]# ls
Makefile       collect.c      macro.c        parseaddr.c    srvrsmtp.c
Makefiles      conf.c         mailq.0        pathnames.h    stab.c
READ_ME        conf.h         mailq.1        queue.c        stats.c
TRACEFLAGS     convtime.c     mailstats.h    readcf.c       sysexits.c
alias.c        daemon.c       main.c         recipient.c    sysexits.h
aliases        deliver.c      makesendmail   safefile.c     trace.c
aliases.0      domain.c       map.c          savemail.c     udb.c
aliases.5      envelope.c     mci.c          sendmail.0     useful.h
arpadate.c     err.c          mime.c         sendmail.8     usersmtp.c
cdefs.h        headers.c      newaliases.0   sendmail.h     util.c
clock.c        ldap_map.h     newaliases.1   sendmail.hf    version.c
```

Thankfully, Eric Allman and the `sendmail` crew have done a fantastic job of making the installation process very straightforward. To compile your new version of `sendmail`, simply run the following (from the `sendmail` `src` directory):

```
[root@gonzo src]# ./Build
```

And then watch it build.

This creates a directory `obj.*` that contains the result of the compilation (so you can build `sendmail` for different machines or operating systems in the same sources). Also check the BuildTools/Site and BuildTools/OS directories for further configuration.

Caution

Before you install the new `sendmail` configuration, be sure to make a backup of any files you are going to replace, especially the old `sendmail` daemon you have. In the event that the new `sendmail` doesn't work for you, you will need to restore the old versions while you troubleshoot the new version.

To install the new version of the `sendmail` executable, first stop the currently running daemon with the following command:

```
[root@gonzo src]# /etc/rc.d/init.d/sendmail stop
```

Then type this:

```
[root@gonzo src]# ./Build install
```

With everything in place, you can restart the new daemon with the following:

```
[root@gonzo src]# /etc/rc.d/init.d/sendmail restart
```

sendmail.cf: The Configuration File

With the advent of V.8, `sendmail` has shipped with a quick and easy way to automatically create a `sendmail.cf` file for you. In fact, it is highly recommended that you do *not* create or modify any `sendmail.cf` files manually. You can safely skip this section if you aren't interested in the gory details regarding the `sendmail.cf` file. (I discuss the easy way to configure `sendmail` in the next section.)

The `sendmail.cf` file provides `sendmail` with its brains, and because it's so important, this section covers it in fairly excruciating detail. Don't worry if you don't understand everything in this section the first time through. It will make more sense upon rereading and after you've had a chance to play with some configuration files of your own.

`sendmail`'s power lies in its flexibility, which comes from its configuration file, `sendmail.cf`. `sendmail.cf` statements compose a cryptic programming language that doesn't inspire much confidence at first glance (but C language code probably didn't either, the first time you saw it). However, learning the `sendmail.cf` language isn't very hard, and you won't have to learn the nitty-gritty details unless you plan to write a `sendmail.cf` from scratch—a bad idea at best.

General Form of the Configuration File

Each line of the configuration file begins with a single command character that indicates the function and syntax of that line. Lines beginning with a # are comments, and blank lines are ignored. Lines beginning with a space or tab are continuations of the preceding line, although you should usually avoid continuations.

Table 10.1 shows the command characters and their functions as well as an example of their usage. This table is split into three parts corresponding to the three main functions of a configuration file, which are covered later in the section "A Functional Description of the Configuration File."

10

SMTP AND PROTOCOLS

TABLE 10.1 `sendmail.cf` Command Characters

Command Character	*Command Syntax and Example*	*Function*
#	# comments are ignored	A comment line. Always use lots of comments.
	`# Standard RFC822 parsing`	
D	`DX string`	Defines a macro X to have the string value *string*.
	`DMmailhub.gonzo.gov`	
D	`D{MacroName}value`	Defines long macro {MacroName} to have the value, *value*, then referenced later with ${MacroName}.
	`D{Relay}mailhub.gonzo.gov`	
C	`CX word1, word2`, and so on	Defines a class X as *word1*, *word2*, and so on.
	`Cwlocalhost myuucpname`	
F	`FX/path/to/a/file`	Defines a class X by reading it from a file.
	`Fw/etc/mail/host_aliases`	
H	`H?mailerflag?name:template`	Defines a mail header.
	`H?F?From: $q`	
O	`OX option arguments`	Sets option X. Most command-line options can be set in `sendmail.cf`.
	`OL9` # sets the log level to 9.	
P	`Pclass=nn`	Sets mail delivery precedence based on the class of the mail.
	`Pjunk=-100`	
V	`Vn`	Tells V.8 `sendmail` the version level of the configuration file.
	`V3`	
K	`Kname class arguments`	Defines a key file (database map).
	`Kuucphosts hash /etc/mail/uucphsts`	
M	`Mname,field_1=value_1,...`	Defines a mailer.
	`Mprog,P=/bin/sh,F=lsD, 0A=sh -c $u`	

TABLE 10.1 continued

Command Character	Command Syntax and Example	Function
S	S*nn* S22	Begins a new rule set.
R	R*lhs rhs comment* R$+ $:$>22 call ruleset 22	Defines a matching/rewriting rule.

A Functional Description of the Configuration File

A configuration file does three things. First, it sets the environment for sendmail by telling it which options you want set and the locations of the files and databases it uses.

Second, a configuration file defines the characteristics of the mailers (delivery agents or MTAs) that sendmail uses after it decides where to route a letter. All configuration files must define local and program mailers to handle delivery to users on the local host, most of them also define one or more SMTP mailers, and sites that must handle UUCP mail define UUCP mailers.

Third, a configuration file specifies rulesets that rewrite sender and recipient addresses and select mailers. All rulesets are user-defined, but some have special meaning to sendmail. Ruleset 0, for example, is used to select a mailer. Rulesets 0, 1, 2, 3, and 4 all have special meaning to sendmail and are processed in a particular order (see the section "The S and R Operators: Rulesets and Rewriting Rules" later in this chapter).

The following sections cover the operators in more detail, in the order in which they appear in Table 10.1.

The D Operator: Macros

Macros are like shell variables. After you define a macro's value, you can refer to it later in the configuration file and its value will be substituted for the macro. For example, a configuration file might have many lines that mention the hypothetical mail hub mailer.gonzo.gov. Rather than type that name over and over, you can define a macro R (for relay mailer) as follows:

```
DRmailer.gonzo.gov
```

When sendmail encounters an $R in sendmail.cf, it substitutes the string mailer.gonzo.gov.

Macro names can be more than one character. You could, for example, define

```
D{Relay}mailer.gonzo.gov
```

then refer to it later with

```
${Relay}
```

Quite a few macros are defined by `sendmail` and shouldn't be redefined except to work around broken software. `sendmail` uses lowercase letters for its predefined macros. Uppercase letters can be used freely. V.8 `sendmail`'s predefined macros are fully documented in section 5.1.2 of the SIOG.

The C and F Operators: Classes

Classes are similar to macros but are used for different purposes in rewriting rules (see "The S and R Operators: Rulesets and Rewriting Rules" later in this chapter). As with macros, classes are named by single characters. Lowercase letters are reserved for `sendmail` and uppercase letters for user-defined classes. A class contains one or more words. For example, you could define a class H containing all the hosts in the local domain as follows:

```
CH larry moe curly
```

For convenience, large classes can be continued on subsequent lines. The following definition of the class H is the same as the preceding one:

```
CH larry
CH moe
CH curly
```

You can also define a class by reading its words from a file:

```
CF/usr/local/lib/localhosts
```

If the file `/usr/local/lib/localhosts` contains the words `larry`, `moe`, and `curly`, one per line, this definition is equivalent to the preceding two.

Why use macros and classes? The best reason is that they centralize information in the configuration file. In the preceding example, if you decide to change the name of the mail hub from `mailer.gonzo.gov` to `mailhub.gonzo.gov`, you have to change only the definition of the $R macro remedy for the configuration file to work as before. If the name `mailer.gonzo.gov` is scattered throughout the file, you might forget to change it in some places. Also, if important information is centralized, you can comment it extensively in a single place. Because configuration files tend to be obscure at best, a liberal dose of comments is a good antidote to that sinking feeling you get six months later, when you wonder why you made a change.

The H Operator: Header Definitions

You probably won't want to change the header definitions given in the V.8 sendmail configuration files because they already follow accepted standards. Here are some sample headers:

```
H?D?Date: $a
H?F?Resent-From: $q
H?F?From: $q
H?x?Full-Name: $x
```

Note that header definitions can use macros, which are expanded when inserted into a letter. For example, the $x macro used in the preceding Full-Name: header definition expands to the full name of the sender.

The optional ?mailerflag? construct tells sendmail to insert a header only if the chosen mailer has that mailer flag set (see "The M Operator: Mailer Definitions" later in this chapter).

Suppose the definition of your local mailer has a flag Q, and sendmail selects that mailer to deliver a letter. If your configuration file contains a header definition like the following one, sendmail inserts that header into letters delivered through the local mailer, substituting the value of the macro $F:

```
H?Q?X-Fruit-of-the-day: $F
```

Why would you use the ?mailerflag? feature? Different protocols can require different mail headers. Because they also need different mailers, you can define appropriate mailer flags for each in the mailer definition and use the ?mailerflag? construct in the header definition to tell sendmail whether to insert the header.

The O Operator: Setting Options

sendmail has many options that change its operation or tell it the location of files it uses. Most of them can be given either on the command line or in the configuration file. For example, you can specify the location of the aliases file in either place. To specify the aliases file on the command line, you use the -o option:

```
$ /usr/sbin/sendmail -oA/etc/aliases [other arguments...]
```

To do the same thing in the configuration file, you include a line like this:

```
OA/etc/aliases
```

Either use is equivalent, but options such as the location of the aliases file rarely change, and most people set them in sendmail.cf. The V.8 sendmail options are fully described in the SIOG.

The P Operator: Mail Precedence

Users can include mail headers indicating the relative importance of their mail, and sendmail can use those headers to decide the priority of competing messages. Precedences for V.8 sendmail are given as follows:

```
Pspecial-delivery=100
Pfirst-class=0
Plist=-30
Pbulk=-60
Pjunk=-100
```

If users who run large mailing lists include the header Precedence: bulk in their letters, sendmail gives them a lower priority than letters with the header Precedence: first-class.

The V Operator: `sendmail.cf` Version Levels

As V.8 sendmail evolves, its author adds new features. The V operator tells V.8 sendmail which features it should expect to find in your configuration file. Older versions of sendmail don't understand this command. The SIOG explains the configuration file version levels in detail.

> **Note**
>
> The configuration file version level does not correspond to the sendmail version level. V.8 sendmail understands versions 1 through 5 of configuration files, and no such thing as a version 8 configuration file exists.

The K Operator: Key Files

sendmail has always used keyed databases—for example, the aliases databases. Given the key postmaster, sendmail looks up the data associated with that key and returns the names of the accounts to which the postmaster's mail should be delivered. V.8 sendmail extends this concept to arbitrary databases, including NIS maps (Sun's Network Information Service, formerly known as Yellow Pages or YP; see Chapter 15, "NIS: Network Information Service," for details). The K operator tells sendmail the location of the database, its class, and how to access it. V.8 sendmail supports the following classes of user-defined databases: dbm, btree, hash, and NIS. The default used when compiling under Linux is one of the hash or btree formats. See the SIOG for the lowdown on key files.

The M Operator: Mailer Definitions

Mailers are either MTAs or final delivery agents. Recall that the aliases file enables you to send mail to a login name (which might be aliased to a remote user), a program, or a file. A special mailer can be defined for each purpose, and even though the SMTP MTA is built in, it must have a mailer definition to tailor sendmail's SMTP operations.

Mailer definitions are important because all recipient addresses must resolve to a mailer in ruleset 0. Resolving to a mailer is just another name for sendmail's main function, mail routing. For example, resolving to the local mailer routes the letter to a local user via the final delivery agent defined in that mailer (such as /bin/mail), and resolving to the SMTP mailer routes the letter to another host via sendmail's built-in SMTP transport, as defined in the SMTP mailer.

A concrete example of a mailer definition will make this information clearer. Because sendmail requires a local mailer definition, look at the following:

```
Mlocal, P=/bin/mail, F=lsDFMfSn, S=10, R=20, A=mail -d $u
```

All mailer definitions begin with the M operator and the name of the mailer—in this case, local. Other fields follow, separated by commas. Each field consists of a field name and its value, separated by an equal sign (=). The allowable fields are explained in section 5.1.4 of the SIOG.

In the preceding local mailer definition, the P= equivalence gives the pathname of the program to run to deliver the mail, /bin/mail. The F= field gives the sendmail flags for the local mailer (see also "The H Operator: Header Definitions" earlier in the chapter.) These flags are not passed to the command mentioned in the P= field but are used by sendmail to modify its operation, depending on the mailer it chooses. For example, sendmail usually drops its superuser status before invoking mailers, but you can use the S mailer flag to tell sendmail to retain this status for certain mailers.

The S= and R= fields specify rulesets for sendmail to use in rewriting sender and recipient addresses. Because you can give different R= and S= flags for each mailer you define, you can rewrite addresses differently for each mailer. For example, if one of your UUCP neighbors runs obsolete software that doesn't understand domain addressing, you might declare a special mailer just for that site and write mailer-specific rulesets to convert addresses into a form its mailer can understand.

The S= and R= fields can also specify different rulesets to rewrite the envelope and header addresses . A specification such as S=21/31 tells sendmail to use ruleset 21 to rewrite sender envelope addresses and ruleset 31 to rewrite sender header addresses. This capability comes in handy for mailers that require addresses to be presented differently in the envelope than in the headers.

The A= field gives the argument vector (command line) for the program that will be run—in this case, /bin/mail. In this example, sendmail runs the command as mail -d $u, expanding the $u macro to the name of the user to whom the mail should be delivered:

```
/bin/mail -d joe
```

You could type this same expanded command to your shell at a command prompt.

You might want to use many other mailer flags to tune mailers—for example, to limit the maximum message size on a per-mailer basis. These flags are all documented in section 5.1.4 of the SIOG.

The S and R Operators: Rulesets and Rewriting Rules

A configuration file is composed of a series of rulesets, which are somewhat like subroutines in a program. Rulesets are used to detect bad addresses, to rewrite addresses into forms that remote mailers can understand, and to route mail to one of sendmail's internal mailers (see the previous section, "The M Operator: Mailer Definitions").

sendmail passes addresses to rulesets according to a built-in order. Rulesets also can call other rulesets not in the built-in order. The built-in order varies depending on whether the address being handled is a sender or receiver address and which mailer has been chosen to deliver the letter.

Rulesets are announced by the S command, which is followed by a number to identify the ruleset. sendmail collects subsequent R (rule) lines until it finds another S operator or the end of the configuration file. The following example defines ruleset 11:

```
# Ruleset 11
S11
R$+        $: $>22 $1      call ruleset 22
```

This ruleset doesn't do much that is useful. The important point to note is that sendmail collects ruleset number 11, which is composed of a single rule.

sendmail's Built-In Ruleset Processing Rules

sendmail uses a three-track approach to processing addresses: one to choose a delivery agent, another to process sender addresses, and another for receiver addresses.

All addresses are first sent through ruleset 3 for preprocessing into a canonical form that makes them easy for other rulesets to handle. Regardless of the complexity of the address, ruleset 3's job is to decide the next host to which a letter should be sent. Ruleset 3 tries to locate that host in the address and mark it within angle brackets. In the simplest case, an address like joe@gonzo.gov becomes joe<@gonzo.gov>.

Ruleset 0 then determines the correct delivery agent (mailer) to use for each recipient. For example, a letter from `betty@whizzer.com` to `joe@gonzo.gov` (an Internet site) and `pinhead!zippy` (an old-style UUCP site) requires two different mailers: an SMTP mailer for `gonzo.gov` and an old-style UUCP mailer for `pinhead`. Mailer selection determines later processing of sender and recipient addresses because the rulesets given in the `S=` and `R=` mailer flags vary from mailer to mailer.

Addresses sent through ruleset 0 must resolve to a mailer. This means that when an address matches the `lhs`, the `rhs` gives a triple of the mailer, user, and host. The `rhs` tells `sendmail` what to do with addresses that match the pattern specified by the `lhs`. The following line shows the syntax for a rule that resolves to a mailer:

```
Rlhs      $#mailer $@host $:user   your comment here...
```

The mailer is the name of one of the mailers you've defined in an `M` command—for example, `smtp`. The host and user are usually positional macros taken from the `lhs` match (see "The Right-Hand Side (`rhs`) of Rules" later in the chapter).

After `sendmail` selects a mailer in ruleset 0, it processes sender addresses through ruleset 1 (often empty) and then sends them to the ruleset given in the `S=` flag for that mailer.

Similarly, `sendmail` sends recipient addresses through ruleset 2 (also often empty) and then to the ruleset mentioned in the `R=` mailer flag.

Finally, `sendmail` post-processes all addresses in ruleset 4, which (among other things) removes the angle brackets inserted by ruleset 3.

Why do mailers have different `S=` and `R=` flags? Consider the previous example of the letter sent to `joe@gonzo.gov` and `pinhead!zippy`. If `betty@whizzer.com` sends the mail, her address must appear in a different form to each recipient. For Joe, it should be a domain address, `betty@whizzer.com`. For Zippy, because pinhead expects old-style UUCP addresses, the return address should be `whizzer!betty`. Joe's address must also be rewritten for the `pinhead` UUCP mailer, and Joe's copy must include an address for Zippy that his mailer can handle.

Processing Rules Within Rulesets

`sendmail` passes an address to a ruleset and then processes it through each rule line by line. If the `lhs` of a rule matches the address, it is rewritten by the `rhs`. If it doesn't match, `sendmail` continues to the next rule until it reaches the end of the ruleset. At the end of the ruleset, `sendmail` returns the rewritten address to the calling ruleset or to the next ruleset in its built-in execution sequence.

If an address matches the `lhs` and is rewritten by the `rhs`, the rule is tried again—an implicit loop (but see the "`$:` and `$@`: Altering a Ruleset's Evaluation" section for exceptions).

As shown in Table 10.1, each rewriting rule is introduced by the R command and has three fields—the left-hand side (lhs, or matching side), the right-hand side (rhs, or rewriting side), and an optional comment—which must be separated from one another by tab characters:

```
Rlhs      rhs        comment
```

Parsing: Turning Addresses into Tokens

sendmail parses addresses and the lhs of rules into tokens and then matches the address and the lhs token by token. The macro $o contains the characters that sendmail uses to separate an address into tokens. It's often defined like this:

```
# address delimiter characters
Do.:%@!^/[]
```

All the characters in $o are both token separators and tokens. sendmail takes an address such as rae@rainbow.org and breaks it into tokens according to the characters in the o macro, like this:

```
"rae"      "@"      "rainbow".      "."      "org"
```

sendmail also parses the lhs of rewriting rules into tokens so they can be compared one by one with the input address to see whether they match. For example, the lhs $-@rainbow.org is parsed as follows:

```
"$-"       "@"       "rainbow"      "."      "org"
```

(Don't worry about the $- just yet. It's a pattern-matching operator, similar to a shell wildcard, that matches any single token and is covered later in the section "The Left-Hand Side (lhs) of Rules.") Now you can put the two together to show how sendmail decides whether an address matches the lhs of a rule:

```
"rae"      "@"       "rainbow"      "."      "org"
"$-"       "@"       "rainbow"      "."      "org"
```

In this case, each token from the address matches with the pattern-matching operator ($-) matching rae, so the address matches and sendmail will use the rhs to rewrite the address.

Consider the effect (usually bad) of changing the value of $o. As shown previously, sendmail breaks the address rae@rainbow.org into five tokens. However, if the @ character were not in $o, the address would be parsed quite differently, into only three tokens:

```
"rae@rainbow"      "."      "org"
```

You can see that changing $o has a drastic effect on sendmail's address parsing, and you should leave it alone until you know what you're doing. Even then, you probably won't want to change it because the V.8 sendmail configuration files already have it correctly defined for standard RFC 822 and RFC 976 address interpretation.

The Left-Hand Side (lhs) of Rules

The lhs is a pattern against which sendmail matches the input address. The lhs can contain ordinary text or any of the pattern-matching operators shown in Table 10.2.

TABLE 10.2   lhs Pattern-Matching Operators

Operator	Meaning
$-	Matches exactly one token.
$+	Matches one or more tokens.
$*	Matches zero or more tokens.
$@	Matches the null input (used to call the error mailer).

The values of macros and classes are matched in the lhs with the operators shown in Table 10.3.

TABLE 10.3   lhs Macro and Class-Matching Operators

Operator	Meaning
$X	Matches the value of macro X.
$=C	Matches any word in class C.
$~C	Matches if token is not in class C.

The pattern-, macro-, and class-matching operators are necessary because most rules must match many different input addresses. For example, a rule might need to match all addresses that end with gonzo.gov and begin with one or more of anything.

The Right-Hand Side (rhs) of Rules

The rhs of a rewriting rule tells sendmail how to rewrite an address that matches the lhs. The rhs can include text, macros, and positional references to matches in the lhs. When a pattern-matching operator from Table 10.2 matches the input, sendmail assigns it to a numeric macro $n corresponding to the position it matches in the lhs. For example, suppose the address joe@pc1.gonzo.gov is passed to the following rule:

```
R$+ @ $+       $: $1 < @ $2 >              focus on domain
```

In this example, joe matches $+ (one or more of anything), so sendmail assigns the string joe to $1. The @ in the address matches the @ in the lhs, but constant strings are not assigned to positional macros. The tokens in the string pc1.gonzo.gov match the second $+ and are assigned to $2. The address is rewritten as $1<@$2>, or joe<@pc1.gonzo.gov>.

10

SMTP AND PROTOCOLS

| 296 | *Configuring Services*
|-----|
| | **PART II** |

$: and $@: Altering a Ruleset's Evaluation

Consider the following rule:

```
R$*   $: $1 < @ $j > add local domain
```

After rewriting an address in the rhs, sendmail tries to match the rewritten address with the lhs of the current rule. Because $* matches zero or more of anything, what prevents sendmail from going into an infinite loop on this rule? After all, no matter how the rhs rewrites the address, it will always match $*.

The $: preface to the rhs comes to the rescue, telling sendmail to evaluate the rule only once.

Sometimes you might want a ruleset to terminate immediately and return the address to the calling ruleset or the next ruleset in sendmail's built-in sequence. Prefacing a rule's rhs with $@ causes sendmail to exit the ruleset immediately after rewriting the address in the rhs.

$>: Calling Another Ruleset

A ruleset can pass an address to another ruleset by using the $> preface to the rhs. Consider the following rule:

```
R$*        $: $>66 $1         call ruleset 66
```

The lhs $* matches zero or more of anything, so sendmail always does the rhs. As you learned in the preceding section, the $: prevents the rule from being evaluated more than once. The $>66 $1 calls ruleset 66 with $1 as its input address. Because the $1 matches whatever was in the lhs, this rule simply passes the entirety of the current input address to ruleset 66. Whatever ruleset 66 returns is passed to the next rule in the ruleset.

Testing Rules and Rulesets: The -bt, -d, and -C Options

Debugging sendmail.cf can be a tricky business. Fortunately, sendmail provides several ways to test rulesets before you install them.

> **Note**
>
> The examples in this section assume that your system has a working sendmail. If not, try running these examples again after you have installed V.8 sendmail. Keep in mind that you can press Ctrl+D at any point in the tests to exit testing.

The `-bt` option tells `sendmail` to enter its rule-testing mode:

```
$ /usr/sbin/sendmail -bt
ADDRESS TEST MODE (ruleset 3 NOT automatically invoked)
Enter <ruleset> <address>
>
```

Note

Notice the warning `ruleset 3 NOT automatically invoked`. Older versions of
`sendmail` ran ruleset 3 automatically when in address test mode, which made
sense because `sendmail` sends all addresses through ruleset 3 anyway. V.8
`sendmail` does not, but invoking ruleset 3 manually is a good idea because later
rulesets expect the address to be in canonical form.

The > prompt means `sendmail` is waiting for you to enter one or more ruleset numbers,
separated by commas, and an address. Try your login name with rulesets 3 and 0. The
result should look something like this:

```
> 3,0 joe
rewrite: ruleset  3   input: joe
rewrite: ruleset  3 returns: joe
rewrite: ruleset  0   input: joe
rewrite: ruleset  3   input: joe
rewrite: ruleset  3 returns: joe
rewrite: ruleset  6   input: joe
rewrite: ruleset  6 returns: joe
rewrite: ruleset  0 returns: $# local $: joe
>
```

The output shows how `sendmail` processes the input address `joe` in each ruleset. Each
line of output is identified with the number of the ruleset processing it, the input address,
and the address that the ruleset returns. The > is a second prompt indicating that `sendmail`
is waiting for another line of input. When you're done testing, just press Ctrl+D.

Indentation and blank lines better show the flow of processing in this example:

```
rewrite: ruleset  3   input: joe
rewrite: ruleset  3 returns: joe

rewrite: ruleset  0   input: joe

    rewrite: ruleset  3   input: joe
    rewrite: ruleset  3 returns: joe

    rewrite: ruleset  6   input: joe
    rewrite: ruleset  6 returns: joe

rewrite: ruleset  0 returns: $# local $: joe
```

The rulesets called were 3 and 0, in that order. Ruleset 3 was processed and returned the value `joe`, and then `sendmail` called ruleset 0. Ruleset 0 called ruleset 3 again and then ruleset 6, an example of how a ruleset can call another one by using $>. Neither ruleset 3 nor ruleset 6 rewrote the input address. Finally, ruleset 0 resolved to a mailer, as it must.

Often you need more detail than `-bt` provides—usually just before you tear out a large handful of hair because you don't understand why an address doesn't match the `lhs` of a rule. You can remain hirsute because `sendmail` has verbose debugging built into most of its code.

You use the `-d` option to turn on `sendmail`'s verbose debugging. This option is followed by a numeric code that indicates which section of debugging code to turn on and at what level. The following example shows how to run `sendmail` in one of its debugging modes and the output it produces:

```
$ /usr/sbin/sendmail -bt -d21.12
ADDRESS TEST MODE (ruleset 3 NOT automatically invoked)
Enter <ruleset> <address>
> 3,0 joe
rewrite: ruleset  3   input: joe
--trying rule: $* < > $*
-- rule fails
--trying rule: $* < $* < $* < $+ > $* > $* > $*
-- rule fails
[etc.]
```

The `-d21.12` in the preceding example tells `sendmail` to turn on level 12 debugging in section 21 of its code. The same command with the option `-d21.36` gives more verbose output (debug level 36 instead of 12).

Note

You can combine one or more debugging specifications separated by commas, as in `-d21.12,14.2`, which turns on level 12 debugging in section 21 and level 2 debugging in section 14. You can also give a range of debugging sections, as in `-d1-10.35`, which turns on debugging in sections 1 through 10 at level 35. The specification `-d0-91.104` turns on all sections of V.8 `sendmail`'s debugging code at the highest debugging levels and produces thousands of lines of output for a single address.

The `-d` option is not limited to use with `sendmail`'s address testing mode (`-bt`). You can also use it to see how `sendmail` processes rulesets while sending a letter, as the following example shows:

```
$ /usr/sbin/sendmail -d21.36 joe@gonzo.gov < /tmp/letter
[lots and lots of output...]
```

Unfortunately, the SIOG doesn't tell you which numbers correspond to which sections of code. Instead, the author suggests that keeping such documentation current is a lot of work (which it is), and that you should look at the code itself to discover the correct debugging formulas.

The function tTd() is the one to look for. For example, suppose you want to turn on debugging in sendmail's address-parsing code. The source file parseaddr.c contains most of this code, and the following command finds the allowable debugging levels:

```
$ egrep tTd parseaddr.c
        if (tTd(20, 1))
[...]
        if (tTd(24, 4))
        if (tTd(22, 11))
[etc.]
```

The egrep output shows that debugging specifications such as -d20.1, -d24.4, and -d22.11 (and others) will make sense to sendmail.

If perusing thousands of lines of C code doesn't appeal to you, the O'Reilly book, *sendmail*, Second Edition, documents the debugging flags for sendmail. Note that the book only covers up to sendmail-8.8; small differences in detail could exist but it is still a good reference.

The -C option enables you to test new configuration files before you install them, which is always a good idea. If you want to test a different file, use -C*/path/to/the/file*. You can combine it with the -bt and -d flags. For example, a common invocation for testing new configuration files is

```
/usr/sbin/sendmail -Ctest.cf -bt -d21.12
```

Caution

For security, sendmail drops its superuser permissions when you use the -C option. You should perform final testing of configuration files as the superuser to ensure that your testing is compatible with sendmail's normal operating mode.

Automatically Generating the sendmail.cf File

Luckily, these days no one has to manually edit a sendmail.cf file. Enter the following command:

```
[root@gonzo / ]# rpm -q sendmail-cf
sendmail-cf-8.11.0-8
```

If you get similar output, your configuration and macro files are already installed under the directory `/usr/lib/sendmail-cf`. Otherwise, you will have to install the relevant RPM from your Red Hat CD-ROMs or download the RPM from the Red Hat FTP site (`ftp://ftp.redhat.com`) or one of the many mirrors around the world.

A master Makefile exists in `/usr/lib/sendmail-cf/cf`, which makes a `sendmail.cf` file from a `sendmail.mc` file using the m4 macro processor. The `mc` file is what is edited to create your site-specific `sendmail.cf` file. You will need to check that you have the m4 package installed:

```
[root@gonzo /]# rpm -q m4
m4-1.4.1-3
```

If you get output similar to this (you might have different version numbers, but that's okay), m4 is available on your system. Otherwise, the m4 RPM will be on your Red Hat CD-ROMs.

The `/usr/lib/sendmail-cf` directory will look something like this:

```
[root@gonzo /usr/lib]# ls sendmail-cf/
README          cf        feature    m4        ostype     siteconfig
README.check    domain    hack       mailer    sh
```

The `README` file is worth reading. It contains information on the different features that you can add into your `mc` file, as well as other important information, including a description of the anti-spam features that have made it into the later versions of `sendmail`.

Creating a `sendmail.cf` for your site is a matter of changing to the `cf` directory and selecting an appropriate template. The `ls` should produce a listing similar to

```
[root@gonzo /usr/lib/sendmail-cf]# cd cf
[root@gonzo /usr/lib/sendmail-cf/cf]#  ls
Makefile              generic-hpux10.mc       obj
Makefile.dist         generic-hpux9.mc        python.cs.mc
chez.cs.mc            generic-nextstep3.3.mc  redhat.cf
clientproto.mc        generic-osf1.mc         redhat.mc
cs-hpux10.mc          generic-solaris2.mc     s2k-osf1.mc
cs-hpux9.mc           generic-sunos4.1.mc     s2k-ultrix4.mc
cs-osf1.mc            generic-ultrix4.mc      tcpproto.mc
cs-solaris2.mc        huginn.cs.mc            ucbarpa.mc
cs-sunos4.1.mc        knecht.mc               ucbvax.mc
cs-ultrix4.mc         mail.cs.mc              uucpproto.mc
cyrusproto.mc         mail.eecs.mc            vangogh.cs.mc
generic-bsd4.4.mc     mailspool.cs.mc
```

These are all the different `mc` files you can choose from to create your `cf` file. The `redhat.mc` file is the one you probably should edit. I suggest copying it to another name:

```
[root@gonzo /usr/lib/sendmail-cf/cf]# cp redhat.mc gonzo.mc
```

I will now give you a brief explanation of the various parts of this sample `mc` file:

```
divert(-1)
include(`../m4/cf.m4`)
```

These are directives that the m4 processor needs to process the file. You will find similar entries in some of the other `mc` files.

```
define(`confDEF_USER_ID`,``8:12``)
OSTYPE(`linux`)
undefine(`UUCP_RELAY`)
undefine(`BITNET_RELAY`)
```

The `define` indicates that you want to change a setting in `sendmail`, such as maximum hops allowed for a message or the maximum message size. In this case you're defining which UID and group to run the `sendmail` program as while it is not in privileged mode (running as `root`). All possible parameters you can define are listed in the README file.

Different UNIX operating systems have different conventions for where to place files and which flags to give mailers. This is what the `OSTYPE` macro is for. In the example, `sendmail` should use the Linux conventions for file locations.

The two `undefine`s remove the capability for this `sendmail` host to accept UUCP and BITNET addressed mail.

```
FEATURE(redirect)
FEATURE(always_add_domain)
FEATURE(use_cw_file)
FEATURE(local_procmail)
```

The `FEATURE` macros allow you to add the various `sendmail` features that your site requires.

The `redirect` feature rejects all mail addressed to `address.REDIRECT` with a `551 User not local; please try <address>` message. That way, if Joe leaves the Gonzo company to go to Whizzer Inc., the email administrator at Gonzo can alias Joe to `joe@whizzer.com.REDIRECT` as a courtesy so Joe's friends and work contacts can reach him at his new job.

The second feature, `always_add_domain`, always appends the fully qualified domain name of the local host, even on locally delivered mail whose To: address is unqualified. For example, if I address mail to `joe` instead of `joe@gonzo.gov`, `sendmail` will automatically append `@gonzo.gov` to the To: header before delivery.

10

SMTP AND PROTOCOLS

The use_cw_file feature tells sendmail to look in the file /etc/sendmail.cw for alternate names for the local host. For example, if gonzo.gov also is a primary MX for the hiking club, hikers.org, both gonzo.gov and hikers.org will have entries in the sendmail.cw file.

The next feature indicates that procmail is to be used as the local mailer:

```
MAILER(procmail)
MAILER(smtp)
```

The two MAILER lines define only two mailers, procmail and SMTP. Remember, procmail was defined to be used as the local mailer. It must be defined here also, and SMTP is undefined as the mailer for remote mail deliveries.

```
HACK(check_mail3,`hash -a@JUNK /etc/mail/deny`)
HACK(use_ip,`/etc/mail/ip_allow`)
HACK(use_names,`/etc/mail/name_allow`)
HACK(use_relayto,`/etc/mail/relay_allow`)
HACK(check_rcpt4)
HACK(check_relay3)
```

As of the V8.9 series of sendmail, relaying by external hosts is denied by default. This is to stop other hosts from using your mailhost as a relay point for distributing junk mail (spam) or for other purposes. The HACKs allow you to specify which hosts are allowed to use your mail server as a relay point and which machines on the Internet to never accept email from. This is especially handy if you and your users keep getting spam from the same hosts. Read the /usr/lib/sendmail-cf/README.check file, which describes all the available HACKs and how to use them.

> **Tip**
>
> Suppose your users receive a lot of advertisements via email (or SPAM) and they complain about it to you. Suppose all the SPAM comes from the same hosts. What you can do is stop this host from sending *any* email to your site. This is done by editing the file /etc/mail/deny and adding an entry such as "192.168.1.2 We do not accept mail from spammers." Then create the database for sendmail to use by typing in the command # makemap hash /etc/mail/deny.db < /etc/mail/deny.
>
> You will need to use nslookup to look up the IP address of the spamming host to put in the deny file. When the host corresponding to the IP address of 192.168.1.2 tries to talk to your sendmail process, it will get an error code as well as a configurable textual reason for the connection being denied.

As you can see, the supplied `redhat.mc` file provides a fairly good template for your own `mc` file. You have already copied it to `gonzo.mc`. All you need to do now is add two more items and then you can create the `cf` file `sendmail` can use. Add the following after the list of `FEATURE`s:

```
FEATURE(masquerade_envelope)
MASQUERADE_AS(gonzo.gov)
```

These lines assume that your Gonzo mail host is called `mail.gonzo.gov`. Without these lines, all email you send out from your mail host will have a From: address in the envelope and message body that looks something like `joe@mail.gonzo.gov`. It would be nice to hide which host you sent the mail from and have the recipient From: address read something like `joe@gonzo.gov`. That is what the `MASQUERADE_AS` line does. The `masquerade_envelope` feature causes the message envelope From: header to be similarly masqueraded.

All that you need to do now is build the `sendmail` configuration file:

```
[root@gondor cf]# make gonzo.cf
rm -f gondor.cf
m4 ../m4/cf.m4 gondor.mc > gonzo.cf
chmod 444 gonzo.cf
```

If you are using GNU Make, which is almost certainly the case if you are running Red Hat, you will get an error after typing in the `make` command. Try `make -f Makefile.dist gonzo.cf` instead. If the `make` is successful, a `gondor.cf` file will appear in your `cf` directory. Congratulations, you have created your very first `sendmail.cf` file!

And After All That an Even Easier Method Still

A frequent comment in Perl circles is "there's more than one way to do it." It's yet another way Perl shows its roots so I offer one last method for configuring `sendmail` courtesy of the hard work of Donncha O Caoimh of the Irish Linux Users Group (`http://www.linux.ie/`). His `installsendmail` script is available at `http://cork.linux.ie/projects/install-sendmail/` and works by asking users (you'll be prompted for the `root` password when it's time to update system files, but don't run it as `root`) a series of questions to configure their systems according to their needs. There are informative `README` and `INSTALL` files included and they should be read before using the script. A sample session with the version from March 13, 2000 follows:

```
[kevin@moo kevin]$ wget http://cork.linux.ie/projects/
➥install-sendmail/install-sendmail-5.3.1.tar.gz
--21:18:24--  http://cork.linux.ie:80/projects/install-sendmail/
➥install-sendmail-5.3.1.tar.gz
```

```
                    => `install-sendmail-5.3.1.tar.gz`
Connecting to cork.linux.ie:80... connected!
HTTP request sent, awaiting response... 200 OK
Length: 39,807 [application/x-tar]

    0K -> .......... .......... .......... ........        [100%]

21:18:30 (7.78 KB/s) - `install-sendmail-5.3.1.tar.gz` saved [39807/39807]

[kevin@moo kevin]$ cp ~kevin/install-sendmail-5.3.1.tar.gz .
[kevin@moo kevin]$ tar zxf install-sendmail-5.3.1.tar.gz
[kevin@moo kevin]$ cd install-sendmail-5.3.1
[kevin@moo install-sendmail-5.3.1]$ ./install-sendmail -c
```

It then asks the following questions:

```
Which language do you wish to use? English(1)
1.1 What address do you want all the emails from your machine to have? gonzo.gov
1.2 Will all mail for gonzo.gov come to this machine? n
2.1 Do you want your outgoing email to be sent via an outside email server?
If you're on a modem dial-up connection you probably should say Y here. y
2.1.1 Where do you send your email? (outgoing smtp server, probably your ISP)
[smtp.isp.com]? mail.gonzo.gov
2.2. Queue remote mail? If you have a dial-up connection, you can compose mail
when you're offline, then "queue" it for delivery when you're connected.
(You'll have to run "usr/bin/sendmail -q" to deliver the mail, however.)
Local mail (mail to people who login to your machine) will still be delivered
as normal. If you answer "no" to this question, all mail will be delivered
immediately, rather than queued. This might cause your machine to dial-up your
connection, even at peak times.
Would you like to queue remote mail? y
3.1 Will you be serving mail to a local network? n
4. Virtual Domain Support
4.1 Do you need this feature? I'll provide a way for you to
enter aliases too. n
5. Generics Table Support
5.1 Do you want to map local email addresses to new ones? y
5.1.1 Enter the local username you want to map.
Type "none" when you're finished.
[bob]? kevin
5.1.1 What address should people see when veep writes an email?
[dennis@someplace.org]? caimhin@gonzo.gov
5.1.2 Enter the local username you want to map.
Type "none" when you're finished.
[]? none
6. Incoming Mail Servers
6.1 Do you want Fetchmail support? y
6. Incoming Mail Servers

6.1.1 Enter a pop server you poll for mail. Type "none" when you're finished.
[pop.isp.com]? pop.gonzo.gov
```

```
6.1.2 What username do you use to login to pop.gonzo.gov?
[alan]? caoimhin
6.1.3 What password do you use to login to pop.gonzo.gov?
[password]? moo
6.1.4 What user should receive the mail for caoimhin?
[bob]? kevin
6.1.5 What protocol does pop.gonzo.gov use? (POP3, IMAP, AUTO)
[pop3]? imap
6.1.2 Enter a pop server you poll for mail. Type "none" when you're finished.
[pop.telebot.com]? none
```

At this point it will ask for the `root` password to install the files. Afterwards you should restart `sendmail` with

```
/etc/init.d/sendmail restart
```

This is an excellent tool for users new to `sendmail` on home systems. The previous sections cover the methods that should be used by admins of corporate and university systems.

Testing `sendmail` and `sendmail.cf`

Before you install a new or modified `sendmail.cf`, you must test it thoroughly. Even small, apparently innocuous changes can lead to disaster, and people get really irate when you mess up the mail system.

The first step in testing is to create a list of addresses that you know should work at your site. For example, at `gonzo.gov`, an Internet site without UUCP connections, the following addresses must work:

```
joe
joe@pc1.gonzo.gov
joe@gonzo.gov
```

If `gonzo.gov` has a UUCP link, those addresses must also be tested. Other addresses to consider include the various kinds of aliases (for example, `postmaster`, an `:include:` list, an alias that mails to a file, and one that mails to a program), nonlocal addresses, source-routed addresses, and so on. If you want to be thorough, you can create a test address for each legal address format in RFC 822.

Now that you have your list of test addresses, you can use the `-C` and `-bt` options to see what happens. At a minimum, you should run the addresses through rulesets 3 and 0 to make sure they are routed to the correct mailer. An easy way to do so is to create a file containing the ruleset invocations and test addresses and then run `sendmail` on it. For example, if the file `addr.test` contains the lines

```
3,0 joe
3,0 joe@pc1.gonzo.gov
3,0 joe@gonzo.gov
```

you can test your configuration file `test.cf` by typing

```
$ /usr/sbin/sendmail -Ctest.cf -bt < addr.test
rewrite: ruleset  3    input: joe
rewrite: ruleset  3 returns: joe
[etc.]
```

You also might want to follow one or more addresses through the complete rewriting process. For example, if an address resolves to the `smtp` mailer and that mailer specifies `R=21`, you can test recipient address rewriting by using `3,2,21,4` *test_address*.

If the `sendmail.cf` appears to work correctly so far, you're ready to move on to sending some real letters. You can do so by using a command like the following:

```
$ /usr/sbin/sendmail -v -oQ/tmp -Ctest.cf recipient < /dev/null
```

The `-v` option tells `sendmail` to be verbose so you can see what's happening. Depending on whether the delivery is local or remote, you can see something as simple as `joe...` `Sent` or an entire SMTP dialog. The `-o` sets an option that overrides what is in the `sendmail.cf` file. You can also use `-O` for long options.

The `-oQ/tmp` tells `sendmail` to use `/tmp` as its queue directory. Using this option is necessary because `sendmail` drops its superuser permissions when run with the `-C` option and can't write queue files into the normal mail queue directory. Because you are using the `-C` and `-oQ` options, `sendmail` also includes the following warning headers in the letter to help alert the recipient of possible mail forgery:

```
X-Authentication-Warning: gonzo.gov: Processed from queue /tmp
X-Authentication-Warning: gonzo.gov: Processed by joe with -C srvr.cf
```

`sendmail` also inserts the header `Apparently-to: joe` because, although you specified a recipient on the command line, none was listed in the body of the letter. In this case, the letter's body was taken from the empty file `/dev/null`, so no To: header was available. If you do your testing as the superuser, you can skip the `-oQ` argument and `sendmail` won't insert the warning headers. You can avoid the `Apparently-to:` header by creating a file like

```
To: recipient

testing
```

and using it as input instead of `/dev/null`.

The recipient should be you, so you can inspect the headers of the letter for correctness. In particular, return address lines must include an FQDN (Fully Qualified Domain Name) for SMTP mail. That is, a header such as `From: joe@gonzo` is incorrect because it doesn't include the domain part of the name, but a header such as `From: joe@gonzo.gov` is fine.

You should repeat this testing for the same variety of addresses you used in the first tests. You might have to create special aliases that point to you for some of the testing.

The amount of testing you do depends on the complexity of your site and the amount of experience you have, but a beginning system administrator should test very thoroughly, even for apparently simple installations.

When you are absolutely sure that the sendmail.cf file is correct, you can copy it into place in the /etc directory:

```
[root@gonzo cf]# cp /etc/sendmail.cf /etc/sendmail.cf.bak
[root@gonzo cf]# cp gonzo.cf /etc/sendmail.cf
```

The first copy backs up your current sendmail configuration in case you need to get it back for any reason. Then you can stop and start sendmail or find the process ID and send it a HUP signal. This causes sendmail to reread its configuration file:

```
[root@gonzo cf]# /etc/rc.d/init.d/sendmail restart
```

Common sendmail Configuration Mistakes

There are three main common configuration errors when you are setting up a sendmail-based mail server.

The first is not having an alias for the postmaster user. All bounced messages get sent to this alias, which should point to a user who regularly reads his mail. When you get bounced messages for your site, you should READ them! Most of the time it helps you diagnose a problem before the users notice it and start complaining. It is also a widely known alias that Internet users commonly mail to if they need to contact an email administrator for a particular domain name.

The second is having an incorrectly configured sendmail.cw file. This file should list all the domain names for which the server is responsible for receiving mail.

The third is due to incorrectly configured DNS entries. Most of the time sites have incorrect secondary MX records, which is of no use if your main email server goes down for a period of time. Usually your ISP will be happy to act as a secondary MX for your site.

POP

As much as you might love Linux, the reality is that you must contend with other operating systems out there. Even worse, many of them aren't even UNIX-based. Although the Linux community has forgiven the users of other operating systems, there is still a long way to go before complete assimilation happens. In the meantime, the best thing to do is to use tools to tie the two worlds together.

The following sections cover the integration of the most-used application of any network: electronic mail. Because UNIX and other operating systems have very different views of how email should be handled, the Post Office Protocol (POP) was created. This protocol abstracts the details of email to a system-independent level so anyone who writes a POP client can communicate with a POP server.

> **Note**
>
> The latest version of POP is POP3. POP2 was originally published as RFC 918 in October 1984 and was superceded by RFC 937 in February 1985. POP3 was originally published as RFCs 1081 and 1082 in November 1988. RFC 1081 was superceded by RFC 1225 in May 1991. In June 1993, RFC 1460 superceded RFC 1225, and in November 1994, RFC 1725 made the standards track and rendered RFC 1460 obsolete.

Configuring a POP Server

The POP server you will configure on the sample system is packaged as part of the freely available IMAP package. (Setting up IMAP is discussed in the next section.) This package was developed at the University of Washington (`ftp://ftp.cac.washington.edu/imap`). If you want, you can use the Eudora Light email package available from Qualcomm (`ftp://ftp.qualcomm.com/eudora/eudoralight/`). Like the UW POP package, Eudora Light is available for free. (The Professional version does cost money, however.) Later on in the chapter, I'll show you how to configure your Netscape browser for both POP and IMAP email retrieval.

Red Hat has prepared an RPM of the UW IMAP package. It's available on the CD-ROMs (`imap-4.7c2-12.i386.rpm`), or you can fetch it from Red Hat's FTP site at `ftp://ftp.redhat.com`. To install it from the CD-ROMs, simply run

```
rpm -i imap-4.7c2-12.i386.rpm
```

The `rpm` command then installs three programs (found in `/usr/sbin/`), imapd, ipop2d, and ipop3d, as well as the manual pages. You will not need to worry about using ipop2d because it implements the earlier POP2 specification. Almost every POP client available these days knows how to talk POP3.

Configuring `ipop3d`

Most of the `ipop3d` options are configured at compile time. Therefore, you don't have much of a say in how things are done unless you want to compile the package yourself.

If you are interested in pursuing that route, you can fetch the complete package (which is version 4.7 at the time of this writing) from UW's FTP site at ftp://ftp.cac. washington.edu/imap/imap-4.7.tar.Z. However, it is highly recommended that you stick with the source RPM that is distributed on your Red Hat CD-ROMs because it contains all the patches and other modifications that Red Hat applied to the original codebase.

Using ipop3d gives you the following capabilities:

- Refusal to retrieve mail for anyone whose UID is root.
- Verbose logging to syslog.
- Support for CRAM-MD5 and APOP for user authentication. For these to be enabled, the file /etc/cram-md5.pwd must exist (see the section on setting up APOP support for details).

To allow ipop3d to start from xinetd, edit the /etc/xinetd/ipop3 file and make sure it contains the following:

```
service pop3
{
        disable         = no
        socket_type     = stream
        wait            = no
        user            = root
        server          = /usr/sbin/ipop3d
        log_on_success  += USERID
        log_on_failure  += USERID
}
```

Don't forget to send the HUP signal to xinetd. You can do so by issuing the following command:

```
# /etc/init.d/xinet reload
```

Now you're ready to test the connection. At a command prompt, enter

```
$ telnet popserver pop-3
```

popserver is the name of the machine running the ipop3d program. The pop-3 at the end is what Telnet will reference in your /etc/services file for port 110. You should get a response similar to the following:

```
+OK POP3 popserver.gonzo.gov v6.50 server ready
```

This result means that the POP server has responded and is awaiting an instruction. (Typically, this job is transparently done by the client mail reader.) If you want to test the authentication service, try to log in as yourself and see whether the service registers your current email box. For example, to log in as sshah with the password mars1031, enter

```
user sshah
+OK User name accepted, password please
pass mars1031
+OK Mailbox open, 90 messages
quit
+OK Sayonara
```

The first line, user sshah, tells the POP server that the user for whom it will be checking mail is sshah. The response from the server is an acknowledgment that the username sshah is accepted, and that a password is required to access the mailbox. You can then type **pass mars1031**, where mars1031 is the password for the sshah user. The server acknowledges the correct password and username pair with a statement indicating that 90 messages are currently in user sshah's mail queue. Because you don't want to actually read the mail this way, enter **quit** to terminate the session. The server sends a sign-off message and drops the connection.

How APOP Works

By default, the POP server sends all passwords in *cleartext* (not encrypted). If you're security-conscious, using cleartext passwords over your network is obviously a bad idea and tighter control is needed on authentication. This is where APOP support comes in. APOP is a more security-minded way of authenticating users because the passwords are already encrypted before they're sent over the network.

It works like this: The server issues a *challenge* to a connecting client. The client appends the user's password to the challenge, then encrypts it using MD5—this is called a *hash*—and sends the hash back to the server. The server then compares the client's response with its own calculated value of the checksum (challenge + user password). If there is a match, the client is then authenticated and logged on to the POP3 server.

As you can see, the advantage of this method is that rather than the plaintext password being transmitted in the clear, all that is transferred is a hash of text that means absolutely nothing to a cracker sniffing the network. If implemented correctly, the probability of the same challenge being issued twice by the server is very small! This stops cold the possibility of a replay attack, whereby the attacker grabs an MD5 hash that has come across the wire and tries to use it to log in to someone else's POP3 account.

Setting Up APOP Authentication

Luckily, ipop3d supports APOP. The APOP username and password information is in the /etc/cram-md5.pwd file. Because this database is kept in a cleartext format, you need to make absolutely sure that it has the permissions 0400 (chmod 0400 /etc/cram-md5.pwd).

When you installed `ipop3d`, the `/etc/cram-md5.pwd` database was not created. You will need to create the file with your favorite editor and put some entries in, similar to

```
# CRAM-MD5 authentication database
# Entries are in form <user><tab><password>
# Lines starting with "#" are comments

fred     rubble
wilma    flintstone
barny    beret
betty    wired
```

Obviously, putting any plaintext passwords in any file is bad practice—this is one of the downfalls of the `ipop3d` software. Hopefully, at some point in the future encryption will be added to the APOP database. But in the meantime, you must continue to make sure that the file has the correct permissions. Additionally, it is not recommended that your users use the same password for APOP email access that they use to log in to the server (the password that is specified in `/etc/passwd`).

IMAP

As noted at the beginning of the chapter, POP was a good first step to enable people on non-UNIX operating systems to read their UNIX-based email. But as time went on and distributed computing really took off, the deficiencies stood out. The POP server would not keep the read or unread state of messages. Messages would be downloaded to the user's PC and deleted off the server, so when the user moved to another PC, he had to move his mailbox between the two different machines. In this day and age of remote communication, people found that accessing email from home over a modem connection could be painfully slow if there were many messages to download, and they could not access the email folders they created on their work PC from home.

The IMAP protocol now allows people to store all their folders *online*. This makes it possible to access your email on your laptop while travelling, at home, or at work without having to transfer the messages back and forth. It works by transferring all the message headers of the folder you are reading. Then, using your IMAP client software, you can select a message and it will appear on your screen. The main advantage, of course, is that the messages are left on the server so you can access them wherever you happen to be.

Similarly to the POP3 protocol, IMAP (also commonly referred to as IMAP4) is also an RFC standard, so it's a transparent protocol that can be added to any messaging system. There are IMAP implementations for not just UNIX systems, but for Microsoft Exchange, Novell Groupwise, and countless others.

10

SMTP AND PROTOCOLS

Configuring an IMAP Server

Configuring an IMAP server on your Red Hat Linux system is relatively straightforward. You need to make sure that the `imapd` RPM is installed:

```
[root@gonzo /] # rpm -q imap
imap-4.7c2-3
```

If you get similar output, you are in business. Otherwise, you will need to install `imapd`, which is on your Red Hat Linux CD-ROMs.

You also need to check that `imapd` is not disabled in your `/etc/xinetd.d/imap` file. It should have the following contents:

```
service imap
{
        disable         = no
        socket_type     = stream
        wait            = no
        user            = root
        server          = /usr/sbin/imapd
        log_on_success  += DURATION USERID
        log_on_failure  += USERID
}
```

If you need to change it then have `xinetd` reload its configuration files, which you can do like so:

```
[root@gonzo /] # /etc/init.d/xinet reload
```

By now, `imapd` is running and you should be able to connect to it. This is similar to the way you tested the connection to your POP server in the previous section.

Type in the following:

telnet imapserver imap

`imapserver` is the name of the machine running the `imapd` program. You should get a response similar to the following:

```
* OK imapserver IMAP4rev1 v11.241 server ready
```

This result means the IMAP server has responded and is awaiting an instruction (again, this is normally done by the client mail reader). If you want to test the authentication service, try to log in as yourself and see whether the service registers your current email box. For example, to log in as `sshah` with the password `mars1031`, enter

A001 user sshah mars1031
A001 OK LOGIN completed

You are now logged in to your IMAP server. Since you were just testing, you can log out now by entering this:

```
A002 logout
* BYE imapserver IMAP4rev1 server terminating connection
```

Your IMAP server is now set up and ready to use!

Mail Retrieval

With `imapd` set up on your server, you can access your mail using numerous methods. You can use a command-line program such as Pine on the Linux console, an IMAP-compliant Windows or Macintosh-based email client (a list of which can be found at `http://www.imap.org/products.html`), or Netscape Communicator, which is available as part of the Red Hat Linux distribution.

Configuring Netscape for POP3 or IMAP Retrieval

It's fairly simple to set up Netscape to talk to your mail server. You just need to tell it your IMAP or POP server name, your login name, and if you want to use IMAP, the sub-directory in your home directory on the server where your folders are kept.

Start off by logging in to your account and creating a directory called `Mail`:

```
[fred@gonzo] $ mkdir Mail
```

You will use this directory to store your mail folders so they can be accessed by both your local email client and remote IMAP client.

Now start up Netscape. Just type in **netscape** and it should start up. If you get a `command not found` error, you will need to install it from your Red Hat CD-ROMs.

Click the Communicator menu and select Messenger Mailbox. This will bring up the Netscape messaging system. Now click on Edit, Preferences, and click Identity in the left half of the screen. You will be faced with a dialog box like that shown in Figure 10.3.

Put your real name in. This name is what will be placed in the From: header for email messages you send out. Also, fill in your correct email address. This is the address that people will see in the From: header.

Click Mail Servers and you will see a window similar to Figure 10.4.

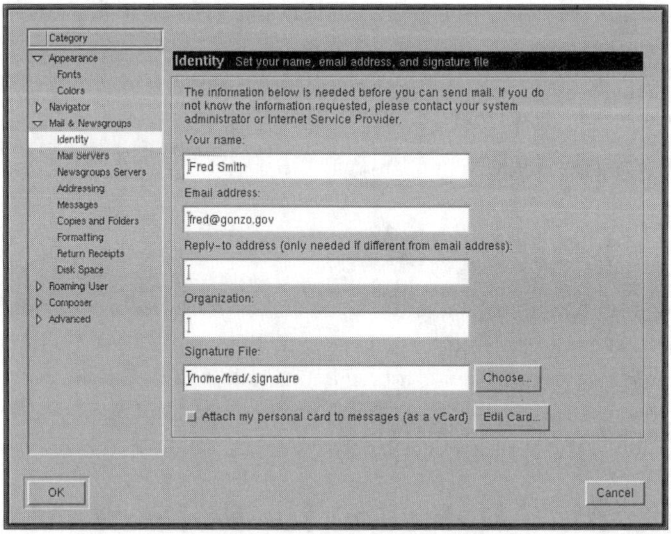

FIGURE 10.3

Setting your identity with Netscape Messenger.

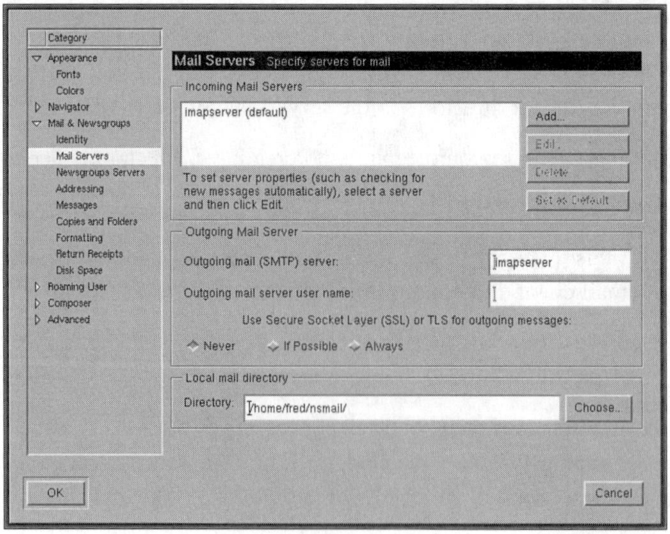

FIGURE 10.4

Setting your Mail Servers details with Netscape Messenger.

In the first text box, enter the username that you use on your mail server. Now you need to enter your outgoing (SMTP) server name. Delete the given Incoming mail server and click Add. That will bring up a screen similar to Figure 10.5. Enter the incoming server name (these two are usually the same). Directly below the information you just entered, you can choose the incoming mail server type. For demonstration purposes, choose IMAP—but you can just as easily choose POP3 if you don't want or need all the neat

IMAP features. Using the tabs across the top, you can set the features that protocol supports such as choosing to move your deleted messages into your Messenger trashcan, selecting SSL encryption if your IMAP server supports it, or selecting Set New Folders for Offline Download. This allows you to download messages so they physically reside on your local PC as well as the server for offline reading.

If you're using IMAP there is one final option that needs to be set before you can begin reading your email with Messenger. Click the Advanced Options tab and, in the IMAP server directory, enter the directory you created at the start of this section (`Mail`). This is the directory that Messenger will use for your online mail folders. Click OK, click OK again, and click the Get Msg button. Messenger will ask for your password and then will begin to download all your email message headers and display them for easy browsing. You can then easily switch to different folders using the drop-down box just under the toolbar.

fetchmail

`fetchmail` is best described with an example. Say your email is stored for you at your ISP. To access your mail using conventional means, such as with Netscape Messenger, you set it up for POP3 access. That way, when you dial in it will download all your messages to your personal Linux account so you can read, reply, and sort through your messages as you please.

The `fetchmail` paradigm is slightly different. Instead of downloading your mail using your mail reader, `fetchmail` is executed as a separate program whose sole purpose is to log in to your POP3 or IMAP server and download all your messages. But that's not all it does! As it downloads your mail, each message is passed on to your regular Mail Delivery Agent (MDA). If you use `sendmail`, `qmail`, `smail`, or some other SMTP-compatible mail server, all the messages are passed to port 25 on your local Linux machine, just as if you were permanently connected on the Internet and email was arriving directly to your machine. Once the mail is delivered to your mail spool file (`/var/spool/mail/<username>`), you can read it using conventional methods, such as command-line mail, `elm`, `pine`, or even Netscape Messenger on a Windows or Macintosh machine elsewhere on your local LAN—long after you have disconnected from your ISP!

This method of mail pickup provides numerous benefits. If you use `procmail` scripts to filter incoming messages as they arrive and your `sendmail` is configured to use `procmail` as the local delivery mailer, your messages will be filtered correctly. Again, if you are using `sendmail` and you have a `.forward` file in your home directory, it will be processed.

`fetchmail` is a very powerful program, and it has many advanced features that we will not go into here. But if you want more information on what it offers, there is a reasonable amount of documentation in `/usr/doc/fetchmail-x.y.z` (x, y, and z are the version numbers of the version you have installed).

To check if `fetchmail` is installed on your system, enter the following command:

```
[root@gonzo /] # rpm -q fetchmail
fetchmail-5.5.0-2
```

If similar output appears, you are in business. Otherwise, install it from your Red Hat CD-ROMs using a similar command to

```
[root@gonzo /] # rpm -i fetchmail-5.5.0-2.i386.rpm
```

Configuring `fetchmail` for POP3 or IMAP Retrieval

When `fetchmail` executes, it searches for a `.fetchmailrc` file in your home directory. This file usually contains all the options that are needed to log in to your ISP's POP or IMAP server. Anything that can be specified in this `rc` file can also be specified on the command line, but it is usually easier to put all the options you regularly use in a `.fetchmailrc` file. To start off, create a configuration file to collect your mail from your ISP's POP3 server. It is fairly simple:

```
poll pop.isp.net protocol pop3 username joe password secret123
```

This is fairly self-explanatory. `poll` signifies the hostname to contact, `protocol` gives the protocol that you want to use to connect, `username` specifies your POP3 username, and `password` indicates that your password follows. If you want, you can leave your password out. If you choose to do it this way, you will be asked for a password when `fetchmail` connects to your POP3 server.

Similarly, it is not hard to guess how to configure `fetchmail` to retrieve your mail from an IMAP server:

```
poll imap.isp.net protocol imap username joe password secret123
```

For security, you should also make sure you have the correct permissions on your
.fetchmailrc file:

```
$ chmod 0400 .fetchmailrc
```

You can also start up fetchmail as a daemon and it can automatically check your mail
once every *n* seconds with the option -d. For example, to check your mail automatically
every minute and put fetchmail in the background, use the following command:

```
$ fetchmail -d 60 &
```

To help diagnose mistakes, the -v option comes in handy. It outputs diagnostic information to the screen as it works to help you narrow down a problem.

fetchmail has an excellent manual page for more details on how to configure some of
the more advanced options. There are also numerous resources on the Internet, such as
http://www.tuxedo.org/~esr/fetchmail.

The easiest way to configure fetchmail is via fetchmailconf:

```
[root@gonzo /] # rpm -q fetchmailconf
fetchmailconf-5.5.0-2
```

Then make sure you're running the X Window System and run fetchmailconf in your
normal user account. A GUI will come up that will give you access to almost every configuration option.

Summary

In this chapter you learned how to install, set up, configure, and test sendmail, ipop3d,
and imapd, as well as to retrieve your mail using Netscape and fetchmail. The key
things to remember about this process follow:

- An MTA is a Mail Transfer Agent (which actually routes and delivers mail), and an
  MUA is a Mail User Agent (which is what the user uses to access mail after it has
  been delivered). sendmail is an MTA *only*.

- The Simple Mail Transfer Protocol (SMTP) is the actual protocol used to transfer
  mail. sendmail is a program that uses this protocol to communicate with other
  mail servers. Other mail servers don't need to run sendmail, but they do need to
  communicate via SMTP.

- sendmail does *not* deliver mail once it has reached the destination system. A special program that's local to the system, such as /bin/mail or /usr/bin/procmail,
  is used to perform the delivery functions.

10

**SMTP AND
PROTOCOLS**

- The aliases file can remap email addresses to other usernames, redirect mail to files, or pass on email messages to another program for processing. Remember to run the `newaliases` program every time you change the alias file.

- `sendmail` is a large program with a history of security problems. Hence, be sure to keep up with the security bulletins. The security section at `http://www.lwn.net` (Linux Weekly News) is worth checking regularly, as well as `ftp://updates.redhat.com` (or mirrors) for security updates to your particular distribution.

- Whenever a new version of `sendmail` is released, download it from `ftp.sendmail.org` and install it.

- The Post Office Protocol (POP) is a protocol for allowing client machines to connect to a mail server and transfer mail. POP is not responsible for delivering mail to other users or systems.

- Although POP isn't nearly as large or complex as `sendmail`, it does have the potential for security problems (as does any Internet-accessible service). Watch for security announcements and upgrade accordingly.

- APOP is the means by which the POP protocol accepts passwords in an encrypted format.

- The Internet Message Access Protocol (IMAP) is a protocol for allowing client machines to connect to a mail server and access your email without having to download all your waiting messages at once. It also allows easy remote access to email when you are constantly moving around, by allowing you to manipulate mail folders on your mail server.

- Netscape Messenger can be configured to talk to either a POP or an IMAP server quite easily.

- `fetchmail` is an alternative method to process your mail from either a POP or an IMAP server.

- `fetchmail` passes mail to your local Mail Transfer Agent (MTA) for processing—`sendmail`, for example.

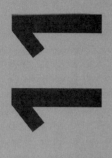

FTP

IN THIS CHAPTER

Using the File Transfer Protocol (FTP) is a popular way to transfer files from machine to machine across a network. Clients and servers have been written for all the popular platforms, thereby often making FTP the most convenient way of performing file transfers.

You can configure FTP servers one of two ways. The first is as a private, user-only site, which is the default configuration for the FTP server. A private FTP server allows only system users to connect via FTP and access their files. You can place access controls to either deny or grant access to specific users.

The other kind of FTP server is anonymous. An anonymous FTP server allows anyone on the network to connect to it and transfer files without having an account. Because of the potential security risks involved with this setup, you should allow access only to certain directories on the system.

> **Caution**
>
> Configuring an anonymous FTP server can pose a security risk. Because server software is inherently complex, it can contain bugs that allow unauthorized users to access your system. The authors of the FTP server configured in this chapter have gone to great lengths to avoid this possibility; however, no one can ever be 100% sure.
>
> If you decide to establish an anonymous FTP server, be sure to keep a careful eye on security announcements from the Computer Emergency Response Team (http://www.cert.org) and update the server software whenever security issues arise.

Depending on which packages you chose to install during the installation, you might already have the FTP server software installed. To determine whether you do, check for the /usr/sbin/in.ftpd file. If it is there, you have the necessary software. If it isn't there, the next section explains how to locate and install it.

Getting and Installing the FTP Server

Red Hat Linux uses the freely available wu-ftpd server. This server comes as an RPM (Red Hat Package Manager) and will be installed during installation. If you decide you want to run an FTP server but did not install the RPM, fetch wu-ftpd-2.6.1-6. i386.rpm from the CD-ROMs or check http://www.redhat.com for the latest edition.

To install the RPM, mount your Red Hat CD-ROM and as root run the following:

```
# rpm -ivh /mnt/cdrom/RedHat/RPMS/wu-ftpd*.rpm
```

If you plan to offer an anonymously accessible site, be sure to install anonftp-3.0-a. i386.rpm from the CD-ROMs as well. As always, you can check for the latest version at http://www.redhat.com.

To install the anonymous FTP file, log in as root and run the following:

```
# rpm -ivh anonftp*.rpm
```

Now you have a working anonymous FTP server. Of course, you should also have an active Internet network connection and a valid host and domain name for a truly public server. See Chapter 14, "Domain Name Service and Dynamic Host Configuration Protocol," for details about Domain Name Service (DNS).

Note

Although the anonftp package contains the files necessary to set up anonymous FTP service and the wu-ftpd rpm file contains the FTP daemon, you'll find the FTP client program in the ftp-0.17-6.i386.rpm package. Install all three RPMs for complete service.

Although you can find the latest version of wuftpd at ftp://ftp.wu-ftpd.org/ pub/wu-ftpd, you should periodically check Red Hat's Web site for RPM updates to Linux FTP software, especially if you allow public access to your computer over the Internet. Many newer versions of Red Hat's Linux networking or communications software contain security fixes or other enhancements that are designed to protect your computers from intruders. Also check the file named CHANGES under the /usr/share/doc/wu-ftpd-2.6.1 directory for details about new fixes.

To test whether the installation worked, simply use the FTP client and connect to your machine. For the sample FTP server, vaio, you would respond to the following:

```
# ftp vaio.home.org
Connected to vaio.home.org.
220 vaio.home.org FTP server (Version wu-2.6.1(1)
➥Mon Jul 24 01:59:25 EDT 2000) ready.
Name (vaio.home.org:bball): anonymous
331 Guest login ok, send your complete e-mail address as password.
Password: bball@tux.org
230 Guest login ok, access restrictions apply.
Remote system type is UNIX.
Using binary mode to transfer files.
```

```
ftp> ls
200 PORT command successful.
150 Opening ASCII mode data connection for directory listing.
total 32
d--x--x--x   2 root     root           4096 Aug  9 15:08 bin
d--x--x--x   2 root     root           4096 Aug  9 15:08 etc
drwxr-xr-x   2 root     root           4096 Aug  9 15:08 lib
drwxr-xr-x   2 root     50             4096 Jul 12 11:31 pub
226 Transfer complete.
ftp>
```

As you can see, after you log in, you'll be in the /home/ftp directory. To quit the FTP client software, simply type **bye** or **quit** at the ftp> prompt. If you want to test the private FTP server, rerun the FTP client but use your login instead of the anonymous login. Here's an example:

```
# ftp vaio.home.org
Connected to vaio.home.org.
220 vaio.home.org FTP server (Version wu-2.6.1(1)
Mon Jul 24 01:59:25 EDT 2000) ready.
Name (vaio.home.org:bball): bball
331 Password required for bball.
Password: mypassword
230 User bball logged in.
Remote system type is UNIX.
Using binary mode to transfer files.
ftp> ls
200 PORT command successful.
150 Opening ASCII mode data connection for directory listing.
total 8856
-rw-rw-r--   1 500      500           500309 Aug 16 15:53 06fig01.pcx
-rw-rw-r--   1 500      500           480674 Aug 16 16:30 06fig02.pcx
-rw-rw-r--   1 500      500           496037 Aug 16 16:10 06fig03.pcx
-rw-rw-r--   1 500      500           361017 Aug 15 13:16 28fig12.pcx
drwxr-xr-x   4 500      500             4096 Aug 21 09:30 Desktop
drwxrwxr-x   5 500      500             4096 Aug 10 00:40 GNUstep
-rw-rw-r--   1 root     root             101 Aug 16 15:42 mychat
-rw-rw-r--   1 root     root             144 Aug 16 15:44 out.txt
-rw-rw-r--   1 500      500           176463 Aug 16 14:59 ppp-2.3.11-7.i386.rpm
226 Transfer complete.
ftp>
```

As you can see, when you log in with a registered username and password, you'll be placed in your home directory on the remote computer.

> **Tip**
>
> If you don't have access to a network, you can test your FTP server by using the hostname *localhost*. You must have an active loopback interface (usually configured by default when you install Red Hat Linux), and enabled by the `/etc/rc.d/init.d/network` script.

How the FTP Server Works

FTP service is controlled from the `/etc/inetd.conf` file and is automatically invoked whenever someone connects to the FTP port. (Ports are logical associations from a network connection to a specific service. For example, port 21 associates to FTP, port 23 associates to Telnet, and so on.) When a connection is detected, the FTP daemon (`/usr/sbin/in.ftpd`) is invoked and the session begins. The default `/etc/inetd.conf` file installed with your Red Hat distribution contains the necessary line for this step to occur.

After the server is invoked, the client needs to provide a username and corresponding password. Two special usernames—anonymous and `ftp`—have been set aside for the purpose of allowing access to the public files. Any other access requires the user to have an account on the server.

If a user accesses the server using an account, an additional check is performed to ensure that the user has a valid shell. If the user doesn't, access is denied to the system. This check is useful if you want to limit user access to a server (for example, POP mail) and do not want users logging in via Telnet or FTP. Valid shells are listed in the your system's `/etc/shells` file. If you install a new shell, be sure to add it to your `/etc/shells` listing so people using that shell can connect to the system via FTP.

Users accessing your system's FTP server are placed in their home directories when they first log in. At that point, they can change to any directories on the system to which they have permission. Anonymous users, on the other hand, have several restrictions.

Anonymous users are placed in the home directory for the FTP users. By default, this directory is set to `/home/ftp` by the anonftp RPM package. Note that other Linux distributions may use a different default FTP directory! After the users get there, the FTP server executes a `chroot` system call, effectively changing the program's `root` directory to the FTP users' directories. Access is denied to any other directories in the system, including `/bin`, `/etc`, and `/lib`. This change in the `root` directory prevents the server from seeing `/etc/passwd`, `/etc/group`, and other necessary binaries (such as `/bin/ls`). To make up

for this change, the server package creates `bin`, `etc`, and `lib` directories under
`/home/ftp`. This is where necessary libraries and programs (such as `ls`) are placed; it's
also where the server software can access them even after the `chroot` system call has
been made.

For security reasons, files placed under the `/home/ftp` directory have their permissions
set such that only the server can see them. (This is done automatically during anonftp's
install.) Any other directories created under `/home/ftp` should be set up so they are
world-readable. Most anonymous FTP sites place such files under the `pub` subdirectory.

Configuring Your FTP Server

Although the default configuration of the FTP server is reasonably secure, you can fine-
tune access rights by editing the following files:

- `/etc/ftpaccess`
- `/etc/ftpconversions`
- `/etc/ftphosts`
- `/var/log/xferlog`

With all these files, you can control who connects to your server, when they can connect,
and where they can connect from. For security, you can create an audit trail of what they
do after connecting. The `ftpaccess` file is the most significant of these because it contains the most configuration options; however, misconfiguring any of the others can lead
to denied service.

Tip

When editing any of the files in the `/etc` directory (FTP related or not), comment the file liberally and keep backups of original or previously working configuration files. Keeping an edit history at the end of the file—listing who last
edited the file, with date, time, and content information—is a good way to
track down problems as well as the source of those problems.

Controlling Access—The `/etc/ftpaccess` File

The `/etc/ftpaccess` file is the primary means of controlling who can access your
server. Each line in the file either defines an attribute or sets its value.

The following commands control access:

- class
- autogroup
- deny
- guestgroup
- limit
- loginfails
- private

The following commands control the information the server shares with clients:

- banner
- email
- message
- readme

These commands control logging capabilities:

- log commands
- log security
- log syslog
- log transfers

The following are miscellaneous commands:

- alias
- cdpath
- compress
- tar
- shutdown

Permissions controls are set by the following commands:

- chmod
- delete
- overwrite
- rename
- umask

- `passwd-check`
- `path-filter`
- `upload`

Controlling User Access

The ability to control user access to your site is a critical component in fine-tuning your anonymous FTP server. The commands described in the following sections define the criteria used to determine in which group each user should be placed.

class

The `class` command defines a class of users who can access your FTP server. You can define as many classes as you want. Each `class` line comes in this form:

```
class classname typelist addrglob [addrglob ...]
```

classname is the name of the class you are defining, *typelist* is the type of user you are allowing into the class, and *addrglob* is the range of IP addresses allowed access to that class.

The *typelist* is a comma-delimited list in which each entry has one of three values: anonymous, guest, or real. Anonymous users are, of course, any who connect to the server as user `anonymous` or `ftp` and want to access only publicly available files. Guest users are special because they do not have accounts on the system per se, but they do have special access to key parts of the guest group. (See the description of the `guestgroup` command later in this chapter for additional details.) Real users must have accounts on the FTP server and are authenticated accordingly.

addrglob takes the form of a regular expression where * implies all sites. Several *addrglob*s can be associated with a particular class.

The following line defines the class anonclass, which contains only anonymous users:

```
class anonclass anonymous *
```

These users can originate their connections from anywhere on the network. On the other hand, this line allows only real users who have accounts on the FTP server to access their accounts via FTP if they are coming from the Local Area Network (LAN):

```
class localclass real 192.168.42.*
```

By default, Red Hat Linux calls `ftpd` with the `-a` option, which enables use of `/etc/ftpaccess`. This means you'll need, at a minimum, the `all` class definition (for real, guest, and anonymous) found in `/etc/ftpaccess`.

autogroup

The autogroup command provides tighter controls of anonymous users by automatically assigning them a certain group permission when they log in. The format of the autogroup line follows:

```
autogroup groupname class [class ...]
```

groupname is the name of the group to which you want the anonymous users set and *class* is the name of a class that is defined by using the class command. You can have multiple *class* entries for an autogroup. Only the anonymous users referenced in *class* will be affected by autogroup.

Remember, the group to which you are providing user permission must be in the /etc/group file.

deny

The deny command enables you to explicitly deny service to certain hosts based on their names, their IP addresses, or whether their hostnames can be reverse-resolved via DNS. The format of the deny command is as follows:

```
deny addrglob message_file
```

addrglob is a regular expression containing the addresses that are to be denied and *message_file* is the filename containing a message that should be displayed to the hosts when they connect.

The following is a sample deny line:

```
deny evilhacker.domain.com /home/ftp/.message.no.evil.hackers
```

This line displays the contents of the file /home/ftp/.message.no.evil.hackers to anyone trying to connect via FTP from evilhacker.domain.com. To deny users access based on whether their IP addresses can be reverse-resolved to their hostnames, use the string !nameserved for the *addrglob* entry.

guestgroup

The guestgroup command is useful when you want to provide your real users with restrictive FTP privileges. The format of the command is as follows:

```
guestgroup groupname [groupname ...]
```

groupname is the name of the restricted group (as taken from /etc/group).

When a user's group is restricted, the user is treated much like an anonymous visitor; thus, the user's account requires the same setups used for anonymous visitors. Also, the user's password entry is a little different in the directory field.

The field for the user's home directory is broken up by the `/./` characters. The effective `root` directory is listed before the split characters, and the user's relative home directory is listed after the split characters. For example, consider the following password entry:

```
user1:encrypted password:500:128:User 1:/home/ftp/./user1:/bin/false
```

Here, `/home/ftp` is the user's new relative `root` directory (the `bin`, `etc`, `pub`, and `lib` directories are under the `/home/ftp` directory by default with Red Hat Linux), and `/home/ftp/user1` is the user's home directory. Note that the `false` command is used when `user1` logs in; although the `ftpaccess` man page documents the use of `/etc/ftponly`, this command will not be found with Red Hat Linux—use of the `false` command is considered an acceptable substitute (don't forget to put `/bin/false` in your system's `/etc/shells` file).

limit

The `limit` command enables you to control the number of users according to class and time of day. This is especially useful if you have a popular archive but the system needs to be available to your users during business hours. The format of the `limit` command is as follows:

```
limit class n times message_file
```

`class` is the class to limit, `n` is the maximum number of people allowed in that class, `times` is the time during which the limit is in effect, and `message_file` is the file that will be displayed to the client when the maximum limit is reached.

The format of the `times` parameter is somewhat complex. The parameter is in the form of a comma-delimited string, where each option is for a separate day. The days Sunday through Saturday take the form `Su`, `Mo`, `Tu`, `We`, `Th`, `Fr`, and `Sa`, respectively, and all the weekdays can be referenced as `Wk`. Time should be kept in military format without a colon separating the hours and minutes. A range is specified by the dash character.

For example, to limit the class `anonfolks` to 10 users from Monday through Thursday, all day, and Friday from midnight to 5 p.m., you would use the following `limit` line:

```
limit anonfolks 10 MoTuWeTh,Fr0000-1700 /home/ftp/.message.too_many
```

If the limit is reached in this case, the file `/home/ftp/.message.too_many` is displayed to the connecting user.

loginfails

The `loginfails` command enables you to disconnect clients after they've reached your predetermined number of failed login attempts. By default, this number is five; however, you can set it by using this command:

```
loginfails n
```

n is the number of attempts. For example, the following line disconnects a user from the FTP server after three failed attempts:

```
loginfails 3
```

private

You might find it convenient to share files with other users via FTP without placing the file in a 100% public place or giving these users a real account on the server. The clients use the SITE GROUP and SITE GPASS commands so they can change to privileged groups that require passwords.

To provide your FTP server with this capability, set the private flag by using this command:

```
private switch
```

switch is either YES (to turn it on) or NO (to turn it off).

Because passwords are required for these special groups, you must use the /etc/ ftpgroups file. The format of an access group in /etc/ftpgroups follows:

```
access_group_name:encrypted_password:real_group
```

access_group_name is the name the client uses to reference the special group, *encrypted_password* is the password users need to supply (via SITE GPASS) access the group, and *real_group* is the actual group referenced in the /etc/group file.

Tip

To create the *encrypted_password* entry, use the UNIX crypt function. To simplify generation of the encrypted password, use the following Perl script:

```perl
#!/usr/bin/perl
srand( time() ^ ($$ + ($$ << 15)));
@salts= ('46' .. '57','65' .. '90','97' .. '122');
print "Enter password to encrypt: ";
chop ($password=<STDIN>);
print "The encrypted password is: ",crypt ( $password,
  ( chr ($salts[int(rand $#salts+1)] ) .
    chr ( $salts[int(rand $#salts+1) ] ))), "\n";
```

Controlling Banner Messages

The commands in this section enable you to provide messages to FTP users when they connect to your site or when they specify a special action. These commands are a great way to make your site self-documenting.

banner

The banner command displays a sign onscreen before the client provides a login and password combination. This is an important opportunity to display your server's security policies, where to upload software, and instructions for anonymous users regarding login procedures and software location. The format of this command follows:

```
banner path
```

path is the full pathname of the file you want to display. Consider this example:

```
banner /home/ftp/.banner
```

email

The email command specifies the site maintainer's email address. Some error messages or information requests provide this email address on demand. The default value in the /etc/ftpaccess file is root@localhost.

The format of the email command is:

```
email address
```

address is the full email address of the site maintainer.

It is recommended that you create an email alias "FTP" that forwards to the system administrators. Also, it's a good idea to provide this kind of information in the sign-on banner, so users know whom to contact if they cannot log in to the system.

message

The message command sets up special messages that are sent to the clients when they log in or when they change to a certain directory. You can specify multiple messages. Here's the format of this command:

```
message path when {class ...}
```

path is the full pathname to the file that will be displayed, *when* is the condition under which to display the message, and *class* is a list of classes to which this message command applies.

The *when* parameter should take one of two forms: either LOGIN or CWD=*dir*. If it is LOGIN, the message is displayed upon a successful login. If the parameter is set to CWD=*dir*, the message is displayed when clients enter the *dir* directory.

The *class* parameter is optional. You can list multiple classes for a specific message. This capability is useful, for example, if you want specific messages sent only to anonymous users.

The message file itself (specified by *path*) can contain special flags that the FTP server substitutes with the appropriate information at runtime. These case-sensitive options are as follows:

Option	Description
%I	Local time
%F	Free space in the partition where *dir* is located
%C	Current working directory
%E	Site maintainer's email address (specified by the email command)
%R	Client hostname
%L	Server hostname
%U	Username provided at login time
%M	Maximum number of users allowed in the specified class
%N	Current number of users in specified class

Remember, when messages are triggered by an anonymous user, the message path needs to be relative to the anonymous FTP directory.

The default message command defined in /etc/ftpaccess is as follows:

```
message /welcome.msg    login
```

No message file is defined. Use your favorite text editor to create your own welcome message and type in the following:

```
Welcome to %L, %U,
you are %N out of %M users.
It is %T.
```

This message will print the hostname, login name, and tell the user the user's number, along with the local time. Save the file under the /home/ftp directory. When an anonymous user logs in, the user will see this:

```
230-Welcome to thinkpad.home.org, anonymous
230-you are 1 out of unlimited users.
230-It is Thu June 29 14:27:02 2000.
230-
230-
```

readme

The readme command specifies the conditions under which clients are notified that a certain file in their current directory was last modified. This command looks like this:

```
readme path when class
```

path is the name of the file about which you want to alert the clients (for example, README), *when* is similar to the *when* in the message command, and *class* is the classes for which this command applies. The *when* and *class* parameters are optional.

Remember, when you're specifying a path for anonymous users, the file must be relative to the anonymous FTP directory.

Controlling Logging

As with any complex network service, security quickly becomes an issue. To contend with possible threats, you must track connections and their corresponding commands. Use the following commands to determine how much, if any, logging should be done by the server software.

log commands

For security purposes, you probably want to log the actions of your FTP users. The log commands option enables you to do this. Each command invoked by the clients is sent to your log file. The format looks like this:

```
log commands typelist
```

typelist is a comma-separated list specifying which kinds of users should be logged. The three kinds of users recognized are anonymous, guest, and real. (See the description of the class command earlier in this chapter for each user type's description.) For example, to log all the actions of anonymous and guest users, specify the following:

```
log commands anonymous,guest
```

log transfers

If you want to log only clients' file transfers (rather than logging their entire sessions with the log commands statement), use log transfers. This command's format looks like this:

```
log transfers typelist directions
```

typelist is a comma-separated list specifying which kinds of users should be logged (anonymous, guest, or real), and *directions* is a comma-separated list specifying which direction the transfer must take in order to be logged. The two directions you can choose to log are inbound and outbound.

For example, to log all anonymous transfers that are both inbound and outbound, use

```
log transfers anonymous inbound,outbound
```

The resulting logs are stored in /var/log/xferlog.

Miscellaneous Server Commands

The following set of commands provides some miscellaneous configuration items. Each command adds a good deal of flexibility to the server, making it that much more useful to you as its administrator.

alias

The `alias` command defines directory aliases for your FTP clients. These aliases are activated when the clients use the `cd` command and specify an alias. This capability is useful for providing shortcuts to often-requested files. This command's format looks like this:

```
alias string dir
```

`string` is the alias and `dir` is the actual directory to which the users should be transferred. The following is an example of this command:

```
alias orb_discography /pub/music/ambient/orb_discography
```

Hence, if clients connect and use the command `cd orb_discography`, they are automatically moved to the `/pub/music/ambient/orb_discography` directory, regardless of their current locations.

cdpath

Similar to the UNIX PATH environment variable, the `cdpath` command establishes a list of paths to check whenever clients invoke the `cd` command. The format of the `cdpath` command follows:

```
cdpath dir
```

`dir` is the server directory that will be checked whenever clients use the `cd` command. Remember, for security reasons, specify directories relative to the FTP home directory for your anonymous users. An example of the `cdpath` command is

```
cdpath /pub/music
cdpath /pub/coffee
```

If clients type the command `cd instant`, the server examines the directories in the following order:

1. `./instant`
2. Aliases called `instant` (for more information, see the description of `alias` earlier in this chapter)
3. `/pub/music/instant`
4. `/pub/coffee/instant`

compress

The `wu-ftpd` server offers a special `compress` feature that enables the server to compress or decompress a file before transmission. With this capability, a client who might not have the necessary software to decompress a file can still fetch it in a usable form. (For example, a file on your server is compressed using gzip, and a Windows client machine needs to get it but does not have the DOS version of gzip available.)

The `compress` command's format follows:

`compress switch classglob`

`switch` is either YES (to turn on this feature) or NO (to turn it off). `classglob` is a comma-separated list of classes to which this compress option applies.

There is, of course, a catch to using this command. You need to configure the `/etc/ftpconversions` file so the server knows which programs to use for certain file extensions. The default configuration supports compression by either `/bin/compress` or `/bin/gzip`.

For more information, see "Converting Files On-the-Fly—The `/etc/ftpconversions` File" later in this chapter.

tar

Almost identical to the `compress` option, `tar` specifies whether the server will tar and untar files for a client on demand. The format of this command is

`tar switch classglob`

`switch` is either YES (to turn it on) or NO (to turn it off). The `classglob` option is a comma-separated list of classes that is specified by the `tar` command.

Like the `compress` command, this feature is controlled by the `/etc/ftpconversions` file. For more information, see the section on `/etc/ftpconversions` later in this chapter.

shutdown

The `shutdown` command tells the server to periodically check for a particular file to see whether the server will be shut down. By default, the RPMs you installed invoke the FTP server whenever there is a request for a connection; therefore, you don't really need `shutdown`. On the other hand, if you intend to change the system so the server software is constantly running in the background, you might want to use `shutdown` to perform clean shutdowns and to notify users accessing the site.

The format of the `shutdown` command is

`shutdown path`

path is the full path of the file that contains shutdown information. When that file does become available, it is parsed out and the information gained from it dictates the behavior of the shutdown process, as well as the behavior of the `ftpshut` program (discussed later in this chapter). Although there isn't any standard place for storing this file, you might find it logical to keep it in `/etc/ftpshutdown` with the other FTP configuration files. Make sure the file is readable by `root`.

The format of the file is as follows:

```
year month day hour minute deny_offset disconnect_offset text
```

year is any year after 1970; *month* is from 0 to 11 to represent January to December, respectively; *day* is from 0 to 30; *hour* is from 0 to 23; and *minute* is from 0 to 59. The *deny_offset* parameter specifies the time at which the server should stop accepting new connections in the form HHMM, where HH is the hour in military format and MM is the minute. *disconnect_offset* is the time at which existing connections are dropped; it is also in the form HHMM.

The *text* parameter is a free-form text block displayed to users to alert them of the impending shutdown. The text can follow the format of the `message` command (see the description of this command earlier in the chapter) and can have the following special character sequences available:

Option	Description
%s	The time the system will shut down
%r	The time new connections will be denied
%d	The time current connections will be dropped

Controlling Permissions

Along with controlling logins and maintaining logs, you will need to tightly control the permissions of the files placed in the archive. The following commands specify what permissions should be set under certain conditions.

chmod

The `chmod` command determines whether a client has authorization to change permissions on the server's files by using the client's `chmod` command. This command's format is

```
chmod switch typelist
```

switch is either YES (to turn it on) or NO (to turn it off). *typelist* is the comma-separated list of user types affected by this command. The user types available are anonymous, guest, and real.

delete

The `delete` command tells the server whether FTP clients are authorized to delete files that reside on the server. This command looks like this:

```
delete switch typelist
```

`switch` is either `YES` (to turn it on) or `NO` (to turn it off). `typelist` is the comma-separated list of user types affected by this command. The user types available are anonymous, guest, and real.

overwrite

To control whether FTP clients can upload files and replace existing files on the server, use the `overwrite` command. This command's format is

```
overwrite switch typelist
```

`switch` is either `YES` (to turn it on) or `NO` (to turn it off). `typelist` is the comma-separated list of user types affected by this command. The user types available are anonymous, guest, and real.

rename

Client FTP software can send a `rename` request to the server to rename files. The `rename` command determines whether this request is acceptable. The format of this command follows:

```
rename switch typelist
```

`switch` is either `YES` (to turn it on) or `NO` (to turn it off). `typelist` is the comma-separated list of user types affected by this command. The user types available are anonymous, guest, and real.

umask

The `umask` command determines whether clients can change their default permissions in a fashion similar to the `umask` shell command. The format of the `umask` command looks like this:

```
umask switch typelist
```

`switch` is either `YES` (to turn it on) or `NO` (to turn it off). `typelist` is the comma-separated list of user types affected by this command. The user types available are anonymous, guest, and real.

passwd-check

Providing a valid email address as a password is considered good manners when connecting to an anonymous FTP site. The `passwd-check` command lets you determine how strictly you regulate the string submitted as an anonymous user's email address. The format of this command follows:

```
passwd-check strictness enforcement
```

strictness is one of three possible strings: none, trivial, or rfc822; and *enforcement* is one of two possible strings: warn or enforce.

If you select none for *strictness*, the password isn't checked. trivial is slightly more demanding, requiring that at least @ appears in the password. rfc822 is most strict, requiring the email address to comply with the RFC 822 "Message Header Standard" (for example, bball@tux.org).

By using warn as the *enforcement*, the users are warned if they fail to comply with the strictness requirement, but they can still connect. enforce, on the other hand, denies connection until users submit acceptable passwords.

path-filter

If you allow users to upload files to your server via FTP, you might want to set acceptable filenames (for example, control characters in filenames are not acceptable). You can enforce this restriction by using the path-filter command. This is the command's format:

```
path-filter typelist mesg allowed-regexp denied-regexp
```

typelist is a comma-separated list of users that are affected by this command; the user types available are anonymous, guest, and real. *mesg* is the filename of the message that will be displayed if the file does not meet this criteria. *allowed-regexp* is the regular expression the filename must meet in order to be approved for uploading. *denied-regexp* is the regular expression that, if met, causes the file to be explicitly denied; *denied-regexp* is an optional parameter.

```
path-filter anonymous,guest /ftp/.badfilename UL* gif$
```

This code displays the file /ftp/.badfilename to anonymous or guest users if they upload a file that doesn't begin with the string UL or that ends with the string gif.

upload

You can use the upload command, along with path-filter, to control the files that are placed on your server. The upload command determines the client's permissions for placing a file in a specific directory. This command also determines the file's permissions once it is placed in that directory. The format of upload is

```
upload directory dirglob switch owner group mode mkdir
```

directory is the directory that is affected by this command, *dirglob* is the regular expression used to determine whether a subdirectory under *directory* is a valid place to make an upload, and *switch* is either YES or NO, thereby establishing that an upload either can or cannot occur there. The *owner*, *group*, and *mode* parameters establish the file's owner, group, and permissions after the file is placed on the server. Finally, you can specify the *mkdir* option as either dirs (*is* able to create subdirectories under the specified directory) or nodirs (is *not* able to do this).

Here is a sample entry:

```
upload /home/ftp * no
upload /home/ftp /incoming yes ftp ftp 0775 nodirs
```

This example specifies that the /home/ftp/incoming directory (/incoming to the anonymous client) is the only location in which a file can be placed. After the file is placed in this directory, its owner becomes ftp, group ftp, and the permission is 775. The nodirs option at the end of the second line prevents the anonymous client from creating subdirectories under /incoming.

> **Tip**
>
> It is recommended that you set uploads to group ownership by ftp with a 775 file permission. This allows read-only access, so the /incoming directory doesn't become a trading ground for questionable material—for example, illegal software.

Converting Files On-the-Fly—The /etc/ftpconversions File

The format of the /etc/ftpconversions file is

```
1:2:3:4:5:6:7:8
```

where 1 is the strip prefix, 2 is the strip postfix, 3 is an add-on prefix, 4 is an add-on postfix, 5 is the external command to invoke to perform the conversion, 6 is the type of file, 7 is the option information used for logging, and 8 is a description of the action.

Confused? Don't be. Each option is actually quite simple. The following sections describe them one at a time.

The Strip Prefix

The *strip prefix* is the string at the beginning of a filename that should be removed when the file is fetched. For example, if you want a special action taken on files beginning with discography., where that prefix is removed after the action, you would specify discography. for this option. When clients specify filenames, they should not include the strip prefix. That is, if a file is called `discography.orb` and a client issues the command `get orb`, the server performs the optional command on the file and then transfers the results to the client. Although documented, this feature is not currently supported.

The Strip Postfix

The *strip postfix* is the string at the end of the filename that should be removed when the file is fetched. The strip postfix is typically used to remove the trailing `.gz` from a gzipped file that is being decompressed before being transferred back to the client.

The Add-On Prefix

An *add-on prefix* is the string inserted before the filename when a file is transferred either to or from the server. For example, you might want to insert the string `uppercase.` to all files being pulled from the server that are being converted to uppercase. Although documented, this feature, like the strip prefix, is not currently supported.

The Add-On Postfix

An *add-on postfix* is the string appended to a filename after an operation on the file is complete. This type of postfix is commonly used when the client issues the command `get largefile.gz`, where the actual filename is only `largefile`; in this case, the server compresses the file using gzip and then performs the transfer.

The `external` Command

The key component of each line is the `external` command. This entry specifies the program to be run when a file is transferred to or from the server. As the file is transferred, it is filtered through the program where downloads (files sent to the client) need to be sent to the standard out, and uploads (files sent to the server) will be coming from the standard in. For example, if you want to provide decompression with gzip for files being downloaded, the entry would look like the following:

```
gzip -cd %s
```

The `%s` in the line tells the server to substitute the filename that is being requested by the user.

Conversion Examples

You'll find additional conversion entries in an example `ftpconversions` file under the `/usr/share/doc/wu-ftp/2.6.1/examples` directory, including at least two for calculating file checksums. Examples of all other configuration and control files are also included.

The Type of File Field

The type of file field for /etc/ftpconversions is a list of possible filetypes that can be acted on, with type names separated by the pipe symbol (|). The three file types recognized are T_REG, T_ASCII, and T_DIR, which represent regular files, ASCII files, and directories, respectively. An example of this entry is T_REG | T_ASCII.

The Options Field

The options field of /etc/ftpconversions is similar to the type of file field in that it is composed of a list of names separated by the pipe symbol (|). The three types of options supported are O_COMPRESS, O_UNCOMPRESS, and O_TAR, which specify whether the command compresses files, decompresses files, or uses the tar command. An example entry is O_COMPRESS | O_TAR, which says the file is both compressed and tarred.

The Description of the Conversion

The last parameter of /etc/ftpconversions, the description of the conversion, is a free-form entry in which you can describe the type of conversion.

Example of an /etc/ftpconversions Entry

The following is a sample entry that compresses files using gzip on demand. This would allow someone who wants to get the file orb_discography.tar to instead request the file orb_discography.tar.gz and have the server compress the file by using gzip before sending it him. The configuration line that does this is as follows:

```
: : :.gz:/bin/gzip -9 -c %s:T_REG:O_COMPRESS:GZIP
```

The first two parameters are not necessary because you don't want to remove anything from the filename before sending it to the requester. The third parameter is empty because you don't want to add any strings to the beginning of the filename before sending it. The fourth parameter, though, does have the string .gz, which adds the .gz suffix to the file before sending it. The fifth parameter is the actual command used to compress the file, where the -9 option tells gzip to compress the file as much as it can, -c sends the compressed file to the standard output, and %s is replaced by the server from which the filename is requested (for example, orb_discography.tar). T_REG in the sixth parameter tells the server to treat the file as a normal file rather than an ASCII file or directory. The second-to-last parameter, O_COMPRESS, tells the server that the action being taken is file compression. The last parameter is simply a comment for the administrator so she can quickly determine the action being taken.

Configuring Host Access—The `/etc/ftphosts` File

The `/etc/ftphosts` file establishes rules on a per-user basis, determining whether or not users are allowed to log in from specific hosts.

Each line in the file can be one of two commands:

```
allow username addrglob
```

```
deny username addrglob
```

The `allow` command allows the user specified in *username* to connect via FTP from the explicitly listed addresses in *addrglob*. You can list multiple addresses.

The `deny` command explicitly denies the specified user *username* (or denies anonymous access where *username* is *ftp*) access from the sites listed in *addrglob*. You can list multiple sites.

The FTP Log File—`/var/log/xferlog`

Although `/var/log/xferlog` isn't a configuration file, it plays an important role because all the logs generated by the FTP server are stored in this file. Each line of the log file is described in Table 11.1.

TABLE 11.1   `/var/log/xferlog` Fields

Log Field	Definition
current-time	The current time in DDD MMM dd hh:mm:ss YYYY format, where DDD is the day of the week, MMM is the month, dd is the day of the month, hh:mm:ss is the time in military format, and YYYY is the year.
transfer-time	The total time in seconds spent transferring the file.
remote-host	The hostname of the client that initiated the transfer.
file-size	The size of the file that was transferred.
filename	The name of the file that was transferred.
transfer-type	The type of transfer done, where a is an ASCII transfer and b is a binary transfer.
special-action-flag	A list of actions taken on the file by the server, where C means the file was compressed, U means the file was uncompressed, T means the file was tarred, and - means no action was taken.

TABLE 11.1   continued

Log Field	Definition
direction	A flag indicating whether the file was outgoing or incoming, represented by o or i, respectively.
access-mode	The type of user who performed the action, where a is anonymous, g is a guest, and r is a real user.
username	The local username if the user was of type real.
service-name	The name of the service being invoked (most often FTP).
authentication-method	The type of authentication used: 0 means no authentication was done (anonymous user) and 1 means the user was validated with RFC-931. Authentication Server Protocol.
authenticated-user-id	The username by which this transfer was authenticated.
completion-status	(c)omplete or (i)ncomplete file transfer status.

FTP Administrative Tools

Several are available to help you administer your FTP server. These tools were automatically installed as part of the wu-ftp package when the server was installed. These utilities help you see the current status of the server and control its shutdown procedure:

- ftprestart
- ftpshut
- ftpwho
- ftpcount

ftprestart

The ftprestart command performs the reverse of the ftpshut command, and is used to restart an FTP server that has been shut down. The format of ftprestart is as follows:

```
ftprestart -V
```

The -V option merely prints a version number.

ftpshut

The ftpshut command eases shutdown procedures of the FTP server. This capability, of course, applies only if you are running the server all the time—instead of leaving it to be invoked from inetd as needed. The format of ftpshut is as follows:

```
ftpshut -l login-minutes -d drop-minutes time warning message
```

login-minutes is the number of minutes before server shutdown that the server will begin refusing new FTP transactions. *drop-minutes* is the number of minutes before server shutdown that the server will begin dropping existing connections. The default value for *login-minutes* is 10, and the default for *drop-minutes* is 5.

time is the time at which the server will be shut down. You can specify this time one of three ways. The first is to specify the time in military format without the colon (for example, 0312 to indicate 3:12 a.m.). The second is to specify the number of minutes to wait before shutting down. The format of this method is +*min*, where *min* is the number of minutes to wait (for example, +60 shuts the server down in 60 minutes). The last option is the most drastic; if you specify the string now, the server shuts down immediately.

warning message is the message displayed to all FTP clients, instructing them that the server will be shut down. See the description of the shutdown command for the /etc/ftpaccess file earlier in this chapter for details on the formatting available for the warning message.

ftpwho

ftpwho displays all the active FTP users on the system. The output of the command is in the format of the /bin/ps command. The format of this command follows:

```
pid tty stat time connection details
```

pid is the process ID of the FTP daemon handling the transfer; *tty* is always a question mark (?) because the connection is coming from FTP, not Telnet; *stat* is the status of that particular instance of the daemon, where S means it's sleeping, Z means it has crashed (gone *zombie*), and R means it's the currently running process. *time* indicates how much actual CPU time that instance of the FTP has taken. Finally, *connection details* tells where the connection is coming from, who the user is, and that user's current function.

The following is an example of output from ftpwho:

```
Service class all:
  1184 ?        SN     0:00 ftpd: dell.home.org: anonymous/horsey@sawbill.com:
➥ IDLE
  1181 ?        SN     0:00 ftpd: green.home.org: bball: IDLE
    -   2 users (-1 maximum)
```

Here you can see that two users are logged in. (An unlimited number of users are allowed to connect). The first user is an anonymous user who claims to be horsey@ sawbill.com and is currently not performing any functions. The second user, who has the username bball, is currently also idle.

ftpcount

`ftpcount`, which is a simplified version of `ftpwho`, shows the current total of users in each class defined in `/etc/ftpaccess`. A sample output from `ftpcount` shows the following:

```
Service class all                 -   2 users ( -1 maximum)
```

Using FTP Clients

This section introduces you to several of the FTP clients included with Red Hat Linux. Although the venerable `ftp` command has remained the standard network file transfer utility and tool of choice for millions of users worldwide, there's always room for improvement. However, the `ftp` command has a number of features of which many users might not be aware.

Most new and experienced Red Hat Linux users know how to access remote FTP servers by using `ftp` on the command line along with the name of a remote computer (as described at the beginning of this chapter). You can also speed up anonymous log-ins by using FTP's `-a` command-line option. However, later versions of the `ftp` command will also log in and retrieve files with a single command line. To do this, use FTP's auto-fetch capability. Specify an FTP address on the command line with your login, password, name of the computer, and the complete path to the location of a desired file. (You can also use wildcards to retrieve multiple files at one time.) Construct a command line like this:

```
# ftp ftp://bball:mypassword@aptiva.home.org/home/bball/happy2.jpg
Connected to aptiva.home.org.
220 aptiva.home.org FTP server (Version wu-2.4.2-academ[BETA-18](1)
 Mon Aug 3 19:17:20 EDT 1998) ready.
Remote system type is UNIX.
Using binary mode to transfer files.
331 Password required for bball.
230 User bball logged in.
200 Type set to I.
250 CWD command successful.
250 CWD command successful.
Retrieving home/bball/happy2.jpg
local: happy2.jpg remote: happy2.jpg
227 Entering Passive Mode (192,168,2,36,4,226)
150 Opening BINARY mode data connection for happy2.jpg (34636 bytes).
100% |*******************************************| 34636       00:00 ETA
226 Transfer complete.
34636 bytes received in 0.02 seconds (1.76 MB/s)
221 Goodbye.
```

As you can see, ftp logged into the remote computer with a name and password, retrieved the file happy2.jpg, and then disconnected. Another ftp command feature is the .netrc, and you can use it to accomplish the same task as the preceding command-line example. First, use your favorite text editor to create the file .netrc in your home directory. Then enter a series of auto-login lines like this:

```
machine aptiva.home.org
login bball
password mypassword
macdef init
get happy2.jpg
bye
```

The first line in the file uses the machine keyword to specify a remote computer. The next two lines specify your remote login and password. The macdef and init keywords specify immediate execution of the init macro. Any FTP commands placed following these keywords and two blank lines will be executed. In this example, the get command is used to retrieve the file happy2.jpg, and the bye command is used to quit the connection.

Save the .netrc file and exit your editor. Next, use the chmod command to give the file read and write permissions of 600, like this:

```
# chmod 600 .netrc
```

Finally, to test your .netrc file, use ftp with the hostname of the remote computer on the command line, like this:

```
# ftp aptiva
Connected to aptiva.home.org.
220 aptiva.home.org FTP server (Version wu-2.4.2-academ[BETA-18](1)
 Mon Aug 3 19:17:20 EDT 1998) ready.
331 Password required for bball.
230 User bball logged in.
get happy2.jpg
local: happy2.jpg remote: happy2.jpg
227 Entering Passive Mode (192,168,2,36,5,0)
150 Opening ASCII mode data connection for happy2.jpg (34636 bytes).
100% |*****************************************| 34718        00:00 ETA
226 Transfer complete.
34718 bytes received in 0.05 seconds (696.50 KB/s)
bye
221 Goodbye.
```

As you can see, the .netrc file connected, logged in, retrieved the file, and quit the connection. You can use this approach to regularly retrieve files from remote computers (such as weather maps), to regularly upload files to remote sites (such as Web-page directories), or to automate other file transfer tasks (such as regular, remote transfers of system logs through crontab entries).

Getting Files with the `wget` Command

The `wget` command, like `ftp`, may be used to retrieve files quickly and easily with a single command line. However, `wget` may also be used to retrieve files using Hypertext Transfer Protocol (HTTP) by using a Uniform Resource Locator (URL) like this:

```
# wget http://www.tux.org/~bball/index.html
--13:21:23-- http://www.tux.org:80/%7Ebball/index.html
           => `index.html'
Connecting to www.tux.org:80... connected!
HTTP request sent, awaiting response.... 200 OK
Length: 6,054 [text/html]
    OK -> .....                                  [100%]
13:21:25 (6.54 KB/s) - `index.html' save [6054/6054]
```

In this example, the file `index.html` is retrieved via HTTP from a Web site. The `wget` command may also be used with the `ftp://URL` form to retrieve files and can quickly mirror FTP sites. For more details, use the `info` command to read `wget`'s info file.

autoexpect

The tool-rich Linux environment features many different software tools (such as the `expect` interpreter) you can use to accomplish difficult tasks. Yet another way to automate file transfers(and other tasks) is with the `autoexpect` command. The `autoexpect` command will create an `expect` script to accomplish tasks performed during an `autoexpect` session.

To automate an FTP transfer, use the `autoexpect` command's `-f` command-line option, followed by the name of the desired command, and an initial command line, like this:

```
# autoexpect -f eftp ftp aptiva.home.org
autoexpect started, file is eftp
Connected to aptiva.home.org.
220 aptiva.home.org FTP server (Version wu-2.4.2-academ[BETA-18](1)
Mon Aug 3 19:17:20 EDT 1998) ready.
Name (aptiva:): bball
bball
331 Password required for bball.
Password:mypassword

230 User bball logged in.
Remote system type is UNIX.
Using binary mode to transfer files.
ftp> get happy2.jpg
get happy2.jpg
local: happy2.jpg remote: happy2.jpg
227 Entering Passive Mode (192,168,2,36,5,64)
150 Opening BINARY mode data connection for happy2.jpg (34636 bytes).
```

```
100%  |**************************************************| 34636          00:00 ETA
226 Transfer complete.
34636 bytes received in 0.03 seconds (1.10 MB/s)
ftp> bye
bye
221 Goodbye.
autoexpect done, file is eftp
```

This session will create an executable file named eftp, which will connect to the remote computer, log in, retrieve the file happy2.jpg, and then disconnect. To perform the automatic FTP session, type **eftp** on the command line like this:

```
# ./eftp
```

> ### Tip
>
> If the generated program works too fast, open the file (it is an expect command script) and look for this line:
>
> ```
> set force_conservative 0   ;# set to 1 to force conservative mode even if
>                            ;# script wasn't run conservatively originally
> ```
>
> Change the force_conservative setting to 1 and then save the file. This will slow the script, to allow for slower connections.

ncftp

The ncftp command is another attempt at improving the ftp command. This program features utilities that help when building shell scripts to automate file retrieval, and offers a pseudo-graphical interface for FTP transfer from the shell command line. According to NcFTP's author, Mike Gleason, this command has a number of unique features:

- Auto-resume downloads
- Background processing
- Bookmarks
- Cached directory listings
- Command-line editing
- Downloading entire directory trees
- Filename completion
- Host redialing
- Progress meters
- Working with firewalls, proxies, and more

In its simplest form, ncftp may be used just like the ftp command, with the name of a remote computer:

```
# ncftp aptiva.home.org
```

For more details about ncftp, see its man page or documentation under the /usr/doc/ncftp directory.

xtp

Like ftp and ncftp, John Cristy's xtp command may be used to log in and automatically retrieve one or more files from remote computers. For example, use the xtp command with a complete FTP command-line address like this:

```
# xtp ftp://bball:mypasswd@aptiva.home.org//home/bball/happy2.jpg
```

This will log in to the remote FTP server with your username and password, then retrieve the file happy2.jpg and quit the connection. The xtp command has a number of command-line options. For details, use a Web browser such as the text-only lynx browser to read xtp's online documentation, like this:

```
# lynx /usr/share/Image*/www/xtp.html
```

Although xtp's online documentation is included with Red Hat Linux, you'll have to go to http://www.wizards.dupont.com/cristy/www/xtp.html for more information or to ftp://ftp.wizards.dupont.com to download a copy.

gftp

Brian Masney's gFTP client is an easy-to-use interface to FTP file transfers. You can start this client during your Enlightenment X11 session by clicking the Main Menu button in your GNOME Panel, selecting Internet, and then clicking the gftp menu item. You can also start the gftp command from the command line and specify a remote computer, like this:

```
# gftp aptiva.home.org
```

The gFTP client will start as shown in Figure 11.1.

Like other FTP clients, the gftp command supports direct logins. The general syntax for the gftp command line is this:

```
# gftp [[ftp://][user:pass@]ftp-site[:port][/directory]]
```

Figure 11.1

The gFTP *client supports FTP file transfers with the click of a mouse, and it even supports drag-and-drop file transfers.*

This shows that you can use optional keywords, such as ftp://, along with a username, password, particular port number for the remote FTP server, and a destination directory for file transfers. Using this syntax, you can start an FTP session in your directory on a remote computer, like this:

```
# gftp ftp://bball:mypasswd@aptiva.home.org/home/bball
```

This will log you in to your remote computer and use a home directory for file transfers.

The gFTP main window (refer to Figure 11.1) features a menu bar with six drop-down menus, two directory windows for the local computer (on the left) and the remote computer (on the right), a progress window (showing the Filename, Progress, and Hostname of the computer), and a scrolling session window showing current activity.

The FTP menu is used to specify the type of file transfers and other options. The Local menu manipulates files and directories, while the Remote menu connects, disconnects, changes servers, and manipulates remote files and directories. The Transfers menu controls the transfer session and uploads (or downloads) files. The Logging menu can be used to keep track of your FTP session. The Tools menu compares the local and remote directories and highlights files that aren't found in both windows. This can make synchronizing file directories between computers a snap!

After you connect, files are transferred between the local and remote computers by clicking a file, and then clicking the appropriate direction arrow in the gFTP dialog box. This sends (or receives) files between computers. Another feature of gFTP, when used during

GNOME-enabled X11 sessions, is drag and drop. This means that you can transfer files to a remote computer by clicking and dragging a file from the desktop of the GNU Midnight Commander, and then releasing the file onto the remote computer's file listing window.

Aside from a short man page and README file under the `/usr/share/doc/` `gftp-2.0-7b` directory, you won't find any documentation for the gFTP client on your system. For the latest developments concerning gFTP, go to `http://gftp.seul.org`.

Using the `kfm` Command

Built-in network connectivity and utility are some of the newest features brought to the graphical desktop with the advent of today's sophisticated X11 window managers and environments. One of the major benefits of using the K Desktop Environment and GNOME-aware window managers with X11 is that you can combine the drag-and-drop features of a desktop file manager with the FTP and HTTP protocols to quickly and easily download, transfer, and view files.

For example, if you have an active Internet connection and use KDE, you can use the `kfm` client to perform FTP file transfers using drag and drop. Open a `kfm` window, such as your home directory, and then type in a remote URL using the FTP form in the Location: field of the client, like this:

```
ftp://ftp.tux.org
```

After you press Enter, you'll be logged into the site. You can then click to select a file, drag its name to your desktop (or another folder), select Copy from the pop-up menu, and then watch the progress of the download, as shown in Figure 11.2.

FIGURE 11.2

The kfm client supports FTP file transfers and drag-and-drop objects over an active network!

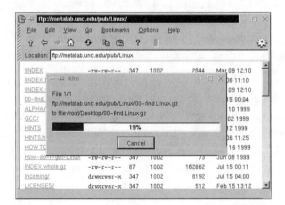

You can also use multiple selections to download multiple files, or just create symbolic links! If you just create a symbolic link to a file, such as a graphic, when you click on the link on your desktop, and have an active Internet connection, the file will be downloaded and displayed automatically!

Summary

You might think the proliferation of the World Wide Web would make FTP servers extinct; however, that is not the case. People are still deploying FTP sites in full force because of the ease with which they can be established and maintained. No cute HTML, no extra work—just put the file in the right place for downloading and let people get it.

The wealth of FTP clients and transfer tools available for Linux will make the job of transferring a large number of files between computers on a network a lot easier.

This chapter covered, in great detail, configuring the wu-ftpd server. The key points to remember when working with the FTP server are as follows:

- Keep a good watch on security announcements related to FTP servers, especially the wu-ftpd server.

- Monitor your logs for suspicious activity.

- Test your configuration carefully. With a large number of options available, make sure your server behaves the way you intended.

- When setting up file owners and permissions, be sure the permissions are correct.

- Use plenty of messages to help make your server self-documenting to outside users.

Apache Server

This chapter covers the installation, configuration, and administration of the Apache Web server.

Apache is the most widely used Web server on the Internet today, according to the NetCraft survey of Web sites. The name "Apache" appeared during the early development of the software because it was "a patchy" server, made out of patches for the freely available source code of the NCSA HTTPd Web server. For a while after the NCSA HTTPd project was discontinued, a number of people wrote a variety of patches for the code, either to fix bugs or to add features that they wanted. There was a lot of this code floating around and people were freely sharing it, but it was completely unmanaged. After a while, Bob Behlendorf and Cliff Skolnick set up a centralized repository of these patches, and the Apache project was born. The project is still composed of a rather small core group of programmers, but anyone is welcome to submit patches to the group for possible inclusion in the code.

In the last couple of years, there has been a surge of interest in the Apache project, partially buoyed by the new interest in Open Source. It's also due, in part, to IBM's commitment to support and use Apache as the basis for the company's Web offerings. They have dedicated substantial resources to the project because it made more sense to use an established, proven Web server than to try to write their own. The consequences of this interest have been a stable version for the Windows NT operating system and an accelerated release schedule.

In mid-1999 The Apache Software Foundation was incorporated as a not-for-profit company. A board of directors, who are elected on an annual basis by the ASF members, oversees the company. This company provides a foundation for several different Open Source Software development projects—including the Apache Web Server project.

The best places to find out about Apache are the Apache Group's Web site, `http://www.apache.org/`, and the Apache Week Web site, `http://www.apacheweek.com/`, where you can subscribe to receive Apache Week by email to keep up on the latest developments in the project.

Tip

In addition to the extensive online documentation, you will also find the complete documentation for Apache in the HTML directory of your Apache server. You can access this documentation by looking at `http://localhost/manual/` on your new Red Hat system, with one of the Web browsers included on your system. If you do not find Apache's documentation at this location, you may have to install it yourself. You install it like this (the version number can vary):

```
rpm -Uvh apache-manual-1.3.12-25.i386.rpm
```

Red Hat ships with as recent a version of Apache as possible, but it quickly gets old due to Apache's rapid release schedule. You can obtain Apache as an RPM (Red Hat Package Manager) installation file in the /pub/redhat/current area of Red Hat's FTP server, or you can get the source code from the Apache Web site and, in true Linux tradition, build it for yourself.

This chapter covers version 1.3.12, which ships with Red Hat 7.

Server Installation

You can install Apache from RPMs or by building the source code yourself. The Apache source builds on just about any UNIX-like operating system, and also on Win32.

If you are about to install a new version of Apache, it is probably a good idea to shut down the old server. Even if it is unlikely that the old server will interfere with the installation procedure, shutting it down ensures that there will be no problems. If you do not know how to stop Apache, look at the section "Starting and Stopping the Server" later in this chapter.

Installing from the RPM

You can find the Apache RPM either on the Red Hat Linux installation media, on the Red Hat FTP server, or one of its many mirror sites. You will want to check the updates.redhat.com FTP site (or one of the mirrors) as often as possible. In the directory corresponding to your Red Hat version you will from time to time find updates for Apache. These can be important updates that fix bugs or security breaches. When an updated version comes out, you will want to install it as quickly as possible in order to be secure.

> **Note**
>
> If you want as recent a version as possible you might want to look into Red Hat's Rawhide distribution, also available on their FTP server. This distribution is experimental and always contains the latest versions of all RPMs. However, do note that the Apache package might depend on new functionality available in other RPMs in the Rawhide distribution. Therefore, you might need to install many new RPMs to be able to use packages from Rawhide. If you want to use an Apache version from the Rawhide distribution, it might be a better option to download the source code RPM, or SRPM as they are called, and compile it yourself—that way you should be able to avoid dependencies on other, new packages.

Caution

You should be wary of installing experimental packages, especially on servers that are used in "real life." Very carefully test the packages beforehand!

After you have obtained an Apache RPM, you can install it with the command-line `rpm` tool by typing the following:

`rpm -Uvh latest_apache.rpm`

where `latest_apache.rpm` is the name of the latest Apache RPM.

For more information on installing packages with RPM, see Chapter 21, "Linux System Administration."

The Apache RPM installs files in the following directories:

- `/etc/httpd/conf`—This directory contains all the Apache configuration files, which include `access.conf`, `httpd.conf`, and `srm.conf`. See the section on configuration files later in this chapter.

- `/etc/rc.d/`—The tree under this directory contains the system startup scripts. The Apache RPM installs a complete set for the Web server. These scripts, which you can use to start and stop the server from the command line, will also automatically start and stop the server when the computer is halted, started, or rebooted. See Chapter 9, "System Startup and Shutdown," for information about these startup scripts.

- `/var/www`—The RPM installs the default server icons, CGI programs, and HTML files in this location. If you want to keep Web content elsewhere, you can do so by making the appropriate changes in the server configuration files.

- `/var/www/html/manual/`—If you have installed the apache-manual RPM, you will find a copy of the Apache documentation in HTML format here. You can access it with a Web browser by going to `http://localhost/manual/`.

- `/usr/share/man`—The RPM contains manual pages, which are placed in this directory.

- `/usr/sbin`—The executable programs are placed in this directory. This includes the server executable itself, as well as various utilities.

- `/usr/bin`—Some of the utilities from the Apache package are placed here—for example, the `htpasswd` program, which is used for generating authentication password files.

- /var/log/http—The server log files are placed in this directory. By default, there are two log files—access_log and error_log—but you can define any number of custom logs containing a variety of information. See the section on logging later in this chapter.

- /usr/src/redhat/SOURCES/—This directory contains a tar archive containing the source code for Apache, and in some cases patches for the source. You must have installed the Apache SRPM for these files to be created.

When Apache is being run, it will also create files in the following directories:

- /var/run/lock—The startup script adds a lock file, called httpd.

- /var/run—Apache will create a file, httpd.pid, containing the process ID of Apache's parent process.

> **Note**
>
> If you are upgrading to a newer version of Apache, RPM will not write over your current configuration files. RPM moves your current files and appends the extension .rpmnew to them. For example, srm.conf becomes srm.conf.rpmnew.

Building the Source Yourself

There are several ways in which you can obtain the source code for Apache. The Red Hat distribution has SRPMs containing the source of Apache, which sometimes include patches to make it work better with Red Hat's distribution. The most up-to-date versions are found at ftp://updates.redhat.com. When you install one of these SRPMs, a tar archive containing the Apache source will be created in /usr/src/redhat/SOURCES/. You can also download the source directly from http://www.apache.org/.

Once you have a tar file, you will need to unroll it in a temporary directory somewhere nice, like /tmp. This will create a directory called apache_*version_number*, where *version_number* is the version that you have downloaded (for example, apache_1.3.12).

There are two ways to compile the source—the old, familiar way (at least, to those of us who have been using Apache for many years) and the new, easy way.

The Easy Way

To build Apache the easy way, just run the ./configure in the directory just created. You can provide it with a --prefix argument to install in a directory other than the default, which is /usr/local/apache/.

```
./configure --prefix=/preferred/directory/
```

This will create a file called `Configuration` in the `src/` subdirectory. It also generates the makefile that will be used to compile the server code.

Once this step is done, type **make** to compile the server code. After the compilation is completed type **make install** to install the server. You can now configure the server via the configuration files. See the section "Runtime Server Configuration Settings" for more information.

> **Note**
>
> The Apache Autoconf-style interface (APACI), described here, is only available in version 1.3 and later.

The Advanced Way

If you want to do things the old-fashioned way, or you just want more control over the way that your server is built, follow these steps:

1. In the source directory, copy the file `Configuration.tmpl` to `Configuration` and open up `Configuration` with your favorite editor.
2. Modify the compiler flags if, and only if, you know what you're doing. Uncomment those modules that you would like included, comment out modules that you don't want, or add lines for custom modules that you have written or acquired elsewhere.
3. Run the `Configure` script to create the `Makefile`.
4. Finally, compile and install the server with **make** and **make install**.

> **Tip**
>
> You may want to symlink, using the `ln` command, the existing file locations (listed in the RPM installation section earlier in this chapter) to the new locations of the files because the default install locations are not the same as when the RPM installs the files. Failure to do this could result in your Web server process not being started automatically at system startup.
>
> I would strongly recommend that you stick with the RPM version of Apache until you really know your way around what happens at system startup.

File Locations After Manual Installation

As of version 1.3.4, all of the files are placed in various subdirectories of
/usr/local/apache (or whatever directory you specified with the --prefix parameter).
Before version 1.3.4, files were placed in /usr/local/etc/httpd.

The following is a list of those directories that are used by Apache, as well as brief comments on their usage.

- /usr/local/apache/conf—This directory contains all the Apache configuration files, which include access.conf, httpd.conf, and srm.conf. See the section on configuration files later in this chapter.

- /usr/local/apache—The cgi-bin, icons, and htdocs subdirectories contain the CGI programs, standard icons, and default HTML documents, respectively.

- /usr/local/apache/bin—The executable programs are placed in this directory.

- /usr/local/apache/logs—The server log files are placed in this directory. By default, there are two log files—access_log and error_log—but you can define any number of custom logs containing a variety of information. See the section on logging later in this chapter.

Runtime Server Configuration Settings

At this point, you have successfully installed the Apache server one way or another. It will run, but perhaps not quite the way that you want it to. This section talks about configuring the server so that it works exactly how you want it to work.

Traditionally, Apache had the runtime configurations in three files: httpd.conf, access.conf, and srm.conf. This was mainly because that's how the config files were written for NCSA, and Apache grew out of NCSA. And although there was some logic behind the original decision to split configuration options into three files, this made less and less sense over time—especially since you could put any configuration option in any file and it would work.

So, starting with Apache 1.3.4, the runtime configurations are stored in just one file—httpd.conf. The other files are still there, but they contain only a comment telling you that the files are there for purely historical reasons and that you should really put all of your configuration files in httpd.conf.

> **Note**
>
> You can still use the three-configuration-file approach if you really want to. It makes sense to some people. However, the distinction between what should go in one file or another has become increasingly blurred over the years.
>
> If you want to keep using the three-file system, I've noted when these files appeared in `srm.conf` or `access.conf` prior to version 1.3.4.

Apache reads the data from the configuration file(s) when the parent process is started (or restarted). You can also cause the Apache process to reload configuration information with the command `/etc/rc.d/init.d/httpd reload`. This is discussed later in the section "Starting and Stopping the Server."

You perform runtime configuration of your server with *configuration directives*, which are commands that set some option. You use them to tell the server about various options that you want to enable, such as the location of files important to the server configuration and operation. Configuration directives follow this syntax:

```
directive option option...
```

You specify one directive per line. Some directives only set a value such as a filename, whereas others let you specify various options. Some special directives, called *sections*, look like HTML tags. Section directives are surrounded by angle brackets, such as `<directive>`. Sections usually enclose a group of directives that apply only to the directory specified in the section:

```
<Directory somedir/in/your/tree>
  directive option option
  directive option option
</Directory>
```

All sections are closed with a matching section tag that looks like `</directive>`. Note that section tags, like any other directives, are specified one per line.

Editing `httpd.conf`

Most of the default settings in the config files are okay to keep, particularly if you have installed the server in a default location and are not doing anything unusual on your server. In general, if you don't understand what a particular directive is for, you should leave it set to the default value.

Table 12.1 lists some of the settings that you *might* want to change.

TABLE 12.1 Some Commonly Used Configuration Directives

Directive	*Description*
ServerType	This is mentioned more as a curiosity than anything else. The two server types are standalone and inetd. You will want this to be standalone in almost every imaginable case. Setting the ServerType to inetd will cause a new server to be spawned to handle every incoming HTTP request. That server will then die off immediately when the request has been served. This is presumably useful for testing configuration changes because the configuration files will be reloaded each time a new server process is spawned. Of course, this is extremely slow, since you have the overhead of server startup with every request.
ServerRoot	This directive sets the absolute path to your server directory. This directive tells the server where to find all the resources and configuration files. Many of these resources are specified in the configuration files relative to the ServerRoot directory.
	Your ServerRoot directive should be set to /etc/httpd if you installed the RPM and /usr/local/apache (or whatever directory you chose when you compiled Apache) if you installed from the source.
Port	The Port directive indicates which port you want your server to run on. By default, this is set to 80, which is the standard HTTP port number. You may want to run your server on another port, such as for running a test server that you don't want people to find by accident. Don't confuse this with real security! See the section "Authentication and Access Control" for more information on how to secure parts of your Web server.
User and Group	The User and Group directives should be set to the UID and group ID (GID) that the server will use to process requests. There are generally two ways to set this up. The most common way is to set user to nobody and group to nobody. The other way, which is used in Red Hat, is to set them to a user with few or no privileges. In this case, they are set to user apache and group apache. As you can imagine, this is a user defined specifically to run Apache. If you want to use a different UID or GID, you need to be aware that the server will run with the permissions of the user and group set here. This means that in the event of a security breach, whether on the server or (more likely) in your own CGI programs, those programs will run with the assigned UID. If the server runs as root or some other privileged user, someone can exploit the security holes and do nasty things to your site. Always think in terms of the specified user running a command like rm -rf /, since that would wipe all files from your system. That should convince you that leaving this as a user with no privileges is probably a good thing.

TABLE 12.1   continued

Directive	Description
	Instead of specifying the User and Group directives using names, you can specify them using the UID and GID numbers. If you use numbers, be sure that the numbers you specify correspond to the user and group you want and that they are preceded by the pound (#) symbol.

Here's how these directives look if specified by name:

```
User nobody

Group nogroup
```

Here's the same specification by UID and GID:

```
User #-1

Group #-1
```

Directive	Description
ServerAdmin	The ServerAdmin directive should be set to the address of the Webmaster managing the server. It should be a valid email address or alias, such as *webmaster@gnulix.org*. Setting this value to a valid address is important because this address will be returned to a visitor when a problem occurs on the server.
ServerName	The ServerName directive sets the hostname the server will return. Set it to a fully qualified domain name (FQDN). For example, set it to *www.your.domain* rather than simply *www*. This is particularly important if this machine will be accessible from the Internet rather than just on your local network. You really do not need to set this unless you want a different name returned than the machine's canonical name. If this value is not set, the server will figure out the name by itself and set it to its canonical name. However, you might want the server to return a friendlier address, such as *www.your.domain*. Whatever you do, ServerName should be a real Domain Name System (DNS) name for your network. If you are administering your own DNS, remember to add an alias for your host. If someone else manages the DNS for you, ask that person to set this name for you.
DocumentRoot	Set this directive to the absolute path of your document tree, which is the top directory from which Apache will serve files. By default, it is set to /var/www/html or, if you built the source code yourself, /usr/local/apache/htdocs (if you did not choose another directory when you compiled Apache). Prior to version 1.3.4, this directive appears in srm.conf.

TABLE 12.1 continued

Directive	Description
UserDir	This directive defines the directory relative to a local user's home directory where that user can put public HTML documents. It's relative because each user will have his or her own HTML directory. The default setting for this directive is `public_html`. So, each user will be able to create a directory called `public_html` under his or her home directory, and HTML documents placed in that directory will be available as `http://servername/~username`, where *username* is the username of the particular user. Prior to version 1.3.4, this directive appears in `srm.conf`.
DirectoryIndex	The `DirectoryIndex` directive indicates which file should be served as the index for a directory, such as which file should be served if the URL `http://gnulix.org/SomeDirectory/` is requested. It is often useful to put a list of files here so that, in the event that `index.html` (the default values) is not found, another file can be served instead. The most useful application of this is to have a CGI program run as the default action in a directory. If you also have users who make their Web pages on Windows, you might want to add `index.htm` as well. In this case, the directive would look like `DirectoryIndex index.html index.cgi index.htm`. Prior to version 1.3.4, this directive appears in `srm.conf`.

Caution

Allowing individual users to put Web content on your server poses several important security considerations. If you are operating a Web server on the Internet rather than on a private network, you should read the WWW Security FAQ by Lincoln Stein. You can find a copy at `http://www.w3.org/Security/Faq/www-security-faq.html`.

.htaccess Files

Almost any directive that appears in the configuration files can appear in an `.htaccess` file. This file, specified in the `AccessFileName` directive in `httpd.conf` (or `srm.conf` prior to version 1.3.4) sets configurations on a per-directory basis. As the system administrator, you can specify both the name of this file and which of the server configurations may be overridden by the contents of this file. This is especially useful for sites where there are multiple content providers and you want to control what these people can do with their space.

12

APACHE SERVER

To limit what .htaccess files can override, you need to use the AllowOverride directive. This can be set globally or per directory. To configure which options are available by default, you need to use the Options directive.

> **Note**
>
> Prior to version 1.3.4, these directives appear in the access.conf file.

For example, in your httpd.conf file, you will see the following:

```
# Each directory to which Apache has access can be configured with respect
# to which services and features are allowed and/or disabled in that
# directory (and its subdirectories).
#
# First, we configure the "default" to be a very restrictive set of
# permissions.
#
<Directory />
    Options FollowSymLinks
    AllowOverride None
</Directory>
```

Options Directives

Options can be None, All, or any combination of Indexes, Includes, FollowSymLinks, ExecCGI, or MultiViews. MultiViews is not included in All and must be specified explicitly. These options are explained in Table 12.2.

TABLE 12.2 Switches Used by the Options Directive

Switch	Description
None	None of the available options are enabled for this directory.
All	All of the available options, except for MultiViews, are enabled for this directory.
Indexes	In the absence of an index.html file or another DirectoryIndex file, a listing of the files in the directory will be generated as an HTML page for display to the user.
Includes	Server-Side Includes (SSIs) are permitted in this directory. This can also be written as IncludesNoExec if you want to allow includes, but don't want to allow the exec option in these includes. For security reasons, this is usually a good idea in directories over which you do not have complete control, such as UserDir directories.

TABLE 12.2 continued

Switch	Description
FollowSymLinks	Allows access to directories that are symbolically linked to a document directory. This is usually a bad idea, and you should not set this globally for the whole server. You might want to set this for individual directories, but only if you have a really good reason to do so. This option is a potential security risk because it allows Web users to escape from the document directory, and it could potentially allow them access to portions of your filesystem where you really don't want people poking around.
ExecCGI	CGI programs are permitted in this directory, even if it is not a ScriptAlias-ed directory.
MultiViews	This is part of the mod_negotiation module. When the document that the client requests is not found, the server tries to figure out which document best suits the client's requirements. See http://localhost/manuals/mod/mod_negotiation.html for your local copy of the Apache documentation.

12

APACHE SERVER

Note

These directives also affect all subdirectories of the specified directory.

AllowOverrides Directives

The AllowOverrides directives specify which options .htaccess files can override. You can set this per directory. For example, you can have different standards about what can be overridden in the main document root and in UserDir directories.

This capability is particularly useful for user directories, where the user does not have access to the main server configuration files.

AllowOverrides can be set to All or any combination of Options, FileInfo, AuthConfig, and Limit. These options are explained in Table 12.3.

TABLE 12.3 Switches Used by the AllowOverrides Directive

Switch	Description
Options	The .htaccess file can add options not listed in the Options directive for this directory.
FileInfo	The .htaccess file can include directives for modifying document type information.
AuthConfig	The .htaccess file may contain authorization directives.
Limit	The .htaccess file may contain allow, deny, and order directives.

Authentication and Access Control

There will be times when you have material on your Web site that is not supposed to be available for the general public. You need to be able to lock out these areas somehow and only provide the means to unlock them to the right users. There are several ways in which you can accomplish this type of access, authentication, and authorization with Apache. You can use different criteria to control access to these sections, from simply checking the client's IP address or hostname to asking for a username and password. This section briefly covers some of these methods.

Access Restrictions with `allow` and `deny`

One of the simplest ways to provide access to a specific group of users is to restrict accesses based on IP addresses or hostnames. Apache uses the `allow` and `deny` directives to accomplish this. Both of these directives take an address expression as a parameter. See the following list for possible values and usage of the address expression:

- `all` can be used to affect all hosts.
- A host or domain name, which can either be a partially or a fully qualified domain name. For example: `test.gnulix.org` or `gnulix.org`.
- An IP address, which can be either full or partial. For example: `212.85.67` or `212.85.67.66`.
- A network/netmask pair, such as `212.85.67.0/255.255.255.0`.
- A network address specified in CIDR format. For example, `212.85.67.0/24`. This is the CIDR notation for the same network and netmask that was used in the previous example.

If you have the choice, it is preferable to base your access control on IP addresses, rather than hostnames. This is faster, because no name lookups are necessary—the IP address of the client is included with each request.

There is also another way to use `allow` and `deny`. Apart from specifying a hostname or an IP address, you can also check for the existence of a specific environment variable. For example, the following statement will deny access to a request with a context that contains an environment variable named NOACCESS:

```
deny from env=NOACCESS
```

The default behavior of Apache is to apply all the `deny` directives first and then check the `allow` directives. If you want to change this order you can use the `order` statement. There are three different ways in which Apache may interpret this statement:

- `Order deny,allow`—The deny directives are evaluated before `allow`. If a host is not specifically denied access it will be allowed to access the resource. This is the default ordering if nothing else is specified.

- `Order allow,deny`—All `allow` directives are evaluated before deny. If a host is not specifically allowed access it will be denied access to the resource.

- `Order mutual-failure`—Only hosts that are specified in an `allow` directive and at the same time do not appear in a `deny` directive will be allowed access. If a host does not appear in either directive it will not be granted access.

Consider this example. Suppose you only wanted to allow persons from within your own domain to access the `server-status` resource on your Web. If your domain were named `gnulix.org` you would add something along these lines in your configuration file:

```
<Location /server-status>
    SetHandler server-status
    Order deny,allow
    Deny from all
    Allow from gnulix.org
</Location>
```

Authentication

Authentication is the process of ensuring that visitors really are who they claim to be. By specifying that only certain users are allowed to access an area, Apache will request that the client authenticate itself before granting access. See Figure 12.1 for an example of how an authentication dialog might look if you are using the `konqueror` browser.

FIGURE 12.1

The authentication dialog.

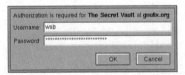

There are several methods of authentication in Apache. We will cover the most common method: Basic authentication. Using this method a user will be required to supply a user-name and a password to access the protected resources. Apache will then verify that the user is allowed to access the resource in question. Should this be the case the password will be verified. If this also checks out, the user will have been authorized and the request will be served.

HTTP is a stateless protocol, therefore the authentication information must be included with each request. This means that each request to a password-protected area will be larger and therefore somewhat slower. Taking this into account, it is a good idea to protect only those areas that absolutely need it.

In order to use Basic authentication you will need a file that lists which users are allowed to access the resources. This list will consist of a plain text file containing name and password pairs. It looks very much like the user file of your Linux system—that is, `/etc/passwd`. In fact, you could actually use this as a user list for authentication. But this is a very bad idea!

> **Caution**
>
> When you are using Basic authentication, passwords and usernames are sent as base64-encoded text from the client to the server—which is just as readable as plain text. The username and password are included in each request that is sent to the server. So anyone who might be snooping on Net traffic could be able to get hold of this information!

To create a user file for Apache, use the `htpasswd` command. This is included with the Apache package and if you installed using the RPMs it will be found in `/usr/bin`. Running `htpasswd` without any options will produce the following output:

```
Usage:
        htpasswd [-cmdps] passwordfile username
        htpasswd -b[cmdps] passwordfile username password

 -c  Create a new file.
 -m  Force MD5 encryption of the password.
 -d  Force CRYPT encryption of the password (default).
 -p  Do not encrypt the password (plaintext).
 -s  Force SHA encryption of the password.
 -b  Use the password from the command line rather than prompting for it.
On Windows and TPF systems the '-m' flag is used by default.
On all other systems, the '-p' flag will probably not work.
```

As you can see, it is not a very difficult command to use. For example, to create a new user file named `gnulixusers` with a user named `wsb` you would need do something like this:

```
htpasswd -c gnulixusers wsb
```

You would then be prompted for a password for the user. To add more users you would repeat the same procedure, only omitting the `-c` flag.

You can also create user group files. The format of these files is more or less like the `/etc/groups`. The first entry on a line is the group name. A colon follows this and then a list of all users is specified, separated by spaces. For example, an entry might look like this:

```
gnulickers: wsb pgj jp ajje nadia rkr hak
```

Now that you know how to create a user file, it is time to look at how Apache might use this to protect Web resources. First of all you will want to point Apache to the user file. You do this with the `AuthUserFile` directive. As its parameter the directive takes the file path to the user file. If it is not absolute—that is, beginning with a /—it will be assumed that it is relative to the `ServerRoot`. Using the `AuthGroupFile` directive, you can specify a group file in the same manner.

The next directive you need to use is `AuthType`. This sets the type of authentication to be used for this resource. Because this section is looking at how to use Basic authentication, this will be set to `Basic`.

Now you need to decide which realm the resource is to belong to. This is used to group different resources that will share the same users for authorization. The realm can consist of just about any string. The realm will be shown in the Authentication dialog on the user's Web browser. Therefore, it is best to set the realm string to something informative. The realm is defined with the `AuthName` directive.

Finally, you need to state what type of users are required for the resource. You do this with the `require` directive. There are three ways to use this directive:

- If you specify `valid-user` as an option, any user in the user file will be allowed to access the resource (that is, provided he or she also entered the correct password).
- You can specify a list of users who are allowed access with the `users` option.
- You can specify a list of groups with the `group` option. Entries in the group list as well as the user list are separated by a space.

Returning to the `server-status` example from earlier, instead of letting users access the `server-status` resource based on hostname, change it to require that they be authenticated. You can do this with the following entry in the configuration file:

```
<Location /server-status>
    SetHandler server-status
    AuthType Basic
    AuthName "Server status"
    AuthUserFile "gnulixusers"
    Require valid-user
</Location>
```

Final Words on Access Control

If you have host-based as well as user-based protection on a resource, the default behavior of Apache is to require that the requester satisfy both controls. But you want to mix host-based and user-based protection and allow access to a resource if either method succeeds. You can do this using the `satisfy` directive. This can either be set to `All` (this is the default) or Any. When set to All, all access control methods must be satisfied before the resource is served. If it is set to Any, the resource is served if any of the access conditions are met.

Here's another example. Once again using the previous server-status example, this time combine access methods so that all users from the Gnulix domain are allowed access and those from outside the domain must identify themselves before gaining access. You can do this with the following:

```
<Location /server-status>
    SetHandler server-status
    Order deny,allow
    Deny from all
    Allow from gnulix.org
    AuthType Basic
    AuthName "Server status"
    AuthUserFile "gnulixusers"
    Require valid-user
    Satisfy Any
</Location>
```

There are more ways to protect material on you Web server, but the methods discussed here should get you started and will probably be more than adequate for most circumstances. Look to Apache's online documentation for more examples of how to secure areas of your site.

Apache Modules

Apache is built upon a modular concept. At its core there is little functionality. Modules are added in order to implement more advanced features and functionality. Each module solves a well-defined problem by adding the extra features that are needed. Using this concept, you can more or less tailor Apache server to suit your exact needs.

There are close to 40 modules included with the basic Apache server. Many more are available from other developers. There is a repository for add-on modules for Apache called The Apache Module Registry, and it can be found at http://modules.apache.org/.

Each module adds new directives that can be used in your configuration files. As you might guess, there are far too many extra commands, switches, and options to describe them all in this chapter. Therefore, this section will only briefly describe those modules that are available with Red Hat's Apache installation. If you need further information on how to use a module, please refer to the online documentation for the server that is included with the Red Hat distribution or look at the Apache Groups Web site. Local copies of this documentation are located at http://localhost/manual/.

Following is an alphabetical list of those modules that are included with Red Hat's Apache RPM.

mod_access

This module gives you the ability to control access to areas on your Web server based on IP addresses, hostnames, and/or environment variables. You will be able to grant or deny access to any part of your Web server depending on those criteria. It is possible to use partial hostnames or subsets of IP addresses as access qualifiers. For example, you might want to allow anyone from within your own domain to access certain areas of your Web. See the section "Authentication and Access Control" for more information.

mod_actions

This module provides the ability to dynamically execute scripts based on the type of HTTP request. You will be able to map the execution of CGI scripts to MIME content types or request methods.

mod_alias

There are times when you need to manipulate the URLs of incoming HTTP requests. You might want to redirect the client's request to another URL, or you may want to map a part of the filesystem into your Web hierarchy. For example:

```
Alias /images/ /home/wsb/graphics/
```

This example would fetch contents from the `/home/wsb/graphics` directory for any URL that starts with `/images/`. This will be done without the client knowing anything about it. If you use a redirection, the client will be instructed to go to another URL to find the requested content.

For more advanced URL manipulation, look at `mod_rewrite` also.

mod_asis

Using this module you will be able to specify in fine detail all information that is to be included in a response. This will completely bypass any headers that Apache might otherwise have added to the response. All files with an `.asis` extension will be sent straight through to the client without any changes.

As a short example, assume that you have moved the contents from one location to another on your site. Now you need to inform people who try to access this resource that it has moved, as well as redirect them to the new location automatically. To do this you might add something like the following code into a file with an `.asis` extension.

```
Status: 301 No more old stuff!
Location: http://gnulix.org/newstuff/
Content-type: text/html

<HTML>
 <HEAD>
  <TITLE>We've moved...</TITLE>
 </HEAD>
 <BODY>
   <P>We've moved the old stuff and now you'll find it at:</P>
   <A HREF="http://gnulix.org/newstuff/">New stuff</A>!.
 </BODY>
</HTML>
```

mod_auth

This is the simplest of all user authentication schemes available for Apache, and as such it is often referred to as Basic authentication. This scheme is based on storing usernames and encrypted passwords in a text file. This file looks very much like UNIX's /etc/passwd file. These files are created with the htpasswd command. See the section "Authentication and Access Control" for more information about this subject.

mod_auth_anon

This module provides anonymous authentication similar to that of anonymous FTP. The module will allow you to define user IDs of those who are to be handled as guest users. When such a user tries to log on, she will be prompted for her email address as her password. It is possible to have Apache check the password to ensure that it is a (more or less) proper email address. Basically it ensures that there is an @ character and at least one . character in the password.

mod_auth_db

This module is very much like the mod_auth module. Rather than keeping the user data in a plain text file it uses Berkeley DB files.

mod_auth_digest

This is an extension of the basic mod_auth module. Instead of sending the user information in plain text it will be sent via the MD5 Digest Authentication process. This authentication scheme is defined in RFC 2617. This is a much more secure way of sending user data over the Internet compared to using Basic authentication. Unfortunately, not all Web browsers support this authentication scheme.

To create password files for use with `mod_auth_dbm` you will need to use the `htdigest` utility. It has more or less the same functionality as the `htpasswd` utility. See the man page of `htdigest` for further information.

> **Caution**
>
> This module is still considered experimental!

mod_autoindex

If you have not provided a default HTML file for a directory and have enabled directory indexing, this module will dynamically create a file list for the directory in question. This list will be rendered in a user-friendly manner similar to those lists that FTP provides. There are many options that will provide you with the ability to fine-tune every aspect of the look and feel of the directory listing.

mod_bandwidth

This module provides bandwidth usage limitation. It enables basic traffic shaping for replies so that the server will not become overloaded when there are too many requests. This can be applied either to parts of the server or the whole server. You may apply the module based on file size, location or domain of the client, and the location or directory of the requested material.

This is one of the third-party modules that Red Hat has added that are generally not part of the Apache distribution.

mod_cern_meta

This module gives you the ability to add additional HTTP headers to each HTTP response. You can configure Apache so that the contents of files with certain extensions, usually `.meta`, will be included together with any other HTTP headers that Apache generates.

mod_cgi

This module allows you to execute CGI scripts on you server. See the section on dynamic content for more information about how to use CGIs.

mod_digest

This module is being deprecated and will be replaced by `mod_auth_digest`. Therefore, you are probably better off using that module instead.

mod_dir

This is used to determine which files are returned automatically when a user tries to access a directory. The default is `index.html`. If you have users who create Web pages on Windows systems you will probably want to include `index.htm` as well like this:

```
DirectoryIndex index.html index.htm
```

mod_env

This module allows you to control how environment variables are passed to CGI and SSI scripts.

mod_example

This is only a demo module. Its main purpose is for people to study its source code and learn how to code new modules for Apache.

mod_expires

Use this module if you want to add an expire date to content on your site. This is accomplished by adding an Expires header to the HTTP response. Content that has expired will not be cached by Web browsers or cache servers.

mod_headers

This is a very useful module that allows you to manipulate the HTTP headers of your server's responses. You can replace, add, merge, or delete headers as you see fit. The module supplies a directive for this called `Header`. Ordering of the `Header` directive is important. A `set` followed by an `unset` for the same HTTP header will remove the header altogether. You can place `Header` directives almost anywhere within your configuration files. These directives are then processed in the following order:

1. Core Server
2. Virtual Host
3. `<Directory>` and `.htaccess` files
4. `<Location>`
5. `<Files>`

mod_imap

This module provides for server-side handling of image map files. Clickable regions are defined in a .map file. There are six directives available for use in the .map file. These are used to describe the layout of the clickable regions as well as which URLs they lead to.

mod_include

This enables the use of Server-Side Includes on your server. See the section "Dynamic Content" later in the chapter for more information about how to use SSI.

mod_info

The mod_info module provides comprehensive information about your server's configuration. For example, it will display all the modules that are installed, as well as all the directives that are used in its configuration files.

mod_log_agent

This enables you to log the content of the UserAgent header from HTTP requests. Using this information allows you to see which Web browsers visitors to your site are using.

mod_log_config

This module allows you to define how your log files should look. See the section "Logging" for further information about this subject.

mod_log_referer

This enables you to log the referer part of an HTTP request.

> **Note**
>
> As of Apache 1.3.5, this module is deprecated. Use the CustomLog directives instead. See the section on logging for more information on CustomLog.

mod_mime

This module tries to determine the MIME type of files from their extensions.

mod_mime_magic

This module tries to determine the MIME type of files by examining portions of their content.

mod_mmap_static

This module uses the mmap() function to map static pages into system memory. This is used to reduce the server latency introduced by disk access. Because these pages are cached within system memory, the server will need to be restarted if the pages are updated on disk.

> **Caution**
>
> This module is still considered experimental!

mod_negotiation

Using this module it is possible to select one of several document versions that best suits the client's capabilities. There are several options to select which criteria to use in the negotiation process. You can, for example, choose among different languages, graphics file formats, and compression methods.

mod_proxy

This module implements proxy and caching capabilities for an Apache server. It can proxy and cache FTP, CONNECT, HTTP/0.9, and HTTP/1.0 requests. This is not an ideal solution for sites that have a large number of users and therefore have very high proxy and cache requirements. However, it is more than adequate for a small number of users.

mod_put

This module implements the PUT and DELETE methods from the HTTP/1.1 protocol.

> **Caution**
>
> Because this module grants people write access, you will have to ensure that write access is limited only to trusted users!

This is one of the third-party modules that Red Hat has added. These are generally not part of the Apache distribution.

mod_rewrite

This is the Swiss army knife of URL manipulation. It allows you to perform any imaginable manipulation of URLs using powerful regular expressions. It provides rewrites, redirection, proxying, and so on. There is very little that you cannot accomplish using this module.

See `http://localhost/manual/misc/rewriteguide.html` for a cookbook, which will give you a very good overview of what this module is capable of.

mod_setenvif

This module allows you to manipulate environment variables. Using regular expressions it is possible to conditionally change the content of environment variables. The order in which `SetEnvIf` directives appear in the configuration files is important. It is possible that each `SetEnvIf` directive may reset an earlier `SetEnvIf` directive when used on the same environment variable. Be sure to keep that in mind when using the directives from this module.

mod_speling

This module automatically corrects minor typos in URLs. If no file matches the requested URL, this module will build a list of the files in the requested directory and will extract those files that are the closest matches. It will try to correct only one spelling mistake.

mod_status

This module creates a Web page containing a plethora of information about a running Apache server. The page will contain information about the internal status as well as statistics about the running Apache processes. This can be a great aid when you are trying to configure your server for maximum performance. It is also a good indicator when something is amiss with your Apache server.

mod_throttle

This module provides you with the possibility to throttle incoming requests so that the server will not become overloaded when there are too many requests. You may throttle requests directed either to a certain user's material or to a specific virtual host.

12

APACHE SERVER

You can access the documentation for this module at
`http://www.snert.com/Software/Throttle/`.

This is one of the third-party modules that Red Hat has added. These are generally not
part of the Apache distribution.

mod_unique_id

This module generates a unique request identifier for every incoming request. This ID
will be put into the `UNIQUE_ID` environment variable.

mod_userdir

This module enables you to map a subdirectory in each user's home directory into your
Web tree. The module provides several different ways to accomplish this.

mod_usertrack

This module generates a cookie for each user session. This can be used to track the
user's click stream within your Web tree. You will need to enable a custom log that logs
this cookie into a log file.

mod_vhost_alias

This module provides excellent support for dynamically configured mass virtual hosting.
It is especially useful for ISPs with very many virtual hosts. However, for the average
user Apache's ordinary virtual hosting support should prove to be more than sufficient.

There are two ways to host virtual hosts on an Apache server. You can either have one IP
address with multiple CNAMEs, or you can have multiple IP addresses with one name
per address. Apache has different sets of directives to handle each of these options.

Virtual Hosting

One of the more popular services to provide with a Web server is to host a virtual
domain, also known as a virtual host. This is a complete Web site with its own domain
name, as if it were a standalone machine, but it's hosted on the same machine as other
Web sites. Apache implements this capability in a simple way with directives in the
`httpd.conf` configuration file.

A new way to dynamically host virtual servers was recently added. This is enabled using
the `mod_vhost_alias` module. The module is primarily intended for ISPs and similar
large sites that host a large number of virtual sites. This is a module for more advanced

use, and as such it goes outside the scope of this introductory chapter. Instead, this section concentrates on the traditional ways of hosting virtual servers.

> **Note**
>
> For information on setting up your Linux machine with multiple IP addresses or giving your Linux machine multiple CNAMEs, see Chapter 14, "Domain Name Service and Dynamic Host Configuration Protocol."

Address-Based Virtual Hosts

Once you have configured your Linux machine with multiple IP addresses, setting up Apache to serve them as different Web sites is quite simple. You need only put a `VirtualHost` directive in your `httpd.conf` file for each of the addresses that you want to make an independent Web site:

```
<VirtualHost gnulix.org>
ServerName gnulix.org
DocumentRoot /home/virtual/gnulix/public_html
TransferLog /home/virtual/gnulix/logs/access_log
ErrorLog /home/virtual/gnulix/logs/error_log
</VirtualHost>
```

It is recommended that you use the IP address, rather than the hostname, in the `VirtualHost` tag.

You may specify any configuration directives within the `<VirtualHost>` tags. For example, you may want to set `AllowOverrides` directives differently for virtual hosts than you do for your main server. Any directives that are not specified default to the settings for the main server.

The directives that cannot be set in `VirtualHost` sections are `ServerType`, `StartServers`, `MaxSpareServers`, `MinSpareServers`, `MaxRequestsPerChild`, `BindAddress`, `Listen`, `PidFile`, `TypesConfig`, `ServerRoot`, and `NameVirtualHost`.

Name-Based Virtual Hosts

Name-based virtual hosts allow you to run more than one host on the same IP address. You need to add the additional names to your DNS as CNAMEs of the machine in question. When an HTTP client (Web browser) requests a document from your server, it sends with the request a variable indicating the server name from which it is requesting the document. Based on this variable, the server determines from which of the virtual hosts it should serve content.

> **Note**
>
> Some older browsers are unable to see name-based virtual hosts because this is a feature of HTTP 1.1, and those older browsers are strictly HTTP 1.0-compliant. However, many other older browsers are partially HTTP 1.1-compliant, and this is one of the parts of HTTP 1.1 that most browsers have supported for a while.

Name-based virtual hosts require just one step more than IP address-based virtual hosts. You first need to indicate which IP address has the multiple DNS names on it. This is done with the NameVirtualHost directive:

```
NameVirtualHost 212.85.67.67
```

You then need to have a section for each name on that address, setting the configuration for that name. As with IP-based virtual hosts, you only need to set those configurations that need to be different for the host. You must set the ServerName directive because that is the only thing that distinguishes one host from another:

```
<VirtualHost 212.85.67.67>
ServerName bugserver.gnulix.org
ServerAlias bugserver
DocumentRoot /home/bugserver/htdocs
ScriptAlias /home/bugserver/cgi-bin
TransferLog /home/bugserver/logs/access_log
</VirtualHost>

<VirtualHost 212.85.67.67>
ServerName pts.gnulix.org
ServerAlias pts
DocumentRoot /home/pts/htdocs
ScriptAlias /home/pts/cgi-bin
TransferLot /home/pts/logs/access_log
ErrorLog /home/pts/logs/error_log
</VirtualHost>
```

> **Tip**
>
> If you are hosting Web sites on an intranet or internal network, there is often a chance that users will use the shortened name of the machine rather than the fully qualified domain name. For example, they might type http://bugserver/index.html in their browser location field rather than http://bugserver.gnulix.org/index.html. In that case, Apache will not recognize that those two addresses should go to the same virtual host. You could get

> around this by setting up VirtualHost directives for both bugserver and
> bugserver.gnulix.org, but the easy way around this is to use the ServerAlias
> directive, which lists all valid aliases for the machine:
>
> ```
> ServerAlias bugserver
> ```

Logging

Apache provides for logging just about any information you might be interested in from Web accesses. There are two standard log files that are generated when you run your Apache server—access_log and error_log. All logs except for the error_log (by default, this is just the access_log) are generated in a format specified by the CustomLog and LogFormat directives. These directives appear in your httpd.conf file.

A new log format can be defined with the LogFormat directive:

```
LogFormat "%h %l %u %t \"%r\" %>s %b" common
```

The common log format is a good starting place for creating your own custom log formats. Note that most of the log analysis tools available will assume that you are using the common log format or the combined log format, both of which are defined in the default configuration files.

The following variables are available for LogFormat statements:

%a	Remote IP address.
%A	Local IP address.
%b	Bytes sent, excluding HTTP headers. This is shown in CLF format. For a request without any data content, a "-" will be shown instead of 0.
%B	Bytes sent, excluding HTTP headers.
%{VARIABLE}e	The contents of the environment variable VARIABLE.
%f	Filename.
%h	Remote host.
%H	Request protocol.
%{HEADER}i	The contents of HEADER; header line(s) in the request sent to the server.
%l	Remote logname (from identd, if supplied).
%m	Request method.
%{NOTE}n	The contents of note NOTE from another module.

12

APACHE SERVER

%{HEADER}o	The contents of HEADER; header line(s) in the reply.
%p	The canonical port of the server serving the request.
%P	The process ID of the child that serviced the request.
%q	The contents of the query string, prepended with a ? character. If there is no query string this will evaluate to an empty string.
%r	First line of request.
%s	Status. For requests that were internally redirected, this is the status of the *original* request—%>s for the last.
%t	Time, in common log format time format.
%{format}t	The time, in the form given by format, which should be in strftime(3) format. See the section "Basic SSI Directives" for a complete list of available formatting options.
%T	The time taken to serve the request, in seconds.
%u	Remote user from auth; may be bogus if return status (%s) is 401.
%U	The URL path requested.
%V	The server name according to the UseCanonicalName directive.
%v	The canonical ServerName of the server serving the request.

In each variable, you can put a conditional in front of the variable that will determine whether the variable is displayed. If it is not displayed, - will be displayed instead. These conditionals are in the form of a list of numerical return values. For example, %!401u will display the value of REMOTE_USER unless the return code is 401.

You can then specify the location and format of a log file using the CustomLog directive:

```
CustomLog logs/access_log common
```

If it is not specified as an absolute path, the location of the log file is assumed to be relative to the ServerRoot.

Dynamic Content

The most common way to provide dynamic content on Web sites is with CGI (Common Gateway Interface) programs. The CGI is a specification of communication between server processes (such as programs that generate dynamic documents) and the server itself. Server-Side Includes (SSIs) allow output from CGI programs, or other programs, to be inserted into existing HTML pages.

Another way to add dynamic content to your Web site is to use PHP. This is an HTML-embedded scripting language that was designed specifically for Web usage. The PHP module for Apache is one of the most popular third-party modules available.

CGI

By default, you may put any CGI program in the `ScriptAlias` directory on your server. These programs must be executable by the user as which the server is running. This usually means that you will need to change the mode of the files to 555 so that the user whom Apache is running as can execute them. The default in Red Hat is that Apache runs as a user named `apache`.

```
chmod 555 program.cgi
```

In order to execute CGI programs outside of the `ScriptAlias` directory, you will need to enable the `ExecCGI` option for that directory. This is done either in your `httpd.conf` file (`access.conf` prior to version 1.3.4) or in an `.htaccess` file in the directory.

CGI programs can be written in any language. The most popular languages for CGI programming are Perl and C. You may want to pick up a good book on CGI programming, such as *CGI Programming With Perl, Second Edition*, since this is not intended to be a CGI book.

To test whether you have CGI configured correctly, try the CGI program in Listing 12.1, written in Perl, which displays the values of the HTTP environment variables.

LISTING 12.1   environment.pl

```
#!/usr/bin/perl -w

print <<EOF;
"Content-type: text/html

<HTML>
 <HEAD>
  <TITLE>Simple CGI program</TITLE>
 </HEAD>
 <BODY>
EOF
for (keys %ENV)    {
    print "  $_ = $ENV{$_}<BR>\n";
}
print <<EOF;
 </BODY>
</HTML>
EOF
```

If you are going to be writing CGI programs in Perl, you may want to look at the CGI modules that come bundled with Perl. There is also an extensive module library for Perl, which contains many modules designed to be used when writing CGIs. The archive can be accessed at `http://www.cpan.org`.

If you are using many CGIs written in Perl you may want to look into the `mod_perl` module. It embeds a Perl interpreter within the Apache server. This will result in faster execution times for your CGIs because there will be no need to start up a new Perl interpreter for each request. However, this will make the memory footprint of each Apache process much larger.

SSI

Server-Side Includes (SSIs) are directives written directly into an HTML page, which the server parses when the page is served to the Web client. They can be used to include other files, the output from programs, or environment variables.

The most common way to enable SSI is to indicate that files with a certain filename extension (typically `.shtml`) are to be parsed by the server when they are served. This is accomplished with the following lines in your `httpd.conf` file (`srm.conf` prior to version 1.3.4):

```
# To use server-parsed HTML files
#
#AddType text/html .shtml
#AddHandler server-parsed .shtml
```

If you uncomment the `AddType` and `AddHandler` lines, you will tell the server to parse all `.shtml` files for SSI directives.

The less commonly used, but in my opinion much better, way of enabling SSI is with the `XBitHack` directive. `XBitHack` can be set to a value of on or off, and can be set in either your configuration file or in `.htaccess` files. If the `XBitHack` directive is on, it indicates that all files with the user execute bit set should be parsed for SSI directives. This has two main advantages. One is that you do not need to rename a file, and change all links to that file, simply because you want to add a little dynamic content to it. The other reason is more cosmetic—users looking at your Web content cannot tell by looking at the filename that you are generating a page dynamically, and so your wizardry is just that tiny bit more impressive.

Another positive side effect of using `XBitHack` is that it enables you to control how clients should cache your page. Usually pages containing SSI statements will not contain a `Last-modified` HTTP header. Therefore they will not be cached by proxies nor Web browsers. If you enable `XBitHack`, the `group-execute` bit for files will control whether or not a `Last-modified` header should be generated. It will be set to the same value as the last modified time of the file. Be sure to use this only on files that really are supposed to be cached.

In addition to these directives, the following directive must be specified for directories where you want to permit SSI.

```
Options Includes
```

This may be set in the server configuration file or in an `.htaccess` file.

Basic SSI Directives

SSI directives look rather like HTML comment tags. The syntax is as follows:

```
<!--#element attribute=value attribute=value ... -->
```

The `element` can be one of the following:

config   This lets you set various configuration options regarding how the document parsing is handled. Because the page is parsed from top to bottom, `config` directives should appear at the top of the HTML document. There are three configurations that can be set with this command:

errmsg   Sets the error message that is returned to the client if something goes wrong while parsing the document. This is usually [`an error occurred while processing this directive`], but it can be set to anything with this directive.

Example: `<!--#config errmsg="[It's broken, dude]" -->`

sizefmt   Sets the format used to display file sizes. You can set the value to `bytes` to display the exact file size in bytes, or `abbrev` to display the size in KB or MB.

Example: `<!--#config sizefmt="bytes" -->`

timefmt   Sets the format used to display times. The format of the value is the same as is used in the `strftime` function used by C (and Perl) to display dates, shown in the following table.

%%	Format
%a	Day of the week abbr.
%A	Day of the week
%b	Month abbr.

%%	Format
%B	Month
%c	ctime format: `Sat Nov 19 21:05:57 1994`
%d	Numeric day of the month
%e	DD
%D	MM/DD/YY
%h	Month abbr.
%H	Hour, 24-hour clock, leading 0's
%I	Hour, 12-hour clock, leading 0's
%j	Day of the year
%k	Hour
%l	Hour, 12-hour clock
%m	Month number, starting with 1
%M	Minute, leading 0's
%n	NEWLINE
%o	Ornate day of month—1st, 2nd, 25th, and so on
%p	AM or PM
%r	Time format: `09:05:57 PM`
%R	Time format: `21:05`
%S	Seconds, leading 0's
%t	Tab
%T	Time format: `21:05:57`
%U	Week number; Sunday as first day of week
%w	Day of the week, numerically; Sunday == 0
%W	Week number; Monday as first day of week
%x	Date format: `11/19/94`
%X	Time format: `21:05:57`
%y	Year (2 digits)
%Y	Year (4 digits)
%Z	Time zone in ASCII, such as PST

echo   Displays any one of the include variables, listed below. Times are displayed in the time format specified by `timefmt`. The variable to be displayed is indicated with the `var` attribute.

DATE_GMT	The current date in Greenwich Mean Time.
DATE_LOCAL	The current date in the local time zone.
DOCUMENT_NAME	The filename (excluding directories) of the document requested by the user.
DOCUMENT_URI	The (%-decoded) URL path of the document requested by the user. Note that in the case of nested include files, this is not the URL for the current document.
LAST_MODIFIED	The last modification date of the document requested by the user.

exec   Executes a shell command or a CGI program, depending on the parameters provided. Valid attributes are `cgi` and `cmd`.

cgi	The URL of a CGI program to be executed. The URL needs to be a local CGI, not one located on another machine. The CGI program is passed the QUERY_STRING and PATH_INFO that were originally passed to the requested document, so the URL specified cannot contain this information. You should really use `include virtual` instead of this directive.
cmd	A shell command to be executed. The results will be displayed on the HTML page.

fsize   Displays the size of a file specified by either the `file` or `virtual` attribute. Size is displayed as specified with the `sizefmt` directive.

file	The path (filesystem path) to a file, either relative to the `root` if the value starts with /, or relative to the current directory if not.
virtual	The relative URL path to a file.

flastmod   Displays the last modified date of a file. The desired file is specified as with the `fsize` directive.

include   Includes the contents of a file. The file is specified with the `file` and `virtual` attributes, as with `fsize` and `flastmod`. If the file specified is a CGI program and `IncludesNOEXEC` is not set, the program will be executed and the results displayed. This is to be used in preference to the `exec` directive. You can pass a QUERY_STRING with this directive, which you cannot do with the `exec` directive.

`printenv` Displays all existing variables. There are no attributes.

Example: `<!--#printenv -->`

`set` Sets the value of a variable. Attributes are `var` and `value`.

Example: `<!--#set var="animal" value="cow" -->`

> **Note**
>
> All defined CGI environment variables are also allowed as `include` variables.

> **Note**
>
> In your configuration files (or in .htaccess), you can specify `Options IncludesNOEXEC` to disallow the `exec` directive, as this is the least secure of the SSI directives. Be especially cautious when Web users are able to create content (like a guest book or discussion board) and these options are enabled!

These variables can be used elsewhere with some of the following directives.

Flow Control

Using the variables set with the `set` directive and the various environment variables and include variables, there is a limited flow control syntax that can be used to generate a certain amount of dynamic content on server-parsed pages.

The syntax of the `if/else` functions is as follows:

```
<!--#if expr="test_condition" -->
<!--#elif expr="test_condition" -->
<!--#else -->
<!--#endif -->
```

`expr` can be a string, which is considered true if non-empty, or a variety of comparisons between two strings. Available comparison operators are =, !=, <, <=, >, and >=. If the second string has the format /string/, the strings are compared with regular expressions. Multiple comparisons can be strung together with && (AND) and || (OR). Any text appearing between the if/elif/else directives will be displayed on the resulting page. An example of such a flow structure follows:

```
<!--#set var="agent" value="$HTTP_USER_AGENT" -->
<!--#if expr="$agent = /Mozilla/" -->
Mozilla!
```

```
<!--#else -->
Something else!
<!--#endif -->
```

This code will display "Mozilla!" if you are using a browser that passes `Mozilla` as part of its `USER_AGENT` string, and "Something else!" otherwise.

PHP

PHP can to some extent be seen as a mixture of the CGI and SSI. It is embedded in HTML as is SSI, but it provides full and rich language features. The syntax of PHP is largely inspired by C and Perl. There are also several PHP-specific features. It allows developers to rapidly design and write applications for usage on the Web.

You can use PHP with Apache in two ways. The first approach is to use it as a script engine that is run as a CGI program—much the same way as Perl is commonly used for CGIs. The other, and far superior, way is to use the `mod_php` approach. This will embed PHP within Apache. Therefore, there will be no overhead to start up PHP when an application is run. It will, however, add to the memory footprint of the Apache processes.

The `mod_php` module is included in the Red Hat distribution. You can test if it has been installed properly on your system by using this code snippet in your Web.

```
<HTML>
 <HEAD>
 <TITLE>Testing PHP</TITLE>
 </HEAD>
 <BODY>
  <H1>Testing PHP</H1>
  <P>If you have PHP installed, you'll get a greeting;</P>
  <?php print "Hello world!"; ?>
 </BODY>
</HTML>
```

PHP has far too many features to go into it in this chapter, especially since this is not a chapter on programming. However, there are several excellent PHP resources available online. The best place to start is `http://www.php.net`.

Starting and Stopping the Server

At this point, you have your Apache server installed and configured the way you want it. It's time to start it up for the first time.

Starting the Server Manually

The Apache server, httpd, has a few command-line options you can use to set some defaults specifying where httpd will read its configuration directives. The Apache httpd exccutable understands the following options:

```
httpd [-D name][-d directory] [-f file]
          [-C "directive"] [-c "directive"]
          [-v] [-V] [-h] [-l] [-L] [-S] [-t] [-T]
```

The -D option defines a name for use with <IfDefine name> directives in your configuration files. This allows you to conditionally include or exclude sections of your configuration when starting the server.

The -d option overrides the location of the *ServerRoot* directory. It sets the initial value of the *ServerRoot* variable (the directory where the Apache server is installed) to whichever path you specify. This default is usually read from the ServerRoot directive in httpd.conf.

The -f flag specifies the location of the main configuration file, conf/httpd.conf. It reads and executes the configuration commands found in *ConfigurationFile* on startup. If the *ConfigurationFile* is not an absolute path (it doesn't begin with a /), its location is assumed to be relative to the path specified in the *ServerRoot* directive in httpd.conf. By default, this value is set to *ServerRoot*/conf/httpd.conf.

The -v option prints the development version of the Apache server and terminates the process.

The -V option shows all of the settings that were in effect when the server was compiled.

The -h option prints the following usage information for the server:

```
Usage: httpd [-D name] [-d directory] [-f file]
             [-C "directive"] [-c "directive"]
             [-v] [-V] [-h] [-l] [-L] [-S] [-t] [-T]
Options:
  -D name         : define a name for use in <IfDefine name> directives
  -d directory    : specify an alternate initial ServerRoot
  -f file         : specify an alternate ServerConfigFile
  -C "directive"  : process directive before reading config files
  -c "directive"  : process directive after  reading config files
  -v              : show version number
  -V              : show compile settings
  -h              : list available command line options (this page)
  -l              : list compiled-in modules
  -L              : list available configuration directives
  -S              : show parsed settings (currently only vhost settings)
  -t              : run syntax check for config files (with docroot check)
  -T              : run syntax check for config files (without docroot check)
```

The -l option lists those modules that are compiled into your Apache server.

The -L option lists all of the configuration directives that are available with the modules that are compiled into your Apache server.

The -S option lists the virtual host settings for the server.

The -t option is extremely useful. It runs a syntax check on your configuration files. It's a good idea to run this check before restarting your server, once you have made changes to your configuration files. Performing such a test is especially important because an error in the configuration file might result in your server shutting down when you try to restart it.

The -T option is the same as the -t option, but it does not check the configured document roots.

> **Note**
>
> When you start the server manually from the command line, you need to do so as root. There are two main reasons for this:
>
> - If your standalone server uses the default HTTP port (port 80), only the superuser can bind to Internet ports that are lower than 1024.
> - Only processes owned by root can change their UID and GID as specified by the User and Group directives. If you start the server under another UID, it will run with the permissions of the user starting the process.

The /etc/rc.d httpd Scripts

Red Hat Linux uses scripts in the /etc/rc.d directory to control the startup and shutdown of various services, including the Apache Web server. The main script installed for the Apache Web server is /etc/rc.d/init.d/httpd and it is shown in Listing 12.2.

> **Note**
>
> /etc/rc.d/init.d/httpd is a shell script and is not the same as the Apache server located in /usr/sbin. That is, /usr/sbin/httpd is the program executable file, and /etc/rc.d/init.d/httpd is a shell script that helps control that program. See Chapter 9, "System Startup and Shutdown," for more information.

12

APACHE SERVER

You can use the following options to control the Web server:

- `start`—The system uses this option to start the Web server during boot up. You, as `root`, can also use this script to start the server.

- `stop`—The system uses this option to stop the server gracefully. You should use this script, rather than the `kill` command, to stop the server.

- `reload`—You can use this option to send the `HUP` signal to the `httpd` server to have it reread the configuration files after modification.

- `restart`—This option is a convenient way to stop and then immediately start the Web server. If the `httpd` server was not running, it will be started.

- `condrestart`—The same as the `restart` parameter, except that it will only restart the `httpd` server if it is actually running.

- `status`—This option indicates whether the server is running, and if it is, it provides the various PIDs for each instance of the server.

For example, to check on the current status, use the command

`/etc/rc.d/init.d/httpd status`

which prints the following for me:

```
httpd (pid 8643 8642 6510 6102 6101 6100 6099 6323 6322 6098 6097 6096
➥ 6095 362 6094 6093) is running...
```

This indicates that the Web server is running; in fact, there are 16 instances of the server currently running.

> **Tip**
>
> Use the `reload` option if you are making many changes to the various server configuration files. This saves time when you're stopping and starting the server by having the system simply reread the configuration files.

LISTING 12.2   `/etc/rc.d/init.d/http`

```
#!/bin/sh
#
# Startup script for the Apache Web Server
#
# chkconfig: 345 85 15
# description: Apache is a World Wide Web server.  It is used to serve \
#              HTML files and CGI.
# processname: httpd
# pidfile: /var/run/httpd.pid
# config: /etc/httpd/conf/access.conf
```

LISTING 12.2 continued

```
# config: /etc/httpd/conf/httpd.conf
# config: /etc/httpd/conf/srm.conf


# Source function library.
. /etc/rc.d/init.d/functions

# See how we were called.
case "$1" in
  start)
        echo -n "Starting httpd: "
        daemon httpd
        echo
        touch /var/lock/subsys/httpd
        ;;
  stop)
        echo -n "Shutting down http: "
        killproc httpd
        echo
        rm -f /var/lock/subsys/httpd
        rm -f /var/run/httpd.pid
        ;;
  status)
        status httpd
        ;;
  restart)
        $0 stop
        $0 start
        ;;
  reload)
        echo -n "Reloading httpd: "
        killproc httpd -HUP
        echo
        ;;
  *)
        echo "Usage: $0 {start|stop|restart|reload|status}"
        exit 1
esac

exit 0
```

Configuration File Listings

What follows are complete listings of the server configuration files for Apache version 1.3.12. If you have a different version of the server installed, or even if you have this version installed, you may notice some differences between your configuration files and the ones listed here. Some of these differences will simply be the differences between my system and yours. Others are places where I have set parameters differently.

Listing 12.3 shows the server configuration file.

LISTING 12.3   conf/httpd.conf

```
##
## httpd.conf -- Apache HTTP server configuration file
##


#
# Based upon the NCSA server configuration files originally by Rob McCool.
#
# This is the main Apache server configuration file.  It contains the
# configuration directives that give the server its instructions.
# See <URL:http://www.apache.org/docs/> for detailed information about
# the directives.
#
# Do NOT simply read the instructions in here without understanding
# what they do.  They're here only as hints or reminders.  If you are unsure
# consult the online docs. You have been warned.
#
# After this file is processed, the server will look for and process
# /usr/conf/srm.conf and then /usr/conf/access.conf
# unless you have overridden these with ResourceConfig and/or
# AccessConfig directives here.
#
# The configuration directives are grouped into three basic sections:
#  1. Directives that control the operation of the Apache server process as a
#     whole (the 'global environment').
#  2. Directives that define the parameters of the 'main' or 'default' server,
#     which responds to requests that aren't handled by a virtual host.
#     These directives also provide default values for the settings
#     of all virtual hosts.
#  3. Settings for virtual hosts, which allow Web requests to be sent to
#     different IP addresses or hostnames and have them handled by the
#     same Apache server process.
#
# Configuration and logfile names: If the filenames you specify for many
# of the server's control files begin with "/" (or "drive:/" for Win32), the
# server will use that explicit path.  If the filenames do *not* begin
# with "/", the value of ServerRoot is prepended -- so "logs/foo.log"
# with ServerRoot set to "/usr/local/apache" will be interpreted by the
# server as "/usr/local/apache/logs/foo.log".
#

### Section 1: Global Environment
#
# The directives in this section affect the overall operation of Apache,
# such as the number of concurrent requests it can handle or where it
# can find its configuration files.
#
```

LISTING 12.3 continued

```
#
# ServerType is either inetd, or standalone.  Inetd mode is only supported on
# Unix platforms.
#
ServerType standalone

#
# ServerRoot: The top of the directory tree under which the server's
# configuration, error, and log files are kept.
#
# NOTE!  If you intend to place this on an NFS (or otherwise network)
# mounted filesystem then please read the LockFile documentation
# (available at <URL:http://www.apache.org/docs/mod/core.html#lockfile>);
# you will save yourself a lot of trouble.
#
# Do NOT add a slash at the end of the directory path.
#
ServerRoot "/etc/httpd"

#
# The LockFile directive sets the path to the lockfile used when Apache
# is compiled with either USE_FCNTL_SERIALIZED_ACCEPT or
# USE_FLOCK_SERIALIZED_ACCEPT. This directive should normally be left at
# its default value. The main reason for changing it is if the logs
# directory is NFS mounted, since the lockfile MUST BE STORED ON A LOCAL
# DISK. The PID of the main server process is automatically appended to
# the filename.
#
LockFile /var/lock/httpd.lock

#
# PidFile: The file in which the server should record its process
# identification number when it starts.
#
PidFile /var/run/httpd.pid

#
# ScoreBoardFile: File used to store internal server process information.
# Not all architectures require this.  But if yours does (you'll know because
# this file will be  created when you run Apache) then you *must* ensure that
# no two invocations of Apache share the same scoreboard file.
#
ScoreBoardFile /var/run/httpd.scoreboard

#
# In the standard configuration, the server will process this file,
# srm.conf, and access.conf in that order.  The latter two files are
# now distributed empty, as it is recommended that all directives
# be kept in a single file for simplicity.  The commented-out values
```

LISTING 12.3   continued

```
# below are the built-in defaults.  You can have the server ignore
# these files altogether by using "/dev/null" (for Unix) or
# "nul" (for Win32) for the arguments to the directives.
#
#ResourceConfig conf/srm.conf
#AccessConfig conf/access.conf

#
# Timeout: The number of seconds before receives and sends time out.
#
Timeout 300

#
# KeepAlive: Whether or not to allow persistent connections (more than
# one request per connection). Set to "Off" to deactivate.
#
KeepAlive On

#
# MaxKeepAliveRequests: The maximum number of requests to allow
# during a persistent connection. Set to 0 to allow an unlimited amount.
# We recommend you leave this number high, for maximum performance.
#
MaxKeepAliveRequests 100

#
# KeepAliveTimeout: Number of seconds to wait for the next request from the
# same client on the same connection.
#
KeepAliveTimeout 15

#
# Server-pool size regulation.  Rather than making you guess how many
# server processes you need, Apache dynamically adapts to the load it
# sees --- that is, it tries to maintain enough server processes to
# handle the current load, plus a few spare servers to handle transient
# load spikes (e.g., multiple simultaneous requests from a single
# Netscape browser).
#
# It does this by periodically checking how many servers are waiting
# for a request.  If there are fewer than MinSpareServers, it creates
# a new spare.  If there are more than MaxSpareServers, some of the
# spares die off.  The default values are probably OK for most sites.
#
MinSpareServers 5
MaxSpareServers 20

#
```

LISTING 12.3 continued

```
# Number of servers to start initially --- should be a reasonable ballpark
# figure.
#
StartServers 8

#
# Limit on total number of servers running, i.e., limit on the number
# of clients who can simultaneously connect --- if this limit is ever
# reached, clients will be LOCKED OUT, so it should NOT BE SET TOO LOW.
# It is intended mainly as a brake to keep a runaway server from taking
# the system with it as it spirals down...
#
MaxClients 150

#
# MaxRequestsPerChild: the number of requests each child process is
# allowed to process before the child dies.  The child will exit so
# as to avoid problems after prolonged use when Apache (and maybe the
# libraries it uses) leak memory or other resources.  On most systems, this
# isn't really needed, but a few (such as Solaris) do have notable leaks
# in the libraries. For these platforms, set to something like 10000
# or so; a setting of 0 means unlimited.
#
# NOTE: This value does not include keepalive requests after the initial
#       request per connection. For example, if a child process handles
#       an initial request and 10 subsequent "keptalive" requests, it
#       would only count as 1 request towards this limit.
#
MaxRequestsPerChild 100

#
# Listen: Allows you to bind Apache to specific IP addresses and/or
# ports, in addition to the default. See also the <VirtualHost>
# directive.
#
#Listen 3000
#Listen 12.34.56.78:80
Listen 80

#
# BindAddress: You can support virtual hosts with this option. This directive
# is used to tell the server which IP address to listen to. It can either
# contain "*", an IP address, or a fully qualified Internet domain name.
# See also the <VirtualHost> and Listen directives.
#
#BindAddress *

#
# Dynamic Shared Object (DSO) Support
#
```

LISTING 12.3   continued

```
# To be able to use the functionality of a module which was built as a DSO you
# have to place corresponding `LoadModule' lines at this location so the
# directives contained in it are actually available _before_ they are used.
# Please read the file README.DSO in the Apache 1.3 distribution for more
# details about the DSO mechanism and run `httpd -l' for the list of already
# built-in (statically linked and thus always available) modules in your httpd
# binary.
#
# Note: The order in which modules are loaded is important.  Don't change
# the order below without expert advice.
#
# Example:
# LoadModule foo_module modules/mod_foo.so

#LoadModule mmap_static_module modules/mod_mmap_static.so
LoadModule vhost_alias_module modules/mod_vhost_alias.so
LoadModule env_module          modules/mod_env.so
LoadModule config_log_module   modules/mod_log_config.so
LoadModule agent_log_module    modules/mod_log_agent.so
LoadModule referer_log_module modules/mod_log_referer.so
#LoadModule mime_magic_module   modules/mod_mime_magic.so
LoadModule mime_module         modules/mod_mime.so
LoadModule negotiation_module modules/mod_negotiation.so
LoadModule status_module       modules/mod_status.so
LoadModule info_module         modules/mod_info.so
LoadModule includes_module     modules/mod_include.so
LoadModule autoindex_module    modules/mod_autoindex.so
LoadModule dir_module          modules/mod_dir.so
LoadModule cgi_module          modules/mod_cgi.so
LoadModule asis_module         modules/mod_asis.so
LoadModule imap_module         modules/mod_imap.so
LoadModule action_module       modules/mod_actions.so
#LoadModule speling_module      modules/mod_speling.so
LoadModule userdir_module      modules/mod_userdir.so
LoadModule alias_module        modules/mod_alias.so
LoadModule rewrite_module      modules/mod_rewrite.so
LoadModule access_module       modules/mod_access.so
#LoadModule auth_module         modules/mod_auth.so
#LoadModule anon_auth_module    modules/mod_auth_anon.so
#LoadModule db_auth_module      modules/mod_auth_db.so
#LoadModule digest_module       modules/mod_digest.so
#LoadModule proxy_module        modules/libproxy.so
#LoadModule cern_meta_module    modules/mod_cern_meta.so
LoadModule expires_module      modules/mod_expires.so
LoadModule headers_module      modules/mod_headers.so
#LoadModule usertrack_module    modules/mod_usertrack.so
#LoadModule example_module      modules/mod_example.so
#LoadModule unique_id_module    modules/mod_unique_id.so
LoadModule setenvif_module     modules/mod_setenvif.so
```

LISTING 12.3 continued

```
#LoadModule bandwidth_module    modules/mod_bandwidth.so
#LoadModule put_module          modules/mod_put.so
<IfDefine HAVE_PERL>
LoadModule perl_module          modules/libperl.so
</IfDefine>
<IfDefine HAVE_PHP>
LoadModule php_module           modules/mod_php.so
</IfDefine>
<IfDefine HAVE_PHP3>
LoadModule php3_module          modules/libphp3.so
</IfDefine>
<IfDefine HAVE_PHP4>
LoadModule php4_module          modules/libphp4.so
</IfDefine>
<IfDefine HAVE_DAV>
LoadModule dav_module           modules/libdav.so
</IfDefine>
<IfDefine HAVE_ROAMING>
LoadModule roaming_module       modules/mod_roaming.so
</IfDefine>
<IfDefine HAVE_SSL>
LoadModule ssl_module           modules/libssl.so
</IfDefine>

#   Reconstruction of the complete module list from all available modules
#   (static and shared ones) to achieve correct module execution order.
#   [WHENEVER YOU CHANGE THE LOADMODULE SECTION ABOVE UPDATE THIS, TOO]
ClearModuleList
#AddModule mod_mmap_static.c
AddModule mod_vhost_alias.c
AddModule mod_env.c
AddModule mod_log_config.c
AddModule mod_log_agent.c
AddModule mod_log_referer.c
#AddModule mod_mime_magic.c
AddModule mod_mime.c
AddModule mod_negotiation.c
AddModule mod_status.c
AddModule mod_info.c
AddModule mod_include.c
AddModule mod_autoindex.c
AddModule mod_dir.c
AddModule mod_cgi.c
AddModule mod_asis.c
AddModule mod_imap.c
AddModule mod_actions.c
#AddModule mod_speling.c
AddModule mod_userdir.c
AddModule mod_alias.c
```

12

APACHE SERVER

LISTING 12.3   continued

```
AddModule mod_rewrite.c
AddModule mod_access.c
#AddModule mod_auth.c
#AddModule mod_auth_anon.c
#AddModule mod_auth_db.c
#AddModule mod_digest.c
#AddModule mod_proxy.c
#AddModule mod_cern_meta.c
AddModule mod_expires.c
AddModule mod_headers.c
#AddModule mod_usertrack.c
#AddModule mod_example.c
#AddModule mod_unique_id.c
AddModule mod_so.c
AddModule mod_setenvif.c
#AddModule mod_bandwidth.c
#AddModule mod_put.c
<IfDefine HAVE_PERL>
AddModule mod_perl.c
</IfDefine>
<IfDefine HAVE_PHP>
AddModule mod_php.c
</IfDefine>
<IfDefine HAVE_PHP3>
AddModule mod_php3.c
</IfDefine>
<IfDefine HAVE_PHP4>
AddModule mod_php4.c
</IfDefine>
<IfDefine HAVE_DAV>
AddModule mod_dav.c
</IfDefine>
<IfDefine HAVE_ROAMING>
AddModule mod_roaming.c
</IfDefine>
<IfDefine HAVE_SSL>
AddModule mod_ssl.c
</IfDefine>

#
# ExtendedStatus: controls whether Apache will generate "full" status
# information (ExtendedStatus On) or just basic information (ExtendedStatus
# Off) when the "server-status" handler is called. The default is Off.
#
#ExtendedStatus On

### Section 2: 'Main' server configuration
#
# The directives in this section set up the values used by the 'main'
```

LISTING 12.3   continued

```
# server, which responds to any requests that aren't handled by a
# <VirtualHost> definition.  These values also provide defaults for
# any <VirtualHost> containers you may define later in the file.
#
# All of these directives may appear inside <VirtualHost> containers,
# in which case these default settings will be overridden for the
# virtual host being defined.
#


#
# If your ServerType directive (set earlier in the 'Global Environment'
# section) is set to "inetd", the next few directives don't have any
# effect since their settings are defined by the inetd configuration.
# Skip ahead to the ServerAdmin directive.
#


#
# Port: The port to which the standalone server listens. For
# ports < 1023, you will need httpd to be run as root initially.
#
Port 80


#
# If you wish httpd to run as a different user or group, you must run
# httpd as root initially and it will switch.
#
# User/Group: The name (or #number) of the user/group to run httpd as.
#  . On SCO (ODT 3) use "User nouser" and "Group nogroup".
#  . On HPUX you may not be able to use shared memory as nobody, and the
#    suggested workaround is to create a user www and use that user.
#  NOTE that some kernels refuse to setgid(Group) or semctl(IPC_SET)
#  when the value of (unsigned)Group is above 60000;
#  don't use Group nobody on these systems!
#
User apache
Group apache


#
# ServerAdmin: Your address, where problems with the server should be
# e-mailed.  This address appears on some server-generated pages, such
# as error documents.
#
ServerAdmin webmaster@gnulix.org


#
# ServerName: allows you to set a host name which is sent back to clients for
# your server if it's different than the one the program would get (i.e., use
# "www" instead of the host's real name).
#
```

LISTING 12.3   continued

```
# Note: You cannot just invent host names and hope they work. The name you
# define here must be a valid DNS name for your host. If you don't understand
# this, ask your network administrator.
# If your host doesn't have a registered DNS name, enter its IP address here.
# You will have to access it by its address (e.g., http://123.45.67.89/)
# anyway, and this will make redirections work in a sensible way.
#
#ServerName localhost


#
# DocumentRoot: The directory out of which you will serve your
# documents. By default, all requests are taken from this directory, but
# symbolic links and aliases may be used to point to other locations.
#
DocumentRoot "/var/www/html"


#
# Each directory to which Apache has access, can be configured with respect
# to which services and features are allowed and/or disabled in that
# directory (and its subdirectories).
#
# First, we configure the "default" to be a very restrictive set of
# permissions.
#
<Directory />
    Options FollowSymLinks
    AllowOverride None
</Directory>


#
# Note that from this point forward you must specifically allow
# particular features to be enabled - so if something's not working as
# you might expect, make sure that you have specifically enabled it
# below.
#


#
# This should be changed to whatever you set DocumentRoot to.
#
<Directory "/var/www/html">


#
# This may also be "None", "All", or any combination of "Indexes",
# "Includes", "FollowSymLinks", "ExecCGI", or "MultiViews".
#
# Note that "MultiViews" must be named *explicitly* --- "Options All"
# doesn't give it to you.
#
    Options Indexes Includes FollowSymLinks
```

LISTING 12.3   continued

```
#
# This controls which options the .htaccess files in directories can
# override. Can also be "All", or any combination of "Options", "FileInfo",
# "AuthConfig", and "Limit"
#
    AllowOverride None

#
# Controls who can get stuff from this server.
#
    Order allow,deny
    Allow from all
</Directory>

#
# UserDir: The name of the directory which is appended onto a user's home
# directory if a ~user request is received.
#
UserDir public_html

#
# Control access to UserDir directories.  The following is an example
# for a site where these directories are restricted to read-only.
#
#<Directory /home/*/public_html>
#    AllowOverride FileInfo AuthConfig Limit
#    Options MultiViews Indexes SymLinksIfOwnerMatch IncludesNoExec
#    <Limit GET POST OPTIONS PROPFIND>
#        Order allow,deny
#        Allow from all
#    </Limit>
#    <Limit PUT DELETE PATCH PROPPATCH MKCOL COPY MOVE LOCK UNLOCK>
#        Order deny,allow
#        Deny from all
#    </Limit>
#</Directory>

#
# DirectoryIndex: Name of the file or files to use as a pre-written HTML
# directory index.  Separate multiple entries with spaces.
#
DirectoryIndex index.html index.htm index.shtml index.cgi

#
# AccessFileName: The name of the file to look for in each directory
# for access control information.
#
AccessFileName .htaccess
```

LISTING 12.3   continued

```
#
# The following lines prevent .htaccess files from being viewed by
# Web clients.  Since .htaccess files often contain authorization
# information, access is disallowed for security reasons.  Comment
# these lines out if you want Web visitors to see the contents of
# .htaccess files.  If you change the AccessFileName directive above,
# be sure to make the corresponding changes here.
#
# Also, folks tend to use names such as .htpasswd for password
# files, so this will protect those as well.
#
<Files ~ "^\.ht">
    Order allow,deny
    Deny from all
</Files>

#
# CacheNegotiatedDocs: By default, Apache sends "Pragma: no-cache" with each
# document that was negotiated on the basis of content. This asks proxy
# servers not to cache the document. Uncommenting the following line disables
# this behavior, and proxies will be allowed to cache the documents.
#
#CacheNegotiatedDocs

#
# UseCanonicalName:  (new for 1.3)  With this setting turned on, whenever
# Apache needs to construct a self-referencing URL (a URL that refers back
# to the server the response is coming from) it will use ServerName and
# Port to form a "canonical" name.  With this setting off, Apache will
# use the hostname:port that the client supplied, when possible.  This
# also affects SERVER_NAME and SERVER_PORT in CGI scripts.
#
UseCanonicalName On

#
# TypesConfig describes where the mime.types file (or equivalent) is
# to be found.
#
TypesConfig /etc/mime.types

#
# DefaultType is the default MIME type the server will use for a document
# if it cannot otherwise determine one, such as from filename extensions.
# If your server contains mostly text or HTML documents, "text/plain" is
# a good value.  If most of your content is binary, such as applications
# or images, you may want to use "application/octet-stream" instead to
# keep browsers from trying to display binary files as though they are
# text.
#
```

LISTING 12.3   continued

```
DefaultType text/plain

#
# The mod_mime_magic module allows the server to use various hints from the
# contents of the file itself to determine its type.  The MIMEMagicFile
# directive tells the module where the hint definitions are located.
# mod_mime_magic is not part of the default server (you have to add
# it yourself with a LoadModule [see the DSO paragraph in the 'Global
# Environment' section], or recompile the server and include mod_mime_magic
# as part of the configuration), so it's enclosed in an <IfModule> container.
# This means that the MIMEMagicFile directive will only be processed if the
# module is part of the server.
#
<IfModule mod_mime_magic.c>
    MIMEMagicFile share/magic
</IfModule>

#
# HostnameLookups: Log the names of clients or just their IP addresses
# e.g., www.apache.org (on) or 204.62.129.132 (off).
# The default is off because it'd be overall better for the net if people
# had to knowingly turn this feature on, since enabling it means that
# each client request will result in AT LEAST one lookup request to the
# nameserver.
#
HostnameLookups Off

#
# ErrorLog: The location of the error log file.
# If you do not specify an ErrorLog directive within a <VirtualHost>
# container, error messages relating to that virtual host will be
# logged here.  If you *do* define an error logfile for a <VirtualHost>
# container, that host's errors will be logged there and not here.
#
ErrorLog /var/log/httpd/error_log

#
# LogLevel: Control the number of messages logged to the error_log.
# Possible values include: debug, info, notice, warn, error, crit,
# alert, emerg.
#
LogLevel warn

#
# The following directives define some format nicknames for use with
# a CustomLog directive (see below).
#
LogFormat "%h %l %u %t \"%r\" %>s %b \"%{Referer}i\" \"%{User-Agent}i\""
➥ combined
```

LISTING 12.3   continued

```
LogFormat "%h %l %u %t \"%r\" %>s %b" common
LogFormat "%{Referer}i -> %U" referer
LogFormat "%{User-agent}i" agent

#
# The location and format of the access logfile (Common Logfile Format).
# If you do not define any access logfiles within a <VirtualHost>
# container, they will be logged here.  Contrariwise, if you *do*
# define per-<VirtualHost> access logfiles, transactions will be
# logged therein and *not* in this file.
#
CustomLog /var/log/httpd/access_log common

#
# If you would like to have agent and referer logfiles, uncomment the
# following directives.
#
#CustomLog /var/log/httpd/referer_log referer
#CustomLog /var/log/httpd/agent_log agent

#
# If you prefer a single logfile with access, agent, and referer information
# (Combined Logfile Format) you can use the following directive.
#
#CustomLog /var/log/httpd/access_log combined

#
# Optionally add a line containing the server version and virtual host
# name to server-generated pages (error documents, FTP directory listings,
# mod_status and mod_info output etc., but not CGI generated documents).
# Set to "EMail" to also include a mailto: link to the ServerAdmin.
# Set to one of:  On | Off | EMail
#
ServerSignature On

#
# Aliases: Add here as many aliases as you need (with no limit). The format is
# Alias fakename realname
#
# Note that if you include a trailing / on fakename then the server will
# require it to be present in the URL.  So "/icons" isn't aliased in this
# example, only "/icons/"..
#
Alias /icons/ "/var/www/icons/"

<Directory "/var/www/icons">
    Options Indexes MultiViews
    AllowOverride None
    Order allow,deny
    Allow from all
```

LISTING 12.3   continued

```
</Directory>

#
# ScriptAlias: This controls which directories contain server scripts.
# ScriptAliases are essentially the same as Aliases, except that
# documents in the realname directory are treated as applications and
# run by the server when requested rather than as documents sent to the client.
# The same rules about trailing "/" apply to ScriptAlias directives as to
# Alias.
#
ScriptAlias /cgi-bin/ "/var/www/cgi-bin/"


#
# "/var/www/cgi-bin" should be changed to whatever your ScriptAliased
# CGI directory exists, if you have that configured.
#
<Directory "/var/www/cgi-bin">
    AllowOverride None
    Options ExecCGI
    Order allow,deny
    Allow from all
</Directory>


#
# Redirect allows you to tell clients about documents which used to exist in
# your server's namespace, but do not anymore. This allows you to tell the
# clients where to look for the relocated document.
# Format: Redirect old-URI new-URL
#


#
# Directives controlling the display of server-generated directory listings.
#


#
# FancyIndexing: whether you want fancy directory indexing or standard
#
IndexOptions FancyIndexing


#
# AddIcon* directives tell the server which icon to show for different
# files or filename extensions.  These are only displayed for
# FancyIndexed directories.
#
AddIconByEncoding (CMP,/icons/compressed.gif) x-compress x-gzip

AddIconByType (TXT,/icons/text.gif) text/*
AddIconByType (IMG,/icons/image2.gif) image/*
AddIconByType (SND,/icons/sound2.gif) audio/*
AddIconByType (VID,/icons/movie.gif) video/*
```

LISTING 12.3   continued

```
AddIcon /icons/binary.gif .bin .exe
AddIcon /icons/binhex.gif .hqx
AddIcon /icons/tar.gif .tar
AddIcon /icons/world2.gif .wrl .wrl.gz .vrml .vrm .iv
AddIcon /icons/compressed.gif .Z .z .tgz .gz .zip
AddIcon /icons/a.gif .ps .ai .eps
AddIcon /icons/layout.gif .html .shtml .htm .pdf
AddIcon /icons/text.gif .txt
AddIcon /icons/c.gif .c
AddIcon /icons/p.gif .pl .py
AddIcon /icons/f.gif .for
AddIcon /icons/dvi.gif .dvi
AddIcon /icons/uuencoded.gif .uu
AddIcon /icons/script.gif .conf .sh .shar .csh .ksh .tcl
AddIcon /icons/tex.gif .tex
AddIcon /icons/bomb.gif core

AddIcon /icons/back.gif ..
AddIcon /icons/hand.right.gif README
AddIcon /icons/folder.gif ^^DIRECTORY^^
AddIcon /icons/blank.gif ^^BLANKICON^^

#
# DefaultIcon: which icon to show for files which do not have an icon
# explicitly set.
#
DefaultIcon /icons/unknown.gif

#
# AddDescription: allows you to place a short description after a file in
# server-generated indexes.  These are only displayed for FancyIndexed
# directories.
# Format: AddDescription "description" filename
#
#AddDescription "GZIP compressed document" .gz
#AddDescription "tar archive" .tar
#AddDescription "GZIP compressed tar archive" .tgz

#
# ReadmeName: the name of the README file the server will look for by
# default, and append to directory listings.
#
# HeaderName: the name of a file which should be prepended to
# directory indexes.
#
# The server will first look for name.html and include it if found.
# If name.html doesn't exist, the server will then look for name.txt
# and include it as plaintext if found.
#
```

LISTING 12.3   continued

```
ReadmeName README
HeaderName HEADER

#
# IndexIgnore: a set of filenames which directory indexing should ignore
# and not include in the listing.  Shell-style wildcarding is permitted.
#
IndexIgnore .??* *~ *# HEADER* README* RCS CVS *,v *,t

#
# AddEncoding: allows you to have certain browsers (Mosaic/X 2.1+) uncompress
# information on the fly. Note: Not all browsers support this.
# Despite the name similarity, the following Add* directives have nothing
# to do with the FancyIndexing customization directives above.
#
AddEncoding x-compress Z
AddEncoding x-gzip gz tgz

#
# AddLanguage: allows you to specify the language of a document. You can
# then use content negotiation to give a browser a file in a language
# it can understand.  Note that the suffix does not have to be the same
# as the language keyword --- those with documents in Polish (whose
# net-standard language code is pl) may wish to use "AddLanguage pl .po"
# to avoid the ambiguity with the common suffix for perl scripts.
#
AddLanguage en .en
AddLanguage fr .fr
AddLanguage de .de
AddLanguage da .da
AddLanguage el .el
AddLanguage it .it

#
# LanguagePriority: allows you to give precedence to some languages
# in case of a tie during content negotiation.
# Just list the languages in decreasing order of preference.
#
LanguagePriority en fr de

#
# AddType: allows you to tweak mime.types without actually editing it, or to
# make certain files to be certain types.
#
# The following is for PHP4 (conficts with PHP/FI, below):
<IfModule mod_php4.c>
  AddType application/x-httpd-php .php4 .php3 .phtml .php
  AddType application/x-httpd-php-source .phps
</IfModule>
```

LISTING 12.3   continued

```
# The following is for PHP3:
<IfModule mod_php3.c>
  AddType application/x-httpd-php3 .php3
  AddType application/x-httpd-php3-source .phps
</IfModule>

# The following is for PHP/FI (PHP2):
<IfModule mod_php.c>
  AddType application/x-httpd-php .phtml
</IfModule>

AddType application/x-tar .tgz

#
# AddHandler: allows you to map certain file extensions to "handlers",
# actions unrelated to filetype. These can be either built into the server
# or added with the Action command (see below)
#
# If you want to use server side includes, or CGI outside
# ScriptAliased directories, uncomment the following lines.
#
# To use CGI scripts:
#
#AddHandler cgi-script .cgi

#
# To use server-parsed HTML files
#
AddType text/html .shtml
AddHandler server-parsed .shtml

#
# Uncomment the following line to enable Apache's send-asis HTTP file
# feature
#
#AddHandler send-as-is asis

#
# If you wish to use server-parsed imagemap files, use
#
AddHandler imap-file map

#
# To enable type maps, you might want to use
#
#AddHandler type-map var

#
# Action: lets you define media types that will execute a script whenever
```

LISTING 12.3   continued

```
# a matching file is called. This eliminates the need for repeated URL
# pathnames for oft-used CGI file processors.
# Format: Action media/type /cgi-script/location
# Format: Action handler-name /cgi-script/location
#

#
# MetaDir: specifies the name of the directory in which Apache can find
# meta information files. These files contain additional HTTP headers
# to include when sending the document
#
#MetaDir .web

#
# MetaSuffix: specifies the file name suffix for the file containing the
# meta information.
#
#MetaSuffix .meta

#
# Customizable error response (Apache style)
#   these come in three flavors
#
#     1) plain text
#ErrorDocument 500 "The server made a boo boo.
#   n.b.  the (") marks it as text, it does not get output
#
#     2) local redirects
#ErrorDocument 404 /missing.html
#   to redirect to local URL /missing.html
#ErrorDocument 404 /cgi-bin/missing_handler.pl
#   N.B.: You can redirect to a script or a document using server-side-includes.
#
#     3) external redirects
#ErrorDocument 402 http://some.other_server.com/subscription_info.html
#   N.B.: Many of the environment variables associated with the original
#   request will *not* be available to such a script.

#
# The following directives modify normal HTTP response behavior.
# The first directive disables keepalive for Netscape 2.x and browsers that
# spoof it. There are known problems with these browser implementations.
# The second directive is for Microsoft Internet Explorer 4.0b2
# which has a broken HTTP/1.1 implementation and does not properly
# support keepalive when it is used on 301 or 302 (redirect) responses.
#
BrowserMatch "Mozilla/2" nokeepalive
BrowserMatch "MSIE 4\.0b2;" nokeepalive downgrade-1.0 force-response-1.0

#
```

LISTING 12.3   continued

```
# The following directive disables HTTP/1.1 responses to browsers which
# are in violation of the HTTP/1.0 spec by not being able to grok a
# basic 1.1 response.
#
BrowserMatch "RealPlayer 4\.0" force-response-1.0
BrowserMatch "Java/1\.0" force-response-1.0
BrowserMatch "JDK/1\.0" force-response-1.0


# If the perl module is installed, this will be enabled.
<IfModule mod_perl.c>
  Alias /perl/ /var/www/perl/
  <Location /perl>
    SetHandler perl-script
    PerlHandler Apache::Registry
    Options +ExecCGI
  </Location>
</IfModule>


#
# Allow http put (such as Netscape Gold's publish feature)
# Use htpasswd to generate /etc/httpd/conf/passwd.
# You must unremark these two lines at the top of this file as well:
#LoadModule put_module          modules/mod_put.so
#AddModule mod_put.c
#
#Alias /upload /tmp
#<Location /upload>
#    EnablePut On
#    AuthType Basic
#    AuthName Temporary
#    AuthUserFile /etc/httpd/conf/passwd
#    EnableDelete Off
#    umask 007
#    <Limit PUT>
#        require valid-user
#    </Limit>
#</Location>


#
# Allow server status reports, with the URL of http://servername/server-status
# Change the ".your_domain.com" to match your domain to enable.
#
<Location /server-status>
    SetHandler server-status
    Order deny,allow
    Deny from all
    Allow from gnulix.org
</Location>
```

LISTING 12.3   continued

```
#
# Allow remote server configuration reports, with the URL of
#  http://servername/server-info (requires that mod_info.c be loaded).
# Change the ".your_domain.com" to match your domain to enable.
#
<Location /server-info>
    SetHandler server-info
    Order deny,allow
    Deny from all
    Allow from gnulix.org
</Location>

# Allow access to local system documentation from localhost
Alias /doc/ /usr/share/doc/
<Location /doc>
  order deny,allow
  deny from all
  allow from localhost
  Options Indexes FollowSymLinks
</Location>

#
# There have been reports of people trying to abuse an old bug from pre-1.1
# days.  This bug involved a CGI script distributed as a part of Apache.
# By uncommenting these lines you can redirect these attacks to a logging
# script on phf.apache.org.  Or, you can record them yourself, using the script
# support/phf_abuse_log.cgi.
#
#<Location /cgi-bin/phf*>
#    Deny from all
#    ErrorDocument 403 http://phf.apache.org/phf_abuse_log.cgi
#</Location>

#
# Proxy Server directives. Uncomment the following lines to
# enable the proxy server:
#
#<IfModule mod_proxy.c>
#ProxyRequests On
#
#<Directory proxy:*>
#    Order deny,allow
#    Deny from all
#    Allow from .your_domain.com
#</Directory>

#
# Enable/disable the handling of HTTP/1.1 "Via:" headers.
# ("Full" adds the server version; "Block" removes all outgoing Via: headers)
```

12

APACHE SERVER

LISTING 12.3   continued

```
# Set to one of: Off | On | Full | Block
#
#ProxyVia On


#
# To enable the cache as well, edit and uncomment the following lines:
# (no cacheing without CacheRoot)
#
#CacheRoot "/var/cache/httpd"
#CacheSize 5
#CacheGcInterval 4
#CacheMaxExpire 24
#CacheLastModifiedFactor 0.1
#CacheDefaultExpire 1
#NoCache a_domain.com another_domain.edu joes.garage_sale.com

#</IfModule>
# End of proxy directives.

### Section 3: Virtual Hosts
#
# VirtualHost: If you want to maintain multiple domains/hostnames on your
# machine you can setup VirtualHost containers for them.
# Please see the documentation at <URL:http://www.apache.org/docs/vhosts/>
# for further details before you try to setup virtual hosts.
# You may use the command line option '-S' to verify your virtual host
# configuration.

#
# If you want to use name-based virtual hosts you need to define at
# least one IP address (and port number) for them.
#
#NameVirtualHost 12.34.56.78:80
#NameVirtualHost 12.34.56.78

#
# VirtualHost example:
# Almost any Apache directive may go into a VirtualHost container.
#
#<VirtualHost ip.address.of.host.some_domain.com>
#    ServerAdmin webmaster@host.some_domain.com
#    DocumentRoot /www/docs/host.some_domain.com
#    ServerName host.some_domain.com
#    ErrorLog logs/host.some_domain.com-error_log
#    CustomLog logs/host.some_domain.com-access_log common
#</VirtualHost>

#<VirtualHost _default_:*>
#</VirtualHost>
```

LISTING 12.3   continued

```
<IfDefine HAVE_SSL>
##
## SSL Virtual Host Context
##

#  Apache will only listen on port 80 by default.  Defining the virtual server
#  (below) won't make it automatically listen on the virtual server's port.
Listen 443

<VirtualHost _default_:443>

#  General setup for the virtual host
DocumentRoot "/var/www/html"

#   SSL Engine Switch:
#   Enable/Disable SSL for this virtual host.
SSLEngine on

#   SSL Cipher Suite:
#   List the ciphers that the client is permitted to negotiate.
#   See the mod_ssl documentation for a complete list.
#SSLCipherSuite ALL:!ADH:RC4+RSA:+HIGH:+MEDIUM:+LOW:+SSLv2:+EXP:+eNULL

#   Server Certificate:
#   Point SSLCertificateFile at a PEM encoded certificate.  If
#   the certificate is encrypted, then you will be prompted for a
#   pass phrase.  Note that a kill -HUP will prompt again. A test
#   certificate can be generated with `make certificate' under
#   built time. Keep in mind that if you've both a RSA and a DSA
#   certificate you can configure both in parallel (to also allow
#   the use of DSA ciphers, etc.)
SSLCertificateFile /etc/httpd/conf/ssl.crt/server.crt
#SSLCertificateFile /etc/httpd/conf/ssl.crt/server-dsa.crt

#   Server Private Key:
#   If the key is not combined with the certificate, use this
#   directive to point at the key file.  Keep in mind that if
#   you've both a RSA and a DSA private key you can configure
#   both in parallel (to also allow the use of DSA ciphers, etc.)
SSLCertificateKeyFile /etc/httpd/conf/ssl.key/server.key
#SSLCertificateKeyFile /etc/httpd/conf/ssl.key/server-dsa.key

#   Server Certificate Chain:
#   Point SSLCertificateChainFile at a file containing the
#   concatenation of PEM encoded CA certificates which form the
#   certificate chain for the server certificate. Alternatively
#   the referenced file can be the same as SSLCertificateFile
#   when the CA certificates are directly appended to the server
#   certificate for convenience.
#SSLCertificateChainFile /etc/httpd/conf/ssl.crt/ca.crt
```

12

APACHE SERVER

LISTING 12.3   continued

```
#    Certificate Authority (CA):
#    Set the CA certificate verification path where to find CA
#    certificates for client authentication or alternatively one
#    huge file containing all of them (file must be PEM encoded)
#    Note: Inside SSLCACertificatePath you need hash symlinks
#          to point to the certificate files. Use the provided
#          Makefile to update the hash symlinks after changes.
#SSLCACertificatePath /etc/httpd/conf/ssl.crt
#SSLCACertificateFile /etc/httpd/conf/ssl.crt/ca-bundle.crt

#    Certificate Revocation Lists (CRL):
#    Set the CA revocation path where to find CA CRLs for client
#    authentication or alternatively one huge file containing all
#    of them (file must be PEM encoded)
#    Note: Inside SSLCARevocationPath you need hash symlinks
#          to point to the certificate files. Use the provided
#          Makefile to update the hash symlinks after changes.
#SSLCARevocationPath /etc/httpd/conf/ssl.crl
#SSLCARevocationFile /etc/httpd/conf/ssl.crl/ca-bundle.crl
#    Client Authentication (Type):
#    Client certificate verification type and depth.  Types are
#    none, optional, require and optional_no_ca.  Depth is a
#    number which specifies how deeply to verify the certificate
#    issuer chain before deciding the certificate is not valid.
#SSLVerifyClient require
#SSLVerifyDepth  10

#    Access Control:
#    With SSLRequire you can do per-directory access control based
#    on arbitrary complex boolean expressions containing server
#    variable checks and other lookup directives.  The syntax is a
#    mixture between C and Perl.  See the mod_ssl documentation
#    for more details.
#<Location />
#SSLRequire (     %{SSL_CIPHER} !~ m/^(EXP|NULL)-/ \
#            and %{SSL_CLIENT_S_DN_O} eq "Snake Oil, Ltd." \
#            and %{SSL_CLIENT_S_DN_OU} in {"Staff", "CA", "Dev"} \
#            and %{TIME_WDAY} >= 1 and %{TIME_WDAY} <= 5 \
#            and %{TIME_HOUR} >= 8 and %{TIME_HOUR} <= 20      ) \
#            or %{REMOTE_ADDR} =~ m/^192\.76\.162\.[0-9]+$/
#</Location>
#    SSL Engine Options:
#    Set various options for the SSL engine.
#    o FakeBasicAuth:
#      Translate the client X.509 into a Basic Authorisation.  This means that
#      the standard Auth/DBMAuth methods can be used for access control.  The
#      user name is the `one line' version of the client's X.509 certificate.
#      Note that no password is obtained from the user. Every entry in the user
```

LISTING 12.3   continued

```
#       file needs this password: `xxj31ZMTZzkVA`.
#    o ExportCertData:
#       This exports two additional environment variables: SSL_CLIENT_CERT and
#       SSL_SERVER_CERT. These contain the PEM-encoded certificates of the
#       server (always existing) and the client (only existing when client
#       authentication is used). This can be used to import the certificates
#       into CGI scripts.
#    o StdEnvVars:
#       This exports the standard SSL/TLS related `SSL_*` environment variables.
#       Per default this exportation is switched off for performance reasons,
#       because the extraction step is an expensive operation and is usually
#       useless for serving static content. So one usually enables the
#       exportation for CGI and SSI requests only.
#    o CompatEnvVars:
#       This exports obsolete environment variables for backward compatibility
#       to Apache-SSL 1.x, mod_ssl 2.0.x, Sioux 1.0 and Stronghold 2.x. Use this
#       to provide compatibility to existing CGI scripts.
#    o StrictRequire:
#       This denies access when "SSLRequireSSL" or "SSLRequire" applied even
#       under a "Satisfy any" situation, i.e. when it applies access is denied
#       and no other module can change it.
#    o OptRenegotiate:
#       This enables optimized SSL connection renegotiation handling when SSL
#       directives are used in per-directory context.
#SSLOptions +FakeBasicAuth +ExportCertData +CompatEnvVars +StrictRequire
<Files ~ "\.(cgi|shtml)$">
    SSLOptions +StdEnvVars
</Files>
<Directory "/var/www/cgi-bin">
    SSLOptions +StdEnvVars
</Directory>

#    Notice: Most problems of broken clients are also related to the HTTP
#    keep-alive facility, so you usually additionally want to disable
#    keep-alive for those clients, too. Use variable "nokeepalive" for this.
SetEnvIf User-Agent ".*MSIE.*" nokeepalive ssl-unclean-shutdown

#    Per-Server Logging:
#    The home of a custom SSL log file. Use this when you want a
#    compact non-error SSL logfile on a virtual host basis.
CustomLog /var/log/httpd/ssl_request_log \
        "%t %h %{SSL_PROTOCOL}x %{SSL_CIPHER}x \"%r\" %b"

</VirtualHost>

</IfDefine>
```

12

APACHE SERVER

Listing 12.4 shows `srm.conf`, which is basically empty.

LISTING 12.4   conf/srm.conf

```
##
## srm.conf -- Apache HTTP server configuration file
##


#
# This is the default file for the ResourceConfig directive in httpd.conf.
# It is processed after httpd.conf but before access.conf.
#
# To avoid confusion, it is recommended that you put all of your
# Apache server directives into the httpd.conf file and leave this
# one essentially empty.
#
```

Listing 12.5 shows the global access configuration file.

LISTING 12.5   conf/access.conf

```
##
## access.conf -- Apache HTTP server configuration file
##


#
# This is the default file for the AccessConfig directive in httpd.conf.
# It is processed after httpd.conf and srm.conf.
#
# To avoid confusion, it is recommended that you put all of your
# Apache server directives into the httpd.conf file and leave this
# one essentially empty.
#
#
# This is the default file for the AccessConfig directive in httpd.conf.
# It is processed after httpd.conf and srm.conf.
#
# To avoid confusion, it is recommended that you put all of your
# Apache server directives into the httpd.conf file and leave this
# one essentially empty.
#
```

Summary

There are still some things that you can do to further customize your Web server, but by this point you should at least have a functional server.

There is a plethora of Apache documentation online. For more information about Apache and the subjects discussed in this chapter, look at some of the following resources:

Extensive documentation and information about Apache: The Apache Project Web site at `http://www.apache.org/`.

Breaking news about Apache, and great technical articles: ApacheWeek at `http://www.apacheweek.com/`.

Another good Apache site, with original content as well as links to Apache-related stories on other sites: Apache Today at `http://apachetoday.com/`.

HTML, CGI, and related subjects: The HTML Writers Guild at `http://www.hwg.org/`.

Available add-on modules for Apache: The Apache Module Registry at `http://modules.apache.org/`.

There are also several good books about Apache. For example, *Apache Server Unleashed*, ISBN 0-672-31808-3.

12

APACHE SERVER

Internet News

CHAPTER 13

IN THIS CHAPTER

Usenet newsgroups are a fascinating and informative source of information, entertainment, news, and general chat. Usenet is one of the oldest components of the Internet and was popular long before the World Wide Web came on the scene. Usenet is still the most popular aspect of the Internet in terms of user interaction, offering a dynamic and often controversial forum for discussion on any subject.

Usenet newsgroups now number well over 100,000 groups dedicated to many different subjects. A full download of an average day's newsgroup postings takes several hundred megabytes of disk space and associated transfer time. Obviously, if you are going to access Usenet over anything slower than a T1 (1.544MBps) line, you have to be selective in what you download. An analog modem simply can't download the entire Usenet feed in a reasonable time. Selective access to newsgroups suits most users, however, because few (if any) users actually read all the postings on Usenet every day!

Providing access to the Usenet newsgroups is a natural purpose for Linux because newsgroups evolved under UNIX. To provide Usenet newsgroup access for yourself and anyone else accessing your machine, you need to set up newsgroup software on your system and get access to a source for downloading newsgroups. Any connection to the Internet gives you access to newsgroups, whether directly through your own gateway, through a news forwarding service, or through a third-party access service. Most Internet service providers (ISPs) can offer news access to you as part of their basic service. You choose which newsgroups you may be interested in from the complete list of all those available, and those groups are transferred to your machine for reading. If you want to access a newsgroup you didn't download, a quick connection to your ISP lets you sample the postings.

In this chapter you will learn how to configure your Linux machine to download newsgroups from your Internet connection. You will also see how to easily configure your Red Hat machine as a caching news server with Leafnode+. Finally, you will see how to install and configure one of the most popular newsreaders, trn. A *newsreader* is what users need to read postings in a newsgroup. There are several alternatives available for Linux access to newsgroups, so I chose the most common method to give you a taste of how to configure your Red Hat system as a news server.

Linux and Newsgroups

There are three main ways to download newsgroups onto your Linux system: INN, C News, and Leafnode+. INN (Internet News) implements the NNTP (Network News Transfer Protocol), which is widely used over TCP/IP connections to ISPs or the Internet. INN is the most flexible and configurable method of downloading entire newsgroups and works especially well on larger sites that have high-speed connections to the Internet or those sites where a lot of news is transferred (for example, large educational institutions).

C News was designed for downloading news through UUCP (UNIX to UNIX Copy) connections. Leafnode+ is probably the best choice for most sites, especially those that do not have the bandwidth to download all the news that your organization requires. Because INN is included with most Linux systems, that's the choice discussed first; a discussion about using Leafnode+ as a money-saving and time-saving alternative method to provide news for your users follows that.

Rich Salz developed INN to provide a complete Usenet package. One of INN's attractions is that it doesn't care whether you are using TCP/IP or UUCP to transfer your newsgroups. INN handles both methods equally well. INN handles the NNTP protocol for transferring news with the innd server process and provides newsreading services as a separate server, nntrpd, which is executed when it detects a connection on the news TCP/IP port (119).

How a Newsfeed Works

Usenet newsgroup postings are sent from machine to machine across the Internet all the time. To send mail from one system to another, Usenet uses a technique called flooding. *Flooding* happens when one machine connects to another and essentially transfers all the postings in the newsgroups as one big block of data. The receiving machine then connects to another machine and repeats the process. In this way, all the postings in the newsgroups are transferred across the entire Internet. This is much better than maintaining a single source of newsgroup information on a server isolated somewhere on the Internet. Each machine that participates in the flooding has a list of all other machines that can send or receive newsgroup postings. Each connection is called a *newsfeed*. When you connect to an ISP and download newsgroup postings, you are creating a newsfeed between your machine and the ISP's, which in turn has a newsfeed to another machine somewhere on the Internet.

Every time a new posting is added (or *posted*) to a newsgroup, the newsfeeds are used to transfer that posting. Each article has a list of all the machines that have received the posting, so it is easy to avoid transferring the same new posting to every machine on the Internet many times. The list of machines that have received the posting is called the *path*. Each posting also has a unique message ID, which prevents duplicate postings.

Preventing Duplicate News Postings

When you connect to your ISP and request newsgroup updates, one of two methods is often used to ensure you don't get duplicate postings when you use your newsreader. The most common technique is called *ihave/sendme*, which informs the machine at the other end of your newsfeed (such as your ISP's server) which message IDs you already have and which are lacking. At that point only the missing postings are transferred to your Linux machine.

13

INTERNET NEWS

The ihave/sendme protocol is excellent for updating a few newsgroups but starts to bog down dramatically when handling very large volumes of newsgroups. For this reason, a method called batching is used to transfer large newsgroup feeds. With *batching*, everything on one end of the newsfeed is transferred as a block. Your machine then sorts through the download, discarding any duplicates. Batching adds more overhead to your local Linux machine than ihave/sendme, but involves a lot less messaging between the two ends of the newsfeeds.

Pushing and Pulling the News

Two other terms are used to describe the transfer of newsgroup postings from one machine to another, and these terms apply especially to smaller systems that don't download the entire newsfeed every day. Your system can download articles from the newsfeed using the ihave/sendme protocol, a technique called *pushing* the news. Alternatively, your machine can request specific postings or entire newsgroups from the newsfeed based on the post's arrival date, a technique called *pulling* the news.

Alternative Methods to Downloading Newsgroups

Before looking at how to download Usenet newsgroups to your machine, there is one alternative you might want to consider. If you don't use Usenet a lot or have limited connection time to the newsfeed, consider interacting with a news server on a remote network. This method lets you read the postings on that server instead of downloading them to your machine. Many ISPs allow you to choose whether to download newsgroups to your machine or to read them on their news server. Obviously, if you are reading on the server, you must be connected all the time. This might be a better choice, however, if you do not often surf Usenet or you have limited disk space on your machine. Another alternative is to read news via the Web at http://www.deja.com/usenet/. This very powerful Web site contains almost all the newsgroups from around the world and offers a strong search facility. If you are looking to solve a particular problem, chances are you will find an answer if you do a search there.

INN Hardware and Software Requirements

INN doesn't impose too many hardware requirements; most Linux-capable hardware is sufficient to run INN. If you do download a lot of newsgroup postings, however, slow processors will be affected. Because INN often works in the background, your foreground tasks get slower while INN crunches away in the background. This is usually not a problem with 80486 or better CPUs running Red Hat Linux.

There are no extra RAM requirements for INN, although the more RAM, the better, to avoid swapping. If you download only a dozen newsgroups a day, Linux needs no extra RAM. You should have swap space allocated on your system as a RAM overflow, but there is no need to expand swap space just for INN unless the existing swap space is very small (less than half your physical RAM, for example).

Disk space may be a problem if you don't have a lot to spare. Downloading newsgroups can eat up disk space at an alarming rate, even if you download only a few groups a day. Because newsgroup postings are not automatically deleted after you read them, the effect is cumulative. This is especially a problem with newsgroups that contain binary information such as compiled programs or pictures. A typical newsgroup download can range from a few kilobytes to several gigabytes. Some of the binary newsgroups get many gigabytes daily, all of which accumulate over a week or so to huge amounts of disk space. It is not unusual for a day's complete download of all the newsgroups to take up several hundred gigabytes of disk space, so you must be careful about which newsgroups you choose to download.

Modems are another issue, and the speed of your modem directly impacts how many newsgroups you can download in a reasonable amount of time. Obviously, the faster your modem, the better. A 56Kbps modem will download much more data in a minute than a 9,600bps modem. That doesn't mean you need to junk your existing slower modems and replace them. The determining factor for your connection is the amount of data you will be transferring. If you download less than a dozen non-binary newsgroups a day, a 9,600bps modem is just fine. When you start downloading megabytes of data a day, as often happens with binary-laden newsgroups, you need a much faster connection to keep the download time to a minimum. Any of today's 56Kbps modems will suit your purposes for typical Usenet downloads of a few dozen non-binary newsgroups. When you start downloading large amounts of news, you should look at faster connections such as ISDN (128Kbps), T1 (1.544Mbps), or T3 (45Mbps). Cable modems and ADSL can usually download at a speed between that of ISDN and a T1 connection. However, be aware that disk and CPU requirements go up with the more groups downloaded and the more readers using your news server. Also remember that some companies will charge bandwidth fees for many higher-speed options.

Software requirements for INN are simple: You need INN and a configured connection to a newsfeed source (such as UUCP or TCP/IP to an ISP). INN is supplied with Red Hat Linux, and you can also obtain it from most Linux FTP and Web sites.

13

INTERNET NEWS

An Introduction to INN

INN was designed for handling news on very large systems with complex connections and configuration problems. INN contains an NNTP component but is noticeably faster when downloading and handling newsgroups than NNTP alone. Luckily, INN can be quickly configured for most basic Linux setups. I look at setting up INN on a typical Red Hat Linux system using a dial-up connection to an ISP using TCP/IP because this is the most common configuration. One problem with INN is a lack of good documentation. To date, no one has spent the time to produce a good public domain HOW-TO file about configuring and maintaining INN on Linux systems, but there is an INN FAQ, among other things, available from the INN home page at `http://www.isc.org/inn.html`.

INN uses a daemon called `innd` to control its behavior. Another daemon, `nnrpd`, is used to provide newsreader services. After INN is installed it will start automatically at boot. Every time a user launches a newsreader, a copy of `nnrpd` is started.

Installing INN

To install INN, you can start with either the source code (usually obtained from a Web or FTP site) or a precompiled binary included in the Red Hat INN package. Precompiled binaries are much easier because they save the hassle of running a C compiler to produce the binary from source code.

> **Note**
>
> If you are working with INN source code instead of a precompiled binary, you should carefully read any README files included in the source distribution. They describe the steps involved in compiling the INN software for your system. A makefile accompanies the source code and will almost certainly need modification to suit your system. With the latest INN distribution, however, a configure script gets run before compilation, which takes care of most configuration options. The version of INN shipping with Red Hat Linux when this chapter was written was 2.2.3.

To install your precompiled INN binaries on the system and properly configure it for secure operation, follow these steps:

1. Check your `/etc/passwd` file for a user called `news`. If one does not exist, create the `news` user. The user `news` should belong to a group called `news`. The home directory can be anything, and the startup command should be `blank` or something

like /bin/false for security reasons—no one should ever need to actively log in as the news user. Neither of these parameters is used by the system. The news user is created to allow INN to run as a non-root login for better system security. This account should exist by default on Red Hat systems. Also make sure that the Password field is filled by an asterisk (*) in /etc/passwd (or if shadow passwords are in use it should be an x in /etc/passwd and an asterisk in /etc/shadow). This makes doubly sure that no one can log in interactively as the news user.

2. Check the /etc/group file for a group called news. If one does not exist, create it. The news login should be the only user in the news group. Providing a dedicated group for INN access enhances system security. This group should exist by default on Red Hat systems.

3. INN often sends mail to the news logins, so you might want to create an alias for the usernames news and usenet to root, postmaster, or to whatever other login you want these messages to be sent. The alias file is kept in /etc/aliases. When you add aliases, make sure to run the /usr/bin/newaliases command afterward so that the added aliases will take effect.

4. Check to see if INN is already installed on your system by typing this code:

```
rpm -q inn
```

If no installed package is found, you'll need to install INN and probably the clean-feed package as well. To install cleanfeed, do the following:

```
rpm -i cleanfeed-0.95.7b-9.noarch.rpm
```

Install the INN package from the directory containing RPM files by issuing the following command:

```
rpm -i inn-2.2.3-3.i386.rpm
```

Installing the package should cause the creation of two files called /etc/init.d/innd and /etc/rc.news. These files will be used by init to start news services each time you boot. Once installed, they are executed automatically during the boot process unless explicitly disabled or removed.

5. The INN RPM file will install INN and newsgroup support under the /usr hierarchy (mainly in /usr/lib and /usr/bin). In previous versions of Red Hat Linux these files were located under /usr/lib/news.

6. The INN RPM will install the INN configuration files into the /etc/news directory and will add several files to the /etc/cron.* directories to be run by cron. The /etc/cron.daily/inn-cron-expire file calls the news.daily program once per day to expire (remove) old articles and to clean and maintain the INN logs. The /etc/cron.hourly/inn-cron-rnews file downloads new articles to your system once per day. The /etc/cron.hourly/inn-cron-nntpsend file sends articles created on your system to your outgoing news server once every hour.

After the INN package has successfully been installed, you can start news services by typing this code:

```
/etc/init.d/innd start
```

7. If you are uncomfortable starting INN on a running system, you can reboot your machine now. INN should start automatically as a part of the boot process.

The INN Startup Files

When the INN RPM is installed, it should automatically install the important INN startup files, /etc/init.d/innd (shown in Listing 13.1) and /usr/bin/rc.news.

LISTING 13.1   Contents of /etc/init.d/innd

```
#! /bin/sh
#
# innd          InterNet News System
#
# chkconfig: 345 95 05
# description: inn is the most popular server for Usenet news. It allows \
#              you to setup local news servers. It can be difficult to \
#              set up properly though, so be sure to read /usr/doc/inn* \
#              before trying.
# processname: innd
# pidfile: /var/run/news/innd.pid

# Source function library.
. /etc/init.d/functions

# Get config.
. /etc/sysconfig/network

# Check that networking is up.
if [ ${NETWORKING} = "no" ]
then
    exit 0
fi

[ -d /etc/news ] || exit 0
[ -d /var/spool/news ] || exit 0

RETVAL=0

start() {
        echo -n "Starting INND system: "
        daemon --user news /etc/rc.news
```

LISTING 13.1 continued

```
        RETVAL=$?
        [ $RETVAL -eq 0 ] && touch /var/lock/subsys/innd
        echo
        return $RETVAL
}

stop() {
        if [ -f /var/run/news/innd.pid ]
        then
                echo -n "Stopping INND service: "
                killproc innd
                RETVAL=$?
                [ $RETVAL -eq 0 ] && rm -f /var/run/news/innd.pid
                echo
        fi
        if [ -f /var/run/news/innwatch.pid ]
        then
                echo -n "Stopping INNWatch service: "
                killproc innwatch -9
                RETVAL=$?
                [ $RETVAL -eq 0 ] && rm -f /var/run/news/innwatch.pid
                echo
        fi
        if [ -f /var/run/news/innfeed.pid ]
        then
                echo -n "Stopping INNFeed service: "
                killproc innfeed -9
                RETVAL=$?
                [ $RETVAL -eq 0 ] && rm -f /var/run/news/innfeed.pid
                echo
        fi
        if [ -f /var/run/news/actived.pid ]
        then
                echo -n "Stopping INN actived service: "
                killproc actived -9
                RETVAL=$?
                [ $RETVAL -eq 0 ] && rm -f /var/run/news/actived.pid
                echo
        fi
        [ $RETVAL -eq 0 ] && rm -f /var/lock/subsys/innd /var/lock/news/*
        return $RETVAL
}

reload() {
        echo -n "Reloading INN Service: "
        killproc innd -HUP
```

LISTING 13.1   continued

```
        RETVAL=$?
        return $RETVAL
}

restart() {
        stop
        start
}

# See how we were called.
case "$1" in
  start)
        start
        ;;
  stop)
        stop
        ;;
  status)
        status innd
        ;;
  reload)
        reload
        ;;
  restart)
        stop
        start
        ;;
  condrestart)
        if [ -f /var/lock/subsys/innd ]; then
            restart
        fi
        ;;
  *)
        echo "Usage: $0 {start|stop|status|restart|condrestart}"
        exit 1
        ;;
esac

exit $RETVAL
```

It is a pretty standard control file—very similar to all the others in the /etc/init.d directory. It starts off by checking that all the various networking services are running; then, depending on what argument is passed to it (start, stop, status, or restart), it performs the appropriate action. Most of the work is performed in the rc.news file, an example of which is displayed in Listing 13.2.

LISTING 13.2 Contents of /etc/rc.news

```
#!/bin/sh
## $Revision: 1.22.2.1 $
## News boot script.  Runs as "news" user.  Requires inndstart be
## setuid root.  Run from rc.whatever as:
##      su news -c /path/to/rc.news >/dev/console


. /usr/lib/innshellvars

AZ=ABCDEFGHIJKLMNOPQRSTUVWXYZ
az=abcdefghijklmnopqrstuvwxyz
## Pick ${INND} or ${INNDSTART}
WHAT=${INNDSTART}
## Set to true or false
: ${DOINNWATCH:=true}
DOINNWATCH=`echo ${DOINNWATCH} | tr ${AZ} ${az}`
if [ -z "${DOINNWATCH}" \
     -o "${DOINNWATCH}" = "on" \
     -o "${DOINNWATCH}" = "true" \
     -o "${DOINNWATCH}" = "yes" ]; then
    DOINNWATCH=true
else
    DOINNWATCH=false
fi


: ${DOCNFSSTAT:=false}
DOCNFSSTAT=`echo ${DOCNFSSTAT} | tr ${AZ} ${az}`
if [ -z "${DOCNFSSTAT}" \
     -o "${DOCNFSSTAT}" = "on" \
     -o "${DOCNFSSTAT}" = "true" \
     -o "${DOCNFSSTAT}" = "yes" ]; then
    DOCNFSSTAT=true
else
    DOCNFSSTAT=false
fi

MAIL="${MAILCMD} -s 'Boot-time Usenet warning on `hostname`' ${NEWSMASTER}"

## RFLAG is set below; set INNFLAGS in inn.conf(5)
RFLAG=""

## Clean shutdown or already running?
if [ -f ${SERVERPID} ] ; then
    if kill -0 `cat ${SERVERPID}` 2>/dev/null; then
    echo 'INND is running'
    exit 0
    fi
    echo 'INND:  PID file exists -- unclean shutdown!'
    RFLAG="-r"
fi
```

13

INTERNET NEWS

LISTING **13.2**   continued

```
if [ ! -f ${PATHDB}/.news.daily ] ; then
    case `find ${PATHBIN}/innd -mtime +1 -print 2>/dev/null` in
    "")
    ;;
    *)
    echo 'No .news.daily file; need to run news.daily?' | eval ${MAIL}
    ;;
    esac
else
    case `find${PATHDB}/.news.daily -mtime +1 -print 2>/dev/null` in
    "")
    ;;
    *)
    echo 'Old .news.daily file; need to run news.daily?' | eval ${MAIL}
    ;;
    esac
fi

## Active file recovery.
if [ ! -s ${ACTIVE} ] ; then
    if [ -s ${NEWACTIVE} ] ; then
    mv ${NEWACTIVE} ${ACTIVE}
    else
    if [ -s ${OLDACTIVE} ] ; then
        cp ${OLDACTIVE} ${ACTIVE}
    else
        echo 'INND:   No active file!'
        exit 1
    fi
    fi
    RFLAG="-r"
    # You might want to rebuild the DBZ database, too:
    #cd ${PATHDB} \
    #       && makehistory -r \
    #       && mv history.n.dir history.dir \
    #       && mv history.n.index history.index \
    #       && mv history.n.hash history.hash
fi

## Remove temporary batchfiles and lock files.
( cd ${BATCH} && rm -f bch* )
( cd ${LOCKS} && rm -f LOCK* )
( cd ${TEMPSOCKDIR} && rm -f ${TEMPSOCK} )
rm -f ${NEWSCONTROL} ${NNTPCONNECT} ${SERVERPID}

## Start the show.
echo 'Starting innd.'
eval ${WHAT} ${RFLAG} ${INNFLAGS}
```

LISTING 13.2   continued

```
# Gee, looks like lisp, doesn't it?
${DOINNWATCH} && {
    echo "Scheduled start of ${INNWATCH}."
    ( sleep 60 ; ${INNWATCH} ) &
}

${DOCNFSSTAT} && {
    echo "Scheduled start of cnfsstat."
    ( sleep 60 ; ${PATHBIN}/cnfsstat -s -l ) &
}

RMFILE=${MOST_LOGS}/expire.rm
for F in ${RMFILE} ${RMFILE}.*; do
    if [ -f $F -a -s $F ] ; then
    echo "Removing articles from pre-downtime expire run (${F})."
    (
        echo 'System shut down during expire.' \
        'Unlinking articles listed in'
        echo ${F}
    ) | eval ${MAIL}
    ${PATHBIN}/expirerm ${F}
    fi
done &
```

This script performs numerous housekeeping chores, which include checking that the news.daily script (which takes care of things such as article expiration) has been run recently and actually starting INN.

After the INN package is installed and ready to go, you need to check the configuration information to make sure everything will run smoothly when innd or nntpd (the NNTP daemon) connect to the newsfeed.

Note

INN is very particular about its user and group setup and file permissions in general. As a general rule, don't modify any INN file permissions at all; you may otherwise find the package ceases to work properly.

Configuring INN

Configuring INN can take hours because it is a complex package that allows many news-feeds at once. Don't worry; for a simple connection to an ISP through TCP/IP or UUCP, you can configure INN in a few minutes. Most of the work was done when you installed the package.

When changing configuration files it is always advisable to back up the copies. If it's a personal system, just copy them with the same name with the extension `.orig` or `.bak` appended. If there are multiple admins on the machine, adding your login name helps the other admins know who did what. Follow these steps to check and configure your INN setup, being careful to back up any files changed and preserve permissions as you go:

1. Edit the `/etc/news/incoming.conf` file. This file lists all the newsfeeds that your system connects to and is read by the INN daemon. Enter the names or IP addresses of the newsfeed machines using the following as an example:

   ```
   peer newsfeed {
       hostname:      news.isp.net
   }
   ```

   Because most systems will have only a single newsfeed, you will only need one `peer` entry. If your newsfeed requires a password, add another parameter `password:` with the appropriate password after the colon. There are many other parameters that can be specified on a per-newsfeed basis. For a full list see the `incoming.conf(5)` manual page.

2. If you allow other machines on your local area network or machines connecting through a remote access server on your machine to read news collected by your system, you need to add their names to the `/etc/news/nnrp.access` file. This file is read when the `nnrpd` daemon starts for each person invoking a newsreader. The `nnrp.access` file contains a list of all the machines that are allowed to read news from your server and follows this syntax:

   name:perms:user:password:newsgroup

   name is the address of the machine that you are allowing to read news. (You can use wildcards to allow entire subnets.) *perms* is the permissions and has one of the following values: `Read` (for read-only access), `Post` (to allow posting of messages), or `Read Post` (for both `Read` and `Post`). *user* authenticates a username before it is allowed to post, and *password* accomplishes the same task. To prevent a user from posting messages through your server, leave *user* and *password* as spaces so they can't be matched.

   newsgroup is a pattern of newsgroup names that can be either read or not read, depending on how you set up the contents. Access to newsgroups uses wildcards, so `comp*` allows access to all newsgroups starting with `comp`, whereas `!sex` disables access to any newsgroups starting with the word `sex`. The default setting in the `nnrp.access` file is to prevent all access. To allow all users in the domain `tpci.com` to read and post news with no authentication required, add this line to `nnrp.access`:

   .tpci.com:Read Post:::

To open the news system to everyone on your system regardless of domain name, use an asterisk instead of a domain name.

3. The file `inn.conf` should be in your `/etc/news` directory. You should probably change the line with `organization` in it to the following:

organization: Your company name

This specifies the default `organization:` header entry when your users post an article to your news server.

Of course, if you are setting up INN to get news from your ISP's news server, your ISP would have to set up its end with the newsgroups that you want your users to be able to access. Remember that news takes up a lot of bandwidth, so try to minimize the amount of news you download.

Another common task is to set up a local newsgroup. This might be used by a company to discuss projects, or by a school to discuss classes. This common task is covered in part six of the INN FAQ. The entire FAQ can be found in `/usr/share/doc/inn-2.2.2/faq`. To do this, make sure that INN is up by running `/etc/init.d/innd status`. Add the group by typing **ctlinnd newgroup foozle.widgets**. Add the following to `/etc/news/newsfeeds`:

```
ME:!foozle.*::
out.going.site:*,!foozle.*:Tf,Wnm
```

Then add a descriptive entry to `/var/lib/news/newsgroups` and you're done. Replace "foozle" and "out.going.site" with the group hierarchy name you'd like to use and the name of your peering site.

After setting the `incoming.conf`, `nnrp.access`, and `inn.conf` files and notifying your ISP that you want to access its NNTP service, you should be able to use INN to download news and access it with a newsreader. (This assumes you've granted yourself permission in the `nnrp.access` file.) A lot of complexity can be introduced into INN's configuration file, but keeping it simple tends to be the best method. As your experience grows, you can modify the behavior of the newsfeeds; you should start, however, with as simple an access approach as possible to allow testing of the news system first. After setting up INN, the next step is to provide users with a newsreader.

Introduction to Leafnode+

As mentioned before, many companies and individuals run a news cache of some sort instead of getting a full newsfeed. This saves time and money. The news cache described in this chapter is very simple to set up and maintain, and is called Leafnode+. At the time of this writing, Leafnode+ was not shipping with Red Hat, but it is easily downloadable from `http://www.io.com/~kazushi/leafnode+/`. Leafnode+ is from the same project as Leafnode—`http://www.leafnode.org/`—and the projects are intending to merge eventually. Both offer very similar features, but the authors developed them in different ways.

How Leafnode+ Works

Leafnode+ was designed to look like a regular NNRP-based server that any newsreader can connect to—but with a difference! You specify in the configuration a default news server that Leafnode+ gets its articles from; this is normally your ISP's news server. At this point you run fetchnews, which is the utility that downloads news articles and posts any messages you've written. On its first run it will build up a list of groups to put in the active list. However, it won't download any articles; it only presents "psuedo articles" to inform you that it has registered your interest in the group. For example, if you are reading the `comp.os.linux.announce` newsgroup, the first time you read it you'll find a single article informing you that Leafnode+ knows of your interest and will start fetching that group for you. When fetchnews runs again, and for as long as you read to that group, that newsgroup will be retrieved.

Articles are stored locally, and so is the news server's active list. The *active list* is the current newsgroup listing for that particular news server. This is useful because the list doesn't have to be refetched every time you open your newsreader.

Another useful Leafnode+ feature is that it can connect to multiple news servers. There are a number of public news servers on the Internet that are usually related to a particular topic. As an example, Microsoft provides a news server called `msnews.microsoft.com` and has specific newsgroups on Microsoft-related topics. (Newsgroups are named `microsoft.*`.). Similarly, Red Hat has a news server called `news.redhat.com`. (Newsgroups are named `redhat.*`.). To make full use of this neat feature, you can configure Leafnode+ to talk to specific servers and link newsgroups with these servers. When you use the newsreader, it makes browsing through all the different groups on all the different news servers transparent and it caches it all for you!

Leafnode+ is best suited to small installations of a few dozen users. It is well suited to dial-up users and makes news reading simple in such situations.

Downloading and Configuring Leafnode+

Since Leafnode+ is not part of the standard Red Hat 7 distribution, you have to download it. This is a pretty simple process, since there is already an RPM included on the CD-ROMs with this book. If you feel adventurous you can have a go at downloading the newer version, compiling and installing it yourself. It would be wise to check both `http://www.leafnode.org/` and `http://www.io.com/~kazushi/leafnode+/` to see the status of the projects.

Install it with this command:

```
rpm -i  leafnode+-2.10-1.i386.rpm
```

This installs the configuration files under `/etc/leafnode.conf`, some documentation in `/usr/doc/leafnode+-2.10`, and the binaries that do all the work in `/usr/sbin`. Of course, the appropriate startup files are installed in the `/etc/rc.d` tree.

Edit the `/etc/leafnode.conf` file and add in your news server. There are several examples provided. In the simplest case the file would contain

```
server = news.isp.net
username = username
password = password
timeout_short = 7
timeout_long = 21
timeout_active = 14
maxcount = 2000
```

At that point run fetchnews as the news user. Assuming a `root` shell type

```
su news -c /usr/sbin/fetchnews
```

This will run for a while—it's downloading your news active list. Once that is complete, run your newsreader and read the psuedo articles that Leafnode+ provides. After you've visited all the newsgroups you are interested in, run fetchnews again in the same manner.

Leafnode+ actually consists of a set of three binaries. The install process configures two of the three binaries. One is `texpire`, which expires old news articles and is configured to run daily. Another is `leafnode`, which acts like a news server for your newsreader and is run from inetd. Lastly, there's fetchnews. Because this is the most dynamic part, you're left to configure that on your own based on your needs. You can have it run every hour out of `cron`, as part of your `ppp-up` script, or run it by hand. Remember, fetchnews also delivers the articles you post. The more often it runs, the quicker your posts propagate and new news is delivered, but for cost reasons it's wise to run it less often in dial-on-demand situations.

When you have fetchnews configured to your liking, you can forget about Leafnode+. That is, with one caveat—it can consume a large number of inodes so make sure the partition it's on (usually `/var`) has enough inodes.

Introduction to trn

There are many newsreaders available for Linux systems, but trn remains the perennial favorite. This is an old package but is simple to use as well as fast and efficient. You might not need a newsreader at all if you have Web services on your system. Many Web browsers allow access to newsgroups either in your own news directory or through a connection to an ISP's newsfeed.

The primary advantage of trn over the earlier rn (read news) package is that trn lets you follow threads. A *thread* in a newsgroup is a continuing discussion with one primary subject. Before trn came along, you had to read news consecutively from first to last, trying to assemble several different conversations into logical groups as you went. When trn became available, you could start with one thread, read all the postings about that subject, and then move on to another subject, regardless of the chronological order in which the postings were made.

Threads are usually handled automatically without requiring any special user interaction, although there is some work performed behind the scenes on your newsfeed. Some newsgroups do not support threading, but most do. If threads are available, you can follow the thread from start to finish, or jump out and change threads at any time.

Installing and Configuring trn

The trn newsreader is easy to install as a binary package; an RPM is included with Red Hat Linux. Type the following to see if trn is already installed on your system:

```
rpm -q trn
```

If no package by that name is found, you can install the trn package from the directory containing RPM files by issuing the following command:

```
rpm -i trn-3.6-25.i386.rpm
```

There really is no special configuration required for trn to run. When the binary is available on your system, it will check for the newsgroup information in /var/lib/news and present it to you. In the past, trn wasn't capable of forming threads on its own. Because of this, external threading utilities such as mthreads or overview were once popular. As of version 3.0, however, trn supports direct threading without the need for external thread utilities. Most users now use trn as a standalone program.

Summary

In this chapter you learned how to install and configure the Internet News service, INN, and how to set up a simpler and more personal NNRP server using Leafnode+. The steps involved may seem a little overwhelming, but if you take them slowly and check everything carefully, you'll be surprised how little time it takes to have a functional newsfeed on your Linux machine. Remember that you do need a connection available to a newsfeed before you complete and test the INN configuration.

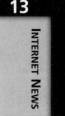

CHAPTER 14

Domain Name Service and Dynamic Host Configuration Protocol

IN THIS CHAPTER

Referring to hosts by their IP addresses is convenient for computers, but humans have an easier time working with names. Obviously, we need some sort of translation table to convert IP addresses to hostnames. With millions of machines on the Internet and new ones popping up every day, it would be impossible for everyone to keep this sort of table up-to-date. This is where DNS comes in.

The Domain Name Service (DNS) is the system by which each site maintains its own mapping of IP addresses to machine names. Each site puts this mapping into a publicly accessible database, so anyone can find the IP address corresponding to a hostname in the site simply by querying the site's database.

To access this database, you need to run a DNS server for your site. A DNS server is also known as a nameserver (NS). These servers come in three varieties:

- Master (also called *primary*)
- Slave (also called *secondary*)
- Caching

If you are connecting to an existing network (through your school or company network, for example), you only need to run a caching server. On the other hand, if you are setting up a new site to be accessed through the Internet, you need to set up a primary server. Secondary servers eliminate the single point of failure represented by a lone master server and also share the query load.

This chapter shows how to configure each of these nameservers and gives you an overview of the tasks involved in maintaining a DNS database.

A Brief History of the Internet

To understand the Domain Name System, it is important to know a little about the history of the Internet and its precursor, ARPAnet.

The Internet began in the late 1960s as an experimental wide area computer network funded by the Department of Defense's Advanced Research Projects Agency (ARPA). This network, called ARPAnet, was intended to allow government scientists and engineers to share expensive computing resources. During this period, only government users and a handful of computers were ever connected to ARPAnet. It remained that way until the early 1980s.

In the early 1980s, two main developments led to the popularization of ARPAnet. The first was the development of the Transmission Control Protocol and the Internet Protocol (TCP/IP). TCP/IP standardized connectivity to ARPAnet for all computers. The second was U.C. Berkeley's version of UNIX, known as BSD, which was the first UNIX distribution to include TCP/IP as a networking layer. Because BSD was available to other universities at minimal cost, the number of computers connecting to ARPAnet soared.

All of a sudden, thousands of computers were connected to a network that had been designed to handle just a few computers. In many cases, these new computers were simultaneously connected to a university network and to ARPAnet. At this point, it was decided that the original ARPAnet would become the backbone of the entire network, which was called the Internet.

In 1988, the Defense Department decided the ARPAnet project had continued long enough and stopped funding it. The National Science Foundation (NSF) then supported the Internet until 1995, when private companies such as BBNPlanet, MCI, and Sprint took over the backbone.

Now millions of computers and millions of users are on the Internet, and the numbers keep rising.

The `hosts.txt` File

In the early days, when there were only a few hundred computers connected to ARPAnet, every computer had a file called `hosts.txt`. UNIX modified the name to `/etc/hosts`. This file contained all the information about every host on the network, including the name-to-address mapping. With so few computers, the file was small and could be maintained easily.

The maintenance of the `hosts.txt` file was the responsibility of SRI-NIC, located at the Stanford Research Institute in Menlo Park, California. When administrators wanted a change to the `hosts.txt` file, they emailed the request to SRI-NIC (Stanford Research Institute Network Information Center), which incorporated the request, once or twice a week. This meant that the administrators also had to periodically compare their `hosts.txt` file against the SRI-NIC `hosts.txt` file and, if the files were different, the administrators had to `ftp` a new copy of the file.

As the Internet started to grow, the idea of centrally administering hostnames and deploying the `hosts.txt` file became a major issue. Every time a new host was added, a change had to be made to the central version and every other host on ARPAnet had to get the new version of the file.

In the early 1980s, SRI-NIC called for the design of a distributed database to replace the `hosts.txt` file. The new system was known as the Domain Name System (DNS). ARPAnet switched to DNS in September 1984, and it has been the standard method for publishing and retrieving hostname information on the Internet ever since.

14

DNS AND DHCP

DNS is a distributed database built on a hierarchical domain structure that solves the inefficiencies inherent in a large monolithic file such as `hosts.txt`. Under DNS, every computer that connects to the Internet does so from an Internet domain. Each Internet domain has a nameserver that maintains a database of the hosts in its domain and handles requests for hostnames. When a domain becomes too large for a single point of management, subdomains can be delegated to reduce the administrative burden.

The `/etc/hosts` File

Although DNS is the primary means of name resolution, the `/etc/hosts` file is still found on most machines. It can help to speed up the IP address lookup of frequently requested addresses, such as the IP address of the local machine. Also, during boot time, machines need to know the mapping of some hostnames to IP addresses (for example, your NIS servers) before DNS can be referenced. The IP address-to-hostname mapping for these hosts is kept in the `/etc/hosts` file.

The following is a sample `/etc/hosts` file:

```
# IP Address     Hostname      Alias
127.0.0.1        localhost
192.168.100.7    vestax        www
192.168.100.8    mailhub       mailhub.domain.cxm
192.168.100.6    technics
```

The leftmost column is the IP address to be resolved. The next column is the hostname corresponding to that IP address. Any subsequent columns are aliases for that host. In the second line, for example, the address `192.168.100.7` is for the host `vestax`. Another name for `vestax` is `www`. The domain name is automatically appended to the hostname by the system. However, many people append it themselves for clarity (for example, `www.domain.cxm`).

Note

Use of the `.cxm` domain name prevents conflict with any existing `.com` domain. For that reason, all examples in this chapter use the `.cxm` top level domain.

At the very least, you need the entries for

- Localhost
- Your NIS server (if you use NIS or NIS+)
- Any systems from which you NFS mount disks
- The host itself

In this example, `localhost` is the first line, followed by `vestax`, which is a WWW server. The machine `mailhub` is used by `sendmail` for mail transfers. Finally, there is `technics`, the name of the machine from which the `/etc/hosts` file came.

BIND 8

Most DNS implementations, including the one shipping with Red Hat Linux, use BIND, which stands for Berkeley Internet Name Domain. In the late 1990s, BIND underwent a major version change, from version 4.x.x to version 8.x.x. Red Hat Linux 7 ships with BIND version 8.2.2.

BIND version 8 represents a substantial improvement over its version 4 predecessors. There are several security improvements, including restriction of queries and/or zone transfers to and from specific IP addresses/subnets. Note that some of these security improvements existed in the latest of the version 4 series BIND implementations. Version 8 uses a new, easier boot file (`named.conf`) syntax. Version 4 and before used semicolons to comment out lines in the boot file. Version 8 doesn't tolerate semicolons as comments in the boot file, but it gives the administrator three excellent new choices:

```
/* C type comments for multi line comments */
// C++ comments are great for single line or partial line
# Shell type comments are familiar to Unix admins
```

Note

The preceding comments are used in the boot file. The zone data files still use semicolons as comments.

14

DNS AND DHCP

The comment change brings up the fact that BIND 8 configuration files are absolutely incompatible with their BIND 4 predecessors. Although there are scripts to convert the configuration files, the quickest option is likely to be rewriting the files. Because BIND 8 configuration files are more straightforward than BIND 4, this rewrite should be a fairly simple task for all but the most complex setups.

By default, BIND 8 has the DNS boot file `/etc/named.conf`. Version 4 implementations default to the boot file `/etc/named.boot`. Red Hat 7 comes with an `/etc/named.boot` file, but that file has no effect on any system set up with the DNS that ships with Red Hat 7.

BIND 8 has hostname checking, which might break with naming conventions accepted by older BIND versions. If you encounter this problem when converting to BIND 8, you can temporarily turn hostname checking off with the following three lines in the `options` section of `named.conf`:

```
check -names master ignore;
check -names slave ignore;
check -names response ignore;
```

Because BIND 8 comes with Red Hat Linux 7, and because it's easier and more secure, BIND 8 is covered exclusively in this chapter.

A Word About This Chapter's Examples

The examples in this chapter were created to illustrate specific points and to allow you to safely run them on a two-computer network. To accomplish this with minimal risk to the worldwide DNS system or your company's DNS system, all examples use the imaginary top-level domain name `.cxm`.

In addition, all examples use private IP subnet `192.168.100`. This is one of the subnets set aside for local, non-Internet use. You can see the complete list of private IP subnets in RFC 1918, mirrored at `http://www.isi.edu/in-notes/rfc1918.txt`. If, by chance, your company already uses the `192.168.100` numbers for in-house IP addresses, you must pick another private subnet for this chapter's examples.

If running this chapter's examples happens to release any information to a higher level or the worldwide DNS, the bogus top level domain and the private IP numbers would instantly brand it as garbage to be ignored. Of course, if you're doing a genuine Internet-connected DNS instead of the chapter examples, use the domain name and IP address assigned to your organization by the proper authorities.

DNS is complex, and it is one of the few systems on your network that depends intimately on the correct working of machines elsewhere. Likewise, machines elsewhere depend intimately on the correct working of your DNS system. In the world of real top-level domains and public IP addressees, an unnoticed error in your DNS setup can cause serious problems for other people thousands of miles away, which in turn may cause serious problems for you.

When doing real-world DNS, please keep these rules in mind:

- Do not set up DNS for a zone until you have received delegation of authority over that zone.
- Always make sure your reverse and forward zones agree with each other.

- Always maintain at least one secondary DNS server over a zone to avoid having a single point of failure.

- Check and recheck your setup for errors.

In order to best illustrate specific points, this chapter's examples do not consistently follow all these rules. I suggest that if you want to run this chapter's examples, you do so on a pair of machines not presently serving DNS for your organization, and make sure to use the bogus `.cxm` top-level domain and the private `192.168.100` subnet.

Note

Any time you observe excessively slow `telnet` connections (greater than 5 seconds to get the logon prompt), suspect dysfunctional DNS resolution, probably reverse resolution. In such cases, it's simple to configure forward and reverse resolution by following the instructions in the "Configuring DNS Server Master Zones" section later in this chapter.

Caution

Before editing any configuration file, back it up. Original distribution or installation-default files should be backed up to files with `.org` appended to the end (such as `resolv.conf.org`). Other revisions can be backed up with the naming convention of your choice, as long as they don't overwrite the `.org` files. Take care never to change or overwrite an `.org` file.

Important DNS Facts and Concepts

There are several vital DNS facts and concepts. Knowledge of these facts and concepts are essential for fast and effortless configuration of DNS, as well as for effective DNS troubleshooting. The most important are discussed in this section.

The DNS Client and Server Are Distinct

Every network-enabled Linux computer has DNS client software, commonly called the *resolver*. The DNS client software simply queries its assigned DNS servers in the order they appear in the `/etc/resolv.conf` file. A computer's DNS client can be assigned a server on the same computer, on another computer, or sometimes on one of each.

DNS servers are machines configured to return query data. The DNS server software relies on the `/etc/named.conf` file and the files pointed to by the zone references in that file. Clients ask, and servers answer (sometimes after asking other servers).

Confusion can arise, however, when a single computer has both a DNS client and server, with the client pointing to the server. The client and server can appear as one entity, with the resulting confusion. So always remember that `/etc/resolv.conf` pertains to the DNS client or resolver. All the other files, like `/etc/named.conf` and the files it references, pertain to the DNS server.

DNS Terminology

Table 14.1 is a limited glossary of DNS terminology.

TABLE 14.1   Glossary of Essential DNS Terminology

Term	Definition
DNS client	The software component on all networked computers that finds the IP address for a name (or vice versa) by asking its assigned DNS server(s). On Red Hat Linux machines, the client gets its configuration information from `/etc/resolv.conf`. Sometimes the term *DNS client* is used to refer to the computer itself.
Resolver	For practical purposes, a synonym for *DNS client*.
DNS server	The software component that returns the name-to-IP translation (or vice versa) to the inquiring client. The DNS server may ask other DNS servers for help in doing this. On Red Hat Linux 7 machines, the server gets its configuration from `/etc/named.conf` and the files' `named.conf` references. On Red Hat Linux machines used as DNS servers, DNS services are provided by a daemon called `named`.
Resolve	To convert a name to an IP address, or vice versa. Resolving is done by DNS and sometimes by other software.
Zone	A subdomain or subnet over which a DNS server has authority.
Master	A nameserver with authority over a zone that derives its data from local zone data files. Note that a nameserver can be master for some zones and slave for others.
Primary	A synonym for *master*.
Slave	A nameserver with authority for a zone that derives its data from another nameserver in a zone transfer. The other nameserver can be a master or another slave. Once the information is derived, it is stored locally so it can function even if its source goes down. Note that a nameserver can be master for some zones and slave for others.
Secondary	A synonym for *slave*.
Zone transfer	A transfer of zone data from a master or slave DNS server to a slave DNS server. The receiving slave initiates the zone transfer after exceeding the refresh time or upon notification from the sending server that the data has changed.

DNS Maps Names to IP Numbers and Vice Versa

DNS maps names to IP numbers and vice versa. That's all it does. This is a vital concept to understand.

Almost everything you can do with a fully qualified domain name, URL, or any other name resolvable to an IP address, you can do with that IP address. And if you use IP addresses, you needn't use DNS (except for a few reverse DNS situations). For the most part, if a command doesn't work with the IP address, the fault is not with DNS but with a lower-level network function. Trying commands with IP addresses instead of domain names and URLs is a great troubleshooting test.

The Forward and Reverse Zones Must Be Kept in Sync

The forward and reverse zones must be kept in sync. If a host changes IP addresses, that fact must be recorded in both the forward and the reverse zone data files and the serial number for each incremented. Failure to keep forward and reverse zones in sync can cause a variety of hard to solve problems, possibly worldwide.

The `HUP` Signal Versus Restart

According to most literature, including the `named` man page, `named` can be forced to reload its zone data files by the following command:

```
# kill -HUP `cat /var/run/named.pid`
```

Unfortunately, this doesn't always work. A test that doesn't do what the troubleshooter thinks it does can waste hours. Therefore, the recommended way to get the zone data files to reload is with a restart:

```
# /etc/rc.d/init.d/named restart
```

Restarting loses accumulated cache and eliminates DNS service during the restart process (20 seconds to 4 minutes). If that is unacceptable, you can try the `HUP` signal, but be very careful to verify that it does what you think it will. You can view the current `named` database and cache by sending `named` an `INT` signal. This is explained in the section "Troubleshooting DNS," later in this chapter.

The `in-addr.arpa` Domain

All reverse mappings exist in the `in-addr.arpa` domain, thereby eliminating any possible confusion regarding the number's purpose. The network and subnetwork parts of the IP address are placed in reverse order to follow the standard way domain names are written. Domain names describe the hostname, the subnetwork, and then the network, whereas IP addresses describe the network, the subnetwork, and finally the hostname. Placing the IP address in reverse order follows the convention established by the actual host and network names.

Host Naming Schemes

It is common for sites to pick a naming scheme for all of their hosts. This tends to make it easier to remember names, especially as the site grows in size. For example, the east wing of the office might use famous music bands to name their machines, and the west wing might use the names of *Star Trek* characters. This also makes it easier to locate a machine by its name.

Configuring the DNS Client: `/etc/resolv.conf`

Every machine in your network is a DNS client. Each DNS client runs resolver code to query DNS servers. The resolver gets its configuration from file `/etc/resolv.conf`. To find out which DNS server to use, you need to configure the file `/etc/resolv.conf`. This file should look something like this:

```
search domain.cxm
nameserver 192.168.100.1
```

Here `domain.cxm` is the domain name of the site, and the IP address listed after `nameserver` is the address of the DNS server that should be contacted. You can have up to three nameserver entries, each of which will be tried sequentially until one of them returns an answer. In PPP-connected machines, one or more of the nameservers can be at the ISP, relieving the local DNS server of work and decreasing traffic on the phone line.

> **Note**
>
> You must supply the nameserver's IP address, not its hostname. After all, how is the resolver going to know what the nameserver's IP address is until it finds the nameserver?

If you were to delete the `search domain.cxm` line, the result would be an inability to look up a host without its complete domain name. For instance, the following would fail if the search line were deleted:

```
$ nslookup mainserv
```

However, the following would still succeed:

```
$ nslookup mainserv.domain.cxm
```

The `/etc/host.conf` Order Statement

A client computer can choose its method of name resolution or specify a hierarchy of methods to use. This is done with the `order` statement in `/etc/host.conf`. One very efficient and reliable hierarchy is to try the `/etc/hosts` file first and then try DNS. This has two advantages:

- An `/etc/hosts` lookup is very fast.
- The computer can look itself up when DNS is down.

To accomplish this, make sure the following line is in `/etc/host.conf`:

```
order hosts,bind
```

The Software of DNS

To configure a DNS for your site, you need to be familiar with the following tools:

- `named`
- The resolver library
- `nslookup`
- `traceroute`

named

The `named` daemon needs to run on DNS servers to handle queries. If `named` cannot answer a query, it forwards the request to a server that can. Along with queries, `named` is responsible for performing zone transfers. Zone transferring is the method by which changed DNS information is propagated across the Internet. If you didn't install the `named` daemon with the Red Hat 7 operating system, you need to install it from the BIND distribution, available from `http://www.redhat.com`. It is also on one of the CD-ROMs that comes with this book. The filename is

```
bind-8.2.2_P5-24.i386.rpm
```

The `named` daemon is normally started at bootup. Here are the commands to manually start, stop, and restart `named`, respectively:

```
/etc/rc.d/init.d/named start
/etc/rc.d/init.d/named stop
/etc/rc.d/init.d/named restart
```

After you make any change to `/etc/named.conf` or any of the files referenced by `named.conf`, you must restart `named` before the changes will take effect.

14

DNS AND DHCP

> **Note**
>
> nslookup delivers many powerful features when used interactively. It can also lead to frustrating hangs. For enhanced troubleshooting, learn about nslookup from its man page.

The Resolver Library

The resolver library enables client programs to perform DNS queries. This library is built into the standard library under Linux. The resolver library takes its configuration information from /etc/resolv.conf.

nslookup

The nslookup command is a utility invoked from the command line to ensure that both the resolver and the DNS server being queried are configured correctly. It does this by resolving either a hostname into an IP address or an IP address into a domain name. To use nslookup, simply provide the address you want to resolve as a command-line argument. For example, here is the one-argument version:

```
# nslookup mydesk.domain.cxm
```

On a properly configured DNS, the result should look something like this:

```
# nslookup mydesk.domain.cxm
Server:  mainserv.domain.cxm
Address:  192.168.100.1

Name:    mydesk.domain.cxm
Address:  192.168.100.2
```

The two-argument version specifies the IP address of the DNS server as the second argument. In the absence of the second argument, the first server line in /etc/resolv.conf is used. Here's a two-argument example:

```
# nslookup mydesk.domain.cxm 192.168.100.1
```

The two-argument command returns the exact same output as the one-argument version. The two-argument version is used when reverse DNS isn't functioning correctly or if /etc/resolv.conf has been temporarily renamed or deleted.

traceroute

The traceroute utility enables you to determine the path a packet is taking across your network and into other networks. This is very useful for debugging network connection problems, especially when you suspect the trouble is located in someone else's network.

Using the ICMP protocol (Internet Control Message Protocol, the same protocol as used by `ping`), `traceroute` looks up each machine along the path to a destination host and displays the corresponding name and IP address for that site. Along with each name is the number of milliseconds that each of the three tiers took to get to the destination.

Preceding each name is a number that indicates the distance to that host in terms of *hops*. The number of hops to a host indicates the number of intermediate machines that had to process the packet. As you can guess, a machine that is one or two hops away is usually much closer than a machine that is 30 hops away.

To use `traceroute`, give the destination hostname or IP address as a command-line argument. For example:

```
# traceroute www.hyperreal.org
```

This should return something similar to the following:

```
traceroute to hyperreal.org (204.62.130.147), 30 hops max, 40 byte
➥packets
 1  fe0-0.cr1.NUQ.globalcenter.net (205.216.146.77)  0.829 ms  0.764
➥ms  0.519 ms
 2  pos6-0.cr2.SNV.globalcenter.net (206.251.0.30)  1.930 ms  1.839 ms
➥1.887 ms
 3  fe1-0.br2.SNV.globalcenter.net (206.251.5.2)  2.760 ms  2.779 ms
➥2.517 ms
 4  sl-stk-17-H10/0-T3.sprintlink.net (144.228.147.9)  5.117 ms  6.160
➥ms  6.109 ms
 5  sl-stk-14-F0/0.sprintlink.net (144.228.40.14)  5.453 ms  5.985 ms
➥6.157 ms
 6  sl-wired-2-S0-T1.sprintlink.net (144.228.144.138)  10.987 ms
➥25.130 ms  11.831 ms
 7  sf2-s0.wired.net (205.227.206.22)  30.453 ms  15.800 ms  21.220 ms
 8  taz.hyperreal.org (204.62.130.147)  16.745 ms  14.914 ms  13.018 ms
```

14

DNS AND DHCP

> **Note**
>
> Using a hostname for `traceroute` or `ping` might appear to hang if the name can't be resolved. It's best to learn a few strategic IP addresses (like your ISP's DNS, WWW, default gateway, and so on) and check those if hostnames appear to fail.

If you see any star characters (such as *) instead of a hostname, that machine is probably unavailable. This could be due to a variety of reasons, with network failure and firewall protection being the most common. Also, be sure to note the time it takes to get from one site to another. If you feel that your connection is excessively slow, it might be just one connection in the middle that is slowing you down and not the site itself.

By using `traceroute`, you can also get a good measure of the connectivity of a site. If you are in the process of evaluating an ISP, try doing a `traceroute` from its site to a number of other sites, especially to large communications companies such as Sprint and MCI. Count how many hops, and how much time per hop, it takes to reach its network.

DNS Server Configuration Files

The DNS server is a potentially complex system configured by a surprisingly straightforward set of files. These files consist of a single boot file and several zone data files, each of which is pointed to by a zone record in the boot file. This section discusses these files and their features, syntax, and conventions.

The DNS Boot File: `/etc/named.conf`

The `/etc/named.conf` file is read in when `named` is started. Boot file comments can be done in three different ways:

```
/* C style comments can comment out multiple lines */
// C++ style comments comment one or fractional lines
# Shellscript style comments function like C++ style
```

Other statements take the form

```
keyword {statement; statement; ...; statement;};
```

Because everything in this file is brace-, space-, and semicolon-delimited, multiple spacing and line breaks do not affect its functionality.

> **Caution**
>
> Bugs caused by syntax errors in the `named` files are hard to detect. Often there are no symptoms, and even when symptoms are observable, the messages are often cryptic and hard to trace to the bug. So it is imperative to check the files carefully.

The two most common section-starting keywords in `named.conf` are `options` and `zone`. Listing 14.1 is a `named.conf` that does reverse DNS on its loopback and its `eth0`, and does forward DNS on `domain.cxm`.

LISTING 14.1   Example `named.conf` File

```
options {
  directory "/var/named";         #referred files in /var/named
};

zone "." {
  type hint;                      #hints for caching
  file "named.ca";                #root servers file in
};                                #   /var/named/named.ca

zone "0.0.127.in-addr.arpa" {     #reverse on loopback
  type master;
  file "named.local";
};

zone "100.168.192.in-addr.arpa" { #reverse on eth0 subnet
  type master;                    #file is on this host
  file "named.192.168.100";       #rev dns file
};

zone "domain.cxm" {               #DNS for all hosts this domain
  type master;                    #file is on this host
  file "named.domain.cxm";        #dns file for domain
};
```

The `options` section holds information that's global to the entire DNS server. This one contains a single piece of information, the `directory` statement, which tells `named` the location of any filenames mentioned in the configuration.

`zone "."` is the caching zone. A caching zone isn't a master or slave, but rather a set of hints for the server software to use; hence the `type hints;` statement. The file for `zone "."` is `named.ca`, which was created by Red Hat's installation. `named.ca` contains a list of all the root DNS servers on the Internet. These root servers are needed to prime `named`'s cache. You can get the latest list of root servers from the InterNIC at

`ftp://rs.internic.net/domain/named.cache`

Each zone has a `type` statement indicating `master`, `slave`, or `hint` and a `file` statement pointing to the file containing data for the zone. Files of type `slave` have a nested `master` section. This will be demonstrated in the section "Adding a Slave DNS Server," later in this chapter.

Each zone section defines a zone of authority, which is usually a domain, a subdomain or, in the case of reverse DNS, a subnet. Almost every zone defines a file from which it derives its information. Every zone has a `type` statement.

notify

Another statement appearing frequently in zones and the `options` section is the `notify` statement, which can be `notify yes;` or `notify no;`. The default is yes, so there's no reason to put in a `notify yes;` except for documentation. If `notify` is yes, the zone's slaves are informed of zone data changes so they can initiate a zone transfer. If it's no, no notification is given. `notify no;` is often inserted to prevent bogus domains (like `domain.cxm`) from hitting real Internet nameservers. Note that if a `notify` statement appears in the `options` section, it serves as the default for all zones but is specified to be overridden by any zone-specific `notify` statement.

forwarders

With a `forwarders` statement in the `options` section, you can specify one or more name-servers to send queries that can't be resolved locally:

```
options {
  forwarders { 192.168.100.10; 192.168.100.20; };
  ...
```

This sends unresolved queries to the two servers mentioned instead of sending them to the local caching DNS. This can be advantageous when there's a premium on outside traffic. If all internal servers resolve outside names via one or two servers, those servers build up huge caches, meaning that more queries are resolved inside the building walls. Otherwise, all the servers might be making identical queries to the outside world.

If for some reason the forwarder cannot answer the query, the query is tried via the normal server-caching DNS. To absolutely forbid any remote query from a DNS server, place a `forward-only;` statement right below the `forwarders` statement. Doing this makes the forwarder server(s) a single point of failure, so it's not recommended.

DNS Zone Data Files

Zone data files are pointed to by the file statements in the boot file's zone sections and contain all data about the zone. The first thing to understand is that the syntax of a zone data file is totally different from the syntax of the boot file `named.conf`.

Zone Data File Syntax Is Totally Different from Boot File Syntax

It's important to remember that the syntax of the zone data files is not the same as that of the DNS boot file (`named.conf`). The zone data file comment character is the semicolon. For each line, DNS will fail if the `name` data item has spaces before it.

> **Note**
>
> The name data item is normally the first on the line and must not be preceded with spaces. However, occasionally the name data item can be absent from the line, giving the appearance of space before the first data item. What's really happening is that the name data item was left off the line, allowing it to default to the name data item in the nearest previous line containing a name data item. For all practical purposes, the next data item after the name is either the word IN or a number representing a "Time To Live" (followed by IN). Knowing this can help you avoid much confusion.

Zone Data File Naming Conventions

A zone data file can be given any name. For maintainability, however, a naming convention should be used. The conventions used in this chapter are outlined in the following paragraphs.

The cache (root server) data file is called named.ca because the Red Hat installation created it with that name. For the same reason, the reverse DNS file for the loopback at 127.0.0.1 is called named.local.

Master forward DNS data files are the word named, followed by a period, followed by the entire domain name. For instance, the master forward DNS data file for domain domain.cxm is called named.domain.cxm.

Master reverse DNS zone data files are the word named, followed by a period, followed by the IP number of the subnet. For instance, the reverse DNS zone data file for subnet 192.168.100 is named.192.168.100. Many people reverse the IP address to match the 100.168.192.in-addr.arpa statement. The naming convention is entirely up to you.

Zone Data Substitutions

As mentioned previously, the file statement in the named.conf zone record points to the zone data file describing the domain named in the zone. Because the domain is specified by the named.conf zone record, that domain is substituted for the @ symbol anywhere that symbol appears in the zone data file. The same is true for reverse DNS subnets. Furthermore, in the zone data file, any name not ending in a period is assumed to be relative to the domain specified in named.conf. For instance, if the domain specified in named.conf is domain.cxm and the name mainserv appears unterminated by a period inside the zone data file, the word mainserv means the same as the absolute version, mainserv.domain.cxm. (note the terminating period).

Zone Data File Components

The zone's file line in the /etc/named.conf file points to a file containing the information that named needs in order to answer queries on the zone's domain. The file format for these configuration files is a bit tricky, unfortunately, and requires care when you're setting it up. Be especially careful with periods—a misplaced period can quickly become difficult to track down.

The format of each line in the configuration file is as follows:

```
name     IN    record_type    data
```

Here *name* is the hostname you are dealing with. Any hostnames that do not end in a period have the domain name appended to them automatically.

The second column, IN, is actually a parameter telling named to use the Internet class of records. There are two other classes, CH and HS, but they're almost never used.

The third and fourth columns, *record_type* and *data*, indicate what kind of record you're dealing with and the parameters associated with it, respectively. There are 10 possible records:

SOA	Start of authority
NS	Nameserver
A	Address record
PTR	Pointer record
MX	Mail exchanger
CNAME	Canonical name
RP and TXT	The documentation entries
HINFO	Host information
NULL	Null resource record with no format or data

SOA: Start of Authority

The SOA record starts the description of a site's DNS entries. The format of this entry is as follows:

```
domain.cxm. IN SOA ns1.domain.cxm. hostmaster.domain.cxm. (
     2000070100      ; serial number, YYYYMMDDxx
     10800           ; refresh rate in seconds (3 hours)
     1800            ; retry in seconds (30 minutes)
     1209600         ; expire in seconds (2 weeks)
     604800 )        ; minimum in seconds (1 week)
```

The first line begins with the domain for which this SOA record is authoritative. In most real zone data files, the hard-coded `domain.cxm.` in the first column would be replaced by the @ symbol. This first data item is followed by `IN`, to indicate that the Internet standard is being used, and `SOA`, to indicate start of authority. The column after `SOA` is the primary nameserver for this domain. Finally, the last column specifies the email address for the person in charge. Note that the email address is not in the standard *user@domain.cxm* form, but has a period instead of the @ symbol. A good practice is to create the mail alias `hostmaster` at your site and have all mail sent to it and forwarded to the appropriate people.

At the end of the first line is an open parenthesis. This tells `named` that the line continues onto the next line, thereby making the file easier to read.

The five values presented in subsequent lines detail the characteristics of this record. The first line is the record's serial number. Whenever you make a change to any entry in this file, you need to increment this value so secondary servers know to perform zone transfers. Typically, the current date in the form `YYYYMMDDxx` is used, where `YYYY` is the year, `MM` is the month, `DD` is the day, and `xx` is the revision done that day. This allows for multiple revisions in one day.

The second value is the refresh rate in seconds. This value tells the slave DNS servers how often they should query the master server to see if the records have been updated.

The third value is the retry rate in seconds. If the secondary server tries to contact the primary DNS server to check for updates but cannot contact it, the secondary server tries again after *retry* seconds.

When secondary servers have cached the entry, the fourth value indicates to them that if they cannot contact the primary server for an update, they should discard the value after the specified number of seconds. One to two weeks is a good value for this.

The final value, the `minimum` entry, tells caching servers how long they should wait before expiring the entry if they cannot contact the primary DNS server. Five to seven days is a good guideline for this entry.

Don't forget to place a closing parenthesis after the fifth value.

NS: Nameserver

The NS record specifies the authoritative nameservers for a given domain. For example:

```
IN NS    ns1.domain.cxm.
IN NS    ns2.domain.cxm.
```

Note that if the NS records directly follow the SOA record, you do not need to specify the name field in the DNS record. In that case, the NS records will assume the same name field as the SOA record.

14

DNS AND DHCP

In this example, the domain, `domain.cxm`, has two nameservers, `ns1.domain.cxm.` and `ns2.domain.cxm.`. These are fully qualified hostnames, so they need to have the period as the suffix. Without the period, `named` would evaluate their value to be `ns1.domain.cxm.domain.cxm`, which is *not* what you're looking for.

A: Address Record

The address record is used for providing translations from hostnames to IP addresses. There should be an `A` record for each machine that needs a publicly-resolvable hostname. A sample entry using the `A` record is

```
mydesk    IN A       192.168.100.2
```

In this example, the address is specified for the host `mydesk`. Because this hostname is not suffixed by a period, `named` assumes it is in the same domain as the current `SOA` record. Thus, the hostname is `mydesk.domain.cxm`.

PTR: Pointer Record

The pointer record, also known as the reverse resolution record, tells `named` how to turn an IP address into a hostname. `PTR` records are a little odd in that they should not be in the same `SOA` as your `A` records. Instead, they appear in an `in-addr.arpa` subdomain `SOA`.

A `PTR` record looks like this:

```
2.100.168.192.  IN PTR  mydesk.domain.cxm.
```

Notice that the IP address to be reverse-resolved is in reverse order and is suffixed with a period.

MX: Mail Exchanger

The mail exchanger record enables you to specify which host on your network is in charge of receiving mail from the outside. `sendmail` uses this record to determine the correct machine to which mail needs to be sent. The format of an `MX` record looks like this:

```
domain.cxm.   IN MX 10    mailhub
              IN MX 50    mailhub2
```

The first column indicates the hostname for which mail is received. In this case, it's `domain.cxm`. Based on the previous examples, you might have noticed that you have yet to specify a machine that answers to `domain.cxm.`, but the sample `MX` record shows that you can accept mail for it. This is an important feature of DNS; you can specify a hostname for which you accept mail even if that hostname doesn't have an `A` record.

As expected, the IN class is the second column. The third column specifies that this line is an MX record. The number after the MX indicates a priority level for that entry. Lower numbers mean higher priority. In this example, sendmail will try to communicate with mailhub first. If it cannot successfully communicate with mailhub, it will try mailhub2.

CNAME: Canonical Name

The CNAME record makes it possible to alias hostnames via DNS. This is useful for giving common names to servers. For example, we are used to Web servers having the hostname www, as in www.domain.cxm. However, you might not want to name the Web server using this convention at all. On many sites, the machines have a theme to the naming of hosts, and placing www in the middle of that might appear awkward.

To use a CNAME, you must have another record for that host—such as an A or MX record—that specifies its real name. For example:

```
mydesk      IN A        192.168.100.2
www      IN CNAME    mydesk
```

In this example, mydesk is the real name of the server and www is its alias.

RP and TXT: The Documentation Entries

Providing contact information as part of your database is often useful—not just as comments, but as actual records that can be queried by others. You can accomplish this by using the RP and TXT records.

TXT records are freeform text entries in which you can place any information you see fit. Most often, you will only want to give contact information. Each TXT record must be tied to a particular hostname. For example:

```
domain.cxm.   IN TXT "Contact: Heidi S."
              IN TXT "Systems Administrator/Ring Master"
              IN TXT "Voice: (800) 555-1212"
```

Because TXT records are freeform, you're not forced to place contact information there. As a result, the RP record was created, which explicitly states who is the person responsible for the specified host. For example:

```
domain.cxm.      IN RP heidis.domain.cxm. domain.cxm.
```

The first column states the domain for which the responsible party is set. The second column, IN, defines this record to use the Internet class. RP designates this to be a responsible party record. The fourth column specifies the email address of the person who is actually responsible. Notice that the @ symbol has been replaced by a period in this address, much as in the SOA record. The last column specifies a TXT record that gives additional information. In this example, it points back to the TXT record for domain.cxm.

HINFO: Host Information

These records list various host information, such as CPU type and operating system.

NULL: Null Resource Record

An empty record containing neither format nor data. According to RFC 1035, this can be thought of as a "user defined" record that can contain absolutely anything as long as it's not more than 65535 "octets," which are basically bytes in this context.

Other Resource Records

The DNS standard has other types of resource records. To see the full list, see RFC 1035 and some of the other RFCs that updated it. You can find RFC 1035 at `http://ietf.` `org/rfc/rfc1035.txt`. To see the entire list of RFCs, listing replacements and updates, go to `ftp://ftp.isi.edu/in-notes/rfc-index.txt`.

Configuring `resolv.conf` with `linuxconf`

The `/etc/resolv.conf` file contains the configuration for the DNS client (resolver). It typically looks something like this:

```
search domain.cxm
nameserver 192.168.211.34
nameserver 192.168.100.1
```

> **Caution**
>
> Before editing any configuration file, with an editor or with a tool like · `linuxconf`, back it up. Original distribution or installation-default files should be backed up to files with `.org` appended to the end (such as `resolv.conf.` `org`). Other revisions can be backed up with the naming convention of your choice, as long as they don't overwrite the `.org` files. Take care never to change or overwrite an `.org` file.
>
> Note that with tools like `linuxconf`, it's not always possible to predict every configuration file that will be affected. Do your best to back up files you believe will be affected.

In the preceding `/etc/resolv.conf`, typically the first nameserver address is that of the ISP's DNS server, while the second is that of your local LAN. Sometimes they're reversed, or sometimes only the local LAN number is used (in which case all DNS resolution is through either the local DNS or local caching DNS). The search line is important in that it's what enables lookup of a hostname without fully qualifying the domain. For instance, execute the following command:

```
$ nslookup mydesk
Server:  mainserv.domain.cxm
Address:  192.168.100.1

Name:    mydesk.domain.cxm
Address:  192.168.100.2

$
```

You can experiment by commenting out the search line in /etc/resolv.conf, after which the exact same command fails:

```
$ nslookup mydesk
Server:  mainserv.domain.cxm
Address:  192.168.100.1

***mainserv.domain.cxm can't find mydesk: No response from server
$
```

Even after commenting out the search line, you can still look up the fully qualified domain name (FQDN), as shown by the following command:

```
$ nslookup mydesk.domain.cxm
Server:  mainserv.domain.cxm
Address:  192.168.100.1

Name:    mydesk.domain.cxm
Address:  192.168.100.2

$
```

Many administrators prefer to directly edit /etc/resolv.conf. However, the linuxconf utility provides a convenient edit method. In linuxconf, choose Networking, Name Server Specification (DNS) to access the Resolver configuration screen. Be sure to check the DNS Is Required for Normal Operation check box. Place your list of DNS servers, in the order you want them tried, in the text boxes titled IP of Name Server 1 through IP of Name Server 3. Note that the second and third name servers are optional.

The Resolver configuration screen, accessible from Linuxconf, is shown in Figure 14.1.

Note that this figure is for the sylvia computer rather than mainserv, revealing the fact that both are set up the same way. Both are resolved from 192.168.100.1 (mainserv) and search domain domain.cxm. The Search Domain 1 through Search Domain 4 fields are optional, and if you enter info in them, they are written to /etc/resolv.conf as search lines. As previously discussed, search lines enable searching by a hostname

14

DNS AND DHCP

without a domain name. Multiple search lines are sometimes handy to search for a host in multiple domains. For instance, if `domain.cxm` has a subdomain called `subdomain.domain.cxm`, and if hostnames are unique on both, it might be handy to include both in search lines. However, if there's a chance that the same hostname exists on both domains, it's better to have only one search line.

FIGURE 14.1

The Resolver con-figuration screen.

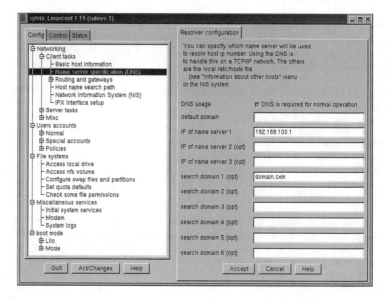

The one other field on this form is the Default Domain field. If entered, it specifies a string to append to all hostnames. As such it's very similar to the search lines. Note that the default domain can be defined outside `/etc/resolv.conf`. For instance, if a fully qualified domain name is given as an argument to the hostname command, everything to the right of the first dot is considered the default domain. It can also be defined in the `.rhosts` file. In practice on Red Hat machines, the default domain is rendered unnecessary by using a search line instead.

A Trivial Caching DNS

A normal Red Hat 7 installation includes a caching DNS implementation. Depending on the exact install method, and post-install configuration activities, this installation-default setup may have a flaw, making it excessively slow on any reverse DNS lookup (more on reverse DNS later in the "Configuring DNS Server Master Zones" section of this chapter). This problem can be verified by using `telnet` to access the newly installed machine. If this flaw exists, `telnet` will typically take 30 seconds or more to ask for the username and may time out entirely. Note that it's possible for slow `telnet` to be caused by flawed forward (name to number) resolution, although this is less common.

The following code contains the installation-default `/etc/resolv.conf` file for the new host:

```
search domain.cxm
nameserver 192.168.100.1
```

The `resolv.conf` file configures the DNS client, not the DNS server, even though in many cases they coexist on the same computer. The first line of `resolv.conf` defines `domain.cxm` as the client's default domain. That's the domain that's appended to machine names. The second line defines the IP address of the DNS server used by the client.

Listing 14.2 contains the installation-default `/etc/named.conf` file for the new host.

LISTING 14.2 The `/etc/named.conf` File

```
// generated by named-bootconf.pl

options {
        directory "/var/named";
        /*
         * If there is a firewall between you and nameservers you want
         * to talk to, you might need to uncomment the query-source
         * directive below.  Previous versions of BIND always asked
         * questions using port 53, but BIND 8.1 uses an unprivileged
         * port by default.
         */
        // query-source address * port 53;
};

//
// a caching only nameserver config
//
zone "." {
        type hint;
        file "named.ca";
};

zone "0.0.127.in-addr.arpa" {
        type master;
        file "named.local";
};
```

14

DNS AND DHCP

In this file, anything preceded by `//` or enclosed in `/* */` is a comment. In English, the preceding file says the following:

- All zone data files mentioned in `named.conf` shall be relative to directory `/var/named`.

- zone `"."` is the root of the DNS tree, hints to which are given in file `named.ca`, which is a list of the root servers.

- Any IP address in subnet `127.0.0` shall be resolved according to zone data file `named.local`, which is used, but not created, by the DNS server. Had it been `type slave` instead of `type master`, the file would have been created by the DNS server out of data from a zone transfer from a master zone on another computer.

When you're working with `named.conf`, remember that syntax is important. Make sure all quotes, braces, and semicolons are in place. If you prefer, everything between braces may be placed on a single line.

Testing Your Caching DNS

First, verify that `telnet` logs in properly. Run this command on another machine:

```
# telnet 192.168.100.1
```

If it takes about a second for the username prompt to appear, so far so good. If it takes 20 seconds or more, there's still a reverse DNS problem.

> **Note**
>
> The `telnet` program is the "miner's canary" of reverse DNS. If there's a reverse DNS problem, `telnet` will hang or be extremely slow. Other programs can hang, with much worse consequences, because of bad reverse DNS. `sendmail` is one such program.
>
> In the case of `sendmail`, it's possible the hang will prevent successful boot, requiring a repair expedition with boot and rescue disks. Other programs that are sometimes run on bootup can also hang on bad reverse DNS. This is why it's vital to have `telnet` working properly before you shut down or reboot the system.
>
> If for some reason you can't repair reverse DNS before rebooting, temporarily rename `/etc/resolv.conf` before booting, and then rename it after.
>
> The easiest way to repair your reverse and forward DNS resolution is to follow the instructions in the "Configuring DNS Server Master Zones" section later in this chapter, and then test with `nslookup` and maybe `dnswalk`. The `dnswalk` utility is discussed in the "Troubleshooting DNS" section of this chapter.

Testing Non-Local Lookup

The time has come to test the lookup capability of your caching DNS. Although a caching-only DNS server cannot provide lookup for the local network, it can refer any queries for the Internet at large to the proper Internet DNS servers. You'll remember that /var/named/named.ca was simply a list of the world's root DNS servers. These servers are "consulted" unless your cache "remembers" a lower-level server that's authoritative over the domain.

Start by verifying a good Internet connection with the ping command. Remember that DNS cannot work without a good network connection. ping the IP addresses of several Web sites that are known to be up most of the time. If you cannot ping these addresses, look for network, PPP, or routing problems.

If you're using PPP, sometimes you'll need to make a new default route corresponding to your PPP.

With PPP connections, routing is often the cause. While pppd is running, start with the ifconfig ppp0 command:

```
# /sbin/ifconfig ppp0
ppp0      Link encap:Point-to-Point Protocol
          inet addr:10.37.60.188  P-t-P:10.1.1.1  Mask:255.255.255.255
          UP POINTOPOINT RUNNING NOARP MULTICAST  MTU:1500  Metric:1
          RX packets:7 errors:0 dropped:0 overruns:0 frame:0
          TX packets:7 errors:0 dropped:0 overruns:0 carrier:0
          collisions:0 txqueuelen:10
```

If you can ping the ppp0 inet address and the IP address following P-t-P (which stands for Point To Point) but cannot ping other Internet addresses, suspect routing. With pppd running, issue this command:

```
# /sbin/route add default gw 10.1.1.1 ppp0
```

Obviously, substitute the P-t-P address given by the ifconfig command. Try your ping again.

Once you can ping using IP addresses, you're ready to test your caching DNS itself by accessing a URL with ping. Try this command:

```
# ping www.mcp.com
```

If all is well, the preceding ping command will display replies from www.mcp.com. If not, carefully review the files and commands discussed up to this point. Once you can ping the URL, you know your caching DNS works.

14

DNS AND DHCP

If you have lynx installed, you can actually use it to browse the Web:

```
# lynx http://www.mcp.com
```

After a suitable delay, the Macmillan Publishing Web site should appear in your lynx browser.

Addressing Special PPP Considerations

The preceding was an example. To reduce bandwidth, in real life you'd let your ISP do all your DNS by telling your DNS client that the nameserver is the ISP's nameserver. Simply put a

```
nameserver ###.###.###.###
```

line in your /etc/resolv.conf file above all other nameserver lines. The ###.###.###.### represents your ISP's primary DNS. You can also place the secondary DNS there. However, your DNS client will honor only three nameserver lines.

If you find that the additional nameserver(s) slows your normal network activities, you can have two different files you copy to /etc/resolv.conf: one for when you're online and one for when you're not.

Caching Server Summary

As installed, Red Hat 7 comes configured as a caching server. Depending on the installation procedures and post-installation configuration activities, it's possible that a reverse DNS flaw, or even a forward DNS flaw, can cause problems on programs like telnet, ftp, and sendmail. In such a case, the simple addition of reverse DNS resolution for the network subnet, or possibly forward DNS resolution for the domain, gives you a completely functioning caching-only server capable of resolving all Internet domain names, but not any that are declared locally.

Caching-only servers are the simplest and least authoritative of the three server types. The other two, master and slave, are discussed in the sections "Configuring DNS Server Master Zones" and "Adding a Slave DNS Server."

Configuring DNS Server Master Zones

As mentioned earlier, DNS comes in three flavors:

- Master (also called primary)
- Slave (also called secondary)
- Caching-only

We discussed creating a caching-only server earlier in the chapter. Caching-only servers cannot answer queries, but can only pass those queries on to other servers with master or slave zones that are authoritative over the domain in question. However, all DNS servers should be configured to perform caching functions.

Now let's turn our attention to adding DNS server master zones. A DNS server master zone can answer queries about its domain without querying other servers, because its data resides on the local hard disk. A DNS server master zone is considered to have the most up-to-date records for all the hosts in that domain.

Adding Local Domain Resolution

Earlier in the chapter you created a caching-only DNS residing on the hypothetical host `mainserv` at address `192.168.100.1` in domain `domain.cxm`. Assume that this same subnet has host `mydesk` at `192.168.100.2`. It's an easy task to add local domain resolution, using master zones. Here is the basic procedure:

1. Add master zone `domain.cxm` to `named.conf`, pointing to zone data file `named.domain.cxm`.

2. Add master zone `100.168.192-in-addr.arpa` to `named.conf`, pointing to zone data file `named.192.168.100`.

3. Create zone data file `named.domain.cxm`, resolving both hosts, `sendmail` and `www`.

4. Create reverse zone data file `named.192.168.100`, resolving both IP addresses.

5. Restart `named`.

6. Test and troubleshoot.

> **Note**
>
> Anytime you modify a zone data file, you must be sure to increment that file's serial number. The serial number is the first number after the first opening parenthesis and is usually expressed as `yyyymmdd##` to give you 100 chances per day to increase it.
>
> Never use a serial number greater than 2147483647, because it will overflow the 32-bit internal representation of the serial number. This would produce a very hard-to-find bug, as your secondaries get bogus serials and won't update as needed. Fortunately, this will no longer be an issue by the year 2147 because compilers and operating systems will accommodate much bigger numbers than 32 bits.
>
> Obviously, serial numbers must never be more than 10 digits and must never include non-numerics.

14

DNS AND DHCP

> Failure to increment it will result in various slave and cache DNS servers failing to pick up your modifications. It must be incremented, not changed to a lesser value.
>
> When you're creating a brand new zone data file, the best practice is to set its serial number to the present date, revision 0. For instance, if you create it on February 21, 2002, the serial number for the new file should be 2002022100.

Add Zone `domain.cxm` to `named.conf`

Add the following code to `/etc/named.conf`:

```
zone "domain.cxm" {            #DNS for all host this domain
  type master;                 #file on this host
  file "named.domain.cxm";     #dns file for domain
};
```

This says to refer any name or FQDN in domain `domain.cxm` to the data in `named.domain.cxm`, which, due to the `type master;` statement, is input to the DNS server, not output from it and not an intermediate file. Note that the text to the right of the pound signs (#) are comments. Next, create file `named.domain.cxm`.

Add Master Zone `100.168.192-in-addr.arpa` to `named.conf`

Add the following code to `/etc/named.conf`:

```
zone "100.168.192.in-addr.arpa" {   #DNS for all IP's in subnet
      type master;                  #file on this host
      file "named.192.168.100";     #DNS file for this subnet
};
```

The preceding says to refer any IP address in the 192.168.100 subnet to the data in `named.192.168.100`, which resides in `/var/named` as specified by `directory` clause in the `options` statement of `/etc/named.conf`. See Listing 14.1 in the section "DNS Server Configuration Files" earlier in this chapter.

Create Zone Data File `named.domain.cxm`

Create the following `/var/named/named.domain.cxm`:

```
@       IN      SOA     mainserv.domain.cxm. hostmaster.domain.cxm.  (
                                2000072001 ; Serial
                                28800      ; Refresh
                                14400      ; Retry
                                3600000    ; Expire
                                86400 )    ; Minimum
```

```
                  IN    NS          mainserv
                  IN    MX 10       mainserv

mainserv          IN    A           192.168.100.1
mydesk            IN    A           192.168.100.2
www               IN    CNAME       mainserv
```

Nameserver `mainserv.domain.cxm` has authority over zone `@`, which, via the zone call in `named.conf`, is set to `domain.cxm`. The information between the parentheses contains timing details explained earlier in this chapter. A single nameserver (`NS`) for `@` (`domain.cxm`) is at `mainserv`. `mainserv` handles the mail (`MX`) for `domain.cxm`. The `mainserv` and `mydesk` hosts in `domain.cxm` have addresses `192.168.100.1` and `192.168.100.2`, respectively. Alias `www` refers to `mainserv`, which by a previous line is set to `192.168.100.1`.

The `IN NS` and `IN MX` statements have no name identifier in column 1. An `IN` item lacking a name identifier defaults to the name identifier of the last statement possessing an identifier, which in this case is the top line.

The preceding zone data file is built for simplicity. Real-life servers have an `ns IN A 192.168.100.1` type line so they can call the nameserver `ns` in all files. That way, if the nameserver is changed from `mainserv` to `mydesk`, the only required change in any file is the `ns IN A` line. Real-life zones also have at least two `IN NS` lines, so if one nameserver goes down, the other one picks up the slack.

Note that syntax is important, especially because zone data file syntax is different from boot file syntax. All name identifiers must be in column 1. All periods (`.`) are vital because a name ending in a period is considered absolute, while a name not ending in a period is considered relative to the `@` symbol, which is substituted by the domain from the `named.conf` zone record.

Create Reverse Zone Data File `named.192.168.100`

Create the following `named.192.168.100`:

```
@      IN    SOA     mainserv.domain.cxm. hostmaster.domain.cxm. (
                            2000072001  ; Serial
                            28800       ; Refresh
                            14400       ; Retry
                            3600000     ; Expire
                            86400 )     ; Minimum
       IN    NS      mainserv.domain.cxm.

1      IN    PTR     mainserv.domain.cxm.
2      IN    PTR     mydesk.domain.cxm.
```

14

DNS AND DHCP

In the preceding, the @ at the start stands for what was called from /etc/named.conf, in this case 100.168.192.in-addr.arpa. The 1 and 2 in the name field at the bottom are prepended to that, so the full reverse domains are 1.100.168.192.in-addr.arpa, which resolves to mainserv.domain.cxm, and 2.100.168.192.in-addr.arpa, which resolves to mydesk.domain.cxm.

Restart named, and then Test and Troubleshoot

Restart with this command:

```
# /etc/rc.d/init.d/named restart
```

It could take a few minutes for this command to finish.

Once it finishes, test it. First, try accessing the machine with telnet and make sure you get the login: prompt within a second or two. If telnet hangs, investigate your reverse DNS zones and reverse DNS zone data files.

Next, try running the following commands:

```
ping 192.168.100.1
ping 192.168.100.2
```

Do each ping from each server. If any IP ping fails, there's a network connectivity problem that must be solved before you attempt to activate DNS. Once connectivity is proved, do the following:

```
ping mainserv
ping mydesk
ping mainserv.domain.cxm.
ping mydesk.domain.cxm.
ping www.domain.cxm.
```

> **Note**
>
> If the fully qualified domain names (that is, mydesk.domain.cxm) succeed but the server names (that is, mainserv) fail, check to make sure you have the proper search statement in /etc/resolv.conf. It's the search domain.cxm line that enables resolution of the hostname alone.

If the preceding ping commands succeed, it confirms a working DNS. If not, troubleshoot (covered later in this section). The following nslookup commands add further confirmation if they succeed, don't hang, and deliver the right IP address:

```
nslookup mainserv
nslookup mydesk
```

```
nslookup mainserv.domain.cxm.
nslookup mydesk.domain.cxm.
nslookup www.domain.cxm.
nslookup 192.168.100.1
nslookup 192.168.100.2
```

Each command should quickly deliver the expected results. If you have `sendmail` up and running, test the `IN MX` statements with email operations.

Troubleshooting is essentially the process of elimination. Try to determine whether it's the forward or reverse lookup that is giving you problems. Try to narrow it down to a single domain, server, or IP. Use `ping` to make sure you have network connectivity.

Adding Virtual Domain Resolution

Not all IP addresses denote actual hardware. Some are alias addresses intended to represent Web sites. These Web sites are sometimes granted individual alias IP addresses. Here are the steps to add a virtual domain (in the existing subnet):

1. Create the zone in `named.conf`.
2. Create a new zone data file.
3. Add an `IN PTR` line to the existing reverse DNS file for the subnet.
4. Restart `named`.

In the following example, add domain `vdomain.cxm` at IP address `192.168.100.101`. This IP address is created by the following command:

```
# /sbin/ifconfig eth0:0 192.168.100.101 netmask 255.255.255.0
```

This IP is made into a virtual host Web site in `/etc/httpd/conf/httpd.conf`, so all it needs is a domain name. Assuming you want to give `192.168.100.101` the name `vdomain.cxm`, add the following zone to `named.conf`:

```
zone "vdomain.cxm" {          #DNS for virtual domain
  type master;                #file is on this host
  file "named.vdomain.cxm";   #dns file for domain
};
```

As you can see, the zone data file is `named.vdomain.cxm`. Create that file as follows:

```
@       IN      SOA     mainserv.domain.cxm. hostmaster.domain.cxm.  (
                                2000072001 ; Serial
                                28800      ; Refresh
                                14400      ; Retry
                                3600000    ; Expire
                                86400 )    ; Minimum
```

14

DNS AND DHCP

```
                  IN    NS          mainserv.domain.cxm.

@                 IN    A           192.168.100.101
www               IN    CNAME       @
```

Read the preceding as follows: `mainserv.domain.cxm` has authority over @ (vdomain.cxm). The nameserver for @ is `mainserv.domain.cxm`, and `vdomain.cxm` (@) has the address `192.168.100.101`, as does `www.vdomain.cxm`.

The reason both `vdomain.cxm` and `www.vdomain.cxm` are resolved is so they can be accessed as `http://vdomain.cxm` or `http://www.vdomain.cxm`.

Now add the reverse DNS for the virtual domain with this line in `named.192.168.100`:

```
101    IN    PTR      vdomain.cxm.
```

> **Note**
>
> The preceding example placed the virtual domain in the host's subnet. It can be in a different subnet (and often is). In that case, a new reverse DNS zone data file must be set up for the additional subnet, and several routing and forwarding steps must be taken so the different subnet is visible to browsers around the world.

Once again, test your work with `nslookup` and any other DNS diagnostic tools you might be using.

Delegating Authority

With millions of domain names and URLs on the Internet, the only way to keep track is with a distributed system. DNS implements this distribution through delegation to subdomains.

This section implements a trivial delegation whose purpose is illustrative only. No `MX`, no `CNAME`, no secondary server, not even reverse DNS. Just the same subnet as the rest of the examples in this chapter.

Imagine that a new department, called Subdomain, wants to administer its own DNS. That makes less work for the `domain.cxm` administrators. Table 14.2 shows that the department has four hosts.

TABLE 14.2   The Subdomain Department's Servers

Host	IP
sylvia	192.168.100.40
brett	192.168.100.41
rena	192.168.100.42
valerie	192.168.100.43

So from a DNS point of view, the four hosts are `sylvia.subdomain.domain.cxm`, `brett.subdomain.domain.cxm`, `rena.subdomain.domain.cxm`, and `valerie.subdomain.domain.cxm`. The nameserver for `subdomain.domain.cxm` is on host `sylvia`. Here is a synopsis of the steps to take to accomplish this:

1. Add authority for `subdomain.domain.cxm` on `sylvia`.

2. Test the `subdomain.domain.cxm` local resolution.

3. Delegate from `mainserv` to `sylvia` for the subdomain.

4. Test the `subdomain.domain.cxm` delegation.

Add Authority for `subdomain.domain.cxm` on `sylvia`

Start by adding a zone for the subdomain. Simply add this code to `sylvia`'s `/etc/named.conf`:

```
zone "subdomain.domain.cxm" {
  type master;
  file "named.subdomain.domain.cxm";
};
```

Next, make the zone data file, `named.subdomain.domain.cxm` in the `/var/named` directory. Here's the file:

```
@ IN SOA sylvia.subdomain.domain.cxm. hostmaster.subdomain.domain.cxm. (
                        2000072001 ; Serial
                        28800      ; Refresh
                        14400      ; Retry
                        3600000    ; Expire
                        86400 )    ; Minimum

            IN    NS        sylvia.subdomain.domain.cxm.
sylvia      IN    A         192.168.100.40
brett       IN    A         192.168.100.41
rena        IN    A         192.168.100.42
valerie     IN    A         192.168.100.43
```

14

DNS AND DHCP

Finally, make sure that there's reverse DNS resolution for sylvia and that you can quickly access sylvia with telnet. You don't need to provide reverse DNS for other hosts, just sylvia. (Review the "Configuring DNS Server Master Zones" section earlier in this chapter, if necessary.) Remember that the same reverse resolution problems that can delay or time-out telnet can prevent booting in certain situations.

When you can quickly access sylvia with telnet, restart named on sylvia with this command:

```
# /etc/rc.d/init.d/named restart
```

Test the subdomain.domain.cxm Local Resolution

This implementation has no reverse DNS for brett, rena, and valerie, so nslookup might fail. Use ping to test instead. ping all four hosts. The results should resolve to the correct IP addresses, similar to the following example:

```
# ping sylvia.subdomain.domain.cxm
PING sylvia.subdomain.domain.cxm (192.168.100.40): 56 data bytes
64 bytes from 192.168.100.40: icmp_seq=0 ttl=255 time=0.398 ms
--- sylvia.subdomain.domain.cxm ping statistics ---
2 packets transmitted, 2 packets received, 0% packet loss
round-trip min/avg/max = 0.235/0.316/0.398 ms

# ping brett.subdomain.domain.cxm
PING brett.subdomain.domain.cxm (192.168.100.41): 56 data bytes
64 bytes from 192.168.100.41: icmp_seq=0 ttl=255 time=0.479 ms
--- brett.subdomain.domain.cxm ping statistics ---
2 packets transmitted, 2 packets received, 0% packet loss
round-trip min/avg/max = 0.242/0.360/0.479 ms

# ping rena.subdomain.domain.cxm
PING rena.subdomain.domain.cxm (192.168.100.42): 56 data bytes
64 bytes from 192.168.100.42: icmp_seq=0 ttl=255 time=0.482 ms
--- rena.subdomain.domain.cxm ping statistics ---
2 packets transmitted, 2 packets received, 0% packet loss
round-trip min/avg/max = 0.244/0.363/0.482 ms

# ping valerie.subdomain.domain.cxm
PING valerie.subdomain.domain.cxm (192.168.100.43): 56 data bytes
64 bytes from 192.168.100.43: icmp_seq=0 ttl=255 time=0.471 ms
--- valerie.subdomain.domain.cxm ping statistics ---
2 packets transmitted, 2 packets received, 0% packet loss
round-trip min/avg/max = 0.234/0.352/0.471 ms
```

Once the DNS server on sylvia can resolve its hostnames to IP addresses, it's time to delegate from mainserv.

Delegate from `mainserv` to `sylvia` for the Subdomain

Add the following two lines to `mainserv`'s `/var/named/named.domain.cxm` under all other NS statements (to prevent breaking default names):

```
subdomain          IN   NS        sylvia.subdomain.domain.cxm.
sylvia.subdomain   IN   A         192.168.100.40
```

These lines say that `sylvia.subdomain.domain.cxm` is the nameserver for domain `subdomain.domain.cxm.`. (Remember that `subdomain` without a period is the same as `subdomain.domain.cxm.`.) Because `sylvia.subdomain.domain.cxm.` has been mentioned, it must be locally resolved to an IP address. Hence the second line.

However, notice that there is no reference to `brett`, `rena`, or `valerie` anywhere on the `mainserv` server. That work is done on `sylvia`. This is the beauty of delegation. The `subdomain` subdomain could have 200 hosts and 1,000 subdomains below it, and you could pass on queries with just these two lines.

To finish the job, increment the serial number, save the file, and restart `named`.

Test the `subdomain.domain.cxm` Delegation

Start by `ping`ing `sylvia.subdomain.domain.cxm` (be sure to fully resolve it). If that doesn't work, there's a problem with the local DNS. Examine `named.domain.cxm`.

Once you can `ping sylvia.subdomain.domain.cxm`, try pinging `brett.subdomain.domain.cxm`. If that doesn't work, make sure it works on `sylvia` itself. Troubleshoot accordingly.

Once you can `ping` all `subdomain.domain.cxm` hosts from `mainserv`, you know you've performed DNS delegation.

14

DNS AND DHCP

> **Note**
>
> To make the point as simply as possible, the preceding example did not implement reverse DNS or subnet splitting. In real life, the subdomain would probably be on a different subnet. In that case, reverse DNS could be implemented and delegated in pretty much the same way as forward DNS, but using subdomains of the `in-addr.arpa` domain in reverse DNS zone definition files on the domain and subdomain hosts.

Adding a Slave DNS Server

The Internet would be an unpleasant place without slave servers. Slaves receive their data directly from a master DNS server, from a slave receiving data directly from a master, or maybe even from something more removed than that. Thus, you can control a large number of slaves by administering a single master.

The process of receiving that data is called a *zone transfer*. Zone transfers happen automatically when either of the following two events occurs:

- The zone's refresh time is exceeded (the refresh time is the second number in the zone data file's SOA list).

- The slave is listed as an NS server in the referring master or slave's zone data record, and neither the zone in named.conf nor the options section contains a notify no statement. The administrator changes the master's zone record, increments its serial number (the first number in the zone data file's SOA list), and restarts named. This is called NOTIFY.

> **Note**
>
> NOTIFY (the second event) works only with BIND 8 and higher servers and slaves.

The point is, with only one master to maintain, you can control a large number of slave DNS servers, making it practical to spread the work among numerous servers in different parts of the world.

Spreading the work is one advantage of slave DNS servers. A second advantage is that it's an easy way to create a second DNS server for each zone, enhancing reliability through redundancy while keeping only one point of administration. Note that although slave servers get their data from the master, they write it to disk, so they continue to provide DNS services even if the master goes down.

In this section you'll create a slave DNS server for the domain.cxm and 100.168.192 (reverse DNS) zones on host mydesk. Here's a synopsis of how it's done:

1. On mydesk named.conf, add slave zones domain.cxm and 100.168.192. in-addr.arpa.

2. Restart named on mydesk.

3. On mainserv named.domain.cxm, add mydesk as a second nameserver.

4. On mainserv named.192.168.100, add mydesk as a second nameserver.

5. Restart named on `mainserv`.

6. Test.

> **Note**
>
> If domain.cxm were a legitimate domain in the worldwide DNS system, the master and any slaves would need to be delegated authority from above before they would work as DNS servers. However, because domain.cxm is a bogus domain constructed for this example, it is not necessary in this case.

Adding Slave Zones to mydesk

Add the following zones to /etc/named.conf on server mydesk:

```
zone "100.168.192.in-addr.arpa" {
  type slave;
  file "slave.192.168.100";
  masters {192.168.100.1;};
};

zone "domain.cxm" {
  type slave;
  file "slave.domain.cxm";
  masters {192.168.100.1;};
};
```

On each one, the `file` statement names the file in which to write data obtained from the master and from which to answer queries. The `masters {192.168.100.1;};` statement (and be sure to punctuate it *exactly* that way) tells named to acquire data from 192.168.100.1 whenever the refresh time is exceeded or whenever it's hit with a NOTIFY from 192.168.100.1, whichever comes first. The `type slave` statement tells named that this zone is allowed to do zone transfers to obtain the data from 192.168.100.1.

Notice that the files start with the word `slave` instead of named. This convention allows the administrator to refresh all slave zones with an `rm slave.*` command and a named `restart` command. Unlike the master zone data files, these slave zone data files are not maintained by humans and can be regenerated by the server. Contrast this with deleting a master's zone data file, which would be disastrous. Of course, if the master is down, deleting the slave files would be equally disastrous, so take care before you delete any slave zone data file.

Once the slave zones have been added, simply restart named with this command:

```
# /etc/rc.d/init.d/named restart
```

14

DNS AND DHCP

The `named` daemon will create the slave zone data files and will in fact act as a slave DNS server in every respect except for receiving `NOTIFY` statements (the master doesn't yet know about this slave server).

So it's perfectly possible to set up a slave to a master without the master knowing it. Because of the extra traffic burden placed on the master, this is not proper DNS etiquette. The administrator of the master should be informed of all slaves.

The master can defend itself against unauthorized slaves by limiting the servers that can receive zone transfers. Just put one of the following statements in `named.conf`'s zone section(s) or in the global section:

```
allow-transfer {192.168.100.2; };   #only mydesk can be slave
```

or

```
allow-transfer {192.168.100.2; 192.168.100.10};   #both
```

or

```
allow-transfer {192.168.100/24; };   #only hosts on subnet
```

Verify the existence of files `/var/named/slave.domain.cxm` and `/var/named/slave.192.168.100`. If they exist, verify that this list of commands quickly gives the expected output:

```
nslookup mainserv 192.168.100.2
nslookup mydesk 192.168.100.2
nslookup mainserv.domain.cxm 192.168.100.2
nslookup mydesk.domain.cxm 192.168.100.2
nslookup 192.168.100.1 192.168.100.2
nslookup 192.168.100.2 192.168.100.2
```

In the next section, you'll make the master aware of the slaves so it can send the `NOTIFY` statements upon modification and restart.

Adding Second Nameservers to `mainserv`

Add the following line below the `IN NS` statement in `named.domain.cxm`:

```
        IN    NS         mydesk
```

Before you save your work and exit, be sure to increment the serial number (the first number in the parenthesized `SOA` list).

Now add this line below the `IN NS` statement in `named.192.168.100`:

```
        IN    NS    192.168.100.2.
```

Remember that the address of `mydesk.domain.cxm` is `192.168.100.2`. Once again, be sure to increment the serial number. The incremented serial number is what tells the slave it needs to do the zone transfer.

Finally, restart the `mainserv` DNS server with this command.

```
# /etc/rc.d/init.d/named restart
```

The addition of the `NS` record enables `NOTIFY` statements to be sent to the DNS server on `mydesk`, causing that server to initiate a zone transfer. The new `NS` record also enables `mydesk` to be used as a backup nameserver.

To verify that the slave zones are working, do the following shell commands and make sure you get the expected output:

```
nslookup mainserv 192.168.100.2
nslookup mydesk 192.168.100.2
nslookup mainserv.domain.cxm 192.168.100.2
nslookup mydesk.domain.cxm 192.168.100.2
nslookup 192.168.100.1 192.168.100.2
nslookup 192.168.100.2 192.168.100.2
```

DNS slaves and their zone transfers, together with delegation, give DNS the power to serve millions of URLs.

Troubleshooting DNS

Many DNS troubleshooting techniques were discussed previously in this chapter, such as using the `telnet` program to detect reverse-DNS problems. Other troubleshooting options include script programs and named logging options.

Using Scripting to Stress-Test Your DNS Setup

You can make two handy scripts to stress-test your DNS setup. They can be named anything, but this example calls them `check1` and `check`. The `check1` script simply records the results of an `nslookup` in file `junk.jnk`, while `check` calls `check1` for each domain and IP under consideration. Here's the code for `check1`:

```
echo "nslookup $1 $2" >> junk.jnk
nslookup $1 $2 >> junk.jnk
echo " " >> junk.jnk
echo " " >> junk.jnk
```

`check1` simply writes the `nslookup` of its arguments to a file. `check` takes a single argument that, if present, it passes as arg2 to various `check1` calls. Here's the code for `check`:

```
rm junk.jnk
./check1 mainserv $1
./check1 mydesk $1
./check1 mainserv.domain.cxm $1
./check1 mydesk.domain.cxm $1
./check1 www.domain.cxm $1
./check1 192.168.100.1 $1
./check1 192.168.100.2 $1
less junk.jnk
```

The preceding script should run quickly and produce the right output. If not, there is a problem. By selectively commenting out lines of the check script, you can narrow down the scope of the problem.

The nslookup program delivers many powerful features when used interactively. It can also lead to frustrating hangs. For enhanced troubleshooting, learn about nslookup from its man page.

Debugging with Dumps and Logs

One of the main debugging tools you have with named is having the daemon dump its cached database to a text file. To have named dump its cache, you must send the daemon an INT signal. The file /var/run/named.pid contains the process ID of named. The following command sends the INT signal to named:

 # kill -INT `cat /var/run/named.pid`

The file /var/named/named_dump.db will contain the cache information that was dumped. The cache file will look similar to a zone database file.

The named daemon also supports debug logging. To start the daemon logging, send the daemon a USR1 signal like this:

 # kill -USR1 `cat /var/run/named.pid`

The logging information is logged in the /var/named/named.run file. If the USR1 signal is sent to the daemon, the verbosity of the logging information increases. In fact, it's so verbose that you'll need to search for strings like error and not found. To reset the debug level to 0, send the daemon a USR2 signal.

The HUP signal can be sent to the named daemon each time a zone database is changed, and theoretically the HUP signal rereads the databases without having to kill and restart the named daemon. But in fact, sometimes the HUP signal doesn't always work as advertised. The following example sends the HUP signal to named:

 # kill -HUP `cat /var/run/named.pid`

> **Caution**
>
> If alterations are made to the /etc/named.conf file, the named daemon must be stopped and restarted before you can see the changes.
>
> In any situation, if you want to make sure that all files are read and loaded, use this command:
>
> **# /etc/rc.d/init.d/named restart**

Another great debugging technique, especially after you've restarted named, is to look at the system log. You can find what file contains the appropriate log by looking in /etc/syslog.conf. Default for Red Hat 7 is /var/log/messages. Because you're interested only in recent messages, grab the tail end of the file with this command:

 # tail -n 400 /var/log/messages | less -N

All log entries have date and time, so if need be you can read back more than 400 lines. Look especially for error, not found, no such, fail, and so on. Carefully evaluate any error messages and try to figure out what they mean and what caused them.

Checking Your DNS Configuration with dnswalk

I find dnswalk an indispensable tool. It checks your DNS configuration very thoroughly. It's the DNS equivalent of C's lint utility or Samba's testparm utility. Using dnswalk first can easily save hours of troubleshooting, so it's worth the few minutes it takes to install and use it.

The dnswalk utility depends on the perl-Net-DNS tool, so the latter must be installed first. When using the Red Hat distribution, the easiest installation is via rpm. First, obtain these two files from the net:

ftp://rufus.w3.org/linux/contrib/libc5/i386/perl-Net-DNS-0.12-1.i386.rpm

ftp://rufus.w3.org/linux/contrib/noarch/noarch/dnswalk-2.0.2-1.noarch.rpm

Now install them with the following two commands:

 # rpm -ivh perl-Net-DNS-0.12-1.i386.rpm

 # rpm -ivh dnswalk-2.0.2-1.noarch.rpm

> **Note**
>
> If you prefer to compile, build, and install from source code, you can get the source at http://www.visi.com/~barr/dnswalk/.

14

DNS AND DHCP

It's essential to install them in the preceding order, because `dnswalk` depends on perl-Net-DNS. The `dnswalk` executable, which is really a Perl program, is installed in `/usr/sbin` directory. `dnswalk` is used by naming a domain as the sole argument. The domain must end in a dot (`.`). The following is an example:

```
# dnswalk domain.cxm.
Checking domain.cxm.
BAD: domain.cxm. has only one authoritative nameserver
Getting zone transfer of domain.cxm. from mainserv.domain.cxm...done.
SOA=mainserv.domain.cxm contact=hostmaster.domain.cxm
0 failures, 0 warnings, 1 errors.
#
```

You'll note that the only error it finds is the lack of a secondary DNS server. Most examples in this chapter define only one DNS server. In the following example, `named.domain.cxm` has been changed so that `mydesk.domain.cxm` resolves to `192.168.100.22`, but the reverse lookup in `named.192.168.100` is left at `192.168.100.2`. This is a forward/reverse mismatch—a serious problem that would have been very difficult to diagnose with tools like `nslookup`:

```
# dnswalk domain.cxm.
Checking domain.cxm.
BAD: domain.cxm. has only one authoritative nameserver
Getting zone transfer of domain.cxm. from mainserv.domain.cxm...done.
SOA=mainserv.domain.cxm contact=hostmaster.domain.cxm
WARN: mydesk.domain.cxm A 192.168.100.22: no PTR record
0 failures, 1 warnings, 1 errors.
#
```

In the preceding code, note the "`no PTR record`" warning, indicating that there's no reverse DNS for `192.168.100.22`.

If you configure DNS on anything more than the most casual basis, `dnswalk` is a vital investment. Use it early and often.

DNS Resources

Although this chapter covers the most-needed DNS information, a complete discussion of DNS could easily fill a large book. Here are some further sources of DNS documentation:

- `/usr/share/doc/bind-8.2.2_P5/`—Note that the exact directory name might be different, depending on your Red Hat distribution. This directory contains `CHANGES`, `INSTALL`, `TODO`, and `Version`. It also contains directories `bog/`, `html/`, `misc/`, `notes/`, `rfc/`, and `tmac/`. The `html/` and `rfc/` directories are especially interesting.

- `http://www.isc.org/products/BIND/bind4.html`—Documentation for the old BIND 4.

- `http://www.dns.net/dnsrd/`—The DNS Resources directory.

- `http://www.isc.org/bind.html`—Internet Software Consortium's BIND page, with BIND downloads and links to other valuable information. This page includes links to the Bind Operations Guide, in (BIND 4) HTML, Postscript, and Lineprinter.

Automatically Configuring Clients with DHCP

DHCP stands for Dynamic Host Configuration Protocol. It's a protocol to configure hosts (computers) dynamically, meaning that unconfigured client computers can be plugged into a DHCP served LAN, and will be given an IP address, a DNS server address, a WINS server address, and many other configuration items that would otherwise need to be manually configured by the network administrator. The administrator's sole network configuration task is to make sure each client has a unique hostname.

Obviously, this can save many weeks of configuration over the lifetime of a medium-sized LAN. It also makes renumbering a cinch when the LAN's network address or netmask is changed. DHCP can be used to automatically reconfigure LAN clients to accommodate changes in DNS and WINS server addresses.

Configuring a DHCP Server

The first step is to see whether DHCP is already in service. Use the following command:

```
# ps ax | grep dhcpd
```

If you see an instance of dhcpd running, you know it's already configured and running. Otherwise, you'll need to configure dhcpd. It's an easy task.

The first step is to try running dhcpd in the foreground, and observe the error messages (if any):

```
# dhcpd -f
Internet Software Consortium DHCP Server 2.0
Copyright 1995, 1996, 1997, 1998, 1999 The Internet Software Consortium.
All rights reserved.

Please contribute if you find this software useful.
For info, please visit http://www.isc.org/dhcp-contrib.html
```

14

DNS AND DHCP

```
Can't open /etc/dhcpd.conf: No such file or directory
exiting.
#
```

In the preceding example, notice the error stating it can't find /etc/dhcpd.conf. If you get this error, the next step is to create the file. The following is a simple example dhcpd.conf for a server at 192.168.100.1:

```
subnet 192.168.100.0 netmask 255.255.255.0 {
    range 192.168.100.200 192.168.100.240;
        option subnet-mask 255.255.255.0;
        option broadcast-address 192.168.100.255;
        option routers 192.168.100.1;
        option domain-name-servers 192.168.100.1;
        option domain-name "domain.cxm";
        option ip-forwarding on;
        option netbios-node-type 8;
}
```

The preceding specifies that any client in the 192.168.100.0/24 subnet will be given an IP address in the 192.168.100.200-240 range, broadcast address 192.168.100.255, default route 192.168.100.1, DNS (equivalent of resolv.conf) at 192.168.100.1, domain name domain.cxm, ip forwarding is on. The netbios-node-type 8 refers to a client netbios node type H, which instructs the client to attempt netbios resolution first through unicast, and then on failure by broadcast. This is the widely preferred method.

Note that the preceding is an extremely simple dhcpd.conf. They can get much more complex. Several subnets can be served, either on separate physical networks or sharing a network. Groups of subnets can share properties. Individual hosts can be configured centrally, using only their MAC addresses as identification, and they can, if desired, be allocated hostnames centrally. DHCP can even be configured to reject requests from hosts not already listed in dhcpd.conf, although that eliminates some of the "plug and connect" functionality.

DHCP is incredibly powerful and flexible. To learn more about it, consult the following man pages:

- dhcpd
- dhcpd.conf
- dhcp-options
- dhcpd.leases
- dhclient
- dhcrelay

After /etc/dhcpd.conf has been created, once again try running the daemon in the foreground:

```
# dhcpd -f
Internet Software Consortium DHCP Server 2.0
Copyright 1995, 1996, 1997, 1998, 1999 The Internet Software Consortium.
All rights reserved.

Please contribute if you find this software useful.
For info, please visit http://www.isc.org/dhcp-contrib.html

Can't open lease database /var/lib/dhcp/dhcpd.leases: No such file or director
y -- check for failed database rewrite attempt!
Please read the dhcpd.leases manual page if you.
don't know what to do about this.
exiting.
#
```

In the preceding example, notice the error stating it can't open lease database /var/lib/dhcp/dhcpd.leases. You must create the directory, mode 755 all the way down the tree. Then, create an empty dhcpd.leases with the following command:

```
# touch /var/lib/dhcp/dhcpd.leases
```

Now dhcpd should run, as shown in the following example:

```
# dhcpd -f
Internet Software Consortium DHCP Server 2.0
Copyright 1995, 1996, 1997, 1998, 1999 The Internet Software Consortium.
All rights reserved.

Please contribute if you find this software useful.
For info, please visit http://www.isc.org/dhcp-contrib.html

Listening on LPF/eth0/00:a0:c9:e8:20:3c/192.168.100.0
Sending on   LPF/eth0/00:a0:c9:e8:20:3c/192.168.100.0
Sending on   Socket/fallback/fallback-net
```

Notice in the preceding that this time dhcpd listens and sends on sockets, and runs continuously. You can run DHCP server with the dhcpd -f command whenever you need to troubleshoot. However, you'll typically run it in the background. Press Ctrl+C to terminate dhcpd, and then run it as a daemon with the following command:

```
# /etc/rc.d/init.d/dhcpd restart
Shutting down dhcpd: [FAILED]
Starting dhcpd: [  OK  ]
#
```

The failure on shutdown is due to the fact that it wasn't running in the first place. The final step is to configure the server to run dhcpd on reboot. That's accomplished with

14

DNS AND DHCP

linuxconf, Control Panel, Control Service Activity, dhcpd. Press Enter to obtain the Service dhcpd screen. Check the Automatic check box on the Startup line, check the check boxes for Level 3 and Level 5, then click the Accept button, and quit all the way out of linuxconf. The next time you reboot, dhcpd will run automatically.

Once the dhcp server is up and running, clients must be told to use the server's information. The next section describes how to set up a client to use the server's information.

Configuring a Linux-Based DHCP Client

Setting a Linux client as a DHCP client requires addition or modification of one line in one file. The file is /etc/sysconfig/network-scripts/ifcfg-eth0. The line you change looks like this:

BOOTPROTO=static

If that line exists, it specifies that the eth0 interface's IP address is a static address, specified by other lines in the file. To make the client a DHCP client, change the line as follows, or if it doesn't exist, add the following line:

BOOTPROTO=dhcp

Then restart the client's network interface with the following command:

/etc/rc.d/init.d/network restart

If you execute the ifconfig command on the client, you'll see that the client's IP address is now an address from the range specified by the server's dhcpd.conf file. To switch back to static addressing, change back to BOOTPROTO=static and restart the network.

You can also use linuxconf to switch between static and DHCP addressing. The menu sequence is Networking, Basic Host Information, look for the Config Mode radio buttons, and enable the one saying Dhcp. Unfortunately, linuxconf needlessly changes several other lines in the ifcfg-eth0 and several other files. The least invasive method of switching between static and DHCP boot protocols is to manually edit ifcfg-eth0.

> **Note**
>
> The preceding discussion assumes that the client computer interfaces with the network through its eth0 network card. If it interfaces through eth1, the file to edit would be ifcfg-eth1.

Tracking DHCP Server Changes

As mentioned earlier, a prime benefit of DHCP is central administration of client network properties. Imagine your organization decides they need the subnet of your current LAN somewhere else, so you have to renumber the LAN. With statically configured clients, you'd need to walk to every client and change several parameters. But if they receive their network parameters via DHCP, the clients change automatically. Almost.

Each client must be told to release and renew its current DHCP lease. The renewal transfers the new information.

One way of releasing and renewing is simply rebooting the client. In the Linux world rebooting is considered bad form, so you can simply restart the network to release and renew your DHCP lease. The following command, run on the client, restarts the client's network interface on the client:

```
# /etc/rc.d/init.d/network restart
```

Configuring a Windows-Based DHCP Client

Configuring a Windows-based DHCP client is almost as easy as configuring a Linux-based DHCP client. First, pull up the Network dialog box by right-clicking any Network Neighborhood icon and choosing Properties. In the list box on the Configuration tab, choose TCP/IP->Ethernet adapter (exact wording depends on the adapter) and then click the Properties button. You're then brought to the TCP/IP Properties dialog box.

On the IP Address tab, check the Obtain an IP Address Automatically radio button. Then, on the WINS Configuration tab, check the Use DHCP for WINS Resolution radio button. Click OK all the way out, and answer "yes" when asked if you want to reboot. When the computer reboots, its IP address will be assigned by the DHCP server. All parameters set in dhcpd.conf on the DHCP server will likewise override those set on the Windows client. Thus, parameters like the DNS configuration can be set up centrally.

Releasing and Renewing Your DHCP Lease

Unlike Linux, Windows does not release and renew on reboot. This means that even after the DHCP server has its IP address range modified, the Windows client continues on with the old address until the DHCP lease expires. This is clearly a problem.

Windows offers a way to release and renew the DHCP lease through a program called winipcfg.exe, located in the C:\windows\system directory. Simply run winipcfg.exe, select the ethernet adapter from the drop-down list, click the Release button, and then click Renew.

14

DNS AND DHCP

> **Note**
>
> The `winipcfg.exe` drop-down list typically contains two choices, one for the ppp interface and one for the Ethernet interface. On clients with multiple ethernet cards, it contains a choice for each ethernet card.

Summary

This chapter covered the historical motivations for the creation of DNS. You saw the different types of nameservers and a sample DNS query. You learned how to create and maintain DNS database files. In addition, you learned how to build a caching-only server and master and slave zones, how to create zones for virtual domains, and how to delegate authority. This chapter also included a review of essential DNS troubleshooting tools. With the material in this chapter, you should have a good idea of how to implement DNS throughout your local network.

Finally, this chapter covered DHCP, a protocol that enables central administration of a LAN's client Ethernet addresses, DNS servers, WINS servers, and many more client network configuration parameters. DHCP is configured by editing the `dhcpd.conf` file.

NIS: Network Information Service

CHAPTER 15

The Network Information Service (NIS) is a simple, generic client/server database system. Under Linux, however, the most common use for it is sharing password and group files across a network. This chapter covers the setup of both master and slave NIS servers, as well as the configuration needed for clients to use them.

NIS, developed by Sun Microsystems as part of its SunOS operating system, was originally known as *The Yellow Pages*, or *YP* for short. Unfortunately, the name Yellow Pages had already been trademarked, and the resulting lawsuit forced the name change to NIS. You will soon discover that all the NIS commands are still prefixed with yp.

The NIS protocol was made public and implementations of it quickly spread to other variations of UNIX. Linux has supported NIS from its onset. Because Linux follows the NIS standard, it can work with other flavors of UNIX as either the NIS server or client.

Understanding NIS

As you configure your network, you will find that some of your configuration files are not host specific, but they require frequent updating. /etc/passwd and /etc/group are two that come to mind. NIS enables you to set up a master server where these files are stored and then configure each machine on your network as clients to this server. Whenever a client needs to fetch an entry from the /etc/passwd file, it consults the NIS server instead.

Two prerequisites must be met in order for a file to be sharable via NIS. First, the file must be tabular with at least one entry that is unique across the entire file. In the /etc/passwd file, this entry is either the login or UID. Second, the file in its raw form must be a straight text file.

With the criteria met, the files are converted into DBM files, a simple database format allowing for quick searches. You must create a separate DBM for each key to be searched. In the /etc/passwd file, for instance, you need the database to be searchable by login and by UID. The result is two DBM files, passwd.byname and passwd.byuid.

The original text file, along with the DBM files created from it, is maintained at the NIS master server. Clients that connect to the server to obtain information do not cache any returned results.

NIS Domains

NIS servers and clients must be in the same NIS domain to communicate with one another. Note that the NIS domain is not the same as a DNS domain, although it is valid for them to share the same name.

> **Tip**
>
> You should maintain separate names for your NIS and DNS domains for two reasons. First, it is easier for you to differentiate what you're talking about when discussing problems with anyone else. Second, having separate names makes it more difficult for potential intruders to understand the internal workings of your machines from the outside.

Both the clients and servers bind themselves to a domain; hence, a client can only belong to one NIS domain at a given time. Once bound, clients send a broadcast to find the NIS server for the given domain.

The Different Servers

So far, you might have noticed that I've referenced the NIS server explicitly as the *master* server. The two kinds of NIS servers are master servers and slave servers.

Master NIS servers are the actual truth holders. They contain the text files used to generate the DBM files, and any changes to the database must be made to these files.

Slave NIS servers are designed to supplement master NIS servers by taking some of the load off. When a file is updated on the server, a server push is initiated and the slave NIS server gets an updated copy of the DBM files.

> **Caution**
>
> Like any network service, NIS might have bugs that can allow unauthorized access to your system. It is prudent to keep track of security reports and obtain patches when they become available. The two best places to start are the Computer Emergency Response Team Web site at www.cert.org and the comp.os.linux.announce newsgroup. Both provide a moderated source of information that you can use to maintain your system.

Installing the Software

If you didn't install the NIS software during the initial setup process, you need to install it now. Start by mounting the Red Hat CD-ROM. The following assumes that the CD-ROM is mounted on the /mnt/cdrom directory.

15

NIS: NETWORK
INFORMATION
SERVICE

Access the /mnt/cdrom/RedHat/RPMS directory:

```
[root@server /root]# cd /mnt/cdrom/RedHat/RPMS
```

Install the RPMS yp-tools-2.4-4.i386.rpm, ypbind-1.6-11.i386.rpm, and ypserv-1.3.11-9.i386.rpm with the following commands:

```
[root@server RPMS]# rpm -i yp-tools-2.4-4.i386.rpm
[root@server RPMS]# rpm -i ypbind-1.6-11.i386.rpm
[root@server RPMS]# rpm -i ypserv-1.3.11-9.i386.rpm
```

After the software is installed, the next step is configuring the master NIS server.

Configuring a Master NIS Server

Before you configure the server software, you need to decide whether you are going to set up any slave servers. If you are, you need to know their hostnames before continuing. Along with the names of your NIS servers, you need to decide on a NIS domain name at this point. Remember that this domain name is not the same as your DNS domain name and for clarity should be set differently. Also, the names must be in the /etc/hosts file.

With this information, you are ready to begin. First, you need to set the domain name with the domainname command:

```
[root@vestax /etc]# domainname audionet.domain.com
```

Although this will work for the moment, you do need to change a startup configuration file so that this happens every time your system reboots. The /etc/init.d/ypserv script that was installed as part of the RPM looks for the domain name to be set in the /etc/sysconfig/network file. Simply add the following line:

```
NISDOMAIN="audionet.domain.com"
```

With the domain name set, you can decide what files you want to share via NIS, as well as their filenames. You do this by editing /var/yp/Makefile. As the name implies, NIS maintains its maps by using the make utility. Although familiarity with how this tool works is useful, it isn't mandatory in order to configure NIS.

Begin by loading /var/yp/Makefile into your favorite editor. Scroll past the lines that read as follows:

```
# These are files from which the NIS databases are built. You may edit
# these to taste in the event that you wish to keep your NIS source files
# separate from your NIS server's actual configuration files.
```

Below this segment of text, you will see lines that resemble the following:

```
GROUP      = $(YPPWDDIR)/group
PASSWD     = $(YPPWDDIR)/passwd
etc...
```

> **Note**
>
> As you scroll down the file, you will notice several parameters you can set to alter the behavior of the NIS server. For the time being, you probably shouldn't alter anything except for those items discussed in this section. If you are feeling adventurous, read the comments associated with each line and have fun with it.

This section tells NIS where your database files are located. The $(YPPWDDIR) string is a variable that was set to /etc at the top of the Makefile. Although it is possible to change this to another directory, you should probably keep it there for consistency. The string that comes after $(YPPWDDIR) is the name of the file in /etc that will become shared through NIS. Most of these entries can remain the same. The few that you want to change are GROUP, PASSWD, SHADOW, ALIASES, and possibly HOSTS.

The GROUP line shows that the file for controlling group information is at /etc/group. You might want to keep your local group file on the server separate from your NIS group file because your local group file could contain server-specific groups that you don't want to share across NIS, such as the www group for your Web server.

The same holds true for the other lines as well, especially the PASSWD line. A simple convention you can use to indicate that the file is being shared across NIS is to suffix it with a .yp. The resulting line looks something like the following:

```
PASSWD       = $(YPPWDDIR)/passwd.yp
```

> **Note**
>
> By default, the NIS server will not distribute any password entries with a UID or GID below 500. To change this, look for the line reading MINUID=500 in the makefile. Right below it is MINGID=500. Changing their values will change the minimum UIDs and GIDs. Unless you already have a UID/GID numbering system that includes values below 500, you will probably want to keep this setting as is.

15

NIS: NETWORK INFORMATION SERVICE

With the filenames you want set, you can now determine which files to distribute. Scroll down the makefile past the following block:

```
# If you don't want some of these maps built, feel free to comment
# them out of this list.
```

Your cursor should be at the following line:

```
all:  passwd group hosts rpc services netid protocols mail \
      # netgrp shadow publickey networks ethers bootparams printcap \
      # amd.home auto.master auto.home auto.local passwd.adjunct \
      # timezone locale netmasks
```

This line specifies which maps will be made available via NIS. The # symbol before netgrp is the comment symbol. The second and third lines are commented out.

Before making any changes to this line, you should make a copy of it and comment the copy out. The result looks something like the following:

```
#all:  passwd group hosts rpc services netid protocols mail \
      # netgrp shadow publickey networks ethers bootparams printcap \
      # amd.home auto.master auto.home auto.local passwd.adjunct \
      # timezone locale netmasks

all:  passwd group hosts rpc services netid protocols mail \
      # netgrp shadow publickey networks ethers bootparams printcap \
      # amd.home auto.master auto.home auto.local passwd.adjunct \
      # timezone locale netmasks
```

By commenting out the line, you can retain a copy of it just in case something goes wrong. You can always refer to the copy and see how the line looked before things were changed. With the copy in place, go ahead and begin your changes.

The only files you need to distribute for your network are passwd, group, hosts, rpc, services, netid, protocols, and mail. This distribution is already set, so you don't need to change anything.

Note

What are those other lines for? Good question! They are other databases that some sites distribute as well. As you need specific entries in that list, you can simply uncomment them and include them for distribution to your clients. At some sites, NIS is used to distribute other kinds of information, so you can create custom entries. You can even use NIS to make a company-wide telephone directory.

Unless you are comfortable with makefiles, you should leave the remainder of the file alone. Save the makefile and quit the editor. You'll need to make sure that the ypserv daemon is running before proceeding any further. To ensure that it is running, execute the following:

```
/etc/init.d/ypserv start
```

You are ready to initialize your NIS database with the /usr/lib/yp/ypinit -m command. When invoked, this command prompts for the name of any NIS slave servers you want to set up. For this example, select denon to be the slave NIS server.

Remember that you do not have to set up a slave NIS server. Setting up a slave server is only useful if you have a large number of NIS clients and you need to distribute the load they generate.

If you have not already set your domain name, the following initialization will error out with a message that says, "The local host's domain name hasn't been set. Please set it.". To initialize the master server, use the following:

```
[root@vestax /root]# /usr/lib/yp/ypinit -m
At this point, we have to construct a list of the hosts which will run NIS
servers. vestax is in the list of NIS server hosts. Please continue to add
the names for the other hosts, one per line. When you are done with the
list, type a <control D>.

     next host to add:  vestax
     next host to add:  denon
     next host to add: <CTRL-D>
The current list of NIS servers looks like this:

vestax
denon

Is this correct?  [y/n: y]   y
We need some minutes to build the databases...
Building /var/yp/audionet.domain.com/ypservers...
Running /var/yp/Makefile...
NIS Map update started on Tuesday July 25 22:35:21 PDT 2000
make[1]: Entering directory '/var/yp/audionet.domain.com'
Updating passwd.byname...
Updating passwd.byuid...
Updating hosts.byname...
Updating hosts.byaddy...
Updating group.byname...
Updating group.bygid...
Updating netid.byname...
```

```
Updating protocols.bynumber...
Updating protocols.byname...
Updating rpc.byname...
Updating rpc.bynumber...
Updating services.byname...
Updating mail.aliases...
gmake[1]: Leaving directory '/var/yp/audionet.domain.com'
NIS Map update completed
```

If anywhere in the middle of the output, you receive a message like the following instead,

```
make[1]:***No rule to make target '/etc/shadow', needed by 'shadow.byname'.
➥ Stop.
make[1]: Leaving directory '/var/yp/audionet.domain.com'
```

it means that you are missing one of the files you listed in the makefile. Check that you edited the makefile as you intended, and then make sure that the files you selected to be shared via NIS actually do exist. After you've made sure of these, you do not need to rerun ypinit but instead can simply rerun cd /var/yp;make.

The hosts that you add are put into the file /var/yp/ypservers. As an alternative to running the ypinit command, you can manually edit the /var/yp/ypservers file and then run make using the preceding sequence.

Starting the Daemons on Boot

To start the NIS server automatically at boot time, you need to create a symbolic link from the runlevel 3 startup directory. To do this, type the following:

```
[root@client /root]# cd /etc/rc3.d
[root@client rc3.d]# ln -s ../init.d/ypserv S60ypserv
```

The yppasswdd daemon allows users from NIS clients to change their passwords on the NIS server. To start this program automatically at boot time, you need to type the following:

```
[root@client /root]# cd /etc/rc3.d
[root@client rc3.d]# ln -s ../init.d/yppasswdd S61yppasswdd
```

If you want to start the daemons by hand so you don't need to reboot, simply run the following:

```
[root@client /root]# /etc/init.d/ypserv start
[root@client /root]# /etc/init.d/yppasswdd start
```

You now have a NIS master server. Time to test the work with a NIS client.

Configuring a NIS Client

Compared to configuring a NIS server, NIS clients are trivial. You must deal with three files, /etc/yp.conf, /etc/sysconfig/network, and /etc/nsswitch.conf.

There are two ways you can edit these files. You can edit them manually or you can use linuxconf. The most accurate way to make the changes is to edit the files manually. However, if you are a beginner and not used to editing configuration files, perhaps you should use linuxconf the first couple of times until you come to grips with what is happening.

Configuring a NIS Client with linuxconf

Type **linuxconf** at the command prompt. Then go to Networking, Client Tasks, and then Network Information System (NIS).

You are asked for the NIS domain name and for the name of the NIS server. Enter the domain name, that is, audionet.domain.com.

You are asked to enter the name of the NIS server. You have two choices here. You can leave the entry blank, in which case the client will just send a broadcast message to the network and it will bind to the first server to respond. The second option is to specify the name of the server; if you do this the client will always bind to that server. Basically, if there is only one NIS server for that domain, specify the name of it; if there are more than one, then leave the entry blank.

Now click Accept, then Act Changes, and then Quit.

linuxconf has now done two things. It has added an entry in the /etc/sysconfig/network file:

`NISDOMAIN="audionet.domain.com"`

This file is checked when the computer boots and it sets the domainname from this entry.

If you specified a NIS server, an entry will have been added to /etc/yp.conf such as

`ypserver vestax.audionet.domain.com`

If you did not specify a NIS server, the /etc/yp.conf file will not have been changed at all. This may not work; you may need to add an entry to /etc/yp.conf such as

`domain NISDOMAIN broadcast`

where NISDOMAIN is the domain name that you have chosen, in this case audionet.domain.com.

That's two of the three files dealt with. The last file to deal with is /etc/nsswitch.conf. This file is more involved than the other two but a default file comes with Red Hat Linux 7 and for most users this file will be perfectly acceptable. There is a section under "Configuring a NIS Client Manually" later in this chapter describing how to edit this file.

Now that you have made all the necessary changes to all the relevant files there is only one thing left to do. You must set up the client daemon to automatically start at boot time. You do this by creating a symbolic link from /etc/rc3.d/S63ypbind to /etc/init.d/ypbind. The exact commands are as follows.

```
[root@client /root]# cd /etc/rc3.d
[root@client rc3.d]# ln -s ../init.d/ypbind S63ypbind
```

Configuring a NIS Client Manually

The first file to edit is /etc/yp.conf. The entries in this file are used for the initial binding. Use one of the following valid entries:

domain NISDOMAIN server HOSTNAME

Use server HOSTNAME for the domain NISDOMAIN. You could have more than one entry of this type for a single domain.

domain NISDOMAIN broadcast

Use broadcast on the local net for domain NISDOMAIN. Use this option if there is more than one NIS server on the network.

ypserver HOSTNAME

Use server HOSTNAME for the local domain. The IP address of the server must be listed in /etc/hosts.

The second file to edit is /etc/sysconfig/network. This file is used to set the NIS domain name at boot time. To do this, simply add this line:

NISDOMAIN="*domainname*"

domainname is the same as specified in the /etc/yp.conf file (in this case, audionet.domain.com).

The last file that needs to be changed is /etc/nsswitch.conf. This is slightly more involved than the previous files; however, a default file comes with the Red Hat installation. This file is used to configure which services are used to determine information such as hostnames, password files, and group files.

Begin by opening /etc/nsswitch.conf with your favorite editor. Scroll past the comments (those lines beginning with the # symbol). You should see something like this:

```
passwd:     files nisplus nis
shadow:     files nisplus nis
group:      files nisplus nis

hosts:      files nisplus nis dns

services:      nisplus [NOTFOUND=return] files
etc...
```

The first column indicates the file in question. In the first line, this is passwd. The next column indicates the source for the file. This can be one of six options listed in Table 15.1.

TABLE 15.1   Editing /etc/nsswitch.conf

Option	Description
nis	Uses NIS to determine this information.
yp	Uses NIS to determine this information (alias for nis).
Dns	Uses DNS to determine this information (only applicable to hosts).
files	Uses the file on the local machine to determine this information (for example, /etc/passwd).
[NOTFOUND=return]	Stops searching if the information has not been found yet.
nisplus	Uses NIS+.

The order in which these are placed in the /etc/nsswitch.conf file determines the search order used by the system. For example, in the hosts line, the order of the entries is files nis dns, indicating that hostnames are first searched for in the /etc/hosts file, then via NIS in the map hosts.byname, and finally by DNS via the DNS server specified in /etc/resolv.conf.

In almost all instances, you want to search the local file before searching through NIS or DNS. This allows a machine to have local characteristics (such as a special user listed in /etc/passwd) while still using the network services being offered. The notable exception to this is the netgroup file that by its very nature should come from NIS.

Modify the order of your searches to suit your site's needs and save the configuration file.

Now that all the files are in place, set up the client daemon to automatically start at boot time. You do this by creating a symbolic link from /etc/rc.3/S63ypbind to /etc/init.d/ypbind. The exact commands are as follows:

```
[root@client /root]# cd /etc/rc3.d
[root@client rc3.d]# ln -s ../init.d/ypbind S63ypbind
```

Testing the Client

Because of the way NIS works under Red Hat, you do not need to reboot to start NIS client functions. To see if you can communicate with the NIS server, start by setting the domain name by hand. You can do so with the following command:

```
[root@client /root]# domainname nis_domain
```

nis_domain is the NIS domain name. In the test case, it is audionet.domain.com. Start the NIS client daemon, ypbind, with this command:

```
[root@client /root]# /etc/init.d/ypbind start
```

With the NIS client and server configured, you are ready to test your work:

```
ypcat passwd
```

If your configuration is working, you should see the contents of your NIS server's /etc/passwd.yp file displayed on your screen (assuming, of course, that you chose that file to be shared via NIS for your passwd file). If you receive a message such as

```
No such map passwd.byname.
➥ Reason: can't bind to a server which serves domain
```

you need to double-check that your files have been properly configured.

Tip

As a precautionary measure, you should schedule a reboot while you are with the machine to ensure that it does start and configure the NIS information correctly. After all, your users will not be happy if after a power failure, your machine does not come back up correctly without assistance.

Configuring a NIS Secondary Server

After you've decided to configure a machine as a NIS secondary server, you start by configuring it as a NIS client machine. Verify that you can access the server maps via the
ypcat command.

Now you are ready to tell the master server that a slave server exists. To do this, edit the
/var/yp/ypservers file so that the slave server you are setting up is included in the list.
Now make sure you are in /var/yp and then run a make. If you configured your master
server with the name of the slave server during the ypinit -m phase, you do not need to
do this.

On the slave server make sure that the ypserv daemon is installed. If it is not, you will
need to install this from the RPM.

```
[root@client /root]# cd /mnt/cdrom/Redhat/RPMS
[root@client RPMS]# rpm -I ypserv*
```

You will have to make the ypserv daemon start at boot time. The commands to do this are

```
[root@client /root]# cd /etc/rc3.d
[root@client rc3.d]# ln -s ../init.d/ypserv S60ypserv
```

You can now initialize the slave server by running the command

```
/usr/lib/yp/ypinit -s master
```

master is the hostname for the NIS master server. In this example, it's vestax. The output should look something like the following:

```
We will need some minutes to copy the databases from vestax.
Transferring mail.aliases...
Trying ypxfrd ... not running
Transferring services.byname...
Trying ypxfrd ... not running
Transferring rpc.bynumber...
Trying ypxfrd ... not running
[etc...]

denon.domain.com's NIS database has been set up.
If there were warnings, please figure out what went wrong, and fix it.

At this point, make sure that /etc/passwd and /etc/group have
been edited so that when the NIS is activated, the databases you
have just created will be used, instead of the /etc ASCII files.
```

15

NIS: NETWORK
INFORMATION
SERVICE

Don't worry about the `Trying ypxfrd...not running` message. This happens because you haven't set the NIS master server to run the YP map transfer daemon `rpc.ypxfrd`. In fact, you never set it up to do so; instead, use a server push method where the NIS master server pushes the maps to all the NIS slaves whenever there is an update.

To set the NIS master to do the actual push, you need to change its makefile a little. On the master server, edit the makefile so that the line `NOPUSH="True"` is changed to read **`NOPUSH="false"`** and the line that reads `DOMAIN = 'basename \'pwd\''` is changed to **`DOMAIN = '/bin/domainname'`**.

Now for the big test: On the NIS master server, run `cd /var/yp;make all` to force all the maps to be rebuilt and pushed. The output should look something like the following:

```
Updating passwd.byname....
Pushed passwd.byname map.
Updating passwd.byuid...
Pushed passwd.byuid map.
Updating hosts.byname...
Pushed hosts.byname.
Updating hosts.byaddr...
Pushed hosts.byaddr.
[etc...]
```

If you get an error like the following:

```
Could not read ypservers map: 3 Can't bind to server which serves this domain
```

you will have to set up the master server as a client also. Change the `/etc/yp.conf` file to point to the server, in this case `vestax.audionet.domain.com`. Add an entry to the `/etc/sysconfig/network` file such as `NISDOMAIN=nisdomain` where *nisdomain* is your domain, in this example `audionet.domain.com`. Don't forget to start the `ypbind` daemon also.

On the NIS slave server, change the `/etc/yp.conf` file so that the `ypserver` is set to point to the slave server. Run the command `ypcat passwd` and see whether your NIS password file is displayed. If so, you're set. The NIS slave server is configured.

If you're having problems, trace through your steps. Also be sure to reboot the machine and see if your NIS slave server still works correctly. If it doesn't come back up, be sure that the changes you made to the boot sequence when installing `ypserv` were correct.

> **Tip**
>
> If your NIS client or slave server seems to have a hard time finding other hosts on the network, be sure that the /etc/nsswitch.conf file is set to resolve hosts by file before NIS. Then be sure that all the important hosts needed for the NIS servers to set themselves up are in their own local /etc/hosts file.

Using NISisms in Your /etc/passwd File

The most popular use of NIS is to keep a global user database so that it is possible to grant access to any machine at your site to any user. Under Red Hat Linux, this behavior is implicit for all NIS clients.

Sometimes, however, you do not want everyone accessing certain systems, such as those used by personnel. You can fix this access by using the special token + in your /etc/passwd file. By default, NIS clients have the line +:::::: at the end of their /etc/passwd file, thereby allowing everyone in NIS to log in to the system. To arrange that the host remains a NIS client but does not grant everyone permission, change the line to read +::::::/bin/false. This will allow only people with actual entries in the /etc/passwd file for that host (for example, root) to log in.

To allow a specific person to log in to a host, you can add a line to the /etc/passwd file granting this access. The format of the line is +*username*:::::: where *username* is the login of the user you want to grant access to. NIS will automatically grab the user's passwd entry from the NIS server and use the correct information for determining the user information (for example, UID, GID, GECOS, and so on). You can override particular fields by inserting the new value in the +*username*:::::: entry. For example, if the user sshah uses /usr/local/bin/tcsh as his shell but the host he needs to log in to keeps it in /bin/tcsh, you can set his /etc/passwd entry to +sshah::::::/bin/tcsh.

Using Netgroups

Netgroups are a great way to identify people and machines under nice, neat names for access control. A good example of using this feature is for a site where users are not allowed to log in to server machines. You can create a netgroup for the system administrators and let in members of the group through a special entry in the /etc/passwd file.

15

NIS: NETWORK INFORMATION SERVICE

Netgroup information is kept in the /etc/netgroup file and shared via NIS.

The format of a netgroups file is as follows:

```
groupname member-list
```

groupname is the name of the group being defined, and the *member-list* consists of other group names or tuples of specific data. Each entry in the *member-list* is separated by a whitespace.

A tuple containing specific data comes in this form:

```
(hostname, username, domain name)
```

hostname is the name of the machine for which that entry is valid, *username* is the login of the person being referenced, and *domain name* is the NIS domain name. Any entry left blank is considered a wildcard; for example, (technics,,,) implies everybody on the host technics. An entry with a dash in it (-) means that there are no valid values for that entry. For example, (-,sshah,) implies the user sshah and nothing else. This is useful for generating a list of users or machine names for use in other netgroups.

In files where netgroups are supported (such as /etc/passwd), you reference them by placing an @ sign in front of them. If you want to give the netgroup sysadmins consisting of (-,sshah,) (-,heidis,) permission to log in to a server, you add this line to your /etc/passwd file:

```
+@sysadmins
```

An example of a full netgroups file follows:

```
sysadmins     (-,sshah,) (-,heidis,) (-,jnguyen,) (-,mpham,)
servers       (numark,-,) (vestax,-,)
clients       (denon,-,) (technics,-,) (mtx,-,)
research-1    (-,boson,) (-,jyom,) (-,weals,) (-,jaffe,)
research-2    (-,sangeet,) (-,mona,) (-,paresh,) (-,manjari,) (-,jagdish,)
consultants   (-,arturo,)
allusers         sysadmins research-1 research-2 consultants
allhosts         servers clients
```

As a general rule, the line lengths should be no more than 1,024 characters. Although the system has no problems with the greater line lengths, it is difficult to edit the file because vi, view, and perhaps other editors have a 1,024-character line-length limitation.

Some Troubleshooting Tips

If the NIS software isn't behaving as you think it should, you can check a few things:

- Make sure the processes are running. Use `ps auxw` to list all the running processes. Make sure you see the appropriate processes running, regardless of whether the machine is a client, a server, or both.

- Check system logs (in `/var/log`) to see if there are any messages indicating peripheral problems that could be affecting your configuration.

- If the processes appear to be running but are not responsive, kill them and restart them. In some rare circumstances, the daemon may be misbehaving and may need to be restarted.

- Make sure `/etc/nsswitch.conf` is configured properly. This is a common problem.

- If you are trying to start the daemons by hand, make sure you are logged in as `root`.

When encountering problems, slow down, take a short break, and then retrace your steps. It's amazing how often simply slowing down helps you find problems.

Summary

This chapter covered the installation and configuration of NIS master servers, secondary servers, and clients. In addition to the setup of NIS itself, common "NISisms" and netgroups were discussed. The lessons learned from these sections put a powerful tool in your hands.

Some key points to remember:

- Use `ypinit` to set up NIS master servers and secondary servers.
- The `/var/yp` directory contains the makefile necessary to update NIS information.
- Consider separating NIS files from your regular system files for clarity.
- NIS servers need the `ypserv` daemon.
- NIS clients need the `ypbind` daemon.
- `yppasswdd` allows users on NIS clients to change their passwords.
- Schedule a reboot to test all your changes.

Although it isn't the most exciting feature to come along in recent history, NIS is one of the most useful of the core network services. In conjunction with other services, NIS gives you the ability to create a seamless system for all of your users.

15

NIS: NETWORK INFORMATION SERVICE

NFS: Network Filesystem

CHAPTER 16

The Network Filesystem, or NFS, is the means by which UNIX systems share their disk resources. What makes NFS really useful is its capability to function in a heterogeneous environment. Most UNIX variants, if not all, support NFS, and you can find NFS support for Microsoft Windows inexpensively, making it a good choice for sharing disks.

NFS was originally developed by Sun Microsystems during the 1980s. Sun shared its design and made the protocol a standard, which eliminated any interoperability conflicts with other operating systems. Linux supported NFS before version 1.0 was released.

A key feature of NFS is its robust nature. It is a *stateless protocol*, meaning that each request made between the client and server is complete in itself and does not require knowledge of prior transactions. Because of this, NFS cannot tell the difference between a very slow host and a host that has failed altogether. This allows servers to go down and come back up without having to reboot the clients. If this doesn't make much sense, don't worry about it. Understanding the underlying protocol isn't necessary for you to set up and successfully run an NFS server.

> **Note**
>
> In Chapter 17, "Samba," you'll read about how Linux can share its disks with Windows machines. NFS and Samba are *not* the same. They are two different protocols with two fundamentally different views on how disks should be shared. One of the many things that makes Linux great is its capability to support both means of sharing disks at the same time. In fact, it's common for Linux servers to share disks with each other through NFS and with Windows-based clients with Samba at the same time.

> **Caution**
>
> Unfortunately, NFS's design is insecure by nature. Although taking some steps to protect yourself from the evil hacker pretending to be a common user provides a moderate level of security, there is not much more you can do. Any time you share a disk with another machine via NFS, you need to give the users of that machine (especially the root user) a certain amount of trust. If you believe that the person you are sharing the disk with is untrustworthy, you need to explore alternatives to NFS for sharing data and disk space.
>
> Keep up with security bulletins from both Red Hat and the Computer Emergency Response Team (CERT). You can find these bulletins on Red Hat's site at www.redhat.com, CERT's site at www.cert.org, or the moderated newsgroup comp.security.announce.

Installing NFS

Before you begin installing NFS, make sure that your network setup is functioning correctly and that the server and clients can ping each other. Setting up your network is explained in Chapter 20, "TCP/IP Network Management."

Although the NFS software comes preinstalled with Red Hat Linux, you need to be aware of what the software is and what each specific program does. This is important when you are troubleshooting problems and configuring NFS-related tools such as the automounter.

Three programs provide NFS server services:

* `rpc.portmapper`—This program does not directly provide NFS services itself; however, it maps calls made from other machines to the correct NFS daemons.

* `rpc.nfsd`—This daemon translates the NFS requests into actual requests on the local filesystem.

* `rpc.mountd`—This daemon services requests to mount and unmount filesystems.

> **Note**
>
> The `rpc.nfsd` and `rpc.mountd` programs need only run on your NFS servers. In fact, you might find it prudent not to run them at all on your client machines, for security concerns and to free resources that might otherwise be consumed by them. NFS clients do not need any special NFS software to run. They should run the `rpc.portmapper` program, however, because it provides RPC functionality to programs other than NFS.

By default, these programs are installed and loaded at boot time. To check for this, use the `rpcinfo` command as follows:

```
rpcinfo -p
```

This will display all the registered RPC programs running on your system. To check which RPC programs are registered on a remote host, use

```
rpcinfo -p hostname
```

where *hostname* is the name of the remote host you want to check. The output for a Linux host running NFS looks something like the following:

```
[root@vestax /root]# rpcinfo -p
  program  vers  proto   port
   100000     2    tcp    111       portmapper
   100000     2    udp    111       portmapper
```

```
100005    1    udp    821    mountd
100005    1    tcp    823    mountd
100003    2    udp   2049    nfs
100003    2    tcp   2049    nfs
```

Starting and Stopping the NFS Daemons

You might run across instances when you need to stop NFS and restart it later. You can do this by using the startup scripts that are executed at boot time and shutdown. NFS's scripts are in /etc/init.d. To start the NFS services, run the following as root:

[root@vestax /root]# /etc/init.d/nfs start

To stop NFS services, run the following as root:

[root@vestax /root]# /etc/init.d/nfs stop

Status of NFS

There are other options that can be used with NFS to do other tasks. For example, you can get a status of NFS by running the following command:

[root@vestax /root]# /etc/init.d/nfs status

This returns output that is something like this:

```
rpc.statd (pid 965) is runnning...
rpc.mountd (pid 987) is running...
rpc.nfsd is stopped
nfsd (pid 366) is running...
rpc.rquotad (pid 976) is running...
```

Configuring NFS Servers and Clients

The two key files to NFS are /etc/exports and /etc/fstab. The exports file is configured on the server side and specifies which directories are to be shared with which clients and each client's access rights. The fstab file is configured on the client side and specifies which servers to contact for certain directories, as well as where to place them in the directory tree.

Setting Up the /etc/exports File

The /etc/exports file specifies which directories to share with which hosts on the network. You only need to set up this file on your NFS servers.

The /etc/exports file follows this format:

```
/directory/to/export    host1(permissions) host2(permissions)
                        ↪host3(permissions) host4(permissions)
#
# Comments begin with the pound sign and must be at the start of
# the line
#
/another/dir/to/export  host2(permissions) host5(permissions)
```

> **Note**
>
> There is a sample /etc/exports at the end of the chapter.

In this example, /directory/to/export is the directory you want to make available to other machines on the network. You must supply the absolute pathname for this entry. On the same line, you list the hosts and which permissions they have to access. If the list is longer than the line size permits, you can use the standard backslash (\) continuation character to continue on the next line.

You specify the names of the hosts in four ways:

- Their direct hostname.
- Using @*group,* where *group* is the specific netgroup. Wildcard hosts in the group are ignored.
- Wildcards in the hostname. The asterisk (*) can match an entire network. For example, *.engr.widgets.com matches all hosts that end in .engr.widgets.com.
- IP subnets can be matched with address/netmask combinations. For example, to match everything in the 192.168.42.0 network where the netmask is 255.255.255.0, you use 192.168.42.0/24 (that is, IP/netmask bits).

Each host is given a set of access permissions. The most significant ones are

- rw—Read and write access.
- ro—Read-only access.

- sync—This option requests that all file writes be committed to disk before the write request completes. The data is safer with this option because it is written to the disk more often; however, it does put more of a strain on the system's resources. By default this option is turned off and the server writes the data whenever it deems necessary.

- no_subtree_check—This option disables subtree checking. Subtree checking can improve reliability on directories that are exported as read-only or directories where files aren't often renamed. A good example of this is /usr. Subtree checking should be disabled on directories where files are frequently renamed. Home directories should have subtree checking disabled. Subtree checking is enabled by default.

- no_root_squash—Acknowledge and trust the client's root account.

If you are familiar with the export file configurations of other flavors of UNIX, you know that this process is not similar. Whether one is better than the other is a holy war discussion best left to Usenet newsgroups.

After you set up your /etc/exports file, run the exportfs command with the -r option:

```
exportfs -r
```

This sends the appropriate signals to the rpc.nfsd and rpc.mountd daemons to reread the /etc/exports file and update their internal tables.

Tip

It is considered a good convention to place all the directories you want to export in the /export hierarchy. This makes the intent clear and self-documenting. If you need the directory to also exist elsewhere in the directory tree, use symbolic links. For example, if your server is exporting its /usr/local hierarchy, you should place the directory in /export, thereby creating /export/usr/local. Because the server itself will need access to the /export/usr/local directory, you should create a symbolic link from /usr/local that points to the real location, /export/usr/local.

Tip

If you have an error in your /etc/exports file, it is reported when NFS starts up in syslog. Syslog is explained in Chapter 21, "Linux System Administration."

Using mount to Mount an Exported Filesystem

To mount a filesystem, use the mount command:

```
mount servername:/exported/dir /dir/to/mount
```

servername is the name of the server from which you want to mount a filesystem, */exported/dir* is the directory listed in its /etc/exports file, and */dir/to/mount* is the location on your local machine where you want to mount the filesystem. For example, to mount /export/home from the NFS server denon to the directory /home, use

```
mount denon:/export/home /home
```

Remember that the directory must exist in your local filesystem before anything can be mounted there.

You can pass options to the mount command. The most important characteristics are specified in the -o options. These characteristics are listed in Table 16.1.

TABLE 16.1   Arguments to mount

Characteristic	Description
rw	Read/write.
ro	Read-only.
bg	Background mount. Should the mount initially fail (the server is down, for instance), the mount process will place itself in the background and continue trying until it is successful. This is useful for filesystems mounted at boot time because it keeps the system from hanging at that mount if the server is down.
intr	Interruptible mount. If a process is pending I/O on a mounted partition, it will allow the process to be interrupted and the I/O call to be dropped.
soft	By default, NFS operations are hard, meaning that they require the server to acknowledge completion before returning to the calling process. The soft option allows the NFS client to return a failure to the calling process after retrans number of retries.
retrans	Specifies the maximum number of retried transmissions to a soft-mounted filesystem.
wsize	Specifies the number of bytes to be written across the network at once. The default is 8192 (for example, wsize=2048). You shouldn't change this value unless you are sure of what you are doing. Setting this value too low or too high can have a negative impact on your system's performance.
rsize	Specifies the number of bytes to be read across the network at once. Like wsize, the default is 8,192 bytes. The same warning applies as well: Changing the value without understanding its effect can have a negative impact on your system's performance.

Here's an example of these parameters in use:

```
mount -o rw,bg,intr,soft,retrans=6 denon:/export/home /home
```

> **Note**
>
> There are many more options to the `mount` command, but you will rarely see them. See the man page for `mount` for additional details.

> **Caution**
>
> Solaris NFS clients talking to Linux NFS servers seems to bring out a bug in the Linux NFS implementation. If you suddenly notice normal files being treated as directories or other such unusual behavior, change the `wsize` and `rsize` to 2048 when mounting the directory. This appears to fix the problem without hurting performance too drastically.

Unmounting a Filesystem

To unmount the filesystem, use the `umount` command:

```
umount /home
```

This will unmount the `/home` filesystem.

There is a caveat, of course. If users are using files on a mounted filesystem, you cannot unmount it. All files must be closed before the unmount can happen, which can be tricky on a large system, to say the least. There are three ways to handle this:

- Use the `lsof` program (available at `ftp://vic.cc.purdue.edu/pub/tools/unix/lsof`) to list the users and their open files on a given filesystem. Then, either wait until they are done, beg and plead for them to leave, or kill their processes. Then you can unmount the filesystem. This isn't the most desirable way to achieve an unmount, but you'll find that this is often the path you need to take.

- Use `umount` with the `-f` option to force the filesystem to unmount. This is often a bad idea because it confuses the programs (and users) who are accessing the filesystem. Files in memory that have not been committed to disk might be lost.

- Bring the system to single-user mode and then unmount the filesystem. Although this is the greatest inconvenience of the three, it is the safest way because no one loses any work. Unfortunately, on a large server, you'll have some angry users to contend with. (Welcome to system administration!)

Configuring the `/etc/fstab` File to Mount Filesystems Automatically

At boot time, the system will automatically mount the `root` filesystem with read-only privileges. This allows it to load the kernel and read critical startup files. However, after the system has bootstrapped itself, it will need guidance. Although it is possible for you to jump in and mount all the filesystems, it isn't realistic because you then have to finish bootstrapping the machine yourself. Even worse, the system might not come back online by itself.

To get around this, Linux uses a special file called `/etc/fstab`. This file lists all the partitions that need to be mounted at boot time and the directory where they need to be mounted. Along with that information, you can pass parameters to the `mount` command.

> **Note**
>
> NFS servers can also be NFS clients. For example, a Web server that exports part of its archive to, say, an FTP server, can NFS mount from the server containing home directories at the same time.

Each filesystem to be mounted is listed in the `fstab` file in the following format:

```
/dev/device        /dir/to/mount      ftype parameters fs_freq fs_passno
```

An example would look like this:

```
server:/usr/local/pub    /pub    nfs    rsize=8192,wsize=8192,timeo=14,intr
```

> **Note**
>
> There is a sample `/etc/fstab` at the end of the chapter.

The following items make up this line:

- `/dev/device`—The device to be mounted. In the case of mounting NFS filesystems, this comes in the form of *servername:/dir/exported*, where *servername* is the name of the NFS server and */dir/exported* is the directory that is exported from the NFS server. For example, `denon:/export/home`, where `denon` is the hostname of your NFS server and `/export/home` is the directory that is specified in the `/etc/exports` directory as being shared.
- `/dir/to/mount`—The location at which the filesystem should be mounted on your directory tree.

- ftype—The filesystem type. Usually, this is ext2 for your local filesystems. However, NFS mounts should use the NFS filesystem type.

- parameters—These are the parameters you passed to mount using the -o option. They follow the same comma-delimited format. A sample entry looks like rw,intr,bg.

- fs_freq—This is used by dump to determine whether a filesystem needs to be dumped.

- fs_passno—This is used by the fsck program to determine the order to check disks at boot time. The root filesystem should be set to 1, and other filesystems should have a 2. Filesystems on the same drive will be checked sequentially, but filesystems on different drives will be checked at the same time.

Any lines in the fstab file that start with the pound symbol (#) are considered comments and are ignored.

If you need to mount a new filesystem while the machine is live, you must perform the mount by hand. If you want this mount to be active automatically the next time the system is rebooted, you should add it to the fstab file.

There are two notable partitions that don't follow the same set of rules as normal partitions. They are the swap partition and /proc, which use filesystem types swap and proc, respectively.

You do not mount the swap partition using the mount command. It is instead managed by the swapon command. For a swap partition to be mounted, you must list it in the fstab file. Once it is there, use swapon with the -a parameter. The /proc filesystem is even stranger because it really isn't a filesystem. It is an interface to the kernel abstracted into a filesystem format. Take a peek into it for a large amount of useful information regarding the inner workings of the kernel.

Tip

If you need to remount a filesystem that already has an entry in the fstab file, you don't need to type the mount command with all the parameters. Instead, simply pass the directory to mount as the parameter, as in

    mount /dir/to/mount

where /dir/to/mount is the directory that needs to be mounted. mount will automatically look to the fstab file for all the details, such as which partition to mount and which options to use.

If you need to remount a large number of filesystems that are already listed in the `fstab` file, you can use the `-a` option in `mount` to remount all the entries in `fstab`:

```
mount -a
```

If it finds that a filesystem is already mounted, no action on that filesystem is performed. If it finds that an entry is not mounted, on the other hand, it will automatically mount it with the appropriate parameters.

Caution

When you are setting up servers that mount filesystems from other servers, be wary of *cross mounting*. Cross mounting happens when two servers mount each other's filesystems. This can be dangerous if you do not configure the `/etc/fstab` file to mount these systems in the background (via the `bg` option), because it is possible for these two machines to deadlock during their boot sequence as each host waits for the other to respond.

For example, let's say you want `host1` to mount `/export/usr/local` from `host2` and `host2` to mount `/export/home/admin` from `host1`. If both machines are restarted after a power outage, `host1` will try to mount the directory from `host2` before turning on its own NFS services. At the same time, `host2` is trying to mount the directory from `host1` before it turns on its NFS services. The result is that each machine waits forever for the other machine to start.

If you use the `bg` option in the `/etc/fstab` entry for both hosts, they would fail on the initial mount, place the mount in the background, and continue booting. Eventually, both machines would start their NFS daemons and allow each other to mount their respective directories.

Exporting Filesystems with `linuxconf`

`linuxconf` is a very handy tool for setting up NFS shares as it saves you having to learn the exact syntax that is used in `/etc/exports`.

Type **linuxconf** at the prompt. Go to Networking, Server Tasks, and then Exported File Systems (NFS).

You are presented with a list of all the paths you are currently exporting (see Figure 16.1). Obviously at present the list is empty. For each path that you want to export you will add it here. Each of these is then added to /etc/exports. Click Add, and the dialog box shown in Figure 16.2 displays.

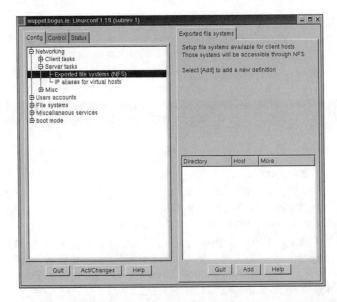

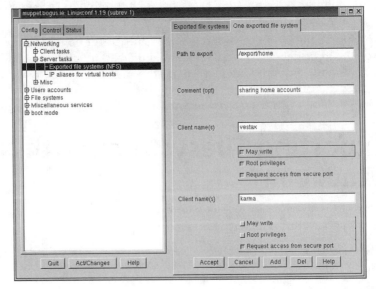

Under Path to Export enter the full path to the directory you want to export. There is a place to enter a comment; this is optional. You are asked for the Client name(s) to export to. There are four types of entries that you can use here. These were explained earlier, in the section "Setting Up the /etc/exports File."

You are presented with options for the share. If you select May Write, the user on the client will be able to write to files in the exported directory providing that the file's permissions allow them to do so. Root Privileges gives root on the client root privileges in the exported directory. This puts a lot of trust in root on the client machine. You can leave Request Access from Secure Port selected.

You may of course want to have different permissions for different clients. That is why there is more than one place to enter a client name and its permissions. By default there are two places for entering a client and its permissions. You can have as many as you wish—just click Add and another entry will be created.

Now save your changes and exit linuxconf. Make sure to accept changes whenever presented with the option.

Complete Sample Configuration Files

Listing 16.1 contains a complete /etc/exports file for a server.

LISTING 16.1   A Complete /etc/exports File

```
#
# /etc/exports for denon
#
# Share the home dirs:
/export/home        technics(rw) pioneer(rw) vestax(rw)
                    ➥atus(rw) rane(rw)

#
# Share local software
#
/export/usr/local   technics(rw,no_root_squash)
                    ➥vestax(rw,no_root_squash)
                    ➥pioneer(rw,no_root_squash)
                    ➥atus(rw,no_root_squash)
                    ➥rane(rw,no_root_squash)
```

Listing 16.2 contains a complete /etc/fstab file for a client.

LISTING 16.2 A Complete /etc/fstab File

```
#
# /etc/fstab for technics
#
/dev/hdb2                /                         ext2      defaults      1 1
/dev/hda8                /home                     ext2      defaults      1 2
/dev/hda7                swap                      swap      defaults      0 0
/dev/fd0                 /mnt/floppy               ext2      noauto        0 0
/dev/cdrom               /mnt/cdrom                iso9660   noauto,ro     0 0
none                     /proc                     proc      defaults      0 0
none                     /dev/pts                  devpts    mode=0622     0 0
```

You can also manually mount a filesystem. This is especially important if you want to mount a floppy disk as an msdos filesystem. The following command will mount a floppy disk to /mnt/floppy. Remember to unmount the disk before removing it.

mount /dev/fd0 /mnt/floppy

Unmounting is just a simple command:

umount /mnt/floppy

Summary

In this chapter you learned how to start and stop NFS servers, mount and unmount directories, and create and maintain the configuration files for clients and servers.

NFS, a rather straightforward tool, is one of the power features that lets you work not only with other Linux systems, but with other variants of UNIX as well. From a user's standpoint, it provides a seamless bridge between clients and servers so that they can keep to their tasks instead of trying to remember the drive letter for their home directory.

Samba

CHAPTER

17

IN THIS CHAPTER

This chapter gives you the information you need to install, configure, and use the Samba suite of Session Message Block (SMB) protocol services under Linux. With Samba, you can share a Linux filesystem with Windows 95, 98, 2000, or NT. You can share a Windows 95, 98, or NT FAT filesystem with Linux. You can also share printers connected to either Linux or a system with Windows 95, 98, 2000, or NT.

SMB is the protocol used by Microsoft's operating systems to share files and printer services. Microsoft and Intel developed the SMB protocol system in 1987, and later, Andrew Tridgell created an SMB implementation for various UNIX systems and Linux.

> **Note**
>
> Common Internet File System (CIFS) is a protocol that is basically an updated SMB. Samba works perfectly with CIFS. For the rest of this chapter the protocol will be referred to as "SMB." Most Linux and UNIX system administrators refer to both protocols as "SMB."

The Samba suite of SMB protocol utilities consists of several components. The `smbd` daemon provides the file and print services to SMB clients, such as Windows NT, LAN Manager, Windows for Workgroups, or other Linux and UNIX clients. The configuration file for this daemon is described in `smb.conf`. The `nmbd` daemon provides NetBIOS nameserving and browsing support. You can also run `nmbd` interactively to query other name service daemons.

The SMB client program (`smbclient`) implements a simple FTP-like client on a Linux or UNIX box. The SMB mounting program (`smbmount`) enables mounting of server directories on a Linux or UNIX box. The `testparm` utility allows you to test your `smb.conf` configuration file. The `smbstatus` utility tells you who is currently using the `smbd` server.

SWAT is a Web-based interface to the `smb.conf` Samba configuration file. SWAT is described in this chapter.

In the Red Hat 7 distribution, these files can be found in the following directories:

```
smbd and nmbd: /usr/sbin
smbclient, smbmount, testparm, smbstatus: /usr/bin
smb.conf: /etc/samba
```

Installing Samba

You can install Samba during the Red Hat installation from the CD-ROM or later using RPM. If you need to install the package, first download the current version from Red Hat's Web site (http://www.redhat.com) or locate the package on your CD-ROM. You can then install the package (the current stable version is samba-2.0.7-21ssl.i386.rpm) with the following command:

```
# rpm -ivh samba-2.0.7-21ssl.i386.rpm
```

The package should contain all the files needed to run Samba, including the two primary programs (smbd and nmbd).

Getting a Simple Samba Setup Running

Samba can be very complex, so it's important to get the simplest possible implementation of Samba running before making major configuration changes.

17

SAMBA

Caution

I experienced a rare intermittent problem with Samba in which neither Linux nor Windows clients could connect to the server. The Linux clients reported the following error:

```
error connecting to 192.168.100.3:139 (Connection refused)
Connection to mydesk failed
```

After placing the following two lines in the [global] section of my smb.conf and restarting Samba, the symptom disappeared:

```
netbios name=mydesk
encrypt passwords=yes
```

Surprisingly, removing those lines and restarting Samba again did not resurrect the symptom, so with no current way to reproduce the symptom, no definitive diagnosis is possible.

If you experience a refused connection on port 139, start by verifying that the daemons are running using the following command:

```
$ ps ax | grep –i mbd
```

If the daemons are running, explicitly configure `netbios name` to the Samba server's hostname, and explicitly configure encrypted passwords to yes. If your clients can't use encryption, you can troubleshoot further, but getting Samba running is an important first step.

In addition, it's a good idea to check `http://www.redhat.com` for updates, errata, and bug fixes.

The main configuration file, `smb.conf`, is located in the `/etc/samba` directory of your Red Hat Samba server. It is used by the Samba server software (`smbd`) to determine directories and printers, and to determine security options for those directories and printers.

Note

Many changes to the `smb.conf` file will not be recognized until the Samba server is restarted. The command to restart the Samba server is

`$ /etc/rc.d/init.d/smb restart`

The ; character at the beginning of an `smb.conf` line indicates that the line is a comment that is to be ignored when processed by the Samba server. The # character does the same thing. Customarily, the ; character is used to comment out option lines, whereas the # is used at the beginning of lines that are truly comments.

The `smb.conf` file layout consists of a series of named sections. Each section starts with its name in brackets, such as `[global]`. Within each section, the parameters are specified by key/value pairs, such as `comment = Red Hat Samba Server`.

`smb.conf` consists of three special sections and zero or more custom sections. The special sections are `[global]`, `[homes]`, and `[printers]`. Before I describe them in detail, let's look at getting a minimally running Samba.

Caution

Be sure to back up the original `/etc/samba/smb.conf` file before making your first modification.

First, make sure whatever username is used on the test client also exists on the Linux box. Add the user and password with the `adduser` and `passwd` commands.

> **Note**
>
> Samba works only on functioning networks. To prevent frustration, always make sure the client and server can ping each other's IP address before attempting any Samba configuration or testing. Also, attempt to ping the server's hostname from the client to determine what to expect from smbclient or smbmount commands using the hostname instead of the IP address.

Testing with a Linux Client

The default /etc/samba/smb.conf should be sufficient to run a simple Samba test with a Linux client. Run the following command:

```
# smbclient '//192.168.100.1/homes' -U myuid
```

Note that this example uses 192.168.100.1 as the Samba server's IP address. Substitute the IP address of your Samba server. Any name resolving to that same IP address can be used in its place. The preceding example uses myuid for the username; please substitute whatever username the client is logged in under. homes represents the [homes] section of smb.conf.

You are asked for a password. Type the user's password. If the server password is different from the client password, use the server password. If all is well, you are greeted by the following prompt:

```
smb: \>
```

Type **ls** and press Enter. You'll get a directory listing that includes the file .bash_profile. You have proven that you have a simple Samba running.

If you get an error message that resembles the following one, it probably indicates that the smb daemon is not running on the server.

```
error connecting to 192.168.100.1:139 (Connection refused)
```

Run the daemon with this command on the Samba server:

```
$ /etc/rc.d/init.d/smb restart
```

> **Note**
>
> For the rest of this chapter, the term "restart Samba" refers to running the preceding command, which restarts the Samba daemons.

You see a [FAILED] on smbd shutdown (it wasn't running in the first place); you'll see an [OK] on the subsequent smb start. Use linuxconf, choosing Control, Control Panel, Control Service Activity on the linuxconf menu to make sure the smb daemon is enabled on reboot.

Testing with a Windows Client

Samba is what makes a Linux computer show up in a Windows Network Neighborhood. What shows up in Network Neighborhood is the workgroup name attached to workgroup= in the [global] section of the Samba server's /etc/samba/smb.conf. Samba works best with workgroup names that are all capital letters, eight characters or fewer, and do not contain spaces.

Next, in the [global] section, temporarily uncomment password level and username level. Make password level equal to the longest likely password on this system, and username level equal to the longest likely username. These specify how many characters are non–case-sensitive, which is very important with non–case-sensitive SMB clients such as Windows.

Note

The changes to username and password levels are typically not required, and significantly slow authentication. The preceding suggestion is simply to temporarily eliminate any possible case sensitivity problems. Once the system is working perfectly, you'll want to re-comment the password and user levels.

Whenever there's a troubleshooting question involving case sensitivity for users and passwords, you can once again uncomment them and re-comment them upon resolution.

Now decide whether to use clear passwords or encrypted passwords and how to implement that decision. Early Windows SMB clients defaulted to clear text passwords. Beginning with Windows 95 OEM Service Release 2, Windows defaulted to encrypted passwords. All Windows 98 clients default to encrypted. Likewise, the default behavior changed from clear text to encrypted in Windows NT 4 Service Pack 3.

Encrypted passwords are not enabled in the Red Hat Linux 7 default smb.conf. For Windows versions 95-OSR2 and later, and Windows NT version 4 Service Pack 3, either each encrypted text client must be changed to clear-text passwords, or the server's smb.conf must be changed to enable encrypted passwords. In addition, any clear-text clients must be changed to encrypted passwords. A discussion of each technique follows.

> **Note**
>
> The documentation packaged with Red Hat 7 contains detailed discussions of plain versus encrypted passwords and their ramifications. See these documents:
>
> `/usr/share/doc/samba-2.0.7/docs/textdocs/Win95.txt`
>
> `/usr/share/doc/samba-2.0.7/docs/textdocs/WinNT.txt`
>
> `/usr/share/doc/samba-2.0.7/docs/textdocs/ENCRYPTION.txt`
>
> Windows NT users, please note that NT SMB clients present some additional challenges. Be sure to read these three documents carefully if you are having problems with Windows NT SMB clients.
>
> For Windows 2000, be sure to see `http://us1.samba.org/samba/ftp/docs/Win2000_PlainPassword.reg`.

Enabling Encrypted Passwords on the Server

In the [global] section, uncomment encrypt passwords = yes. Assuming the client username is myuid, perform the following command:

```
# smbpasswd -a myuid
```

> **Note**
>
> The preceding command fails unless the SMB password file, /etc/samba/smbpasswd, exists. The easiest way to use the touch command is as follows:
>
> ```
> # touch /etc/samba/smbpasswd
> ```
>
> Note that in other Linux distributions, or in Samba implementations compiled from source, the location of smbpasswd may be different.

Type in the password. If the password is not the same as it is on the client, the user will be prompted for the password the first time he accesses the Samba server.

You can even enable or disable password encryption on a client-by-client basis. To do so, you need to make a small include file for each client. The config file must contain the client's netbios name in the filename, and must contain an encrypt parameter in the file. For instance, if there are two clients, win98box and win95box, and win95box does not use encryption, here's the proper win95box.encrypt:

```
encrypt passwords=no
```

Likewise, `win98box.encrypt` looks like this:

```
encrypt passwords=yes
```

Finally, place the following statement in the `[global]` section of `smb.conf`:

```
include=%m.encrypt
```

The client's netbios name is substituted for `%m`. Restart Samba, and note that the `win95box` client doesn't use encryption, but the `win98box` client does.

Disabling Encrypted Passwords on the Windows Client

If your situation precludes enabling encrypted passwords on the server, they can also be disabled on the client to match the server.

Caution

This technique requires editing the Windows Registry, which involves significant risk, including risk of data loss and OS inoperability. If possible, it's preferable to handle this issue on the server, as explained previously.

On Windows 9x machines, in regedit, navigate to `[HKEY_LOCAL_MACHINE\System\CurrentControlSet\Services\VxD\VNETSUP]`. If it contains an object called `EnablePlainTextPassword`, set that object's value to 1. If it does not contain that object, create that object as a `DWORD` and give it a value of 1. Exit regedit and reboot the Windows machine. For Windows NT and Windows 2000 machines, see `NT4_PlainPassword.reg` and `Win2000_PlainPassword.reg`, respectively, in the `/usr/share/doc/samba-2.0.7/docs` directory.

The Proof: Network Neighborhood

Restart Samba with this command:

```
# /etc/rc.d/init.d/smb restart
```

Ideally, once you've completed configuration and rebooted, the server's workgroup (defined in `[global]`, `workgroup=`) should simply appear inside the Entire Network folder of Network Neighborhood. Double-clicking the workgroup should produce an icon for the server, which, if double-clicked, produces an icon for the user directory described in the `[homes]` section. Files in that directory should appear when that directory's icon is double-clicked. Note that files beginning with a dot (such as `.bash_profile`) are

17

considered hidden by Windows and can be viewed only if the folder's Windows Explorer view properties are set to see all files.

The preceding paragraph describes the ideal outcome. Often there are difficulties—even if you've set up everything exactly right. First, it can take Windows over a minute (sometimes several minutes) to find out that the server's Samba configuration has been changed and restarted. Sites with an NT PDC/Samba combo have been known to take upwards of an hour to recognize smb.conf Samba server changes. There are often password difficulties resulting from Windows being non–case sensitive and Linux being case sensitive. There may be problems with name resolution. Of course, there could be a basic network problem.

None of this presents a major obstacle. Take a few minutes' break to make sure Windows has gotten the word. You may want to reboot Windows. Make sure you have a network by confirming that the client and server can ping each other's IP address.

It's often helpful to use Start, Find, Computer to try to find the server's IP address. Note that the capability to find the server is not absolutely essential to complete Samba use; find is not equivalent to ping. Remember to refresh the various Network Neighborhood screens often (with F5).

It's often easier to access a Samba server from the Windows command line. Assuming server mainserv, workgroup MYGROUP, try the net view and net use commands:

```
N:\>net view \\mainserv
Shared resources at \\MAINSERV

Sharename   Type        Comment
-------------------------------------------
slitt       Disk        Home Directories
The command was completed successfully.

N:\>
```

The preceding command browses the Samba server for shares, a sort of command-line equivalent to Network Neighborhood.

```
N:\>net use x: \\mainserv\homes
The command was completed successfully.

N:\>
```

The preceding command maps drive x: to the user's home share. This can be verified with a directory listing of x:.

```
N:\>net use x: /delete
The command was completed successfully.

N:\>
```

The preceding deletes the drive mapping, once again verified by a directory listing, which gives an "Invalid drive specification" error.

```
N:\>net view /workgroup:MYGROUP
Servers available in workgroup MYGROUP.
Server name          Remark
-----------------------------------------
\\MAINSERV            Samba Server
\\MYDESK              Mydesk, Mandrake
The command was completed successfully.

N:\>
```

The preceding browses the entire workgroup for servers. This is an important command because often it triggers a browser election. Browser elections are beyond the scope of this chapter, but if you can't see your Samba server in Network Neighborhood, issuing the preceding command can sometimes fix that problem by triggering a browser election.

If problems continue, temporarily set username level and password level to 128 (overkill) and make sure they're uncommented. Make sure your client and server agree on the use of encrypted or clear-text passwords, as described earlier this chapter. Restart Samba on the server:

```
# /etc/rc.d/init.d/smb restart
```

In case of persistent problems, always remember you can use the smbclient utility on the server to deduce whether it's a problem on the Samba server or somewhere else (network or Windows). Remember to consider password encryption.

If problems continue, it's time to view the documentation in the /usr/share/doc/samba-2.0.7/docs/ tree. It's important to have a simple Samba working before attempting serious configuration. Once a working Samba has been established, it's a good idea to back up /etc/samba/smb.conf (but be sure not to overwrite the backup of the original that came with Red Hat Linux 7).

Configuring Samba

Samba has hundreds of configuration options. This chapter discusses those options most likely to be useful.

> **Note**
>
> Andrew Tridgell has written an excellent diagnostic procedure, called DIAGNOSIS.txt, for Samba. On the Red Hat 7 distribution it's available at /usr/share/doc/samba-2.0.7/docs/textdocs/DIAGNOSIS.txt.
>
> It's excellent for troubleshooting tough Samba problems.

The [global] Section

The [global] section controls parameters for the entire SMB server. It also provides default values for the other sections:

```
[global]

# workgroup = NT-Domain-Name or Workgroup-Name
   workgroup = MYGROUP
```

Workgroup= specifies the workgroup. Try to keep it all uppercase, fewer than nine characters, and without spaces.

```
# server string is the equivalent of the NT Description field
   server string = Samba Server
```

server string= specifies a human-readable string used to identify the server in the client's user interface. server string= goes in the [global] section. Note the similarity to the comment= option, which identifies individual shares in the client's user interface.

```
;   hosts allow = 192.168.1. 192.168.2. 127.
```

If uncommented, the hosts allow= line restricts Samba access to certain subnets: a handy security measure. Multiple subnets are separated by spaces. Class C subnets have three numbers and three dots, class B two numbers and two dots, and class A one number and one dot.

```
# if you want to automatically load your printer list rather
# than setting them up individually then you'll need this
   printcap name = /etc/printcap
   load printers = yes
```

The preceding enables printing without fuss, and is uncommented by default.

```
# It should not be necessary to spell out the print system type unless
# yours is non-standard. Currently supported print systems include:
# bsd, sysv, plp, lprng, aix, hpux, qnx
;   printing = bsd
```

It should not be necessary to uncomment the preceding code on a Red Hat Linux server.

```
# Uncomment this if you want a guest account, you must add this to /etc/passwd
# otherwise the user "nobody" is used
;   guest account = pcguest
```

The preceding, if uncommented, defines a guest account for clients logged in as a user not known to the Samba server.

```
# Password Level allows matching of _n_ characters of the password for
# all combinations of upper and lower case.
;   password level = 8
;   username level = 8
```

17

SAMBA

Uncomment these to help troubleshoot problems with connection by Windows clients. Set to the length of the longest likely password and username, respectively. As you learned earlier in the chapter, they control non–case sensitivity. For instance, a value of 8 means the first eight characters of the password will be compared without case sensitivity to the entered password. If the problem goes away, there may be a problem with case sensitivity. Once problems have been corrected, it's best to re-comment these two lines because case-insensitive authentication is slow.

```
# You may wish to use password encryption. Please read
# ENCRYPTION.txt, Win95.txt and WinNT.txt in the Samba documentation.
# Do not enable this option unless you have read those documents
;  encrypt passwords = yes
;  smb passwd file = /etc/samba/smbpasswd
```

Passwords are encrypted by default for Windows 95 OSR2 and beyond, but are clear text for earlier versions. To allow Windows-encrypted passwords to work with Samba, the encrypt passwords=yes line must be uncommented, and smb encrypted passwords added on the server with the smbpasswd -a command. Here is an example:

```
# smbpasswd -a valerie
```

The preceding command adds SMB user valerie (who should already have a Linux user ID) to the smb-encrypted password file, and allows you to give Valerie a password.

```
# Enable this if you want Samba to be a domain logon server for
# Windows95 workstations.
;   domain logons = yes

# if you enable domain logons then you may want a per-machine or
# per user logon script
# run a specific logon batch file per workstation (machine)
;   logon script = %m.bat
# run a specific logon batch file per username
;   logon script = %U.bat
```

The preceding deals with giving users individual login scripts and making Samba a domain server for Windows 9x clients. Windows NT and 2000 clients can also log in to Samba servers if the Samba server is set up as a PDC (Primary Domain Controller). Note, however, that the version of Samba included with Red Hat 7 cannot be effectively set up as a PDC, so a different version would need to be downloaded. *Samba Unleashed* offers the complete procedures to set up a Samba server as a PDC.

The [homes] Section

The [homes] section allows network clients to connect to a user's home directory on your server without having an explicit entry in the smb.conf file. When a service request is made, the Samba server searches the smb.conf file for the specific section corresponding

to the service request. If the service is not found, Samba checks whether there is a
[homes] section. If the [homes] section exists, the password file is searched to find the
home directory for the user making the request. Once this directory is found, the system
shares it with the network:

```
[homes]
   browseable = no
   writable = yes
```

The preceding is the simplest usable [homes] share. The browseable=no entry instructs
the SMB client not to list the share in a browser (such as Windows Explorer). However,
[homes] is a special case. The user share it represents will be visible in the client browse
list even if [homes] contains browseable=no. If [homes] were to contain
browseable=yes, a share called homes would actually appear in the client browse list.
The writable=yes entry enables the user to write to the directory, which is typically the
desired situation in home directories.

> **Note**
>
> The writable= parameter has two synonyms, writeable= and write ok=, and
> one inverse synonym, read only=. Thus, these four lines perform identically:
>
>   writable=yes
>   writeable=yes
>   write ok=yes
>   read only=no

In general, Samba has excellent defaults, making the preceding [homes] configuration
practical. The following [homes] share contains additional parameters:

```
[homes]
   comment = Home Directories
   browseable = no
   read only = no
   path = %H/smbtree
   create mode = 0750
```

The comment entry is a human-readable share identification string to be displayed by the
client user interface. Note that comment= is similar to server string=, but the latter is
only valid in the [global] section. The read only= parameter is an inverse synonym of
writable=, and was explained previously. Also explained previously was the
browseable= parameter.

Note the `path=` entry. Because Samba is primarily a file server, it's probably undesirable to have the user access config files in his home directory (`.bash_profile`, for instance). `%H` is a macro indicating the user's home directory, while `smbtree` is a directory under the user's home directory. To implement this as a policy, the system administrator must, of course, create a script to create the subdirectory upon addition of each new user. The directory can also be created by a `root preexec=script` parameter, which is explained in the `smb.conf` man page.

> **Caution**
>
> Linux and Windows use a different linefeed sequence in text files. When editing a file through Samba, the text file protocol is determined by the OS of the client. This means that if the same file is edited by clients of both operating systems, corruption can result.

The final entry sets the file permissions for any files created on the shared directory.

The [printers] Section

There are two ways Samba can make printers available. One is to create a specific share section with a `print ok=yes` line, a specific printcap printer specified by a `printer name=` line, and possibly a list of valid users. The other way is to let the `[printers]` section do most of the work, and list all printcap-defined printers to the client.

> **Note**
>
> This section mentions `/etc/printcap`, *printcap*, and *printcap printers* several times. `/etc/printcap` is a file defining all the Linux system's printers. A *printcap printer* is a printer defined by name in `/etc/printcap`.
>
> It is possible to edit `/etc/printcap` with an editor, but `/etc/printcap` has a tricky layout and syntax. The preferred way is to use `printtool`, which works in Linux's X environment. Use `printtool &` to access `printtool`.
>
> For further information about Linux printers and printing and the `/etc/printcap` file, see Chapter 19, "Printing with Linux." For `printcap` specifics, see the `printcap` command man page.

The following two lines sufficiently allow use of all printcap-defined printers on SMB clients:

```
[printers]
path = /var/spool/samba
```

The simplest case of a dedicated print share follows:

```
[vals_lp]
print ok = yes
printer name = lp_mine
path = /home/everyone
```

In the dedicated print share, `print ok=yes` (or the `printable=yes` synonym) is necessary. It's also necessary to name the printer with the `printer name=` line. The intent of `[printers]` is accessibility to all users with valid IDs. The intent of a special printer is typically to restrict access to a user or group, implying that it would be a good idea to add a `valid users=` line to the dedicated printer share. Beyond that, the `[printers]` section and dedicated print shares function pretty much the same.

The `[printers]` section defines how printing services are controlled if no specific entries are found in the `smb.conf` file. As with the `[homes]` section, if no specific entry is found for a printing service, Samba uses the `[printers]` section (if it's present) to allow a user to connect to any printer defined in `/etc/printcap`:

```
[printers]
   comment = All Printers
   path = /var/spool/samba
   browseable = no
   printable = yes
# Set public = yes to allow user 'guest account' to print
   public = no
   writable = no
   create mode = 0700
```

The `comment`, `browseable`, and `create mode` entries mean the same as those discussed earlier in the `[homes]` section. Note that `browseable=no` applies to the `[printers]` section, not to the printcap printers, which are listed in the SMB client's front end as a consequence of the `[printers]` section. If `browseable=` were `yes`, a share called `printers` would be listed on the client. That's clearly not what's needed.

The `path` entry indicates the location of the spool directory to be used when servicing a print request via SMB. Print files are stored there prior to transfer to the printcap-defined printer's spool directory.

The `printable` value, if `yes`, indicates that this printer resource can be used to print. It must be set to `yes` in any printer share, including `[printers]`. The `public` entry controls whether the guest account can print. The `writable=no` entry assures that the only things written to the spool directory are spool files handled by printing functions.

The `create mode=0700` specifies that all files are created with all rights for the user, and not for anyone else. This prevents different print jobs having the same filename from inadvertently overwriting each other.

17

SAMBA

Samba Printer Troubleshooting Tips

Samba printer shares (including [printers]) usually work the first time. When they don't, it's important to remember a printer share won't work without a working Samba [global] section and a working printcap printer, and Samba won't work without a working network.

> **Note**
>
> The following troubleshooting tips work not only for the [printers] section, but also for any dedicated printer shares. Dedicated printer shares all have print ok=yes, and they have a printer name= option as well.

Therefore, before troubleshooting any printer share including [printers], make sure the client and server machines can ping each other's IP address. If not, troubleshoot the network.

Next, make sure you can see the [global] defined workgroup in the client listing (Network Neighborhood or **smbclient -NL Ipaddress**). If not, troubleshoot Samba as a whole before working on the printer. Use testparm (discussed later this chapter) to verify that smb.conf is internally consistent.

Next, make sure the printcap printer works properly. The printcap name can be deduced from the share's printer name= option. If there's no printer name= in the share, it can be deduced from the client request. Perform the following:

```
# lpr -P printcap_printer_name /etc/fstab
```

This should print /etc/fstab to the physical printer defined as printcap_printer_name in /etc/printcap. /etc/fstab is an ideal test file because it's short and exists on all Red Hat Linux machines. Once the machines can ping each other, the client can see the workgroup defined in the [global] section, and you can print to the printcap printer, you're ready to troubleshoot the Samba printer share.

Many Samba printer problems occur because the default printer command doesn't work. This is especially true if the printcap printer is a network printer instead of a local printer. First try putting the following line in the printer share:

```
print command = lpr -P %p %s; rm %s
```

The command will print the file %s (the spool file passed from the client) to printer %p (the printer name passed from the client). You'll notice this is the same command done in the printcap printer test described previously, so it should work.

If it still doesn't work, verify that the `path=` entry points to a directory to which the user has read and write access. Make sure that any printer `name=` entry points to a working printer defined in `/etc/printcap`. Make sure the entry has a `printable=yes` or `print ok=yes` entry; otherwise, it's not a Samba printer share. If the printer share has a `valid users=` entry, make sure the user in question is one of those users.

If it still isn't working, it's time to install your own test point. Temporarily create directory `/home/freeall` with mode `777` (all can read, write, and execute), comment out any `print command=` line in `smb.conf`, and add the following line:

print command = cp %s /home/freeall/%p.tst;rm %s

This copies the file to be printed to a file in `/home/freeall` with the same filename as the printcap printer with the extension `.tst`. This gives several pieces of information. First, the filename tells you what printer it's trying to print to. You can check `/etc/printcap` or `printtool` for the existence of that printer. You can print that file and see if it comes out properly.

If the file does not exist, you know something's wrong on the client side of the `print` command. Be sure to check the queue on the client to see if it's getting stuck. Sometimes a single failure on the server can jam the client queue. Also be sure that all users can read, write, and execute directory `/home/freeall`; the print will otherwise bomb on permissions. Once the problem is resolved, be sure to remove the `/home/freeall` test directory you created for security reasons.

Another handy troubleshooting tool is checking the Samba logs. They usually contain useful error messages. If the log file is not defined in the `[global]` section of `smb.conf`, look in the `/var/log/samba` directory.

Beyond these tips, remember that troubleshooting is simply a matter of keeping a cool head and narrowing the scope of the problem.

Configuring a Samba File Server with `linuxconf`

On Red Hat machines, you can always start Samba with the following command:

 # /etc/rc.d/init.d/smb restart

However, for servers regularly running Samba it's desirable to have Samba start upon boot. That can be done quite easily from `linuxconf`, using the menu selection Control Panel, Control Service Activity. When presented with a list of services, highlight SMB and press Enter. On the top line check Startup Automatic. Then place an X in Level 3 and Level 5 so that it starts up in network/text and network/GUI mode.

Tab down to the Accept button and press Enter, then tab to the Quit button and press Enter to leave the service list. Next arrow up to Activate Configuration at the top of the Control Panel menu and press Enter. Either the changes are made, or a screen appears giving you the opportunity to activate the changes or preview what has to be done. Highlight Activate the Changes and press Enter. The changes are written to disk, and the Control Panel menu reappears. At this point you can tab to the Quit button and press Enter to leave the Control Panel, and then quit all the way out of linuxconf.

Reboot the machine to test whether in fact Samba started automatically. The following command yields the needed information:

```
# ps ax | grep mbd
16789 ?         S       0:00 smbd -D
16799 ?         S       0:00 nmbd -D
16802 ?         S       0:00 smbd -D
17236 pts/2     S       0:00 grep mbd
#
```

If one or more copies of smbd and one or more copies of nmbd are running, Samba is running.

Sharing Files and Print Services

After configuring your defaults for the Samba server, you can create specific shared directories limited to certain groups of people or available to everyone. For example, say you want to make a directory available to only one user. To do so, you would create a new section and fill in the needed information. Typically, you'll need to specify the user, directory path, and configuration information to the SMB server, as shown here:

```
[jacksdir]
comment = Jack's remote source code directory
path = /usr/local/src
valid users = tackett
browseable = yes
public = no
writable = yes
create mode = 0700
```

This sample section creates a shared directory called jacksdir. It's best to keep share names to under nine characters to avoid warnings in the testparm utility, and to avoid problems on older SMB clients incapable of using longer share names. The path to the directory on the local server is /usr/local/src. Because the browseable entry is set to yes, jacksdir will show up in the client's network browse list (such as Windows Explorer). However, because the public entry is set to no and the valid users entry lists only tackett, only the user tackett can access this directory using Samba. You can grant access to more users and to groups by specifying them (using an at sign prepended to the group name) in the `valid users` entry. Here's the `valid users=` line after giving group `devel` access:

```
valid users = tackett, @devel
```

> **Note**
>
> The @ in @devel is a group designator, telling Samba that devel is a group. There are actually three group designators: @, +, and &. @ is interpreted as a NIS netgroup if possible, and if not, a group on the local machine. & is interpreted only as a NIS group, and + is interpreted only as a group on the local machine. Most people simply use @. You can find out all the details by searching "invalid users" in the `smb.conf` man page.

A printer share is created by placing a `print ok=yes` (or synonym) and a `printer name=` in the share. Here is an example:

```
[vals_lp]
print ok = yes
printer name = lp_mine
path = /home/everyone
valid users = valerie, @devel
browseable = yes
```

Here is a printer that is listed as `vals_lp` on the client because of the `browseable=yes`. It prints out of printcap printer `lp_mine`. Its spool directory is `/home/everyone`, and valid users are `valerie` and the `devel` group.

The primary differences between a printer share like this and the `[printers]` section is that the `[printers]` section displays all printcap printers without being browseable, whereas a printer share such as the preceding displays only the printer whose value appears in the `printer name=` option, and then only if a `browseable=yes` option appears. The `[printers]` section does not have or require a `printer name=` option because its purpose is to display all printers to the client and allow the client access to all printers.

All the same Samba printer troubleshooting tips previously listed in the `[printers]` section of this chapter apply to printer shares.

Optimizing Samba Performance

Samba performs excellently, so performance usually isn't an issue. If performance becomes an issue, there are several options to evaluate.

> **Note**
>
> The author tested all of the following Samba configuration performance enhancement techniques and was unable to attain any significant performance gains on an underloaded Samba server with a Celeron 333, 64MB of RAM, a 7200rpm 14.4GB disk, and 100Mb wiring, using a test of copying a 20MB file back and forth. The conclusion is that gains depend on many factors, including but not limited to system load. These techniques will not help if the bottleneck is the wire, which appears to be the case on the author's setup.

Samba's defaults yield excellent performance. However, the Samba 2.0.7 default is `level2 oplocks=no`. You can substantially boost performance of a share whose primary file access is read, and that has little write contention, by setting it to `yes`.

Level 2 oplocks are an opportunistic locking mechanism enabling the file to be cached, for read access, on the client. This greatly decreases traffic over the wire. However, if even one client requests write access for the file, all the clients must reread the file.

Make sure to retain the default `oplocks=yes` unless files are edited directly on the UNIX box, in which case the client caching would result in a versioning problem. You should also turn off `oplocks` on unstable networks, but most Linux/Samba served networks are extremely stable.

Modern Samba versions, including the one shipped with Red Hat 7, default to `wide links=yes`. It is slightly more secure to set this to `no`, but setting it to `no` creates a substantial performance decrease. To minimize that decrease, be sure that `getwd cache=yes`, which is already the default. The combination of `wide links=no` and `getwd cache=no` significantly reduces performance.

Last but not least, the `smb.conf` shipping with Red Hat 7 contains the following parameter:

```
socket options = TCP_NODELAY SO_RCVBUF=8192 SO_SNDBUF=8192
```

Unless you have a specific reason to do otherwise, the preceding should be the setting of the `socket options=` parameter on Red Hat 7 Samba servers.

Tweaks to virtual memory utilization may also improve Samba performance by tuning Linux to optimally handle Samba. Two tweaks specifically have been documented.

> **Caution**
>
> Do not attempt the following `bdflush` and `buffermem` tweaks without first consulting and understanding the contents of file `/usr/share/doc/kernel-doc-2.2.10/sysctl/vm.txt` (this file is also located at `/usr/src/linux-2.2.16/Documentation/sysctl/vm.txt`). Each of the values are explained in that document.

```
# echo "80 500 64 64 80 6000 6000 1884 2" >/proc/sys/vm/bdflush

# echo "60 80 80" >/proc/sys/vm/buffermem
```

Some other possible enhancement techniques include faster network hardware and wiring, a better server hard disk, more server memory, or a server CPU upgrade.

The bottom line is that performance is bottleneck-limited, so to improve performance, it's essential to locate the performance bottleneck. A performance enhancement plan can be made once that's done. Until the bottleneck is located, speculation makes little sense.

One of the best bottleneck analysis techniques is deliberately slowing a suspected bottleneck. If system throughput slows proportionately, you've found a bottleneck. If system throughput slows only slightly, continue looking.

Testing Your Configuration

After creating the configuration file, you should test it for correctness. Start by making sure the client and server can ping each other's IP address. Without a functioning network, Samba will not work.

Next, use the `testparm` program. `testparm` is a simple test program that checks the `/etc/samba/smb.conf` configuration file for internal correctness. If this program reports no problems, you can use the configuration file with confidence that `smbd` will successfully load the configuration file.

> **Caution**
>
> Using `testparm` is not a guarantee that the services specified in the configuration file will be available or will operate as expected. This kind of testing guarantees only that Samba is able to read and understand the configuration file.

testparm has the following command line:

```
testparm [configfile [hostname hostip]]
```

configfile indicates the location of the smb.conf file if it is not in the default location (/etc/samba/smb.conf). The *hostname hostip* optional parameter instructs testparm to see whether the host has access to the services provided in the smb.conf file. If you specify *hostname*, you must specify the IP number of that host as well. Otherwise, the results will be unpredictable.

The following illustrates sample output from running testparm. If there are any errors, the program reports them, along with a specific error message:

```
# testparm smb.conf ntackett 209.42.203.236
Load smb config files from smb.conf
Processing section "[homes]"
Processing section "[printers]"
Loaded services file OK.
Allow connection from ntackett (209.42.203.236) to homes
Allow connection from ntackett (209.42.203.236) to printers
Allow connection from ntackett (209.42.203.236) to lp
```

Testing with smbstatus

The smbstatus program reports on current Samba connections. smbstatus has the following command line:

```
# smbstatus [-d] [-p] [-s configfile]
```

configfile is by default /etc/samba/smb.conf. -d provides verbose output, and -p provides a list of current SMB processes. The -p option is useful if you are writing shell scripts using smbstatus. Following is sample output:

```
# smbstatus

Samba version 2.0.7
Service     uid     gid     pid     machine
--------------------------------------------------
spec_dir    myuid   myuid   4381    p2300    (192.168.100.201)
➥ Thu May  6 22: 18:31 1999

No locked files

Share mode memory usage (bytes):
    1048464(99%) free + 56(0%) used + 56(0%) overhead = 1048576(100%) total
```

Running the Samba Server

The Samba server consists of two daemons, smbd and nmbd. The smbd daemon provides the file and print sharing services. The nmbd daemon provides NetBIOS name server support.

You can run the Samba server either from the init scripts or from inetd (or xinetd) as a system service. Because Red Hat by default starts SMB services from the init scripts each time you boot, rather than as a service from inetd, you can use this command to start or stop the SMB server:

```
# /etc/rc.d/init.d/smb start|stop
```

Using the init scripts provides better response to SMB requests rather than continuously spawning the programs from inetd.

17

SAMBA

> **Caution**
>
> The smb script in the /etc/rc.d/init.d directory was placed there by the Samba .rpm file and is deleted when you uninstall Samba using rpm. Always back up this file before uninstalling Samba, or installing a different version of Samba.

Accessing Shares

Samba shares can be accessed by SMB clients on Windows and Linux platforms. Windows access is via Network Neighborhood and Windows Explorer, as well as the net view and net use commands from the DOS prompt. Linux access is via the smbclient and smbmount commands.

Using smbclient on a Linux Client

The smbclient program allows Linux users to access SMB shares on other machines (typically Windows). If you want to access files on other Linux boxes, you can use a variety of methods including FTP, NFS, and the r-commands, such as rcp.

smbclient provides an FTP-like interface that allows you to transfer files with a network share on another computer running an SMB server. Unlike NFS, smbclient does not allow you to mount another share as a local directory. smbmount, which is discussed later in this chapter, provides the capability to mount smb shares.

smbclient provides command-line options to query a server for the shared directories available or to exchange files. For more information on all the command-line options, consult the man page for smbclient. Use the following command to list all available shares on the machine 192.168.100.1:

$ smbclient -NL 192.168.100.1

Any name resolving to the IP address can be substituted for the IP address. The -N parameter tells smbclient not to query for a password if one isn't needed, and the -L parameter requests the list.

To transfer a file, you must first connect to the Samba server using the following command:

$ smbclient //192.168.100.1/homes -U tackett

The parameter //192.168.100.1/homes specifies the remote service on the other machine. This is typically either a filesystem directory or a printer. Any name resolving to the IP address can be substituted for the IP address. The -U option enables you to specify the username you want to connect with. There are many additional smbclient command configurations; see the smbclient man page for full details. The smbclient utility prompts you for a password if this account requires one and then places you at this prompt:

smb: \

\ indicates the current working directory.

From this command line, you can issue the commands shown in Table 17.1 to transfer and work with files.

TABLE 17.1   smbclient Commands

Command	Parameters	Description
? or help	[command]	Provides a help message on command or in general if no command is specified.
!	[shell command]	Executes the specified shell command or drops the user to a shell prompt.
cd	[directory]	Changes to the specified directory on the server machine (not the local machine). If no directory is specified, smbclient reports the current working directory.

TABLE 17.1 continued

Command	Parameters	Description
lcd	[directory]	Changes to the specified directory on the local machine. If no directory is specified, smbclient will report the current working directory on the local machine.
del	[files]	The specified files on the server are deleted if the user has permission to do so. Files can include wildcard characters.
dir or ls	[files]	Lists the indicated files. You can also use the command ls to get a list of files.
exit or quit	none	Exits from the smbclient program.
get	[remotefile] [local name]	Retrieves the specified *remotefile* and saves the file on the local server. If *local name* is specified, the copied file will be saved with this filename rather than the filename on the remote server.
mget	[files]	Copies all the indicated files, including those matching any wildcards, to the local machine.
md or mkdir	[directory]	Creates the specified directory on the remote machine.
rd or rmdir	[directory]	Removes the specified directory on the remote machine.
put	[localfile] [remotename]	Copies the specified file from the local machine to the server.
mput	[files]	Copies all the specified files from the local machine to the server.
print	[file]	Prints the specified file on the remote machine.
queue	none	Displays all the print jobs queued on the remote server.

You can specify the password on the command line by appending a percent sign to the username followed by the password:

```
$ smbclient //192.168.100.1/homes -U tackett%tackettspassword
```

Although the preceding command is convenient, many versions of UNIX show the password portion of the command in clear text in a ps command. Default Red Hat Linux 7 installations show the password as a string of X characters, but in security-critical environments, or where someone might be looking over your shoulder, it's better to let smbclient prompt for the password and accept it silently.

Mounting Shares on a Linux Client

To make life even easier, the smbmount command enables you to mount a Samba share to a local directory. To experiment with this, create an /mnt/test directory on your local workstation. Now run the following command as user root, or quoted in the tail of an su -c command:

```
# mount -t smbfs //192.168.100.1/homes /mnt/test -o
➥username=myuid,dmask=777,fmask=777
```

This command is an smbmount command, even though it looks like an ordinary mount command. The -t smbfs tells the mount command to call smbmount to do the work. The preceding command grants all rights to anyone, via the dmask= and fmask= arguments. These arguments can be tuned to give proper access.

> **Note**
>
> The syntax of the smbmount command has changed extensively since the version that shipped with Red Hat 6. Running smbmount without arguments yields an excellent syntax guide.

Another syntax is the following:

```
# smbmount //192.168.100.1/homes /mnt/test -o username=myuid,dmask=777,fmask=777
```

This calls smbmount directly, but the syntax using the Linux mount command is preferred.

Assume the command is given on the local workstation, and that workstation already contains a /mnt/test directory. Further assume a Samba server at 192.168.100.1, accessible to the workstation via the network. Note that any name resolving to the IP address can be substituted for the IP address. Running the preceding command on the local machine mounts to local directory /mnt/test the share defined in the [homes] section, logged in as user myuid.

To unmount it, simply run this command as user root, or quoted in the tail of an su -c command:

```
# umount /mnt/test
```

This capability is not limited to the user's home directory. It can be used on any share in smb.conf on the Samba server.

You can also use `smbmount` to mount shared Windows resources on a Linux computer. The following mounts Windows 98 share `menudata` on existing Linux directory `/mnt/test`:

```
# mount -t smbfs //wincli/menudata /mnt/test
```

This must be done as `root`. You'll be asked for a password. Be sure to input the password of the share, because Windows 9x sharing is share mode, not user mode. To mount NT or Windows 2000 shares, use the `-U` option followed by a valid username on the Windows computer. That user must have rights to the share. Furthermore, be sure you can resolve the Windows machine by name (that is, `WINCLI`) in DNS, or the preceding command may fail or hang. Also, be sure that `/mnt/test` exists, or you'll receive an error message saying `Could not resolve mount point /mnt/test`.

Common `smb.conf` Options

There are hundreds of Samba options. For complete documentation, view the `smb.conf` man page with this command:

```
$ man smb.conf
```

An understanding of a few options suffices for most tasks. A discussion of those options and conventions follows. Note that many options are followed by (G) or (S), meaning they are intended for the `[global]` section or a share section, respectively.

Special Conventions

Many options expecting users as the value can also take groups. In these cases the value is the group name preceded by an at sign. For instance, group `acct` can be represented as `@acct`. The `@` specifies to look for the group first in NIS, then in the local machine. Prepending `&` says interpret as a NIS group only, and prepending `+` specifies local group only.

Several substitution characters can be used in `smb.conf`. They are all explained on the `smb.conf` man page. Two, `%u` and `%H`, are especially useful. `%u` will be substituted with the username, whereas `%H` will be substituted with the user's home directory. For instance, here's a share giving a document directory below `/home/everyone` to every user, as long as the sysadmin has created a directory with the user's username below `/home/everyone`:

```
[everyone]
comment = Accessible to everyone
path = /home/everyone/%u
browsable = yes
public = no
writeable = yes
create mode = 700
```

The preceding works only if `root` creates the user's subdirectory, mode `0700`, and changes group and owner to that of the user. This is not the best way to accomplish this task. It's merely a demonstration of the `%u` substitution. Note that the directory creation could also be accomplished with a `root preexec=` script.

`read only=` Versus `writeable=` Versus `writable=` Versus `write ok=` (S)

`writeable=`, `writable=`, and `write ok=` are synonyms, meaning they completely substitute for each other. `read only=` is an inverted synonym for `writeable=`, `writable=`, and `write ok=`, meaning that a `read only=yes` substitutes for a `writeable=no`, and a `read only=no` substitutes for a `writeable=yes`, and so on. Only one of these four options needs to specify whether a share is writeable. If this option is specified in the `[global]` section, it serves as a default for all shares. (This is true of all options that can be put in share definitions.) Note that these options can be overridden by the `write list=` option.

```
read only=no
writeable=yes
writable=yes
write ok=yes
```

All four mean the same thing and are interchangeable. The default is `read only=yes`.

`valid users=` (S)

The lack of this option or a blank value following the equal sign in any share makes the share accessible to everyone (probably not what you want). To limit access, place a comma-delimited list of valid users after the equal sign:

```
valid users = myuid, tackett, @acct
```

This option gives access to users `myuid` and `tackett`, and group `acct`. This option is overridden by the `invalid users=` option.

`invalid users=` (S)

This is a list of users who cannot access this share. This list overrides any users in the `valid users=` option for the share.

```
[ateam]
valid users = myuid,tackett,art
invalid users = myuid,tackett
```

This `smb.conf` snippet allows only `art` to access `[ateam]`.

read list= (S)

The value is a list of users to be given read-only access. This overrides any `read only=`, `writeable=`, and so on, restricting the listed users to read-only access. If any user on the `read list=` list is also on the `write list=` option for the share, `read list=` is overridden and that user can write in the directory.

Does `read list=` override `valid users=`? That's an interesting question. When a user not appearing in an existing `valid users=` list for the share appears in the `read list=` list, that user is prompted for a password. No matter whose password is input, the user is kicked out. This behavior is exactly mirrored by Samba's `smbclient` program and Windows Network Neighborhood. Here is an example:

```
[spec_dir]
path = /home/everyone/spec
valid users = valerie,tackett
writeable = yes
read list = valerie,tackett,myuid
write list = tackett
```

In this example, the `/home/everyone/spec` directory can be read by `valerie` and `tackett`, but not by `myuid` (no `valid users=` entry for `myuid`). User `valerie` cannot write the directory because her entry in `read list=` overrides the `writeable=` option. However, `tackett` can write it because his `write list=` entry overrides his `read list=` entry.

write list= (S)

Any share can have a list of users who can write to that share, no matter what the `writeable=` or `read list=` options say. Here's an example giving write access to `[billsdir]` for `bill`, `tackett`, and `myuid`, in spite of the fact that the directory is optioned to be read-only:

```
[billsdir]
valid users = bill, tackett, myuid
read only = yes
write list = bill, tackett, myuid
```

path= (S)

This is the directory accessed through the share. In the case of a print share, it's the spool directory (spool here before submitting to the printcap printer, which may also have its own spool). Note that if the `[global]` section contains a `root=`, `root dir=`, or `root directory=`, the `path=` will be relative to the directory specified as the root.

create mask= and create mode= (S)

These two are synonyms. They specify the maximum permissions for a newly created file. The DOS permissions (read-only, hidden, and so on) will further restrict it. The default is 744, meaning user gets all rights, but group and other get only read. If the owner later marks the file read-only from DOS, the file's actual mode on the Linux box is changed to 544 to reflect the loss of write permissions.

browseable= (S)

The browseable= entry instructs the SMB client whether to list the share in an SMB client's browser (such as Windows Explorer). It does not grant access to users not in the valid users= list, nor does browseable=no deny access to users in the valid users= list.

If set to yes, the existence of the share can be seen even by those without rights to the share. If set to no, it cannot be seen even by those in the valid users= list. However, in clients that allow a user to access a share not listed (smbclient and net use, for instance), browseable=no does not prevent a valid user from accessing the share, as long as the user enters the proper command with the proper share name. For instance, look at the following smb.conf share:

```
[valsdir]
comment = Valerie's special directory
path = /home/everyone/valsdir
browseable = no
valid users = valerie
```

Execute the following command:

```
$ smbclient -NL 192.168.100.1
```

This is the yield:

```
Sharename       Type        Comment
---------       ----        -------
    everyone    Disk        Accessible to everyone
    IPC$        IPC         IPC Service (Jacks Samba Server)
    jacksdir    Disk        Jack's remote source code directory
    lp          Printer
    myuidx      Disk        Myuid's remote source code directory
    spec_dir    Disk
    valerie     Disk        Home Directories
```

Notice that share valsdir is not listed. That's because it's not browseable. However, access is not affected on SMB clients allowing a user to access an unlisted share by name. For instance, in SMB client smbclient, user valerie can issue the following command:

```
$ smbclient //192.168.100.1/valsdir -U valerie
```

This will bring up an `smbclient` prompt allowing user `valerie` to read and write to `/home/everyone/valsdir`. In Windows, map the share to a drive letter with the following command:

```
C:\> net use x: \\192.168.100.1\valsdir
```

In summary, `browseable=` governs the visibility, not the accessibility, of the resource. However, some SMB clients (such as Windows Network Neighborhood and Windows Explorer) make access of unlisted shares non-obvious.

The default for `browseable=` is yes. If you are in tight security situations where listing on the client is not desired, you must insert a `browseable=no` line to make it invisible to the client browser. Note that the `smb.conf` that ships with Red Hat Linux 7 contains a `browseable=no` line in `[homes]`, `[Profiles]` (commented out), and `[printers]`.

printable= (S)

This allows printing from the share, so it should be used on any share that's a printer, and not used on other shares. In the `[printers]` section, `printable=` defaults to yes. Everywhere else it defaults to no.

hosts allow= Versus hosts deny= Versus allow hosts= Versus deny hosts= (S)

`hosts allow=` governs which hosts or subnets can access a share. If this option is used in the `[global]` section, it becomes the default for all shares. If this option is used, it denies entry to all hosts or subnets not specifically allowed. Use this code to allow a single host:

```
hosts allow = 192.168.100.201
```

To allow an entire subnet, use its address and subnet mask:

```
hosts allow = 192.168.100./255.255.255.0
```

`hosts allow=` overrides any `hosts deny=` options, which simply deny access to a host or subnet. `allow hosts=` is a synonym of `hosts allow=`, and `deny hosts=` is a synonym of `hosts deny=`.

public= and guest ok= (S)

These two are synonyms, with `guest ok=` preferred in SWAT (Samba Web Administration Tool). The purpose of this option is to allow those without a login on the server to access a share. This is a security compromise that sometimes makes sense on a printer. Care must be used to avoid the possibility of allowing a hostile exploit. For that reason the default is no.

comment= (S) and server string= (G)

These two are related in that they both provide human-readable strings to identify Samba resources in an SMB client's user interface. comment= describes a share, whereas server string= goes in the [global] section and describes the entire Samba server.

domain logons= (G)

This defaults to no, but if set to yes, the Samba server is allowed to serve as a domain server for a Windows 95/98 workgroup. This is different from a Windows NT domain.

encrypt passwords= and smb passwd file= (G)

These options are vital to serving Windows clients, and are discussed extensively earlier in this chapter. Defaults are encrypt passwords=no and smb passwd file=/etc/samba/smbpasswd.

> **Note**
>
> Different Samba distributions have different default values of smb passwd file=. When in doubt, grep the output of testparm (on an empty file) to find the default.

config file= (G)

This is a method of specifying a Samba configuration file other than /etc/samba/smb.conf. When Samba encounters this option, it reloads all parameters from the specified file.

hosts equiv= (G)

This dangerous option points to a file containing hosts and users allowed to log in without a password. This is obviously an extreme security risk. The default is none, and the best policy is to leave this option absent from smb.conf.

interfaces= (G)

This becomes necessary when the server serves multiple subnets. Here's an example:

```
interfaces = 192.168.2.10/24 192.168.3.10/24
```

A /24 is a subnet mask. 24 represents 24 bits of 1s, or 255.255.255.0. Thus, the example would serve subnets 192.168.2 and 192.168.3. Normal subnet notations with four dot-delimited numbers can also be used after the slash.

load printers= (G)

This defaults to yes. A yes value loads all printers in printcap for Samba browsing.

null passwords= (G)

This option defaults to no, meaning no user with a zero-length password on the server can log in to Samba. Setting this to yes is an obvious security risk.

password level and username level (G)

These determine the level of non–case sensitivity of username and password comparisons. The default is 0, meaning the client-provided password or username is first compared with case sensitivity against the copy on the server, and that the client username or password is converted to lowercase and compared to the copy on the server if that fails.

In troubleshooting Samba connection problems from Windows clients, it's often handy to set these options high (such as 24) to see if that fixes the problem. Although this represents a minor security problem and also slows initial connection, it often solves the problem. Once problems have been fixed, you should re-comment these two options to beef up security and speed authentication.

Connection problems from Windows clients also are often solved with the encrypt passwords= and smb passwd file= options.

security= (G)

Default is security=user, which enforces security by user and password. This is generally the best choice, with excellent security and predictability.

security=server and security=domain are used primarily when password authentication is actually done by yet another machine. security=domain is used to join Samba to an NT domain. security=share offers less security and less predictable operation, but is sometimes a logical choice in less security-intense situations such as if most of the client usernames don't exist on the server, or if most usage is by printers not requiring passwords.

This topic is important, and is discussed further in documents /usr/share/doc/ samba-2.0.7/docs/textdocs/security_level.txt and /usr/share/doc/ samba-2.0.7/docs/textdocs/DOMAIN_MEMBER.txt.

workgroup= (G)

This is the workgroup in which the server appears, and also controls the domain name used with the security=domain setting. The default is WORKGROUP, but Red Hat 7–supplied smb.conf contains the line workgroup=MYGROUP.

netbios name= (G)

Samba's default behavior is to use the host's hostname as the SMB netbios name. But that default does not always work properly. It's an excellent idea to hard-code the text of the hostname in this parameter. For instance, if the Samba server's hostname is `mainserv`, the following is recommended:

```
netbios name=mainserv
```

wins support= (G)

This specifies that the Samba server also serves as a Windows WINS server. WINS is part of Windows' name resolution system. Every network should have a WINS server, so if you have no NT or Windows 2000 computers acting as a WINS server, you should enable this option. Note, however, that this should *never* be set if you have another WINS server on your network. Do not confuse this option with `wins server=`, which simply points to another server acting as the WINS server.

wins server= (G)

This *does not* make the Samba box a WINS server. Instead, it refers WINS requests to a different host acting as a WINS server. This is important in multi-subnetted networks.

local master= (G)

This defaults to `yes`, so it's not normally necessary or desirable to set it to `no`. However, if you want to prevent the Samba server from becoming a browse master on its subnet, setting this to `no` is the way to do it. Note that a `yes` value does not specify that the Samba server will be a browse master, only that it will compete with other hosts, in a browser election, to become the local browse master. The winner is decided by the greatest value of `os level=` and other criteria.

preferred master= (G)

This defaults to `no`. If set to `yes`, it does two things. First, it gives the Samba server a slight advantage in winning a browser election. More importantly, it triggers a browser election within thirty seconds of a Samba restart. This guarantees that an election selects a host (not necessarily this one) as a local master browser, thereby preventing those pesky situations in which Network Neighborhood doesn't recognize a share for several minutes or upwards of an hour. There should be only one Samba server set as preferred master, because if there are more they will fight a "browser war" with each other. In browser wars the loser calls for another election, and elections can happen as frequently as every 30 seconds. This brings performance to a standstill.

It's recommended that the host with `preferred master=yes` also set `domain master=yes`.

domain master= (G)

Defaulting to `no`, this option specifies that Samba create a WAN-wide browser on this host. Always set this true on multi-subnet networks not containing a Windows PDC. It's recommended to set this option to `yes` if specifying `preferred master=yes`.

os level= (G)

Default is `20`. The (commented out) option in the default Red Hat 7 `smb.conf` is set at `33`. When a browser election takes place, every possible browse master (including those on Windows computers) is queried for its os level. The one with the highest level wins. In the event of a tie, other factors, such as `preferred master=`, are taken into account. Setting this to `65` should beat out all Windows 9x, NT, and Windows 2000 servers.

> **Note**
>
> The guaranteed sufficient value of the os level= parameter will change as Microsoft modifies its operating system. Therefore, in troubleshooting any problem in which the Samba server does not become the master browser, temporarily set os level=255. Once all problems have been solved, try reducing it to 129, 65, or even 34. Note that the BROWSING.txt documentation states that 34 will beat all other Samba servers, but that documentation was written in April 2000, and technology can change quickly.

domain logons= (G)

Setting this to `yes` enables your Samba server to authenticate Windows clients upon logon, not just upon access of files stored on the Samba server.

Samba Resources

With Red Hat Linux 7 installed, you have access to voluminous Samba documentation. Every program has its own man page, available with the Linux command:

```
#man programname
```

programname is `smbtar`, `smbmount`, or the like.

17

SAMBA

There is also text-based hyperlink help available with the `info` program:

```
#info programname
```

programname is smbtar, smbmount, or the like.

You can find text format Samba documentation in directory /usr/share/doc/ samba-2.0.7/docs/textdocs. You can find Samba documentation in HTML form in directory /usr/share/doc/samba-2.0.7/docs/htmldocs.

As of Samba version 2 and later, a great source of documentation is SWAT. SWAT is discussed later in this chapter. If SWAT is enabled on your server, it's a highly organized source of Samba documentation. Users other than root can take advantage of SWAT's documentation, although only user root can alter a properly permissioned smb.conf configuration through SWAT.

Samba Applications Documentation Sources

Samba is a suite of programs (listed in Table 17.2) designed to give all necessary client and server access to SMB on your Linux-based computer. Each program has a man page and an info page.

TABLE 17.2   Programs Composing the Samba Suite

Program	Description
smbd	The daemon that provides the file and print services to SMB clients, such as Windows for Workgroups, Windows NT, or LanManager. (The configuration file for this daemon is described in smb.conf.)
nmbd	The daemon that provides NetBIOS nameserving and browsing support.
smbclient	This program implements an FTP-like client that is useful for accessing SMB shares on other compatible servers.
testparm	This utility enables you to test the /etc/samba/smb.conf configuration file.
smbstatus	This utility enables you to tell who is currently using the smbd server.
smbpasswd	This utility changes a user's SMB password in the smbpasswd file.
smbrun	This is an interface program between smbd and external programs.
smbtar	This is a shell script for backing up SMB shares directly to a UNIX-based tape drive.
smbmount	Use this utility to mount an SMB filesystem.
smbmnt	Called by smbmount to do the work. Generally not called directly.
smbumount	A utility that unmounts an SMB filesystem.

Configuration Option Documentation

Samba has hundreds of configuration options. For complete information, search for these three strings on the smb.conf man page: "COMPLETE LIST OF GLOBAL PARAMETERS", "COMPLETE LIST OF SERVICE PARAMETERS", and "EXPLANATION OF EACH PARAMETER". All the same information is accessible in the smb.conf info page.

Other Documentation

The smb.conf file supports a number of variable substitutions. The %H and %u substitutions were discussed earlier in this chapter. For a complete list and description of these substitutions, search the smb.conf man page for the phrase "VARIABLE SUBSTITUTIONS".

The smb.conf file has several options related to name mangling. *Name mangling* is a method of interfacing between old DOS 8.3 filename conventions and modern file naming conventions. It also relates to case sensitivity, default case, and the like. To see a complete treatise on the subject, search for the string "NAME MANGLING" in the smb.conf man page.

Last but not least, *Samba Unleashed* provides extremely deep and broad coverage of Samba.

Using Samba as a Logon Server

Samba can be used to authenticate logons on Windows 9x, NT, and 2000 computers. Windows 2000 must have NetBIOS over TCP/IP enabled to interact with Samba.

This section gives instructions for setting up Samba to authenticate logons on Windows 9x clients. The version of Samba shipped with Red Hat Linux 7 is not well suited to authenticate logons on NT or Win2K hosts. Those hosts require Samba running as a PDC. PDC functionality is best accomplished with the Samba_TNG version of Samba, which can be downloaded from www.samba.org.

Samba can do all of the following:

- Replace the Windows client's logon mechanism with centralized authentication.
- Supply a logon script.
- Centrally administrate per-user Windows profiles.

Windows profiles are beyond the scope of this chapter. You can get profile details from:

- *Samba Unleashed*
- /usr/share/doc/samba-2.0.7/docs/textdocs/PROFILES.txt
- /usr/share/doc/samba-2.0.7/docs/textdocs/DOMAIN.txt

Basic Windows 9x Logon Authentication

In the following sample `smb.conf`, the server's hostname is `mainserv`, the workgroup is MYGROUP, the Windows 9x clients all use encrypted passwords, and there is no WINS server or domain controller other than the Samba server:

```
[global]
netbios name=mainserv
workgroup=MYGROUP
encrypt passwords=yes

wins support=yes
preferred master=yes
domain master=yes
domain logons=yes

[homes]
writeable=yes
```

Restart Samba and you now have a server capable of assuming the logon authentication duties for Windows 9x clients. The next step is to set up the clients and users.

Each potential user must have a valid UNIX account and a valid `smbpasswd` entry. Assuming the user has a valid UNIX account, setting up the `smbpasswd` entry is simply a matter of doing the following as `root`:

```
# smbpasswd -a slitt
```

The preceding adds an `smbpasswd` entry for user `slitt` by prompting for the password and a password confirmation. The password should be the same as used on the client.

Now that the user is taken care of, modify the client computer to authenticate against Samba instead of locally. On the Windows 9x client, right-click any Network Neighborhood icon and choose Properties to pull up the Network dialog box. Select the Configuration tab, and highlight Client for Microsoft Networks in the The Following Network Components Are Installed drop-down list, and click the Properties button to bring up the Client for Microsoft Networks Properties dialog box.

Check the Logon to Windows NT Domain checkbox, type the workgroup name of the Samba server (which should match the client) in the Windows NT Domain text box, and check the Logon and Restore Network Connections radio button. Click OK all the way out of all dialog boxes, and answer affirmatively when asked if you want to restart the computer.

Upon restart, the Windows logon screen contains a third field, the domain. In the domain field, type in the workgroup name for the Samba server (which should already match the client workgroup name on the identification tab of the Network dialog box). If all is well, you're logged in.

If not, verify that the user and password used on the Windows client is matched by a user/password combination in smbpasswd. You can verify that you're really authenticating on the server by changing the password on the server, using the smbpasswd command, and then verifying that client logons now fail. Naturally, the original password must then be restored.

Enabling a Server-Hosted Logon Script

It's very handy to implement a server-hosted logon script. This section outlines a simple scheme, administered only by user root.

Start by creating directory /home/netlogon/scripts, owner and group root, mode 755.

Add the following to the smb.conf [global] section:

```
logon script=scripts\%U.bat
```

> **Caution**
>
> Danger of time waste! Much time is wasted troubleshooting logon script problems resulting from treating logon scripts as UNIX files. Symptoms resulting from this mistake are elusive to track.
>
> Always use backslashes (never forward slashes) in the logon script= parameter. Always use backslashes in commands within the logon script. Most elusive, always save the logon script as a DOS format file, with CRLF line separators. Within the vi editor, this can be accomplished by executing the following command before writing your file:
>
> ```
> :set fileformat=dos
> ```
>
> At the risk of beating a dead horse, logon script problems resulting from forward slashes and UNIX style files can bite you over and over again, costing up to an hour each time. The best prevention is to be very aware of this, and check at the first sign of problems with logon scripts.

The preceding Samba parameter specifies that the logon script is a .bat file with a filename identical to the user, located in the scripts directory below the special [netlogon] share.

Create the [netlogon] share as follows:

```
[netlogon]
path=/home/netlogon
writeable=no
guest ok=no
oplocks=no
```

Next, assuming you'll log on to the client as user `myuid`, create the following `/home/netlogon/scripts/myuid.bat`:

```
echo This is user myuid
c:\windows\command\choice.com
```

Restart Samba and log on. If all is well, upon client logon a DOS command prompt appears announcing that this is user `myuid`, and prompting for a `Y` or `N` keypress, after which the logon process completes.

Samba Troubleshooting Tips

A detailed description of the troubleshooting process used in Samba diagnosis is beyond the scope of this chapter. Suffice it to say that you diagnose Samba problems using a narrowing process similar to other troubleshooting tasks. This section gives a few handy tips for quick diagnosis of Samba problems.

Use `testparm` Early and Often

The `testparm` utility tests your `smb.conf` file for legal syntax, printing out errors and warnings for illegal syntaxes. The 15 seconds it takes is well worth the reduction in troubleshooting time. Many problems revealed by `testparm` are difficult to pinpoint with other tests.

Another great use for `testparm` is finding Samba's defaults. Start by creating an empty file called `empty.fil`. Then, to find the default for the `preferred master=` parameter, execute the following command:

```
$ testparm -s empty.fil | grep -i "preferred master"
        preferred master = No
$
```

The preceding command reveals the default to be `No`.

Use `DIAGNOSIS.txt`

This is a predefined diagnostic written by Andrew Tridgell, the originator of Samba. Following the steps of this file yields a remarkably quick pinpointing of the cause of Samba problems. Better still, it provides a common symptom description tool for everyone, so a simple "it failed on step 7 of DIAGNOSIS.txt" replaces paragraphs of text. On your Red Hat 7 distribution, this file is available at `/usr/share/doc/samba-2.0.7/docs/textdocs/DIAGNOSIS.txt`.

Understand the Access Hierarchy

Samba requires a functioning network, meaning you can't Samba if you can't ping. A "Samba problem" is not really a Samba problem if you can't ping—it's a network problem.

Likewise, you can't browse on a Windows client if you can't browse (via `smbclient -NL servername`) on the Linux server. So if Windows browsing doesn't work, check browsing on the server.

Additionally, you can't browse in Network Neighborhood if you can't browse in the Windows command environment via the `net view \\servername` command. The bottom line is to be conscious of the following access hierarchy:

- You must be able to `ping` to be able to browse on the server.
- You must be able to browse on the server to browse on the Windows client's command line.
- You must be able to browse on the Windows client's command line to be able to browse in Network Neighborhood or Windows Explorer.

Look at the Log Files

Samba writes its activity to its log files. The default location for its log files on a Samba server are contained in directory `/var/log/samba`. By viewing these logs you can look back in time to see what transpired during the error.

Additionally, most Samba software can be run at higher error levels such that more debugging information is written to the logs. This can greatly aid diagnosis. See the various man pages for methods of increasing error levels.

Use SWAT to Reduce Your `smb.conf` File

Comments are nice documentation, and so are parameters explicitly set to their default values. But too much of such "readability" makes for an incredibly unwieldy and therefore unreadable `smb.conf`. Sometimes it's nice to get rid of all the comments and the parameters set explicitly to their default values. SWAT does just that. Simply back up your existing `smb.conf` (this is a must), and then run SWAT as `root`, enter the global page, and click the `Commit Changes` button. All comments and explicitly specified defaults disappear, leaving just the system's distinctive features.

Making a Sure-Fire Browser `smb.conf`

Sometimes you just can't see the Samba server from your Windows 9x machines. This is especially prevalent when there is no WINS server, domain master, or PDC on the network. If there are no NT or Windows 2000 servers (or clients acting as WINS servers or

PDCs), you can guarantee the Samba box becomes a WINS server and browse master by including the following:

```
os level=65
preferred master=yes
domain master=yes
```

> **Caution**
>
> Never use the preceding settings on a network that has an NT or Win2K master browser, WINS server, or PDC. To do so will cause serious network problems.

Also, make sure to set the `netbios name=` parameter to the hostname of the Samba server, and to set the `workgroup=` parameter to the workgroup of the client computers.

Keep a Cool Head

Troubleshooting is easy with the right attitude. Simply hunt down the root cause with a "just the facts" attitude. You can see a detailed description of troubleshooting and troubleshooting processes at `http://www.troubleshooters.com/tuni.htm`.

Samba Security

Lock up your `smb.conf` file, and throw away the key. Giving a person write access to `smb.conf` is as good as giving him the root password. Here's why.

Imagine a disgruntled employee writing a script that backs up `/etc/passwd` and then creates an `/etc/passwd` file with no root password. He logs in as `root`, without a password, and now has control of your system. He restores the original `/etc/passwd` and changes the password again.

But of course the script mentioned in the preceding paragraph won't work unless he's running as `root`. So he writes the script, manages to get write access to `smb.conf`, and adds a new share with a `root preexec=` option pointing to his mischievous script. He then accesses his new share through Samba, and immediately logs in as `root` and changes the password. He covers his tracks, and owns the system. Unbelievably, he didn't need to restart Samba to accomplish this exploit.

The `root preexec=` and `root postexec=` parameters run the commands specified by their values as `root`. This functionality cannot be turned off without a source code change to Samba. Therefore, the utmost care must be taken to grant `smb.conf` write access only to those who can be trusted with the `root` password. Making `smb.conf` owner `root`, group `root`, file mode 644 should do the trick.

> **Caution**
>
> It might seem a good idea to make the file mode 664, and then give a select group access to smb.conf. Unfortunately, older versions of SWAT enabled complete read/write access to an smb.conf that was owned by root, group root, and file mode 660 or 664. The SWAT that comes with Red Hat 7 does not have this flaw, but a cracker might be able to install the older SWAT on the system, after which he could exploit this flaw.

SWAT Precautions

SWAT is the smb.conf configuration program with a browser interface, discussed later in the section titled "Using SWAT for Web-Based Samba Configuration." The preceding caution statement highlights one of the security issues with SWAT. There are others. All passwords given to SWAT are sent in the clear, so they can be sniffed. That's why it's best to allow SWAT only from localhost.

Another SWAT precaution is to shut down all sessions of your browser after completing your SWAT work. A SWAT authentication remains good as long as there's a session of the browser. That means you could finish your SWAT work, navigate out of the SWAT Web pages, and even close the browser. But if there are other copies of the browser running, a sneaky co-worker could sit down at your computer, navigate to http://192.168.100.1:901 (or wherever your Samba server resides), and install a mischievous root preexec= parameter while you're gone.

Considerations for Special Parameters

Several parameters deserve a security mention. Certainly the hosts equiv= parameter should never be used, because it specifies a file listing hosts and users who are allowed on without passwords.

In anything but the most trusting environments, or servers with nothing but printers, security=share should not be used because passwords relate to shares, not users. That means when an employee leaves, he leaves with the passwords to the shares. It also means that passwords are known far and wide.

Watch out for the admin users= parameter. It grants users listed in its value total access to the share's entire tree. Although they are confined to that tree, they can still do plenty of damage if mistakes are made. Don't use admin users= unless you have a very good reason to do so, and can't do what is needed any other way.

The `valid users=` parameter is a good thing. It restricts share access to those on its list. Because groups can be put in that list, you should use a `valid users=` parameter in all shares except those you truly want to be universally accessible, or in special shares like `[homes]`, `[printers]`, and `[netlogon]`.

Use `writeable=`, `read list=`, and `write list=` to determine which users and groups have write access.

The `hosts allow=` parameter can limit access to certain subnets or hosts. Use it.

This Is the Tip of the Iceberg

Security is an immense subject. This section has presented a few of the most obvious security issues. There are hundreds of other issues, including password synchronization, LDAP, NIS, SSL, Kerberos, checking the authenticity of your Samba source code or RPM package, and much, much more. *Samba Unleashed* contains an entire chapter on Samba security, and for the system administrator needing to lock things down really tight, there's plenty to learn beyond that.

Using SWAT for Web-Based Samba Configuration

SWAT is a Web-based tool to provide local or remote, password-guarded Samba administration from any browser that can access the server. SWAT is new with Samba 2 and is included in Red Hat 7, which ships with Samba 2.0.7.

> **Caution**
>
> Configuring with SWAT will dramatically change your `smb.conf` file. It will eliminate all comments, eliminate `include=` and `copy=` options, eliminate many options already set to the default, and change options to more common synonyms (and in some cases to inverse synonyms, simultaneously reversing the value).
>
> Always back up `smb.conf` before configuring with SWAT. A SWAT-configured `smb.conf` file is much shorter, making it more readable. However, the loss of comments and self-documenting default-configured options can make it less readable. If you've tailored your `smb.conf` for readability and self-documentation, you may want to refrain from using SWAT.

SWAT is a convenience that can improve security by making errors less likely. It dramatically changes `smb.conf`, however, and it can cause a security breach if not used carefully.

Activating SWAT on Your Server

Red Hat 7 comes with SWAT disabled. To enable it, the `disable = yes` line in `/etc/xinetd.d/swat` must be commented out. Also, depending on the state of your system's name resolution it might not work simply because `xinetd` cannot resolve `localhost` to a number. As discussed in Chapter 20, "TCP/IP Network Management," Red Hat 7 uses `xinetd` instead of the older `inetd` to start various services.

Start by accessing either localhost or your Samba server's IP address as an http URL from either Netscape or `lynx`. If you receive an error message saying `Unexpected network read error; connection aborted.` in `lynx`, or `A network error occurred while netscape was receiving data. (Network Error: Connection reset by peer)` `Try connecting again`, it's likely you're being stopped by security. As a temporary diagnostic, disable host checking by doing the following:

1. Verify that `/etc/services` contains the following line. The line should not be commented.

   ```
   swat            901/tcp
   ```

2. Comment out the following line in `/etc/xinetd.d/swat`:

   ```
   disable = yes
   ```

3. VERY TEMPORARILY comment out the following line in `/etc/xinetd.d/swat`:

   ```
   only_from = localhost
   ```

4. Find the PID of `xinetd` using `ps ax | grep xinetd`.

5. Send a `SIGUSR1` signal to `xinetd` with the following command:

   ```
   # kill -s SIGUSR1 PID
   ```

This procedure should successfully enable SWAT on a typically installed Red Hat 7 server from absolutely any IP address. Obviously, commenting out the `only_from =` line is a serious security violation. It's just a temporary diagnostic test. If the URL now asks you for a username and password (`lynx` first throws an `Access without authorization denied--retrying` error, then asks for the username and password), that means the problem was host checking. Now it's time to fix it correctly.

The original line was as follows:

```
only_from = localhost
```

Unless your system can correctly resolve the name `localhost`, the preceding line causes the discussed error. To resolve this error, simply uncomment the `only from=` line and replace `localhost` with `127.0.0.1`. If you want to also access SWAT from machines on your local subnet (in all but the smallest, most trusting organizations that's a bad idea), you can add your subnet. For instance, if your network is `192.168.100`, the following line enables access from both `localhost` and from your subnet:

```
only_from = 127.0.0.1 192.168.100.0
```

Notice once again that `localhost` is specified by number, not name. Notice that the `0` in the second IP address serves as a wildcard indicating it's really a subnet, and allowing access from anyone on that subnet. Note further that the two IP addresses are separated by a space, not a comma.

The next step is to access Samba configuration through SWAT.

Configuring `smb.conf` from Your Browser Using SWAT

> **Caution**
>
> After completing your SWAT work, you must close all browsers on your workstation. All open browsers will "remember" the password, allowing anyone with physical access to your workstation (or server terminal) access to Samba configuration, including password administration.
>
> Additionally, if SWAT is used on a browser at a remote workstation, passwords are sent across the wire as clear text and can be sniffed.
>
> For best security, use SWAT only on the server's terminal, and when done, close all browsers. For best security, configure `/etc/xinetd.d/swat` to accept queries only from `127.0.0.1`.

From your favorite browser (Netscape Navigator, Microsoft Internet Explorer, or `lynx`) navigate to port 901 of the server's IP address:

```
# lynx http://192.168.100.1:901
```

Or, if you're on the console, it's safer to access it as `localhost`:

```
# lynx http://localhost:901
```

The browser asks for a username and password. To enable read-write access, use `root` and root's password. Once authenticated, a page appears with links for HOME, GLOBALS, SHARES, PRINTERS, STATUS, VIEW, and PASSWORD. Choosing GLOBALS, SHARES, or PRINTERS brings up a page in which you can edit options. Each contains a button that can be toggled between Advanced View and Basic View, with Advanced View showing every possible configuration option. Note that with the SHARES and PRINTERS pages, you'll need to choose the share or printer from a drop-down list and then click the Choose button before you can edit the share or printer.

Assuming you're logged in to SWAT as root, a Commit Changes button will be visible. After making changes, clicking this button will write smb.conf. If you click the Reset Values button, the options will revert to values in the present smb.conf file.

> **Note**
>
> Some smb.conf changes take effect immediately, but to ensure that all changes take effect, you must restart smbd with the following command:
>
> # /etc/rc.d/init.d/smb restart

The SWAT page contains voluminous, well-organized documentation, available even to those not logged in as root, and therefore unable to change the configuration.

Using Samba as a Linux Migration Tool

Some computer users want to migrate completely to Linux, leaving Windows behind. For such users, Samba is an indispensable migration tool. This discussion assumes the user has separate Windows and Linux boxes, network connected, and the Linux box is running Samba.

The first step is to decide the structure of your data tree on the Linux box. For backup and tracking purposes, many consider it best to have all real data in the data tree, leaving the home directory for temporary work. An excellent plan is to put all data under a directory called /d, and place all data accessed exclusively with Windows-based programs in subdirectory /d/w.

The next step, and it's absolutely vital to do this before transferring any files, is to have a working backup system for the /d tree. See Chapter 22, "Backup and Restore."

17

SAMBA

Creating the Data Directory Share

Now the first step of the transition is simply moving data files to directories under the /d/w directory, and accessing them via Samba with the same Windows programs as always. The Samba share for /d looks like this, assuming it's to be used only by user myuid:

```
[d]
comment=Linux Data Directory
path=/d
writeable=yes
valid users=myuid
```

Naturally, in the preceding example the /d directory should be owned by myuid, and the file mode of /d should be 0700. Slightly more complex is the situation in which several people need to access and modify the files. In such a case, add all such people in a group (let's call it hometeam). Make /d owned by root with group hometeam and make the file mode for /d 770. Now anyone from group hometeam has total access to the directory. Next, create the [d] share as follows:

```
[d]
comment=Linux Data Directory
path=/d
writeable=yes
valid users=@hometeam
force group=hometeam
create mode=660
directory mode=770
oplocks=no
```

In the preceding share definition, anyone in group hometeam, but nobody else, can access the share through Samba. The force group=hometeam statement sets the group to hometeam for files newly created through Samba. Otherwise, each file's group would be set to the primary group of the user that created the file. Thus, the force group= hometeam line enables different users to edit each other's files.

The create mode=660 sets the mode on files created through Samba to 660 so anyone in the file's group (which of course was set to hometeam by the force group=) can read and write the file. The directory mode=770 is done for similar reasons.

Finally, the oplocks=no prevents on-client caching. This is desirable if and only if files are expected to be edited on both the server and the client, because doing so with on-client caching would create corruption. In a Windows-to-Linux transition, it's very likely that files will be edited on both sides.

The Early Transition

The earliest part of the transition is simply moving data from the Windows hard disk to the /d/w directory, and accessing it using the same programs as always. This data migration needn't be done in a single step, as long as there's an organized method to keep track of what has and hasn't been moved. It might be tempting to leave copies of the original files in the original Windows directory, but this practice would lead to a version control nightmare. Instead, keep Windows copies under something like a c:\moved directory. Once you're confident that the files on the Linux side are correct and are being regularly backed up, you can delete their Windows hard disk counterparts with confidence.

The next step is to edit the data with Linux programs. For instance, you might use Gimp instead of Paint Shop Pro to edit .jpg files. Once you start editing some of a directory's files using Linux-based software, it's best to move it to an appropriate directory under /d, rather than /d/w.

Eliminating Those Pesky DOS Carriage Returns from Text Files

In text files, DOS and Windows delineate lines with a carriage return line feed combination (CRLF). Linux (and all UNIX and UNIX workalikes) use only a line feed (LF). Before working on a text file on the Linux box, you should convert it to the Linux line feed–only format. The following is a simple script to convert DOS format files to UNIX format:

```
#!/bin/sh
while [ $1 ]; do {
        echo Converting $1
        cp $1 $1.dos
        touch -r $1 $1.dos
        cat $1.dos | sed s/^M$//g > $1
        touch -r $1.dos $1
        shift
}
done
```

Caution

In the preceding script, all occurrences of ^M are a single Ctrl+M character, not a caret followed by an uppercase M. You can make a Ctrl+M character by pressing Ctrl+V followed by Ctrl+M.

The preceding script works on single files and on wildcards. It converts each file from DOS to UNIX file format, keeping a backup (which gets overwritten the next time the script runs) as a .dos file, and retains the original file date and time due to the touch commands.

> **Caution**
>
> Never run the preceding script against binary files, because it will irretrievably corrupt a binary file.
>
> The preceding script is the simplest possible. This script can corrupt text files in certain situations, such as when existing backup files cannot be overwritten, as well as other situations. Before adopting it, you should test to determine that it meets your needs. Be careful with the preceding script.
>
> Always back up a directory before running this script on any files in that directory.

The Migration Endgame

Once you've begun using Linux programs to edit your data, you might notice that it's inconvenient to continually move from one computer to the other. VNC to the rescue. VNC is a GUI-aware remote access program similar to PC-Anywhere, except that it works on Windows, Linux, UNIX, and most UNIX workalikes.

By running VNC server (WinVNC.exe) on your Windows box and vncviewer on your Linux box, you can operate your Windows box from your Linux box, and never need to switch chairs (unless you need to insert a CD, power down, and the like). The vncviewer program comes ready to run on your Linux box, and you can download the Windows VNC server from http://www.uk.research.att.com/vnc/index.html. Install the Windows VNC server per the downloaded instructions, and then to access the Windows box from your Linux box, simply execute the following command in a GUI terminal on the Linux box:

```
$ vncviewer 192.168.100.5:0
```

The preceding command assumes the Windows box is at 192.168.100.5. You're asked to enter the same password you configured on the VNC server on the Windows box, after which your Linux box appears to "turn into" a Windows box. Be sure to use the F8 key to view the popup menu, from which you can toggle full screen mode, send an F8 character to the Windows app, send a Ctrl+Alt+Delete to the Windows machine, and other handy tricks.

There's more information on setting up VNC in Chapter 28, "Emulators, Tools, and Window Clients," and at http://www.troubleshooters.com/tpromag/200006/200006.htm#_vnc, and detailed VNC information at http://www.uk.research.att.com/vnc/index.html.

Summary

Samba enables a Linux computer to act as a secure, sophisticated file and print server. At this point, you should have a properly configured Samba server up and running and should have learned the commands and options that make that Samba server practical. You have learned several tips on troubleshooting your Samba setup.

Several advanced options are available for Samba and the various programs that make up the Samba suite. Finally, you can find a large amount of information on Samba at `http://www.samba.org`.

System
Administration and
Management

PART

III

IN THIS PART

Linux Filesystems, Disks, and Other Devices

One of the simplest and most elegant aspects of UNIX design is the way almost everything is represented as a file. Even the devices on which files are stored are represented as files.

Hardware devices are associated with drivers that provide a file interface; the special files representing hardware devices (or just *devices*) are kept in the directory /dev.

Basic Concepts of Devices

Devices are either block devices or character devices. A *character device* is one from which you can read a sequence of characters—for example, the sequence of keys typed at a keyboard or the sequence of bytes sent over a serial line. Character devices are sometimes referred to as *sequentially accessed devices*. A *block device* is one that stores data and offers access to all parts of it equally; diskettes and hard disks are block devices. Block devices are sometimes called *random access devices*.

When you perform some operation on a file, the kernel can tell that the file involved is a device by looking at its file mode (not its location). Different major and minor device numbers distinguishes the device nodes. The *major device number* indicates to the kernel which of its drivers the device node represents. For example in Linux, a block device with major number 3 is an IDE disk drive, and one with the major device number 8 is a SCSI disk. Each driver is responsible for several instances of the hardware it drives, and these are indicated by the value of the minor device number. For example, the SCSI disk with the minor number 0 represents the whole "first" SCSI disk, and the minor numbers 1 to 15 represent 15 possible partitions on it. The ls command prints the major and minor device numbers for you:

```
ls -l --sort=none /dev/sda{,[0-9],[0-9][0-9]} /dev/sdb
brw-rw----   1 root     disk       8,   0 Jul  4 08:22 /dev/sda
brw-rw----   1 root     disk       8,   1 Jul  4 08:22 /dev/sda1
brw-rw----   1 root     disk       8,   2 Jul  4 08:22 /dev/sda2
brw-rw----   1 root     disk       8,   3 Jul  4 08:22 /dev/sda3
brw-rw----   1 root     disk       8,   4 Jul  4 08:22 /dev/sda4
brw-rw----   1 root     disk       8,   5 Jul  4 08:22 /dev/sda5
brw-rw----   1 root     disk       8,   6 Jul  4 08:22 /dev/sda6
brw-rw----   1 root     disk       8,   7 Jul  4 08:22 /dev/sda7
brw-rw----   1 root     disk       8,   8 Jul  4 08:22 /dev/sda8
brw-rw----   1 root     disk       8,   9 Jul  4 08:22 /dev/sda9
brw-rw----   1 root     disk       8,  10 Jul  4 08:22 /dev/sda10
brw-rw----   1 root     disk       8,  11 Jul  4 08:22 /dev/sda11
brw-rw----   1 root     disk       8,  12 Jul  4 08:22 /dev/sda12
brw-rw----   1 root     disk       8,  13 Jul  4 08:22 /dev/sda13
brw-rw----   1 root     disk       8,  14 Jul  4 08:22 /dev/sda14
brw-rw----   1 root     disk       8,  15 Jul  4 08:22 /dev/sda15
brw-rw----   1 root     disk       8,  16 Jul  4 08:22 /dev/sdb
```

The somewhat obscure option (`--sort=none`) with this `ls -l` command ensures that the devices are presented in correct order. If you use only `ls -l`, the entries are sorted alphabetically, and `/dev/sda10` comes before `/dev/sda2`.

The `b` at the far left of the output of this command indicates that each of these entries is a block device. (Character devices are indicated by a `c`.) The major and minor device numbers appear just before the time field, separated by commas. (This is the position normally occupied in `ls -l` output by the file's size.)are associated with drivers that provide a file interfac

Character Devices

There are many character devices on a Linux system. On my system there are over 1600 devices marked as character devices in `/dev`. To see how many character devices there are on your system, use the following:

```
$ ls -l /dev/|grep ^c|wc -l
```

Character devices all deal with data one character at a time and process them sequentially. For example, the keyboard device will interpret each key as it is typed and if you want to "move" within this character stream it would only be possible to move forward (since each keystroke is lost as you process it). Also, you could only skip forward by actually reading and discarding keystrokes.

One good example of a character device is `/dev/audio`. This enables you to output data to your sound card. Each byte that is sent to it will be handled by the device drive and then sent to the actual hardware of the sound card. Because this is a pure character device, there are no random access capabilities of this device. To "rewind" a sound, you need to resend the file to the device again.

Block Devices

If you had just one file of data to store, you could put it directly on a block device and read it back. Block devices have a fixed capacity, however, and you would need some method of marking the end of your data. Block devices behave in most respects just like ordinary files, except that although an ordinary file has a length determined by how much data is in it, the "length" of a block device is its total capacity. If you write a megabyte to a 100MB block device and read back its contents, you get the 1MB of data followed by 99MB of its previous contents. Bearing in mind this restriction, several UNIX utilities encode the amount of data available in the file's data rather than the file's total length. Hence, they are suitable for storing data directly on block devices—for example, `tar` and `cpio`, which are suitable for everybody, and `dump`, which is suitable only for the system administrator (because it requires read access to the block device underlying the data to be backed up). To back up the entire contents of your home directory to diskettes, you type the following:

```
$ find $HOME -print0 | cpio --create -0 --format=crc >/dev/fd0
```

The `-print0` and `-0` options for `find` and `cpio` ensure that the names of the files to be backed up are separated by ASCII NULLs, rather than newlines. This ensures that any filenames containing a newline are correctly backed up.

> **Note**
>
> The only characters that are illegal in UNIX filenames are the slash and the ASCII NULL.

Most of the backup utilities for Linux are written specifically to write their backups to any kind of file; in fact, they were designed for sequentially accessed character devices, such as tape drives. See Chapter 22, "Backup and Restore," for more information about the various backup programs that are available for Linux.

Filesystems

When you have more than one item of data, it is necessary to have some method of organizing files on the block device. These methods are called *filesystems*. Linux enables you to choose any organizational method to marshal your files on its storage device. For example, you can use the MS-DOS filesystem on a diskette or the faster `ext2` filesystem on your hard disk.

Many different filesystems are supported by Linux; the `ext2` filesystem is the most used because it is designed for Linux and is very efficient. Other filesystems are used for compatibility with other systems; for example, it's common to use the `msdos` and `vfat` filesystems on diskettes; these are the native filesystems of MS-DOS and Windows 95. Under Red Hat Linux 7, some filesystems are built in to the kernel:

```
$ cat /proc/filesystems

        ext2
nodev   proc
        iso9660
nodev   devpts
```

Some filesystems are available as loadable modules:

```
$ ls -x /lib/modules/`uname -r`/fs
```

```
autofs.o          binfmt_aout.o      binfmt_java.o      binfmt_misc.o
coda.o            fat.o              hfs.o              hpfs.o
lockd.o           minix.o            msdos.o            ncpfs.o
nfs.o             nfsd.o             nls_cp437.o        nls_cp737.o
nls_cp775.o       nls_cp850.o        nls_cp852.o        nls_cp855.o
nls_cp857.o       nls_cp860.o        nls_cp861.o        nls_cp862.o
nls_cp863.o       nls_cp864.o        nls_cp865.o        nls_cp866.o
nls_cp869.o       nls_cp874.o        nls_cp932.o        nls_cp936.o
nls_cp949.o       nls_cp950.o        nls_iso8859-1.o    nls_iso8859-14.o
nls_iso8859-15.o  nls_iso8859-2.o    nls_iso8859-3.o    nls_iso8859-4.o
nls_iso8859-5.o   nls_iso8859-6.o    nls_iso8859-7.o    nls_iso8859-8.o
nls_iso8859-9.o   nls_koi8-r.o       romfs.o            smbfs.o
sysv.o            ufs.o              umsdos.o           vfat.o
```

Some of these (nfs, ncpfs, and smbfs) are network filesystems that don't depend on block devices. Network filesystems are covered in Chapter 16 "NFS: Network Filesystem" and Chapter 17, "Samba." Other filesystems are supported by Linux but are not provided by the standard kernel.

The mount Command

Use the mount command to mount a block device onto the filesystem. You need to specify what device contains the filesystem, what type it is, and where in the directory hierarchy to mount it.

A mount command looks like this:

```
mount -t type -o options device mount-point
```

device should either be a block device or if it contains a colon it can be the name of another machine from which to mount a filesystem (see Chapter 16). The *mount-point* should be an existing directory (or you get an error); the filesystem will appear at this position. (Anything previously in that directory will be hidden.) The filesystem type and options are optional, and the variety and meaning of options depend on the type of filesystem being mounted. If the filesystem you want to mount is specified in the /etc/fstab file, you need to specify only the mount point or the device name; the other details are read from /etc/fstab by mount.

> **Tip**
>
> When you are browsing the filesystem, it is not always easy to quickly see the difference between an empty device and a mount point on which no device has been mounted. A good way to make this simpler is to create a file called `filesystem not mounted` in each directory that is to serve as a mount point. You will then immediately see whether or not there is a device mounted on the mount point.

Here is an example of the `mount` command being used:

```
# ls /mnt/floppy
filesystem not mounted
# mount -t vfat /dev/fd1 /mnt/floppy
mount: block device /dev/fd1 is write-protected, mounting read-only
# ls /mnt/floppy
grub-0.4.tar.gz
# umount /mnt/floppy
# ls /mnt/floppy
filesystem not mounted
```

In this example, I listed the files in my `/mnt/floppy` mount point. I saw that no diskette was mounted, so I mounted a diskette containing a `vfat` filesystem at the mount point. I got an informational message telling me that the diskette was write-protected; if the diskette had not been write-protected, there would have been no message. The directory `/mnt/floppy` already existed. I used `ls` to see what was on the disk and unmounted it again using the `umount` command. I then ran `ls` again, and the response I got was simply the name of a file that I leave in the directory `/mnt/floppy` on my hard disk to remind me that there currently is nothing mounted there. This hint enables me to distinguish a written diskette from an empty diskette that is mounted. You can also use the `df` command to see what filesystems are mounted. For example:

```
# mount -t vfat /dev/fd0 /mnt/floppy
# df /mnt/floppy/
Filesystem         1k-blocks      Used Available Use% Mounted on
/dev/fd0               1423         0      1423   0% /mnt/floppy
# umount /mnt/floppy
# df /mnt/floppy/
Filesystem         1k-blocks      Used Available Use% Mounted on
/dev/hda6           2028066   1850753     72493  96% /
```

As you see from the example, when a device is mounted on a mount point, `df` will output statistics for that device; otherwise it will output statistics about the device upon which the directory resides.

Mounting a vfat diskette as we did earlier causes the Linux kernel to automatically load the vfat driver into the kernel while it is needed. The kernel module handler loads these drivers, and when they become unused after the filesystem is unmounted, they are unloaded to recover the memory that they occupied. See Chapter 27, "Configuring and Building Kernels," for more information about kernel modules.

Potential Problems with mount

Any one of several things can cause the mount command to fail, for example:

- **Incorrect device name**—It is possible to specify an incorrect device name (that is, a device file that does not exist or one for which a driver is not available in the kernel or for which the hardware is not present).

- **Unreadable devices**—Devices can be unreadable either because the devices themselves are bad (for example, empty diskette drives or bad media) or because you have insufficient permissions to mount them. Filesystems, other than those sanctioned by the administrator by listing them with the option user in /etc/fstab, are forbidden to ordinary users and require root privilege to mount them.

- **Bad mount point**—Trying to mount a device at a mount point that does not already exist will not work.

- **Other errors**—Still more error conditions are possible but unlikely (for example, exceeding the compiled-in limit to the number of mounted filesystems) or self-explanatory (for example, most usage errors for the mount command itself). There are some more unlikely error messages that chiefly relate to the loopback devices.

When you mount a filesystem, the mount point (the point at which the filesystem is to be mounted) must be a directory. This directory doesn't have to be empty, but after the filesystem is mounted, anything underneath it is inaccessible. Linux provides a *singly rooted* filesystem, which is in contrast to those operating systems that give each filesystem a separate drive letter. This is more flexible because the size of each block device (hard disk or whatever) is hidden from programs, and things can be moved around. For example, if you have some software that expects to be installed in /opt/umsp, you can install it in /big-disk/stuff/umsp and make /opt/umsp a symbolic link. There is also no need to edit a myriad of configuration files that are using the wrong drive letter after you install a new disk drive.

Many options govern how a mounted filesystem behaves; for example, it can be mounted read-only. There are options for filesystems such as msdos that don't have any concept of users. The filesystems enable you to give each file a particular file mode (for security or to allow access by everyone). When you mount an nfs filesystem, there is so much flexibility available that the options have a separate manual page (man nfs), although the defaults are perfectly reasonable. The nfs filesystem is explained in more detail in Chapter 16.

Table 18.1 contains options useful for mount in alphabetical order. Unless otherwise indicated, these options are valid for all filesystem types, although asking for asynchronous writes to a CD-ROM is no use. Options applicable only to NFS filesystems are not listed here; refer to the nfs command manual page for those.

TABLE 18.1   mount Options

Option	Description
async	Write requests for the filesystem normally should wait until the data has reached the hardware; with this option, the program continues immediately instead. This does mean that the system is slightly more prone to data loss in the event of a system crash, but on the other hand, crashes are rare with Linux. This option speeds up NFS filesystems to a startling extent. The opposite of this option is sync.
auto	Indicates to mount that it should mount the device when given the -a flag. This flag is used by the startup scripts to make sure that all the required filesystems are mounted at boot time. The opposite of this option is noauto.
defaults	Turns on the options rw, suid, dev, exec, auto, nouser, and async.
dev	Allows device nodes on the system to be used. Access to devices is completely determined by access rights to the on-disk device node. Hence, if you mount an ext2 filesystem on a diskette and you have previously placed a writable /dev/kmem device file on the disk, then you've just gained read/write access to kernel memory. System administrators generally prevent this from happening by mounting removable filesystems with the nodev mount option.
exec	Indicates to the kernel that it should allow the execution of programs on the filesystem. It is more usual to use the negated version of exec—that is, noexec—which indicates to the kernel that execution of programs on this filesystem shouldn't be allowed. This is generally used as a security precaution or for NFS filesystems mounted from another machine that contains executable files of a format unsuitable for this machine (for example, intended for a different CPU).
noauto	Opposite of auto.
nodev	Opposite of dev.
noexec	Opposite of exec.
nosuid	Opposite of suid.
nouser	Opposite of user.
remount	Allows the mount command to change the flags for an already-mounted filesystem without interrupting its use. You can't unmount a filesystem that is currently in use, and this option is basically a workaround. The system startup scripts, for example, use the command mount -n -o remount,ro / to change the root filesystem from read-only (it starts off this way) to read/write (its normal state). The -n option indicates to mount that it shouldn't update /etc/fstab because it can't do this while the root filesystem is still read-only.

TABLE 18.1   continued

Option	Description
ro	Mounts the filesystem read-only. This is the opposite of the option rw.
rw	Mounts the filesystem read/write. This is the opposite of the option ro.
suid	Allows the set user ID and set group ID file mode bits to take effect. The opposite of this option is nosuid. The nosuid option is more usual; it is used for the same sorts of reasons that nodev is used.
sync	All write operations cause the calling program to wait until the data has been committed to the hardware. This mode of operation is slower but a little more reliable than its opposite, asynchronous I/O, which is indicated by the option async.
user	Allows ordinary users to mount the filesystem. When there is a user option in /etc/fstab, ordinary users indicate which filesystem they want to mount or unmount by giving the device name or mount point; all the other relevant information is taken from the /etc/fstab file. For security reasons, user implies the noexec, nosuid, and nodev options.

> **Note**
>
> One of the defaults for filesystems is that they are mounted async. This matters in that the operating system will return control before it actually reads or writes a file. Many people have erred by pulling a diskette out of the drive too soon, causing a read or write to be aborted and errors to occur.

18

LINUX FILESYSTEMS, DISKS, AND OTHER DEVICES

Options are processed by the mount command in the order they appear on the command line (or in /etc/fstab). Thus, it is possible to allow users to mount a filesystem and then run set user ID executables by using the options user, suid in that order. Using them in reverse order (suid, user) wouldn't work because the user option would turn off the suid option again.

There are many other options available, but they are all specific to particular filesystems. All the valid options for mount are detailed in its manual page. An example is the umask flag for the vfat and fat filesystems, which allows you to make all the files on your MS-DOS or Windows partitions readable (or even writable if you prefer) for all the users on your Linux system.

Mounting with the User Mount Tool

This graphical tool is good for quickly mounting and unmounting filesystems. This is especially useful for diskette and CD-ROM filesystems. Figure 18.1 shows the user mount tool. You will note that the floppy drive is mounted, but that the CD-ROM is not.

FIGURE 18.1

The user mount tool.

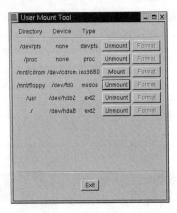

The user mount tool reads /etc/fstab to get the information for mounting. This means that by default, the floppy drive is of type ext2. This setting is great for Linux, but does not allow it to be used in a DOS setting. I have found that by changing the /etc/fstab entry for the floppy drive to the type msdos, I gain greater flexibility in the use of my diskettes as I switch between systems.

Setting Up Filesystems

There are several ways of changing the entries in the /etc/fstab file. The first is to edit the file manually using your favorite editor. This assumes that you are a flawless typist and know all of the different options. Of course, knowing how to edit the file by hand means you do not have to have the X Window System running. I will also discuss how to administer filesystems with the fsconf utility (/sbin/fsconf) and linuxconf (/sbin/linuxconf). These utilities can be run in several ways; they both have a GUI interface, a text mode, and a curses-based interface.

Editing /etc/fstab Manually

The filesystem table /etc/fstab is just a text file; it is designed to have a specific format that is readable by humans and not just computers. It is separated into columns by tabs or spaces. You can edit it with your favorite text editor; it doesn't matter which. You must take care, however, if you modify it by hand because removing or corrupting an entry will make the system unable to mount that filesystem the next time it boots. For this reason, I make a point of saving previous versions of this file using the Revision Control System (a very useful program; see the manual page for rcs).

A sample /etc/fstab looks like this:

```
#
# /etc/fstab
#
# You should be using fstool (control-panel) to edit this!
#
#<device> <mountpoint> <filesystemtype> <options>     <dump> <fsckorder>

/dev/hda1    /             ext2     defaults        1      1
/dev/hdb5    /home         ext2     defaults,rw     1      2
/dev/hda3    /usr          ext2     defaults        1      2
/dev/hdb1    /usr/src      ext2     defaults        1      3

/dev/hdc     /mnt/cdrom    iso9660  user,noauto,ro  0      0
/dev/sbpcd0  /mnt/pcd      iso9660  user,noauto,ro  0      0
/dev/fd1     /mnt/floppy   vfat     user,noauto     0      0

/proc        /proc         proc     defaults
/dev/hda2    none          swap     sw
```

The first four entries are the ext2 filesystems composing the sample Linux system. When Linux is booted, the root filesystem is mounted first; all the other local (that is, non-network) filesystems are mounted next. Filesystems appear in /etc/fstab in the order they are mounted; /usr must appear before /usr/src, for example, because the mount point for one filesystem exists on the other. The following three filesystems are all removable filesystems (two CD-ROMs and a floppy drive). These have the noauto option set so that they are not automatically mounted at boot time. The removable devices have the user option set so that I can mount and unmount them without having to use su all the time. The CD-ROMs have the filesystem type iso9660, which is the standard filesystem for CD-ROMs, and the floppy drive has the filesystem type vfat because I often use it for interchanging data with MS-DOS and Windows systems.

The last two filesystems are special; the first (/proc) is a special filesystem provided by the kernel as a way of providing information about the system to user programs. The information in the /proc filesystem is used to make utilities such as ps, top, xload, free, netstat, and so on work. Some of the "files" in /proc are really enormous (for example, /proc/kcore). Don't worry; no disk space is wasted. All the information in the /proc filesystem is generated on-the-fly by the Linux kernel as you read it. You can tell that they are not real files because, for example, root can't give them away with chown.

The final "filesystem" isn't a filesystem at all; it is an entry that indicates a disk partition used as swap space. Swap partitions are used to implement virtual memory. Files can also be used for swap space. The names of the swap files go in the first column where the device name usually goes.

The two numeric columns on the right relate to the operation of the dump and fsck commands. The dump command compares the number in column 5 (the *dump interval*) with the number of days since that filesystem was last backed up. This way it can inform the system administrator that the filesystem needs to be backed up. Other backup software— for example, AMANDA—can also use this field for the same purpose. (Refer to Chapter 22 for more information on AMANDA.) Filesystems without a dump interval field are assumed to have a dump interval of 0, denoting "never dump." For more information, see the manual page for dump.

The sixth column is the fsck pass and indicates which filesystems can be checked in parallel at boot time. The root filesystem is always checked first, but after that, separate drives can be checked simultaneously because Linux is a multitasking operating system. There is no point, however, in checking two filesystems on the same hard drive at the same time because this results in a lot of extra disk head movement and wasted time. All the filesystems that have the same pass number are checked in parallel from 1 upward. Filesystems with a 0 or missing pass number (such as the floppy and CD-ROM drives) are not checked at all.

Creating New Filesystems

When you install Red Hat Linux, the installation process makes some new filesystems and sets up the system to use them.

Many operating systems don't distinguish between the preparation of the device's surface to receive data (formatting) and the building of new filesystems. Linux does distinguish between the two, principally because only diskettes need formatting and also because Linux offers as many as half a dozen different filesystems that can be created (on any block device). Separately providing the facility of formatting diskettes in each of these programs is poor design and requires you to learn a different way of doing it for each kind of new filesystem. The process of formatting diskettes is dealt with separately. (See the section "Floppy Disk Drivers" later in this chapter for more information.)

Filesystems are initially built by a program that opens the block device and writes some structural data to it so that when the kernel tries to mount the filesystem, the device contains the image of a pristine filesystem. This means that both the kernel and the program used to make the filesystem must agree on the correct filesystem structure.

Linux provides a generic command, mkfs, that enables you to make a filesystem on a block device. In fact, because UNIX manages almost all resources with the same set of operations, mkfs can be used to generate a filesystem inside an ordinary file! Because this is unusual, mkfs asks for confirmation before proceeding. When this is done, you can even mount the resulting filesystem using the loop device. (See the section "Mounting Filesystems on Files" later in this chapter for more information.)

Because of the tremendous variety of filesystems available, almost all the work of building the new filesystem is delegated to a separate program for each; however, the generic mkfs program provides a single interface for invoking them all. It's not uncommon to pass options to the top-level mkfs (for example, -V to make it show what commands it executes or -c to make it check the device for bad blocks). The generic mkfs program also enables you to pass options to the filesystem-specific mkfs. Most of these filesystem-dependent options have sensible defaults, and you normally do not want to change them. The only options you might want to pass to mke2fs, which builds ext2 filesystems, are -m and -i. The -m option specifies how much of the filesystem is reserved for root's use (for example, for working space when the system disk would otherwise have filled completely). The -i option is more rarely exercised and is used for setting the balance between inodes and disk blocks; it is related to the expected average file size. As stated previously, the defaults are reasonable for most purposes, so these options are used only in special circumstances:

```
# mkfs -t ext2 /dev/fd0
mke2fs 1.18, 11-Nov-1999 for EXT2 FS 0.5b, 95/08/09
Filesystem label=
OS type: Linux
Block size=1024 (log=0)
Fragment size=1024 (log=0)
184 inodes, 1440 blocks
72 blocks (5.00%) reserved for the super user
First data block=1
1 block group
8192 blocks per group, 8192 fragments per group
184 inodes per group

Writing inode tables: done
Writing superblocks and filesystem accounting information: done
# mount /dev/fd0 /mnt/floppy/
# ls -la /mnt/floppy/
total 17
drwxr-xr-x    3 root     root         1024 Jul 31 04:24 .
drwxr-xr-x    4 root     root         4096 Jul 23 09:56 ..
drwxr-xr-x    2 root     root        12288 Jul 31 04:24 lost+found
# umount /mnt/floppy/
```

18

LINUX FILESYSTEMS,
DISKS, AND OTHER
DEVICES

Here, you see the creating and mounting of an ext2 filesystem on a diskette. The structure of the filesystem as specified by the program's defaults are shown. There is no volume label, and there are 4,096 bytes (4KB) per inode ($360 \times 4 = 1,440$). The block size is 1KB, and 5% of the disk is reserved for root. These are the defaults (which are explained in the manual page for mke2fs). After you have created a filesystem, you can use dumpe2fs to display information about an ext2 filesystem, but remember to pipe the result through a pager such as less because this output can be very long.

After creating the filesystem on this diskette, you can include it in the filesystem table by changing the existing line referring to a vfat filesystem on /dev/fd1 to the following:

```
/dev/fd1      /mnt/floppy     ext2    user,sync,errors=continue 0 0
```

The first three columns are the device, mount point, and filesystem type, as shown previously. The options column is more complex than previous ones. The user option indicates that users are allowed to mount this filesystem. The sync option indicates that programs writing to this filesystem wait while each write finishes and only then continue. This might seem obvious, but it is not the normal state of affairs. The kernel normally manages filesystem writes in such a way as to provide high performance. (Data still gets written to the device, of course, but it doesn't necessarily happen immediately.) This is perfect for fixed devices such as hard disks, but for low-capacity removable devices such as diskettes, it's less beneficial. Normally, you write a few files to a diskette and then unmount it and take it away. The unmount operation must wait until all data has been written to the device before it can finish (and the disk can then be removed). Having to wait like this is off-putting, and there is always the risk that someone might copy a file to the diskette, wait for the disk light to go out, and remove it. With asynchronous writes, some buffered data might not have yet been written to disk. Hence, synchronous writes are safer for removable media.

The ext2 filesystem has a configurable strategy for errors. If an ext2 filesystem encounters an error (for example, a bad disk block) there are three possible responses to the error:

- **Remount the device read-only**—For filesystems that contain mostly unessential data (for example, /tmp, /var/tmp, or news spools), remounting the filesystem read-only so that it can be fixed with fsck is often the best choice.

- **Panic**—Continuing regardless of potentially corrupted system configuration files is unwise, so a *kernel panic* (a controlled crash—emergency landing, if you prefer) can sometimes be appropriate.

- **Ignore it**—Causing a system shutdown if a diskette has a bad sector is a little excessive, so the continue option tells the kernel to carry on regardless in this situation. If this actually does happen, the best thing to do is to use the -c option of e2fsck, for example, with fsck -t ext2 -c /dev/fd1. This runs e2fsck, giving it the -c option, which invokes the command badblocks to test the device for bad disk blocks. After this is done, e2fsck does its best to recover from the situation.

Creating and Editing Filesystems Graphically with `fsconf` and `linuxconf`

The `fsconf` utility allows you to edit, add, or delete mounts. When you invoke the filesystem configurator, you are given the choice of five tasks (see Figure 18.2).

FIGURE 18.2

The `fsconfig` tool—top level.

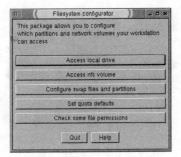

If you look at Figure 18.3 you will notice that `linuxconf` uses the same menu layout as `fsconf`.

FIGURE 18.3

The `linuxconf` tool—top level.

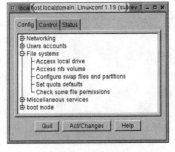

Each of these utilities is detailed here.

Access Local Drive

The first option you see is Access Local Drive. As you can see from Figure 18.4, this option shows the current local filesystems.

In Figure 18.5 you will find the same dialog for `linuxconf`.

You get the Volume Specification window, as seen in Figure 18.6, when you click Add. Both `linuxconf` and `fsconf` supply exactly the same GUI for these options (see Figure 18.6).

FIGURE 18.4

Accessing the Local Volume in fsconf.

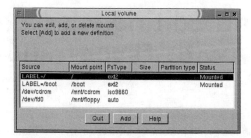

FIGURE 18.5

Accessing the Local Volume in linuxconf.

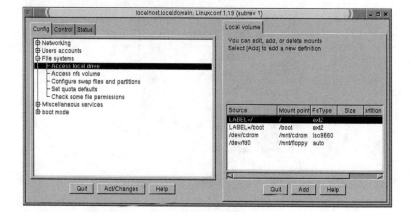

FIGURE 18.6

The Volume Specification window.

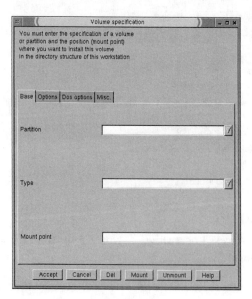

You will notice that both the Partition and Type input boxes are drop-down menus. Clicking their arrows allows you to select from a list of possible values.

Figure 18.7 shows the screen with the partitions selected. The window gives you a list of all of your current partitions.

FIGURE 18.7

Volume Specification—list of current partitions.

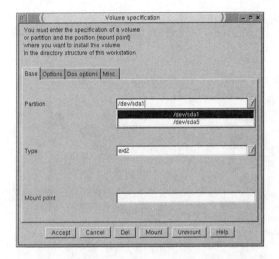

The screen showing the volume type is shown here as Figure 18.8.

FIGURE 18.8

Volume Specification— Volume Type.

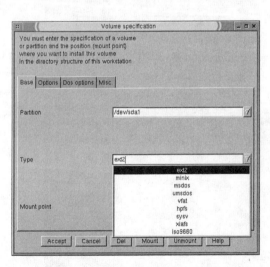

As you can see from the list, you have a good set of options to choose from, and you don't have to remember whether it is called MS DOS or just DOS!

The DOS option is here because DOS and OS/2 are single-user systems, whereas Linux is a multiuser system. DOS and OS/2, therefore, have no means of assigning ownership of files. To get around this problem, and to keep everyone from seeing everyone else's DOS files, Linux allows entire filesystems to be mounted with the user and group IDs defined with the default you set here.

Just like many other screens, this one also has drop-down menus that allow you to choose the default user ID, the default group ID, and the translation mode. This can be seen in Figure 18.9.

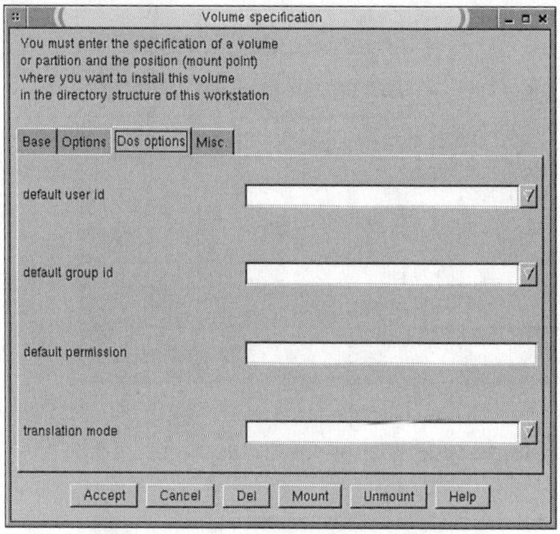

FIGURE 18.9

Volume Specification— DOS Options.

The translation mode can be a bit confusing. There are three options and they're shown in Figure 18.10.

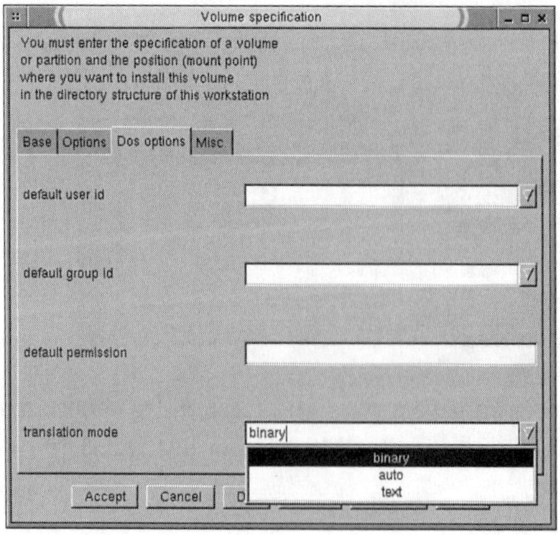

FIGURE 18.10

Volume Specification— Translation Mode.

These options are binary, auto, and text. Text files are stored differently in DOS than in Linux. In Linux, the end-of-file marker is a single ASCII line feed. In DOS, the end-of-file marker is an ASCII carriage return followed by an ASCII line feed. The three options listed allow for translation from one type of system to the other. *Binary* indicates no translation. *Auto* means to translate all files that are not named to indicate that they are an executable, program code, graphics, TeX, or an archive file. Executable files have an extension of BIN, COM, EXE, or SYS. Program code has an extension of APP, DLL, DRV, LIB, OBJ, OVL, OVR, or PIF. Graphic files have an extension of BMP, GIF, GL, JPG, PCX, and TIF. TeX files end in DVI, GF, PX, PXL, TFM, and VF. Archive files traditionally have an extension of ARC, ARJ, DEB, GZ, LHA, LZH, TAR, TAZ, TPZ, TZ, TZP, Z, ZIP, and ZOO. Finally, *text* means to translate all files regardless of type. This third option can cause problems if you accidentally translate a file that should not be translated.

Repairing Filesystems

Some disk data is kept in memory temporarily before being written to disk for performance reasons. (See the earlier discussion of the sync mount option.) If the kernel does not have an opportunity to actually write this data, the filesystem can become corrupted. This can happen in several ways, for example:

- The storage device (for example, a diskette) can be manually removed before the kernel has finished with it.
- The system might suffer a power loss.
- The Linux kernel locks up or reboots the system. Thankfully this is a very rare occurrence.
- The user might mistakenly turn off the power or accidentally press the Reset button.

As part of the boot process, Linux runs the fsck program, whose job it is to check and repair filesystems. Most of the time, the boot follows a controlled shutdown (see the manual page for shutdown), and in this case, the filesystems will have been unmounted before the reboot. In this case, fsck says that they are "clean." It knows this because before unmounting them, the kernel writes a special signature on the filesystem to indicate that the data is intact. When the filesystem is mounted again for writing, this signature is removed.

If, on the other hand, one of the disasters listed takes place, the filesystems will not be marked "clean;" when fsck is invoked, as usual, it will notice this and begin a full check of the filesystem. This also occurs if you specify the -f flag to fsck. To prevent errors creeping up on it, fsck also enforces a periodic check; a full check is done at an interval specified on the filesystem itself (usually every 20 boots or 6 months, whichever comes sooner), even if it were unmounted cleanly.

The boot process (see Chapter 9, "System Startup and Shutdown") checks the `root` filesystem and then mounts it read/write. (It's mounted read-only by the kernel; `fsck` asks for confirmation before operating on a read/write filesystem, and this is not desirable for an unattended reboot.) First, the `root` filesystem is checked with the following command:

```
fsck -V -a /
```

Executing this command checks all the other filesystems:

```
fsck -R -A -V -a
```

These options specify that all the filesystems should be checked (`-A`) except the `root` filesystem, which doesn't need checking a second time (`-R`), and that operations produce informational messages about what it is doing as it goes (`-V`), but that the process should not be interactive (`-a`). The latter is specified because, for example, there might not be anyone present to answer any questions from `fsck`.

In the case of serious filesystem corruption, the approach breaks down because there are some things that `fsck` will not do to a filesystem without your permission. In this case, it returns an error value to its caller (the startup script), and the startup script spawns a shell to allow the administrator to run `fsck` interactively. When this happens, this message appears:

```
***An error occurred during the file system check.
***Dropping you to a shell; the system will reboot
***when you leave the shell.
Give root password for maintenance
(or type Control-D for normal startup):
```

This is a troubling event, particularly because it might well appear if you have other problems with the system—for example, a lockup (leading you to press the Reset button) or a spontaneous reboot. None of the online manuals are guaranteed to be available at this stage because they might be stored on the filesystem whose check failed. This prompt is issued if the `root` filesystem check failed or the filesystem check failed for any of the other disk filesystems.

When the automatic `fsck` fails, you need to log in by specifying the `root` password and run the `fsck` program manually. When you have typed in the `root` password, you are presented with the following prompt:

```
(Repair filesystem) #
```

You might worry about what command to enter here or indeed what to do at all. At least one of the filesystems needs to be checked, but which one? The preceding messages from `fsck` should indicate which, but it isn't necessary to go hunting for them. You can give `fsck` a set of options that tells it to check everything manually, and this is a good fallback:

```
fsck -A -V ; echo == $? ==
```

This is the same command as the previous one, but the `-R` option is missing, in case the `root` filesystem needs to be checked, and the `-a` option is missing, so `fsck` is in its interactive mode. This might enable a check to succeed just because it can now ask you questions. The purpose of the `echo == $? ==` command is to unambiguously interpret the outcome of the `fsck` operation. If the value printed between the equal signs is less than 4, all is well. If this value is 4 or more, more recovery measures are needed. The meanings of the various values follow:

0	No errors
1	Filesystem errors corrected
2	System should be rebooted
4	Filesystem errors left uncorrected
8	Operational error
16	Usage or syntax error
128	Shared library error

If this does not work, it might be because of a *corrupted superblock*; `fsck` starts its disk check and if this is corrupted, it can't start. By good design, the `ext2` filesystem has many backup superblocks scattered regularly throughout the filesystem. Suppose the command announces that it has failed to clean some particular filesystem—for example, `/dev/sda1`. You can start `fsck` again using a backup superblock by using the following command:

```
fsck -t ext2 -b 8193 /dev/sda1
```

`8193` is the block number for the first backup superblock. This backup superblock is at the start of block group 1. (The first is numbered `0`.) There are more backup superblocks at the start of block group 2 (16385) and block group 3 (24577); they are spaced at intervals of 8,192 blocks. If you made a filesystem with settings other than the defaults, these might change. `mke2fs` lists the superblocks that it creates as it goes, so that is a good time to pay attention if you're not using the default settings. There are further things you can attempt if `fsck` is still not succeeding, but these situations are rare and usually indicate hardware problems so severe that they prevent the proper operation of `fsck`. Examples include broken wires in the IDE connector cable and similar nasty problems. If this command still fails, you might seek expert help or fix the disk in a different machine.

These extreme measures are unlikely; a manual `fsck`, in the unusual circumstance where it is actually required, almost always fixes things. After the manual `fsck` has worked, the `root` shell that the startup scripts provide has done its purpose. Type **exit** to exit it. At this point, to make sure that everything goes according to plan, the boot process is started again from the beginning. This second time around, the filesystems should all be error-free and the system should boot normally.

Various Kinds of Hardware

There are block devices under Linux for representing all sorts of random access devices: diskettes, hard disks (XT, EIDE, and SCSI), Zip drives, CD-ROM drives, RAM disks, and loopback devices.

Hard Disks

Hard disks are large enough to make it useful to keep different filesystems on different parts of the hard disk. The scheme for dividing these disks is called *partitioning*. Although it is common for computers running MS- DOS to have only one partition, it is possible to have several different partitions on each disk. The summary of how the disk is partitioned is kept in its *partition table*.

The Partition Table

A hard disk might be divided like this:

```
$ fdisk -l
Disk /dev/hda: 128 heads, 63 sectors, 970 cylinders
Units = cylinders of 8064 * 512 bytes

   Device Boot    Start      End    Blocks   Id  System
/dev/hda1    *        1      177    713632+   6  FAT16
/dev/hda2            179      970   3193344    5  Extended
/dev/hda3            178      178      4032    a  OS/2 Boot Manager
/dev/hda5            179      696   2088544+   6  FAT16
/dev/hda6            920      970    205600+   6  FAT16
/dev/hda7            697      762    266080+  82  Linux swap
/dev/hda8            763      919    632992+  83  Linux

Disk /dev/hdb: 255 heads, 63 sectors, 523 cylinders
Units = cylinders of 16065 * 512 bytes

   Device Boot    Start      End    Blocks   Id  System
/dev/hdb1    *        2      383   3068415    5  Extended
/dev/hdb2            384      523   1124550   83  Linux
/dev/hdb5              2      192   1534176    6  FAT16
/dev/hdb6            193      383   1534176    6  FAT16
```

Note that the partitions on the first disk have names starting with /dev/hda and those on the second have names starting with /dev/hdb. The number of the partition follows these prefixes.

Note

All is not quite as simple as it could be in the partition table, however. Early hard disk drives on PCs were quite small (about 10MB), so you were limited to a small number of partitions, and the format of the partition table originally allowed for only four partitions. Later on, this was too great a restriction, and the *extended partition* was introduced as a workaround.

Inside each extended partition is another partition table. This enables the extended partition to be divided, in the same way, into four *logical partitions*. Partitions that aren't inside an extended partition are sometimes referred to as *primary partitions*.

Disk Geometry

The units of the table in the last section are *cylinders*. The partition table allocates a consecutive block of cylinders to each partition. The term *cylinder* itself dates from the days when it was possible to remove a disk pack from a UNIX machine and point to the various parts. That can't be done here, so here's another way of looking at it.

Imagine that a hard disk is in fact a stack of pizzas. Each of the pizzas is a *platter*, a disk-shaped surface with a magnetic coating designed to hold magnetic encodings. Both sides of these platters are used. These platters rotate around the spindle, like the spindle in a record player. The hard disk has a movable arm containing several *disk heads*. Each side of each platter has a separate disk head. If you were to put your fingers between the pizzas while keeping them straight, your fingers are the same as the arrangement of the heads on the arm. All the parts of the platters that the heads pass over in one rotation of the disk is called a *cylinder*. The parts of a single platter that one head passes over in one rotation is called a *track*. Each track is divided into *sectors*, as if the pizzas had been already sliced for you. The layout of a disk, its *geometry*, is described by the number of cylinders, heads, and sectors comprising the disk. Another important feature is the rotational speed of the disk; generally, the faster it is, the faster the hard disk can read or write data.

Note

IBM PCs with older BIOSs can have difficulty with large disks; see the Linux Large-Disk mini HOWTO (if you installed the HOWTOs).

Floppy Disk Drivers

Diskettes, sometimes referred to as floppy disks, are removable low-capacity storage media. As storage devices, they are far slower than hard disks, but they have the advantage of being removable, which makes them good media for transporting modest amounts of data.

The block devices corresponding to the floppy disks drivers, as they are called for legacy reasons, begin with the letters fd; /dev/fd0 is the first, and any additional ones have increasing numbers. There are many possible formats for a diskette, and the kernel needs to know the format (geometry) of a disk to access it properly. Linux can usually work out the correct format, so the automatic devices /dev/fd0 (plus /dev/fd1 and so on for extra floppy drives) are usually sufficient. If for some reason it is necessary to specify the exact format, further device names are provided. The device /dev/fd0H1440, for example, denotes a 1.44MB high-density diskette. There are many more devices indicating obscure formats, both older lower-capacity formats and other nonstandard extra–high-capacity formats. You can even create your own diskette formats using the setfdprm program.

The most common reason to use the specific-format device names is that you are formatting a diskette for the first time. In this situation, the disk is not yet readable, so the kernel will not be able to autoprobe it for an existing format. You need to use the name, for example /dev/fd0H1440, to denote a high-density 3.5-inch disk in the first floppy drive. For device names representing other formats, refer to the fd manual page. Section 4 of the manual is devoted to devices.

The process of formatting a diskette is completely destructive to the data on it, and because it requires writing to the actual device itself, it requires root privileges. It is done like this:

```
# fdformat /dev/fd0H1440
Double-sided, 80 tracks, 18 sec/track. Total capacity 1440 kB.
Formatting ... done
Verifying ... done
```

After you have formatted a floppy, don't forget to use mkfs to build a filesystem on it. (See the section "Creating New Filesystems" earlier in this chapter.)

If you have the X Window System running, you can use the user mount tool previously discussed in this chapter to accomplish the same tasks.

CD-ROM Drives

CD-ROM drives are fundamentally another kind of read-only block device. They are mounted in just the same way as other block devices. CD-ROMs almost always contain standard ISO 9660 filesystems, often with some optional extensions. There is no reason, however, why you should not use any other filesystem. Once you have mounted your CD-ROM, it behaves like any other read-only filesystem.

You can set up and mount your CD-ROM drive using the Red Hat File System Manager, as explained previously, or by using the `mount` command:

```
# mount -t iso9660 /dev/cdrom /mnt/cdrom
```

The directory `/mnt/cdrom` is a common place to mount your CD-ROM drive under Red Hat Linux.

The device name `/dev/cdrom` is commonly used as a symbolic link to the actual device name corresponding to the CD-ROM. This is because at the time the CD-ROM drive became available for the PC, there was no cheap standard interface for these devices. Each manufacturer chose or invented an interfacing scheme that was incompatible with everyone else's. For this reason, there are about a dozen different drivers for CD-ROM drives available in the Linux kernel. SCSI would have been a sensible standard to use, but although SCSI CD-ROM drives are available, they're not particularly popular.

The ATAPI standard arrived in time to ensure that all non-SCSI CD-ROM drives at quad speed or faster use a standard interface, so the situation is far simpler for new CD-ROM drives. Support for ATAPI CD-ROMs is handled by one driver for all drives. The ATAPI standard also provides for very large hard disk drives and tape drives. ATAPI CD-ROM drives are attached to IDE interfaces, just like hard disks, and they have the same set of device names as hard disk devices.

Because CD-ROMs come already written, there is no need to partition them. They are accessed using the device names for whole-disk devices: `/dev/hda`, `/dev/hdb`, and so on.

The ISO 9660 standard specifies a standard format for the layout of data on CD-ROMs. It restricts filenames to no more than 32 characters, for example. Most CD-ROMs are written with very short filenames for compatibility with MS-DOS. To support certain UNIX features such as symbolic links and long filenames, developers created a set of extensions called *Rock Ridge*, and the Linux kernel will automatically detect and use the Rock Ridge extensions.

CD-ROM drives also usually support the playing of audio CDs, and there are many Linux programs for controlling the CD-ROM drive in the same way as you might control a CD player. The multimedia package on the Red Hat 7 CD-ROMs contains the `xplaycd` program for playing CDs. To make it work, you need to set the `/dev/cdrom` symbolic link to point to your real CD-ROM device.

If you have the X Window System running, you can use the user mount tool previously discussed in this chapter to accomplish the same tasks by clicking buttons.

RAID

RAID is an acronym for Redundant Array of Inexpensive Disks. Using RAID it is possible to combine several disks in various ways and access them as one. In fact, under Linux it is possible to include just about any kind of block devices in a RAID set. There are several different levels of RAID; each level offers different ways of combining the underlying devices. The following RAID levels are the most used with Linux:

- Linear or appending—This will combine two or more disks, or devices, into one logical device that appears to be one single disk for all intents and purposes. As one device is filled with data, writing will commence on the next device in the set.

- RAID 0 or striping—This works similarly to the linear mode. The difference is that accesses are done in parallel to the devices in the RAID set. Because accesses are done in parallel, performance is generally improved.

- RAID 1 or mirroring—This mode will maintain exact copies of the data from the main device on all the other devices in the RAID set. This means that the devices must be of the same size; if there is a difference the RAID set will only use as much space as is available on the smallest device. If one of the disks breaks down, you will have a copy of the data available on the other devices.

- RAID 4 or striping with parity—This RAID level is quite similar to RAID 1; however, instead of mirroring the entire disk only parity information is mirrored and only onto one other device. The other devices in the set will be used the same way as in RAID 0. If one of the disks in the set breaks down, the parity information can be used in the process of reconstructing the data. This RAID level is not used very often.

- RAID 5 or striping with striped parity—This is the same as RAID 4, except that the parity information is also striped. This eliminates certain bottlenecks that exist in RAID 4. This RAID level is the most commonly used because it offers both high availability and increased performance. However, performance does not increase in all situations.

Linux supports both hardware and software RAID. To use hardware RAID you will need a RAID controller, which is a specialized hard drive interface. This controller creates an array of disks and presents these as a single drive to the operating system. Having these abilities in hardware reduces the load on the system. These kinds of controllers are generally rather expensive. Linux supports a number of RAID controllers. If you are about to purchase one or have access to one, be sure to check `/usr/src/linux/Documentation` to see whether it is supported by Linux. Because different RAID controllers have different user interfaces, we will not cover such controllers here.

As mentioned, Linux also supports software RAID. This offers the same capabilities as the hardware version. The main difference is that it puts a bigger load on the system. Apart from having software RAID support in the Linux kernel, there is a suite of tools to set up and maintain RAID disks on your system.

Don't include IDE disks that are on the same controller in a RAID set. Switching between a slave and a master IDE disk is quite slow. If you have such disks in a RAID set they will constantly need to switch back and forth. This will result in a huge performance hit. Should you also be using disk space on the same disks or controller for swap memory as well, your system can become excruciatingly slow. If you have to use IDE disks for your RAID set, be sure to put them on different IDE interfaces.

The following commands are used to create and use software RAID sets:

- `/sbin/mkraid`—This will create a RAID set. As its parameter you name a RAID set that is specified in `/etc/raidtab` or an alternative configuration file. All data on the devices that are involved will be destroyed.

- `/sbin/raidstart`—This activates the specified RAID set and makes it available for usage as a "normal" block device or disk.

The configuration file for a RAID set is not at all hard to set up. Take a look at Listing 18.1, which is one of the sample configuration files that comes with the RAID tool suite. The usage and format of the options should be pretty obvious.

LISTING 18.1   raid0.conf.sample

```
# Sample raid-0 configuration

raiddev                 /dev/md0

raid-level              0    # it's not obvious but this *must* be
                             # right after raiddev

persistent-superblock   0    # set this to 1 if you want autostart,
                             # BUT SETTING TO 1 WILL DESTROY PREVIOUS
                             # CONTENTS if this is a RAID0 array created
                             # by older raidtools (0.40-0.51) or mdtools!

chunk-size              16

nr-raid-disks           2
nr-spare-disks          0

device                  /dev/hda1
raid-disk               0

device                  /dev/hdb1
raid-disk               1
```

After you have created a RAID set you can use it like you would an ordinary hard disk under Linux. For example, suppose you had just created the RAID set from the previous listing. You would use the mke2fs, if you wanted to use that filesystem, to create a filesystem on your new RAID device. After this you can mount the newly create device on a mount point and use it as you would any other device under Linux.

For more exhaustive coverage of how to use software RAID with Red Hat Linux, see http://www.redhat.com/support/docs/tips/raid/RAID-INDEX.html.

Loopback Devices

Loopback devices enable you to store new filesystems inside regular files. You might want to do this to prepare an emulated hard disk image for DOSEMU, an install disk, or just to try a filesystem of a new type or an ISO9660 CD-ROM image before writing it to the CD writer.

Mounting Filesystems on Files

Under UNIX, you need root permissions to change the system's filesystem structure; even if you own a file and the mount point on which you want to mount it, only root can do this, unless the user option has been specified in /etc/fstab for this filesystem.

When a filesystem is mounted using the loopback driver, the file containing the filesystem plays the role of the block device in the mount command and /etc/fstab. The kernel talks to the block device interface provided by the loopback device driver, and the driver forwards operations to the file:

```
# mount $(pwd)/rtems.iso -t iso9660 -o ro,loop /mnt/test
# ls -F /mnt/test
INSTALL   LICENSE   README   SUPPORT   c/   doc/   rr_moved/
# mount | grep loop | fold -s
/home/james/documents/books/Sams/Linux-Unleashed-2/ch9/tmp/rtems.iso on
/mnt/test type iso9660 (ro,loop=/dev/loop0)
# umount /mnt/test
```

After the loopback filesystem is mounted, it's a normal filesystem.

Using Encrypted Filesystems

Loopback filesystems offer even more features—encryption, for example. A loopback filesystem can be configured to decrypt data from the block device on-the-fly so that the data on the device is useless to people even if they can read it—unless they have the password. The mount command prompts for the password at the appropriate time. To make this work, first you have to use mkfs to generate a filesystem on the encrypted block device; losetup is used to associate a loop device and encryption method with the block device you want to use (in the following case, a floppy drive):

```
# /sbin/losetup -e DES /dev/loop0 /dev/fd1
Password:
Init (up to 16 hex digits):
# /sbin/mkfs -t ext2 -m0 /dev/loop0
mke2fs 1.10, 24-Apr-97 for EXT2 FS 0.5b, 95/08/09
Linux ext2 filesystem format
Filesystem label=
360 inodes, 1440 blocks
0 blocks (0.00) reserved for the super user
First data block=1
Block size=1024 (log=0)
Fragment size=1024 (log=0)
1 block group
8192 blocks per group, 8192 fragments per group
360 inodes per group

Writing inode tables: done
Writing superblocks and filesystem accounting information: done
# losetup -d /dev/loop0
```

As shown previously, losetup's -e option associates an encryption method and block device with a loopback device. The -d option deletes this association and erases the stored encryption key.

When the filesystem has been created on the encrypted device, it can be mounted in a manner similar to the normal case:

```
# /sbin/losetup -d /dev/loop0
# mount /dev/fd1 -t ext2 -o loop=/dev/loop0,encryption=DES /mnt/test
Password:
Init (up to 16 hex digits):
# ls /mnt/test
lost+found
```

Usually, the whole process of using an encrypted filesystem can be set up for ordinary users by adding the appropriate line to /etc/fstab:

```
$ mount /mnt/test
Password:
Init (up to 16 hex digits):
$ ls -ld /mnt/test
drwxrwxrwx  3 james   root     1024 Sep 14 22:04 /mnt/test
```

In this example, root has enabled users to mount encrypted filesystems by including this line in /etc/fstab:

```
/dev/fd1   /mnt/test   ext2   user,loop,encryption=DES
```

18

LINUX FILESYSTEMS, DISKS, AND OTHER DEVICES

Additionally, ownership of the top-level directory on the diskette has been given to the user james because it is presumably his diskette. If root had not done this, james would have been able to mount his filesystem but not read it. It was an essential step, but it turns out that in this example, root has made a fatal mistake. As well as changing the ownership of the filesystem's root directory, root has changed the directory's mode as well. This means that once the unsuspecting james has supplied his secret password, any user on the system can read and write the files on the diskette. This underlines the fact that encryption alone is not sufficient for safety. Careful thought is also essential.

In the previous case, the file ownerships and permissions have turned out to be more of a hindrance than a help. It is probably better to use an MS-DOS filesystem on the encrypted device because ownership is automatically given away to the user mounting the disk and the file modes are set correctly:

```
$ ls -ld /mnt/floppy/
drwxr-xr-x 2 james  users   7168 Jan  1  1970 /mnt/floppy/
```

However, there are still two problems with this strategy. First, it is not possible to make an encrypted filesystem easily on a diskette because the mkfs.msdos program needs to know the geometry for the device on which it is creating the filesystem, and the loopback device drivers don't really have geometries. Second, once your encrypted ext2 filesystem is mounted, the superuser can still read your data.

The encryption methods outlined previously are not available in standard kernels because most useful forms of encryption technology are not legally exportable from the United States. However, they are already available outside the United States at http://www.kerneli.org/

You need to apply these patches to your kernel and recompile it in order to use the DES and IDEA encryption methods with loopback devices.

To summarize, encrypted filesystems can be useful for some kinds of data (for example, for storing digital signatures for important system binaries in such a way that they can't be tampered with), but their usefulness to users other than root is limited. Of course, all the ordinary file encryption mechanisms are still available to and useful for ordinary users.

Other Block Devices

Although hard disks, floppy disks drivers, and CD-ROM drives are probably the most heavily used block devices, there are other kinds of block devices, including RAM disks and Zip drives.

RAM Disks

RAM disks are block devices that store their data in RAM rather than on a disk. This means they are very fast; nevertheless, RAM disks are rarely used with Linux because Linux has a very good disk-caching scheme, which provides most of the speed benefit of a RAM disk but not the fixed cost in memory.

The most common use for RAM disks is to serve as a `root` filesystem while Linux is being installed. A compressed filesystem image is loaded into a RAM disk, and the installation process is run from this disk. The RAM disk's filesystem can be larger than a single diskette because the image is compressed on the diskette.

Although RAM disks are useful with operating systems lacking effective disk buffering, they offer little performance advantage under Linux. If you want to try a RAM disk, they work just like any other block device. For example, to mount a RAM disk as `/tmp`, you add this line to `/etc/fstab`:

```
/dev/ram    /tmp        ext2    defaults    0 0
```

Then you create and mount an `ext` filesystem with the following:

```
/sbin/mkfs -t ext2 /dev/ram
mount /tmp
```

Any performance benefits from doing this are hard to find, but you might find that this helps in unusual circumstances.

The principal advantage of RAM disks is that they provide great flexibility in the boot process. Although it is possible to recompile a kernel including support for your hardware, it makes the initial installation process difficult. Historically, programmers worked around this problem by providing dozens of different installation boot disks, each with support for one or two items of boot hardware (SCSI cards and CD-ROM drives, for example).

A simpler solution is to exploit loadable kernel modules. Instead of having separate boot disks for each type of hardware, all containing different kernels, it is simple to provide just one boot disk containing a modular kernel and the module utilities themselves.

A compressed filesystem is loaded from the diskette into a RAM disk by the kernel loader, LILO, at the same time the kernel is loaded. The kernel mounts this filesystem and runs a program (`/linuxrc`) from it. This program then mounts the "real" `root` filesystem and exits, enabling the kernel to remount the real `root` filesystem on `/`. This system is convenient to set up, and the process of creating initial RAM disks has been automated by Red Hat Software (see the manual page for `mkinitrd`). Red Hat Linux systems whose `root` filesystem is on a SCSI device have a modular kernel and boot by this method.

Zip Drives

Zip drives are drives providing removable cartridges, available in various sizes from 100MB to 250MB. They come in three varieties: parallel port (PPA), IDE, and SCSI. All are supported by Linux. The parallel version is emulated as a SCSI drive but with a proprietary parallel port interface. Hence, it also appears as a SCSI disk.

Because they're just standard (but removable) SCSI or IDE disks, most aspects of their use are similar to those for other block devices. Red Hat Linux 7 comes with support for both the SCSI and PPA varieties. You can find further information in the Zip-Drive mini HOWTO (which explains how to install your Zip drive), and the Zip-Install mini HOWTO, which explains how to install Red Hat Linux onto a Zip drive.

USB Devices

USB is a new standard for connecting devices to your computer. It allows you to connect a variety of devices via a fast serial bus. It can be used with keyboards, Web cameras, network cards, and so on.

USB support was only recently added to Linux. Therefore it is at the moment in a state of flux. There is a lot of work going on to get as many USB devices as possible to work with Linux. Unfortunately, support is slightly immature and there is no way to be sure that a USB device will work with Linux. Therefore, you should check on Linux compatibility before purchasing a USB device. A good resource about Linux USB can be found at `http://www.linux-usb.org/`. There you will also find a list of USB devices known to work with Linux.

If you have USB devices connected to your computer, you can use the `usbview` command to get information about them. This command will list all USB devices that Linux can access and print information about them.

Character Devices

Character devices offer a flow of data that must be read in order. Whereas block devices enable a seek to select the next block of data transferred, for example, from one edge or the other of a diskette, character devices represent hardware that doesn't have this capability. An example is a terminal, for which the next character to be read is whatever key you type at the keyboard.

In fact, because there are only two basic types of devices, block and character, all hardware is represented as one or the other, rather like the animal and vegetable kingdoms of biological classification. Inevitably, this means that a few devices don't quite fit into this classification scheme. Examples include tape drives, generic SCSI devices, and the special memory devices such as `/dev/port` and `/dev/kmem`.

> **Note**
>
> Network interfaces are represented differently (see Chapter 20, "TCP/IP Network Management").

Parallel Ports

Parallel ports are usually used for communicating with printers, although they are versatile enough to support other things too—for example, scanners, Zip drives, CD-ROM drives, and even networking.

The hardware itself offers character-at-a-time communication. The parallel port can provide an interrupt to notify the kernel that it is now ready to output a new character, but because printers are usually not performance-critical on most PCs, this interrupt is often borrowed for use by some other hardware, often sound hardware. This has an unfortunate consequence: The kernel often needs to poll the parallel hardware, so driving a parallel printer often requires more CPU work than it should.

The good news is that if your parallel printer interrupt is not in use by some other hardware, it can be enabled with the printer driver configuration program `tunelp`. The `-i` option for `tunelp` sets the IRQ for use with each printer device. You might set the IRQ for the printer port to 7 like this:

```
# /usr/sbin/tunelp /dev/lp1 -i 7
/dev/lp1 using IRQ 7
```

If this results in the printer ceasing to work, going back to the polling method is easy:

```
# /usr/sbin/tunelp /dev/lp1 -i 0
/dev/lp1 using polling
```

The best way to test a printer port under Red Hat Linux is from the Control Panel's Printer Configuration tool (`/usr/bin/printtool`). The Tests menu offers the option of printing a test page directly to the device rather than via the normal printing system. This is a good starting point. You can find more information on setting up printers in Chapter 19, "Printing with Linux."

Tape Drives

Tape drives provide I/O of a stream of bytes to or from the tape. Although most tape drives can be repositioned (that is, rewound and wound forward like audio or video tapes), this operation is very slow by disk standards. Although access to a random part of the tape is at least feasible, it is very slow, so the character device interface is workable for using tape drives.

For most UNIX workstations, the interface of choice for tape drives is SCSI because this fits in well with the SCSI disks and so on. SCSI provides the capability to plug in a new device and start using it. (Of course, you can't do this with the power on.) SCSI has traditionally been more expensive than most other PC technologies, so it wasn't used for many tape drives developed for use with PCs. Several interfaces have been used for tape drives for IBM PCs:

Type	Device Names	Major Number
SCSI	/dev/st*	9
Floppy	/dev/rft*	27
QIC-02	/dev/rmt	12
IDE	/dev/ht*	37
Parallel Port	(Currently unsupported)	

All these tape drives have the feature that when the device is closed, the tape is rewound. All these drives except the QIC-02 drive have a second device interface with a name prefixed with n—for example /dev/nst0, /dev/nst3, or /dev/nht0. The n-variant of the devices are non-rewinding versions of the tape devices. All tape devices support the magnetic tape control program, mt, which is used for winding tapes past files, rewinding them, and so on. Many commands, particularly the more advanced mt commands, are only available for SCSI tape drives.

Apart from the mt command for the basic control of a tape drive, there are many commands that you can use for storing and retrieving data on tape. Because the character devices are "just files," you could use cat to store data on the tape, but this is not very flexible. A great many programs are particularly or partly designed with tape drives in mind:

tar This is widely used for creating archives in regular files but was originally created for making tape backups. In fact, tar stands for *tape archiver*. Archives made by tar can be read on a wide variety of systems.

cpio Another program principally intended for backups and so on, cpio stands for copy in–out. The GNU version of cpio, which is used by Linux distributions, supports eight different data formats—some of which are varieties of its "native" format, two are varieties of tar archives, and some are obsolete. If you want to unpack an unknown archive, cpio, along with file and dd, is very useful.

dump	The dump utility is of use only to system administrators because it backs up an ext2 filesystem by raw access to the block device on which the filesystem exists. (For this reason, it is better to do this when the filesystem is either not mounted or is mounted read-only.) This has the advantage, among other things, that the access times of the backed-up directories are left unmodified. (GNU tar will also do this.) Although tapes written with dump are not always readable on other versions of UNIX, unlike those written by tar and cpio, dump is a popular choice.
dd	Designed for blockwise I/O, dd is a general-purpose tool for doing file manipulations and can often be useful.
afio	A variant of cpio, afio compresses individual files into the backup. For backups, this is preferable to tar's compression of the whole archive because a small tape error can make a compressed tar archive useless, although a tar archive that isn't compressed doesn't have this vulnerability. afio isn't widely used outside the Linux world.
AMANDA	AMANDA is a powerful backup system that schedules, organizes, and executes backups for you. It uses either tar or dump to do the actual work and will effortlessly allow you to automate all the backups for one machine or a multitude. One of its most useful features is its ability to perform fast backups across the network from several client machines to a single server machine containing a tape drive.
BRU	BRU (Backup and Restore Utility) is a commercial product for making backups.

For more information about some of these tape utilities, see Chapter 22.

18

LINUX FILESYSTEMS, DISKS, AND OTHER DEVICES

Terminals

The *terminal* is the principal mode of communication between the kernel and the user. When you type keystrokes, the terminal driver turns them into input readable by the shell or whatever program you are running.

For many years, UNIX ran only on serial terminals. Although most computers now also have video hardware, the terminal is still a useful concept. Each window in which you can run a shell provides a separate *pseudoterminal*, each one rather like a traditional serial terminal. Terminals are often called ttys because the device nodes for many of them have names like /dev/tty*.

The terminal interface is used to represent serial lines to "real" terminals, to other computers (via modems), mice, printers, and so on. The large variety of hardware addressed by the terminal interface has led to a wide range of capabilities offered by the terminal device driver, and explaining all the facilities offered could easily occupy an entire chapter. This section just offers an overview of the facilities.

For more complete information on terminals and serial I/O, refer to the Linux Documentation Project's excellent HOWTO documents. These are provided on the Red Hat Linux 7 CD-ROM (you need to install them) and are also available on the Web at `http://www.linuxdoc.org/`. Specific HOWTOs dealing with this are the Serial HOWTO and the Serial Port Programming mini-HOWTO. Many documents deal with using modems for networking.

The Terminal Device Driver

The terminal device driver gathers the characters you type at the keyboard and sends them to the program you're working with, after some processing. This processing can involve gathering the characters into batches a line at a time and taking into account the special meanings of some keys you might type.

Some special keys of this sort are used for editing the text that is sent to the program you're interacting with. Much of the time, the terminal driver is building a line of input that it hasn't yet sent to the program receiving your input. Keys that the driver will process specially include the following:

Return (CR) or Line Feed (LF)

CR is usually translated into LF by the terminal driver. (See the `icrnl` option in the manual page for `stty`.) This ends the current line, which is then sent to the application. (It is waiting for terminal input, so it wakes up.)

Backspace/Delete

Only one of these two keys can be selected as the erase key, which erases the previous character typed. For more information, read the Linux Keyboard Setup mini-HOWTO.

End-of-File, Usually Ctrl+D

When a program is reading its standard input from the keyboard and you want to let it know that you've typed everything, you press Ctrl+D. ("Usually" indicates that this option is shell dependent and may differ depending upon which shell you are using.)

Word-Erase, Usually Ctrl+W

This combination deletes the last word you typed.

Kill-Line, Usually Ctrl+U

This kills the entire line of input so that you can start again.

Interrupt, Usually Ctrl+C

This kills the current program. Some programs block this at times when the program might leave the terminal in a strange state if it were unexpectedly killed.

Suspend, Usually Ctrl+Z

This key sends a suspend signal to the program you're using. The result is that the program is stopped temporarily, and you get the shell prompt again. You can then put that program (job) in the background and do something else. See Chapter 25, "Shell Scripting," for more information.

Quit, Usually Ctrl+\ (Ctrl+Backslash)

Sends a Quit signal to the current program; programs that ignore Ctrl+C can often be stopped with Ctrl+\, but programs ignoring Ctrl+C are often doing so for a reason.

Stop, Usually Ctrl+S, and Start, Usually Ctrl+Q

These keys stop and restart terminal output temporarily, which can be useful if a command produces a lot of output, although it can often be more useful to repeat the command and pipe it through `less`.

You can examine many other terminal modes and settings with the `stty` command. This command has a built-in set of sensible settings for terminals, and typing `stty` to find the current settings usually shows you only the differences from its "sane" settings:

```
$ stty
speed 9600 baud; line = 0;
```

Tip

If you ever find that your terminal state is messed up, you can usually fix it with the command $ `stty sane` and Ctrl+J. Note that you finish the command Ctrl+J, rather than Enter (which is the same as Ctrl+M). The `icrnl` option might have been turned off. This is fixed again with `stty sane`. GNU bash will always cope with CRs that have not been converted to LF anyway, but some other programs won't.

If this still doesn't work, and the screen font appears to have been changed, type **echo**, press Ctrl+V and Esc, type **c**, and press Ctrl+J. You press Ctrl+V to make the terminal driver pass the next key without processing. You can get a similar effect by typing **reset** and pressing Ctrl+J, but the program `reset` is only available if the `ncurses` package is installed.

Programs can turn off the processing that the line driver does by default; the resulting behavior (raw mode) allows programs to read unprocessed input from the terminal driver (for example, CR is not mapped to LF), and control characters don't produce the signals described in the table earlier in this section. The `stty sane` command will return things to normal.

Serial Communications

Although the terminal interfaces used most commonly under Linux are the console driver and the pseudo-terminals driven by programs such as `xterm`, `script`, and `expect`, the original terminal interface involved serial communications. In fact, this still lingers; a pseudo-`tty` associated with an `xterm` window still has an associated baud rate as shown in the example in the section "The Terminal Device Driver" earlier in this chapter. Changing this baud rate has no actual effect. For real serial ports, however, the baud rate and many other parameters have a direct relevance. The device nodes relating to the serial ports are composed of two "teams," with the names `/dev/cua*` and `/dev/ttyS*`. Starting with version 2.2 of the kernel, `/dev/ttyS*` is the "correct" name to use. `/dev/cua*` will, most likely, disappear from the next version or two. The device nodes allow you to use the same serial hardware for both incoming and outgoing serial connections.

Configuring the Serial Ports

Serial port configuration is mostly done either with the `stty` command or directly by programs using the interface outlined in the `termios` manual page. The `stty` command offers almost all the configuration possibilities provided by `termios`; however, there are configuration issues for serial hardware that are not addressed by `stty`. The `setserial` command allows the configuration of the correct IRQ settings for each serial port and of extra-fast baud rates that the standard `termios` specification doesn't provide. For more detailed information, refer to the Linux Serial HOWTO and the manual page for `setserial`.

Generic SCSI Devices

Not all SCSI devices are hard disks, CD-ROM drives, or tape drives. Some are optical scanners, CD-ROM recorders, or even electron microscopes. The kernel can't possibly abstract the interfaces for all possible SCSI devices, so it gives user programs direct access to SCSI hardware via the generic SCSI devices. These enable programs to send arbitrary SCSI commands to hardware. Although this arrangement offers the opportunity of wreaking havoc by mistake, it also offers the capability of driving all sorts of interesting hardware, of which the principal examples are CD-ROM recorders. The SCSI device nodes all have names starting with `/dev/sg`. SCSI commands are sent to the devices by writing data to the device, and the results are read back by reading from the device.

CD-ROM Recorders

CD-ROM recorders are devices for recording data on special media that can be read in ordinary CD-ROM drives. There are two stages in the writing of a CD: generating the CD image and writing that image to the media.

The surface of a CD-R (recordable CD) is only writable once, so if mkisofs worked like the other mkfs tools, it would always generate image files representing empty CDs. For this reason, mkisofs populates the filesystem with files as it generates the image file. The same principles apply to CD-RW, which are CD-R that are rewriteable. Under Linux they are treated just as CD-R, the only difference being that you can record over them a second time, or many more times for that matter.

The CD image file is produced by the mkisofs program, which generates the structures for an ISO 9660 filesystem and populates it with the files from a directory tree. CDs are not writable in the same sense as block devices; this is why they are not actually block devices. The image file must be written to the CD-R with a specialized program, cdrecord, which understands all the various proprietary schemes used for driving CD writers. All the CD writers supported by Linux (as of version 2.0.30 of the kernel) are SCSI devices, so the kernel accommodates this by providing access to the generic SCSI device interface that enables a program to send SCSI commands to these devices. However, there is also support for some IDE CD writers, but these are all handled by using a special driver that lets IDE emulate SCSI.

While *burning* (writing) a CD, it is usually important that the flow of data to the writer keeps up with the speed at which the writer is going; otherwise, if the writer runs out of data to write, the CD-R is ruined. For this reason, it is usual to use mkisofs to generate an image file and then separately use cdrecord to write this image file to the CD writer.

It is possible to use a pipe to send the data from mkisofs directly to cdrecord. This often works either because a fast machine can ensure that mkisofs supplies the data fast enough to keep the CD writer busy or because the CD writer is not sensitive to data underruns. (Some of the more expensive ones have internal hard disks or very big RAM caches to which the data is written during an intermediate stage.) This technique is not recommended, however, because the generation of the intermediate image file has other benefits; it enables you to test your CD image before the final writing of the data takes place.

Testing CD Images

Just as you can use mkfs to create a filesystem inside an ordinary file, you can mount filesystems contained in ordinary files by using the loopback device driver described previously. The first example of mounting a loopback filesystem is a demonstration of how you can test a CD image.

18

LINUX FILESYSTEMS, DISKS, AND OTHER DEVICES

Other Character Devices

Several other varieties of character devices, such as /dev/null, are used frequently.

The Controlling Terminal Device—/dev/tty

Most processes have a controlling terminal, particularly if they were started interactively by a user. The *controlling terminal*, which I refer to as simply /dev/tty, is used for initiating a conversation directly with the user (for example, to ask him something). An example is the crypt command:

```
$ fmt diary.txt | crypt | mail -s Diary confidant@linux.org
Enter key:
$
```

Here, the crypt command has opened /dev/tty to obtain a password. It was not able to use its own standard output to issue the prompt and its standard input to read the password because they are being used for the data to be encrypted.

> **Note**
>
> Of course, it's unusual to send email encrypted with crypt. A better choice is probably GnuPG. This is an Open Source replacement for PGP.

More useful examples are commands that need to ask the operator something even if the input and output are redirected. A case in point is the cpio command, which prompts the operator for the name of a new tape device when it runs out of space. See the section "/dev/null and Friends" later in this chapter for another example.

Nonserial Mice

Many computers have bus or PS/2 mice instead of serial mice. This arrangement has the advantage of keeping both of the two standard serial ports free, but the disadvantage of using up another IRQ. These devices are used by gpm and the X Window System, but most other programs don't interact with them directly. Setting up your system with these mice is easy; the Red Hat Linux installation process pretty much takes care of it for you. If you have problems with your mouse, however, you should read the manual page for gpm and the Linux BusMouse HOWTO.

Audio Devices

There are several audio-related device nodes on Linux systems, and they include the following:

`/dev/sndstat`	Indicates the status of the sound driver
`/dev/audio*`	Sun-compatible audio output device
`/dev/dsp*`	Sound sampling device
`/dev/mixer`	For control of the mixer hardware on the sound card
`/dev/music`	A high-level sequencer interface
`/dev/sequencer*`	A low-level sequencer interface
`/dev/midi*`	Direct MIDI port access

Setting up the sound driver under Linux can sometimes be difficult, but the `sndconfig` utility included with Red Hat makes this easier for most cards. If you have problems be sure to check out the Linux Sound HOWTO provides useful advice.

Random Number Devices

Many program features require the generation of apparently random sequences. Examples include games, numerical computations, and various computer-security–related applications. Numerical computing with random numbers requires that the sequence of random numbers be repeatable but also that the sequence "look" random. Games require apparently random numbers, but the quality of the random numbers is not quite as critical as for numerical computation programs. The system libraries produce repeatable sequences of "pseudo-random" numbers that satisfy these requirements well.

On the other hand, in many aspects of computer security, it is advantageous to generate numbers that really are random. Because you can assume that an attacker has access to the same sorts of random number generators that you do, using them is not very safe; an attacker can use these generators to figure out what random number you'll use next. Sequences that are genuinely random must in the end be produced from the real world and not from the internals of some computer program. For this reason, the Linux kernel keeps a supply of random numbers internally. These numbers are derived from very precise timings of the intervals between "random" external events—for example, the user's key presses on the keyboard, mouse events, and even some interrupts (such as from the floppy disk drive and some network cards). These "real" random numbers are used in security-critical contexts—for example, the choosing of TCP sequence numbers.

> **Note**
>
> The Linux kernel uses these methods to produce TCP sequence numbers that are more difficult to guess than those of any other implementation at the time of writing. This improves the security of TCP connections against "hijacking."

The two random number devices differ in what happens when the rate of reading exceeds the rate at which random data is collected inside the kernel. The `/dev/random` device makes the calling program wait until some more randomness arrives, and the `/dev/urandom` device falls back on the difficult-to-guess MD5 hash to produce a stream of random data. When more random information arrives later, it is added to the randomness of `/dev/urandom`. To summarize, `/dev/random` doesn't sacrifice quality in favor of speed, but `/dev/urandom` does.

`/dev/null` and Friends

In the following segment, the special devices `/dev/full` and `/dev/null` first simulate a tape-full condition and then discard the output:

```
$ echo test | cpio -o >/dev/full
Found end of tape.  To continue, type device/file name when ready.
/dev/null
1 blocks
```

In the real world, when the tape on `/dev/st0` becomes full, you probably just change the tape in the drive and type `/dev/st0` a second time. However, `/dev/full` is occasionally useful for testing purposes, and `/dev/null` is used all the time for discarding unwanted output. The device `/dev/full` produces a stream of zero bytes when read. (`/dev/null`, on the other hand, produces no output at all.)

Memory Devices

The memory devices have the same major device number as `/dev/null` and `/dev/full` but are used differently. They are as follows:

`/dev/mem`	Provides access to physical memory
`/dev/kmem`	Provides access to the kernel's virtual memory
`/dev/port`	Provides access to I/O ports

These devices are not frequently used in many programs; the X Window System's X server uses memory mapping on `/dev/mem` to access the video memory, and many programs use `/dev/port` to access I/O ports on those architectures that have a separate I/O space. (Many modern processors do not.)

Virtual Console Screen Devices

The virtual console (VC) screen devices provide read access to the VCs memory. This can be used to get screen capture capabilities for virtual consoles, for example. The devices are not readable by ordinary users; hence, other users cannot eavesdrop on your session.

There are two sets of device nodes for this purpose:

```
$ ls -l /dev/vcs[012] /dev/vcsa[012]
crw--w----  1 root     tty        7,   0 Jul 21 16:29 /dev/vcs0
crw--w----  1 wsb      tty        7,   1 Jul 21 16:29 /dev/vcs1
crw--w----  1 root     tty        7,   2 Jul 21 16:29 /dev/vcs2
crw--w----  1 root     tty        7, 128 Jul 21 16:29 /dev/vcsa0
crw--w----  1 wsb      tty        7, 129 Jul 21 16:29 /dev/vcsa1
crw--w----  1 root     tty        7, 130 Jul 21 16:29 /dev/vcsa2
```

Each set is numbered from 0 to 63, corresponding to the numbering system for the /dev/tty* console devices. The device /dev/vcs0, like the device dev/tty0, always refers to the currently selected VC.

The /dev/vcs* files provide a snapshot of what is in view on the corresponding VC. This snapshot contains no newlines because there are none actually on the screen; after all, a newline character just moves the cursor. To make the captured data into the kind of thing you usually see in text files or send to printers, you need to add newlines in the appropriate places. This can be done with the dd command:

```
$ dd cbs=80 conv=unblock </dev/vcs1 | lpr
```

This example works only if the screen actually is 80 columns wide. This is not always true; the kernel can set up a different video mode at boot time, and you can use the SVGATextMode command to change it at any time.

You can overcome this problem by using the other set of devices, /dev/vcsa*. Reading from these devices gives a header, followed by the screen data with attribute bytes. The header consists of two bytes indicating the screen size (height first), followed by two bytes indicating the cursor position. The screen data is provided at a rate of two bytes per character cell, the first containing the attribute byte and the second containing the character data (as with /dev/vcs*). You can use this data to provide full-color screen dumps and so on. The following script uses a /dev/vcsa device to determine the width of the VC and to get the conversion of the corresponding /dev/vcs device right:

```
#! /bin/sh

#Insist on exactly one argument (the VC number to dump)
[$# -eq 1] || {echo "usage: $0 [vc-number]">2; exit 1}
```

18

LINUX FILESYSTEMS,
DISKS, AND OTHER
DEVICES

```
vc=$1 #Which VC to dump

#Extract the VC's width from the second byte of the vcsa device
#The "unpack" expression extracts the value of the second
#character of the input (the vcsa device).
Width=`dd if=/dev/vcsal bs=1 count=1 skip=1 2>/dev/null|hexdump -e '"%d"'`

#Use dd(1) to convert the output now that we know the width
dd cbs=${width} conv=unblock</dev/vcs${vc} 2>/dev/null
```

Summary

This chapter introduced character and block devices, filesystem administration, and gave an overview of the hardware that can be accessed via the special files in the /dev directory.

One of the difficulties in writing a chapter like this is that things are constantly changing. For example, soon we will be using ext3 instead of ext2 for the standard filesystem type. The kernel maintainers and distribution maintainers are trying to keep things in line enough so that ordinary computer users can use this stuff, but at the same time allow flexibility so that new and improved "stuff" can be designed. Many of the areas that the Linux community has focused on throughout the years have fallen under the section devices and filesystems. Therefore, as the standards switch from using /dev/cua* devices to using /dev/ttyS* devices, and so on, documentation needs to be constantly updated.

In the meantime, programmers are working their penguins to the wing tip trying to design easier tools to help remove some of the difficulty with using and configuring Linux. They have come a long way with tools such as usermount and fsconf, but they still have a long way to go before they are finished.

You can find further information from the Linux Documentation Project material at http://www.linuxdoc.org/. Much of the LDP material is also provided on the CD-ROMs accompanying this book.

CHAPTER 19

Printing with Linux

This chapter shows you how to use printers and printer utilities with Red Hat Linux. Many different programs, files, and directories are integral to supporting printing under Red Hat Linux, but you'll soon find that with little effort, you'll be able to get to work and print nicely formatted documents and graphics.

If you can print to your printer from DOS, Windows 98, NT, or Windows 2000, chances are you'll be able to print under Linux, and you'll probably be pleasantly surprised by the additional printing capabilities you won't find in that proprietary commercial operating system installed on your PC.

As a Red Hat Linux user, you'll be especially pleased because the kind folks in North Carolina have hidden the ugly and gory details of manually installing a printer behind an easy-to-use graphical interface. You'll find the process a snap!

Printer Devices

Under Linux, each piece of your computer's hardware is abstracted to a device file (hopefully with an accompanying device driver in the kernel; see Chapter 18, "Linux Filesystems, Disks, and Other Devices," for more details). Printer devices, traditionally named after line printers, are character mode devices and will be found in the /dev directory. Some of these devices, along with the traditional hardware port assignments, are shown in Table 19.1.

TABLE 19.1 Parallel Printer Devices

Device Name	Printer	Address
/dev/lp0	First parallel printer	0x3bc
/dev/lp1	Second parallel printer	0x378
/dev/lp2	Third parallel printer	0x278

Serial printers are assigned to serial devices, such as /dev/ttySX, where X is a number from 0 to 3. Quite a few tty devices are listed in /dev. Generally, if you're going to use a serial printer, you have to use the setserial command to make sure the printer's serial port is set to the fastest baud rate your printer supports.

In some special cases, such as using an old Apple LaserWriter as a serial printer (it has a Diablo print-wheel emulation mode using the Courier font), you must define your own printer or edit an entry in the /etc/printcap database. Sometimes you can manipulate the printer to get a higher speed. For example, here's a 10-year-old trick, posted to the

comp.laser-printers newsgroup by Dale Carstensen, for increasing the serial port
speed of the Apple LaserWriter Plus to 19200:

```
%!
0000 % Server Password
statusdict begin 25 sccbatch 0 ne exch 19200 ne or
{ serverdict begin oxiteerver} {pop end stop} ifelse
statusdict begin
25 19200 0 setsccbatch
end % noteÑnext line has an actual CTRL-D
```

See Appendix D in the *RedBook*, Adobe's PostScript language reference manual, for
more information about LaserWriters, or peruse comp.laser-printers for hints on setting up your laser printer. Also read the file Psfiles.htm under the /usr/share/
ghostscript/5.50 directory for information about the numerous PostScript printer utilities included in the Ghostscript distribution.

Most desktop users, however, have a printer attached to the parallel printer port, so I'll
first concentrate on /dev/lp.

What Printer Should I Use with Linux?

Nearly any printer that uses your computer's serial or parallel port should work. One
might think that a PostScript printer is the best printer to use with Linux because many
programs and text utilities used with Linux and ported from other UNIX systems output
graphics and text as PostScript. However, another great reason to use Linux, and Red
Hat's distribution of Linux, is that through the magic of software, your $99 inkjet printer
can also print PostScript documents—even in color. That's a bargain!

19

New PPA Printer Support!

Even printers using Printing Performance Architecture (PPA), such as the HP 720,
820, or 1000-series printers, which in the past required a special software driver
available only for Windows, are now supported! Thanks to early efforts by Tim
Norman, even HP 710C, 712C, 720C, 722C, 820Cse, 820Cxi, 1000Cse, and 1000Cxi
printer users can now enjoy printing. Red Hat Linux now incorporates supporting
filters that provide various color modes. See this chapter's section "printtool—
The Red Hat Linux Print System Manager" for details on installing support.

Ghostscript Printing Support

When you use Linux, you'll find excellent support for many different popular printers. Red Hat Linux comes with a special configuration tool, called `printtool`, that directly supports more than 100 printers. The Ghostscript interpreter, included with Red Hat Linux, is an integral part of Linux printing for many users and supports more than 100 different printers. Table 19.2 lists Ghostscript drivers and supported printers.

You can also verify the built-in printer devices in your Red Hat distribution's version of Ghostscript by directly calling the gs interpreter with its `--help` command-line option like this:

```
# gs --help
```

The gs command will output several lines of help text on command-line usage, then list the compiled or built-in printer and graphics devices. You can also get this output by running gs and then using the `devicenames ==` command during an X11 session, like this:

```
# gs
GNU Ghostscript 5.50 (2000-2-13)
Copyright (C) 1998 Aladdin Enterprises, Menlo Park, CA.  All rights
reserved.
This software comes with NO WARRANTY: see the file COPYING for details.
Loading NimbusRomNo9L-Regu font from
/usr/share/fonts/default/Type1/n021003l.pfb... 2184672 863369 1450640
152624 0 done.
Loading NimbusSanL-Regu font from
/usr/share/fonts/default/Type1/n019003l.pfb... 2465960 1103598 1450640
158396 0 done.
GS> devicenames ==
[/dnj650c /mj500c /necp6 /lbp310 /la50 /x11alpha /hl7x0 /djet500 /lp8000
/lp2563 /lp2000 /iwlo /lj5gray /jj100 /tek4696 /lj250 /oki182 /imagen
/cljet5 /pr201 /t4693d4 /lq850 /lips3 /x11mono /ljet3d /fmpr /stcolor
/lips4v /appledmp /x11gray2 /ljet2p /dj505j /sj48 /lips4 /la75plus
/x11cmyk4 /laserjet /mj6000c /oce9050 /lbp320 /la70 /x11cmyk /ljet4pjl
/djet500c /mj700v2c /m8510 /escpage /iwlq /x11 /declj250 /deskjet /xes
...
```

Note that a blank X11 window will open (because the interpreter expects to display a PostScript graphic or document); ignore the window and type the command on the gs command line. After you press Enter, you'll see a list of built-in drivers (not all the output is shown here). For the latest list of supported printers and other information, see Ghostscript's home page at `http://www.cs.wisc.edu/~ghost/printer.html`.

TABLE **19.2**   Ghostscript Drivers and Supported Printers

Driver	Printer(s)
ap3250	Epson AP3250
appledmp	Apple dot matrix printer, ImageWriter
bj10e	Canon BJ10e
bj200	Canon BJC-210, 240, 250, 70, 200
bjc600	Canon BJC-600, 610, 4000, 4100, 4200, 4300, 4550, 210, C2500240, 70
bjc800	BJC-800, 7000
cdeskjet	HP DeskJet 500C
cdj500	HP DeskJet 400, 500C, 540C, 690C, 693C
cdj550	HP DeskJet 550C, 560C, 600, 660C, 682C, 683C, 693C, 694C, 850, 870C
cdjcolor	(24-bit color for cdj500 supported printers)
cdjmono	HP DeskJet 500C, 510, 520, 540C, 693C
cp50	Mitsubishi CP50 printer
deskjet	HP DeskJet, Plus
djet500	HP DeskJet 500, Portable
djet500c	HP DeskJet 500C
dnj650c	HP DesignJet 650C
epson	Epson dot-matrix
eps9mid	Epson compatible 9-pin
eps9high	Epson compatible 9-pin
epsonc	Epson LQ-2550, Fujitsu 2400, 2400, 1200
hl7x0	Brother HL 720, 730
ibmpro	IBM Proprinter
imagen	Imagen ImPress
iwhi	Apple Imagewriter (hi-res)
iwlo	Apple Imagewriter (lo-res)
iwlq	Apple Imagewriter LQ
jetp3852	IBM Jetprinter
la50	DEC LA50
la70	DEC LA70
la75	DEC LA75
la75plus	DEC LA75plus
lbp8	Canon LBP-8II
lips3	Canon LIPS III

19

PRINTING WITH
LINUX

TABLE 19.2   continued

Driver	Printer(s)
lj250	DEC LJ250
lj4dith	HP DeskJet 600, LaserJet 4
ljet2p	HP LaserJet IId, IIp, III
ljet3	HP LaserJet III
ljet3d	HP LaserJet IIId
ljet4	HP DeskJet 600, 870Cse; LaserJet 4, 5, 5L, 6L, Oki OL410ex
ljetplus	HP LaserJet Plus, NEC SuperScript 860
ln03	DEC LN03
lp2563	HP 2563B
lq8000	Epson LP-8000
lq850	Epson LQ850, Canon BJ300
m8510	C. Itoh M8510
necp6	NEC P6, P6+, P60
nwp533	Sony NWP533
oce9050	OCE 9050
oki182	Okidata MicroLine 182
okiibm	Okidata IBM-compatible
paintjet	HP PaintJets
pj	HP PaintJet XL
pjxl	HP PaintJet XL
pjxl300	HP PaintJet XL300, HP DeskJet 600, 1200C, 1600C
r4081	Ricoh 4081, 6000 laser printers
sj48	StarJet 48
sparc	SPARCprinter
stcolor	Epson Stylus Color, Color II, 500, 600, 800
st800	Epson Stylus 800
t4693d2	Textronix 4693d (2-bit)
t4693d4	Textronix 4693d (4-bit)
t4693d8	Textronix 4693d (8-bit)
tek4696	Textronix 4695/4696
uniprint	Canon BJC 610, HP DeskJet 550C, NEC P2X, Epson Stylus Color, II, 500, 600, 800, 1520
xes	Xerox XES 2700, 3700, 4045

Ghostscript has several important uses, such as displaying PostScript documents. But when you print with Red Hat Linux, Ghostscript is used to translate the PostScript output of programs destined for your printer into a usable, printable form, such as a printer control language. In general, if you have a printer that supports some form of printer control language (PCL), you shouldn't have problems.

How Do I Print?

One of the first things you should do before setting up your printer for Linux (especially if it is a parallel-port printer), is to make sure the printer works. First, check to see that your printer is plugged in, turned on, and attached to your computer's parallel port. Pass-through parallel port cables shouldn't pose a problem, but don't expect to be able to use your printer while you're using your CD-ROM, QuickCam, SCSI adapter, tape drive, or SyQuest drive if attached to a pass-through cable.

For starters, try this simple code:

```
# ls >/dev/lp0
```

Chances are your printer will activate and its print head will move, but when you look at the printout, you might see a staircase effect, with each word on a separate line, moving across the page. Don't worry—this is normal and tells you that you can at least access your printer. Later in this chapter, you'll find out how to fine-tune your printing.

New Parallel-Port Drivers

Red Hat Linux uses version 2.2.16 of the Linux kernel. Unlike previous 2.0 versions of the kernel, recent 2.2.X and newer kernels use a different approach to parallel-port initialization, recognition, and configuration. In legacy kernels, parallel-port support was aimed specifically at providing printer support and was "hard-wired" into the kernel. This approach did not cover the needs of the myriad of parallel-port devices on the market. The newer approach, which uses several parallel-port kernel modules, abstracts communication with your computer's hardware to better support a much wider range of devices and provide new features, such as using multiple devices.

As distributed, Red Hat Linux contains a default parallel-port kernel module configuration in /etc/modules.conf. This line enables the low-level parallel-port parport kernel modules to attempt to autodetect any attached printers or devices:

```
alias parport_lowlevel parport_pc
```

19

PRINTING WITH LINUX

You can view the output of these modules with the `dmesg` command following an attempt to print. Look for output similar to this:

```
parport0: PC-style at 0x3bc [SPP,PS2]
parport_probe: succeeded
parport0: Printer, Hewlett-Packard HP DeskJet 340
lp0: using parport0 (polling).
```

This shows that the computer's parallel port was detected, along with an attached printer (HP 340). The attached printer will use `/dev/lp0` as the printer device. You can also use the `lsmod` command to verify that the printer drivers have been loaded following a print job, like this:

```
# lsmod
Module                  Size  Used by
parport_probe           3428  0  (autoclean)
parport_pc              7464  1  (autoclean)
lp                      5416  0  (autoclean)
parport                 7320  1  (autoclean) [parport_probe parport_pc lp]
...
```

The `parport` modules are automatically loaded whenever the `lp.o` kernel module is used. If your parallel port hardware is detected, you can examine the contents of the hardware file under the printer port's device number (such as `/dev/lp0`) like this:

```
# cat /proc/parport/0/hardware
base:   0x3bc
irq:    none
dma:    none
modes:  SPP,PS2
```

You can also use the `parport_pc` kernel module to specify your system's parallel I/O port address and IRQ. Use the `insmod` command to first load the `parport.o` module like this:

```
# insmod parport
```

Next, use the `parport_pc` module, along with its `io` and `irq` options like this:

```
# insmod parport_pc io=0x378 irq=7
```

This will tell the Linux kernel that your computer has a parallel port using the specified address and IRQ. This can be important, especially if you need to custom configure the port for a printer or other device.

You can also try the `tunelp` command, which sets various parameters to "tune" your printer port or lets you know if your printer device is using interrupts or polling for printing. Try using the command with its `-s` or status option like this:

```
# tunelp /dev/lp0 -s
```

You might see this output:

```
/dev/lp0 status is 223, on-line
```

If `tunelp` reports `"No such device or address"`, if you do not find an `lp` character device, and if you cannot load the parport modules, see Chapter 27, "Configuring and Building Kernels," to learn how to build kernel modules for your system.

For details about the new parport drivers, read the file `parport.txt` under the `/usr/share/doc/kernel-doc-2.2.16` directory.

`printtool`—The Red Hat Linux Print System Manager

If you want to install, modify, or delete a local, remote, or LAN printer, you're going to love the `printtool` program. Found in `/usr/bin`, `printtool` is a graphical interface printer setup program you can call up from the command line, from the GNOME or KDE desktop panel, or through the Red Hat `control-panel` program.

The `control-panel` and `printtool` programs require `root` permission and run under X, so you'll have to first fire up X and then type the following from a terminal window:

```
# printtool
```

After you type in `root`'s password and press Enter, the main `printtool` dialog box comes up, as shown in Figure 19.1.

FIGURE 19.1

The printtool *client is used to set up printers for your Red Hat Linux system.*

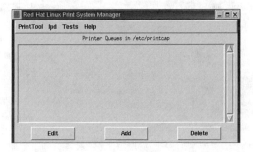

Click the Add button and you'll be asked to select a local, remote, SMB, NCP manager, or "Direct to port" printer (see Figure 19.2).

19

PRINTING WITH LINUX

FIGURE 19.2

The printtool
*client may be used
to define printer
settings for a vari-
ety of printer
types.*

Remote Linux Printers

To set up a remote printer, click the Remote UNIX (lpd) Queue button. You'll see a dialog box like that shown in Figure 19.3.

FIGURE 19.3

The printtool
*Remote Queue
dialog box is used
to set up a remote
printer.*

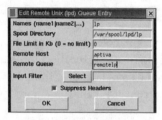

To set up your system to be able to print to a remote printer attached to another Linux
computer on your network, type in the hostname of the remote machine hosting the
printer, then type in the remote print queue's name. Click the Select button. You'll see a
dialog box like that shown in Figure 19.4.

FIGURE 19.4

The printtool
*Configure Filter
dialog box is used
to set filter options
for more than 100
different printers.*

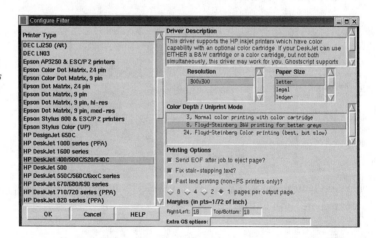

Select the correct printer type, resolution, paper size, and other options. Note that these
settings should match the capabilities of the remote printer! When you've finished selecting the remote printer's options, click OK.

The `printtool` command then creates a simple remote printer entry in your system's printer capability database, `/etc/printcap`. The entry will look something like this:

```
##PRINTTOOL3## REMOTE djet500 300x300 letter {} DeskJet500 8 1
lp:\
        :sd=/var/spool/lpd/lp:\
        :mx#0:\
        :sh:\
        :rm=aptiva.home.org:\
        :rp=remotelp:\
        :if=/var/spool/lpd/lp/filter:
```

The `:rm` and `:rp` entries define the remote host and printer. The remote machine (`aptiva.home.org` in this example) should have a configured printer named `remotelp`, and should also have a properly configured `hosts.lpd` file under the `/etc` directory. For example, to enable printing on the `remotelp` queue from other computers, you should enter a list of allowed remote hostnames (or IP addresses) in aptiva's `/etc/hosts.lpd` file like this:

```
ascentia.home.org
stinky.home.org
192.168.2.38
presario.home.org
hitachi.home.org
```

This allows print jobs from the listed computers. For details about remote printer entries, see the `printcap` man page and look for the `rm` and `rp` capabilities.

> **Note**
>
> There are other, possibly easier ways to print to remote printers, such as using the `rlpr` command. For more information, read Grant Taylor's *Linux Printing HOWTO* available at `http://www.linuxdoc.org`.

After you've created your remote printer, you'll see a remote entry in `printtool`'s main dialog box, as shown in Figure 19.5.

You can test your remote printer by clicking the Tests menu item (as shown in Figure 19.5) and then clicking the ASCII or PostScript test pages. The ASCII test page will print seven lines of test in 10-point Courier to check alignment and proper linefeeds. The PostScript test page will print a page of text, the Red Hat logo, an eight-color or eight-shaded box, and two lined boxes at the one-inch and half-inch margins of your page.

FIGURE 19.5

The printtool *main dialog box may be used to test local or remote printers.*

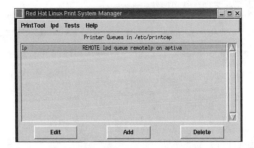

To set up for printing to an SMB printer, you must have Server Message Block services enabled (through the smbd daemon, part of the Samba software package). You must also have the smbclient command and associated smbprint shell script installed under the /usr/bin directory. You must also be connected to a Windows network and have printer sharing enabled under the remote Windows computer.

For example, under Windows 95, navigate to the Network device in the Control Panel (available through the Settings menu item in the Start menu). Click the File and Print Sharing button, select I Want to Be Able to Allow Others to Print to My Printers, and click OK. Click the Identification tab at the top of the Network window, note the name of your computer, and close the window.

After rebooting, open the Printers folder, right-click the printer you would like to share, and select the Sharing menu item. Select Shared As, enter a shared name and a password, and click OK. You need the name and password information when you run printtool. According to printtool, you need the following to set up a LAN printer:

- Printer server name
- Printer server IP number
- Printer name
- Printer user
- Printer password
- Workgroup

This information (which you can also get from the shared printer's Properties menu under Network Neighborhood) is entered in the SMB Printer Entry dialog box that pops up after you select the type of printer you want to set up. You should also select the type of printer through the Select button at the Input Filter field (similar to that shown in Figure 19.4).

Note

Check Chapter 17, "Samba," for information on setting up other services through Server Message Block (SMB) Windows-based networks. Need more detailed instructions on how to print from Red Hat Linux to a printer on a Windows 95/98/NT system or to print on a Linux printer from Windows 95? Browse to http://www.redhat.com/support/docs/tips/Samba-Tips/Samba-Tips.html. You'll also find the latest information about Samba through the central Samba Web page at http://samba.anu.edu.au/samba.

Again, after you fill out your LAN printer's information and click OK, printtool creates a printer entry in /etc/printcap. The printer entry might look something like this:

```
##PRINTTOOL3## SMB cdj500 300x300 letter {} DeskJet500 8 1
lp0:\
    :sd=/var/spool/lpd/lp0:\
    :mx#0:\
    :sh:\
    :af=/var/spool/lpd/lp0/acct:\
    :lp=/dev/null:\
    :if=/var/spool/lpd/lp0/filter:\
```

Note

If you do not select a printing filter for your SMB printer, the smbprint filter specified in your SMB printer's /etc/printcap entry is identical to the smbprint command found under the /usr/bin directory! Also, you'll receive a warning before you create an SMB or NCP printer for Red Hat Linux with printtool. When you use printtool to create an SMB printer entry, a file named .config is created under the printer's /var/spool/lpd directory, or spool directory. This file, which contains the Share (server) name, the printer username, workgroup, and the password, is not encrypted and anyone on your system can read it.

19

PRINTING WITH LINUX

Before you can print to your SMB printer, you should have an active network connection. You can then use the -P option of the lpr command, followed by your new LAN printer's name and the name of the file you'd like to print. Using a /etc/printcap entry for a defined printer lp0, use lpr to print a file called myfile.txt:

```
# lpr -Plp0 myfile.txt
```

You can also use the smbprint command, part of Andrew Tridgell's collection of programs in the Samba software package, to print to a LAN printer. The smbprint command is a shell script, found under the /usr/bin directory, that uses the smbclient command to send files to a shared printer. In fact, a modified version of smbprint is used as Red Hat's printer filter when you create an SMB printer entry with printtool. For details about smbclient, see its man page.

Local Printers

Red Hat's printtool can easily and quickly set up a parallel port printer attached directly to your computer. To do so, run printtool, click the Add button, select Local, and click OK.

Linux then tries to load the parallel printing module, lp.o, and an Info dialog box appears (shown in Figure 19.6). The dialog box tells you what parallel printer devices have been detected. If printtool reports that no device was found, check your /etc/modules.conf entry for the parport driver.

FIGURE 19.6

printtool *will quickly and easily set up local (attached) printers as long as a parallel port is recognized.*

You see an Edit Local Printer Entry dialog box (shown in Figure 19.7) after you click OK. If you'd like to give your printer a name, type a name in the Names field. If you want to limit the size of any spooled printer files (because you don't have enough space on your hard drive), enter a number (such as 1024 for 1MB). After you have finished, click the Select button.

FIGURE 19.7

The printtool *printer device main configuration dialog box allows you to name printers and limit the size of spooled printer files.*

The Configure Filter dialog box appears (as shown in Figure 19.4). When finished selecting your options, click OK. The printer you defined should now appear under the list of Printer Queues in the main `printtool` dialog box. Select it and then choose an ASCII or PostScript test from the Tests menu.

Don't See Your Printer Listed?

If you don't see the exact model of your printer listed in the Configure Filter dialog, don't fret! Chances are very good that your printer works similarly to another printer in the same family line. Unless you have an esoteric printer that requires specialized drivers, many filter entries for printers from the same manufacturer will work just fine. For example, HP 340 printer users may use any of the entries for the HP500 series of printers, and Canon BJC 50 and 80 users can use the Canon BJC 600 entries.

The `printtool` client (written in the Python language) works by first defining your printer and then inserting the definition into an `/etc/printcap` entry, along with a pointer to a filter script (written using `bash`) in the `/var/spool/lpd` directory. The filter and associated scripts reside in a directory, or printer queue, under `/var/spool/lpd`, with either a name you choose or an assigned default.

Customizing RHS Printer Filters

The master set of printer filters, along with definitions of the printer entries in the `printtool` database, reside under the `/usr/lib/rhs/rhs-printfilters` directory. You can change options for your selected printer by editing the file `printerdb`. For example, if you find that you only want black-and-white printing for your HP Deskjet 400, open the `printerdb` file (as root) with your favorite text editor. Scroll through the file until you find the HP 400 entry, like this:

```
StartEntry: DeskJet500
  GSDriver: cdj500
  Description: {HP DeskJet 400/500C/520/540C}
  About: { \
          This driver supports the HP inkjet printers which have \
          color capability with an optional color cartridge. \
          If your DeskJet can use EITHER a B&W cartridge or \
          a color cartridge, but not both simultaneously, \
          this driver may work for you. \
          Ghostscript supports several optional parameters for \
          this driver: see the document 'devices.doc' \
          in the ghostscript directory under /usr/doc. \
```

```
            }
    Resolution: {300} {300} {}
    BitsPerPixel:  {3} {Normal color printing with color cartridge}
    BitsPerPixel:  {8} {Floyd-Steinberg B&W printing for better greys}
    BitsPerPixel: {24} {Floyd-Steinberg Color printing (best, but slow)}
EndEntry
```

To add simple black-and-white printing as an option for this series of printer, add a `BitsPerPixel` entry following the `Resolution:` entry:

```
    BitsPerPixel:  {1} {Normal B&W printing with black cartridge}
```

> **Note**
>
> You can split up the printer filter definitions to create custom entries for different printers, or create your own printer entries by using proper syntax between the `StartEntry:` and `EndEntry` keywords, which provide options prior to printing and translation of your PostScript document by the Ghostscript interpreter. A monochrome-only DeskJet500 entry is included, but you can rename entries to be more specific about the type of printer, and rename entries for printers installed on your LAN. Despite the pointer in the `printerdb` file, details about the Ghostscript options will be found under the `/usr/share/doc/ghostscript-5.50` in the file `Devices.htm`.

As you can see, `printtool` can add, edit, or delete printers. Another nice feature is the capability to assign a size limit to spooled files, which can be helpful if you have limited disk space or don't want users to fill up your filesystem. If you have a printer that requires you to change the print cartridge so that you can print black-and-white or color pages, you'll find `printtool` indispensable. Try it!

Although the current version of `printtool`, 3.48, creates a backup of your `/etc/printcap` database each time you make a change, it does not delete the associated printer queue or spool directory when you delete a printer.

Linux Printing Commands

Of course, you don't have to use the `printtool` command to set up your printer. You can edit `/etc/printcap` directly, but you should know what you're doing and understand `printcap`'s format. This file, an ASCII database of your system's local and networked printers, describes the capabilities of each printer in detail. For full details, see the `printcap` man page for commands and the `termcap` man page for the file's layout.

In fact, you can have multiple entries for each printer, which is helpful if you want to print different size papers, print color or black-and-white documents by switching cartridges, or change printer trays.

Old versions of Red Hat Linux used the 4.3BSD line-printer spooling system. This system has a number of features and associated programs to support background printing, multiple local and networked printers, and control of the printers and queued documents.

The main files used in the older printer spooling system were as follows:

```
/etc/printcap
/usr/sbin/lpd
/usr/sbin/lpc
/usr/bin/lpr
/usr/bin/lprm
/usr/bin/lpq
/dev/printer
```

These files provided the basic features needed to initiate and control print jobs from the command line. See Table 19.3 for a selected list of additional Linux commands you may find helpful when printing.

Red Hat Linux now uses Patrick Powell's LPRng print spooler software, which is descended from the 4.3BSD release but rewritten from the ground up. LPRng offers a host of benefits and features over the previous printer spooling software, such as being distributed under the GNU GPL, backward compatibility, security, diagnostics, and multiple printers on a single queue. In addition to the previously listed commands, LPRng also uses

```
/etc/lpd.conf
/usr/sbin/checkpc
/etc/lpd.perms
/usr/bin/lpstat
```

These additional files are used for site-specific settings, to check or fix LPRng's installation, to set permissions for users, and to report on a printer's status.

When you first boot Linux, the shell script, `lpd` (under `/etc/rc.d/init.d/`) starts `lpd`, the printer daemon. This program, a printer server, runs in the background and waits for print requests. When a request is detected on the print queue, the server connects to the designated printer and passes the document stream through the proper printer filter.

19

PRINTING WITH
LINUX

Print requests are started with the lpr command. For example, the following command line will print your document to a file in the /var/spool/lpd/lp directory using the printer named lp:

```
# lpr -Plp myfile.txt
```

Other print-spooling commands can help track your request. If you're printing a large document or a number of smaller files, you can see a list of print jobs running by using the lpq command. For example, to print a number of files at once to the default printer, use this:

```
# lpr *
```

> **Note**
>
> The LPRng system will only allow printing of 52 files at once. If you want to print more multiple files, you'll need to split up the print job.

Follow that command with this:

```
# lpq
```

This outputs the following:

```
Printer: lp@thinkpad
 Queue: 1 printable job
 Server: pid 3631 active
 Unspooler: pid 3632 active
 Status: processing 'dfB630thinkpad.home.org', size 1309, format 'f', IF filter
'filter' at 17:40:52.610
 Rank   Owner/ID                Class Job Files            Size Time
active root@thinkpad+630          A   630 adsl,amd,anacron,apm 14542 17:40:51
```

This shows quite a bit of information, but the important item to note is the job number (630 in this example). If you want to stop the preceding print job, use the lprm command, followed by the job number, as in the following:

```
# lprm 630
Printer lp@thinkpad:
  checking perms 'root@thinkpad+630'
  dequeued 'root@thinkpad+630'
```

This shows that lprm has removed the spool files and stopped the job. To disable or enable a printer and its spooling queue, rearrange the order of any print jobs, or find out the status of printers, you can use lpc from the command line or interactively, but you must be logged in as root or as a superuser (through the su command).

LPRng's `lpc` command is very comprehensive and offers much more control over system and network printing than the legacy `lpc` command. This command may be used to activate or abort the print server, disable or enable print queuing, hold or release print jobs, and even move print jobs to a different printer! Start `lpc` on the command line like this:

```
# lpc
```

To view the built-in help on command keywords and syntax, type **help** or press ? like this:

```
lpc> help
```

After you press Enter, you'll see several pages of help text for `lpc`'s 30 different commands. A more abbreviated command is LPRng's `lpstat`. Use the command like this:

```
# lpstat
Printer: lp@thinkpad
 Queue: no printable jobs in queue
 Status: subserver pid 3632 exit status 'JABORT' at 17:43:05.111
```

If you have print jobs waiting, you'll see a list of jobs, along with information similar to that returned by `lprm`.

LPRng is documented through its commands' man pages and documentation under the `/usr/share/doc/LPRng-3.6.22` directory. You'll find the latest version and documentation (including an excellent HOWTO document) at `http://www.astart.com/lprng/LPRng.html`.

TABLE 19.3   Selected Printing Commands

Command	Description
cancel	LPRng utility to cancel print service
checkpc	Verifies and fixes LPRng print system files
lpc	Controls program for local and remote printers
lpd	LPRng print server daemon
lpf	General printer filter
lpr	Sends print jobs to printer queue
lprm	Controls print queue
lpstat	Displays specified print service status
mpage	Prints multiple pages of text per sheet
nprint	NetWare print client
pbm2ppa	Converts bitmap to HP PPA format

19

PRINTING WITH
LINUX

TABLE 19.3   continued

Command	Description
pbmto10x	Converts bitmap to Gemini printer graphic
pbmtoepson	Converts bitmap to Epson printer graphic
pbmtoppa	Converts bitmap to HP PPA format
pbmtoptx	Converts bitmap to Printronix printer graphic
pnm2ppa	Converts any map to HP PPA format
pqlist	Lists NetWare print queue
pqrm	Removes jobs from NetWare print queue
pqstat	Lists jobs in NetWare print queue
pr	Formats text files for printing
printmail	Formats mail messages for printing
pserver	NetWare print server
sliceprint	Formats documents with long lines
smbclient	Essential command used by smbprint for printing
smbprint	Shell script for printing to shared printers
testprns	Printer name check utility for Samba
tunelp	Parallel-port hardware utility

Other Helpful Printer Programs and Filters

Printer filters work by defining and inserting printer definitions into your /etc/printcap file. Embedded in each printer description is a pointer (pathname) to a script or program containing the filter to be run before output to the printer. This section introduces several ancillary printer filter systems you can try with Red Hat Linux.

Apsfilter

Even if you're spoiled by the printtool program, you will at times need to use other programs or scripts to help set up or manage printing. If you can't or don't want to run X, but want to easily install printing services for HP or PostScript printers, one great solution is the printing filter package called Apsfilter, by Andreas Klemm and Thomas Bueschgens. Installing Apsfilter is a snap, and it's even easier to use.

Apsfilter works well with all Linux printing applications. Two added benefits are that it prints two formatted pages in Landscape mode on a single page when you print text documents, saving you paper, and "automagically" recognizes the following documents and graphic formats: `fig`, `bmp`, `pbm`, `pnm`, `ppm`, PDF, `tiff`, `jpeg`, `gif`, Sun rasterfile, PostScript, `dvi`, raw ASCII, and `gzip` and `bzip2` compressed files.

You'll find the Apsfilter available through its home page at `http://people.FreeBSD.org/~andreas/apsfilter/index.html`.

magicfilter

Another printer filter similar to Apsfilter is H. Peter Anvin's magicfilter (also maintained by David Frey for the Debian Linux distribution), which detects and converts documents for printing through a combination of a compiled C filter and a printer configuration file. You'll find a copy at `http://www.debian.org/Packages/unstable/text/magicfilter.html`.

LPRMagic

Michele Andreoli's LPRMagic is another printer filter you can set up under Red Hat Linux. All configuration for the filtering is contained in a `/etc/lprMagic.conf` file. Some of the features of LPRMagic include file type recognition (even `.wav` and MIDI!), delayed printing, and Samba and LPRng support. Installation is via a set of shell scripts (executed as `root`). You can download a copy from `http://metalab.unc.edu/pub/Linux/system/printing/`.

HPTools

Have a Hewlett-Packard printer? If so, you might want to try Michael Janson's HPTools to manage your printer's settings. The main tool is the `hpset` command, which sports more than 13 command-line options you can use to control your printer. For example, to save money on print cartridges by using less ink, you can use `hpset` to tell your printer to print in the economy mode with this code:

```
# hpset -c econ | lpr
```

The `hpset` command also has an interactive mode, so you can test your printer, set different default fonts, or perform other software control of your printer, such as bi- or unidirectional printing.

You can find HPTools through its home page at `http://www.uni-karlsruhe.de/~ujps/hptools.html`.

19

PRINTING WITH LINUX

PostScript Printers

If you want a print spooler specifically designed for PostScript printers, give Dave Chappell's PPR a try. PPR works with printers attached to parallel, serial, and AppleTalk (LocalTalk) ports, along with other network interfaces. PPR also works much like other non-PostScript printer filters and converts a number of graphics file formats for printing.

You can find PPR at `ftp://ppr-dist.trincoll.edu/pub/ppr/`.

Infrared Printer Support

If you are fortunate enough to have a printer with infrared support (such as the Canon BJC 50 or BJC 80, HP LaserJet 6MP or HP LaserJet 2100TN) and a Linux system with an infrared port (such as a laptop), here is good news: You can print without a printer cable! Recent efforts in Linux device driver development have yielded infrared printing (and networking) support, and the latest Linux kernels now have IrDA support built in. IrDA support is supplied as a series of loadable kernel modules and support features such as system logging, networking, serial-port emulation, and printing.

You'll definitely need to read Werner Heuser's IR-HOWTO, found at `http://home.snafu.de/wehe/IR-HOWTO.html`. Development of IrDA for Linux is still experimental, but offers the promise of wireless networking, communication, PalmOS support, and of course, printing! The basic steps to enable infrared printing involve

1. Determining the correct `/dev/ttySX` device used by computer for the IrDA port.
2. Enabling your system's infrared port.
3. Creating the correct device(s), using the `irattach` command to start the port, then using the `ircomm` module to connect to the port.
4. Crafting a correct `/etc/modules.conf` entry to enable the port when booting.
5. Ensuring your setup correctly detects and identifies a remote IrDA device.
6. Testing the connectivity of your printer.

After you have configured your system, the easiest way to print to an infrared printer is to create a special printer entry in your `/etc/printcap` printer database with a special name, such as irlp. Laptop users may need to press certain function keys to disable an existing serial port, or to enable an IR port.

To download the latest set of irDA utilities browse to `http://www.cs.uit.no/linux-irda/`. For a detailed description of a working irDA printing system for the Canon BJC 80, browse to Dave Davey's page at `http://www.physiol.usyd.edu.au/daved/linux/bjc-80.html`.

Other Helpful Programs

The following are short descriptions of just a few of the programs offering handy printing services available as part of your Red Hat distribution or available for download. You'll find some of these indispensable.

`pbm` Utilities

To translate or manipulate your graphics files into a multitude of formats or effects for printing, try one of Jef Poskanzer's numerous `pbm` utilities included with Red Hat Linux. At last count there were nearly 100 programs. Use the `apropos` command with the `pbm` and `pnm` keywords for pointers.

gv

Most of the convenience of having PostScript documents print automatically on cheap inkjet printers under Linux derives from Aladdin Enterprises' interpreter, `gs`, or Ghostscript. However, Johannes Plass's X client, `gv`, based on Tim Theisen's much-beloved Ghostview, is another one of those "insanely great" programs that come with nearly every Linux distribution, including Red Hat's.

You can use `gv`, like the older Ghostview, to preview or print `.ps` files. This program features multiple levels of magnification and landscape and portrait modes, and prints PostScript files too.

Troubleshooting and More Information

I'll offer some general tips on troubleshooting printing and then give some pointers to more information. You should not have trouble with printing under Linux, but if you can't seem to get started, try some of these hints:

- Make sure your printer cable is properly connected to your computer and printer.
- Make sure your printer is on.
- Ensure that you have specified `lpd` service. Ensure that the `lpd` daemon is running; you can try using the `ntsysv` command as `root` to ensure the service is started the next time you boot Linux, or you can use the command:

  ```
  # /etc/rc.d/init.d/lpd start
  ```

- Make sure the kernel daemon is active. (This loads the printer driver module when needed.)

19

PRINTING WITH
LINUX

- Ensure you have the `parport.o`, `parport_pc.o`, and `lp.o` modules available and installed on your system. Also ensure you have a correct entry for the parport modules in your `/etc/modules.conf` file.

- Avoid PPA or Windows-only printers if you do not get satisfactory results.

- Make sure you select the correct printer filter for your printer with the `printtool` command, and use different names for local and remote printers.

Still having problems? See the man pages for `tunelp`, `printcap`, `lpd`, `lpr`, `lpq`, `lprm`, and `lpc`. Curiously, there is no man page for the printtool program, but its Help menu shows some general information and troubleshooting tips.

For information about the BSD printing system, read Ralph Campbell's abstract "4.3BSD Line Printer Spooler Manual," which is part of the 4.4BSD *System Manager's Manual*, tabbed section 7.

For an excellent introduction to LPRng, see Patrick Powell's abstract "LPRng—An Enhanced Printer Spooler." This 13-page document, in PostScript or text format, includes the history, architecture, configuration, operation, and algorithm of the spooler software. You can find it or the LPRng FAQ at `http://www.astart.com/lprng/LPRng.html` or look at the files `Intro.txt` or `Intro.ps` in the doc directory of the LPRng sources.

To join the LPRng mailing list, send a subscribe message to `plp-request@iona.ie`.

For detailed information about printing under Linux, read *The Linux Printing HOWTO* by Grant Taylor. *The Linux Printing HOWTO* contains a host of great tips, tricks, traps, and hacks concerning printing under Linux, including setups for serial printers and network printing.

Also read *The Linux Printing Usage HOWTO* by Mark Komarinski (see `http://www.linuxdoc.org`).

Don't forget to peruse the following newsgroups for information about printers, PostScript, or Linux printing:

```
comp.lang.postscript
comp.laser-printers
comp.os.linux.hardware
comp.os.linux.setup
comp.periphs.printers
comp.sources.postscript
comp.sys.hp.hardware
```

Summary

In this chapter you learned about Linux printer devices, how to print simple files, and even a little about infrared printing, the latest Linux development. I've also shown you the RHS Linux Print System Manager and introduced the LPRng print spooler system. Hopefully, you'll also try some of the other printer programs and filters. Use this chapter's information as a starting point to explore the printing features of Red Hat Linux, and push your printer to the max!

TCP/IP Network Management

TCP/IP (Transmission Control Protocol/Internet Protocol) is the most widespread networking protocol in use today, forming the base of many networks, including the Internet. TCP/IP is actually not just one protocol, but is a protocol suite. It is a group of protocols that work together and allow dissimilar systems (systems built by different manufacturers using different operating systems) to talk to each other through a common set of rules (hence the term protocol). It seems appropriate that credit for establishing the original concept of the TCP/IP suite of protocols, and how these protocols should work together, be given to Dr. Vinton Cerf and Robert Kahn. Cerf and Kahn wrote a paper that came out in an engineering journal in May of 1974 entitled "A Protocol for Packet Network Intercommunication." It described how the data packet should be separated, sectioned, constructed, transmitted, and subsequently reassembled. It explained the function of each section of a packet and detailed the size of the packet and the fields therein. It detailed how the data packet should be constructed and what data should be contained in each section. This was a revolution for the computing industry at the time. The Internet Engineering Task Force (IETF) is the body charged with standardizing TCP/IP. IETF standards documents are called *Requests For Comments* or *RFCs*. There are currently a couple of thousand RFCs, although many have become obsolete. To keep track of RFCs, each one is assigned a number that never changes. For example, RFC-796, written in 1981, deals with *Classful* IP network address mappings. RFCs are the last word on Internet standards, and can be found at the IETF's Web site (`http://www.ietf.org`). Like all UNIX systems, Linux has extensive built-in support for TCP/IP. This chapter discusses the essentials needed to understand and configure network services under Linux.

TCP/IP Basics

Before diving headfirst into the TCP/IP network stack, you may want to read up on some TCP/IP basics. If you're familiar with how TCP/IP works and would like to go straight to the nitty-gritty of configuring your Linux system, you can skip this part and jump straight to the "Configuring the Network" section of this chapter. Along the way you will find methods for configuring your network settings manually by editing the files and for using the graphical interface tools provided.

IP Addresses

Every network interface in a TCP/IP network is assigned a unique *IP address*. The IP address is used to identify and differentiate an interface from other interfaces on the network. In the current IPv4 specifications, an IP address is a 32-bit number. Think of this 32-bit number as a sequence of four 8-bit octets. Computers understand base 2 numbers

(1s and 0s), whereas humans tend to think in base 10 (0–9); we then convert each octet to decimal and separate the decimal values with periods. This 32-bit, 4-octet sequence of base 2--11000000 10101000 00000001 00000001--can now be represented as 192.168.1.1.

It is important to carefully select and keep track of IPs that are assigned to network interfaces. If the network is directly connected to the Internet, you may only assign IPs that have been set aside for your network by the Internet Assigned Numbers Authority (IANA). If the network isn't connected to the Internet, or is separated from the Internet by a firewall, addresses should be selected from the block of private network addresses discussed in the next section. The network administrator is the person responsible for assigning IP addresses within an organization. You should contact him before assigning an IP address to any device.

Dividing the Network

As its name implies, IP (Internet Protocol) was designed from the ground up for *internetworking*. This means it was designed for interconnecting networks. Thus, an IP address is divided into two parts: a *network part* and a *host part*. The network part distinguishes one network from another, whereas the host part identifies a particular host within that network.

Netmasks and Network Classes

The network mask (or *netmask*) identifies what part of the IP address represents the network number, and what part represents the host address. The netmask is another 32-bit number that is converted into four 8-bit octets, translated into decimal, and separated by periods (see Figure 20.1). The 1-bits in the netmask designate the network portion of an IP address. The 0-bits in the netmask correlate with the host portion of an IP address. For example, if a network interface were assigned the IP address of 172.17.24.83 (10101100 00010001 00011000 01010011) with a netmask of 255.255.0.0 (11111111 11111111 00000000 00000000), the network part of the IP address would be 172.17, and the unique host address within that network would be 24.83.

FIGURE 20.1

Netmasks help computers and switching equipment make distinctions between hosts and networks.

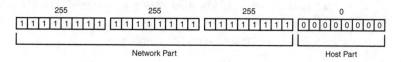

Each logical IP network has a network address and a broadcast address. The network address is used to identify the network itself, and is the lowest number (all 0-bits in the host part) in its respective IP network. The *broadcast address* is a special address that all of the devices in the IP network listen for, and is the highest number (has all 1s in the host part) in its respective IP network. This means that the number of assignable addresses is always two less than the actual range of numbers being used. If you had a network number of 192.168.1.0 and a netmask of 255.255.255.0, your broadcast address would be 192.168.1.255. You would have a maximum of 254 assignable host addresses, even though your actual range of numbers is 0–255.

Historically (due to RFC-796), depending on the first few bits of an IP address, networks were assumed to have default netmasks based on their network *class*. Class A networks have an 8-bit network part and a 24-bit host part. Class B networks have 16 bits each in the network and host parts. Class C networks have a 24-bit network part and an 8-bit host part. Class D networks are considered multicast addresses. See Table 20.1 for the octet-to-network class definition chart.

TABLE 20.1   Network Classes According to RFC-796

First Byte of Address	Default Network Class
1127 (Starts with 0)	A
128191 (Starts with 10)	B
192223 (Starts with 110)	C
224239 (Starts with 1110)	D
240254 (Starts with 1111)	Reserved

CIDR (Classless Interdomain Routing)

Although IP classifications are still used in the networking world, this way of thinking has been obsolete since the release of RFCs 1517, 1518, 1519, and 1520. Those RFCs define CIDR (Classless Interdomain Routing). One of the main reasons CIDR came to be was a lack of an appropriate network class size for a mid-sized company. The class C network, with a maximum of 254 host addresses, is too small; class B, which allows up to 65,534 addresses, is too large for an ethernet's limit of 12,000 attachments. The result is inefficient utilization of class B network numbers.

To begin thinking in terms of CIDR notation, here is a visual exercise that shows you how the netmask for a given range of IPs is calculated.

Assume you want to have communication starting with 10.168.0.0 all the way through 10.168.255.255. Understand that the netmask you use lets the computer know which IP networks to listen to, and which ones to mask out. To see this masking in action you would first need to visualize which bits are common between the two ranges. Wherever the bits match, the corresponding bit in the netmask becomes a 1.

> **Tip**
>
> To simplify the exchange of routing information, and to lower the odds of human error in defining a netmask, it is illegal to have discontiguous 1 bits in the netmask. Once you calculate the first 0 bit in the netmask, all of the remaining bits must be 0.

```
00001010 10101000 00000000 00000000 (10.168.0.0) Start of Range
00001010 10101000 11111111 11111111 (10.168.255.255) End of Range
================================================================
11111111 11111111 00000000 00000000 (255.255.0.0) Netmask
```

> **Tip**
>
> Because this example network starts with a 0 (00001010), it would have traditionally been called a class A network. By using the new rules defined by CIDR, it's now effectively in a class B size.

Instead of representing this network by its network number (lowest IP address of an IP network) and its netmask, in CIDR notation you simply count up all of the on bits (1s) in the netmask and represent this network as 10.168.0.0/16. This network is now said to be a 16-bit network. The traditional class C network is another example of a 16-bit network.

Subnetting

The act of dividing an IP network into smaller subnetworks is called *subnetting*. It is usually done when an organization has a block of addresses that it needs to share between two or more physically separate sites. For example, an organization may request a 24-bit block of addresses for use on the Internet, and then need to share those addresses between two offices. Instead of wasting two full 24-bit networks, you can cut the 24-bit network into two different networks by extending your netmask one more bit. This changes your netmask from 255.255.255.0 (24 1s, a.k.a. /24) to 255.255.255.128 (25 1s, a.k.a. /25). This netmask is applied to both of the newly created networks. Where you once had a network of 192.168.1.0/24, you now have two networks of 192.168.1.0/25 and 192.168.1.128/25. The 192.168.1.0/25 network has a host range of 0–127, where

20

192.168.1.0 is the network number and 192.168.1.127 is the broadcast. The second network has a host range of 128–255, where 192.168.1.128 is the network number and 192.168.1.255 is the broadcast.

To see why this works, try the visualization test shown before on the second network created:

```
11000000 10101000 00000001 10000000 (192.168.1.128)
11000000 10101000 00000001 11111111 (192.168.1.255)
=========================================================
11111111 11111111 11111111 10000000 (255.255.255.128 or 25-bit)
```

Supernetting

As you saw in the subnetting section, you simply added one bit to the network mask to split the network in half. To double the size of a network, you simply take away one bit from the network mask. To continue with the visualization tests, say you are working with the networks of 192.168.126.0/24 and 192.168.127.0/24. Now say you want to be able to have all of the IPs from both 24-bit networks communicate in their own expanded, or *super*, logical IP network. This would define the range of 192.168.126.0–192.168.127.255, which looks like this written out:

```
11000000 10101000 01111110 00000000 (192.168.126.0)
11000000 10101000 01111111 11111111 (192.168.127.255)
=========================================================
11111111 11111111 11111110 00000000 (255.255.254.0 or 23-bit)
```

The resulting netmask has 23 on (1) bits, so the new supernet is represented as 192.168.126.0/23. It has a network number of 192.168.126.0 and a broadcast of 192.168.127.255. There are now 510 assignable IPs in this logical IP network.

This prefix/bit-count notation does not work when joining just any ranges of numbers. For example, look at the range of 192.168.10.0–192.168.13.255:

```
11000000 10101000 00001010 00000000 (192.168.10.0)
11000000 10101000 00001011 00000000 (192.168.11.0)
11000000 10101000 00001100 00000000 (192.168.12.0)
11000000 10101000 00001101 11111111 (192.168.13.255)
=========================================================
11111111 11111111 111111?0 00000000
```

It is illegal to represent this range as 192.168.10.0/22 because it points to a different address range than expected. This can be very confusing to humans, and is bound to lead to error. If you applied the bit count to the address, you're referencing the same network as 192.168.8.0/22. To correctly write out this particular range, you must specify two networks: 192.168.10.0/23 and 192.168.12.0/23. Here's the general rule that lets you know whether the continuous base addresses may be grouped together: For the number X of continuous base addresses to have a common prefix (network number), X must be a power of two, and the last octet containing the network number must be evenly divisible by X.

With that rule in mind, revisit the 192.168.8.0/22 network. To apply the bit count (netmask) against the network prefix (network number), you can write out their binary values and visualize which ranges fall into the mask.

11000000 10101000 00001000 00000000 (192.168.8.0)
11111111 11111111 11111100 00000000 (255.255.252.0 or 22-bits)
==
11000000 10101000 00000111 00000000 (192.168.7.0 is masked out)
11000000 10101000 00001000 00000000 (192.168.8.0 obviously is in)
11000000 10101000 00001001 00000000 (192.168.9.0 is in)
11000000 10101000 00001010 00000000 (192.168.10.0 is in)
11000000 10101000 00001011 00000000 (192.168.11.0 is in)
11000000 10101000 00001100 00000000 (192.168.12.0 is masked out)

In this example, $X=4$, because we're combining four continuous base addresses--4 is a power of two, and 8 (the last octet of the base address) is evenly divisible by 4.

Reserved Network Numbers

There is also a standard reserved block of addresses, defined in RFC-1918, for use in *private networks*. These are networks that will never be connected directly to any public network (specifically the Internet). The private-network addressing standard is shown in Table 20.2.

TABLE 20.2 Private Network Addresses According to RFC-1918

Address Range	Network Class
10.0.0.0–10.255.255.255	A (1 class A network)
172.16.0.0–172.31.255.255	B (16 class B networks)
192.168.0.0–192.168.255.255	C (256 class C networks)

There is another reserved class A network, with addresses in the range of 127.0.0.0–127.255.255.255. This is known as the *loopback* network. It is a virtual network that points to the same host where the packet originates. The usual loopback address in any system is 127.0.0.1. If you want a program to connect to the localhost (the same system) it's running on, you can open a connection to 127.0.0.1. This is useful, for example, when running networking software in a system that isn't connected to a network, or for testing daemons on the local system.

> **Note**
>
> The Class C IP address ranges are intended as private-network addresses for use on internal LANs, especially since the terminals or workstations are not directly connected to the Internet. Most Red Hat Linux users will set up a gateway computer that then forwards or retrieves information for the LAN—this is known as IP masquerading.

Routing

Networks are connected by means of routers. A *router* is a device that has connections to two or more networks and takes care of moving packets between them. When a host sends out a packet whose destination lies in the same network, it sends it directly to the destination host. However, if the packet's destination lies in a different network, it sends the packet to a router so that the router will send it to the correct network. This is why it's so important to set a host's netmask correctly--it's the parameter that tells the host whether to send the packet directly to the destination host or to the router (see Figure 20.2).

FIGURE 20.2

Routers connect networks.

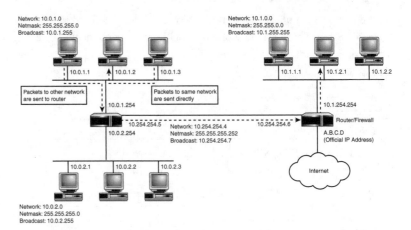

A network usually has a *default router*, which connects it to other networks. In such a setup, all traffic whose destination is outside the local network gets sent to the default router. There may be several routers in a network; for example, one to the Internet and another one to other internal networks. In this case, it may be necessary to use a *static route* to tell the host to send packets destined for specific subnets to a specific router, or use *dynamic routing* by means of a routing daemon (such as `igrpd` or `routed`). These daemons are discussed in the "Network Daemons" section later in this chapter.

The TCP/IP Protocol Suite

TCP/IP is actually not just one protocol, but a protocol suite. At the low level, it's composed of the following protocols:

- IP
- TCP
- UDP

IP is the lowest common denominator of TCP/IP. Every protocol at a higher level must eventually be translated into IP packets. An IP packet is self-contained in the sense that it contains within itself the addresses of its source and destination. However, it may be part of a larger conversation.

TCP is a *connection-based* or *stream-oriented* protocol on top of IP. This means that an application that communicates with another using TCP sends and receives data as a stream of bytes, and the TCP/IP stack takes care of splitting the data into packets and putting the packets back together again in the receiving end. It also ensures that the packets arrive in order and requests retransmission of missing and corrupt packets.

On the other hand, the UDP protocol is a *datagram-based* or *packet-oriented* protocol. It is a connectionless protocol. This protocol does not have built-in checking to ensure that the packets arrive in order, or to check for missing packets. However, due to this missing protocol overhead, UDP can be quite efficient for use with applications that send small amounts of information, or on a network that is fast and reliable, such as Ethernet on a private LAN.

Application-specific protocols work on top of TCP and UDP. Some of these follow:

- SMTP (Simple Mail Transfer Protocol)
- HTTP (Hypertext Transfer Protocol)
- FTP (File Transfer Protocol)
- SNMP (Simple Network Management Protocol)
- NFS (Network Filesystem)

Each has different characteristics, depending on its intended use. Figure 20.3 shows the layers of the TCP/IP suite and the corresponding layers in the OSI reference model. The OSI model was never widely adopted. It consisted of seven layers: application, presentation, session, transport, network, (data) link, and physical.

FIGURE 20.3

TCP/IP is a proto-col suite com-posed of several layers.

Application	Telnet, FTP, HTTP, etc...
Transport	TCP, UDP, etc...
Network	IP and others
Link	Network interface and device driver

Ports

A single computer may host several services. To distinguish one service from the next, something more is needed than just the host's IP address. You use different ports on the computer to respond to specified services (see Figure 20.4). *Ports* are analogous to the jacks in an old-fashioned manual switchboard.

FIGURE 20.4

A single computer may host different services in differ-ent ports.

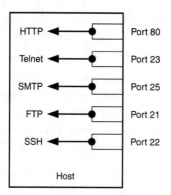

A server daemon can be configured to listen on any port. However, things would be very complicated if this decision were entirely arbitrary, because there would be no easy way of finding out what port a given service was listening on. To help, some *well-known ports* have been defined in RFC-1700. Some of these well-known ports are listed in Table 20.3.

TABLE 20.3   Some Well-Known Port Numbers

Port/Protocol	Name	Use
7/tcp	echo	Echoes everything it receives
13/tcp	daytime	Sends back the current date and time
22/tcp	ssh	Secure Shell
23/tcp	telnet	Remote terminal emulation

TABLE 20.3 continued

Port/Protocol	Name	Use
25/tcp	smtp	Email transfer
53/udp	domain	Domain Name System
80/tcp	www	World Wide Web traffic
110/tcp	pop3	Post Office Protocol, version 3
443/tcp	https	Secure Web traffic

Sockets

In network parlance, a *socket* is a network connection between two processes, which may be running on the same or different computers. Technically, an *open socket* has four parts: source host, source port, destination host, destination port. A *closed socket* has only the source port and source host.

Note that a socket has ports on both sides of the connection. When a client tries to connect to a server, it first asks the system for a *free* port (one that isn't being used by any other program). It then asks the system to connect to a destination host and port using that source port. That is why there can be several programs connected between the same two hosts; for example, a browser can have two or more windows open to the same host. The system keeps track of both the source and the destination port, and has different sockets for each connection.

Configuring the Network

In Red Hat, basic network configuration is generally done at installation time, when configuring the base system, but network interfaces may be added or deleted at any time. As with other UNIX systems, all configuration data is stored in text files in the /etc tree.

An important thing to consider is that Linux, like other UNIX systems, can be reconfigured on-the-fly. In other words, almost any parameter can be changed while the system is operating, without rebooting. This makes it easy to experiment and correct configuration problems. However, if you are new to making permanent configuration changes, it is recommended that you reboot after making any important configuration changes, to ensure the correct configuration will be used when the system reboots.

If you are new to Red Hat Linux and simply want to configure your network to get your system running or to make basic changes to an existing configuration, then the following section is for you. It will quickly outline how to make changes to your network

20

TCP/IP NETWORK MANAGEMENT

configuration without having to edit individual files. If you want to perform more advanced tasks such as setting up routing functions, ipchains, or IP masquerading, then you may want to skip to the next section. This section will walk you through changing and setting hostnames, IP addresses, the default gateway, DNS, and routes to other networks using `linuxconf`.

The next section deals with configuring the network by editing the files stored in `/etc`. NIS is covered in Chapter 15, "NIS: Network Information Service."

Configuration Files

The most important network configuration files in a Linux system follow:

- `/etc/sysconfig/network`
- `/etc/HOSTNAME`
- `/etc/hosts`
- `/etc/services`
- `/etc/host.conf`
- `/etc/nsswitch.conf`
- `/etc/resolv.conf`

Each is covered in turn. All of these files can be modified while a system is running. Modifications (except for `/etc/sysconfig/network`) take place immediately, without having to start or stop any daemons. Note that most of these files accept comments beginning with a hash (#) symbol. Each of these files has an entry in section 5 of the UNIX manual, so you can access them with the `man` command.

Network Setup: `/etc/sysconfig/network`

The network file contains information that will control how other network-related files and daemons get populated. Here is a sample network file:

```
NETWORKING=yes
FORWARD_IPV4=false
HOSTNAME=ltorvalds.tech.access.com
DOMAINNAME=tech.access.com
GATEWAY=205.185.225.1
GATEWAYDEV=eth0
NISDOMAIN=looneytunes
```

This file is best edited through the GUI tool `linuxconf`. This tool requires you to have display access to an X server. If you installed Red Hat Linux 7 and took the defaults, then you will have installed the Gnome desktop. `linuxconf` can be accessed through the Gnome desktop by clicking on the Gnome starting point (that's the little footprint at the bottom left of your screen that looks like the capital letter "G") and following the sequence of menus (Programs, System, Linuxconf).

Hostname: `/etc/HOSTNAME`

The `/etc/HOSTNAME` file contains just one line with the primary name of the host. This file gets its content at boot time from the HOSTNAME line in the `/etc/sysconfig/network` file. This file is used when booting to set the primary hostname of the system. Here's an example of the `/etc/HOSTNAME` file:

`mycomputer`

Using `linuxconf`, the hostname is found under Networking, Client Tasks, Basic Host Information on the Host Name tab. Figure 20.5 shows the field in which this is done. After making changes click the Accept button followed by the Act/Changes button. Click Quit to exit the program.

FIGURE 20.5

The Host Name + Domain field can be used to change both your computer name and your domain.

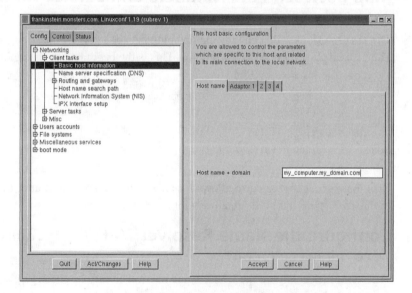

Map Between IP Addresses and Hostnames: `/etc/hosts`

The `/etc/hosts` file contains the mapping between IP addresses and hostnames, and *aliases* for hostnames. IP addresses were designed to be easily readable by computers, but it's hard for people to remember them. That's why the `/etc/hosts` file was created. Here's an example of the `/etc/hosts` file:

```
127.0.0.1      localhost
192.168.1.1    mycomputer
192.168.1.2    server
192.168.1.3    router
192.168.3.45   othercomputer    otheralias
199.183.24.133   www.redhat.com
```

In this case, `othercomputer` also has an alias. It can also be referred to as `otheralias`.

In practice, `/etc/hosts` usually contains the host's name, the localhost entry, and system aliases that the systems administrator commonly uses, although it is perfectly acceptable to maintain a small table of all available hosts on a small LAN in this file. Other host-names are usually resolved using the Internet's Domain Name Service (DNS) possibly provided by a local, but more often, a remote server.. The client portion of DNS is configured in the `/etc/resolv.conf` file.

Map Between Port Numbers and Service Names: `/etc/services`

The `/etc/services` file contains the mapping between port numbers and service names. This is used by several system programs. This is the beginning of the default `/etc/services` file installed by Red Hat:

```
tcpmux      1/tcp                    # TCP port service multiplexer
echo        7/tcp
echo        7/udp
discard     9/tcp      sink null
discard     9/udp      sink null
systat      11/tcp     users
```

Note that `/etc/services` also allows for aliases, which are placed after the port number. In this case, `sink` and `null` are aliases for the `discard` service.

Configure the Name Resolver: `/etc/host.conf` and `/etc/nsswitch.conf`

These two files configure the UNIX name resolver library by specifying where the system will find its name information. `/etc/host.conf` is the file used by version 5 of the libc library, whereas `/etc/nsswitch.conf` is used by version 6 (also known as glibc). The important thing is that some programs will use one and some will use the other, so it's best to have both files configured correctly.

`/etc/host.conf`

The `/etc/host.conf` file specifies the order in which the different name systems (`/etc/hosts` file, DNS, NIS) will be searched when resolving hostnames. Each line of the `/etc/host.conf` file should consist of one of the following directives, followed by a parameter:

Directive	Function
order	Indicates the order in which services will be queried. Its parameter may be any combination of lookup methods separated by commas. The lookup methods supported are bind, hosts, and nis; respectively, DNS, /etc/hosts, and NIS.
trim	Indicates a domain that will be trimmed of the hostname when doing an IP address-to-hostname translation via DNS. trim may be included several times for several domains. trim doesn't affect /etc/hosts or NIS lookups. You should take care that hosts are listed appropriately (with or without full domain names) in the /etc/hosts file and in the NIS tables.
multi	Controls whether a query to the name system will always return only one result, or whether it may return several results. Its parameter may be either on, meaning that several results may be returned when appropriate, or off, meaning that just one result will be returned. Default value is off.
nospoof	Controls a security feature to prevent hostname spoofing. If nospoof is on, after every name-to-IP lookup a reverse IP-to-name lookup will be made. If the names don't match, the operation will fail. Valid parameters are on or off. Default value is off.
alert	If the nospoof directive is on, alert controls whether spoofing attempts will be logged through the syslog facility Default value is off.
reorder	If set to on, all lookups will be reordered so that hosts on the same subnet will be returned first. Default value is off.

This is the default /etc/host.conf file included with Red Hat:

```
order hosts,bind
```

This indicates that lookups will be done first to the /etc/hosts file and then to DNS. If several hosts match, all will be returned. This file is appropriate for most installations, although installations using NIS or where the nospoof behavior is desired will have to modify it.

/etc/nsswitch.conf

The /etc/nsswitch.conf file was originally created by Sun Microsystems to manage the order in which several configuration files are looked for in the system. As such, it includes more functionality than the /etc/host.conf file.

Each line of /etc/nsswitch.conf is either a comment (which starts with a hash sign), or a keyword followed by a colon and a list of methods listed in the order they will be tried.

20

TCP/IP NETWORK MANAGEMENT

Each keyword is the name to one of the /etc files that can be controlled by /etc/nsswitch.conf. The keywords that can be included follow:

Keyword (Filename)	Function
aliases	Mail aliases
passwd	System users
group	User groups
shadow	Shadow passwords
hosts	Hostnames and IP addresses
networks	Network names and numbers
protocols	Network protocols
services	Port numbers and service names
ethers	Ethernet numbers
rpc	Remote Procedure Call names and numbers
netgroup	Networkwide groups

The methods that can be included follow:

Method	Meaning
files	Valid for all keywords except netgroup. Look for record in the corresponding /etc file.
db	Valid for all keywords except netgroup. Look record up in the corresponding database in the /var/db directory. This is useful for extremely long files, such as passwd files with more than 500 entries. To create these files from the standard /etc files, cd into /var/db and run the make command.
compat	Compatibility mode, valid for passwd, group, and shadow files. In this mode, lookups are made first to the corresponding /etc file. If you want to do NIS lookup of the corresponding NIS database, you need to include a line where the first field (username or groupname) is a plus character, followed by an appropriate number of colons (six for /etc/passwd, three for /etc/group, eight for /etc/shadow). For example, in /etc/password, the following line would have to be included at the end:

Method	Meaning
	+:*:::::. The asterisk (*) in this string is representative of an account without a password used for programs that run as a user, but there is no way to log on from a prompt as that user. For example, the *innd* process runs as *news* and retrieves news and stores it in a directory owned by *news* but there is no way to log on as the user *news*.
dns	Valid only for the hosts entry. Lookups are made to the DNS as configured in /etc/resolv.conf.
nis	Valid for all files. Lookups are made to the NIS server if NIS is active.
[*STATUS=action*]	Controls the actions of the Name Service. *STATUS* is one of SUCCESS (operation was successful), NOTFOUND (record was not found), UNAVAIL (selected service was unavailable), or TRYAGAIN (service temporarily unavailable, try again). *action* is one of return (stop lookup and return current status) or continue (continue with next item in this line). For example, a line like hosts: dns nis [NOTFOUND=return] files would result in looking up the host first in DNS and then in NIS. Only if neither of these were available would the /etc/hosts file be used.

This is a typical /etc/nsswitch.conf configured to use the local files for everything, and adds the ability to do DNS-based hostname queries:

```
passwd:         compat
group:          compat
shadow:         compat

hosts:          files dns
networks:       files

protocols:      db files
services:       db files
ethers:         db files
rpc:            db files

netgroup:       db files
```

With this configuration, all names except network names will be looked up first in /var/db (for efficiency). If not found there, it will be looked up in the corresponding /etc files. There are quite a few databases that could be looked up via NIS if an appropriate entry exists in the corresponding database.

Configure the DNS Client: `/etc/resolv.conf`

The `/etc/resolv.conf` file configures the DNS client. It contains the host's domain name search order and the addresses of the DNS servers. Each line should contain a keyword and one or more parameters separated by spaces. The following keywords are valid:

Keyword	Meaning
nameserver	Its single parameter indicates the IP address of the DNS server. There may be several nameserver lines, each with a single IP address. nameservers will be queried in the order they appear in the file. nameservers after the first one will only be queried if the first nameserver doesn't respond.
domain	Its single parameter indicates the host's domain name. This is used by several programs, such as the email system, and is also used when doing a DNS query for a host with no domain name (with no periods, for example). If there's no domain name, the hostname will be used, removing everything before the first dot.
search	Its multiple parameters indicate the domain name search order. If a query is made for a host with no domain name, the host will be looked up consecutively in each of the domains indicated by the search keyword. Note that domain and search are mutually exclusive; if both appear, the last one that appears is used.
sortlist	Allows sorting the returned domain names in a specific order. Its parameters are specified in network/netmask pairs, allowing for arbitrary sorting orders.

There is no generic default `/etc/resolv.conf` file provided with Red Hat. Its contents are built dynamically depending on options given at installation time. This is an example `/etc/resolv.conf` file:

```
search my.domain.com other.domain.com
nameserver 10.1.1.1
nameserver 10.10.10.1
sortlist 10.1.1.0/255.255.255.0 10.0.0.0/255.0.0.0
```

This file indicates that unqualified hosts will be searched first as `host.my.domain.com` and then as `host.other.domain.com`. The nameserver at IP address 10.1.1.1 will be contacted first. If that server doesn't answer after a timeout, the server at 10.10.10.1 will be contacted. If several hosts are returned, the hosts in the class C network 10.1.1.0 will be returned first, followed by any other hosts in the class A network 10.0.0.0, followed by any other hosts.

Again, if you are not comfortable editing the actual configuration file, you may use `linuxconf` to edit the file for you. Just bring up `linuxconf` and select Networking, Client Tasks and click on Name Server Specification (DNS), as shown is Figure 20.6. The default domain is the domain your computer is connected to. The IP of name server 1 is the IP address of the first domain name server in the domain name server search order. You may add up to three of these. Although only one is needed, the more the better. The Search Domain 1 through 6 fields will aid your computer in locating hosts on remote networks. If you are not sure what information to put here, contact your system administrator or the help desk for your Internet service provider.

FIGURE 20.6

Note that only the first two fields are required. The rest are optional.

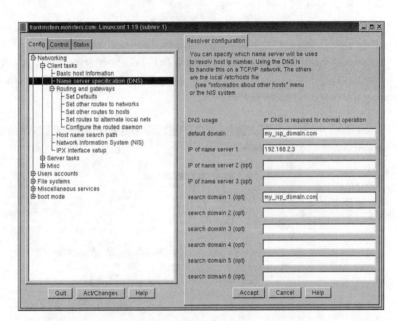

Host Address, Netmask, and Default Router

Like many other UNIX flavors and Linux distributions, Red Hat configures the network automatically during startup. A few pertinent questions are asked during the installation process to set up initial networking devices. But, for the most part, it is very easy to add devices later on, and the system edits all the needed files for you on-the-fly. While logged in as `root` the user can use `linuxconf` to make changes without actually editing the files themselves. This may be the preferable way of making changes to these files for the novice or new user. Figure 20.5, earlier in the chapter, illustrates the first screen the user is shown under the Basic Host Information heading. Once again, the Host Name tab is where you can set your hostname. The tab marked Adaptor 1 is used to configure your ethernet card. The subsequent tabs are for configuring additional ethernet cards. The Adaptor 1 tab is shown in Figure 20.7. You will see there is a button for enabling or disabling the ethernet card. There are buttons for manual, Dhcp, and Bootp configuration modes. Before you go too far, keep in mind that if you are using your computer on a network that uses Dhcp you may click that button and your IP address and network mask will be set for you automatically. There is a field for your Primary Name + Domain, which is the name of your computer and the domain name of the network you are on.

There is also a field for your Aliases. This field is optional. An alias is a nickname you pick for yourself. Put your assigned IP address in the IP Address field. If you selected Dhcp, then once again this is automatically assigned and you need not bother with it. This field contains the IP address assigned to your computer.

The Netmask field is optional and is assigned automatically if you are using the Dhcp mode as well. The Net Device field uniquely identifies your ethernet card to the operating system. Engineers always start counting with the number zero, so if you only have one network card, it will be called eth0 (*eth* being the abbreviation for your ethernet card and *0* being the first designated device).

FIGURE 20.7

If the Dhcp option is selected, the IP Address and Subnet Mask Information fields can be left blank.

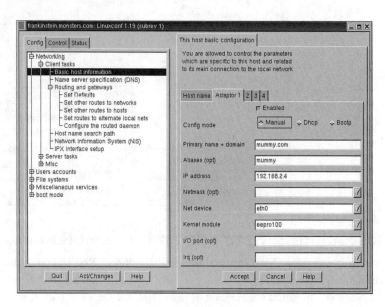

The `/etc/init.d/network` file contains variables specifying the IP address, netmask, network, broadcast address, and default router. This is an example of the relevant section of the file:

```
IPADDR=10.1.1.10
NETMASK=255.255.255.0
NETWORK=10.0.1.0
BROADCAST=10.1.1.255
GATEWAY=10.1.1.1
```

The variable names are self-documenting. The GATEWAY variable specifies the default router.

Configuration Programs

The files detailed in the preceding section serve to configure many general network para meters. Most of these networking options can be modified dynamically just by editing the proper file. linuxconf can be used to do this editing for you. However, linuxconf does not always make the changes dynamically so that changes will take effect immediately. Configuring the host's IP address and routing table dynamically may require special commands.

Configure the Host's Network Interfaces: ifconfig

The /sbin/ifconfig program is used to configure a host's network interfaces. This includes basic configuration such as IP address, netmask and broadcast address, as well as advanced options such as setting the remote address for a point-to-point link (such as a PPP link).

Under Linux, all network interfaces have names composed of the driver name followed by a number. These are some of the network driver names supported by Linux:

Driver Name	Device Type
eth	Ethernet
tr	Token Ring
ppp	Point-to-Point Protocol
slip	Serial Line IP
plip	Parallel Line IP

Interfaces are numbered starting from 0 in the order the kernel finds them, and the devices are created in memory. By default, the Linux kernel will only find one network interface. If you have several network cards, you need to add a line like the following to the /etc/lilo.conf file and then re-run the /sbin/lilo command:

```
append="ether=IRQ,I/O,eth1 ether=IRQ,I/O,eth2"
```

This tells the kernel to add two more Ethernet devices--eth1 and eth2--whose cards are at the IRQ and I/O address specified. If you want the kernel to autoprobe the cards' I/O addresses and IRQs, you can use 0 for IRQ and I/O.

Basic Interface Configuration

This is the basic form of the ifconfig command:

```
ifconfig interface IP-address [netmask netmask] \
➡ broadcast broadcast-address
```

This form of the `ifconfig` command can only be used by `root`. The netmask and broadcast parameters are optional. If they are omitted, `ifconfig` gets their values from the default class for the IP address (see "Netmasks and Network Classes" in this chapter for more details). They should be included if subnetting is being used.

This command will load the proper network driver and configure the interface.

Caution

The command will do exactly as it's told: It won't check whether the broadcast address corresponds to the IP address and netmask supplied, so be careful!

Tip

It's not enough to configure the interface. You need to tell the kernel how to get to the hosts on the network connected to that interface using the `route add` command (see "Manipulating the Routing Table" later in this chapter). You can avoid using the command line by using `linuxconf`. Click on the Adapter 1 tab and you will see the information used by your NIC (Network Interface Card). On this screen you can enable or disable your NIC. You can set the configuration mode of the NIC for Manual (static), Dhcp, or Bootp mode. You can set your hostname, your IP address and mask, specify the name of the network device, and specify the kernel module required for your particular device. If you should require it, you can specify the I/O port number and IRQ setting as well. Once the desired changes have been made, click Accept.

Enabling and Disabling an Interface

An interface can also be temporarily brought down (*deactivated*) and brought back up without having to be reconfigured. This is useful for temporarily disabling a server's network connection (such as when reconfiguring a critical service). This is done with the following commands:

```
ifconfig interface down
ifconfig interface up
```

These forms of the `ifconfig` command can be used only by `root`.

Checking Interface Status

If you want to know the status of a network interface, just issue the command `ifconfig` *interface*. If you want to know the status of all active interfaces, use `ifconfig -a`.

These versions of the `ifconfig` command can be used by any user. They show all of the configuration information for an interface, including its IP address, subnet mask, broadcast address, and physical (hardware) address. (The hardware address is set by the network card's manufacturer.) They also display the interface status, such as whether it is up or down and whether it's a loopback interface. They show other information as well: the *Maximum Transfer Unit* (the size of the largest packet that can be sent through that interface), the network card's I/O address and IRQ number, the number of packets received and sent, and collisions.

You can also check the status of an interface with the `ifconfig -a` command. This prints out all of the interfaces that are currently active with their parameters. Here's an example of the output of `ifconfig -a`:

```
$ /sbin/ifconfig -a
lo        Link encap:Local Loopback
          inet addr:127.0.0.1  Bcast:127.255.255.255  Mask:255.0.0.0
          UP BROADCAST LOOPBACK RUNNING  MTU:3584  Metric:1
          RX packets:1600 errors:0 dropped:0 overruns:0 frame:0
          TX packets:1600 errors:0 dropped:0 overruns:0 carrier:0
          Collisions:0

eth0      Link encap:Ethernet  HWaddr 00:20:87:3E:F0:61
          inet addr:10.0.1.10  Bcast:10.0.1.255  Mask:255.255.255.0
          UP BROADCAST RUNNING MULTICAST  MTU:1500  Metric:1
          RX packets:90506 errors:0 dropped:0 overruns:0 frame:0
          TX packets:92691 errors:0 dropped:0 overruns:0 carrier:1
          Collisions:667
          Interrupt:3 Base address:0x310
```

Network Aliasing--One Interface, Several Addresses

It is sometimes useful for a single network interface to have multiple IP addresses. For example, a server may be running several services, but you may want clients to access different IP addresses for each service to make reconfiguration easier in the future (if you need to split some services off to another server, for example).

Linux, like most other UNIX flavors, provides a feature called *network aliasing*, which does just what its name implies. To be able to use network aliasing, you must have reconfigured and recompiled your kernel, and enabled the Network Aliasing and IP: Aliasing Support options in the Networking Options configuration section. The options can be either compiled into the kernel or compiled as modules.

Once you are running a kernel with aliasing enabled, creating an alias is as easy as issuing a standard `ifconfig` command. All you need to do is append a colon and an alias number to the interface name. Here is an example:

```
ifconfig eth0:0 10.1.1.1 netmask 255.255.255.0 broadcast 10.1.1.255
```

This creates an alias `eth0:0` for Ethernet interface eth0, with the provided parameters.

To automate the creation of an alias each time the host boots, you can add the command to create it to `/etc/init.d/network`.

Other `ifconfig` Options

There are other options to `ifconfig` for some special circumstances:

`ifconfig` *interface* *local-address* `pointtopoint` *remote-address* will enable a Point-to-Point interface--one that connects only to a single other host, not to a network. The interface must also be enabled in the remote host, switching the *local-address* and *remote-address* parameters.

`ifconfig` *interface* *local-address* `tunnel` *remote-address* will create an IPv4 tunnel between two IPv6 networks. IPv4 is the current TCP/IP standard on the Internet. IPv6 is the next-generation IP standard. If there are two IPv6 networks that need to be connected via the Internet, a tunnel that uses the IPv4 protocol must be made.

Manipulating the Routing Table: `route`

The `/sbin/route` command manipulates the kernel's routing table. This table is used by the kernel to see what needs to be done to each packet that leaves the host--whether to send it directly to the destination host or to a gateway, and on which network interface to send it.

The general form of the `route` command follows:

`route` *options* *command* *parameters*

Viewing the Routing Table

The simplest form of the command (with no options and no command) simply outputs the routing table. This form of the command can be used by any user:

```
$ /sbin/route
Kernel IP routing table
Destination     Gateway         Genmask         Flags Metric Ref    Use Iface
localnet        *               255.255.255.0   U     0      0       16 eth0
127.0.0.0       *               255.0.0.0       U     0      0        2 lo
default         router.company. 0.0.0.0         UG    0      0       71 eth0
```

The output has eight columns:

1. The first column (`Destination`) indicates the route destination. The name is substituted if a corresponding entry exists in either `/etc/hosts` or `/etc/networks`. The special name `default` indicates the default gateway.

2. The second column (Gateway) indicates the gateway through which packets to this destination are sent. An asterisk (*) means that packets will be sent directly to the destination host.

3. The third column (Genmask) indicates the netmask that applies to this route. The netmask is applied to the value in the Destination column.

4. The fourth column (Flags) can have several values. The most common flags are

   U   Route is up. This route is enabled.

   H   Target is a host. This is a static route to a specific host (see "Host-Based Static Routes" later in this chapter).

   G   Use a gateway. That packet will not be sent directly to the destination host. The gateway will be used instead.

5. The fifth column (Metric) indicates the distance to the target. This is used by some routing daemons to dynamically calculate the best route to get to a target host.

6. The sixth column (Ref) isn't used in the Linux kernel. In other UNIX systems it indicates the number of references to this route.

7. The seventh column (Use) is the number of times the kernel has performed a lookup for the route.

8. The eighth column (Iface) shows the name of the interface through which packets directed to this route will be sent.

There will always be at least one active route--the localhost route, which is set up in the /etc/init.d/network script. There should also be at least one route per network interface, pointing to the network the interface is connected to.

The -n option modifies the display slightly. It doesn't do host or network name lookups, displaying instead numerical addresses:

```
$ /sbin/route -n
Kernel IP routing table
Destination     Gateway         Genmask         Flags Metric Ref    Use Iface
10.0.1.0        0.0.0.0         255.255.255.0   U     0      0       16 eth0
127.0.0.0       0.0.0.0         255.0.0.0       U     0      0        2 lo
0.0.0.0         10.0.1.254      0.0.0.0         UG    0      0       71 eth0
```

In this case, the default destination and the * gateway are replaced by the address 0.0.0.0. This output format is often more useful than the standard output format because there is no ambiguity as to where things are going.

20

TCP/IP NETWORK
MANAGEMENT

> **Tip**
>
> If you issue a `route` command and it hangs, press Ctrl+C to interrupt it and issue `route -n`. Issuing `route` without the `-n` parameter causes it to do a reverse lookup of every IP in the routing table. If DNS is configured and the host is currently not connected to the network, issuing `route` by itself can take a long time.

Manipulating the Routing Table

The `route` command also adds and removes routes from the routing table. This is done via the following commands:

```
route add|del -net|-host target gw gateway \
➥netmask netmask dev interface
```

The `add` or `del` commands indicate, respectively, whether you want to add or delete a route.

The optional `-net` or `-host` options indicate whether you want to operate on a net or a host route. (See the following "Host-Based Static Routes" section for more information on net or host routes.) Providing it to eliminate any ambiguity is usually best. (For example, the address 10.0.1.0 can be either the network address of a class C network, or the address of a host in a class A or B network.)

The `target` parameter is the host address or network number of the destination. You would use the keyword `default` as the target for setting or deleting the default route.

The optional `gateway` parameter indicates which gateway to use for this route. If omitted, the `route` command assumes that the host or network is connected directly to this host. It's important to add a route to the local network after configuring an interface with `ifconfig`:

```
# /sbin/ifconfig eth0 10.1.1.1 netmask 255.255.255.0 broadcast 10.0.1.255
# /sbin/route add -net 10.1.1.0
```

As its name implies, the optional `netmask` parameter sets the netmask for the route, which will be applied to the `target` address. If omitted, the netmask will be taken either from the default netmask for the IP address or (in the case of routes to local networks) from the interface's netmask. (See "Netmasks and Network Classes" earlier in this chapter for more information on the default netmask.)

The optional `dev` parameter sets the interface on which the packets to this destination will be sent. If omitted, the `route` command checks the current routing table to find which interface has a route to the `gateway`. If no `gateway` is provided, it determines which interface can be used to get directly to the `target`.

> **Warning**
>
> In linuxconf there is a screen called Configure the routed Daemon. This will remain by default in the Does Not Export Any Routes (Silent) mode for most users. Making changes to the way your routed daemon behaves may cause undesirable behavior on the part of your system. Unless you are configuring your system to perform routing functions, leave this alone.

Host-Based Static Routes

Although the route command is most often used to manipulate *network* routes (those that point to a remote network), sometimes it is necessary to add routes to specific hosts. This can be necessary, for example, if a host is connected through a point-to-point link (for example, through a modem or serial cable). See Figure 20.8 for an example.

FIGURE 20.8
Host-based static routes are needed when a host is connected via a point-to-point link.

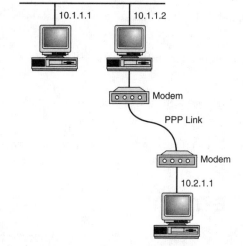

In this example, host 10.1.1.1 won't know how to get to host 10.2.1.1 without the following route command:

```
# /sbin/route add -host 10.2.1.1 gw 10.1.1.2
```

Checking Network Status: netstat

The /bin/netstat command displays the status of all TCP/IP network services. It has several options, depending on the information you want to display.

netstat by itself lists all connected sockets. The -a (all) option lists all open or listening sockets, not just those that have connections. The information listed for each socket includes

- The protocol (tcp or udp).
- Number of bytes currently in the send and receive queues (bytes that the local process hasn't read or that the remote process hasn't acknowledged).
- Addresses of the local and remote hosts. The remote host address is displayed as *:* for sockets that are in LISTEN state.
- Socket state. This can be ESTABLISHED, SYN_SENT, SYN_RECV, FIN_WAIT1, FIN_WAIT2, TIME_WAIT, CLOSED, CLOSE_WAIT, LAST_ACK, LISTEN, CLOSING, or UNKNOWN. In general, the SYN_ states indicate that a connection is in the process of being opened, the _WAIT states indicate the socket is in the process of being closed, ESTABLISHED means the socket is connected, LISTEN means a daemon is waiting for clients to connect, and CLOSED means the socket is unused.

The netstat -e (extended) option lists, in addition to this information, the user currently using the socket.

netstat -r (routes) lists the routing table. It lists the same information as the route command with no parameters.

netstat -i (interfaces) lists the network interfaces and statistics on each interface. It displays the same statistics as the ifconfig argument, but is in table form for easy parsing.

As with the route command, you can also add the -n option to view numeric IP addresses instead of hostnames.

Network Daemons

A *daemon* is a program that waits for another program to ask it to do something. Network daemons in particular are similar to the jacks in an operator's switchboard. They create one or more sockets and listen to those sockets, waiting for another process to connect. In Linux, as with most variants of UNIX, network services can be provided in one of two ways: as standalone daemons where they handle each session themselves or incorporated into another configuration (such as inetd) that handles the connections and disconnections for it.

Standalone TCP/IP Daemons

Originally, all UNIX network servers were standalone daemons. When you wanted to start a server, you ran a program that created the socket and listened to it. Many UNIX server programs still run in this manner. Examples are Squid, the Web cache/proxy server; Samba, the SMB file/print server; Apache, the Web server, and many others (see Chapter 12, "Apache Server," and Chapter 17, "Samba").

Even though they have many functions, most network daemons usually share a few characteristics:

- Their names end with a *d* (for *daemon*).
- They respond to the HUP signal (HANG UP signal; read man 7 signal for more information) by rereading their configuration files. The HUP signal is sent by the kill -HUP command.
- They are usually started at boot time by scripts in the /etc/init.d directory. These scripts minimally accept the start and stop parameters to start and end the daemons. Most of them accept the restart parameter to tell the daemon to reread its configuration files.
- When they receive a request, they create another copy of themselves to service it. Thus, there may be several copies of each daemon running simultaneously at any given time.

Networking Service Control

In the standalone daemon model, each service you run on a server has a corresponding daemon. This poses several problems:

- If you have many services on a server, you need to have many daemons running, even if they are idle. Although inactive daemons will probably be swapped out to disk, they still take up valuable resources, such as virtual memory and process table entries.
- There is no centralized way of modifying the daemons to provide services such as encryption or access control. Each daemon program must be modified to provide these services.
- If a daemon dies because of user or programmer error, the service will not be available until it is restarted. The restart procedure can be automated, but then the program that restarts the daemon can also die.
- Programming a network daemon isn't easy, especially because most daemons must be multithreaded. Being multithreaded enables them to manage several requests at once.

20

TCP/IP NETWORK MANAGEMENT

Eventually someone came up with a solution. How about a single daemon that could be configured to listen to any number of sockets and transfer control to different programs when it was needed? This daemon would also take care of multithreading and of managing the sockets. Thus was born `inetd`, the original so-called "Internet super-server." This is the time we should mention a relatively new addition to Red Hat Linux: `xinetd`. This program is meant to be a secure replacement for `inetd`. Though not completely secure, it is much more secure than `inetd`.

Configuring xinetd

`xinetd` has built-in access control features for stopping connections from undesired clients or only allowing desired connections. It can limit the number of incoming connections, number of incoming connections from specific hosts, or total number of connections for a service. This feature is particularly useful for assistance in thwarting what is known as DdoS (Distributed Denial of Service) attacks. It can limit access to services based on access time of day. `xinetd` can have services bind to specific IPs. This lets you provide different services to internal clients than external clients. `xinetd` is installed at installation time with Red Hat Linux if you select the Everything option for your installation.

When `xinetd` is installed, a Perl script is supplied in the same directory as the `xinetd` binary that conveniently converts an `inetd.conf` into an `xinetd.conf`. It may be run when you are logged in as `root` by typing the string **/usr/sbin/xconv.pl < /etc/inetd.conf > /tmp/xinetd.conf**, where /usr/sbin is your path to the `xinetd` executable. The `xinetd.conf` looks much like a legacy `inetd.conf` file and may be edited much the same as well. As with most subjects with regard to Red Hat Linux, an entire chapter could be written on `xinetd`. You may read more in depth about `xinetd` at `http://www.synack.org/xinetd/`. Here are some of the keywords most commonly used when configuring this new "Super Server":

`wait`	This attribute determines if the service is single-threaded or multi-threaded. If its value is yes the service is single-threaded; this means that `xinetd` will start the server and then it will stop handling requests for the service until the server dies. If the attribute value is no, the service is multithreaded and `xinetd` will keep handling new service requests.
`user`	Determines the `uid` for the server process. The user name must exist in /etc/passwd. This attribute is ineffective if the effective user ID of `xinetd` is not superuser.
`group`	Determines the `gid` for the server process. The group name must exist in /etc/group. If a group is not specified, the group of user will be used (from /etc/passwd). This attribute is ineffective if the effective user ID of `xinetd` is not superuser.

EXIT   Logs the fact that a server exited along with the exit status or the termination signal (the process id is also logged if the PID option is used).

DURATION   Logs the duration of a service session.

Novell Support

There is support built in for the Novell SPX and IPX protocols. The interface setup screen in linuxconf is used for configuring information required to access networked resources on a Novell network using the IPX/SPX protocols. The Enable button on the introductory screen must be pressed in order to use this option. The subsequent information required on the Adapter 1 and Internal Net tabs can be obtained by your Novell network administrator.

You can (as root) control what services are started or not run during bootup by using the ntsysv command. However, you should know that you'll shut off all networking services unless you run xinetd. A much better approach is to edit its configuaration files, found under the /etc directory, and the /etc/xinetd.d directory. For example, here is the default telnet control file under xinetd's /etc/xinetd.d directory:

```
# default: on
# description: The telnet server serves telnet sessions; it uses \
#       unencrypted username/password pairs for authentication.
service telnet
{
        disable = no
        flags          = REUSE
        socket_type    = stream
        wait           = no
        user           = root
        server         = /usr/sbin/in.telnetd
        log_on_failure += USERID
}
```

As you can see, the default state for telnet access is enabled with Red Hat Linux. Your job as a system administrator will be to decide what services to provide on your system.

TCP/IP Troubleshooting Tools

Problems rarely appear once a TCP/IP network is configured. However, networking equipment fails, lines go down, and cables get disconnected. Also, problems can arise during the initial configuration of a networked host.

20

TCP/IP NETWORK
MANAGEMENT

Linux has three basic network troubleshooting tools. Two of them, `ping` and `traceroute`, are concerned with the capability of a host to reach another, while the third one, `tcpdump`, is useful for analyzing the flow of traffic in a network.

ping

The most basic network troubleshooting tool is the `ping` program. Named after the pinging sound made by submarine sonars, `ping` sends out packets to another host and waits for that host to reply to them. `ping` uses ICMP (Internet Control Message Protocol), a protocol that runs over IP and is designed for control messages used for things such as routing and reachability information.

The most common way of using `ping` is to pass it a hostname or address:

```
% ping server.company.com
PING server.company.com (10.0.1.10): 56 data bytes
64 bytes from 10.0.1.10: icmp_seq=0 ttl=245 time=83.239 ms
64 bytes from 10.0.1.10: icmp_seq=1 ttl=245 time=80.808 ms
64 bytes from 10.0.1.10: icmp_seq=2 ttl=245 time=82.994 ms
64 bytes from 10.0.1.10: icmp_seq=3 ttl=245 time=81.635 ms
^C
--- server.company.com ping statistics ---
4 packets transmitted, 4 packets received, 0% packet loss
round-trip min/avg/max = 80.808/82.169/83.239 ms
```

In this case, `ping` pings the target host one time per second, until you press Ctrl+C. At that moment, it prints out the statistics for the run. In the statistics, aside from the number of packets transmitted and received, you can see the minimum, average, and maximum round-trip times, which will help you find out how congested the path to the destination host is at the moment.

`ping` has many options. Here are the most commonly used:

Option	Function
-c *count*	Only sends *count* number of packets instead of pinging forever.
-n	`ping` displays numeric addresses instead of hostnames. Useful when you can't get to the DNS server or when DNS queries take too long.
-r	Record route. Sends an option in every packet that instructs every host between the source and the target to store its IP address in the packet. This way you can see which hosts a packet is going through. However, the packet size is limited to nine hosts. Some systems disregard this option. Because of this, it is better to use `traceroute`.
-q	Quiet output. Outputs just the final statistics.
-v	Verbose. Displays all packets received, not just `ping` responses.

When troubleshooting network problems, you should first ping the IP address of the source host itself. This verifies that the originating network interface is set up correctly. After that, you should try pinging your default gateway, your default gateway's gateway (the next hop out), and so on, until you reach the destination host. That way you can easily isolate where a problem lies. However, once you've verified that you can get to the default gateway, it is better to use the traceroute program (which is described in the following section) to automate the process.

> **Note**
>
> All TCP/IP packets have a field called Time-To-Live, or TTL. This field is decremented once by each router on the network. The packet is discarded the moment it reaches 0. Whereas ping uses a default TTL of 255 (the maximum value), many programs such as telnet and ftp use a smaller TTL (usually 30 or 60). That means that you might be able to ping a host, but not telnet or FTP into it. You may use the -t *ttl* option to ping to set the TTL of the packets it outputs.

---

traceroute

The traceroute program is the workhorse of TCP/IP troubleshooting. It sends out UDP packets with progressively larger TTLs and detects the ICMP responses sent by gateways when they drop the packets. In the end, this maps out the route a packet takes when going from the source host to the target host.

This is how it works: traceroute starts by sending out a packet with a TTL of 1. The packet gets to a gateway, which can be the target host or not. If it is the target host, the gateway sends a response packet. If it isn't the target host, the gateway decrements the TTL. Since the TTL is now 0, the gateway drops the packet and sends back a packet indicating this. Whatever happens, traceroute detects the reply packet. If it has reached the target host, its job is finished. If not (it received notification that the packet was dropped, for instance), it increments the TTL by 1 (its new value is 2) and sends out another packet. This time the first gateway decrements the TTL (to 1) and passes it through to the next gateway. This gateway does the same thing: determines whether it's the destination host and decrements the TTL. This goes on until either you reach the target host or you reach the maximum TTL value (which is 30 by default, but can be changed with the -m *max_ttl* option).

traceroute sends three packets with each TTL and reports the round-trip time taken by each packet. This is useful for detecting network bottlenecks.

`traceroute` is usually used the same way as `ping`--by giving it a destination address. Listing 20.1 shows an example of the output from `traceroute`.

LISTING 20.1 Sample Output from `traceroute`

```
mario@chaos:~ 511 $ /usr/sbin/traceroute www.umbral.com
traceroute to xmaya.umbral.com (207.87.18.30), 30 hops max, 40 byte packets
 1:  master.spin.com.mx (200.13.80.123)   120.75 ms   126.727 ms   109.533 ms
 2:  octopus.spin.com.mx (200.13.81.32)   110.042 ms   104.654 ms   99.599 ms
 3:  200.33.218.161 (200.33.218.161)   119.539 ms   105.697 ms   109.603 ms
 4:  rr1.mexmdf.avantel.net.mx (200.33.209.1)   131.556 ms   112.767 ms 109.6 ms
 5:  bordercore1-hssi0-0.Dallas.cw.net (166.48.77.249)   159.54 ms   155.378 ms 169.598 ms
 6:  core9.Dallas.cw.net (204.70.9.89)   159.483 ms   156.364 ms   159.628 ms
 7:  dfw2-core2-s1-0-0.atlas.digex.net (165.117.59.13)   169.505 ms 156.024 ms   149.628 ms
 8:  lax1-core1-s8-0-0.atlas.digex.net (165.117.50.25)   199.497 ms 194.006 ms   189.621 ms
 9:  sjc4-core2-s5-0-0.atlas.digex.net (165.117.53.74)   199.489 ms
➼    sjc4-core2-s5-1-0.atlas.digex.net (165.117.56.110)   191.025 ms
➼    sjc4-core2-s5-0-0.atlas.digex.net (165.117.53.74)   210.25 ms
10:  sjc4-core6-pos1-1.atlas.digex.net (165.117.59.69)   201.031 ms 196.195 ms   199.584 ms
11:  sjc4-wscore2-p1-0.wsmg.digex.net (199.125.178.37)   360.468 ms 366.267 ms   199.481 ms
12:  sjc4-wscore4-fa1-0.wsmg.digex.net (199.125.178.20)   582.272 ms 207.536 ms   198.275 ms
13:  xmaya.umbral.com (207.87.18.30)   209.457 ms   3076.14 ms *
```

`traceroute` can give you quite a bit of information if you know how to look for it. For example, you can see a few things in Listing 20.1:

- `www.umbral.com` is actually an alias for `xmaya.umbral.com`. `traceroute` always does a reverse DNS lookup and reports the official hostname of the host it's tracing.

- `xmaya.umbral.com` is connected to the Internet through a service provider whose domain is `digex.net` (probably an ISP called Digex). (Lines 7–12 are all in the IP networks belonging to the domain of the last gateway.)

- You are connected to the Internet through an ISP called Spin, which is in Mexico. (Lines 1 and 2 are the first gateway. The domain ends with `.mx`.)

- The digex hosts that appear on line 9 are actually several hosts with the same IP address. This is done for redundancy.

- There seems to be some kind of bottleneck between hosts 10, 11, and 12. Notice how the response time, after slowly growing steadily until line 9, suddenly jumps from about 200 milliseconds to more than 300, and then to more than 500. This might be a temporary bottleneck (caused simply by the traffic load at the moment) or it may be a continuous problem, caused perhaps by a physical media problem or not enough capacity in the link.

As you can see, `traceroute` can be an invaluable tool. Much more information can be gleaned from `traceroute` output; it is best to read the `traceroute(8)` man page for a complete discussion.

tcpdump

`tcpdump` is another invaluable tool for debugging some types of network problems. It basically works as a *packet sniffer*--it listens to the network, looks at any packets that come by (whether destined for the host on which it is running or not), and operates on it. It can store all or just some interesting parts of the traffic it sees, or perform a rudimentary analysis of the information it contains.

`tcpdump` works by setting the network card into what is known as *promiscuous mode*. Normally, a network card will only see packets that are meant for it. However, in promiscuous mode, it will see all packets that pass through the network and pass them to the operating system above. The OS then passes the packets to `tcpdump`, which can then filter and display or store them. Because it modifies the configuration of the network card, `tcpdump` must be run by `root`.

Caution

`tcpdump` is a potential security hole. It falls into the category of programs known as *sniffers*, which listen to the network and can listen to all packets in the network and store them. If users use programs such as Telnet that send passwords in the clear, a cracker might use a sniffer to sniff out their passwords. Because of this, `tcpdump` should never be installed `setuid-root`.

To detect whether a network interface is in promiscuous mode (and thus might have a sniffer running on it), use the `ifconfig` command to display the interface's configuration. The `PROMISC` flag will appear if the interface is in promiscuous mode:

```
# /sbin/ifconfig eth0
eth0      Link encap:Ethernet  HWaddr 00:60:97:3E:F0:61
          inet addr:10.0.1.50  Bcast:10.0.1.255  Mask:255.255.255.0
          UP BROADCAST RUNNING PROMISC MULTICAST  MTU:1500  Metric:1
          RX packets:0 errors:0 dropped:0 overruns:0 frame:0
          TX packets:5 errors:0 dropped:0 overruns:0 carrier:5
          Collisions:0
          Interrupt:3 Base address:0x310
```

If you run `tcpdump` without any arguments, you get a listing of all the packets that pass through the network:

```
# /usr/sbin/tcpdump
tcpdump: listening on eth0
22:46:12.730048 renato.1445323871 > vishnu.nfs: 100 readlink [|nfs]
22:46:12.734224 tumbolia.1012 > vishnu.808: udp 92
22:46:12.746763 tumbolia.22 > atman.1023: P 142299991:142300035(44) ack 3799214339 win 32120 (DF) [tos 0x10]
22:46:12.763684 atman.1023 > tumbolia.22: . ack 44 win 32120 (DF) [tos 0x10]
22:46:12.778100 vishnu.808 > tumbolia.1015: udp 56
22:46:12.780084 gerardo.1448370113 > vishnu.nfs: 124 lookup [|nfs]
22:46:12.780153 tumbolia.22 > atman.1023: P 44:596(552) ack 1 win 32120 (DF) [tos 0x10]
```

The dump will stop when you press Ctrl+C.

As you can see, `tcpdump` by default converts IP addresses to hostnames and port numbers to service names. It also attempts to interpret some packets (such as those where the line ends with `lookup [|nfs]`, which are NFS lookups). In some cases, the number of bytes that `tcpdump` looks at (68) might not be enough to fully decode the packet. In this case, you may use the `-s` option to increase the number (see the `-s` option in Table 20.5).

You don't often want to see all the packets, especially in medium to large networks. Sometimes you want to see all the packets going between two specific hosts, or even those that use a specific service. `tcpdump` takes as a parameter an optional filter expression that will select only certain packets.

`tcpdump`'s filter expressions consist of one or more primitives joined by the keywords `and`, `or`, and `not`. Each primitive consists of a qualifier followed by an ID. A *qualifier* consists of one or more keywords, the most common of which are shown in Table 20.4. The ID specifies the value the corresponding field must have to match the filter.

TABLE 20.4   Most Common `tcpdump` Qualifiers

Qualifier	Matches
`src host`	The IP address of the host from where the packet comes.
`dst host`	The IP address of the host to which the packet is going.
`host`	The IP address of the source or the destination host.
`src port`	The port the packet is coming from.
`dst port`	The port the packet is going to.
`port`	The source or the destination port.
`tcp, udp, or icmp`	The packet's protocol is the specified one.

> ### Tip
>
> One common mistake is to run `tcpdump` through a remote connection, such as when connected through `telnet` or `ssh`, with a filter that includes all the `telnet` or `ssh` packets. An example is including just `host thishost`, where thishost is the host on which `tcpdump` is running. In that case you end up with an incredible amount of output. This is because the first packet that comes through generates output, which is transmitted through the network and captured by `tcpdump`, which generates more output, which is also transmitted through the network, and so on.
>
> To prevent that, be more specific in your filter expressions. For example, you might include the primitive `not port 22` to filter out `ssh` packets.

`tcpdump` also takes several switches, the most common of which are shown in Table 20.5.

TABLE 20.5   Most Common `tcpdump` Switches

Qualifier	Matches
`-c count`	Exit after receiving *count* packets.
`-i interface`	Listen on *interface*. By default, `tcpdump` listens on the first interface found after the loopback interface. You can see the order in which the interfaces are searched using the `ifconfig -a` command.
`-n`	Don't convert numeric addresses and port numbers to host and service names (print numeric output). This eliminates the need for DNS lookups.
`-N`	Print out only the hostname, not its fully qualified domain name. For example, if you give this flag then `tcpdump` will print *redhat* instead of *redhat.com*
`-r file`	Read packets from *file*, which must have been created with the `-w` option.
`-s snaplen`	Grab *snaplen* bytes from each packet. The default is 68, which is enough for IP, ICMP, TCP, and UDP packets. However, for certain protocols (such as DNS and NFS), a *snaplen* of 68 will truncate some protocol information. This is marked by |*protocol*, where the *protocol* indicates the protocol part where truncation occurred.
`-v`	Verbose mode. Print some more information about each packet.
`-vv`	Even more verbose output. Print much more information about each packet.
`-w file`	Capture the packets in *file*.
`-x`	Print out each packet in hex. This will print out either the whole packet or *snaplen* bytes, whichever is less.

Network Security Tools

There are several tools that help you secure your networks. First of all, you must have a firewall to separate your internal network from the Internet and to prevent hackers from getting in. Then there is the problem of getting into your network from the outside, and from your network to the outside world, without leaving a wide-open door for hackers.

You must remember that the most important factor in security is usually the human one. You might have the best firewall in the world, perfectly configured, and an employee might simply copy confidential information to a floppy disk and hand it to a competitor. Security starts with people and with a good security policy. This particular subject cannot be discussed in depth here, however. If you want to learn more (and you should!), an excellent reference is *Maximum Security, Second Edition: A Hacker's Guide to Protecting Your Internet Site and Network*, (ISBN 0-672-31341-3, Sams Publishing).

Firewalls

A *firewall* is a computer that stands between a trusted network (such as your internal network) and an untrusted network (such as the Internet), and controls what traffic passes between them. It is an essential piece of the information security puzzle.

There are two general types of firewalls (which may be combined): application-level firewalls (known as *proxies*), and packet-filtering firewalls. A *packet-filtering firewall* simply allows or disallows packets depending on their content. Most packet-filtering firewalls determine what packets to allow or disallow based on the source or destination addresses, source or destination port, and whether the packet is part of an ongoing conversation.

An application-level firewall or proxy acts as an intermediary between client and server programs. Instead of connecting directly to the server, a client application connects to the proxy and asks it for the information. The proxy opens a connection to the server, sends the request, and continues to pass information back and forth between server and client (see Figure 20.9).

FIGURE 20.9

Packet-filtering versus application-level firewalls.

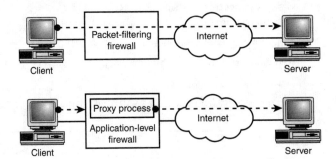

Both types of firewalls have advantages and disadvantages, and many sites implement both. A proxy-based firewall is regarded as being more secure than a packet-filtering firewall, because it does not have complete knowledge of the protocol used by the application.

Another advantage of proxies is that sometimes they may be used to reduce bandwidth usage. For example, an organization may implement a proxy on its firewall that stores the Web pages requested by users. If another user requests the same page again, the proxy can grab it from its local storage and send the page to the user without having to connect to the origin server again. If you multiply this by tens or hundreds of users, you can appreciate the bandwidth savings.

On the other hand, an application-level firewall must be built for each protocol. Thus, there are HTTP proxies, FTP proxies, Telnet proxies, SMTP proxies, and so on. This brings up the problem of *unsupported applications*--applications whose protocols don't have a proxy yet. There are *generic proxies* available, but applications must be modified and recompiled to use them. Since they work on single packets, packet filters are transparent to applications.

A packet-filtering firewall can use additional authentication measures, aside from using just the IP addresses. And a packet-filtering firewall may also do what is known as *network-address translation* or *masquerading*. This means that the firewall converts the source addresses on outgoing packets so the other host thinks it's connecting to the firewall itself, and to the destination addresses on incoming packets so they go to the host that requested the connection initially. This has several advantages. For example, a whole network may connect to the Internet using a single IP address. Also, because internal addresses aren't visible to the outside, hosts on the internal network are more secure against attacks from the outside. The downside to this is that any hosts that provide services to the outside must be outside the firewall; otherwise, the firewall must be specifically configured to pass some packets straight to a particular host.

Linux Firewalling Concepts

The Linux kernel itself contains support for packet filtering and masquerading. This support is provided by the package called IP chains. Installing and configuring IP chains is highly recommended for reasons of security. There is always the danger of some unscrupulous individual breaking into your computer from the Internet or even from within your corporate network. If you take the time to install and configure IP chains properly, you can minimize the danger of this happening. It is widely argued that there is no such thing as a totally secure computer system or network. This may or may not be true. There are merits to each side of the case. Security experts will tell you, however, that the more protection you provide for your system, the more you reduce the chances of your system falling prey to crackers. Providing firewall protection for your system will significantly reduce the likelihood of your system being violated. It's like installing an alarm system on your car. This will not keep your car from being stolen by an individual who is a professional car thief and who has decided he is going to steal your car. What it will do is make the other unprotected cars in the parking lot much more attractive to the thief because they are unprotected and thus much easier to steal. There are also several packages available for proxy-based firewalls, such as the Squid HTTP/FTP proxy cache and the SOCKS proxy.

To determine whether your kernel supports IP chains, look for the file `/proc/net/ip_fwchains`. If the file exists, your current kernel has support for IP chains. If the file doesn't exist, you need to enable the kernel firewall. To do this, you must configure the kernel and enable Network Firewalls and IP: Firewalling. You might also want to enable IP: Always Defragment, IP: Masquerading, and ICMP: Masquerading if you're doing masquerading. After that, recompile and install the kernel and reboot.

Starting with version 2.2 of the Linux kernel, the packet filter is based on the concept of chains, which are configured using the `/usr/sbin/ipchains` utility. If your system doesn't contain this utility, you have to install the `ipchains-1.3.9-17.rpm` from the CD-ROMs.

The `ipchains` tool inserts and deletes rules from the kernel's packet filtering section. Every rule in the kernel's packet filter belongs to a group of rules known as *chains*. Initially, the kernel contains three default chains:

- The *input chain*, which is applied to arriving packets, before passing them to the rest of the kernel or to applications.
- The *output chain*, which is applied to packets just before they leave the host.
- The *forwarding chain*, which is applied to packets that have passed the input chain but whose target host is a different host--for example, when the host is being used as a firewall or router.

When a packet enters a chain, it is tested to determine if it matches each of the rules on the chain. If it does, it is passed to the target of that rule. If it reaches the end of a chain, it is passed to the chain's default target.

A *target* specifies what to do with a packet that matches a particular rule or, in the case of the default targets, that reaches the end of a chain. There are six system targets; they are presented in Table 20.6.

TABLE 20.6 `ipchains` System Targets

Name	Function
ACCEPT	Lets the package through.
DENY	Drops the package silently.
REJECT	Drops the package, notifying the sender.

TABLE 20.6 continued

Name	Function
MASQ	Valid only in the `forward` chain or chains called from it. Masquerades the package.
REDIRECT	Valid only in the `input` chain or chains called from it. Sends the package to a port on the firewall host itself, regardless of its real destination. May be followed by a port specification to redirect the package to a different port regardless of its destination port.
RETURN	Transfers immediately to the end of the current chain; the package will be handled according to the chain's default target.

A target may also be another chain, including a user-defined chain. You may create your own chains at any time, and attach them to any of the predefined chains. The default target of a user-defined chain is always the rule following the one in which the chain is called, so a user-defined chain can be used as a sort of subroutine; you may reuse its rules in several chains. This is useful to reduce the total number of rules and to better document what is happening, since you may name chains after what they do. For example, if a firewall has different rules for two departments (call them the *bosses* and the *masses*), you might define different chains called *bosses* and *masses*, and then simply apply each chain depending on where the packet is coming from.

Building a Firewall with `ipchains`

Consider the network shown in Figure 20.10. There is an internal network using private addresses connected to the public Internet. You want to allow all hosts in the internal network to access the Internet, while providing protection from external hackers. No one needs to access the internal hosts from the outside (thus, this kind of firewall is known as a *one-way firewall*).

FIGURE 20.10

Network setup where all hosts in the internal network have access to the Internet while providing protection from external crackers.

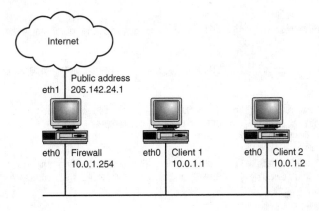

Listing 20.2 shows a shell script that sets up a basic one-way packet-filtering and masquerading firewall using `ipchains`.

LISTING 20.2   A Basic Firewall Using `ipchains`

```
#!/bin/sh -x
# To enable logging if necessary
#LOG=-l

# Constants
ANYWHERE=0.0.0.0/0
EXT_IF=eth0
INT_IF=eth1

# Networks
INTERNAL_NET=10.0.1.0/24
EXTERNAL_ADDR=205.142.24.1/32

# Disable packet forwarding while we set up the firewall
echo 0 > /proc/sys/net/ipv4/ip_forward

# Flush all rules
/sbin/ipchains -F input
/sbin/ipchains -F output
/sbin/ipchains -F forward

# Deny all packets by default - this is a mostly-closed firewall
/sbin/ipchains -P input DENY
/sbin/ipchains -P output DENY
/sbin/ipchains -P forward DENY

# Accept anything to/from localhost
/sbin/ipchains -A input -j ACCEPT -p all -s localhost -d localhost -i lo \
$LOG
/sbin/ipchains -A output -j ACCEPT -p all -s localhost -d localhost -i lo\
 $LOG

# Spoofing protection - deny anything coming from the outside with an \
internal
# address
/sbin/ipchains -A input -j RETURN -p all -s $INTERNAL_NET -d $ANYWHERE -I\
 $EXT_IF $LOG

# Accept TCP packets belonging to already-established connections
/sbin/ipchains -A input -j ACCEPT -p tcp -s $ANYWHERE -d
➥$ME -i $EXT_IF \! -y $LOG

# Accept and masquerade all packets from the inside going anywhere
/sbin/ipchains -A input -j ACCEPT -p all -s $INTERNAL_NET -d $ANYWHERE -I\
 $INT_IF $LOG
```

LISTING 20.2   continued

```
/sbin/ipchains -A forward -j MASQ -p all -s $INTERNAL_NET -d $ANYWHERE -I\
 $INT_IF $LOG

# Accept all TCP packets going to the outside net
/sbin/ipchains -A output -j ACCEPT -p all -s $ME -d $ANYWHERE -i $EXT_IF \
 $LOG

# Accept type 3 ICMP queries (Destination Unreachable)
/sbin/ipchains -A input -j ACCEPT -p icmp -s $ANYWHERE -d $ME -i $EXT_IF \
 --icmp-type destination-unreachable $LOG
/sbin/ipchains -A output -j ACCEPT -p icmp -s $ME -d $ANYWHERE -i $EXT_IF\
 --icmp-type destination-unreachable $LOG

# Catch-all rules to provide logging
/sbin/ipchains -A input -j DENY -l
/sbin/ipchains -A output -j DENY -l
/sbin/ipchains -A forward -j DENY -l

# Enable packet forwarding
echo 1 > /proc/sys/net/ipv4/ip_forward
```

First, you should define a few shell variables to help keep your script readable and manageable. Next, for safety, disable packet forwarding in the kernel now while building the firewall rules. This is important because the first step in actually building the firewall is flushing the system chains, so the system might be left in an insecure state.

There are two broad ways of thinking about firewall policies: mostly-open and mostly-closed. In a *mostly-open firewall*, your system lets everything through except the packets you specify. A *mostly-closed firewall* does the reverse, denying or rejecting everything except that which you specifically allow. This second kind of firewall is usually regarded as more secure, because you know exactly what is going through and won't be subject to future attacks based on now-unused protocols. As you can see in Listing 20.2, to build a mostly-closed firewall you first set the default target of all chains to DENY or REJECT and then add rules to ACCEPT those packets you want to let through. A mostly-open firewall, obviously, is just the opposite: You set the default target to ACCEPT and then add rules to DENY or REJECT those packets you don't want to let through.

You should now add rules for each of the packets you want to let through. Rules are added by executing the ipchains program with parameters that specify the packet characteristics and the action to take. Tables 20.7 and 20.8, respectively, show the commands ipchains will take and its most common options.

20

TCP/IP NETWORK MANAGEMENT

TABLE 20.7   `ipchains` Commands

Command	Action
-A *chain*	Adds rule to *chain*.
-D *chain* [*rulenum*]	Deletes rule number *rulenum* from *chain*. If *rulenum* is omitted, the default is the first rule (number 1).
-I *chain* [*rulenum*]	Inserts rule into *chain* before rule number *rulenum*.
-R *chain* [*rulenum*]	Replaces rule number *rulenum* in *chain*.
-F *chain*	Flushes *chain*. Equivalent to using -D on all rules one by one.
-L *chain*	Lists the rules in *chain*.
-N *chain*	Creates new user-defined chain.
-X *chain*	Deletes user-defined chain.
-P *chain target*	Sets default target for *chain* to *target*.

TABLE 20.8   Most Common `ipchains` Options

Option	Specifies
-s [!] *address*[/*mask*] [!] [*port*[:*port*]]	Source address and port of the packet.
-d [!] *address*[/*mask*] [!] [*port*[:*port*]]	Destination address and port of the packet.
-i [!] *interface*	Interface the packet is arriving on (in the input chain) or leaving on (in the output and forward chains).
-p [!] *protocol*	Packet protocol. It may be any protocol specified in the /etc/protocols file.
-j *target* [*port*]	Target to send the packet to.
[!] -y	Packet is a SYN packet; only for rules that specify -p tcp.
--icmp-type *type*	ICMP type is *type*; only for rules that specify -p icmp.
-l	Log the packet to syslog. -n or --numeric. Used with the -L option. Displays numeric host and port addresses instead of names.

Some of these options allow the use of the ! (short for not) sign. The not sign can be used to negate or reverse the condition. For example, specifying -p ! icmp in a rule will match packets whose protocol is not ICMP to the conditions of this rule.

The source and destination addresses can be specified in several ways. To specify a particular host, you may use its IP address or its hostname. To specify a network, you can either use the CIDR notation, or its normal expanded dotted-quad format. Thus, 1.1.1.0/24 is equivalent to 1.1.1.0/255.255.255.0. Source and destination port numbers can be specified numerically or by service name (mapped from /etc/services). You may also specify a range of ports by using a colon (:) to separate the beginning and ending ports.

The -y option is used when you want to allow TCP connections in one direction only. When building a firewall, for example, you may want to allow your internal hosts to connect to the outside without letting outside agents connect to the internal hosts. Because a connection needs packets going both ways, blocking packets coming from the outside is a naive approach.

The solution is to block just those packets used to initiate a connection. These packets are called SYN packets because they have the SYN flag set in their headers and the FIN and ACK flags cleared. (The *flags* are specific bits set in the packet's header.) If you block any packets with the SYN bit set, your hosts can talk to hosts on the outside without allowing the outside hosts to initiate the connections to your hosts.

The Internet Control Message Protocol (ICMP) is used for control messages, such as host not found or ping responses. It is usually most secure to disable most ICMP messages. However, some message types are needed by various utilities or other parts of the system. The --icmp-type option matches those packets with a specific ICMP message type. For example, ICMP messages such as destination unreachable are used extensively by TCP and UDP. You might also want to allow your internal users to use other utilities such as ping or traceroute. Table 20.9 shows the most common ICMP message types.

TABLE 20.9 The Most Common ICMP Message Types

Number	Name	Required By
0	echo-reply	ping
3	destination-unreachable	Any TCP/UDP traffic
5	redirect	Routing if not running routing daemon
8	echo-request	ping
11	time-exceeded	traceroute

You can find more detailed information on ipchains and its options in the /usr/doc/ipchains-1.3.9/HOWTO.txt file (make sure you installed the HOWTOs).

Proxies

As mentioned, there are two kinds of firewalls: packet-filtering and proxy-based. A basic *packet-filtering firewall* may be complemented with a proxy to enhance its security and, in some cases, cache data to reduce network bandwidth usage.

The most common kind of proxy on the Internet today is the Web-caching proxy. Linux includes a Web-caching proxy called Squid. Run the `rpm -q squid` command to see whether it is installed. If the package isn't installed, you must install the `squid-2.2.STABLE1-1.i386.rpm` file included on the CD-ROMs.

To configure Squid, go to the `/etc/squid` directory and copy the `squid.conf.default` file to `squid.conf`. Edit `squid.conf` to suit your site. The file is extensively commented, so most of its options are self-documenting. They also typically have sensible defaults that you can leave unmodified unless you want to tune the cache. Table 20.10 shows the options you should modify before starting Squid.

TABLE 20.10 Options You Should Modify in `/etc/squid/squid.conf`

Option	Meaning
`cache_dir dirname mbytes level1 level2`	The cache is stored in *dirname*. It occupies at most *mbytes* megabytes of disk space. *dirname* contains *level1* first-level directories, each of which contain *level2* second-level directories. The default values are, respectively, `100`, `16`, and `256`. You should change only the first value to reflect the amount of disk space you want to use for the cache; the second and third values are used for tuning.
`pid_filename filename`	Create *filename* to store the Squid process ID, which is used by the `/etc/rc.d/init.d/squid` script to kill the process when called with the `stop` parameter. You should uncomment this line and leave the value unchanged.
`logfile_rotate nfiles`	When rotating logs, keep *nfiles* archived copies. Although the Squid installation will create a `/etc/logrotate.d/squid` file to handle log rotations, the number of archived copies is modified here.
`ftp_user user@domain.name`	Some FTP sites require that you pass a valid email address as a password. You should modify this parameter so that it contains a valid user ID (usually the site administrator).

TABLE 20.10   continued

Option	Meaning
cache_mgr *user@domain.name*	Email address of the site administrator. This person is emailed if a problem arises with the cache.
cache_effective_user *username*	Squid is usually started from /etc/rc.d/init.d/squid, which is run as root at startup. It is unsafe to run Squid as root, so you must create a new user in /etc/passwd and add its username and group name to the squid.conf file. Squid will set its effective user and group IDs to the ones configured here.
cache_effective_group *groupname*	See cache effective user
err_html_text *html_text*	This should be modified to contain HTML code including the cache administrator's email address. It is added to the end of all error pages presented by Squid to the users.

Once you have configured Squid, you may start it by running /etc/rc.d/init.d/squid start. The first time Squid starts, it will take a long time to create its cache directory hierarchy. Be patient. Squid will log its errors to the /var/log/squid/squid.out, so you can do a tail -f on this file to check whether there are any startup errors.

Secure Remote Access—SSH, the Secure SHell

You have just completely secured your site. You have an airtight firewall in place and have set up your proxy. You have a good security policy and your users have been educated on it. You can sit at your console basking in the feeling of a job well done and use Telnet to log in to one of your servers to start a backup.

What if a few days later you discover your server has been compromised? Someone logged in as root and played amateur sysadmin on it. What could have happened?

This scenario is more common than you might think, and it has bitten many a sysadmin. What happened here was that someone on the internal network was using a *sniffer*, a program that captures all traffic on the LAN. It saw your complete Telnet session, including the server's root password, and reported it to whoever was running the sniffer. That user, armed with the password, went into your server.

The problem with most Internet protocols is that the Internet was initially created without security being a main goal. Most companies today use these same Internet protocols on their internal networks. Even if your network isn't visible from the Internet, don't undervalue the importance of good networkwide security. It has been reported that over 70% of system compromises originate within the firewall, by disgruntled employees, by curious employees who want to see how systems work, or by competitors' spies.

What is a sysadmin to do? Use only the console? What about remote sites that are only connected via the Internet?

Enter the Secure SHell, also known as SSH. *SSH* is a suite of programs that allow you to log on to remote servers and transfer files in a secure manner. It is meant to be a replacement for `rlogin`, `rsh`, `telnet`, and `rcp`, which are insecure because they don't encrypt the data they transfer as it moves from one host to another. SSH, on the other hand, scrambles the data that goes through the network so it is indecipherable to someone using a sniffer. A full discussion of security and encryption technologies is beyond the scope of this book; however, an excellent reference is *Internet Security Professional Reference, Second Edition* (New Riders Publishing, ISBN 1-56205-760-X).

OpenSSH Debuts with Red Hat Linux 7.0

The new version of Red Hat Linux now includes OpenSSH, a collection of free versions of SSH programs inherited from the kind folks at the OpenBSD Project! The suite includes `ssh`, which replaces `telnet`, the `sshd` daemon, and `scp`, which replaces the `ftp` command. You'll also find other utilities included in the distribution, which is composed primarily of the following `.rpm` files:

```
openssh-clients-2.1.1p4-1
openssh-2.1.1p4-1
openssh-askpass-gnome-2.1.1p4-1
openssh-server-2.1.1p4-1
openssh-askpass-2.1.1p4-1
```

For more information, browse to `http://www.openssh.com/`.

With SSH, each host and user has a *private key* and a *public key*. The public key is stored on the server, whereas the private key is kept on the client. Data encrypted with one key can only be decrypted with the other, and vice versa. This means that SSH can be used both for secure communications and for strong authentication, where you need to be sure that the host on the other side of the connection is actually who it claims to be.

Because SSH contains encryption technology, it is illegal to export it from the U.S. `ssh-server` must be installed on the servers (the hosts you are logging on to), `ssh-clients` on the clients (the hosts you are logging on from), and `ssh` on both; `ssh-extras` can be optionally installed on either or both. It is often best to install all packages on all hosts.

The `ssh-server` package contains default `/etc/ssh/sshd_config` and `/etc/ssh/ssh_config` files that work well for most purposes. It also contains an `/etc/rc.d/init.d/sshd` script for starting the sshd daemon when you boot the host. To start the sshd daemon manually, run `/etc/rc.d/init.d/sshd start`. If you want to start it automatically when the server boots, create an appropriate softlink in the `/etc/rc.d/rc?.d` directory that corresponds to your server's `initdefault` runlevel.

The `ssh` and `ssh-clients` packages contain several programs. The most useful are `ssh` and `scp`. `ssh` allows you to log on to a remote host, execute remote programs, and redirect ports from the local host to the remote host and vice versa. `scp`, which allows you to copy files securely from one host to another, is a replacement for the `rcp` program.

The `ssh` Command

The `ssh` command is used to log on to a remote server and execute a command. It has the following syntax:

```
ssh options host options command
```

`ssh` also handles X connection forwarding. Whenever you log on to a remote host using `ssh` from a host that is running X Windows, `sshd` creates a dummy X server and sets the `DISPLAY` variable to point to it. All X traffic going to this dummy server is actually forwarded to the X server on your local host. X authentication is automatically taken care of via `xauth`. That way, the X traffic is also encrypted and secure. You don't have to do anything to make this happen, just log on to the remote server from an X session.

There are many options to the `ssh` command that can be included either before or after the hostname. The most common options to `ssh` are listed in Table 20.11.

TABLE 20.11   Most Common `ssh` Options

Option	Meaning
`-f`	Send process to background after authentication. Useful when you need to enter a password.
`-l user`	Log in as *user* to the remote server.
`-o 'option'`	Set option in the same format as the configuration file. Useful for some options that don't have command-line switch equivalents.
`-v`	Activate verbose mode. Useful for debugging connections.
`-C`	Compress. All data in the connection will be compressed. Useful especially over modem lines. The compression algorithm used is the same one used by `gzip`.

20

TCP/IP NETWORK MANAGEMENT

TABLE 20.11   continued

Option	Meaning
-L port:host:hostport	Forward TCP port *port* to *hostport* on remote host *host*. What this does is open a local server socket on *port* and a socket on the remote host that connects to port *hostport* on *host*. All connections to *port* on the localhost will be forwarded to port *hostport* on *host*.
-R port:host:hostport	The reverse of -L. Forward TCP port *port* on the remote host to port *hostport* on *host*.

Port Forwarding

The -R and -L options deserve special mention. They are useful especially in cases where you need to make a secure "tunnel" through an insecure network (such as the Internet). Consider a case where you have a Web server in California and a database server in Florida. You want the Web server to access the database, but for security purposes you want the communication to be encrypted. Suppose the database listens by default to port 3306. You might run the following shell script on the Web server:

```
#!/bin/sh
while /bin/true
do
  ssh dbserver -L 3306:localhost:3306 sleep 87600
done
```

The while loop is needed because the ssh command (and thus the port forwarding) will run only as long as the command given on the ssh command line specifies. In this case, the sleep 87600 command simply waits for 87,600 seconds (24 hours) before exiting. This command forwards port 3306 of the Web server (where you're running the command) to port 3306 on the localhost of the database server.

If you want to run this script on the database server, you would use the -R option and invert the two port numbers. Since they are the same, the command would be identical except for the option name.

Authentication

This scheme poses a problem, though. The ssh command will ask for the password of the remote user. There are only two ways to automate the password login process:

- Using .rhosts authentication
- Using private/public key authentication

To use .rhosts authentication, you create a .rhosts file in the home directory of the remote user, just as if you were using the rsh command. The difference here is that the remote host will be authenticated by its public key, instead of just by its IP address. Assuming that the command was run by the admin user and that the Web server host is called webserver, the .rhosts file should contain the following line:

```
webserver   admin
```

If you don't like the idea of using a .rhosts file or you are sitting behind a firewall, the only option left is to use private/public keys. What you need to do follows:

1. Log on to the local server.

2. Run the /usr/bin/ssh-keygen program to generate the private and the public keys. They are saved under the user's home directory as .ssh/identity and .ssh/identity.pub, respectively. ssh-keygen asks you for a passphrase, which is used to encrypt the keys and has to be keyed in every time you want to log on remotely. Because the purpose of this is precisely to avoid having to use a password, leave the passphrase blank.

3. Copy the .ssh/identity.pub file to the /tmp directory of the remote server:

   cp $HOME/.ssh/identity.pub remoteserver:/tmp.

4. Log on to the remote server:

   ssh remoteserver.

5. Append the /tmp/identity.pub file to the .ssh/authorized_keys file under the remote user's home directory:

   ```
   cat /tmp/identity.pub >> .ssh/authorized_keys.
   ```

6. Log off the remote server and log back on using ssh. This time ssh shouldn't ask for a password.

Caution

You should never use this procedure with the root user. If you want to use strong authentication when logging in as root, be sure to use a passphrase! The passphrase should be 10–30 characters, and is preferably not a phrase based on words. If you forget the passphrase, you'll have to regenerate the keys.

For this kind of batch process, it is usually best to have a special user whose only function is to perform these processes. If a host is compromised, the attacker will get access only to an unprivileged account.

20

TCP/IP NETWORK
MANAGEMENT

The `ssh_config` and `.ssh/config` Files

The SSH client programs read their configuration from the `/etc/ssh/ssh_config` and the `$HOME/.ssh/config` files. There are many options that can be placed in these files. The most common are shown in Table 20.12.

TABLE 20.12   `ssh_config` Options

Option	Meaning
Host *hostname*	Introduces a new section. The *hostname* is matched against the hostname given on the command line. The options that follow apply to this host until the next `Host` directive. The `?` and `*` characters may be used as wildcards. You may use `Host *` to set defaults that apply to all hosts.
HostName *hostname*	The connection is made to *hostname*. This is useful to create aliases for particular connections (such as with different usernames or for port forwarding).
BatchMode {yes|no}	When set to `yes`, ssh never asks for a password. It fails if it can't log in without a password.
Compression {yes|no}	When set to `yes`, ssh compresses all data transferred to this host. The compression algorithm is the same one used by `gzip`. Equivalent to the `-C` command-line option.
CompressionLevel {1-9}	Specifies how much to compress the data. A `CompressionLevel` of `1` provides the least and fastest compression, whereas a level of `9` provides the most and slowest compression. The default value is `6` and is appropriate for most applications.
User *username*	Log in as *username*. Equivalent to the `-l` command-line option.
LocalForward *port host:hostport*	Forward local *port* to remote *hostport* on *host*. Equivalent to the `-L` command-line option.
RemoteForward *port host:hostport*	Forward remote *port* to local *hostport* on *host*. Equivalent to the `-R` command-line option.

Summary

The networking rules are ever-changing and fast-paced. Becoming a Network Engineer can be a lot of fun and provide a very profitable source of income. This chapter should be all you need to take your first steps in this exciting world of networking. In this chapter, you learned the following:

- The TCP/IP protocol suite forms the basis of the Internet.

- An IP address has a host part and a network part. The decision of which bits are in which part is based on the netmask.

- Routing is the process by which packets travel from one network to another. Most networks have a single default router that connects them to another, upstream network.

- The main tools for troubleshooting TCP/IP problems are `ping`, `traceroute`, and `tcpdump`.

- Linux provides several security tools. The Linux kernel itself provides a firewall, which is configured with ipchains.

Linux System Administration

This chapter focuses on system administration for Red Hat Linux. System administration is the maintenance of a computer system, and the system administrator is the person who maintains the software and hardware for the system. A system administrator can administrate his own local workstation, or he can be responsible for administrating a system with hundreds of users. System administrator duties include hardware configuration, software installation, reconfiguration of the kernel, networking, and anything else that's required to make the system work and to keep it running in a satisfactory manner.

Working as root

In order for the system administrator to perform his many duties, he can assume super-user privileges to perform tasks not normally available to the average user of the system. The superuser performs these tasks as user `root`. `root` is a special user account that is available on every UNIX system. This special user has full access to the system. The system ignores all permissions when responding to commands from the `root` user, providing read, write, and execute permissions to every file and device known to the system.

What does the power of `root` mean in practical terms? The command `rm -rf /` run as `root` could delete the entire system. It also means that `root` has access to all data. Complete access is helpful for backing up and restoring data, performing system maintenance, and even performing security tasks. Many commands, with certain parameters, are ideal to hand off to the users; bringing up print queues is a good example. Unfortunately, with different parameters the same commands could take down the print queues or delete other users' printouts. The `root` account is all-powerful. The `root` user keeps the system up and running as a stable environment; but a `root` user can also destroy the system and all data contained therein.

It is because of this ability to manipulate the system that, as system administrator, you should take great care when you are using the `root` account—not only when you are using and modifying the system, but also when you are changing passwords.

A password is the identification that the operating system uses to determine whether a user attempting to log in with a certain user ID is authorized to use that account. Anyone who knows the `root` password can control the entire system. A user can boot a Red Hat Linux system that is left unsecured from disk and change the `root` password even if he does not know it.

That is correct—you can change the `root` password this easily:

1. Boot the system with the boot disk.
2. Mount the `root` partition.

3. Edit the /etc/passwd file to remove the password for root.

4. Reboot from the hard disk.

5. Set a new password for root.

This process is nice and convenient if the Red Hat system happens to be a system in someone's home with no other purpose than teaching the user how to use Linux. This process is a problem, however, for a Red Hat system used as an ISP in an unsecured location in a public building.

Because of the power of the root account, a user on the system who has access to the root password should not log in directly as root. To perform a task that requires root authority, the user should log in with his regular user account and su to root to perform the task. Then, the user should return to his normal account. This procedure helps ensure two things. First, it keeps the user from accidentally performing actions that he did not intend but are allowed by root. Second, it provides logging. /etc/login.defs is the file that defines, among other things, the su log, the failed login log, and the list of who logged in last. Although logging does not stop an action, it will at least help determine who performed the action.

Performing System Maintenance

The overall function of a system administrator is to keep the system up and running. Not only does this mean applying the latest software updates, adding and replacing hardware, and adding new software, but it also means being part soothsayer, part instructor, and part detective. The system administrator must

- Know where to find things
- Plan processes
- Have a back-out plan and know when to use it
- Make changes in small increments
- Test all changes
- Communicate effectively and in a timely fashion with users

Each of these tasks can be daunting. For example, it takes years of training and practice to understand completely how everything in Linux works, and just about the time you figure out everything, it changes.

The first task is the reason for this book and is covered throughout. The other five items are examined in more detail in the following sections.

Planning Processes

Red Hat is a complex operating system. Many files and processes are dependent upon other files and processes. Therefore, when you are preparing to make a change to the system, it only makes sense to define a process for the task. The amount of planning and documenting required for the task should obviously depend on the complexity of the task, but it should at least touch on the following items:

- Provide a description of the task.
- Provide documentation about how this task is going to affect the system, including, but not limited to, the files and processes affected.
- Plan some way to back out of the change to restore the system to its previous configuration.

Creating a Back-Out Plan

Creating the back-out plan is the most important part of making a change to a system. In determining the back-out plan, consider the time required to perform the task, the time required to test the change, and the time required to back out of the current process and return to the former process. An important part of the back-out plan is a decision point— a predetermined point when you decide to continue with the current process or to implement the back-out plan. This could be a decision based on a time limit, a lack of system resources, malfunctioning equipment, poorly written software, or another problem that requires returning to the former process.

Making Changes in Small Increments

It is easier to back out of small changes than it is to back out of big and multiple changes. It is also easier to plan a series of smaller changes than it is to plan one large change. Diagnosing problems is considerably easier when fewer things are changed than when a large number of things are changed. The job becomes much simpler if you can break a task down into several small tasks, each with individual test plans and back-out plans.

Developing a Test Plan

You must test each system change. Even a small change, such as moving a file from one location to another, should have a test plan. The test plan should be appropriate to the task. In the example of moving a file, the test plan could be as simple as the following:

1. Are users or processes dependent upon the file?
2. If yes, can the users or processes still access the file?

3. If no, make it available (change permissions, add directory to path, create link, and so on).

4. Does the file do what it is supposed to do?

5. If yes, okay; if no, fix and retest.

A task as simple as moving a file requires five steps to properly test. Imagine the difficulty of testing a large change.

Communicating Effectively and in a Timely Manner

Communicating the result of changes to the system is the final element of a successful system change. Success does not necessarily mean that the task was completed without errors. In fact, it could mean that the task could not be completed and the back-out plan was successfully implemented. Communication also means letting the users know in advance about a change that affects them.

Communication, on a larger level, is information passed between one user and another, whether it's one-way communication or a dialog. Although it is imperative to have this communication before, during, and after a system change, communication does not have to stop nor should it stop there. Some system administrators communicate announcements, local news, jokes, and just about anything else to users on a regular basis.

You can use many different tools to communicate with users. To decide which tool to use, you need to determine the purpose of the communication. For example, if you are about to shut down a system, you need to communicate that information only to the users currently logged in to the system. If, on the other hand, you want to announce a birthday, you need to announce that information either to all users or to all users who log in to the system that day. Perhaps a user is remotely logged in to a system and is having problems. A user with only one phone line cannot call in the problem without disconnecting. This situation requires an entirely different form of communication. The following sections discuss several different tools for communication; some are commands, and others are concepts. In addition, examples illustrate which tool is best for that particular need. The following communication tools are discussed in the upcoming sections:

- `write`: One-way communication with another user currently logged in to the system.

- `wall`: One-way communication with all other users currently logged in to the system.

- `talk`: Interactive two-way communication with another user currently logged in to the system.

- mesg: Message reception (talk and write) from other non-root users currently logged in to the system.

- motd: Message of the day received by users when they log in to the system.

- Pre-login message /etc/issue: Displaying the message on a terminal at time of login. Users do not have to log in to see this message.

write

The write command enables a user to write a message to another user's terminal. The syntax is the command followed by the user ID of the person to whom you want to write. This places you in a write shell; you cancel the write shell by pressing Ctrl+C. You type a message and press Enter and the text is displayed on the other user's terminal.

> **Caution**
>
> A message is lost if the sender presses Ctrl+C after typing in the message without pressing Enter.

For example, I tried to write a message to my friend Shaggy.

```
[scooby@cartoons]$ write shaggy
Hello Shaggy.  How are you today?
[scooby@cartoons]$
```

I didn't receive a reply.

I wasn't sure that I was doing it right, so I tried to send a message to myself. Before I did, I turned off my mesg (mesg n). Here's what happened:

```
[scooby@cartoons]$ write scooby
write: you have write permission turned off.
```

As a further test, I turned my mesg on (mesg y) and tried again:

```
[scooby@cartoons]$ mesg y
[scooby@cartoons]$ write scooby

Message from scooby@cartoons on ttyp0 at 20:10 ...
hello
hello
It enters what I type, and then echoes it back to me.
It enters what I type, and then echoes it back to me.
type <ctrl>c
type <ctrl>c
EOF
[scooby@cartoons]$
```

It displayed everything that I typed and then echoed it back to me with `write`. Had this gone to another terminal when I typed and pressed Enter, the message would have been sent to the indicated user.

You will notice that when I received the message, I got an initial line that told me who the message was from, the `tty` (terminal type) I was on, and the time local to the server:

```
Message from scooby@cartoons on ttyp0 at 20:10 ...
```

Pressing Ctrl+C disconnected me from the `write` program, indicated by the last line showing the end of the file (`EOF`).

wall

Administrators sometimes need to send a message to all users currently logged in to the system. This type of communication is typically used when the administrator needs to inform everyone about something that affects them. The `wall` command is typically used when a system is about to shut down. Instead of just blowing everyone off the system, the system administrator might want to give users time to close their applications and save their data.

The `wall` command is short for *write all*. Just like the `write` command, it only sends the text to the terminal, and the computer does not treat the text as input from that user. The standard for `wall` is that it gets its information to display from the user's input. You can either use this method or use a less-than sign to send it information directly from a file.

In the following example, I have a small file that says `system shutting down!` The system was not really shutting down, so I made sure no one was logged in first. When a `wall` command is issued, the output goes to everyone currently logged in, including the person issuing the command.

Here's how I checked to see who was logged in:

```
[scooby@cartoons]$ who
scooby    ttyp1    Aug 24 00:10 (d4.dialup.seanet)
```

I was the only one logged in. Therefore, I issued the following command with the filename:

```
[scooby@cartoons]$ wall < test
Broadcast Message from scooby@cartoons
(/dev/ttyp1) at 0:11 ...
system shutting down!
```

Note that the output indicates that it is a broadcast message from `scooby@cartoons`. It also mentions the terminal I am on and the current time before giving the message. This information is important if something unfortunate were about to happen and a user wanted to respond. If the output were anonymous (as it is when writing to a device), then the people receiving the information would not know to whom to respond.

talk

Writing to a device with `write` or `wall` is strictly one-way communication. One-way communication has benefits as well as drawbacks. For example, what if the person receiving the data wants to respond to the message? She could use a series of `write` commands or the `talk` command. The `talk` command notifies the second person that you want to talk. The command tells the other person what to type in order to finish initializing a `talk` session.

When the session is established, each person receives a split window. When the first person types information on the top window, it is echoed in the bottom window of the second person's display and vice versa. Also, displaying in both windows happens as each letter is typed. As one person types, the other person sees the information.

mesg

The `mesg` command was briefly mentioned in the discussion on `write`. The `mesg` command is used to allow or disallow others from writing or walling messages to you. Of course, `root` overrides the `mesg` authority. The syntax for this command is `mesg y` or `mesg n`. The `y` parameter allows the communication, and the `n` parameter disallows the communication with normal users.

motd

`motd` (*message of the day*) is a good way to pass information on to whomever happens to log in that particular day. Typically, it is a reminder or an announcement of some type. Many companies use it to announce birthdays and other days of significance or to remind users of an event or telephone number to call. `motd` is a good way to communicate if the information is either not that important or only important to a person if he or she has logged in.

`motd` is actually a file that has its contents displayed upon login. The file is kept in the `/etc` directory and is called `motd` (`/etc/motd`). For example, when I log in to my computer, I receive the following message:

```
The system will be down tomorrow for a hardware upgrade.
Hope you are having a great day!
```

> **Note**
>
> `motd` is only seen with a command-line login. This message of the day will not be seen if the user is logging in graphically as with KDE or GNOME.

Pre-Login Message

The /etc/issue file contains the message that is displayed when logging in on the console or a virtual screen (Alt+F1, F2, and so on). The /etc/issue.net file is seen on terminals opened through Telnet. Following the issue statement, the session prompts for the login and password. This pre-login message is a good place to put something that you want everyone to see before they log in to the system. This could include a notice that printers are not working or an explanation of the purpose of the workstation where they are trying to log in. The following example is the pre-login message I get when I log in to my workstation:

```
/etc/issue.net pre-login message
```

```
                                           Technology,Inc.


                        Welcome to Cartoons!



                UNAUTHORIZED USE IS STRICTLY PROHIBITED
```

```
cartoons login:
```

Although the /etc/issue file (and /etc/issue.net file) can be as long as you want it to be, it is best to keep it short. If it is too long, people won't read it, and it will scroll off their screens; those who might have read it will probably not take the time to scroll back to see what, if anything, they missed.

> **Note**
>
> Like motd, the pre-login message is only seen with a command-line login. This pre-login message is not seen if the user is logging in graphically as with KDE or GNOME.

Managing Software with RPM

Years ago, installing software on your Linux box meant untarring a file in your `root` system directory (`/`). Keeping track of what was where and trying to uninstall it was a mess, not to mention even knowing what version of the software you had.

I once removed an old library because I thought it wasn't in use anymore and I needed the disk space. After I deleted the file, half the commands on my system stopped working! Turns out there were dependencies on that library that I didn't know about.

Linux has grown to be much more sophisticated. Now it has package management tools that help you maintain a database of installed software and their files, which allows you to perform powerful queries and verification of your system.

One such tool is the Red Hat Package Manager, which is most commonly referred to as RPM. Some other distributions have their own package management tool, such as debian, but RPM is quickly becoming the standard for many distributions.

Installing

One of the most common tasks that you will use RPM for is installing new software packages. RPM packages typically are in one file having a name such as `banana-1.0-1.i386.rpm`, which includes the package name (`banana`), version (`1.0`), release (`1`), and architecture (`i386`). If you mount your Red Hat Linux CD-ROM and look under the directory `Redhat/RPMS`, you will see the hundreds of software packages that make up the Red Hat Linux distribution.

The typical command to install a package is

```
[root@cartoons]# rpm -ivh banana-1.0-1.i386.rpm
```

> **Note**
>
> To install, upgrade, or uninstall packages, you must be logged in as `root`. The easiest way to become `root` is to type **su**. Then type the `root` password at the shell prompt. However, it isn't necessary to be `root` in order to query and verify packages.

One of the more complex commands allows you to install packages via FTP rather than a CD-ROM or local disk:

```
[root@cartoons]# rpm -i ftp://ftp.redhat.com/pub/RPMS/banana-1.0-1.i386.rpm
```

RPM packages can "depend" on other packages, which means that they require other packages to be installed in order to run properly. If you try to install a package for which there is such an unresolved dependency, you'll see

```
[root@cartoons]# rpm -ivh boat-1.0-1.i386.rpm
failed dependencies:
        banana is needed by boat-1.0-1
[root@cartoons]#
```

To resolve failed dependencies, install the requested packages. If you want to force the installation anyway (a bad idea since the package probably will not run correctly), use the -nodeps option.

Uninstalling

After you have been using your Red Hat Linux system for a period of time, you may decide to remove a package because you never use it or you need to free up some disk space. RPM makes it easy, doing all the hard work for you.

Uninstalling a package is just as simple as installing. You use the following command:

```
[root@cartoons]# rpm -e banana
```

Notice that we used the package name "banana," rather than the name of the original package file banana-1.0-1.i386.rpm.

You can encounter a dependency error when uninstalling a package if some other installed package depends on the one that you are trying to remove. For example:

```
[root@cartoons]# rpm -e banana
 removing these packages would break dependencies:
        banana is needed by boat-1.0-1
[root@cartoons]#
```

You can force RPM to ignore these dependencies by using the -nodeps option, but this option is not recommended because it can leave your system in an unstable state.

Upgrading

Upgrading a package is similar to installing one. The upgrade command is

```
[root@cartoons]# rpm -Uvh banana-2.0-1.i386.rpm
 banana                         #################################
[root@cartoons]#
```

What you don't see on the preceding command is that RPM automatically uninstalled old versions of the banana package. In fact, you may want to always use -U to install packages because it works fine even when there are no previous versions of the package installed. Because RPM performs intelligent upgrading of packages with configuration

files, you may see a message such as `saving /etc/banana.conf as`
`/etc/banana.conf.rpmsave`. This means that during the upgrade, RPM considered your
changes to the existing file to be potentially incompatible with the new configuration file
in the new package. RPM saved your original configuration file and installed a new one.
You should investigate and resolve the differences between the two files as soon as possible to ensure that your system continues to function properly.

Because upgrading is really a combination of uninstalling and installing, you can
encounter regular errors from those modes, plus one additional error: If RPM thinks you
are trying to upgrade to a package with an older version number, you will see

```
[root@cartoons]# rpm -Uvh banana-1.0-1.i386.rpm
  banana    package banana-2.0-1 (which is newer) is already installed
  error: banana-1.0-1.i386.rpm cannot be installed
[root@cartoons]#
```

To cause RPM to upgrade anyway, include `--oldpackage` in the upgrade command:

```
[root@cartoons]# rpm -Uvh --oldpackage banana-1.0-1.i386.rpm
  banana                       ##################################
[root@cartoons]#
```

Querying

You can query the database to find installed packages by using the `rpm -q` command. A
simple use is `rpm -q banana`, which will print the package name, version, and release
number of the installed package banana. For example:

```
[scooby@cartoons]$ rpm -q banana
  banana-2.0-1
[scooby@cartoons]$
```

Package Specification Options

Instead of specifying the package name, you can use the Package Specification Options
with `-q` to specify the package(s) that you want to query. These options include the
following:

- `-a`—Queries all currently installed packages.
- `-f <file>`—Queries the package owning the specified file.
- `-p <packagefile>`—Queries the specified package filename.

Information Options

You can specify what information to display about queried packages. The following
options are used to select the type of information for which you are searching:

- `-i` displays package information such as name, description, release, size, build
  date, install date, vendor, and other miscellaneous information.

- `-l` displays the list of files that the package "owns."

- `-s` displays the state of all the files in the package.

- `-d` displays a list of files marked as documentation (man pages, info pages,
  READMEs, and so on).

- `-c` displays a list of files marked as configuration files. These are the files that you
  change after installation to adapt the package to your system (`sendmail.cf`,
  `passwd`, `inittab`, and so on).

For those options that display file lists, you can add `-v` to the query command to view the
list in the familiar `ls -l` format.

Here's an example of doing a more sophisticated query:

```
[scooby@cartoons]$ rpm -qi kernel
Name        : kernel                      Relocations: (not relocateable)
Version     : 2.2.16                      Vendor: Red Hat, Inc.
Release     : 5.0                 Build Date: Wed 26 Jul 2000 09:13:08 PM EST
Install date: Sat 05 Apr 2000 08:44:13 AM EDT    Build Host: porky.redhat.com
Group       : System Environment/Kernel   Source RPM: kernel-2.2.16-17.src.rpm
Size        : 15122940                    License: GPL
Packager    : Red Hat, Inc. <http://bugzilla.redhat.com/bugzilla>
Summary     : The Linux kernel (the core of the Linux operating system).
Description :
The kernel package contains the Linux kernel (vmlinuz), the core of your
Red Hat Linux operating system.  The kernel handles the basic functions
of the operating system:  memory allocation, process allocation, device
input and output, etc.
```

For more details about using RPM, check out `[scooby@cartoons]$ man rpm`.

Using Gnome-RPM

Red Hat Linux includes a very nice tool named Gnome-RPM that is also referred to as
gnorpm. Gnome-RPM is a Gnome-compliant GUI for the Red Hat package manager.
With Gnome-RPM, you can easily perform many of the same package management tasks
that are available to the command line.

The Gnome-RPM interface, shown in Figure 21.1, has several features:

- **Package Panel**—Located on the left of the UI; it allows you to browse groups of packages.
- **Display Window**—Located on the right of the package panel; it shows the contents of your folders in the panel.
- **Toolbar**—Located above the display and panel; it is a graphical display of package tools.
- **Menu**—Located above the toolbar; it contains text-based commands, as well as help info, preferences, and other settings.
- **Status Bar**—Located beneath the panel and display windows; it shows the total number of selected packages.

FIGURE 21.1

Gnome-RPM.

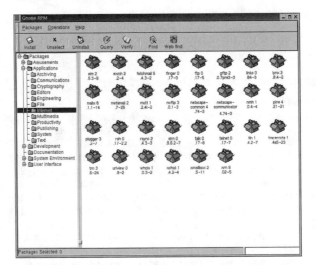

Managing Users and Groups with `linuxconf`

The `linuxconf` command is a highly welcome addition to Red Hat Linux. Having a GUI tool to manage users and groups takes a lot of hassle out of making small changes, but I'm sure that many system administrators still prefer the command-line method.

Creating and Modifying Users

Adding a user is one of the more basic tasks you can perform with `linuxconf`. When you installed Red Hat Linux you should have at least set up one user account. Adding additional users is easy.

To add a new user account, follow these steps:

1. Start `linuxconf`.
2. Click the Config tab.
3. Expand the tree browser under Users Accounts, Normal, User Accounts.
4. Click on User Accounts. You should now see the Users Accounts panel.
5. Click Add.
6. Complete the required fields.
7. Click Accept.

That's all there is to it.

> **Tip**
>
> The user account that you are creating is a login shell account. Although it is not a required field, it is probably a good idea to specify a home directory for your user.

Figure 21.2 shows the User Account Creation tab used for adding a user to `linuxconf`.

FIGURE 21.2

Adding `linuxconf`
user accounts.

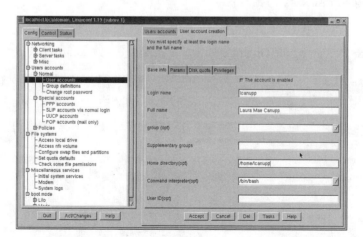

To modify your new user, just go back to the Users Accounts panel and double-click on the user you want to modify from the list. This should bring up a panel that looks like the Add panel from before, but with the appropriate fields already filled in.

Managing Groups with `linuxconf`

A group is a collection of users assembled together for a particular purpose with the intent that the users will share files or resources. This purpose could be job function—programmer, system administrator, accountant, or engineer—or the users could all have access to a special device—scanner, color printer, or modem.

The system does not limit the number of groups. You will notice that many default groups are already defined. These groups were defined when you installed Red Hat Linux.

To add a group:

1. Start `linuxconf`.
2. Click the Config tab.
3. Expand the tree browser under Users Accounts, Normal, Group Definitions.
4. Click on Group Definitions.
5. Click Add.
6. Complete the fields, providing a name for the group.
7. In the Alternate Members field, type the user ID of each user you want to add to this group.
8. Click Accept.

You just defined a new group.

Figure 21.3 shows the Group Specification tab used for adding a group.

FIGURE 21.3

Adding `linuxconf` *groups.*

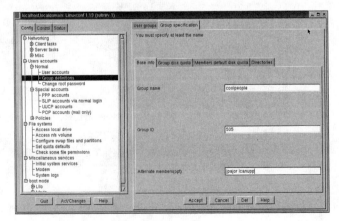

Managing Users and Groups from the Command Line

Although `linuxconf` gives you the option of having a GUI admin tool for managing users and groups, you can also manage users and groups from the command line. This is something Linux is pretty famous for.

Adding Users

The `useradd` command is a command-line utility that you can use to create a new user or to update an existing user. To add new user Barney Rubble to the system, simply `su` to `root` and type:

```
[root@cartoons]# useradd -c "Barney Rubble" -d /home/brubble brubble
```

> **Note**
>
> If you have permission problems or if the command is not found, you may want to make sure that you issue a `su -` command to obtain a `root` login shell.

The `-c` option is the full name of the person. The `-d` option is the home directory that you would want to create for this new user. Lastly, you specify the userid of your new user. Now you can assign a password to the user ID:

```
[root@cartoons]# passwd brubble
Changing password for user brubble
New UNIX password:
```

You could have set the password by including the `-p` option in the `useradd` command, but it requires the encrypted password. The two-step process is a little easier if you are manually creating a new user.

For a more detailed listing of available options for these commands, you can view the man pages for `useradd`.

Changing User Passwords

The user `root` can use the `passwd` command to change the password for any user. If you would like to change the password for the current user logged in, yourself, type **passwd**. For obvious reasons, the system will prompt you for your current password before it assigns you a new one.

Removing Users

You can remove a user with the `userdel` command:

`[root@cartoons]# userdel brubble`

You can use an `-r` option if you would like to remove the user's home directory also:

`[root@cartoons]# userdel -r brubble`

Be careful! This will delete all of the user's data. You may want to back up this data before you remove it.

For a more detailed listing of available options for these commands, you can view the man pages for `userdel`.

Managing Groups from the Command Line

Not only can you manage users from the command line, but Red Hat Linux also provides a couple of utilities for managing groups.

To create a new group you can use the `groupadd` command:

`[root@cartoons]# groupadd newgroup`

You can then add a user to the group with the `usermod` command:

`[root@cartoons]# usermod -G newgroup brubble`

To delete the group use the `groupdel` command:

`[root@cartoons]# groupdel newgroup`

All group commands modify the `/etc/group` file. This is where all group information is stored. If you are brave you can edit the file directly, although it's probably not the best idea to do so because you are more likely to introduce errors in the file than when you use the command-line utilities.

For the format of the `/etc/group` file, each line contains four segments and is delimited by colons:

`group name:password:group ID:users`

If nothing is to be entered into a field, that field is left blank. However, a colon will still delimit the field from the other fields. Table 21.1 contains a short description of each of the fields in the `/etc/group` file.

TABLE 21.1 /etc/group File Fields

Segment	Description
group name	A unique identifier for the group
password	Usually the password is blank, *, or x. By default it is x.
group ID	The unique number that identifies a group to the operating system
users	A list of all user IDs that belong to that group

When adding groups to this file, just follow the format of the existing fields. Add a unique group, assign it a password if necessary, give it a unique group ID, and then list the users associated with that group. The users are separated with commas. If you do not correctly format the line or if the data is incorrect in some other way, the users might not be able to use that group ID.

If the system were using a shadow password system, the password field would be moved to /etc/shadow.group, and an x would be assigned to the field in the /etc/group file.

When finished editing the /etc/group file, double-check its permissions. It should be owned by root, and its group should be root or sys (a group ID of 0). The permissions should be read and write for owner and read for everyone else (644 in hex).

The list of groups does not need to be in a particular order. The order of the list of users in each group is also irrelevant. Red Hat Linux will search the entire file until it comes to the line that it is looking for.

Although users can be in several groups, Linux only allows them to be active in a single group at a given time. The starting group, commonly called the *primary group*, is the group associated with the user in the /etc/passwd file. If a user wants to switch to another group (and he or she is in the group according to /etc/group), the user must issue the newgrp command to switch.

All these commands have man pages where you can read more about them.

Setting Disk Quotas with linuxconf

Most UNIX systems allow administrators to set up disk space limits for users so certain people don't hog all the space on the filesystem. This limit is known as a disk quota.

In order to set disk quotas you must first enable your filesystem for quotas. You can do this relatively easily with linuxconf.

To enable a filesystem for quotas:

1. Start `linuxconf`.

2. Click the Config tab.

3. Expand the tree browser under File Systems, Access Local Drive.

4. Click on Access Local Drive.

   You should now see a panel that looks like Figure 21.4.

FIGURE 21.4

The `linuxconf`
Access Local
Drive panel.

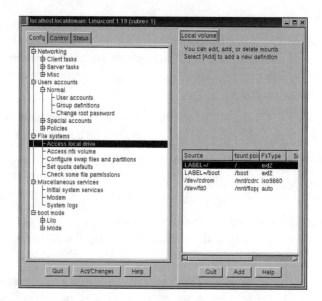

5. Now double-click on the filesystem for which you would like to enable disk quotas.

6. Select the Options tab.

   You should see a panel that looks like Figure 21.5.

7. Choose User Quota Enabled and click Accept.

After you activate the changes, if you go back to User Accounts you will notice when you modify one of your users you can now set a disk space quota for them. You can also specify a default quota for all your users under File Systems, Set Quota Defaults (see Figure 21.6).

FIGURE 21.5

linuxconf *Access Local Drive options.*

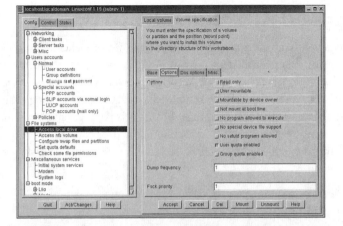

FIGURE 21.6

linuxconf *User Accounts Disk Quota options.*

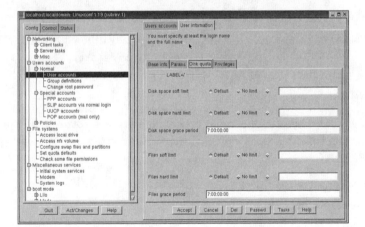

Creating Special Accounts with `linuxconf`

Normal accounts are regular login shell accounts that you can log in to at the console or remote login, if available. You can also use `linuxconf` to create special accounts. The `linuxconf` application allows you to set up special accounts that have limited privileges such as PPP accounts for dial-in access or POP accounts for email. To create special accounts, go to the Config tab under `linuxconf` and select Users Accounts, Special Accounts.

Analyzing Performance

Performance analysis is the process of identifying performance bottlenecks in your system. It involves a number of steps. The first step is to look at the big picture: Is the problem CPU- or I/O-related? If it is a CPU problem, what is the load average? You should probably check what processes are running and what is causing the problem. If it is an I/O problem, is it paging or normal disk I/O? If it is paging, increasing memory might help. You can also try to isolate the program or the user causing the problem. If it is a disk problem, is the disk activity balanced? If you have only one disk, you might want to install a second.

The next section looks at several tools that you can use to determine the answers to the preceding questions.

Determining CPU Usage with `vmstat`

CPU usage is the first test on the list. There are many different ways to obtain a snapshot of the current CPU usage. The one I focus on here is `vmstat`. The `vmstat` command gives you several pieces of data, including CPU usage. The syntax for the command is

```
vmstat interval [count]
```

interval is the number of seconds between reports, and *count* is the total number of reports to give. If the count is not included, `vmstat` will run continuously until you stop it with Ctrl+C or kill the process.

Here is an example of the output from `vmstat`:

```
[scooby@cartoons]$ vmstat 5 5
 procs                    memory    swap       io    system        cpu
 r b w  swpd  free  buff cache si so  bi  bo   in   cs  us sy  id
 0 0 0  1104  1412 10032 36228  0  0  10   8   31   15   7  4  24
 0 0 0  1104  1736 10032 36228  0  0   0   3  111   18   1  1  99
 0 0 0  1104  1816 10032 36228  0  0   0   1  115   23   2  2  96
 0 1 0  1104  1148 10096 36268  8  0   7   4  191  141   4  6  91
 0 0 0  1104  1868  9812 35676  6  0   2  10  148   39  25  4  70
```

The first line of the CPU Usage report displays the average values for each statistic since boot time. It should be ignored. For determining CPU used, you are interested in the last three columns, as indicated by the `cpu` heading. The column names are `us`, `sy`, and `id` (see Table 21.2).

TABLE 21.2   vmstat Fields For CPU Usage

CPU	Description
us	Percentage of CPU cycles spent on performing user tasks.
sy	Percentage of CPU cycles spent as system tasks. These tasks include waiting on I/O, performing general operating system functions, and so on.
id	Percentage of CPU cycles not used. This is the amount of time the system was idle.

A high CPU time (or low idle time) is not necessarily indicative of an overall CPU problem. It could be that a number of batch jobs running just need to be rearranged. To determine whether the system actually has a CPU problem, it is important to monitor the CPU percentages for a significant period of time. If the percentages are high over an extended time, then the system definitely has a problem.

Next, look at a different section of the vmstat output. If the problem is not CPU-related, check whether it is a problem with paging or normal disk I/O. To determine whether it is a memory problem, look at the headings memory and swap:

```
[scooby@cartoons]$ vmstat 5 5
procs                memory      swap        io     system         cpu
r  b  w  swpd  free  buff cache  si so   bi  bo   in   cs  us sy  id
1  0  0  1096  1848  4580 37524  0  0     9   8    8   17   7  3  29
1  0  0  1096  1424  4580 37980  0  0    92  10  125   24  94  4   3
2  0  0  1096   864  4536 38408  0  0   112  31  146   42  93  2   5
2  0  0  1096   732  4360 38480  10 0    98   7  146   48  97  3   1
```

Included in the vmstat output is a "snapshot" table detailing the status of your system's memory (see Table 21.3).

TABLE 21.3   vmstat Fields for Memory and Swap Usage

Memory & Swap	Description
swpd	The amount of virtual memory used (KB)
free	The amount of idle memory (KB)
buff	The amount of memory used as buffers (KB)
cache	The amount of memory left in the cache (KB)
si	The amount of memory swapped in from disk (KB/s)
so	The amount of memory swapped to disk (KB/s)

The most important of these fields is the swap in column. This column shows paging that has previously been swapped out, even if it was done before the vmstat command was issued.

The `io` section is used to determine whether the problem is with blocks sent in or out of the device:

```
[scooby@cartoons]$ vmstat 5 5
 procs                    memory   swap      io    system        cpu
 r b w  swpd  free  buff cache si  so  bi  bo   in  cs  us sy  id
 1 0 0  1096  1848  4580 37524  0   0   9   8    8  17   7  3  29
 1 0 0  1096  1424  4580 37980  0   0  92  10  125  24  94  4   3
 2 0 0  1096   864  4536 38408  0   0 112  31  146  42  93  2   5
 2 0 0  1096   732  4360 38480 10   0  98   7  146  48  97  3   1
```

The `io` section is described in Table 21.4.

TABLE 21.4   `vmstat` Fields for IO

IO	Description
bi	The blocks sent to a block device (blocks/s)
bo	The blocks received from a block device (blocks/s)
cs	The number of context switches per second

These fields run from several to several hundred (maybe even several thousand). If you are having a lot of in and out block transfers, the problem is probably here. Keep in mind, however, that a single reading is not indicative of the system as a whole; it's just a snapshot of the system at that time. Processes can exist in three states: runtime, uninterrupted sleep, and swapped out (see Table 21.5).

TABLE 21.5   `vmstat` Fields for Processor Usage

Processes	Description
r	The number of processes waiting for runtime
b	The number of processes in uninterrupted sleep
w	The number of processes swapped out but otherwise able to run

The number of processes waiting for runtime is a good indication that there is a problem. The more processes waiting, the slower the system. More than likely, you won't look at `vmstat` unless you already know there is a bottleneck somewhere, so the r field doesn't give you much vital information.

Using top to Identify Problems

The `top` command provides another tool for identifying problems with a Linux system. The `top` command displays the top CPU processes. More specifically, `top` provides an ongoing look at processor activity in real time. It displays a listing of the most CPU-intensive tasks on the system and can provide an interactive interface for manipulating processes. The default is to update every five seconds. The following is an example of the output from `top`:

```
 1:36am  up 16 days,  7:50,  3 users,  load average: 1.41, 1.44, 1.21
60 processes: 58 sleeping, 2 running, 0 zombie, 0 stopped
CPU states: 89.0% user,  8.5% system, 92.4% nice,  3.9% idle
Mem:  63420K av, 62892K used,    528K free, 32756K shrd,  6828K buff
Swap: 33228K av,  1096K used, 32132K free                38052K cached
PID USER      PRI  NI  SIZE  RSS SHARE STATE  LIB %CPU %MEM   TIME COMMAND
```

Table 21.6 explains the values output when using the `top` command.

TABLE 21.6 top Fields

Field	Description
up	The time the system has been up and the three load averages for the system. The load averages are the average number of processes ready to run during the last 1, 5, and 15 minutes. This line is just like the output of `uptime`.
processes	The total number of processes running at the time of the last update. This is also broken down into the number of tasks that are running, sleeping, stopped, and zombied.
CPU states	The percentage of CPU time in user mode, system mode, niced tasks, and idle. (*Niced* tasks are only those whose `nice` value is negative.) Time spent in niced tasks is also counted in system and user time, so the total is more than 100 percent.
Mem	Statistics on memory usage, including total available memory, free memory, used memory, shared memory, and memory used for buffers.
Swap	Statistics on swap space, including total swap space, available swap space, and used swap space. This and `Mem` are just like the output of `free`.
PID	The process ID of each task.
USER	The username of the task's owner.
PRI	The priority of the task.
NI	The `nice` value of the task. Negative `nice` values are lower priority.
SIZE	The size of the task's code plus data, plus stack space, in kilobytes.
RSS	The total amount of physical memory used by the task, in kilobytes.
SHARE	The amount of shared memory used by the task.
STATE	The state of the task, either S for sleeping, D for uninterrupted sleep, R for running, Z for zombied, or T for stopped or traced.

TABLE 21.6   continued

Field	Description
TIME	Total CPU time the task has used since it started. If cumulative mode is on, this also includes the CPU time used by the process's children that have died. You can set cumulative mode with the s command-line option or toggle it with the interactive command s.
%CPU	The task's share of the CPU time since the last screen update, expressed as a percentage of total CPU time.
%MEM	The task's share of the physical memory.
COMMAND	The task's command name, which is truncated if tasks have only the name of the program in parentheses (for example, (getty)).

As you can probably tell from the server used to obtain the previously displayed top data, there are no current bottlenecks in the system.

Using free to Show Available Memory

free is another good command for showing the amount of used and free memory:

```
[scooby@cartoons]$ free
             total       used       free     shared    buffers     cached
Mem:         63420      61668       1752      23676      13360      32084
-/+ buffers:            16224      47196
Swap:        33228       1096      32132
```

Table 21.7 describes the values returned when using the free command.

TABLE 21.7   free Fields

Field	Description
Mem	Shows the physical memory.
total	Shows the amount of physical memory not used by the kernel, which is usually about a megabyte.
used	Shows the amount of memory used.
free	Shows the amount of free memory.
shared	Shows the amount of memory shared by several processes.
buffers	Shows the current size of the disk buffer cache.
cached	Shows how much memory has been cached off to disk.
Swap	Shows similar information for the swapped spaces. If this line is all zeros, your swap space is not activated.

To activate a swap space, use the `swapon` command. The `swapon` command tells the kernel that the swap space can be used. The location of the swap space is given as the argument passed to the command. The following example shows starting a temporary swap file:

```
[root@cartoons]# swapon /temporary_swap partition
```

To automatically use swap spaces, list them in the `/etc/fstab` file. The following example lists two swap files for `/etc/fstab`:

```
/dev/hda8 none swap sw 0 0
/swapfile none swap sw 0 0
```

To remove a swap space, use the `swapoff` command. Usually, this is necessary only when using a temporary swap space.

> **Caution**
>
> If swap space is removed, the system will attempt to move any swapped pages into other swap space or to physical memory. If there isn't enough space, the system will freak out but will eventually come back (this is commonly called *thrashing*). The system will be unavailable during the time it is trying to figure out what to do with these extra pages. Also keep in mind that, depending upon how much real memory you have, the system may never figure out what to do with these pages.

Using `renice` to Alter Process Priorities

The `renice` command is used to alter the priority of running processes.

By default in Red Hat Linux, the `nice` value is 0. The range of this is –20 to 20. The lower the value, the faster the process runs. The following example shows how you display the `nice` value by using the `nice` command. My shell is running at the default value of 0. To check this another way, I issue the `ps -l` command. The NI column shows the nice value:

```
[scooby@scooby]$ nice
0
[scooby@cartoons]$ ps -l
  FLAGS    UID   PID  PPID PRI  NI   SIZE  RSS WCHAN       STA TTY TIME COMMAND
    100    759  3138  3137   0   0   1172  636 force_sig   S   p0  0:00 -bash
 100000    759  3307  3138  12   0    956  336             R   p0  0:00 ps -l
```

I can change the nice value by using the renice command. The syntax of the command follows:

```
renice priority [[-p] pid ...] [[-g] pgrp ...] [[-u] user ...]
```

In the following example, the shell's nice value is changed to a value of 5. This means that any process with a lower value will have priority on the system:

```
[scooby@cartoons]$ renice 5 3138
3138: old priority 0, new priority 5
[scooby@cartoons]$ nice
5
[scooby@cartoons]$ ps -l
 FLAGS    UID   PID  PPID PRI  NI   SIZE  RSS WCHAN      STA TTY TIME COMMAND
    100   759  3138  3137   5   5   1172  636 force_sig  S N p0  0:00 -bash
 100000   759  3319  3138  14   5    968  368            R N p0  0:00 ps -l
```

The owner of the process and root have the ability to change the nice value to a higher value. Unfortunately, the reverse is not true:

```
[scooby@cartoons]$ renice -5 3138
renice: 3138: setpriority: Permission denied
```

Only root has the ability to lower a nice value. This means that even though I set my shell to a nice value of 5, I cannot lower it even to the default value.

The renice command is a wonderful way of increasing the apparent speed of the system for certain processes. This is a trade-off, however, because the processes that are raised will now run slower.

One other command that may help as you are trying to troubleshoot your system is the lsof command. The lsof command lists open files. The output includes information about the type of file, the device using the file, its node, and its name.

For more info, see the man pages for these commands.

Understanding Your Security Responsibilities

A system is only as secure as its weakest link, and the system administrator has to be extremely cautious. Keeping on top of possible vulnerabilities is essential, especially if the system contains important data.

Choosing Good Passwords

Choosing a good password is very important. It is important to make sure it doesn't fall into the wrong hands, too! This is especially true for the superuser, root. Imagine someone gains access as superuser to the system. He can do anything he pleases, such as reading everyone's email and files or even erasing the whole system! Passwords should not be easy to guess. Having a password that is your birthday is not a good idea nor is having a password that is all numbers or all letters.

Making Security Updates

Keeping your software up to date is imperative. Every day you hear about vulnerabilities. The older your software is, the more known holes that a hacker can exploit. It is a good idea to periodically check for Red Hat Linux updates and security advisories at `http://www.redhat.com/apps/support/updates.html`. CERT also posts advisories and available updates for many platforms at `http://www.cert.org`.

Getting Help

All system administrators soon realize that they cannot possibly know everything about the operating system; it is too complex and it changes on a regular basis. A good system administrator, however, knows where to turn to get help. Because you are reading this book, you have at least started on your way to becoming a good system administrator. This book unleashes many of the tools and "secrets" of the Red Hat Linux operating system. With a book of this type, the index is very important. A book like this is not bought to be read from cover to cover, like a good C.S. Lewis novel, but is intended to be a resource guide—a place to go to find specific answers to specific questions. The following sections discuss the places you can turn to for help.

Using Man Pages

The man pages are like the Marines: They are your first lines of defense. Man pages contain the online version of the Red Hat Linux reference manuals and provide definitions and explanations of commands. I have referenced them a few times in this chapter. In addition, they provide optional parameters for commands to perform specific functions. Following all of the explanations are examples and other commands that are similar or relate to the command you looked up.

The format of the man pages is as follows:

> Name
> Synopsis
> Description
> Command-Line Options
> See Also
> Bugs

Over time, especially in Linux, people have customized the man pages to include other optional fields. Some of these fields are Author, Sort Keys, Updating, and Notes. The additions have been made to enhance the pages. For example, the Author section many times includes an author's email address, which is handy if the command is not working as you expected it to. (Remember, none of Linux was taken from UNIX, so small differences do exist, even in the "standard" commands.)

Probably the one thing to point out to new man page users is the syntax used for showing the command's synopsis. Several standards are followed in writing commands that are used in the man pages. Here's the synopsis for the ps command:

```
SYNOPSIS
ps  [-]  [lujsvmaxScewhrnu]  [txx]  [O[+|-]k1[[+|-]k2...]]  [pids]
```

Anything in square brackets ([ ]) is optional. Note that the only thing not optional in this command is the command itself. Therefore, you can issue the ps command without any options and you will receive a snapshot of the current processes.

[-] means that the - is an optional argument. Many commercial versions of UNIX require a dash to indicate that what follows are arguments. This is not true for the Red Hat Linux version of the ps command. The next set of characters (between the next set of square brackets) indicates that any of these parameters can be added to the ps command. For example, -la is a common set of parameters to add to the ls command; it displays a long list of all files, including hidden files.

The man pages are not a singular file or directory of Linux manuals. Instead, the man pages are a set of directories, each containing a section of the man pages. These directories contain the raw data for the man pages. Red Hat Linux has eight sections of man pages. In addition, each section has corresponding catn subdirectories that store processed versions of the man pages. When a man page is accessed, the program that formats the man pages saves a copy of the formatted man page in the catn (/var/catman/catn) directories. (This location can be changed in the /etc/man.config file to point to another location.) This saves time in the future; the next time a user requests a man page for a subject that has been accessed before, the formatting does not have to be repeated. Instead, it can be displayed from the previously formatted page. The following shows what information appears within each section:

Section	Content
1	User commands
2	System calls
3	Functions and library routines
4	Special files, device drivers, and hardware

Section	Content
5	Configuration files and file formats
6	Games and demos
7	Miscellaneous: character sets, filesystem types, data type definitions, and so on
8	System administration commands and maintenance commands

The man command searches the sections in a predefined order: 1, 6, 8, 2, 3, 4, 5, and 7. It checks for commands first, followed by system calls and library functions, and then the other sections.

One of the really nice aspects of man pages is that they can be queried using a keyword search. Using the -k option allows you to search the pages for those that contain the specified word. To use this searching capability, you must first issue the command catman -w. This command (which takes a little while to process) indexes the man pages so that the keyword search will work. After running the catman command, the man pages can be searched, as in the following example:

```
[scooby@cartoons]$ man -k show
cnfsstat (8)         - show snapshot of CNFS
dnsdomainname (1)    - show the system's DNS domain name
domainname (1)       - show or set the system's NIS/YP domain name
fbset (8)            - show and modify frame buffer device settings
ftpcount (1)         - show current number of users for each class
ftpwho (1)           - show current process information for each ftp user.
hostname (1)         - show or set the system's host name
last, lastb (1)      - show listing of last logged in users
next (1)             - show the next message
nisdomainname (1)    - show or set system's NIS/YP domain name
nodename (1)         - show or set the system's DECnet node name
nwrights (1)         - Show effective rights for file or directory
prev (1)             - show the previous message
route (8)            - show / manipulate the IP routing table
ruptime (1)          - show host status of local machines
show (1)             - show (display) messages
show (l)             - show run-time parameters for session
```

It also lets you know if it finds no entries, as this example illustrates:

```
[scooby@cartoons]$ man -k Shaggy
Shaggy: nothing appropriate
```

Creating Man Pages

One of the benefits of man pages is that you can add your own local man pages. Adding man pages is a wonderful way of documenting tools that you write for use at your site. There are directories set up specifically for adding local man pages. They are /usr/local/man/manX, where X is the section number.

The simplest way to make a man page is to create a file containing text that describes the command or topic. However, it is fairly easy to make a more elaborate page that looks like a normal man page. Man pages are designed for the `nroff` text formatter and have text and `nroff` directives intermingled.

The best way to figure out what the different directives do is to view a man page and see how it is laid out. To do this with Linux, you must first unzip the file. Once unzipped, the file can be looked at with a text editor. All the different directives begin with a period (or dot). Table 21.8 lists many of the `nroff` directives and explanations of what they do.

TABLE 21.8   `nroff` directives

Directive	Explanation
`.B`	Uses bold type for the text (entire line is bolded).
`.fi`	Starts autofilling the text (adjusting the text on the lines).
`.I`	Uses italicized type for the text (entire line is italicized).
`.IP`	Starts a new indented paragraph.
`.nf`	Stops autofilling the text (adjusting the text on the lines).
`.PP`	Starts a new paragraph.
`.R`	Uses Roman type for text given as its arguments.
`.SH`	Specifies the section heading (names are uppercase by convention).
`.TH`	Specifies the title heading (arguments are command name and section).
`.TP` *n*	Tags the paragraph (uses a hanging indent). The *n* specifies the amount to indent.

When testing the man page, you can simulate an actual man page call to the file with the following command:

```
[scooby@cartoons]$ nroff -man <file> | more
```

The man pages are not the only place where a resourceful system administrator can turn for answers. Also on your system are info pages, and assuming you installed them, HOWTO pages. You also have the Internet, where you can find email services, Web pages describing how to do things, and newsgroups.

Accessing Red Hat Mailing Lists and Newsgroups

Many mailing lists and newsgroups are available to assist you with your problems. After you have been using Linux for a while, you might even be able to answer some questions. Newsgroups are a great source of information. Before I list some newsgroups that are available to you, I want to first mention the Red Hat mailing lists (`http://www.redhat.com/mailing-lists/list_subscribe.html`).

> **Note**
>
> A *newsgroup* is a place where you can download and read postings. When you are on a *mailing list*, you are sent postings either in bulk or as they come in.

These lists are maintained and monitored by Red Hat. Direct from Red Hat's Web page, here are a few of them:

- redhat-list

  For the general discussion of topics related to Red Hat Linux.

- redhat-digest

  The digest version of the redhat-list. Instead of getting mail that goes to the redhat-list as individual messages, subscribers to this list receive periodic volumes that include several postings at once.

- redhat-announce-list

  The most important list; all Red Hat users should make it a point to subscribe. Here, security updates and new RPMs are announced. It is very low traffic and moderated for your convenience.

- redhat-install-list

  For the general discussion of installation-related topics only. This can include appropriate hardware, problems with hardware, package selection, and so on.

- redhat-ppp-list

  For the general discussion of PPP under Red Hat. This includes configuration, installation, changes, and so on.

- redhat-devel-list

  General discussion of software development under Red Hat Linux. This is where we announce the availability of alpha- and beta-quality software that is available for testing purposes (with the exception of RPM, which has its own list).

- sparc-list

  SPARC-specific issues only. This can be kernel development, SILO, and so on.

- axp-list

  Alpha-specific issues only. This can be kernel development, MILO, and so on.

- rpm-list

  Discussion of RPM-related issues. This can be RPM usage in general, RPM development using `rpmlib`, RPM development using shell scripts, porting RPM to non-Linux architectures, and so on.

- cde-list

  CDE discussion only. Mostly related to installation and usage.

- post-only

  This "list" is a fake list. It has no posting address, only a request address (`post-only-request@redhat.com`). You can subscribe to this list to be allowed to post to any of the Red Hat mailing lists without receiving any mail from them. We do not allow posts from folks who aren't subscribed to the list, but people frequently want to read the list via local gateways and don't need to subscribe themselves. This way, you just subscribe to post-only to be allowed to post to any list.

Each of these lists has a subscription address, the list address with `-request` on the end of it. For example, for redhat-list, you send your subscription or unsubscription request to `redhat-list-request@redhat.com`. For the RPM list, you use `rpm-list-request@ redhat.com`. All you need to send is the word `subscribe` in the subject line of your message to subscribe and `unsubscribe` in the subject line to unsubscribe. You can leave the body of the message empty.

> **Note**
>
> To unsubscribe from redhat-digest, send your request to
> `redhat-digest-request@redhat.com`, not `redhat-list-request`.

Accessing Other Newsgroups and Web Pages

Other newsgroups require a newsreader. Most of the current browsers supply some kind of newsreader. There are somewhere around 15,000 to 20,000 newsgroups. Following is a list of some of interest to Linux users:

- `comp.os.linux.advocacy`
- `comp.os.linux.alpha`
- `comp.os.linux.development`
- `comp.os.linux.hardware`
- `comp.os.linux.help`

- comp.os.linux.m68k
- comp.os.linux.misc
- comp.os.linux.networking
- comp.os.linux.portable
- comp.os.linux.powerpc
- comp.os.linux.questions
- comp.os.linux.setup
- comp.os.linux.x

The preceding list consists of just a few of the actual newsgroups that specifically deal with Linux. Most of the others are similar to those listed. It is probably best to scan the newsgroups that you have access to for Linux.

Tip

There is a tool out there on the Web by deja.com that allows you to search the newsgroups. It's very helpful because most likely someone else has already asked your question. Go to `http://www.deja.com/usenet`.

In addition to newsgroups, myriad Web pages are devoted to Linux—Red Hat specifically. When I performed a search on WebCrawler (`http://www.webcrawler.com`) for `Linux`, the search located 17,789 documents; searching on `Linux AND Redhat`, the search located 2640 documents. Considering so many choices and the volatility of the Web, it might be helpful if I point out and briefly describe a few Web resources I believe will be around for a while.

The first one, which should be obvious, is Red Hat's home page at `http://www.redhat.com`. It is, of course, the first place to look for any information concerning Red Hat Linux. Also, for general Linux information, good places to start are `http://www.linux.com` and `http://www.linux.org`.

Another great source for information about Linux (as well as every other type of UNIX) is `http://www.ugu.com`, the UNIX Guru Universe page. According to the site's front page, it is "the largest single point UNIX resource on the Net!" This Web site is highly configurable and provides a great deal of information on everything of value to the UNIX community.

The Linux Documentation Project (`http://www.linuxdoc.org`) has a tremendous number of links, providing everything from general Linux information, to Linux user groups, to Linux development projects. Although I do not think there is much, if anything, unique about this site, it is complete. It has information on just about everything associated with Linux including a large library of HOWTOs to help you do everything from configuring an NFS server to hacking the Linux kernel.

Summary

This chapter gave you a glimpse into the world of system administration. Some of the material presented in this chapter may be overkill for somebody administrating only a few users. For those administrating a large system, the responsibilities are far greater. However, all system administrators need to understand the basics for managing software, managing users, and making sure their system is secure.

Backup and Restore

CHAPTER 22

Depending on how you put Red Hat Linux to work, your system or systems can quickly acquire enormous amounts of valuable data. Data can be in the form of text documents, spreadsheets, graphics, software programs, databases, or numerous large or small files. Data is important because of the time it takes to create it. Even a customized Red Hat Linux system tailored for your computer and peripherals can take time to re-create. If you run a multiuser system, anywhere from 2 to 200 to 2,000 users will depend on you to safeguard their data.

Data can be lost by operator error, bad software, hardware failure, malicious cracking, or natural disaster, but savvy system administrators will devise efficient and inexpensive ways to prevent this. This chapter touches on some basic concepts to keep in mind, and introduces a few software tools included with your Red Hat Linux system that you can use to back up or restore data.

You'll learn about the qualities of a good backup plan, see the process for selecting a reliable backup medium or tool, and learn about different backup strategies.

Successful Backup Considerations

Backups can protect your investment in time and in data, but only if you are successful in backing up and keeping the information; therefore, part of a successful backup procedure is a test strategy to spot-check backups. The easiest way to spot-check your backups is to perform a restore with them, which you should attempt before it is actually needed.

If you automate the backup process, such as through the use of `crontab` scripts, make sure to perform extensive test runs in parallel with sure techniques before relying on automation.

The Difference Between Backup and Archive

You need to understand the difference between a backup and an archive. A good backup strategy involves both forms of data protection. *Backups* are file operations that save your data at regular intervals, either wholly or incrementally (see "Backup Strategies and Operations," later in this chapter). *Archives* are file operations that save your data for long periods of time. For example, the CD-ROM included with this book is an archive of the free portions of the latest Red Hat Linux distribution.

Qualities of a Good Backup

Obviously, in the best of all possible worlds, backups would be perfectly reliable, always available, easy to use, and really fast. In the real world, trade-offs must be made. For example, backups stored offsite are good for disaster recovery, but are not always available.

Above all, backups need to be reliable. A reliable backup medium will last for several years, whereas a reliable archive medium should last much longer. Of course, if the backups are never successfully written to the backup medium, it does not matter how good the medium is, and today's ever-increasing storage requirements can tax even the very best hardware and strategies.

Speed is more or less important, depending on the system and use of the data. If a time window is available when the system is not being used and the backup can be automated, speed is not an issue. On the other hand, restoration might be an issue. The time it takes to restore the data is as important as the need to have the data available.

Availability is a necessary quality. Performing regular backups does no good if, when they are needed, they are unavailable. Backups for disaster recovery may not be available locally and don't always include data timely enough to restore a single file accidentally deleted by a user. A good backup and recovery scheme includes both a local set of backups for day-to-day restores and an offsite set of backups for disaster recovery purposes.

Fast, available, reliable backups are no good if they are not usable. The tools used for backup and restoration need to be easy to use. This is especially important for restoration. In an emergency, the person who normally performs the backup and restores might be unavailable, and a nontechnical user might have to perform the restoration. Obviously, documentation is a part of usability.

Selecting a Backup Medium

Today, many choices of backup media exist, although the three most common types for a long time were floppy disks, tapes, and hard drives. Table 22.1 rates these media—and newer ones such as CD-ROM read-only and CD-RW—in terms of reliability, speed, availability, and usability.

TABLE 22.1   Backup Media Comparison

Medium	Reliability	Speed	Availability	Usability
Floppy disks	Good	Slow	High	Good with small amounts of data; bad with large amounts of data
CD-ROM RO	Good	Medium	High	Read-only media; okay for archives

TABLE 22.1 continued

Medium	Reliability	Speed	Availability	Usability
CD-RW	Good	Medium	Medium	Read-write media; economical for medium-sized systems
DVD	Good	Slow	Low	Expensive
Iomega Zip	Good	Slow	High	100-250MB storage; okay for small systems
Flash ROM	Excellent	Fast	Low	Very expensive; currently limited to less than 1GB
Tapes	Good	Medium/Fast	High	Depending on the size of the tape, can be highly usable; tapes cannot be formatted under Linux
Removable HD	Excellent	Fast	High	Relatively expensive, but available in sizes of 2GB or larger
Hard drives	Excellent	Fast	High	Highly usable

Writable CDs are good for archival purposes, and some formats, such as CD-RW, can be overwritten nearly 1,000 times; however, the expense in time tends to be high if a large number of regular archives or backups must be made. *Flopticals*, with attributes of both floppy and optical disks, tend to have the good qualities of floppy disks and tapes and are good for single file restoration. Flopticals can hold a lot of data, but have not captured the consumer market; they are popular in high-end, large-scale computing operations. More popular removable media are Iomega Zip and Jaz drives, which come in 100MB and 250MB Zip and 1–2GB Jaz form factors. Digital DAT tapes can hold many gigabytes of data, and are also popular.

Selecting a Backup Tool

Many tools are available for making backups. In addition to numerous third-party applications, Red Hat Linux comes with some standard tools for performing this task. This section examines two of them, `tar` and `cpio`.

`tar` and `cpio` are very similar. Both are capable of storing and retrieving data from almost any media. In addition, both `tar` and `cpio` are ideal for small systems, which Red Hat Linux systems often are. For example, the following `tar` command saves all files under /home to the standard output (which can then be redirected to your system's backup device or directory):

```
$ tar c /home >home.tar
```

The c option tells `tar` to create a new archive, and the specified directory is used to gather the files. The output is redirected to the file named `home.tar`.

`cpio`, although similar to the `tar` command, has several advantages. First, it packs data more efficiently. Second, it is designed to back up arbitrary sets of files. (`tar` is designed to back up subdirectories.) Third, `cpio` is designed to handle backups that span over several tapes. Finally, `cpio` skips over bad sections on a tape and continues, but `tar` crashes and burns.

> **Note**
>
> The GNU version of `tar` included with Red Hat Linux has several options useful for multi-volume backup operations. To perform a multivolume backup or restore, use `tar`'s M option on the command line. For example, to create a compressed backup of the `/home` directory via multiple floppy disks, use `tar -cvMf /dev/fd0 /home`.

AMANDA

If you're looking for more sophisticated backup software, you can also try AMANDA, the Advanced Maryland Automatic Network Disk Archiver. This free software, from the University of Maryland at College Park, can be used over a network to back up multiple computer filesystems to a single, large-capacity tape drive. Some features include graceful error recovery, compression, scheduling, encryption, and high-speed backup operation.

Red Hat Linux does not include a copy of AMANDA, which is meant for use with high-capacity tape drives, but which may also be used with floptical, CDR, or CD-RW drives. AMANDA is a sophisticated backup tool with features rivaling those of commercial software backup products. Some of these features include network operation, incremental backups, scheduling, and full dump and restore operations.

You can retrieve a copy of AMANDA from `ftp://ftp.amanda.org/pub/amanda`. The file as distributed by amanda.org will be in a compressed tar archive. Decompress the file and follow instructions for installation. If you'd prefer, you can download a copy in RPM format from `http://rpmfind.net/linux/RPM/amanda.html`.

To use AMANDA, you'll first need to assign correct user and group permissions to a designated holding directory, then create and edit a default configuration file. The configuration file tells AMANDA how much disk space to use, and what type of backup device is available. After initial configuration, AMANDA commands (and options) are generally run using the `su` command like this:

```
# su amanda -c "amandacommand [cmdoptions]"
```

AMANDA is a complex but capable backup system (begging for a graphical interface!). For a short tutorial by John R. Jackson, browse to `http://www.backupcentral.com/amanda.html`. You'll find an FAQ, along with other documentation, and example configuration files under the `/usr/share/doc/amanda-2.4.1p1/` directory. AMANDA Tape Backup information, along with the latest release may be found at `http://sourceforge.net/project/?group_id=120`. For more information, see `http://www.amanda.org`.

Backup Strategies and Operations

The simplest backup strategy is to copy every file from the system to a backup medium. This is called a *full backup*. Full backups by themselves are good for small systems.

The downside of a full backup is that it can be time-consuming. Restoring a single file from a large backup such as a tape archive can be almost too cumbersome to be of value. Sometimes a full backup is the way to go, and sometimes it is not. A good backup and recovery scheme identifies when a full backup is necessary and when incremental backups are preferred.

> **Note**
>
> If you use your Red Hat Linux system for business, you should definitely have a backup strategy. Creating a formal plan to regularly save critical information, such as customer accounts or work projects, is essential to avoid financial disaster. Even more important: After you devise your backup plan, stick to it!

Incremental backups tend to be done more frequently. With an incremental backup, only those files that have changed since the last backup are backed up. Therefore, each incremental builds upon previous incremental backups.

UNIX uses the concept of a backup level to distinguish different kinds of backups. A full backup is designated as a level 0 backup. The other levels indicate the files that have changed since the preceding level. For example, on Sunday evening you might perform a level 0 backup (full backup). Then on Monday night you would perform a level 1 backup, which backs up all files changed since the level 0 backup. Tuesday night would be a level 2 backup, which backs up all files changed since the level 1 backup, and so on. This gives way to two basic backup and recovery strategies. Here is the first:

Sunday	Level 0 backup
Monday	Level 1 backup

Tuesday	Level 1 backup
Wednesday	Level 1 backup
Thursday	Level 1 backup
Friday	Level 1 backup
Saturday	Level 1 backup

The advantage of this backup scheme is that it requires only two sets of backup media. Restoring the full system from the level 0 backup and the previous evening's incremental can perform a complete restore. The negative side is that the amount backed up grows throughout the week, and additional media might be needed to perform the backup. Here is the second strategy:

Sunday	Level 0 backup
Monday	Level 1 backup
Tuesday	Level 2 backup
Wednesday	Level 3 backup
Thursday	Level 4 backup
Friday	Level 5 backup
Saturday	Level 6 backup

The advantage of this backup scheme is that each backup is relatively quick. Also, the backups stay relatively small and easy to manage. The disadvantage is that it requires seven sets of media. Also, you must use all seven sets to do a complete restore.

When deciding which type of backup scheme to use, you need to know how the system is used. Files that change often should be backed up more often than files that rarely change. Some directories, such as /tmp, never need to be backed up.

Performing Backups with `tar` and `cpio`

A full backup with `tar` is as easy as this:

```
$ tar cf backup.tar /
```

This example uses `tar`'s `f` option, followed by the name of the desired backup archive and a designated directory tree to back up. Note that if you have a dual-boot system, and have Windows or another operating system available under the /mnt directory, those systems will also be backed up! You should also know that the GNU `tar` command can also perform on-the-fly compression using `gzip` by including the `z` option like this:

```
$ tar czf backup.tgz /
```

22

BACKUP AND RESTORE

In this example, a compressed archive of the root directory is created and saved in the file named `backup.tgz` (also known as a *compressed tarball*). This is handy for creating single archives of known directories all at once.

An incremental backup takes a bit more work. Fortunately, the `find` command is a wonderful tool to use with backups to find all files that have changed since a certain date. It can also find files that are newer than a specified file. With this information, it is easy to perform an incremental backup. The following command finds all files in the current directory (`.`) that have been modified today and backs up those files with the `tar` command to an archive on `/dev/rmt1`:

```
$ find . -mtime 1 ! -type d | tar cT - >/dev/rmt1
```

The `! -type d` says that if the object found is a directory, don't give it to the `tar` command for archiving. This is done because `tar` follows the directories, and you don't want to back up an entire directory unless everything in it has changed. Of course, the `find` command can also be used for the `cpio` command. The following command performs the same task as the preceding `tar` command, but for the entire filesystem (`/`):

```
$ find / -mtime -1 | cpio -o >/dev/rmt1
```

As mentioned, the `find` command can find files that are newer than a specified file. The `touch` command updates the time of a file and may be used to touch a file after a backup has completed. Then, at the next backup, you simply search for files that are newer than the file you touched. The following example searches for files that are newer than the file `/tmp/last_backup` and performs a `cpio` to archive the data:

```
$ find / -newer /tmp/last_backup -print | cpio -o > /dev/rmt0
```

With `tar`, the same action is completed this way:

```
$ find / -newer /tmp/last_backup | tar cT - >/dev/rmt0
```

> **Note**
>
> You may want to *touch* the file before you start the backup to ensure that the next backup gets any files modified during the current backup.

Once you have found a reliable search command and determined a reliable destination for your backup, you can then automate the process by using a `crontab` setting. For example, one simple approach to back up the `/home` directory each day might be to place your command line (as an executable script) in the `/etc/cron.daily` directory. Red Hat Linux provides (by default) hourly, daily, weekly, and monthly operations in your system's `/etc/crontab` file, which looks like this:

```
...
# run-parts
01 * * * * root run-parts /etc/cron.hourly
02 4 * * * root run-parts /etc/cron.daily
22 4 * * 0 root run-parts /etc/cron.weekly
42 4 1 * * root run-parts /cto/oron.monthly
...
```

If you take a look under the `/etc/cron.daily` directory, you'll see

```
0anacron  logrotate  makewhatis.cron  slocate.cron  tmpwatch
```

These files are executable shell scripts that are run (according to the `/etc/crontab.daily` entry) each day at 4:02 a.m. If your backup operations take too long and can possibly run into the morning work hours, you should adjust this setting, or create your own `/etc/crontab` entry, such as:

```
30 2 * * *     /bin/tar cvzf /backup/daily.tgz /home
```

This example will back up the `/home` directory to the file named `daily.tgz` under the `/backup` directory each morning at 2:30 a.m.

Performing Backups with the taper Script

The `taper` script (`/usr/sbin/taper`), included with Red Hat Linux, is a backup and restore program with a graphical interface you can use to maintain compressed or uncompressed archives on tapes or removable media (even over a network!). Using taper is easy; the format of a `taper` command line looks like this:

```
# taper <-T tape-type> <option> <device>
```

You first need to decide what type of device (or media) you'd like to use with `taper`. This program supports a number of devices, which are listed in Table 22.2 along with the command lines to use.

TABLE 22.2 Device Support by taper

Device	Type	Command Line
/dev/zftape	Floppy tape driver	# taper -T z
/dev/ht0	IDE tape driver	# taper -T i
file	File on hard disk	# taper -T l
/dev/ftape	Floppy tape driver	# taper -T f
/dev/fd0	Removable floppy drive	# taper -T r
/dev/sda4	Removable Zip drive	# taper -T r -b /dev/sda4 (-b denotes the device and archive file)
/dev/sda	SCSI tape drive	# taper -T s

After you start `taper` from the command line of your console or an X11 terminal window (you must be the `root` operator), you'll see a main menu of options to back up, restore, re-create, verify, set preferences, or exit, as shown in Figure 22.1.

FIGURE 22.1

The taper *script offers a graphical interface to back up and restore operations for Linux.*

Navigate through `taper`'s menus with your up or down arrow keys and press the Enter key to make a selection. If you're not sure what keys to use, type a question mark (?) to have `taper` show a concise Help screen.

Start the backup process by selecting files or directories for your backup. First, highlight the Backup Module menu item and then press the Enter key. The `taper` script checks the status of the device you've specified on the command line and then looks for an existing tape archive on the device. If none is found, `taper` asks you to name the volume and then give a name for the new archive. You'll then see a directory listing similar to that in Figure 22.2.

FIGURE 22.2

The taper *script offers selective backup and restoration of your directories or files.*

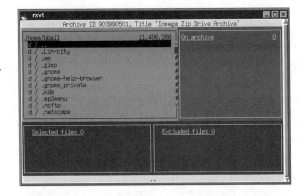

Next, navigate through the listings or directories, using the i or I key to select files or directories to back up. When you finish, press the f or F key to start backing up your files. The `taper` script has many features and can be customized through preference settings in its main menu. For detailed information, see its documentation under the `/usr/share/doc/taper-6.9b` directory.

Restoring Files

Backing up files is a good thing, but backups are like insurance policies. When it is time for them to pay up, you want it all, and you want it now! To get the files, you must restore them. Fortunately, it is not difficult to restore files with either `tar` or `cpio`. The following command restores the file `/home/alana/bethany.txt` from the current archive in the drive:

```
$ tar -xpf /dev/rmt0 /home/alana/bethany.txt
$ cpio -im `*bethany.txt` < /dev/rmt0
```

The `-p` in `tar` and the `-m` in `cpio` ensure that all of the file attributes are restored along with the file. By the way, when you restore directories with `cpio`, the `-d` option creates subdirectories. The `tar` command creates subdirectories automatically.

What Is in the Archive?

When you have an archive on a removable device, you might not know what is on it. Perhaps you are using a multiple-level backup scheme and you don't know which day the file was backed up. Both `tar` and `cpio` offer a way of creating a table of contents for the tape. The most convenient time to create this TOC file, of course, is during the actual backup. The following two lines show how to perform a backup and at the same time create a table of contents file for that archive:

```
$ tar cvf - / > /tmp/backup.Monday.TOC
$ find / -print | cpio -ov > /dev/rmt0 2> /tmp/backup.Monday.TOC
```

The `cpio` backup automatically sends the list to standard error; therefore, this line just captures standard error and saves it as a file. By the way, if the > in the `cpio` command is replaced with the word `tee`, the table of contents is not only written to the file; it is also printed to standard output (the screen). Use a command such as:

```
$ find / -print | cpio -ov | tee >/dev/rmt0 2>/tmp/backup.Monday.TOC
```

22

BACKUP AND
RESTORE

Summary

This chapter introduced some basic backup and recovery tools you can use with Red Hat Linux. Before you blindly back up your system, first sit down and plot a backup strategy. Always assume that the worst can happen! Make a plan to accommodate your users, their needs, and your needs for system integrity. For example, what happens if your system was cracked more than one month ago? Will you be able to backtrack and restore a safe system? Backups are important, but being able to restore the files is more important. Nothing will cause a lump in the throat to appear faster than trying to restore a system, only to find that the backups failed. As with any administrative task performed on a system, backups require a good plan, proper implementation, good documentation, and lots of testing. An occasional spot-check of a backup could save hours, if not days, of time.

System Security

CHAPTER 23

Security is one of the hottest topics in any system debate. How do you make your site more secure? How do you keep the hackers out of your system? How do you make sure your data is safe from intruders? How do you keep your company's secrets a secret?

Your system is as secure as its weakest point. This is an old saying, and one that is still true. I am reminded of an Andy Griffith TV show in which the town drunk (Otis) is sleeping off another episode in the jail. After he is sober, Otis looks around at the bars on the windows, the barred walls, and the gate. "A pretty secure jail," I thought, until the he pushed open the door, said good-bye to Barney, and left. So much for the security!

Many times, systems are as secure as that jail. All the bars and locks are in place, but the door is left open. This chapter takes a look at some of the bars and locks and explains how to lock the door. More importantly, though, it explains how to conduct a security audit and where to go to get more information.

Security comes in many forms. Passwords and file permissions are your first two lines of defense. After that, things get difficult. Security breaches take many forms. To understand your particular system and the security issues relevant to your system, you should first develop a security audit.

Thinking About Security—An Audit

A security audit has three basic parts, each with many issues to think about. First, you need to develop a plan, a set of security aspects to be evaluated. Second, you need to consider the tools available for evaluating the security aspects and choose ones that are suitable for your system. The third part of a security audit is knowledge gathering—not only how to use the system, but what the users are doing with the system, break-in methods for your system, physical security issues, and much more. The following sections look at each of these three pieces of the audit and offer some direction about where to go for more information.

A Security Plan

The plan can be as complex as a formal document or as simple as a few notes scribbled on the back of a dinner napkin. Regardless of the complexity, the plan should at least list what aspects of the system you are going to evaluate and how. This means asking two questions:

- What types of security problems could we have?
- Which ones can we (or should we) attempt to detect or fix?

To answer these questions, a few more questions might be necessary concerning the following areas:

- Accountability
- Change control and tracking
- Data integrity, including backups
- Physical security
- Privacy of data
- System access
- System availability

A more detailed plan can be developed based on discussion of these topics. As always, there will trade-offs; for example, privacy of data could mean that only certain people can log on to the system, which affects system access for the users. System availability is always in conflict with change control. For example, when do you change that failing hard drive on a 24/7 system? The bottom line is that your detailed plan should include a set of goals, a way of tracking the progression of the goals (including changes to the system), and a knowledge base of what types of tools are needed to do the job.

Security Tools

Having the right tools always makes the job easier—especially when you are dealing with security issues. A number of tools are available on the Internet, including tools that check passwords and system security and protect your system. Some major UNIX-oriented security organizations assist the UNIX/Red Hat Linux user groups in discussing, testing, and describing tools available for use. CERT, CIAC, and the Linux Emergency Response Team are excellent sources of information for both beginning and advanced system administrators.

The following list introduces many of the available tools. This should be a good excuse, however, to surf the Net and see what else is available.

cops	A set of programs; each checks a different aspect of security on a UNIX system. If any potential security holes do exist, the results are either mailed or saved to a report file.
courtney	A satan detector. courtney gives the system administrator an early warning of possible network intrusions by detecting and identifying satan's network probing.
crack	A program designed to find standard UNIX eight-character DES-encrypted passwords by standard guessing techniques.
deslogin	A remote login program that can be used safely across insecure networks.

freestone	A portable, fully functional firewall implementation.
ipfilter	A free packet filter that can be incorporated into any of the supported operating systems, providing IP packet-level filtering per interface.
kerberos	A network authentication system for use on physically insecure networks. It allows entities communicating over networks to prove their identities to each other while preventing eavesdropping or reply attacks.
merlin	Takes a popular security tool (such as tiger, tripwire, cops, crack, or spi) and provides it with an easy-to-use, consistent graphical interface, simplifying and enhancing its capabilities.
opie	Provides a one-time password system for POSIX-compliant, UNIX-like operating systems.
Plugslot Ltd.	PCP/PSP UNIX network security and configuration monitor.
rsaref	A cryptographic toolkit providing various functions for the use of digital signatures, data encryption, and supporting areas (PEM encoding, random number generation, and so on).
satan	The security analysis tool for auditing networks. In its simplest (and default) mode, satan gathers as much information about remote hosts and networks as possible by examining such network services as finger, NFS, NIS, ftp, tftp, and rexd.
openssh	Secure shell—a remote login program.
tcp wrappers	Can monitor and control remote access to your local tftp, exec, ftp, rsh, telnet, rlogin, finger, and systat daemon.
tiger	Scans a system for potential security problems.
tis firewall toolkit	Includes enhancements and bug fixes from version 1.2 and new proxies for HTTP/Gopher and X11.
tripwire	Monitors system for security break-in attempts.
xroute	Routes X packets from one machine to another.

As you can see, quite a few tools exist for your use. If you want a good reason for looking at these tools, keep in mind that people trying to break into your system know how to—and do—use these tools. This is where the knowledge comes in.

The expiration of the patent on the RSA public key algorithm and the relaxation of U.S. export controls on encryption software has given Red Hat the opportunity to provide robust tools for security. These include the rpms for openssh (the tool mentioned above as a secure replacement for telnet) and openssl, which is used for adding ssl support to Apache via the mod_ssl rpm.

Knowledge Gathering

Someone once said a little knowledge goes a long way. As stated in the chapter opening, all the bells and whistles can be there, but they do no good if they are not active. It is therefore important that the system staff, the users, and the keepers of the sacred root password all follow the security procedures put in place—and that they gather all the knowledge necessary to adhere to those procedures.

I was at the bank the other day, filling out an application for a car loan. The person assisting me at the bank was at a copy machine in another room (I could see her through the window). Another banking person, obviously new, could be heard from his office, where he was having problems logging in to the bank's computer. He came out and looked around for the bank employee helping me. When he did not see her, I got his attention and pointed him toward the copy area. He thanked me and went to her and asked for the system's password because he could not remember it. She could not remember the password. He went back to his desk, checked a list of telephone numbers hanging on the wall by his phone, entered something into the computer, and was in. About that time, the bank person assisting me came out of the copy area, stuck her head in his office, and said that she recalled the password. He said he had it. She asked if he had done with the password what they normally do. He looked at his phone list and said yes. She left and returned to me at her desk.

This scenario is true. The unfortunate thing about it, besides the fact that at least two customers—the person with the employee trying to log in to the system and I—saw the whole thing, is that they didn't know, nor did they care, that others might be listening. To them it was business as usual. What can be learned from this? Don't write down passwords!

Not only should passwords not be written down, they should not be easily associated with the user. I'll give you two examples that illustrate this point. The first involves a wonderful man with whom I worked on a client site. He has three boys. As a proud father, he talks about them often. When referring to them individually, he uses their first names. When referring to them collectively, he calls them "three boys." His password (he uses the same password for all his accounts) is `threeboys`.

The second example comes from one of the sweetest people I have met in the industry. On this woman's desk is a little stuffed cow named Chelsea. I do not remember the significance of the name, but I remember that she really likes dairy cows. Her password is—you guessed it—`chelsea`. These passwords are probably still `threeboys` and `chelsea`.

File security is another big issue. The use of `umask` (file creation masks) should be mandated. It should also be set to the maximum amount possible. Changing a particular file to give someone else access to it is easy. Knowing who is looking at your files is difficult, if not impossible. The sensitivity of the data, of course, would certainly determine the exact level of security placed on the file. In extremely sensitive cases, such as employees' personnel records, encryption of the files might also be necessary.

After an audit has been done, you should have an excellent idea about what security issues you need to be aware of and which issues you need to track. The next section shows you how to track intruders.

Danger, Will Robinson, Danger!

I used to love watching *Lost in Space*. On that show was a life-sized robot that would declare, "Danger, Will Robinson, danger!" when there was some danger. Unfortunately, no such robot warns of danger on our systems. (Although some tools exist, they are nowhere near as consistent as that robot was!)

If you have a lot of extra disk space, you can turn on auditing, which records all user connects and disconnects from your system. If you don't rely on auditing, you should scan the logs often. A worthwhile alternative might be to write a quick summary script that reports the amount of time each user is on the system.

Unfortunately, there are too many holes to block them all. Measures can be placed to plug the biggest, but the only way to keep a system secure is by locking a computer in a vault, allowing no one access to it and no connectivity outside the vault. The bottom line is that users who want into your system and who are good enough can get in. What you have to do is prepare for the worst.

Preparing for the Worst

The three things that a malicious user can do to a system—short of physically removing it—are stealing data, destroying data (which includes making it inaccessible), and providing easier access for the next time he wants to get into the system. Physically, an intruder can destroy or remove equipment or, if very creative, even add hardware. Short of chaining the system to the desk, retinal scans, card readers, and armed guards, there is not much you can do to prevent theft. Physical security is beyond the scope of this book. What is within the scope of this book is dealing with the data and dealing with additional access measures.

Data should be backed up on a regular basis. The backed-up information, depending on how secure it needs to be, can be kept on a shelf next to the system or in a locked vault at an alternate location. A backup is the best way of retrieving data that has been destroyed.

Most of the time, though, data is not just destroyed. A more common problem is that the data is captured. This could include actual company secrets or system configuration files. Keeping an eye on the system files is very important. Another good idea is to occasionally search for programs that have `suid` or `sgid` capability. It might be wise to search for `suid` and `sgid` files when the system is first installed, so that later searches can be compared to this initial list.

suid and sgid

Many people talk about `suid` (set user ID) and `sgid` (set group ID) without clearly understanding them. The concept behind these powerful and dangerous tools is that a program (not a script) is set to run as the owner or group set for the program—not as the person running the program. For example, say you have a program with `suid` set, and its owner is `root`. Users running the program run that program with the permissions of the owner instead of their own permissions. The `passwd` command is a good example of this. The `/etc/passwd` file is writable by `root` and readable by everyone. The passwd program has `suid` turned on; therefore, anyone can run the passwd program and change her password. Because the program is running as the user `root`, not as the actual user, the `/etc/passwd` file can be written to.

The same concept holds true for `sgid`. Instead of the program running with the permissions and authority of the group associated with the person calling the program, the program is run with the permissions and authority of the group associated with the program.

How to Find `suid` and `sgid` Files

The `find` command once again comes in handy. You can search the entire system with the following command, looking for programs with their `suid` or `sgid` turned on:

```
$ find / -perm -2000 -o -perm -4000 -print
```

Running the preceding `find` command when you first load a system is probably best, saving its output to a file readable only by `root`. Future searches can be performed and compared to this "clean" list of `suid` and `sgid` files to ensure that only the files that are supposed to have these permissions really do. With the current release of Red Hat Linux (version 7), there are approximately 30 files that have either `suid` or `sgid` set, and have either the owner or group of `root`.

Setting `suid` and `sgid`

The set user ID and set group ID can be powerful tools for giving users the ability to perform tasks without the other problems that could arise if a user has the actual permissions of that group or user. However, these can be dangerous tools as well. When considering changing the permissions on a file to be either `suid` or `sgid`, keep in mind these two things:

- Use the lowest permissions needed to accomplish the task.
- Watch for back doors.

Using the lowest permissions means not giving a file an `suid` of `root` if at all possible. Often, a less privileged person can be configured to do the task. The same goes for `sgid`. Many times, setting the group to the appropriate non-sys group accomplishes the same task while limiting other potential problems.

Back doors come in many forms. A program that allows a shell is a back door. Multiple entrances and exits to a program are back doors. Keep in mind that if a user can run an `suid` program set to `root` and the program contains a back door (users can get out of the program to a prompt without actually exiting the program), the system keeps the effective user ID as what the program is set to (`root`). The user now has `root` permissions.

With that said, how do you set a file to have the effective user be the owner of the file? How do you set a file to have the effective group be the group of the file, instead of running as the user ID or the user's group ID of the person invoking the file? The permissions are added with the `chmod` command, as follows:

```
$ chmod u+s file(s)
$ chmod g+s file(s)
```

The first example sets `suid` for the file(s) listed. The second example sets `sgid` for the file(s) listed. Remember, `suid` sets the effective ID of the process to the owner associated with the file, and `sgid` sets the effective group's ID of the process to the group associated with the file. These cannot be set on nonexecutables.

File and Directory Permissions

As I stated in the introduction to this chapter, file and directory permissions are the basics for providing security on a system. These, along with the authentication system, provide the basis for all security. Unfortunately, many people do not know what permissions on directories mean, or they assume that permissions mean the same thing they do on files. The following section describes the permissions on files; after that, the permissions on directories are described.

Files

The permissions for files are split into three sections: the owner of the file, the group associated with the file, and everyone else (the world). Each section has its own set of file permissions, which provide the ability to read, write, and execute (or, of course, to deny the same). These permissions are called a file's *filemode*. Filemodes are set with the `chmod` command.

The object's permissions can be specified in two ways—the numeric coding system or the letter coding system. Using the letter coding system, the three sections are referred to as u for user, g for group, o for other, or a for all three. The three basic types of permissions are r for read, w for write, and x for execute. Combinations of r, w, and x with the three groups provide the permissions for files. In the following example, the owner of the file has read, write, and execute permissions, and everyone else has read access only:

```
$ ls -l test
-rwxr--r--  1 dpitts   users        22 Sep 15 00:49 test
```

The command ls -l tells the computer to give you a long (-l) listing (ls) of the file (test). The resulting line is shown in the second code line and tells you a number of things about the file. First, it tells you the permissions. Next, it tells you how many links the file has. It then tells you who owns the file (dpitts) and what group is associated with the file (users). Following the ownership section, the date and timestamp for the last time the file was modified is given. Finally, the name of the file is listed (test). The permissions are actually made up of four sections. The first section is a single character that identifies the type of object listed. Check Table 23.1 to determine the options for this field.

TABLE 23.1   Object Type Identifier

Character	Description
-	Plain file
b	Block special file
c	Character special file
d	Directory
l	Symbolic link
p	Named pipe
s	Socket

Following the file type identifier are the three sets of permissions: rwx (owner), r-- (group), and r-- (other).

> **Note**
>
> A small explanation needs to be made as to what read, write, and execute actually mean. For files, a user who has *read* permission can see the contents of the file, a user who has *write* permission can write to it, and a user who has *execute* permission can execute the file. If the file to be executed is a script, the user must have read and execute permissions to execute the file. If the file is a binary, just the execute permission is required to execute the file.

Directories

The permissions on a directory are the same as those used by files: read, write, and execute. The actual permissions, however, mean different things. For a directory, read access provides the capability to list the names of the files in the directory but does not allow the other attributes to be seen (owner, group, size, and so on). Write access provides the

23

SYSTEM SECURITY

capability to alter the directory contents. This means the user could create and delete files in the directory. Finally, the execute access enables the user to make the directory the current directory.

Table 23.2 summarizes the differences between the permissions for a file and those for a directory.

TABLE 23.2 File Permissions Versus Directory Permissions

Permission	File	Directory
r	View the contents	Search the contents
w	Alter file contents	Alter directory contents
x	Run executable file	Make it the current directory

Combinations of these permissions also allow certain tasks. For example, I previously mentioned that it takes both read and execute permissions to execute a script. This is because the shell must first read the file to see what to do with it. (Remember that `#! /local/bin/perl` tells the shell to execute the `/local/bin/perl` executable, passing the rest of the file to the executable.) Other combinations allow certain functionality. Table 23.3 describes the combinations of permissions and what they mean, both for a file and for a directory.

TABLE 23.3 Comparison of File and Directory Permission Combinations

Permission	File	Directory
- - -	Cannot do anything with it.	Cannot access it or any of its subdirectories.
r - -	Can see the contents.	Can see the contents.
rw -	Can see and alter the contents.	Can see and alter the contents.
rwx	Can see and change the contents, as well as execute the file.	Can list the contents, add or remove files, and make the directory the current directory (cd to it).
r - x	If a script, can execute it. Otherwise, provides read and execute permission.	Provides capability to change to directory and list contents, but not to delete or add files to directory.
- - x	Can execute if a binary.	Users can execute a binary they already know about.

As stated, the permissions can also be manipulated with a numeric coding system. The basic concept is the same as the letter coding system. As a matter of fact, the permissions look exactly alike—the difference is the way the permissions are identified. The numeric system uses binary counting to determine a value for each permission and sets them. Also, the `find` command can accept the permissions as an argument, using the `-perm` option. In that case, the permissions must be given in their numeric form.

With binary, you count from right to left. Therefore, if you look at a file, you can easily come up with its numeric coding system value. The following file has full permissions for the owner and read permissions for the group and the world:

```
$ ls -la test
-rwxr--r--   1 dpitts    users         22 Sep 15 00:49 test
```

This would be coded as 744. Table 23.4 explains how this number was achieved.

TABLE 23.4 Numeric Permissions

Permission	Value
Read	4
Write	2
Execute	1

Permissions use an additive process; therefore, a person with read, write, and execute permissions to a file would have a 7 (4+2+1). Read and execute would have a value of 5. Remember, there are three sets of values, so each section would have its own value.

Table 23.5 shows both the numeric system and the character system for the permissions.

TABLE 23.5 Comparison of Numeric and Character Permissions

Permission	Numeric	Character
Read-only	4	r--
Write-only	2	-w-
Execute-only	1	--x
Read and write	6	rw-
Read and execute	5	r-x
Read, write, and execute	7	rwx

Permissions can be changed by using the `chmod` command. With the numeric system, the `chmod` command must be given the value for all three fields. Therefore, to change a file to read, write, and execute by everyone, you would issue the following command:

```
$ chmod 777 filename
```

To perform the same task with the character system, you would issue the following command:

```
$ chmod a+rwx filename
```

Of course, more than one type of permission can be specified at one time. The following command adds write access for the owner of the file and adds read and execute access to the group and everyone else:

```
$ chmod u+w,og+rx filename
```

The advantage that the character system provides is that you do not have to know the previous permissions. You can selectively add or remove permissions without worrying about the rest. With the numeric system, each section of users must always be specified. Looking at the preceding example (`chmod u+w,og+rx filename`), an easier way might have been to use the numeric system and replace all those letters with three numbers: `755`. The downside of the character system is apparent when complex changes are being made.

How `suid` and `sgid` Fit into This Picture

The special-purpose access modes `suid` and `sgid` add an extra character to the picture. Before examining what a file looks like with the special access modes, check Table 23.6 for the identifying characters for each of the modes and for a reminder of what they mean.

TABLE 23.6   Special-Purpose Access Modes

Code	Name	Meaning
s	suid	Sets process user ID on execution
s	sgid	Sets process group ID on execution

`suid` and `sgid` are used on executables; therefore, the code is placed where the code for the executable would normally go. The following file has `suid` set:

```
$ ls -la test
-rwsr--r--  1 dpitts    users         22 Sep 15 00:49 test
```

The difference between setting the `suid` and setting the `sgid` is the placement of the code. The same file with `sgid` active would look like this:

```
$ ls -la test
-rwxr-sr--  1 dpitts    users         22 Sep 15 00:49 test
```

To set the suid with the character system, you execute the following command:

```
$ chmod u+s <filename>
```

To set the sgid with the character system, you execute the following command:

```
$ chmod g+s filename
```

To set the suid and the sgid using the numeric system, use these two commands:

```
$ chmod 2### filename
$ chmod 4### filename
```

In both instances, you replace ### with the rest of the values for the permissions. The additive process is used to combine permissions; therefore, the following command adds suid and sgid to a file:

```
$ chmod 6### filename
```

> **Note**
>
> A sticky bit is set by using chmod 1### <filename>. If a *sticky bit* is set, the executable is kept in memory after it has finished executing. The display for a sticky bit is a t, placed in the last field of the permissions. Therefore, a file that has been set to 7777 would have the following permissions: -rwsrwsrwt.

23

The Default Mode for a File or Directory

The default mode for a file or directory is set with the umask, which uses the numeric system to define its value. To set the umask, you must first determine the value you want the files to have. For example, a common file permission set is 644, with which the owner has read and write permission and the rest of the world has read permission. After the value is determined, you subtract it from 777. Keeping the same example of 644, the value would be 133. This value is the umask value. Typically, this value is placed in a system file that is read when a user first logs on. After the value is set, all files created will set their permissions automatically, using this value.

Passwords—A Second Look

The system stores the user's encrypted password in the /etc/passwd file. If the system is using a shadow password system, the value placed in this field is x. A value of * blocks login access to the account, as * is not a valid character for an encrypted field. This field should never be edited by hand (after it is set up). Instead, a program such as passwd should be used so that proper encryption takes place. If this field is changed, the old password is no longer valid and more than likely will have to be changed by `root`.

> **Note**
>
> If the system is using a shadow password system, a separate file, `/etc/shadow`, contains passwords (encrypted, of course).

A *password* should be set up by the user and known only by the user. The system asks for the password, compares the input to the known password, and, if there is a match, confirms the user's identity and lets the user access the system. It cannot be said enough: Do not write down your password. A person who has a user's name and password is, from the system's perspective, that user—and has all of that user's rights and privileges.

Related WWW Sites

Table 23.7 shows Web locations where you can find some of the tools discussed in this chapter. Other Web sites have these tools as well, but these were chosen because they will probably still be around when this book is published and you are looking for the information. It's important, however, to keep up with sites like the BugTraq mailing list or the SecurityFocus site (`http://www.securityfocus.com/`).

TABLE 23.7 WWW Sites for Tools

Tool	Address
cops	`ftp://ftp.cert.org/pub/tools/cops`
courtney	`http://ciac.llnl.gov/ciac/SecurityTools.html`
crack	`ftp://ftp.cerias.purdue.edu/pub/tools/unix/pwdutils/crack`
deslogin	`ftp://ftp.uu.net/pub/security/des`
freestone	`ftp://ftp.soscorp.com/pub/sos/freestone`
ipfilter	`http://cheops.anu.edu.au/~avalon/ip-filter.html`
kerberos	`http://www.contrib.andrew.cmu.edu/usr/db74/kerberos.html`
merlin	`http://ciac.llnl.gov/ciac/SecurityTools.html`
Plugslot Ltd.	`http://www.plugslot.com/`
rsaref	`ftp://ftp.ox.ac.uk/pub/crypto/misc/`
satan	`http://www.fish.com/satan`

TABLE 23.7 continued

Tool	Address
openssh	http://www.openssh.com/
tcp wrappers	ftp://ftp.porcupine.org/pub/security/
telnet (encrypted)	ftp://ftp.tu-chemnitz.de/pub/Local/informatik/sec_tel_ftp/
tiger	ftp://wuarchive.wustl.edu/packages/security/TAMU/
tis firewall toolkit	ftp://ftp.tis.com/pub/firewalls/toolkit/
tripwire	ftp://wuarchive.wustl.edu/packages/security/tripwire/
xroute	ftp://ftp.x.org/contrib/utilities/

Summary

Security is only as good as the users' willingness to follow policy. On many systems and in many companies, this is where the contention comes in. The users just want to get their jobs done. The administrators want to keep undesirables out of the system. The corporate management wants to keep the corporate secrets secret. Security is, in many ways, the hardest area in which to get users to cooperate. It is, in fact, the most important. "Users who write down or share passwords," "poorly written software," and "maliciousness" are usually cited as the biggest security problems.

For the administrator in charge of the system, I can only offer this advice: The best user will only follow the policies you follow. If you have poor security habits, they will be passed along. On the other hand, people generally rise to the minimum level they see exhibited or expected. The job of the administrator is to go beyond the call of duty and gently point out improvements, while at the same time fighting the dragons at the back gate trying to get into the system.

23

SYSTEM SECURITY

Red Hat Development and Productivity

Linux C/C++ Programming Tools

UNIX and Linux shells support a wide range of commands that can be combined, in the form of scripts, into reusable programs. Command scripts for shell programs (and utilities such as gawk and Perl) are all the programming that many users need in order to customize their computing environments.

Script languages have several shortcomings, however. To begin with, the commands a user types into a script are read and evaluated only when the script is being executed. Interpreted languages are flexible and easy to use, but they are inefficient because the commands must be reinterpreted each time the script is executed. Interpreted languages are also ill suited to manipulating the computer's memory and I/O devices directly. Therefore, programs that process scripts (such as the various UNIX/Linux shells, the awk utility, and the Perl interpreter) are themselves written in the C and C++ languages, as are the UNIX and Linux kernels.

Many users find it fairly easy to learn a scripted, interpreted language because the commands usually can be tried out one at a time, with clearly visible results. Learning a language such as C or C++ is more complex and difficult because you must learn to think in terms of machine resources and the way actions are accomplished within the computer, rather than in terms of user-oriented commands. Linux comes with many tools that support program development. Not only are there the C and C++ compilers, but there are also debuggers, project organizing tools, and code management tools. This chapter introduces you to the commands used to compile C and C++ programs along with some of the other tools in the programming environment. Additional resources are listed at the end of the chapter.

Background on the C Language

C is the programming language most frequently associated with UNIX. Since the 1970s, the bulk of the UNIX operating system and its applications have been written in C. Because the C language does not directly rely on any specific hardware architecture, UNIX was one of the first portable operating systems. In other words, the majority of the code that makes up UNIX does not know and does not care which computer it is actually running on. Machine-specific features are isolated in a few modules within the UNIX kernel, which makes it easy for you to modify them when you are porting to a different hardware architecture.

C was first designed by Dennis Ritchie for use with UNIX on DEC PDP-11 computers. The language evolved from Martin Richard's BCPL, and one of its earlier forms was the B language, which was written by Ken Thompson for the DEC PDP-7. The first book on C was *The C Programming Language* by Brian Kernighan and Dennis Ritchie, published in 1978.

In 1983, the American National Standards Institute (ANSI) established a committee to standardize the definition of C. The resulting standard is known as *ANSI C*, and it is the recognized standard for the language, grammar, and a core set of libraries. The syntax is slightly different from the original C language, which is frequently called K&R for Kernighan and Ritchie. There is also an ISO (International Standards Organization) standard that is very similar to the ANSI standard.

It appears that there will be yet another ANSI C standard officially dated 1999 or in the early 2000 years; it is currently known as "C9X."

The C portion of this chapter will primarily address the 1983 ANSI C standard.

Programming in C: Basic Concepts

C is a compiled, third-generation procedural language. *Compiled* means that C code is analyzed, interpreted, and translated into machine instructions at some time prior to the execution of the C program. These steps are carried out by the C compiler and, depending on the complexity of the C program, by the make utility. After the program is compiled, it can be executed over and over without recompilation.

The phrase *third-generation procedural* describes computer languages that clearly distinguish the data used in a program from the actions performed on that data. Programs written in third-generation languages take the form of a series of explicit processing steps, or procedures. These procedures manipulate the contents of data structures by means of explicit references to their locations in memory and manipulate the computer's hardware in response to hardware interrupts.

Elements of the C++ Language

If C is the language most associated with UNIX, C++ is the language that underlies most graphical user interfaces available today.

C++ was originally developed by Dr. Bjarne Stroustrup at the Computer Science Research Center of AT&T's Bell Laboratories (Murray Hill, NJ), also the source of UNIX itself. Dr. Stroustrup's original goal was an object-oriented simulation language. The availability of C compilers for many hardware architectures convinced him to design the language as an extension of C, allowing a preprocessor to translate C++ programs into C for compilation.

After the C language was standardized by a joint committee of the American National Standards Institute and the International Standards Organization in 1989, a new joint committee began the effort to formalize C++ as well. This effort has produced several new features and has significantly refined the interpretation of other language features.

24

Linux C/C++ Programming Tools

Programming in C++: Basic Concepts

C++ is an object-oriented extension to C. Because C++ is a superset of C, C++ compilers will compile C programs correctly, and it is possible to write non–object-oriented code in C++.

The distinction between an object-oriented language and a procedural one can be subtle and hard to grasp, especially with regard to C++, which retains all of C's characteristics and concepts. One way to describe the difference is to say that when programmers code in a procedural language, they specify actions that process the data, whereas when they write object-oriented code, they create data objects that can be requested to perform actions on or with regard to themselves.

Thus, a C function receives one or more values as input, transforms or acts on them in some way, and returns a result. If the values that are passed include pointers, the contents of data variables can be modified by the function. As the standard library routines show, it is likely that the code calling a function will not know, and will not need to know, what steps the function takes when it is invoked. However, such matters as the datatype of the input parameters and the result code are specified when the function is defined and remain invariable throughout program execution.

Functions are associated with C++ objects as well. But the actions performed when an object's function is invoked can automatically differ, perhaps substantially, depending on the specific type of the data structure with which it is associated. This is known as *overloading* function names. Overloading is related to a second characteristic of C++—the fact that functions can be defined as belonging to C++ data structures, an aspect of the wider language feature known as *encapsulation*.

In addition to overloading and encapsulation, object-oriented languages allow programmers to define new abstract data types (including associated functions) and then derive subsequent data types from them. The notion of a new class of data objects, in addition to the built-in classes such as integer, floating-point number, and character, goes beyond the familiar capability to define complex data objects in C. Just as a C data structure that includes an integer element inherits the properties and functions applicable to integers, a C++ class that is derived from another class *inherits* the parent class's functions and properties. When a specific variable or structure (instance) of that class's type is defined, the class (parent or child) is said to be *instantiated*.

File Naming

Most C programs will compile with a C++ compiler if you follow strict ANSI rules. For example, you can compile the standard `hello.c` program (everyone's first program) with the GNU C++ compiler. Typically, you will name the file something like `hello.cc`, `hello.C`, `hello.c++`, or `hello.cxx`. The GNU C++ compiler will accept any of these names.

Project Management Tools

This section introduces some of the programming and project management tools included with Red Hat Linux. You will find tools on this book's CD-ROMs that you can use to help automate your software development projects. If you have some previous UNIX experience, you will be familiar with most of these programs because they are traditional complements to a programmer's suite of software.

If you have programming experience on other software platforms, you will find that these programs are easy to learn. However, mastery will come with experience!

Building Programs with `make`

The `make` command is only one of several programming automation utilities included with Red Hat Linux. You will find others, such as `pmake` (a parallel make), `imake` (a dependency-drive Makefile generator, usually for building X11 applications), `automake`, and one of the newer tools, `autoconf` (which builds shell scripts used to configure program source code packages). Check the man pages for more information.

The `make` command's roots stem from an early version of System V UNIX. The version included with Red Hat Linux is part of the GNU utilities distribution. `Make` is used to automatically handle the building and install of a program, which can be as simple as

```
# make install
```

The magic of `make` is that it will automatically update and build applications. You create this magic through a default file named `Makefile`. However, if you use `make`'s `-f` option, you can specify any Makefile, such as `MyMakeFile`, like this:

```
# make -f MyMakeFile
```

A Makefile is a text file that can contain instructions about which options to pass on to the compiler preprocessor, the compiler, and the linker. The Makefile can also specify which source code files need to be compiled (and the compiler command line) for a particular code module, and which code modules are needed to build the program—a mechanism called *dependency checking*.

Using `make` can also aid in the portability of your program through the use of macros. This allows users of other operating systems to easily configure a program build by specifying local values, such as the names and locations, or *pathnames* of any required

24

LINUX C/C++
PROGRAMMING
TOOLS

software tools. In the following example, macros define the name of the compiler (CC), the installer program (INS), where the program should be installed (INSDIR), where the linker should look for required libraries (LIBDIR), the names of required libraries (LIBS), a source code file (SRC), the intermediate object code file (OBS), and the name of the final program (PROG):

```
# a sample makefile for a skeleton program
CC= gcc
INS= install
INSDIR = /usr/local/bin
LIBDIR= -L/usr/X11R6/lib
LIBS= -lXm -lSM -lICE -lXt -lX11
SRC= skel.c
OBJS= skel.o
PROG= skel

skel:   ${OBJS}
        ${CC} -o ${PROG} ${SRC} ${LIBDIR} ${LIBS}

install: ${PROG}
        ${INS} -g root -o root ${PROG} ${INSDIR}
```

Note

The indented lines in the example above are indented with tabs, not spaces. This is very important to remember. Visually, it is difficult to see the difference but make can tell. When I first started out, I tried spaces and had a tough time figuring out why make kept giving me errors.

Using this approach, you can build the program with

```
# make
```

To build a specified component of your Makefile, use a *target* definition on the command line. To build just the program, use make with the skel target like this:

```
# make skel
```

If you make any changes to any element of a target object, such as a source code file, make will rebuild the target. To build and install the program in one step (using the example), specify the install target like this:

```
# make install
```

Larger software projects may have any number of traditional targets in the Makefile, such as

- test—To run specific tests on the final software.
- man—To process an include troff document with the -man macros.
- clean—To delete any remaining object files.
- archive—To clean up, archive, and compress the entire source code tree.
- bugreport—To automatically collect and then mail build or error logs.

The beauty of the make command is in its flexibility. You can use make with a simple Makefile, or write complex Makefiles containing numerous macros, rules, or commands that work in a single directory or traverse your filesystem recursively to build programs, update your system, and even function as a document management system. The make command will work with nearly any program, including text processing systems such as TeX!

Building Large Applications

C programs can be broken into any number of files, as long as no single function spans more than one file. To compile this program, you compile each source file into an intermediate object before you link all the objects into a single executable. The -c flag tells the compiler to stop at this stage. During the link stage, all the object files should be listed on the command line. Object files are identified by the .o suffix.

Making Libraries with ar

If several different programs use the same functions, they can be combined into a single library archive. The ar command is used to build a library. When this library is included on the compile line, the archive is searched to resolve any external symbols. Listing 24.1 shows an example of building and using a library.

LISTING 24.1 Building a Large Application

```
$ gcc -c sine.c
$ gcc -c cosine.c
$ gcc -c tangent.c
$ ar c libtrig.a sine.o cosine.o tangent.o

$ gcc -c mainprog.c
$ gcc -o mainprog mainprog.o libtrig.a
```

gcc is the command used to invoke the GNU C Compiler. The "GNU C/C++ Compiler Command-Line Switches" section will explain what -c and -o mean.

Large applications can require hundreds of source code files. Compiling and linking these applications can be a complex and error-prone task of its own. The make utility, described previously, is a tool that helps developers organize the process of building the executable form of complex applications from many source files.

Managing Software Projects with RCS and CVS

Although make can be used to manage a software project, larger software projects requiring document management, source code controls, security, and tracking usually use the Revision Control System (RCS) or the Concurrent Versions System (CVS). You will find both of these source code version control utilities on your Red Hat Linux CD-ROMs.

The RCS and CVS systems are used to track changes to multiple versions of files, and they can be used to backtrack or branch off versions of documents inside the scope of a project. The systems are also used to prevent or resolve conflicting entries or (sometimes simultaneously) changes to source code files by numerous developers.

Although RCS and CVS aim to provide similar features, the main difference between the two systems is that RCS uses a locking and unlocking scheme for access, whereas CVS provides a modification and merging approach to working on older, current, or new versions of software. Whereas RCS uses different programs to check in or out of a revision under a directory, CVS uses a number of administrative files in a software *repository* of source code *modules* to merge and resolve change conflicts.

RCS uses at least eight separate programs, including the following:

- ci—Checks in revisions.
- co—Checks out revisions.
- ident—Keyword utility for source files.
- rcs—Changes file attributes.
- rcsclean—Cleans up working files.
- rcsdiff—Revision comparison utility.
- rcsmerge—Merges revisions.
- rlog—Logging and information utility.

Source code control with CVS requires the use of at least six command options on the cvs command line. Some of these commands require additional fields, such as the names of files:

- checkout—Checks out revisions.
- update—Updates your sources with changes by other developers.

- add—Adds new files in cvs records.

- import—Adds new sources into the repository.

- remove—Eliminates files from the repository.

- commit—Publishes changes to other repository developers.

RCS and CVS may be used for more than software development projects. These tools may also be used for document preparation and workgroup editing of documents, and will work with any text files. Both systems use registration and control files to accomplish revision management. Both systems also offer the opportunity to revisit any step or branch in a revision *history*, and to restore previous versions of a project. This mechanism is extremely important in cross-platform development or for software maintenance.

Tracking information is usually contained in separate control files, and each document within a project may contain information automatically updated with each change to a project using a process called *keyword substitution*. CVS can use keywords similar to RCS, which are usually included inside C comment strings (/* */) near the top of a document. A sample of the available keywords includes

- $Author$—Username of person performing last check-in.

- $Date$—Date and time of last check-in.

- $Header$—Inserts the pathname of the document's RCS file, revision number, date and time, author, and state.

- Id—Same as $Header$, but without full pathname.

- $Name$—A symbolic name (see the co man page).

- $Revision$—The assigned revision number (such as 1.1).

- $Source$—RCS file's full pathname.

- $State$—The state of the document, such as Exp for experimental, Rel for released, or Stab for stable.

These keywords may also be used to insert version information into compiled programs by using character strings in program source code. For example, given an extremely short C program named foo.c:

```
/* $Header$ */
#include <stdio.h>
static char rsrcid{} = "$Header$";
main() {
    printf("Hello, Linus!\n");
}
```

24

**LINUX C/C++
PROGRAMMING
TOOLS**

The resulting $Header$ keyword may expand (in an RCS document) to

```
$Header: /home/bball/sw/RCS/foo.c,v 1.1 1999/04/20 15:01:07 root Exp Root $
```

Getting started with RCS is as simple as creating a project directory and an RCS directory under the project directory, and then creating or copying initial source files in the project directory. You then use the `ci` command to check in documents. Getting started with CVS requires you to initialize a repository by first setting the `$CVSROOT` environment variable with the full pathname of the repository and then using the `init` command option with the `cvs` command, like this:

```
# cvs init
```

You will find documentation for RCS and CVS in various man pages, under the `/usr/doc` directories for each of them, and in GNU info documents.

Many organizations use CVS and RCS to manage the source for their projects. There are also commercial code-management (version control) tools that include fancy interfaces, homogenous platform support, and greater flexibility. But those tools require dedicated administrators and significant licensing costs—major disadvantages when compared to RCS or CVS.

Debugging Tools

Debugging is a science and an art unto itself. Sometimes, the simplest tool—the code listing—is best. At other times, however, you need to use other tools. Three of these tools are `lint`, `gprof`, and `gdb`. Other available tools include `escape`, `cxref`, and `cb`. Many UNIX commands have debugging uses.

`lint` is a traditional UNIX command that examines source code for possible problems, but it is not included with Red Hat Linux. The code might meet the standards for C and compile cleanly, but it might not execute correctly. `lint` checks type mismatches and incorrect argument counts on function calls. `lint` also uses the C preprocessor, so you can use command-like options similar to those you would use for `gcc`. The GNU C compiler supports extensive warnings (through the `-Wall` and `-pedantic` options) that might eliminate the need for a separate `lint` command.

> **Note**
>
> If you would like to explore various C syntax-checking programs, navigate to `http://metalab.unc.edu/pub/Linux/devel/lang/c`. One program that closely resembles the traditional `lint` program is `lclint`, found in the `lclint-2.2a-src.tar.gz` file.

The gprof command is used to study how a program is spending its time. If a program is compiled and linked with -p as a flag, a mon.out file is created when it executes, with data on how often each function is called and how much time is spent in each function. gprof parses and displays this data. An analysis of the output generated by gprof helps you determine where performance bottlenecks occur. Whereas using an optimizing compiler can speed up your program, taking the time to use gprof's analysis and revising bottleneck functions will significantly improve program performance.

The third tool is gdb—a symbolic debugger. When a program is compiled with -g, the symbol tables are retained and a symbolic debugger can be used to track program bugs. The basic technique is to invoke gdb after a core dump and get a stack trace. This indicates the source line where the core dump occurred and the functions that were called to reach that line. Often, this is enough to identify the problem. It is not the limit of gdb, though.

gdb also provides an environment for debugging programs interactively. Invoking gdb with a program enables you to set breakpoints, examine variable values, and monitor variables. If you suspect a problem near a line of code, you can set a breakpoint at that line and run the program. When the line is reached, execution is interrupted. You can check variable values, examine the stack trace, and observe the program's environment. You can single-step through the program, checking values. You can resume execution at any point. By using breakpoints, you can discover many of the bugs in your code that you have missed.

There is an X Window version of gdb called xxgdb.

> **Note**
>
> If you browse to http://metalab.unc.edu/pub/Linux/devel/debuggers, you will find at least a dozen different debuggers, including the Data Display Debugger, or ddd, an interface to gdb.

24

Linux C/C++ PROGRAMMING Tools

cpp is another tool that can be used to debug programs. It performs macro replacements, includes headers, and parses the code. The output is the actual module to be compiled. Normally, though, cpp is never executed by the programmer directly. Instead, it is invoked through gcc with either an -E or -P option. -E sends the output directly to the terminal; -P makes a file with an .i suffix.

GNU C/C++ Compiler Command-Line Switches

If you loaded the development tools when you installed Linux (or later using RPM), you should have the GNU C/C++ compiler (gcc). Many different options are available for the GNU C/C++ compiler, and many of them match the C and C++ compilers available on other UNIX systems. Table 24.1 shows the important switches. Look at the man page or info file for gcc for a full list of options and descriptions.

TABLE 24.1 GNU C/C++ Compiler Switches

Switch	Description
-x *language*	Specifies the language (C, C++, Java, and assembler are valid values).
-c	Compiles and assembles only (does not link).
-S	Compiles (does not assemble or link); generates an assembler code (.s) file.
-E	Preprocesses only (does not compile, assemble, or link).
-o *file*	Specifies the output filename (a.out is the default).
-l *library*	Specifies the libraries to use.
-I *directory*	Searches the specified directory for include files.
-w	Inhibits warning messages.
-pedantic	Strict ANSI compliance required.
-Wall	Prints additional warning messages.
-g	Produces debugging information (for use with gdb).
-ggdb	Generates native-format debugging info (and gdb extensions).
-p	Produces information required by gprof.
-pg	Produces information for use by gprof.
-O	Optimizes.

The compilation process takes place in several steps:

1. First, the C preprocessor parses the file. To do so, it sequentially reads the lines, includes header files, and performs macro replacement.

2. The compiler parses the modified code for correct syntax. This builds a symbol table and creates an intermediate object format. Most symbols have specific memory addresses assigned, although symbols defined in other modules, such as external variables, do not.

3. The last compilation stage, linking, ties together different files and libraries and then links the files by resolving the symbols that had not previously been resolved.

New Features of the GNU egcs Compiler System

The egcs (pronounced "eggs") program suite originally was an experimental version of the gcc compiler whose development was first hosted by Cygnus Support (which is now part of Red Hat). Starting with Red Hat 5.1 for Intel, egcs was made available for installation as part of your Red Hat Linux system.

When first being developed, Cygnus described egcs as an experimental step in the development of gcc. Since its first release in late summer 1997, egcs has incorporated many of the latest developments and features from *parallel* development of gcc with many new developments of its own, such as a built-in Fortran 77, Java, and Objective C front ends. Some people have suggested that the name be changed from "Experimental GNU Compiler System" to "Enhanced GNU Compiler System."

> **Note**
>
> You will need to use the gcj front end to the egcs compiler to compile Java language classes. The front-end software and related packages should be included with Red Hat Linux, but you can find out more about egcs Java support by browsing to
>
> http://sources.redhat.com/java/compile.html
>
> Intrepid Linux developers can jump right to the source code tree for the latest egcs and Java support software via the Red Hat Web site.

Although some Linux developers may have felt that development of egcs represented a fork (or split) in gcc compiler development, Cygnus stated that cooperation between the developers of gcc and egcs would prevent this. The hope, according to Cygnus, was that the new compiler architecture and features of egcs would help gcc be the best compiler in the world.

In April 1999, egcs officially became part of future GNU gcc software, and according to Cygnus, the egcs team will be responsible for rolling out future GCC releases. We can only hope that Red Hat will live up to that commitment.

Problems might occur when you are using egcs if you try to build a software package written in C++ that references gcc in its Makefile.

24

LINUX C/C++
PROGRAMMING
TOOLS

The Makefile script may contain names and locations of programs and files used during the build process. The `wmx Makefile` contained the following two definitions:

```
CC    = gcc
CCC   = gcc
```

While this will work if you have only `gcc` installed, if you install the `egcs` suite, you will need to change the name of the designated C++ compiler in your Makefile to `g++`, like this:

```
CC    = gcc
CCC   = g++
```

Just be aware that if you use `egcs` to compile C++ source files (files ending in `.C`, `.cc`, or `.cxx`), you might have to fix the software's Makefile first.

For more information about `egcs` and the latest updates, versions, or feature news about `egcs`, browse to `http://www.gnu.org/software/gcc/gcc.html`. You will find an `egcs` FAQ and pointers to the latest stable `egcs` release, or snapshots of the most recent development version.

Additional Resources

If you are interested in learning more about C and C++, you should look for the following books:

- *Sams Teach Yourself C in 21 Days*, by Peter Aitken and Bradley Jones, Sams Publishing.
- *Sams Teach Yourself C++ for Linux in 21 Days*, by Jesse Liberty and David B. Horvath, CCP, Sams Publishing.
- *C How to Program* and *C++ How to Program*, by H. M. Deitel and P. J. Deitel.
- *The C Programming Language*, by Brian Kernighan and Dennis Ritchie.
- *The Annotated C++ Reference Manual*, by Margaret Ellis and Bjarne Stroustrup.
- *Programming in ANSI C*, by Stephen G. Kochan.

Summary

UNIX was built on the C language. C is a platform-independent, compiled, procedural language based on functions and the capability to derive new, programmer-defined data structures.

C++ extends the capabilities of C by providing the necessary features for object-oriented design and code. C++ compilers such as gcc correctly compile ANSI C code. C++ also provides some features, such as the capability to associate functions with data structures, that do not require the use of full, class-based, object-oriented techniques. For these reasons, the C++ language allows existing UNIX programs to migrate toward the adoption of object orientation over time.

Red Hat Linux is full of tools that make your life as a C/C++ programmer easier. There are tools to create your program (editors), compile it (gcc and egcs), create libraries (ar), control the source (RCS and CVS), build your code (make), debug it (gdb and xxgdb), and finally, determine where inefficiencies lie (gprof). Take advantage of the environment!

CHAPTER 25

Shell Scripting

IN THIS CHAPTER

When you enter commands from the command line, you are entering commands one at a time and getting a response from the system. From time to time, you will need to execute more than one command, one after the other, and get the final result. You can do so with a *shell program* or *shell script*. A shell program is a series of Linux commands and utilities that have been put into a file by using a text editor. When you execute a shell program, the commands are interpreted and executed by Linux one after the other.

You can write shell programs and execute them like any other command under Linux. You can also execute other shell programs from within a shell program if they are in the search path. A shell program is like any other programming language and has its own syntax. You can define variables, assign various values, and so on. These functions are discussed in this chapter.

The Red Hat Linux CD-ROMs that accompany this book come with a rich assortment of capable, flexible, and powerful shells. These shells have numerous built-in commands, configurable command-line prompts, and features such as command-line history and editing. Table 25.1 lists each shell, along with its description and location in your Red Hat Linux filesystem.

TABLE 25.1   Shells with Red Hat Linux

Name	Description	Location
ash	A small shell (sh-like)	/bin/ash
ash.static	A version of ash not dependent on software libraries	/bin/ash.static
bash	The Bourne Again SHell	/bin/bash
bsh	A symbolic link to ash	/bin/bsh
csh	The C shell, a symbolic link to tcsh	/bin/csh
ksh	The public-domain Korn shell	/bin/ksh, /usr/bin/ksh
pdksh	A symbolic link to ksh	/usr/bin/pdksh
rsh	The restricted shell (for network operation)	/usr/bin/rsh
sh	A symbolic link to bash	/bin/sh
tcsh	A csh-compatible shell	/bin/tcsh
zsh	A compatible csh, ksh, and sh shell	/bin/zsh

Creating and Executing a Shell Program

Say you want to set up a number of aliases whenever you log on. Instead of typing all of the aliases every time you log on, you can put them in a file by using a text editor, such as `vi`, and then execute the file.

Here is what is contained in `myenv`, a sample file created for this purpose (for `bash`):

```
#!/bin/sh
alias ll='ls -l'
alias dir='ls'
alias copy='cp'
```

`myenv` can be executed in a variety of ways under Linux.

You can make `myenv` executable by using the `chmod` command, as follows, and then execute it as you would any other native Linux command:

```
# chmod +x myenv
```

This turns on the executable permission of `myenv`. You need to ensure one more thing before you can execute `myenv`—it must be in the search path. You can get the search path by executing

```
# echo $PATH
```

If the directory where the file `myenv` is located is not in the current search path, you must add the directory name in the search path.

Now you can execute the file `myenv` from the command line as if it were a Linux command:

```
# myenv
```

> **Note**
>
> The first line in your shell program should start with a pound sign (#), which tells the shell that the line is a comment. Following the pound sign, you must have an exclamation point (!), which tells the shell to run the command following the exclamation point and to use the rest of the file as input for that command. This is common practice for all shell scripting. For example, if you write a shell script for `bash`, the first line of your script will contain `#!/bin/bash`.

A second way to execute `myenv` under a particular shell, such as `pdksh`, is as follows:

```
# pdksh myenv
```

This invokes a new `pdksh` shell and passes the filename `myenv` as a parameter to execute the file.

> **Note**
>
> The `pdksh` shell, originally created by Eric Gisin, is a public domain version of the `ksh` shell and is found under the `/usr/bin` directory as a symbolic link. In Red Hat Linux, `pdksh` is named `ksh`. Two symbolic links, `/usr/bin/pdksh` and `/usr/bin/ksh`, point to the `pdksh` shell. For more information about `pdksh`, see the `/usr/doc/pdksh` directory or the `ksh` man page.

You can also execute `myenv` from the command line as follows:

Command Line	Environment
`# . myenv`	`pdksh` and `bash`
`# source myenv`	`tcsh`

The dot (`.`) is a way of telling the shell to execute the file `myenv`. In this case, you do not have to ensure that the execute permission of the file has been set. Under `tcsh`, you have to use the `source` command instead of the dot (`.`) command.

After you execute the command `myenv`, you should be able to use `dir` from the command line to get a list of files under the current directory and `ll` to get a list of files with various attributes displayed. However, the best way to use the new commands in `myenv` is to put them into your shell's login or profile file. For Red Hat Linux users, the default shell is `bash`, so make these commands available for everyone on your system by putting them in the `/etc/profile.d` directory. Copy in a `tcsh` version with the file extension `.csh` and the `bash/pdksh` version with a `.sh` file extension.

> **Note**
>
> If you find you'd prefer to use a shell other than `bash` after logging in to Red Hat Linux, use the `chsh` command. You'll be asked for your password and the location and name of the new shell (see Table 25.1). The new shell will become your default shell (but only if its name is in the list of acceptable system shells in `/etc/shells`).

In some instances, you may need to modify how your shell scripts are executed. For example, the majority of shell scripts use a *hash-bang* line at the beginning, like this:

```
#!/bin/sh
```

One of the reasons for this is to control the type of shell used to run the script (in this case, an sh-incantation of bash). Other shells, such as ksh, may respond differently depending on how they're called from a script (hence the reason for symbolic links to different shells).

You may also find different or new environment variables available to your scripts by using different shells. For example, if you launch csh from the bash command line, you'll find at least several new variables, or variables with slightly occluded definitions, such as

 # env
```
...
VENDOR=intel
MACHTYPE=i386
HOSTTYPE=i386-linux
HOST=thinkpad.home.org
```

On the other hand, bash may provide these variables, or variables of the same name with a slightly different definition, such as

 # env
```
...
HOSTTYPE=i386
HOSTNAME=thinkpad.home.org
```

Although the behavior of a bang line is not defined by POSIX, variations of its incantation can be helpful when you're writing shell scripts. As described in the wish man page, you can use a shell to help execute programs called within a shell script without needing to hard-code pathnames of programs. This increases shell script portability.

For example, if you want to use the wish command (a windowing tcl interpreter), your first inclination may be to write

```
#!/usr/local/bin/wish
```

Although this will work on many other operating systems, the script will fail under Linux. However, if you use

```
#!/bin/sh
exec wish "$@"
```

the wish command (as a binary or itself a shell script) can be used. There are other advantages to using this approach. See the wish man page for more information.

Variables

Linux shell programming is a full-fledged programming language and, as such, supports various types of variables. Variables have three major types: environment, built-in, and user.

- *Environment variables* are part of the system environment, and you do not have to define them. You can use them in your shell program. Some of them, such as PATH, can also be modified within a shell program.

- *Built-in variables* are provided by the system. Unlike environment variables, you cannot modify them.

- *User variables* are defined by you when you write a shell script. You can use and modify them at will within the shell program.

A major difference between shell programming and other programming languages is that in shell programming, variables are not typecast. That is, you do not have to specify whether a variable is a number or a string, and so on.

Assigning a Value to a Variable

Say you want to use a variable called lcount to count the number of iterations in a loop within a shell program. You can declare and initialize this variable as follows:

Command	Environment
lcount=0	pdksh and bash
set lcount = 0	tcsh

> **Note**
>
> Under pdksh and bash, you must ensure that the equals sign (=) does not have spaces before and after it.

Shell programming languages do not use typed variables, so the same variable can be used to store an integer value one time and a string another time. This is not recommended, however, and you should be careful not to do this.

To store a string in a variable, you can use the following:

Command	Environment
myname=Sanjiv	pdksh and bash
set myname = Sanjiv	tcsh

The preceding can be used if the string does not have embedded spaces. If a string has embedded spaces, you can do the assignment as follows:

Command	Environment
myname='Sanjiv Guha'	pdksh and bash
set myname = 'Sanjiv Guha'	tcsh

Accessing Variable Values

You can access the value of a variable by prefixing the variable name with a $ (dollar sign). That is, if the variable name is var, you can access the variable by using $var.

If you want to assign the value of var to the variable lcount, you can do so as follows:

Command	Environment
lcount=$var	pdksh and bash
set lcount = $var	tcsh

Positional Parameters

It is possible to write a shell script that takes a number of parameters at the time you invoke it from the command line or from another shell script. These options are supplied to the shell program by Linux as *positional parameters*, which have special names provided by the system. The first parameter is stored in a variable called 1 (number 1) and can be accessed by using $1 within the program. The second parameter is stored in a variable called 2 and can be accessed by using $2 within the program, and so on. One or more of the higher numbered positional parameters can be omitted while you're invoking a shell program.

For example, if a shell program mypgm expects two parameters--such as a first name and a last name--you can invoke the shell program with only one parameter, the first name. However, you cannot invoke it with only the second parameter, the last name.

Here's a shell program called mypgm1, which takes only one parameter (a name) and displays it on the screen:

```
#!/bin/sh
#Name display program
if [ $# -eq 0 ]
then
   echo "Name not provided"
else
   echo "Your name is "$1
fi
```

If you execute `mypgm1` in `pdksh` and `bash` as follows

`# . mypgm1`

you get the following output:

```
Name not provided
```

However, if you execute `mypgm1` as follows

`# . mypgm1 Sanjiv`

you get the following output:

```
Your name is Sanjiv
```

The shell program `mypgm1` also illustrates another aspect of shell programming: the built-in variables. In `mypgm1`, the variable `$#` is a built-in variable and provides the number of positional parameters passed to the shell program.

Built-In Variables

Built-in variables are special variables that Linux provides to you that can be used to make decisions within a program. You cannot modify the values of these variables within the shell program.

Some of these variables are

`$#`	Number of positional parameters passed to the shell program
`$?`	Completion code of the last command or shell program executed within the shell program (returned value)
`$0`	The name of the shell program
`$*`	A single string of all arguments passed at the time of invocation of the shell program

To show these built-in variables in use, here is a sample program called `mypgm2`:

```
#!/bin/sh
#my test program
echo "Number of parameters is "$#
echo "Program name is "$0
echo "Parameters as a single string is "$*
```

If you execute `mypgm2` from the command line in `pdksh` and `bash` as follows

`# . mypgm2 Sanjiv Guha`

you get the following result:

```
Number of parameters is 2
Program name is mypgm2
Parameters as a single string is Sanjiv Guha
```

Special Characters

Some characters have special meaning to Linux shells, so using them as part of variable names or strings causes your program to behave incorrectly. If a string contains such characters, you also have to use escape characters (backslashes) to indicate that the special characters should not be treated as special characters. Some of these characters are shown in Table 25.2.

TABLE 25.2   Special Shell Characters

Character	Explanation
$	Indicates the beginning of a shell variable name
|	Pipes standard output to next command
#	Starts a comment
&	Executes a process in the background
?	Matches one character
*	Matches one or more characters
>	Output redirection operator
<	Input redirection operator
`	Command substitution (the backquote or backtick—the key above the Tab key on most keyboards)
>>	Output redirection operator (to append to a file)
<<	Wait until following end-of-input string (HERE operator)
[ ]	Lists a range of characters
[a-z]	All characters a through z
[a,z]	Characters a or z
. *filename*	Executes ("sources") the file *filename*
Space	Delimiter between two words

A few characters deserve special note. They are the double quotes ("), the single quotes ('), the backslash (\), and the backtick (`), all discussed in the following sections. Also note that you can use input and output redirection from inside your shell scripts. Be sure to use output redirection with care when you're testing your shell programs, because you can easily overwrite files!

Double Quotes

If a string contains embedded spaces, you can enclose the string in double quotes (") so the shell interprets the whole string as one entity instead of more than one. For example, if you assigned the value of abc def (abc followed by one space followed by def) to a variable called x in a shell program as follows, you would get an error because the shell would try to execute def as a separate command.

Command	Environment
x=abc def	pdksh and bash
set x = abc def	tcsh

What you need to do is surround the string in double quotes:

Command	Environment
x="abc def"	pdksh and bash
set x = "abc def"	tcsh

The double quotes resolve all variables within the string. Here is an example for pdksh and bash:

```
var="test string"
newvar="Value of var is $var"
echo $newvar
```

Here is the same example for tcsh:

```
set var = "test string"
set newvar = "Value of var is $var"
echo $newvar
```

If you execute a shell program containing these three lines, you get the following result:

```
Value of var is test string
```

Single Quotes

You can surround a string with single quotes (') to stop the shell from resolving a variable. In the following examples, the double quotes in the preceding examples have been changed to single quotes.

pdksh and bash:

```
var='test string'
newvar='Value of var is $var'
echo $newvar
```

tcsh:

```
set var = 'test string'
set newvar = 'Value of var is $var'
echo $newvar
```

If you execute a shell program containing these three lines, you get the following result:

```
Value of var is $var
```

As you can see, the variable var did not get interpolated.

Backslash

You can use a backslash (\) before a character to stop the shell from interpreting the succeeding character as a special character. Say you want to assign a value of $test to a variable called var. If you use the following command, a null value is stored in var:

Command	Environment
var=$test	pdksh and bash
set var = $test	tcsh

This happens because the shell interprets $test as the value of the variable test. No value has been assigned to test, so var contains null. You should use the following command to correctly store $test in var:

Command	Environment
var=\$test	pdksh and bash
set var = \$test	tcsh

The backslash (\) before the dollar sign ($) signals the shell to interpret the $ as any other ordinary character and not to associate any special meaning to it.

Backtick

You can use the backtick (`) character to signal the shell to execute the string delimited by the backtick. This can be used in shell programs when you want the result of execution of a command to be stored in a variable. For example, if you want to count the number of lines in a file called test.txt in the current directory and store the result in a variable called var, you can use the following command:

Command	Environment
var=`wc -l test.txt`	pdksh and bash
set var = `wc -l test.txt`	tcsh

Comparison of Expressions

The way the logical comparison of two operators (numeric or string) is done varies slightly in different shells. In pdksh and bash, a command called test can be used to achieve comparisons of expressions. In tcsh, you can write an expression to accomplish the same thing.

pdksh and bash

This section covers comparisons using the pdksh or bash shells. Later in the chapter, the section "tcsh" contains a similar discussion for the tcsh shell.

The syntax of the test command is as follows:

```
test expression
```

or

```
[ expression ]
```

Both forms of test commands are processed the same way by pdksh and bash. The test commands support the following types of comparisons:

- String comparison
- Numeric comparison
- File operators
- Logical operators

String Comparison

The following operators can be used to compare two string expressions:

=	To compare whether two strings are equal
!=	To compare whether two strings are not equal
-n	To evaluate whether the string length is greater than zero
-z	To evaluate whether the string length is equal to zero

Next are some examples comparing two strings, string1 and string2, in a shell program called compare1:

```
#!/bin/sh
string1="abc"
string2="abd"
if [ $string1 = $string2 ]; then
    echo "string1 equal to string2"
else
    echo "string1 not equal to string2"
fi
```

```
if [ $string2 != string1 ]; then
   echo "string2 not equal to string1"
else
   echo "string2 equal to string2"
fi

if [ $string1 ]; then
   echo "string1 is not empty"
else
   echo "string1 is empty"
fi

if [ -n $string2 ]; then
   echo "string2 has a length greater than zero"
else
   echo "string2 has length equal to zero"
fi

if [ -z $string1 ]; then
   echo "string1 has a length equal to zero"
else
  echo "string1 has a length greater than zero"
fi
```

If you execute compare1, you get the following result:

```
string1 not equal to string2
string2 not equal to string1
string1 is not empty
string2 has a length greater than zero
string1 has a length greater than zero
```

If two strings are not equal in size, the system pads out the shorter string with trailing spaces for comparison. That is, if the value of string1 is abc and that of string2 is ab, string2 will be padded with a trailing space for comparison purposes--it will have a value of ab .

Number Comparison

The following operators can be used to compare two numbers:

-eq	To compare whether two numbers are equal
-ge	To compare whether one number is greater than or equal to the other number
-le	To compare whether one number is less than or equal to the other number
-ne	To compare whether two numbers are not equal
-gt	To compare whether one number is greater than the other number
-lt	To compare whether one number is less than the other number

The following examples compare two numbers, number1 and number2, in a shell program called compare2:

```
#!/bin/sh
number1=5
number2=10
number3=5

if [ $number1 -eq $number3 ]; then
    echo "number1 is equal to number3"
else
    echo "number1 is not equal to number3"
fi

if [ $number1 -ne $number2 ]; then
    echo "number1 is not equal to number2"
else
    echo "number1 is equal to number2"
fi

if [ $number1 -gt $number2 ]; then
    echo "number1 is greater than number2"
else
    echo "number1 is not greater than number2"
fi

if [ $number1 -ge $number3 ]; then
    echo "number1 is greater than or equal to number3"
else
    echo "number1 is not greater than or equal to number3"
fi

if [ $number1 -lt $number2 ]; then
    echo "number1 is less than number2"
else
    echo "number1 is not less than number2"
fi

if [ $number1 -le $number3 ]; then
    echo "number1 is less than or equal to number3"
else
    echo "number1 is not less than or equal to number3"
fi
```

When you execute the shell program compare2, you get the following results:

```
number1 is equal to number3
number1 is not equal to number2
number1 is not greater than number2
number1 is greater than or equal to number3
number1 is less than number2
number1 is less than or equal to number3
```

File Operators

The following operators can be used as file comparison operators:

-d	To ascertain whether a file is a directory
-f	To ascertain whether a file is a regular file
-r	To ascertain whether read permission is set for a file
-s	To ascertain whether the name of a file has a length greater than zero
-w	To ascertain whether write permission is set for a file
-x	To ascertain whether execute permission is set for a file

Assume that a shell program called compare3 is in a directory with a file called file1 and a subdirectory dir1 under the current directory. Assume file1 has a permission of r-x (read and execute permission) and dir1 has a permission of rwx (read, write, and execute permission). The code for compare3 would look like this:

```
#!/bin/sh
if [ -d $dir1 ]; then
    echo "dir1 is a directory"
else
    echo "dir1 is not a directory"
fi

if [ -f $dir1 ]; then
    echo "file1 is a regular file"
else
    echo "file1 is not a regular file"
fi

if [ -r $file1 ]; then
    echo "file1 has read permission"
else
    echo "file1 does not have read permission"
fi

if [ -w $file1 ]; then
    echo "file1 has write permission"
else
    echo "file1 does not have write permission"
fi

if [ -x $dir1 ]; then
    echo "dir1 has execute permission"
else
    echo "dir1 does not have execute permission"
fi
```

If you execute the file `compare3`, you get the following results:

```
dir1 is a directory
file1 is a regular file
file1 has read permission
file1 does not have write permission
dir1 has execute permission
```

Logical Operators

Logical operators are used to compare expressions using the rules of logic. The characters represent `NOT`, `AND`, and `OR`.

`!`	To negate a logical expression
`-a`	To logically `AND` two logical expressions
`-o`	To logically `OR` two logical expressions

This example named `logic` uses the file and directory mentioned in the previous `compare3` example.

```
#!/bin/sh
if [ -x file1 -a -x dir1 ]; then
    echo file1 and dir1 are executable
else
    echo at least one of file1 or dir1 are not executable
fi

if [ -w file1 -o -w dir1 ]; then
    echo file1 or dir1 are writable
else
    echo neither file1 or dir1 are executable
fi

if [ ! -w file1 ]; then
    echo file1 is not writable
else
    echo file1 is writable
fi
```

If you execute `logic`, it will yield the following result:

```
file1 and dir1 are executable
file1 or dir1 are writable
file1 is not writable
```

tcsh

As stated earlier, the comparisons are different under `tcsh` from what they are under `pdksh` and `bash`. This section explains the same concepts as the section "`pdksh` and `bash`," but it uses the syntax necessary for the `tcsh` shell environment.

String Comparison

The following operators can be used to compare two string expressions:

| == | To compare whether two strings are equal |
| !- | To compare whether two strings are not equal |

The following examples compare two strings, string1 and string2, in the shell program compare1:

```
#!/bin/tcsh
set string1 = "abc"
set string2 = "abd"

if (string1 == string2) then
   echo "string1 equal to string2"
else
   echo "string1 not equal to string2"
endif

if (string2 != string1) then
   echo "string2 not equal to string1"
else
   echo "string2 equal to string1"
endif
```

If you execute compare1, you get the following results:

```
string1 not equal to string2
string2 not equal to string1
```

Number Comparison

These operators can be used to compare two numbers:

>=	To compare whether one number is greater than or equal to the other number
<=	To compare whether one number is less than or equal to the other number
>	To compare whether one number is greater than the other number
<	To compare whether one number is less than the other number

The next examples compare two numbers, number1 and number2, in a shell program called compare2:

```
#!/bin/tcsh
set number1 = 5
set number2 = 10
set number3 = 5
```

25

SHELL SCRIPTING

```
if  ($number1 > $number2)  then
    echo "number1 is greater than number2"
else
    echo "number1 is not greater than number2"
endif

if  ($number1 >= $number3) then
    echo "number1 is greater than or equal to number3"
else
    echo "number1 is not greater than or equal to number3"
endif

if  ($number1 < $number2)  then
    echo "number1 is less than number2"
else
    echo "number1 is not less than number2"
endif

if  ($number1 <= $number3) then
    echo "number1 is less than or equal to number3"
else
    echo "number1 is not less than or equal to number3"
endif
```

Executing the shell program compare2, you get the following results:

```
number1 is not greater than number2
number1 is greater than or equal to number3
number1 is less than number2
number1 is less than or equal to number3
```

File Operators

These operators can be used as file comparison operators:

-d	To ascertain whether a file is a directory
-e	To ascertain whether a file exists
-f	To ascertain whether a file is a regular file
-o	To ascertain whether a user is the owner of a file
-r	To ascertain whether read permission is set for a file
-w	To ascertain whether write permission is set for a file
-x	To ascertain whether execute permission is set for a file
-z	To ascertain whether the file size is zero

The following examples are based on a shell program called compare3, which is in a directory with a file called file1 and a subdirectory dir1 under the current directory. Assume that file1 has a permission of r-x (read and execute permission) and dir1 has a permission of rwx (read, write, and execute permission).

The following is the code for the `compare3` shell program:

```
#!/bin/tcsh
if  (-d dir1) then
    echo "dir1 is a directory"
else
    echo "dir1 is not a directory"
endif

if (-f dir1)  then
    echo "file1 is a regular file"
else
    echo "file1 is not a regular file"
endif

if (-r file1) then
    echo "file1 has read permission"
else
    echo "file1 does not have read permission"
endif

if (-w file1) then
    echo "file1 has write permission"
else
    echo "file1 does not have write permission"
endif

if (-x dir1) then
    echo "dir1 has execute permission"
else
    echo "dir1 does not have execute permission"
endif

if (-z file1) then
    echo "file1 has zero length"
else
    echo "file1 has greater than zero length"
endif
```

If you execute the file `compare3`, you get the following results:

```
dir1 is a directory
file1 is a regular file
file1 has read permission
file1 does not have write permission
dir1 has execute permission
file1 has greater than zero length
```

Logical Operators

Logical operators are used with conditional statements. These operators are used to negate a logical expression or to perform logical ANDs and ORs.

!	To negate a logical expression
&&	To logically AND two logical expressions
||	To logically OR two logical expressions

This example named `logic` uses the file and directory mentioned in the previous compare3 example.

```
#!/bin/tcsh
if ( -x file1 && -x dir1 ) then
    echo file1 and dir1 are executable
else
    echo at least one of file1 or dir1 are not executable
endif

if ( -w file1 || -w dir1 ) then
    echo file1 or dir1 are writable
else
    echo neither file1 or dir1 are executable
endif

if ( ! -w file1 ) then
    echo file1 is not writable
else
    echo file1 is writable
endif
```

If you execute `logic`, it will yield the following result:

```
file1 and dir1 are executable
file1 or dir1 are writable
file1 is not writable
```

Iteration Statements

Iteration statements are used to repeat a series of commands contained within the iteration statement.

The for Statement

The `for` statement has a number of formats. The first format is as follows:

```
for curvar in list
do
    statements
done
```

This form should be used if you want to execute *statements* once for each value in *list*. For each iteration, the current value of the list is assigned to vcurvar. *list* can be a variable containing a number of items or a list of values separated by spaces. This format of the for statement is used by pdksh and bash.

The second format is as follows:

```
for curvar
do
    statements
done
```

In this form, the *statements* are executed once for each of the positional parameters passed to the shell program. For each iteration, the current value of the positional parameter is assigned to the variable curvar.

This form can also be written as follows:

```
for curvar in "$@"
do
    statements
done
```

Remember that $@ gives you a list of positional parameters passed to the shell program, all strung together.

Under tcsh, the for statement is called foreach. The format is as follows:

```
foreach curvar (list)
    statements
end
```

In this form, *statements* are executed once for each value in *list* and, for each iteration, the current value of *list* is assigned to curvar.

Suppose you want to create a backup version of each file in a directory to a subdirectory called backup. You can do the following in pdksh and bash:

```
#!/bin/sh
for filename in `ls`
do
    cp $filename backup/$filename
    if [ $? -ne 0 ]; then
        echo "copy for $filename failed"
    fi
done
```

In the preceding example, a backup copy of each file is created. If the copy fails, a message is generated.

25

SHELL SCRIPTING

The same example in tcsh is as follows:

```
#!/bin/tcsh
foreach filename (`/bin/ls`)
    cp $filename backup/$filename
    if ($? != 0) then
        echo "copy for $filename failed"
    endif
end
```

The while Statement

The while statement can be used to execute a series of commands while a specified condition is true. The loop terminates as soon as the specified condition evaluates to false. It is possible that the loop will not execute at all if the specified condition evaluates to false right at the beginning. You should be careful with the while command because the loop will never terminate if the specified condition never evaluates to false.

In pdksh and bash, the following format is used:

```
while expression
do
    statements
done
```

In tcsh, the following format is used:

```
while (expression)
    Statements
end
```

If you want to add the first five even numbers, you can use the following shell program in pdksh and bash:

```
#!/bin/bash
loopcount=0
result=0
while [ $loopcount -lt 5 ]
do
    loopcount=`expr $loopcount + 1`
    increment=`expr $loopcount \* 2`
    result=`expr $result + $increment`
done

echo "result is $result"
```

In tcsh, this program can be written as follows:

```
#!/bin/tcsh
set loopcount = 0
set result = 0
```

```
while ($loopcount < 5)
    set loopcount = `expr $loopcount + 1`
    set increment = `expr $loopcount \* 2`
    set result = `expr $result + $increment`

end

echo "result is $result"
```

The until Statement

The until statement can be used to execute a series of commands until a specified condition is true. The loop terminates as soon as the specified condition evaluates to true.

In pdksh and bash, the following format is used:

```
until expression
do
    statements
done
```

As you can see, the format is similar to the while statement.

If you want to add the first five even numbers, you can use the following shell program in pdksh and bash:

```
#!/bin/bash
loopcount=0
result=0
until [ $loopcount -ge 5 ]
do
    loopcount=`expr $loopcount + 1`
    increment=`expr $loopcount \* 2`
    result=`expr $result + $increment`
done

echo "result is $result"
```

The example here is identical to the example for the while statement, except the condition being tested is just the opposite of the condition specified in the while statement.

The tcsh command does not support the until statement.

The repeat Statement (tcsh)

The repeat statement is used to execute only one command a fixed number of times.

If you want to print a hyphen (-) 80 times on the screen, you can use the following command:

```
repeat  80 echo '-'
```

The `select` Statement (pdksh)

The `select` statement is used to generate a menu list if you are writing a shell program that expects input from the user online. The format of the `select` statement is as follows:

```
select  item in itemlist
do
     Statements
done
```

`itemlist` is optional. If it's not provided, the system iterates through the entries in `item` one at a time. If `itemlist` is provided, however, the system iterates for each entry in `itemlist` and the current value of `itemlist` is assigned to `item` for each iteration, which then can be used as part of the statements being executed.

If you want to write a menu that gives the user a choice of picking a `Continue` or a `Finish`, you can write the following shell program:

```
#!/bin/bash
select  item in Continue Finish
do
    if [ $item = "Finish" ]; then
       break
    fi
done
```

When the `select` command is executed, the system displays a menu with numeric choices to the user--in this case, 1 for `Continue`, and 2 for `Finish`. If the user chooses 1, the variable `item` contains a value of `Continue`; if the user chooses 2, the variable `item` contains a value of `Finish`. When the user chooses 2, the `if` statement is executed and the loop terminates.

The `shift` Statement

The `shift` statement is used to process the positional parameters, one at a time, from left to right. As you'll remember, the positional parameters are identified as $1, $2, $3, and so on. The effect of the `shift` command is that each positional parameter is moved one position to the left and the current $1 parameter is lost.

The format of the `shift` command is as follows:

```
shift   number
```

The parameter *number* is the number of places to be shifted and is optional. If not specified, the default is 1; that is, the parameters are shifted one position to the left. If specified, the parameters are shifted *number* positions to the left.

The `shift` command is useful when you are writing shell programs in which a user can pass various options. Depending on the specified option, the parameters that follow can mean different things or might not be there at all.

Conditional Statements

Conditional statements are used in shell programs to decide which part of the program to execute depending on specified conditions.

The `if` Statement

The `if` statement evaluates a logical expression to make a decision. An `if` condition has the following format in `pdksh` and `bash`:

```
if [ expression ]; then
    Statements
elif [expression ]; then
    Statements
else
    Statements
fi
```

The `if` conditions can be nested. That is, an `if` condition can contain another `if` condition within it. It is not necessary for an `if` condition to have an `elif` or `else` part. The `else` part is executed if none of the expressions that are specified in the `if` statement and are optional in subsequent `elif` statements are true. The word `fi` is used to indicate the end of the `if` statements, which is very useful if you have nested `if` conditions. In such a case, you should be able to match `fi` to `if` to ensure that all `if` statements are properly coded.

In the following example, a variable `var` can have either of two values: `Yes` or `No`. Any other value is an invalid value. This can be coded as follows:

```
if [ $var = "Yes" ]; then
    echo "Value is Yes"
elif [ $var = "No" ]; then
    echo "Value is No"
else
    echo "Invalid value"
fi
```

In `tcsh`, the `if` statement has two forms. The first form, similar to the one for `pdksh` and `bash`, is as follows:

```
if (expression) then
    Statements
else if (expression) then
    Statements
```

```
else
    Statements
endif
```

The `if` conditions can be nested--that is, an `if` condition can contain another `if` condition within it. It is not necessary for an `if` condition to have an `else` part. The `else` part is executed if none of the expressions specified in any of the `if` statements are true. The optional `if` part of the statement (`else if (expression) then`) is executed if the condition following it is true and the previous `if` statement is not true. The word `endif` is used to indicate the end of the `if` statements, which is very useful if you have nested `if` conditions. In such a case, you should be able to match `endif` to `if` to ensure that all `if` statements are properly coded.

Remember the example of the variable `var` having only two values, `Yes` and `No`, for `pdksh` and `bash`? Here is how it would be coded with `tcsh`:

```
if ($var == "Yes") then
    echo "Value is Yes"
else if ($var == "No" ) then
    echo "Value is No"
else
    echo "Invalid value"
endif
```

The second form of the `if` condition for `tcsh` is as follows:

```
if (expression) command
```

In this format, only a single command can be executed if the expression evaluates to true.

The case Statement

The case statement is used to execute statements depending on a discrete value or a range of values matching the specified variable. In most cases, you can use a case statement instead of an `if` statement if you have a large number of conditions.

The format of a case statement for `pdksh` and `bash` is as follows:

```
case str in
    str1 | str2)
        Statements;;
    str3|str4)
        Statements;;
    *)
        Statements;;
esac
```

You can specify a number of discrete values—such as str1, str2, and so on—for each condition, or you can specify a value with a wildcard. The last condition should be * (asterisk) and is executed if none of the other conditions are met. For each of the specified conditions, all of the associated statements until the double semicolon (;;) are executed.

You can write a script that will echo the name of the month if you provide the month number as a parameter. If you provide a number that is not between 1 and 12, you will get an error message. The script is as follows:

```
#!/bin/sh

case $1 in
    01 | 1) echo "Month is January";;
    02 | 2) echo "Month is February";;
    03 | 3) echo "Month is March";;
    04 | 4) echo "Month is April";;
    05 | 5) echo "Month is May";;
    06 | 6) echo "Month is June";;
    07 | 7) echo "Month is July";;
    08 | 8) echo "Month is August";;
    09 | 9) echo "Month is September";;
    10) echo "Month is October";;
    11) echo "Month is November";;
    12) echo "Month is December";;
    *) echo "Invalid parameter";;
esac
```

You need to end the statements under each condition with a double semicolon(;;). If you do not, the statements under the next condition will also be executed.

The format for a case statement for tcsh is as follows:

```
switch (str)
    case str1|str2:
        Statements
        breaksw
    case str3|str4:
        Statements
        breaksw
    default:
        Statements
        breaksw
endsw
```

You can specify a number of discrete values—such as str1, str2, and so on—for each condition, or you can specify a value with a wildcard. The last condition should be default and is executed if none of the other conditions are met. For each of the specified conditions, all of the associated statements until breaksw are executed.

25

SHELL SCRIPTING

The example that echoes the month when a number is given, shown earlier for pdksh and bash, can be written in tcsh as follows:

```
#!/bin/tcsh

set month = 5
switch  ( $month )
    case 1:
        echo "Month is January"
        breaksw
    case 2:
        echo "Month is February"
        breaksw
    case 3:
        echo "Month is March"
        breaksw
    case 4:
        echo "Month is April"
        breaksw
    case 5:
        echo "Month is May"
        breaksw
    case 6:
        echo "Month is June"
        breaksw
    case 7:
        echo "Month is July";;
        breaksw
    case 8:
        echo "Month is August";;
        breaksw
    case 9:
        echo "Month is September"
        breaksw
    case 10:
        echo "Month is October"
        breaksw
    case 11:
        echo "Month is November"
        breaksw
    case 12:
        echo "Month is December"
        breaksw
    default:
        echo "Oops! Month is Octember!"
        breaksw
endsw
```

You need to end the statements under each condition with breaksw. If you do not, the statements under the next condition will also be executed.

Miscellaneous Statements

You should be aware of two other statements: the `break` statement and the `exit` statement.

The `break` Statement

The `break` statement can be used to terminate an iteration loop, such as a `for`, `until`, or `repeat` command.

The `exit` Statement

`exit` statements can be used to exit a shell program. You can optionally use a number after `exit`. If the current shell program has been called by another shell program, the calling program can check for the code and make a decision accordingly.

Functions

As with other programming languages, shell programs also support *functions*. A function is a piece of a shell program that performs a particular process that can be used more than once in the shell program. Writing a function helps you write shell programs without duplication of code.

The following is the format of a function in `pdksh` and `bash` for function definition:

```
func(){
    Statements
}
```

You can call a function as follows:

```
func param1 param2 param3
```

The parameters *param1*, *param2*, and so on are optional. You can also pass the parameters as a single string--for example, $@. A function can parse the parameters as if they were positional parameters passed to a shell program.

The following example is a function that displays the name of the month or an error message if you pass a month number. Here is the example, in `pdksh` and `bash`:

```
#!/bin/sh
Displaymonth() {
   case $1 in
       01 | 1) echo "Month is January";;
       02 | 2) echo "Month is February";;
       03 | 3) echo "Month is March";;
       04 | 4) echo "Month is April";;
       05 | 5) echo "Month is May";;
```

```
06 |  6) echo "Month is June";;
07 |  7) echo "Month is July";;
08 |  8) echo "Month is August";;
09 |  9) echo "Month is September";;
   10) echo "Month is October";;
   11) echo "Month is November";;
   12) echo "Month is December";;
    *) echo "Invalid parameter";;
 esac
}
```

```
Displaymonth 8
```

The preceding program displays the following:

```
Month is August
```

Summary

This chapter introduced you to the syntax of shell programming and you learned how to write a shell program. Shell programs can be used to write programs that do simple things, such as setting a number of aliases when you log on, or complicated things, such as customizing your shell environment and performing system administration tasks.

Automating Tasks

IN THIS CHAPTER

"[T]he three great virtues of a programmer: *laziness*, *impatience*, and *hubris*."

—Wall and Schwartz, in *Programming Perl*

Automation enlists a machine—a Linux computer, in the present case—to perform jobs. What makes this definition live, however, and the true subject of this chapter, is *attitude*. The most important step you can take in understanding mechanisms of automation under Red Hat Linux is to adopt the attitude that the computer works for you. After you've done that, when you realize you're too lazy to type a telephone number that the machine should already know or too impatient to wait until midnight to start backups, and when you have enough confidence in your own creativity to teach the machine a better way, the technical details will work themselves out. This chapter offers more than a dozen examples of how small, understandable automation initiatives make an immediate difference. Let them lead you to your own successes.

First Example—Automating Data Entry

How can the details work out? Look at an example from the day before I started to write this chapter.

Problem and Solution

A client wanted to enhance an online catalog to include thumbnail pictures of the merchandise. After a bit of confusion about what this really meant, I realized that I needed to update a simple database table of products to include a new column (or attribute or value) that would specify the filenames of the thumbnails. The database management system has a couple of interactive front ends, and I'm a swift typist, so it probably would have been quickest to point and click my way through the 200 picture updates. Did I do that? Of course not—what happened later proved the wisdom of this decision. Instead, I wrote a shell script to automate the update, which is shown in Listing 26.1.

LISTING 26.1   Shell Script That Updates a Database

```
# picture names seem to look like {$DIR/137-13p.jpg,$DIR/201-942f.jpg,...}
# The corresponding products appear to be {137-13P, 201-942F, ...}
DIR=/particular/directory/for/my/client

:       # Will we use .gif-s, also, eventually?  I don't know.
 for F in $DIR/*.jpg
 do
        # BASE will have values {137-13p,201-942f, ...}
```

LISTING 26.1 continued

```
 BASE=`basename $F .jpg`
    # The only suffixes I've encountered are 'p' and 'f', so I'll simply
    #     transform those two.
    # Fxample values for PRODUCT:  {137-13P, 201-942F, ...}
 PRODUCT=`echo $BASE | tr pf PF`
    # one_command is a shell script that passes a line of SQL to the DBMS.
  one_command update catalog set Picture = "'$DIR/$BASE.jpg'"
➥where Product = "'$PRODUCT'"
 done
```

As it turned out, the team decided within a couple days that the pictures needed to be in a different directory, so it was only a few seconds' work to update the penultimate line of the script and add a comment such as this and rerun it:

```
    ...
        # Do *not* include a directory specification in Picture;
➥ that will be known
        #     only at the time the data are retrieved.
    one_command update catalog set Picture = "'$BASE.jpg'" where Product =
➥ "'$PRODUCT'"
 done
```

It's inevitable that we'll someday have more pictures to add to the database or will want reports on orphaned pictures (those that haven't been connected yet to any product). Then this same script, or a close derivative of it, will come into play again.

Analysis of the Implementation

Now work through the example in Listing 26.1 in detail to practice the automation mentality.

Do you understand how the script in Listing 26.1 works? Chapter 25, "Shell Scripting," explains shell processing and Appendix B, "Top Linux Commands and Utilities," presents everything you're likely to need for the most commonly used UNIX utilities. You can always learn more about these by reading the corresponding man pages or any of the fine books available on shell programming. The most certain way to learn, of course, is to experiment on your own. For example, if you have any question about what man tr means by "translation," it's an easy matter to experiment, such as with this:

```
# tr pf PF <<HERE
abcopqOPQ
FfpPab
HERE
```

You can conclude that you're on the right track when you see the following:

```
abcoPqOPQ
FFPPab
```

This is one of the charms of relying on shells for automation; it's easy to bounce between interaction and automation, which shapes a powerful didactic perspective and a check on understanding.

The sample product catalog script in Listing 26.1 is written for sh processing. I strongly recommend this be your target for scripts, rather than ksh, csh, or bash. I prefer any of the latter for interactive command-line use. In automating, however, when I'm often connecting to hosts that don't use Red Hat Linux, availability and esoteric security issues have convinced me to code using constructs that sh—and therefore all the shells—recognize. Default Red Hat Linux installations use a link named /bin/sh that points to /bin/bash. All the work in this chapter is written so that the scripts will function properly no matter what the details are of your host's configuration. Chapter 25 gives more details on the differences among shells.

Did I really include the inline comments, the lines that begin with #, when I first wrote the script in Listing 26.1? Yes. I've made this level of source-code documentation a habit, and it's one I recommend to you. If your life is at all like mine, telephones ring, co-workers chat, and power supplies fail; I find it easier to type this much detail as I'm thinking about it, rather than risk having to re-create my thoughts in case of an interruption. It's also much easier to pick up the work again days or weeks later. Writing for human readability also eases the transition when you pass your work on to others.

Listing 26.1 begins by assigning a shell variable DIR in the third line. It's good practice to make such an assignment, even for a variable (apparently) used only once. It contributes to self-documentation and generally enhances maintainability; it's easy to look at the top of the script and see immediately on what magic words or configuration in the outside environment (/particular/directory/for/my/client in this case; see the third line down) the script depends.

Many of the jobs you'll want to accomplish involve a quantifier: "change all...," "correct every...," and so on. The shell's looping constructs, for and while, are your friends. You'll make almost daily use of them.

basename and tr are universally available and widely used. tr, like many UNIX utilities, expects to read standard input. If you have information in shell variables, you can feed tr the information you want, either through a pipe from echo, as in the example, or an equivalent:

```
echo $VARIABLE | tr [a-z] [A-Z]
```

You can also do it with a so-called HERE document, such as this one:

```
tr [a-z] [A-Z] <<HERE
$VARIABLE
HERE
```

You could perhaps do it by creating a temporary file:

```
echo $VARIABLE >$TMPFILE
tr [a-z] [A-Z] $TMPFILE
```

one_command is a two-line shell script written earlier in the day to process SQL commands. Why not inline the body of that script here? Although technically feasible, I have a strong preference for small, simple programs that are easy to understand and correspondingly easy to implement correctly. one_command already has been verified to do one small job reliably, so the script lets it do that job. This fits with the UNIX tradition that counsels combining robust toolkit pieces to construct grander works.

In fact, notice that the example in Listing 26.1 shows the shell's nature as a "glue" language. There's a small amount of processing within the shell in manipulating filenames, and then most of the work is handed off to other commands; the shell just glues together results. This is typical and is a correct style you should adopt for your own scripting.

Certainly, it was pleasant when the filenames changed and I realized I could rework one word of the script, rather than retype the 200 entries. As satisfying as this was, the total benefit of automation is still more profound. Even greater than saving my time are the improvements in quality, traceability, and reusability this affords. With the script, I control the data entering the database at a higher level and eliminate whole categories of error: mistyping, accidentally pushing a wrong button in a graphical user interface, and so on. Also, the script in Listing 26.1 records my procedure, in case it's later useful to audit the data. Suppose, for example, that next year it's decided I shouldn't have inserted any of these references to the database's Picture attribute. How many will have to be backed out? Useful answers—at most, the count of $DIR/*.jpg—can be read directly from the script; there's no need to rely on memory or speculation.

Tips for Improving Automation Technique

You're in charge of your career in automation. Along with everything else this chapter advises, you'll go furthest if you do the following:

- Improve your automation technique.
- Engineer well.

These tips have specific meaning in the rest of this chapter. Look for ways to apply them in all that follows.

Continuing Education

There are three important ways to improve your skill with automation techniques, which apply equally well whether you're using Perl, cron, Expect, or another mechanism:

- Scan the documentation.
- Read good scripts.
- Practice writing scripts.

Documentation has the reputation of being dry and even unreadable. It's important that you learn how to employ it. All the tools presented here have man pages, which you need to be comfortable using. Read these documents and reread them. Authors of the tools faced many of the challenges you do. Often, reading through the lists of options or keywords, you'll realize that particular capabilities apply exactly to your situation. Study the documentation with this in mind; look for the ideas that you can use. Give particular attention to commands you don't recognize. If some of them—cu or od—are largely superannuated, you'll realize in reading about others—such as tput, ulimit, bc, nice, or wait—that earlier users were confronted with just the situations that confound your own work. Stand on their shoulders and see farther.

> **Note**
>
> Want to know more about a command? There may be two other sources of information besides its man page. Red Hat Linux users should also check the /usr/share/doc directory, where more than 270 programs have individual directories of additional information. You may also find more detailed information about a command if its man page indicates the program is part of the GNU software distribution—the command may be documented with a GNU information page. Information documents reside under the /usr/share/info directory, and you'll find nearly 400 information documents installed on your Red Hat system. Use the info command in this way: info *command*.

It's important to read good programming. Aspiring literary authors find inspiration in Pushkin and Pynchon, not grammar primers; similarly, you'll go furthest when you read the best work of the best programmers. Look in the columns of computer magazines and, most importantly, the archives of software with freely available source code. Good examples of coding occasionally turn up in Usenet discussions. Prize these; read them and learn from the masters.

All the examples in this chapter are written for easy use. They typically do one small task completely; this is one of the best ways to demonstrate a new concept. Although exception handling, and argument validation in particular, is important, covering it is beyond the scope of this chapter.

Crystallize your learning by writing your own scripts. All the documents you read will make more sense after you put the knowledge in place with your own experience.

Good Engineering

The other advice for those pursuing automation is to practice good engineering. This always starts with a clear, well-defined goal. Automation isn't an absolute good; it's only a method for achieving human goals. Part of what you'll learn in working through this chapter is how much, and how little, to automate.

When your goal is set, move as close to it as you can with components that are already written. "Glue" existing programs together with small, understandable scripting modules. Choose meaningful variable names. Define interfaces carefully. Write comments.

Shell Scripts

Although Chapter 25 covers the basic syntax and language of shell programming, look at a few additional examples of scripts that are often useful in day-to-day operation.

Changing Strings in Files with `chstr`

Users who maintain source code, client lists, and other records often want to launch a find-and-replace operation from the command line. It's useful to have a variant of `chstr` on UNIX hosts. Listing 26.2 gives one example.

LISTING 26.2 `chstr`—A Simple Find-and-Replace Operation

```
########
#
# See usage() definition, below, for more details.
#
# This implementation doesn't do well with complicated escape
#     sequences. That has been no more than a minor problem in
#     the real world.
#
########
usage() {
     echo \
"chstr BEFORE AFTER <filenames>
```

LISTING 26.2   continued

```
        changes the first instance of BEFORE to AFTER in each line of
➥ <filenames>,
        and reports on the differences.
Examples:
        chstr TX Texas */addresses.*
        chstr ii counter2 *.c"
        exit 0
}

case $1 in
        -h|-help)       usage;;
esac

if test $# -lt 3
then
        usage
fi

TMPDIR=/tmp
        # It's OK if more than one instance of chstr is run simultaneously.
        #       The TMPFILE names are specific to each invocation, so there's
        #       no conflict.
TMPFILE=$TMPDIR/chstr.$$

BEFORE=$1
AFTER=$2

        # Toss the BEFORE and AFTER arguments out of the argument list.
shift;shift

for FILE in $*
do
        sed -e "s/$BEFORE/$AFTER/" $FILE >$TMPFILE
        echo "$FILE:"
        diff $FILE $TMPFILE
        echo ""
        mv $TMPFILE $FILE
done
```

The preceding chstr script will take its first two arguments as the string to look for and the string to put in its place, respectively. In the script they're in the BEFORE and AFTER variables. The two shift commands move those strings aside from the list of arguments and the rest of the arguments are treated as files. Each file is run through sed to replace $BEFORE with $AFTER and placed in a temporary file. The file is then moved back into place.

Most interactive editors permit a form of global search-and-replace, and some even make it easy to operate on more than one file. Perhaps that's a superior automation for your needs. If not, chstr is a minimal command-line alternative that is maximally simple to use.

> **Note**
>
> Of course, experienced Perl hackers may find Listing 26.2 a bit longer than necessary when nearly the same changes can be accomplished from the command line like this:
>
> `# perl -p -i.tmp -e s/`*beforestr*`/`*afterstr*`/g` *file(s)*
>
> For more information on Perl, see the Perl man pages on your Red Hat system. A good starting point is the perltoc(1) man page.

WWW Retrieval

A question that arises frequently is how to automate retrieval of pages from the World Wide Web. This section shows the simplest of many techniques.

FTP Retrieval

Create a shell script, retrieve_one, with the contents of Listing 26.3 and with execution enabled (that is, command chmod +x retrieve_one).

LISTING 26.3 retrieve_one—Automating FTP *Retrieval*

```
# Usage:  "retrieve_one HOST:FILE" uses anonymous FTP to connect
#      to HOST and retrieve FILE into the local directory.

MY_ACCOUNT=myaccount@myhost.com
HOST=`echo $1 | sed -e "s/:.*//"`
FILE=`echo $1 | sed -e "s/.*://"`
LOCAL_FILE=`basename $FILE`

    # -v:  report all statistics.
    # -n:  connect without interactive user authentication.
ftp -v -n $HOST << SCRIPT
    user anonymous $MY_ACCOUNT
    get $FILE $LOCAL_FILE
    quit
SCRIPT
```

`retrieve_one` is useful for purposes such as ordering a current copy of a FAQ into your local directory; start experimenting with it by making a request with the following:

```
# retrieve_one rtfm.mit.edu:/pub/usenet-by-hierarchy/comp/os/linux/answers/
➥linux/info-sheet
```

Red Hat Linux comes with other utilities you can use for FTP retrieval. See Chapter 11, "FTP," for information about the `ncftp` and `gftp` commands.

HTTP Retrieval

For an HTTP interaction, let the Lynx browser do the bulk of the work. The Lynx browser that accompanies the Red Hat distribution is adequate for all but the most specialized purposes. You can obtain the latest version at `http://lynx.browser.org`. Although most Lynx users think of Lynx as an interactive browser, it's also handy for dropping a copy of the latest headlines, with live links, in a friend's mailbox with this:

```
# lynx -source http://www.cnn.com | mail someone@somewhere.com
```

To create a primitive news update service, script the following and launch it in the background (using the ampersand, &):

```
NEW=/tmp/news.new
OLD=/tmp/news.old
URL=http://www.cnn.com
while true
do
     mv $NEW $OLD
     lynx -dump -nolist $URL >$NEW
     diff $NEW $OLD
          # Wait ten minutes before starting the next comparison.
     sleep 600
done
```

Any changes in the appearance of CNN's home page will appear onscreen every 10 minutes. This simple approach is less practical than you might first expect because CNN periodically shuffles the content without changing the information. It's an instructive example, however, and a starting point from which you can elaborate your own scripts.

Conclusions on Shell Programming

Shells are glue; if there's a way to get an application to perform an action from the command line, there's almost certainly a way to wrap it in a shell script that gives you power over argument validation, iteration, and input-output redirection. These are powerful techniques and well worth the few minutes of study and practice it takes to begin learning them.

Even small automations pay off. My personal rule of thumb is to write tiny disposable one-line shell scripts when I expect to use a sequence even twice during a session. For example, although I have a sophisticated set of reporting commands for analyzing World Wide Web server logs, I also find myself going to the trouble of editing a disposable script such as `/tmp/r9`

```
grep claird `ls -t /usr/cern/log/* | head -1` | grep -v $1 | wc -l
```

to do quick, ad hoc queries on recent hit patterns. This particular example reports on the number of requests for pages that include the string `claird` and exclude the first argument to `/tmp/r9`, in the most recent log.

Scheduling Tasks with cron and at Jobs

Red Hat Linux comes with several utilities that manage the rudiments of job scheduling. `at` schedules a process for later execution, and `cron` (or `crontab`—it has a couple of interfaces, and different engineers use both these names) periodically launches a process. Lastly, for systems that don't stay up all the time there's `anacron`.

The `crond` daemon is started by the `crond` script under the `/etc/rc.d/init.d` directory when you boot Red Hat Linux. This daemon checks your system's `/etc/crontab` file and `/var/spool/cron` directory every minute, looking for assigned tasks at assigned times. As a system administrator, you'll schedule system tasks in `/etc/crontab`. This file initially contains four entries:

```
01 * * * * root run-parts /etc/cron.hourly
02 4 * * * root run-parts /etc/cron.daily
22 4 * * 0 root run-parts /etc/cron.weekly
42 4 1 * * root run-parts /etc/cron.monthly
```

Scripts set to run on an hourly, daily, weekly, or monthly basis will be found under the `/etc` directory as shown. Personal cron tasks, created by using the `crontab` command, are saved under the `/var/spool/cron` directory. Personal at jobs are saved under the `/var/spool/at` directory, and will have group and file ownership of the creator, like this:

```
-rwx------   1 bball    bball        1093 Apr 19 17:47 a0000200eb209c
```

The difference between `crontab` and `at` is that `crontab` should be used to schedule and run periodic, repetitive tasks on a regular basis, whereas at jobs are usually meant to run once at a future time.

> **Note**
>
> The /etc/cron.allow and /etc/cron.deny files control who may use crontab on your system. For details, see the crontab man page. You can also control who can use the at command on your system with the /etc/at.allow and /etc/at.deny files. By default, Red Hat Linux lets anyone use the at and crontab command.

The weakness of cron and at is that they assume the system will always be up. This isn't true for Linux laptop systems, for instance. So by default anacron is installed and set to run at boot time and when apmd resumes (see /etc/sysconfig/apm-scripts/resume for how that's done). Anacron is controlled by the /etc/anacrontab file and is installed to look at the jobs run from the /etc/cron.daily, /etc/cron.weekly, and /etc/cron.monthly directories. So it looks like this:

```
# /etc/anacrontab: configuration file for anacron

# See anacron(8) and anacrontab(5) for details.

SHELL=/bin/sh
PATH=/usr/local/sbin:/usr/local/bin:/sbin:/usr/sbin:/usr/bin

# These entries are useful for a Red Hat Linux system.
1       5       cron.daily      run-parts /etc/cron.daily
7       10      cron.weekly     run-parts /etc/cron.weekly
30      15      cron.monthly    run-parts /etc/cron.monthly
```

What this does is make sure the cron.daily scripts are run once every day (and they're run 5 minutes after anacron is run). The cron.weekly scripts are run 10 minutes after anacron starts if they haven't been run in over a week and the cron.weekly scripts are run 15 minutes after anacron starts if they haven't been run in 30 days. Anacron gets help in determining when a script was last run thanks to the 0anacron script in each of the cron directories above. You'll really notice this if you're a laptop user and always had to update your slocate database by hand!

cron and `find`—Exploring Disk Usage

One eternal reality of system administration is that there's not enough disk space. The following sections offer a couple expedients recommended for keeping on top of what's happening with your system.

Tracking System Core Files

cron use always involves a bit of setup. Although Appendix B gives more details on cron's features and options, I'll go carefully through an example that helps track down core clutter.

You need at least one external file to start using the cron facility. Practice cron concepts by commanding this first:

```
# echo "0,5,10,15,20,25,30,35,40,45,50,55 * * * * date > `tty`"
➥>/tmp/experiment
```

Then specify as follows:

```
# crontab /tmp/experiment
```

Finally, insert this code:

```
# crontab -l
```

The last of these gives you a result that looks something like the following:

```
0,5,10,15,20,25,30,35,40,45,50,55 * * * * date > /dev/ttyxx
```

The current time will appear every five minutes in the window from which you launched this experiment.

For a more useful example, create a /tmp/entry file with this single line:

```
0 2 * * * find / -name "core*" -exec ls -l {} \;
```

Next, use this command:

```
# crontab /tmp/entry
```

The result is that each morning at 2:00, cron launches the core-searching job and emails you the results. This is quite useful because Linux creates files core under certain error conditions. These core images are often large and can easily fill up a distressing amount of space on your disk. With the preceding sequence, you'll have a report in your email inbox each morning, listing exactly the locations and sizes of a collection of files that are likely doing you no good.

Monitoring User Space

Suppose you've experimented a bit and accumulated an inventory of cron jobs to monitor the health of your system. Along with your other jobs, you want your system to tell you every Monday morning at 2:10 which 10 users have the biggest home directory trees (/home/*). First, enter this to capture all the jobs you've scheduled:

```
# crontab -l >/tmp/entries
```

Append this line to the bottom of `/tmp/entries`:

```
10 2 * * 1 du -s /home/* | sort -nr | head -10
```

Make this request and `cron` will email the reports you seek:

```
# crontab /tmp/entries
```

at: Scheduling Future Events

Suppose you write an electronic weekly column on financial cycles in the material world, which you deliver by email. To simplify legal ramifications involving financial markets, you make a point of delivering it at 5:00 Friday afternoon. It's Wednesday now, you've finished your analysis, and you're almost through packing for the vacation you're starting tonight. How do you do right by your subscribers? It only takes three lines of at scripting:

```
# at 17:00 Friday << COMMAND
   mail -s "This week's CYCLES report." mailing_list
➥ < analysis.already_written
COMMAND
```

This schedules the `mail` command for later processing. You can log off from your session and your Linux host will still send the mail at 17:00 Friday, just as you instructed. In fact, you can even shut down your machine after commanding it at ..., and, as long as it's rebooted in time, your scheduled task will still be launched on the schedule you dictated.

Other Mechanisms: Expect, Perl, and More

Are you ready to move beyond the constraints of the UNIX shell? Several alternative technologies are free, easy to install, easy to learn, and more powerful—that is, with richer capabilities and more structured syntax—than the shell. A few examples will suggest what they have to offer.

Expect

Expect, by Don Libes, is scripting language that works with many different programs, and can be used as a powerful software tool for automation. Why? Expect automates interactions, particularly those involving terminal control and time delays, that no other tool has attempted. Many command-line applications have the reputation for being unscriptable because they involve password entry and refuse to accept redirection of standard input for this purpose. That's no problem for the `expect` command, however. Under Red Hat Linux, `expect` is installed under the `/usr/bin` directory, and you'll find documentation in its manual page.

Create a script hold with the contents of Listing 26.4.

LISTING 26.4   hold—A "Keep-Alive" Written in Expect

```
#!/usr/bin/expect

# Usage:  "hold HOST USER PASS".
# Action:  login to node HOST as USER.  Offer a shell prompt for
#     normal usage, and also print to the screen the word HELD
#     every five seconds, to exercise the connection periodically.
#     This is useful for testing and using WANs with short time-outs.
#     You can walk away from the keyboard, and never lose your
#     connection through a time-out.
# WARNING:  the security hazard of passing a password through the
#     command line makes this example only illustrative.  Modify to
#     a particular security situation as appropriate.
set hostname [lindex $argv 0]
set username [lindex $argv 1]
set password [lindex $argv 2]

    # There's trouble if $username's prompt is not set to "...} ".
    #     A more sophisticated manager knows how to look for different
    #     prompts on different hosts.
set prompt_sequence "} "

spawn telnet $hostname

expect "login: "
send "$username\r"
expect "Password:"
send "$password\r"

    # Some hosts don't inquire about TERM.  That's another
    #     complexification to consider before widespread use
    #     of this application is practical.
    # Note use of global [gl] pattern matching to parse "*"
    #     as a wildcard.
expect -gl "TERM = (*)"
send "\r"
expect $prompt_sequence
send "sh -c 'while true; do echo HELD; sleep 5; done'\r"
interact
```

This script starts a telnet session and then keeps the connection open by sending the string "HELD" every five seconds. I work with several telephone lines that are used with short timeouts, as a check on out-of-pocket expenses. I use a variant of the script in Listing 26.4 daily, for I often need that to hold one of the connections open.

Expect is an extension to `tcl`, so it is fully programmable with `tcl` capabilities. For information about `tcl` and `tk` from its author, Dr. John Ousterhout, visit `http://www.sun.com/960710/cover/ousterhout.html`. For more information about Expect, visit `http://expect.nist.gov/`.

> ### Tip
>
> You'll also find the `autoexpect` command included with Red Hat Linux. This command watches an interactive session at the console and then creates an executable program to execute the console session. See Chapter 11 for an example of how to use `autoexpect` to automate an FTP session.

Perl

Some consider Perl the most popular scripting language for Red Hat Linux, apart from the shell. Its power and brevity take on particular value in automation contexts.

> ### Note
>
> For more information about Perl, or to get the latest release, browse `http://www.perl.com` or `http://www.perl.org`.

For example, assume that `/usr/local/bin/modified_directories.pl` contains this code:

```perl
#!/usr/bin/perl
# Usage:  "modified_directories.pl DIR1 DIR2 ... DIRN"
# Output:  a list of all directories in the file systems under
#     DIR1 ... DIRN, collectively.  They appear, sorted by the
#     interval since their last activity, that is, since a file
#     within them was last created, deleted, or renamed.
# Randal Schwartz wrote a related program from which this is
#     descended.
use File::Find;
@directory_list = @ARGV;
# "-M" abbreviates "time since last modification", while
#      "-d" "... is a directory."

find ( sub {
$modification_lapse{$File::Find::name} = -M if -d },
@directory_list );

for ( sort {
$modification_lapse{$a} <=> $modification_lapse{$b}} keys
```

```
%modification_lapse ) {

    # Tabulate the results in nice columns.
    printf "%5d:  %s\n", $modification_lapse{$_}, $_;
}
```

Also assume that you adjoin an entry such as this to your `crontab`:

```
20 2 * * * /usr/local/bin/modified_directories.pl /
```

In this case, each morning you'll receive an email report on the date each directory on your host was last modified. This can be useful both for spotting security issues when read-only directories have been changed (they'll appear unexpectedly at the top of the list) and for identifying dormant domains in the filesystem (at the bottom of the list) that might be liberated for better uses.

Other Tools

Many other general-purpose scripting languages effectively automate operations. Apart from Perl and `tcl`, Python deserves the most attention for several reasons, such as its portability and extensibility.

The next sections describe Python and two other special-purpose tools important in automation: Emacs and `procmail`.

Python

Python can be of special interest to Red Hat Linux users. Python is object-oriented, modern, clean, portable, and particularly easy to maintain. If you are a full-time system administrator looking for a scripting language that will grow with you, consider Python. The official home page for Python is `http://www.python.org`.

Emacs

Emacs is one of the most polarizing lightning rods for religious controversy among computer users. Emacs has many intelligent and zealous users who believe it to be the ideal platform for all automation efforts. Its devotees have developed what was originally a screen editor into a tool with capabilities to manage newsgroup discussion, Web browsing, application development, general-purpose scripting, and much more. For the purposes of this chapter, what you need to know about Emacs follows:

- It's an editor that you ought to try at some point in your career.
- If you favor integrated development environments, Emacs can do almost anything you imagine. As an editor, it emulates any other editor, and its developers ensure that it always offers state-of-the-art capabilities in language-directed formatting, application integration, and development automation.

Even if the "weight" of Emacs sways you against its daily use (it may seem slow on startup and can require quite a bit of education and configuration), keep it in mind as a paragon of how sophisticated programming makes common operations more efficient.

> **Note**
>
> The Emacs editor is included with Red Hat Linux. You can use Emacs with or without the X Window System. Type the word `emacs` on the command line of your console or an X11 terminal window and press the Enter key. Run its built-in tutorial by pressing Ctrl+H and then pressing the T key.

procmail

The most indispensable, most often used Internet function is email. Can email be automated?

Yes—and it's perhaps the single best return on your invested time to do so. Along with aliases, distribution lists, startup configurations, and the plethora of mail agents or clients with their feature sets, you'll want to learn about `procmail`. Suppose you receive a hundred messages a day, that a fifth of them can be handled completely automatically, and that it takes at least three seconds of your time to process a single piece of email; those are conservative estimates. A bit of `procmail` automation will save you at least a minute a day, or six hours a year. Even conservative estimates make it clear that an hour of setting up `procmail` pays for itself many times over.

Along with the man `procmail*` pages (**man -k procmail** for a list), serious study of procmail starts with the page `http://www.faqs.org/faqs/mail/filtering-faq`, Nancy McGough's Filtering Mail FAQ. This gives detailed installation and debugging directions. You'll also find information about `procmail` in the Mail-HOWTO (if you installed the HOWTOs). Because your Red Hat Linux machine will almost certainly have a correctly configured `procmail`, you can immediately begin to program your personal use of it. As a first experiment, create exactly these files.

`~/.procmailrc`, with these contents:

```
VERBOSE=on
MAILDIR=$HOME/mail
PMDIR=$HOME/.procmail
LOGFILE=$PMDIR/log
INCLUDERC=$PMDIR/rc.testing
```

`~/.procmail/rc.testing`, holding this code:

```
:0:
* ^Subject:.*HOT
SPAM.HOT
# chmod 600 ~/. ~/.procmailrc ~/procmail/rc.testing
# chmod a+x ~/.
```

Now exercise your filter with the following:

```
# echo "This message 1." | mail -s "Example of HOT SPAM." YOUR_EMAIL_NAME
# echo "This message 2." | mail -s "Desired message." YOUR_EMAIL_NAME
```

What you now see in your mailbox is only one new item: the one with the subject `Desired message`. You also have a new file in your home directory, `SPAM.HOT`, holding the first message.

`procmail` is a robust, flexible utility you can program to achieve even more useful automations than this. When you gain familiarity with it, it will become natural to construct rules that, for example, automatically discard obvious spam, sort incoming mailing-list traffic, and perhaps even implement pager forwarding, remote system monitoring, or FAQ responding. This can save you considerable time each day.

Internal Scripts

One more element of the automation attitude is to be on the lookout for opportunities within every application you use. Scripting has become a pervasive theme, and almost all common applications have at least a rudimentary macro or scripting capability. IRC users know about bots, Web browsers typically expose at least a couple of scripting interfaces, all modern PPP clients are scriptable, and even such venerable tools as vi and ftp have configuration, shortcut, and macro capabilities that enormously magnify productivity. Even the apm and cardmgr (for PCMCIA cards) will run scripts on certain actions). If you use a tool regularly, take a few minutes to reread its presentation in this volume; chances are you'll come up with a way to make your work easier and more effective.

Concluding Challenge for an Automater—Explaining Value

You've become knowledgeable and experienced in scripting your computer so that it best serves you. You know how to improve your skills in script writing. You've practiced different approaches enough to know how to solve problems efficiently. The final challenge in your automation career is this: How do you explain how good you have become?

This is a serious problem, and, as usual, the solution begins with attitude. You no longer pound at the keyboard to bludgeon technical tasks into submission; you now operate in a more refined way and achieve correspondingly grander results. As an employee, you're much more valuable than the system administrators and programmers who reinvent wheels every day. In your recreational or personal use of Red Hat Linux, the computer is working for you—not the other way around, as it might have been when you started. Your attitude needs to adjust to the reality you've created by improving your productivity. Invest in yourself, whether by attending technical conferences where you can further promote your skills, negotiating a higher salary, or simply taking the time in your computer work to get things right. It's easy in organizations to give attention to crises and reward those visibly coping with emergencies. It takes true leadership to plan ahead, organize work so emergencies don't happen, and use techniques of automation to achieve predictable and manageable results on schedule.

One of the most effective tools you have in taking up this challenge is *quantification*. Keep simple records to demonstrate how much time you put into setting up backups before you learned about cron, or run a simple experiment to compare two ways of approaching an elementary database maintenance operation. Find out how much of your online time goes just to the login process and decide whether scripting that is justified. Chart a class of mistakes that you make and see whether your precision improves as you apply automation ideas.

In all cases, keep in mind that you are efficient, perhaps extraordinarily efficient, because of the knowledge you apply. Automation feels good!

Summary

Automation offers enormous opportunities for using your Linux computer to achieve the goals you set. The examples in this chapter demonstrate that every Linux user can begin immediately to exploit the techniques and attitude of automation. Some of the major automation mechanisms provided by Linux include background processes, scheduling, and sophisticated software tools. As you gain experience by overcoming required administrative tasks, you'll build your own approaches to system administration automation.

Configuring and Building Kernels

The scope of this chapter is forward-looking. Since prebuilt images for the current Red Hat kernels are readily available, and because those ready-made kernels require little more than an rpm -Uvh command, your main use of this chapter may be to build the "canonical" Linux kernel from the sources maintained by Linus Torvalds. With Linux in a transition to new release, this chapter will focus on the canonical 2.4 kernel. Because Linux 2.4 is almost twice the size and has four times the configuration options of Linux 2.2, and because your Red Hat kernel will contain some of these features as vendor patches, some descriptions listed here may be slightly different. This chapter can still guide you through a 2.2 install, but it will tend to tease you with features you can only get through the latest sources.

This is also what Red Hat expects you will do with their 7.1 distribution. Most Linux distributions in late 2000 faced the dilemma to include the nearly finished kernel update, or to stay with the tried and true, and very tired, 2.2 kernel. Red Hat chose a middle path and to prepare you for the jump to 2.4, they have already included most of the requisite software and new system configurations that will ease your transition into 2.4.

This chapter is a guide to configuring the Linux kernel for Intel-based computers and will teach you

- How to obtain and update Linux kernel sources
- How to compile for multiple machines
- How to configure modules
- How to tune virtual memory and filesystem performance using sysctl
- How to add alternate filesystems
- How to add network services
- How to add support for special devices such as video/radio/TV cards, joysticks, and infrared controls
- How to troubleshoot a new kernel

Don't expect to do everything at once. You may only need to consult those few sections on installing your sound or network device. On the other hand, for difficult kernel optimization, advanced networking, or tailoring the kernel for embedded and other special situations, this chapter should give you an overview of what is possible.

Introduction to the Linux Kernel

You may think kernel tuning is no place for the average user. This is both true and false. Like other features of Linux, the possibilities are endless and deep, but you don't need to understand all the gory details of PCI chipsets to tailor a better Linux for your computer.

Armed with nothing more than your computer manuals, you can easily zero in on features you need and leave the very technical tuning for some day down the road. If you know your techie details, Linux will not stand in your way, but if you only know how to run a shell command, you can still build a better Linux.

The first checklist question to ask yourself is, "Do I really need to rebuild the kernel?" The answer is almost always "No." Back in good old UNIX days, this step was so common that most commercial UNIX systems performed an automatic kernel config and install whenever the hardware configuration changed. As recently as 1999, most Linux distributions still required manual recompilation to support some components.

Those were the good old days. Today, your default Red Hat kernel stands an excellent chance of running optimally on your hardware, without *any* source configuration changes. At most, you might fine-tune /etc/modules.conf or set /proc control files. Even if your needs require upgrading to the latest Linux 2.4, you may find it more convenient and just as reliable to fetch the updated binary RPM file.

Do You *Really* Need to Recompile?

There are many ways to modify Linux. Only one of these is to reconfigure and recompile the kernel. Many runtime parameters, such as sound card ports, hard disk geometries, and IRQ assignments, can be set using *bootparams*, the command-line options to the LILO. Many runtime characteristics, even delicate issues such as virtual memory and filesystem behaviors, can be queried and set by shell scripts using the /proc filesystem.

> **Note**
>
> Before you dive in to a complete recompile, you can save a lot of time and bother by investigating these alternative tuning methods.

The kernel installed by your Red Hat RPM file is very flexible and very complete, but one kernel cannot be all things to all people. You may need to trim the size for a small-memory machine, or boost it to handle 16GB, or even just to recompile to take advantage of your particular brand of CPU. At some point, you will want to harness the *real* power of UNIX: the power of choice. Kernel tweaking can be as simple as adding a few boot parameters to set a sound card IRQ, or it can involve picking and choosing from the huge list of modules and kernel options in search of an optimal match. Through the kernel configuration, Linux can be adapted for low memory or huge memory, optimized as a router or firewall, extended to support new hardware and alien filesystems, and can include the largest array of network protocols in the industry.

Understanding the Kernel

The kernel is the innermost layer of the Linux operating system, a thin layer of software between applications and the hardware, and that thing which is most rightly called "Linux." When your computer starts, the BIOS starts the boot loader, the boot loader hands control to the kernel, and the kernel does the rest. It initializes core systems; probes, identifies, and enables your hardware; and initiates the boot scripts. After the boot, the kernel is your gateway to the local machine, managing all resources and tasks, and supplying modules and applications with a uniform interface to services such as task switching, signaling, device I/O, and memory management.

When we say a program "runs on Linux," we mean that it communicates through these kernel interfaces. Because the kernel has been ported to systems from the tiny SH-based handheld computers to the huge S/390 mainframes, any program written on one Linux can be moved to any other platform with relative ease despite the obvious differences in the ways these computers physically handle their memory, disks, and other services. Unlike a portable interpreter such as Java, a Linux program will run optimally as a native application on its new home, depending only on the kernel configuration. Also, because Linux is an implementation of the POSIX standard UNIX interfaces, programs coded for the POSIX standard are also portable to Linux.

Linux is the fastest-growing O/S platform, already rivaling Microsoft Windows/NT and surpassing Novell. Linux is estimated to command *at least* 25% of all servers and 10% of desktops worldwide. There are millions of users deploying Linux in Web servers, edge servers, routers, and embedded systems. Linux is used in the space shuttle, in medicine and telerobotics, and in Hollywood. The reason for this success is not the low price tag: Linux succeeds because it is a solid design that is flexible, friendly to Open Source development, scalable, and portable from handheld computers to mainframes. Simply put, Linux succeeds because it works.

Kernel Modules

Configuring a UNIX kernel means selecting some devices and services and omitting others, and passing configuration values to the included services to more closely match the underlying hardware. Linux 2.0 introduced a middle ground to configuration by allowing for dynamic kernel configuration through the use of modules and `sysctl`. Rather than rebuild the whole kernel when conditions change, the *modular* components let you load and unload services as needed, and the `/proc` interface (`sysctl`) lets you set runtime parameters on-the-fly.

The Linux kernel is now almost completely modular; most components and services can be automatically inserted as needed through the `kmod` and most are generally configured through the `sysctl` interfaces or through setting bootparams in `/etc/modules.conf`.

Modules can dynamically add support for filesystems or network protocols that are only needed only for certain applications and remove the module code while offline.

Module Support in the Red Hat Kernel

Your installed Red Hat kernel and kernel sources will have `sysctl`, the `/proc` filesystem, and kernel module support turned on by default. These features are critical to many userspace applications; think twice before you disable any of these. If you do recompile from the distribution sources, be sure to check the module support settings because some distributions have been sent out with the kernel version number restriction setting; this setting rejects any modules that do not precisely match the kernel version number and is almost certainly not required by your system.

Loadable modules coupled with hardware detection is what lets your Red Hat distribution boot and install on your hardware. A quick look at `/lib/modules` will show many extraneous components. Should your hardware need them, they will already be installed. Modules are also convenient for adding services under tight memory constraints, such as in laptops or embedded systems, and essential where the hardware must be initialized before a service is enabled or where the module must be configured at runtime to support the device; for example, with plug-and-play sound cards where the boot process must initialize the interrupts before the module can be invoked.

The use of kernel modules in Linux also has a political implication: Because module system calls are not considered "linking against the kernel," modules are not bound by the GPL that governs the rest of the kernel sources. Developers are free to create proprietary modules and to distribute these without releasing the source code. This policy has prompted several commercial vendors to provide modules where patent or other licensing issues would otherwise prevent Linux support.

Kernel Bootparams

Almost all kernel modules can be configured at runtime through bootparams statements. These bootparams are generally simple flags and assignment statements that can be entered at the LILO prompt or added into `/etc/lilo.conf` on the append option. For example, if all you need to do is set the proper address for an old SoundBlaster CD-ROM, you can add the line

```
append="sbpcd=0x230,SoundBlaster"
```

to your `/etc/lilo.conf` and re-run `lilo`, or you can give the bootparams when the boot loader prompts.

`LILO: linux sbpcd=0x230,SoundBlaster`

Most kernel services accept bootparams; a complete guide to boot parameters can also be found with the `man bootparam` command.

In addition to the bootparams, most services can be manipulated through `echo`ing values to a `/proc` file; for example, defense against Syn-Cookie attacks is enabled by appending the following line to `/etc/rc.d/rc.local`:

`echo 1 >/proc/sys/net/ipv4/tcp_syncookies`

Note

During a normal boot, there is a short delay after the `LILO` appears. Pressing the Alt key during that delay will change to the `LILO:` prompt and allow you to enter the bootparams. For more information, see the section "Preparing `lilo.conf` for Kernel Updates."

Understanding the Kernel Sources Structure

Linux is "UNIX-like." Linux is not a version of UNIX, but a new OS that aims to be UNIX-interface compatible. Linux is also a large and complex piece of software. The kernel itself contains over 1.7 million lines of source code; by commercial software standards, such a project would take 5 to 10 years and require up to 500 programmers. The methodology of Open Source has been proven through the kernel project: Richard Gooch's Kernel FAQ (`http://www.tux.org/lkml/`) observes that Linux is a little more than eight years old, placing it right on track compared to industrial standards.

Linux is developed by thousands of programmers spread worldwide, and under constant peer review by many thousands more. According to Brooks' Law, communications complexity grows exponentially with the size of the development team, eventually stifling all progress, but the Linux project defeats this law by two clever hacks: Linux is organized into modules and subsystems, and the explosive growth and experimentation on new features is isolated from the mainstream users through a separation into development and production source streams. The modular design distributes communications hierarchically into sub-teams and sub-teams of sub-teams, avoiding the omni-topology that invokes Brooks' Law.

Figure 27.1 shows a package map of the kernel sources. A quick inspection of /usr/src/linux/MAINTAINERS shows almost direct correspondence. The gross structure of Linux partitions the sources by subsystems; since those technologies suit the fancies of the developers, someone with an interest in filesystems may be deeply involved in the /fs package but only marginally involved in /mm.

FIGURE 27.1

Package map of
/usr/src/linux.

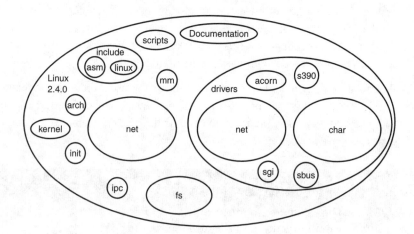

The per-developer partitioning is carried deeper in per-service relationships within the /net and /driver packages. This makes sense when you consider that each service is added and maintained by owners (or vendors) of that hardware who would want to keep their realm of interest localized. This "implementation-oriented" source structure may overlook similarities and opportunities for code re-use, but it is highly pragmatic within the Open Source methodology.

Kernel Version Numbers

Linux kernel version numbers identify the base design and the revision, and also identifies whether you are running an experimental or a production release. The version in use by any Linux system can be queried with uname -a:

```
$ uname -a
Linux kato 2.3.21 #1 Tue Oct 12 16:08:21 EDT 1999 i486 unknown
```

This line identifies that kernel as version 2.3.21 and gives the architecture and the date when the kernel was compiled. The version number contains three parts:

> The major number (2)
>
> The minor number (3)
>
> The current revision (21)

There are enough version-1 Linux machines to be impressive, but they are rare. For practical purposes, the major number is 2; no one is quite sure what change would be big enough to jump to Linux-3, but we might assume it would cease to promise Linux-2 compatibility.

The last number is the incremental patch number and changes with every update. The first important portion of the kernel version number is the middle digit, the "minor" number. *Odd* minor numbers denote "experimental" kernels, the testbed for developers to explore, add new code, and bounce ideas off each other. *Even* minors, on the other hand, carry a stamp of respectability as "production editions."

When a development kernel is ready, it follows the usual process of a feature freeze, then a code freeze, and is then promoted to the next even number. Thus, 2.3.99 became 2.4.0 and was simultaneously branched to become the new development 2.5 source. The road goes ever on.

Newsflash: Development Kernels Can Break

During the rapid development of the odd-minor kernels, you cannot simply jump in and expect to join the other kernel surfers. Although developers try to only release stable code, very often a core change can create havoc for other users. These troubles may be traced to updated libraries, modules, or compiler tools, but sometimes it is just a broken system and the development kernel can strand whole communities of users. Always check the Linux Kernel Web site (http://www.tux.org) or watch the linux-kernel mailing list. If your hardware is not flagged in the trouble reports, pick a development kernel revision that has been stable for at least a few days, and dive in.

Obtaining the Kernel Sources

Every Linux distribution contains kernel sources. Red Hat offers install options to include the kernel headers, and a separate RPM to include the kernel sources. You must install the kernel headers if you plan to compile *any* software; to build the kernel, you must *also* install the kernel-sources RPM, or obtain kernel sources from some other source.

When fetching kernel sources, it is good netiquette to seek a mirror site as close to you as possible. Although famous sites such as Red Hat (ftp://ftp.redhat.com) and kernel.org (ftp://ftp.kernel.org/pub/linux) will have the files you need, you should check http://www.kernel.org for an appropriate mirror site.

Distribution Kernels

Before you replace your kernel sources, be aware that most distributions apply their own patches to the standard Linux sources; Red Hat is no exception to this rule. If you recompile from your official Red Hat source RPM, there may be features missing, modified or added from what is covered in this chapter, and if you obtain canonical sources from the kernel FTP site (ftp://ftp.kernel.org), the resulting kernel may break special features in your distribution.

It is a double edged sword: Using your Red Hat sources means you must rely on Red Hat for all kernel updates whereas the canonical sources are regularly updated by incremental patches that will not apply smoothly to the Red Hat edition. Other authors may also supply patches for special features such as motherboard sensor reading or multiline ppp, and these patches may also fail to apply against the Red Hat edition.

In general, if you need to remain consistent with your Red Hat kit, you should stay with their edition of the kernel source files, but if you need advanced features and timely updates, you should consider migrating to the canonical kernel.org sources.

FTP mirrors partition kernel packages by major and minor version numbers such as /pub/linux/kernel/v2.4. Each directory contains whole-enchilada source tarballs and compressed patch files—if you are jumping up from 2.2 or 2.3, or if you want to start fresh, you need the file named linux-VERSION.tar.gz (or .bz2). Although a lot to download over a modem connection, once you have a standard source tree, you can update incrementally by downloading much smaller patch files.

Before you open *any* .tar file, you should always list the contents to see if the file is complete and to get an overview of the directory structure it will install:

```
$ tar -tzf linux-2.4.5.tar.gz
```

This will print a long list of files, including directories for device drivers, modules, and architecture-dependent code for all the current Linux ports as illustrated in Figure 27.1. The important detail is that the tarball unpacks into a directory called simply linux/.

Symbolic Links to the Kernel Sources

Before you unpack a kernel tarball, create a version-tagged directory and sym-link (`ln -s`) it to the generic `/usr/src/linux` location. For example, if you obtained `linux-2.4.7.tar.gz`, create `/usr/src/linux-2.4.7` and a symlink `/usr/src/linux` before you unpack your kernel sources:

```
cd /usr/src
mkdir linux-2.4.7
ln -s linux-2.4.7 linux
tar xzf linux-2.4.7.tar.gz
```

If `/usr/include/linux` is also symlinked to `/usr/src/linux/include`, your include files will always belong to your current kernel. You can now keep several versions of the kernel, each in its own `/usr/src/linux-X.Y.Z` directory. When you patch your sources, the patch will apply to the appropriate kernel sources through the `linux/` symlink, and you can experiment with multiple versions, quickly switching between them by simply replacing the symlink.

Checklist for Coping with New Kernels

When dealing with new kernels, keep the following items in mind:

- Building and running the kernel depends on the software versions listed in `linux/Documentation/Changes`. Before you compile or run any new kernel, you can save a lot of heartache if you check your system against these version numbers!

- Drivers bundled with Linux may not be the very latest. If you have problems with a particular device, or with very new hardware, search for an update before building your kernel.

- Kernel changes may require changes to your boot scripts, to `/etc/lilo.conf`, or `/etc/modules.conf`. The `linux/Documentation` collection contains many short `README` files on many different parts of the kernel, and each driver subdirectory may also contain additional information on installing or configuring difficult devices. Most kernel modules accept parameters either through the bootparams, through the append line of `/etc/lilo.conf`, or, for dynamically loaded modules, on the `/sbin/insmod` command line or in `/etc/modules.conf`.

- If you give options both in `lilo.conf` and at the `LILO:` prompt, the boot prompt options are *appended* to the end of the append options. This allows you to override installed options at the command line to pre-empt unwanted settings; this is also why many modules also include options to restore their default behavior.

A Script to Check Version Numbers

Checking version numbers against the `Documentation/Changes` file can be tedious, especially if you're like me and can't remember the command syntax for all these commands. The shell script in Listing 27.1 generates a simple list of packages typically included in the Changes list. I originally wrote this as a poor man's version of the `versions` command available on SiliconGraphics IRIX machines.

LISTING 27.1   Shell Script for Extracting Versions

```
#!/bin/sh
echo Versions 0.1 c.1999 by Gary Lawrence Murphy
echo ==========================================================
/sbin/insmod -V 2>&1 | grep version | grep insmod
echo -n GCC:
gcc --version
ld -v
ls -l /lib/libc.so.* | gawk '{print $9 $10 $11;}'
ldd --version 2>&1 | grep ldd
ls -l /usr/lib/libg++.so.* | gawk '{print $9 $10 $11;}'
ps --version
procinfo -v
mount --version
hostname -V
basename --v
/sbin/automount --version
/sbin/showmount --version
bash -version
ncpmount -v
pppd -v
chsh -v
echo ==========================================================
```

Source Tree Patches

Updates are distributed as `patch` files named for the version that results from the patch. For example, an upgrade from 2.4.4 to 2.4.5 will be called `patch-2.4.5.gz`. Patch files are simply context `diff`s, the output of the CVS or UNIX `diff -c` command (see `man diff`) which list the differences from the prior version. The patch is applied by piping the file through the GNU `patch` utility; the `patch` will be given lines of context around the change and told to delete, add, or replace lines in the source files.

Patching Incremental Versions

Patch files can only upgrade by one revision number. Upgrading from 2.4.1 to 2.4.6 will require patches for all intermediate releases. An exception to this rule is the `-ac` series pre-release patches, which are assembled by Alan Cox. These patch files are always accumulative based on the most recent official release. For example, `patch-2.4.1-ac12` might be Alan's twelfth patch on the 2.4.1 release, but it must be applied to a clean 2.4.1 kernel; the patch will fail to upgrade from `patch-2.4.1-ac11`.

Unless you have good reason to suspect otherwise, you should compile and test each incremental revision before applying the next patch. Once a patch is applied, there is no way to undo the changes.

Patch files are also created by comparing the sources of totally clean Linux distributions. Before you run the patch, it is important to back up your `linux/.config` file and then to clean your kernel source tree to the most pristine state using `make mrproper`:

```
cd /usr/src/linux
cp .config /usr/src/config-old
make mrproper
```

This removes any residual generated files from previous compilations as these might interfere with the patch or the subsequent kernel build. Saving any previous `.config` file (which would be otherwise removed by `mrproper`) allows you to bootstrap your next kernel with `make oldconfig`.

There are two things you should know about patch files: They are much smaller than the source tarball (typically a few hundred kilobytes), and they do not always work.

Verifying a Patch Update

After patching your sources, search the kernel tree for reject files (`find . -name "*.rej"`) containing the failed diffs; these are most often the result of some innocuous difference in whitespace or tab stops between the sources owned by the creator of the diff and your own sources. If you find any `*.rej` files, you must *manually* correct the associated source files before you compile.

The `linux/scripts/patch-kernel` is a Perl program that attempts to automate this process. `patch-kernel` will deduce the current source version number and compare this to the patch files found in the current directory. If higher-version patch files are found, the script will step through these sequentially upgrading the sources. Frankly, I have never had much luck with this script, but your mileage may vary.

Once you have patched the sources, you can bootstrap your new kernel configuration by copying your backup `.config` file to `linux/.config` and using `make oldconfig` to migrate the options present in your previous installation, preserving all those fiddly settings that are so often forgotten (such as the IRQ of your sound card!). You will need to monitor this process: `make oldconfig` will stop and prompt for any new options added by the new sources. Once this command has run, use `make xconfig` to recheck the settings, and then compile with any of the `make` build targets.

Upgrades and Modules

Modules are generally loaded automatically via `kmod` or scripted using `/sbin/insmod` program, with the obvious `/sbin/rmmod` to remove them. Other utilities in this suite include `/sbin/depmod` to compute module dependencies and `/sbin/modprobe` to load the module and those upon which it depends.

One of two module things can go wrong with a module when upgrading to a newer kernel:

> The module utilities are incompatible.

> The module dependencies may conflict.

> **Note**
>
> There is a third possibility with pre-2.2 kernels: Module version numbers are mismatched. This happens when the kernel has been compiled with the option to check module version numbers, and those numbers do not exactly match (including the build number). These modules are rejected, and your system may not boot if it depends on some critical module to function. This is no longer an issue because this test is no longer part of the Linux configuration.

The first situation is most likely. The ix386 module utilities have been updated to use PIII instructions and new editions may not have been included in your distribution files. If your module utilities meet the requirements spelled out in `linux/Documentation/Changes`, you will have no problem, but if you do happen to boot a kernel with old module utilities, you can hang your system.

The second problem can hit anyone. This is one of those things that, once you know what has happened, you realize the solution is just common sense. For example, suppose you compile Windows VFAT filesystem support as a module, but then your boot scripts try to use some file from your windows partition prior to the module loading. Or, and more likely, you may accidentally attempt to load modules out of sequence. For instance, you might configure your network support as a module, forgetting that the `httpd` will hang the boot scripts while trying to resolve the hostname, and then inadvertently assign `httpd` an earlier slot in the `/etc/rc.d/rc5.d` boot sequence.

There is only a small overhead in loading and unloading and in the coding of a driver as a module. Unless memory or performance is critical, the code is needed continuously, or the module is required early in the boot process, it can and probably should be compiled as a module.

New Features in 2.4

If you are coming to this chapter from the 2.2 Kernel reference material, you're in for a ride. Systems have changed all over the place. The following is just a partial list of systems that have been added, rewritten, or rethought in the 2.4 kernel:

- Resource Management Subsystem
- Remapped Device Files
- Numerous Changes to the `/proc` Interface
- Support for 4.2 Billion Users
- Memory limit now 16GB
- I2O/PCI Improvements
- Improved Plug-and-Play Support
- Improved Parport Interface
- USB Support
- Extended Joystick Support
- ia64, S/390, and SuperH Ports
- Shared Memory VFS
- Logical Volume Manager
- Single Buffer File Caching
- Raw I/O Devices
- Large-file Filesystems (files > 2GB)
- UDF and UFS Filesystems
- SCSI Subsystem
- Module Access Control
- Network Address Translation (NAT)

- DECNet and ARCNet Support
- Direct Rendering Manager
- Voice Synthesizer Support
- Kernel-level HTTPD
- Documentation/DocBook and docgen

Planned Features for Linux 2.5

Kernels take time to polish for production, and books take time to prepare and print; as a result, there are many features that were either not ready in time to be considered for the 2.4 kernel, or that were not well understood enough to be included in this book prior to press. The following sections are a guess at some of the directions to be taken with 2.5, but do not be surprised if more than one finds its way into an early revision of 2.4.

CML2

If you have ever tried to *add* a new kernel feature, you have already seen why Eric Raymond is spending his flight and hotel time redesigning the kernel configuration tools.

CML2 is the Configuration Modeling Language to succeed the current make xconfig method with a simpler system, is easier to maintain and to program, and will allow module and service developers to specify all dependencies of their code. It may even be possible to specify your hardware to the CML2 interpreter and have it deduce the kernel options without intervention.

Frame Buffers (fbdev)

James Simmons has plans for cleaning up the fbdev layer with a new API, adding support for cards with multiple frame buffers, and adding real multihead support to the console system.

Sound System

Although partially present in 2.4, the next kernel will expand the support for the ALSA sound drivers.

V4L2

The 2.4 kernel contains little in the way of new support for the video and FM radio interface primarily because the developers are reworking the entire system for V4L2; unfortunately, V4L2 was not considered stable enough to be included into the 2.3 development tree and has been pushed back to Linux 2.5.

Memory Management and Memory Devices

Rik van Riel has plans to support allocating very large continuous memory blocks on system initialization, and improved dcache and other improvements to the VM. David Woodhouse is also calling for adding support for flash and other memory device drivers.

Journaling Filesystem

The 2.5 TODO list includes merging in the changes for the ReiserFS and ext3, merging in XFS, HFS+, JFS, and NWFS; whether all of these will happen or if some hybrid occurs remains to be seen.

Configuring the Linux Kernel

Once you know what your new kernel must accomplish and have the sources installed, you are ready to begin creating a customized Linux operating system. Before setting the compile in motion, there are a few last minute details to ensure a successful run, or at least a graceful recovery.

Preparing `lilo.conf` for Kernel Updates

Before you begin, double-check your system against the requirements in `linux/Documentation/Changes`. In particular, ensure you have the correct version of the binutils and the gcc compiler.

You should also create an entry in your `/etc/lilo.conf` to keep your current kernel installed as a backup. In addition to adding a few seconds' delay on the boot prompt with the `delay` parameter (so you can interrupt to add parameters or select an alternate image), add a section for a known stable kernel (such as the original distribution kernel image) and also for the generated backup left behind by the build commands.

```
image=/boot/vmlinuz.orig
        label=stable
        root=/dev/hda3
        append=""
        read-only
image=/boot/vmlinuz.bak
        label=backup
        root=/dev/hda3
        append=""
        read-only
```

Using this configuration, if you have trouble booting from the new kernel, you can enter `stable` at the `LILO:` prompt and boot your original kernel.

The `make bzlilo` compile command will automatically back up the previous kernel from `$(INSTALL_PATH)/vmlinuz` to `$(INSTALL_PATH)/vmlinuz.old` and then run the `lilo` command to install the new kernels. The preceding `/etc/lilo.conf` sections give one more line of defense against a kernel that cannot boot. The fourth section, labeled `backup`, also allows you to make periodic backups of particularly stable development kernels in case repeated compiles leave both `vmlinuz` and `vmlinuz.old` unstable and utility upgrades have cut you off from the original `vmlinuz.orig`. It happens.

Is `lilo.conf` prepared to find the new kernel? Do you have a backup kernel and a boot disk? Do you have enough disk space? These may seem trivial questions, but they are important. An error in any of these may leave your system in an inoperable state and entirely devour your weekend. Even if all you are doing is setting a few `/proc` values or adding a network interface on the boot prompt, it is good defensive driving to consider the recovery plan.

Allow a LILO Delay

While experimenting with kernel options, remember to set the `lilo` delay parameter to give some grace time where you can select an alternative kernel. If your system has a delay of zero seconds, you will not have the opportunity to pre-empt loading the default kernel, and if that kernel is faulty, your only option is to boot from a floppy disk. For more dangerous experiments, `delay` set to -1 will wait indefinitely for a boot parameter.

Configuring with make

The Linux Makefile provides four methods of setting your configuration options:

- `make config`—A command-line terminal program
- `make menuconfig`—An ncurses-based console program
- `make xconfig`—A tk/tcl-based X11 GUI program
- `make oldconfig`—A semi-automatic update program

Why have a command-line interface at all? Suppose you had an autonomous robot submarine or a space probe. Imagine you are in the midst of maneuvers and need a fast kernel reconfig. Simple dumb terminal interfaces can go places other interfaces cannot dream of going! The X11/tk interface may be more elegant and esthetically appealing, but it does require that Tk and X11 are both installed and working.

A forms-based interface is often more comfortable, but X11 is sometimes impractical—for example, while doing remote administration over a slow telnet connection or in a Linux machine for blind users. For these situations, we have the ncurses-based menuconfig. Both the X11 and the ncurses configuration tools offer the same options in the same order, and they have roughly the same capability to navigate backward and forward through the configuration options.

> **Note**
>
> The X and ncurses configuration commands also have the same propensity to allow wildly conflicting kernel options with nary a whisper of dissent... sometime early in 2.5, this will all change with the adoption of Eric Raymond's CML2 Configuration Management Language (see the section "CML2: The Next-Generation Configuration Tool").

To start the configuration, simply go to the /usr/src/linux directory and enter one of the configuration commands. If you choose either of the ncurses or X11 methods, you will see a brief flurry of compiler activity while the user-interface programs compile, and then you will be greeted by an overview screen with all the categories of kernel options.

Those of you who recoil in horror at the thought of a command line can now rest easy. From this point on, those using the xconfig method will be in carpal-tunnel land (a.k.a. "mouse mode") until the configuration is done.

Selecting Configuration Options

Figure 27.2 shows the initial screen as seen in the xconfig display for the 2.4 kernel. 2.2.x kernels are very similar, but with fewer options and minor cosmetic differences. In all of the configuration methods, most kernel options can be set to be included, included as a module, or left out of the compile. On the xconfig and menuconfig screens, there are options to include or exclude complete sections of configuration; disabling these will gray out any dependent options (the dumb-terminal config option will silently skip these sections).

This guide cannot attempt to describe every one of the 1,302 individual options in the Linux kernel; this chapter will only cover the major groups, focus on options of interest to specific applications, and explain some of the implications and configuration options for common Intel-based modules.

FIGURE 27.2

Online Help in
`make xconfig.`

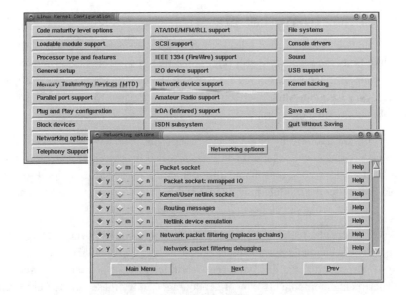

Whether you use the dumb-terminal, ncurses, or X11 method, and whether you are a beginner or advanced user, the most important feature on all the kernel configuration screens is the HELP option. Almost all kernel features are documented right in the configuration screen; whether you are looking at options for installing sound or network support or seeking expert options for filesystems and firewalls, most options carry very reassuring advice: "It is safe to say Y" (or N).

Preparing for a Kernel Configuration

To answer many configuration questions, you must know the insides of your computer. Kernel configuration will ask about network cards, sound cards, PCI chipsets, IDE and SCSI controllers, and a host of other highly personal questions. When in doubt, use the defaults or the recommended option in the associated HELP page.

If you're feeling zealous, keep your computer manuals nearby or run through your first configuration with the panels taken off your computer and a flashlight in hand. You can also find a wealth of information about your hardware by examining the output of the `dmesg` command, or by inspecting `/proc/cpuinfo` and other `/proc` pseudofiles.

It is not absolutely essential that you match your computer chipset perfectly on your first kernel configuration. The defaults normally work very well.

Code Maturity Level

Although a "stable" kernel release such as the 2.4 series is considered to be ready for prime time, the kernel will still offer some features deemed experimental. These may be for supporting new technology for which a standard is not yet set, or they may simply offer new techniques that were considered too essential to omit, but were not completely stable at the time of the release.

This option will also include older kernel options that have been replaced or otherwise considered obsolete. Again, the inference is that these modules were dropped from the mainstream for good reason and although you may need this support to use the kernel on old hardware, the module may be less stable than normally expected, and it may no longer have active developers.

All experimental features are clearly marked; you can only select them if you have specifically enabled experimental services. The experimental code may be essential to your purpose; for example, your real-world testing is essential to the success of these experimental components. You are encouraged to try these new features, report on their results, and file proper bug reports, but do remember these components are not considered stable. We are asked not to flood the mailing lists and newsgroups with complaints, and, if your kernel fails to load or crashes mid-stream, you should suspect experimental modules first, and remove all experimental modules before you suspect you have found a bug among the stable modules.

Processor Type and Features

Most distributions are preset for the safest setting, the old Intel 386 computer. This may be the first kernel option you will change.

Use this option with due caution. Compiling for an advanced CPU may mean your kernel will not boot or will fail on an older machine. This is also true for excluding the floating-point co-processor emulation. A 386-SX may not run if the emulator is missing. Table 27.1 shows the recommended mapping of processor types to processor options.

TABLE 27.1   Intel CPU Kernel Options

Kernel Option	CPU
386	AMD/Cyrix/Intel 386DX/DXL/SL/SLC/SX, Cyrix/TI, 486DLC/DLC2, UMC 486SX-S and NextGen Nx586. Only "386" kernels will run on an i386 machine.
486	MD/Cyrix/IBM/Intel 486DX/DX2/DX4 or SL/SLC/SLC2/SLC3/SX/SX2 and UMC U5D or U5S.
486	AMD/Cyrix/IBM/Intel DX4 or 486DX/DX2/SL/SX/SX2,AMD/Cyrix 5x86, NexGen Nx586 and UMC U5D or U5S.

TABLE 27.1 continued

Kernel Option	CPU
586/K5/5x86/ 6x86/6x86 MX	Generic Pentium, possibly lacking the time stamp counter register.
Pentium/Pentium MMX	Intel Pentium/Pentium MMX, AMD K5, K6 and K63D.
Pentium Pro/ Celeron/ Pentium II	Cyrix/IBM/National Semiconductor 6x86MX, MII and Intel Pentium II/ Pentium Pro.
Pentium III	Intel Pentium III
K6/K6-II/K6-III	AMD K6, K6-II and K6-III
Athelon K7	AMD Athlon
Crusoe	Self-modifying low-power CPU from Transmeta Corp
Winchip-C6	Original IDT Winchip
Winchip-2	IDT Winchip 2
Winchip-2A/3	IDT Winchips with 3dNow!

27

Intel CPU Options: Microcode, MSR, and MTRR

The CPU microcode option is required to use the userspace tools to insert updated microcode into Intel Pentium Pro, Pentium II, Pentium III, and Xeon processors. Note that this uploading is not persistent; rebooting the computer will return to the original microcode and requires re-inserting the update in the boot scripts.

The MSR option will create a /proc entry for the model-specific registers of the Intel CPU, making the RDMSR and WRMSR instructions accessible by userspace programs. These registers provide access to the FPU execution state, the time stamp counters, and performance monitoring.

Detailed information on Intel MSRs can be found in the Pentium Processor User's Manual (http://x86.org/intel.doc/586manuals.htm).

For Pentium II and Pentium Pro machines supporting the Memory Type Range Register (MTRR), Linux can double video transfer performance through the MTRR option. To use MTRR, you must use an X server that can use MTRR through either ioctl() calls or through the /proc/mtrr pseudo-file. You can query your MTRR system through cat /proc/mtrr, and code for manipulating the interface is provided in linux/Documentation/mtrr.txt. An initialization bug on some Symmetric Multi-Processor (SMP) machines can also be corrected by including MTRR support.

High Memory Support

Linux will support up to 64 gigabytes of RAM, but this support must invoke Intel Physical Address Extensions (PAE) to use memory above the 4GB limit. All Intel Pentium series CPUs and the new ia64 support PAE, but enabling this option will crash on CPUs that do not support PAE. For systems with up to 1GB of RAM, no special options are required, and for systems with between 1GB and 4GB of RAM, the 4GB option will split memory into a 3GB space useable by other applications and a 1GB region for internal use by the kernel.

Memory Technology Devices

If your CPU cannot cache all the memory on your machine, you can still use this memory for swap or storage through the Memory Technology Device (MTD) option. This option is primarily intended for "flash" cards and the "disk on a chip" components used in embedded applications, but can also be used to gain access to this inaccessible memory.

SMP and IO-APIC

With the 2.4 kernels, SMP will support up to 16 processors on Intel x86 machines; SMP support for other architectures is still considered experimental.

Symmetric Multi-Processing (SMP) can have some unexpected side effects and enabling this option can restrict the portability of your kernel. Whereas a non-SMP kernel will run on a multi-CPU machine (but will use only one processor), an SMP kernel will slow a single CPU machine, hang on ix486 machines, and different architectures such as Pentium III versus Pentium Pro will not run the same SMP code. SMP will also require the Enhanced Real Time Clock Support and will disable Advanced Power Management; you may also need to set your BIOS options for Unixware. For more information on SMP support, look up the SMP-FAQ (http://www.irisa.fr/prive/mentre/smp-faq/).

The Advanced Programmable Interrupt Controller options APIC and IO-APIC are generally related to SMP machines but may be supported on some single-processor boards; the option will not slow the kernel if your hardware lacks this support, so it is safe to set this option, and this support will be automatically included if you select SMP.

Loadable Module Support

It is hard to imagine a circumstance in which you would not want to include module support and enable the kernel module loader. For most situations, module support allows the kernel to support many devices and filesystems without incurring the overhead of including this support at all times. In some situations, incompatible devices can share ports through the loading and unloading of modules, such as when using a single parallel port for both a printer and for a parallel-port SCSI drive.

Modules are usually loaded by init scripts or other shell scripts that explicitly call the `insmod` and `rmmod` utilities to load and unload modules as needed. Modern kernels automagically load modules as needed through the program specified in `/proc/sys/kernel/modprobe` (usually `/sbin/modprobe`) and then clear out unused modules through explicit calls to `rmmod -a`; this cleanup is often added to the `root` crontab:

```
0-59/5 * * * * /sbin/rmmod --a
```

General Setup

General options setup includes enabling networking, PCI hardware, Microchannel and Parallel ports, Advanced Power Management, and support for ELF, aout, and other binary executables. For most Intel-based Linux systems, the important details here will be the Parport and PCI options. Advanced administrators will probably want to pay close attention to the PCI options and to the new `sysctl` interface.

PCMCIA

New in the 2.4 kernel, support for plug-in devices, typically the "PC-Card" or PCMCIA cards used in laptops, have been folded into the main kernel source tree. If you had previously configured a laptop using the pcmcia-modules package, this will be familiar ground.

Networking Support

Unless you have a very good technical reason (that is, you know what you are doing), you will include networking support. Many applications require this module, even on non-networked machines. You must also ensure your version of net-tools understands the new `/proc/dev/net` (net-tools-1.50 is also required to accommodate IPv6 protocol).

BSD Accounting

BSD Accounting is of most interest to ISPs and others who need to trace and track the use of their systems for billing or other accounting purposes. Adding BSD Accounting will create a special file that logs system process information, allowing compatible software to gather detailed usage information.

SysV IPC (DOSEMU)

Interprocess Communications (IPC) is an MS-DOS protocol for synchronizing and exchanging data between separate programs. If you plan on running the DOSEMU MS-DOS Emulator, you must include IPC. Although, now that kmod has replaced the old

Linux 2.0 `kerneld` dynamic loader and allows the automatic loading and unloading of kernel modules, there is no real need to include IPC in the main kernel; removing kerneld support from the IPC module has also reduced its size by 40%.

`sysctl` Support

Adding `sysctl` provides means for controlling the running kernel either through system calls, or, if the `/proc` filesystem is enabled, through pseudo-files in the `/proc/sys` directory. In the `/proc` interface, the directory is partitioned into several areas that govern different aspects of the kernel:

- `dev/device`—Specific information (for example, `dev/cdrom/info`)
- `fs/control`—Control of specific filesystems, such as setting the number of file-handles and inodes, dentry and quota tuning, and configuring the support for arbitrary binaries (see "Support for Misc Binaries" later in this chapter)
- `kernel/`—Kernel status and tuning
- `net/`—Networking parameters
- `sunrpc/`—SUN Remote Procedure Call (RPC)
- `vm/`—Virtual memory, and buffer and cache management

> **Tip**
>
> The First Rule of Optimization: Don't.
> The Second Rule of Optimization (for experts only): Don't (yet).

These services are both powerful and dangerous. Be sure you know what you are getting into before you fiddle with these files! Kernel parameters include the interpretation of Ctrl+Alt+Delete, the time delay for a reboot after a kernel panic, your system host and domain name, and a number of architecture-dependent features for the Sparc and Mac platforms. The `sunrpc` directory also includes debug flags for kernel hacking of remote procedure calls.

Detailed information on using and interpreting all these features can be found in `linux/Documentation/sysctl/`.

Virtual Memory Tuning Through `sysctl`

Virtual memory tuning allows for hand-optimizing the machine for disk activity. For example, by setting the system's tolerance for dirty memory pages to a higher value, the kernel will have less disk activity (which saves power and improves speed) although it increases the risk of thrashing if real memory becomes scarce). On a very large-memory machine with a lot of memory, the default behavior of the caching algorithm could be modified with

```
echo "80 500 64 64 80 6000 6000 1884 2" >/proc/sys/vm/bdflush
```

This would restrict the flushing of the dirty buffers until memory was 80% full (plus some other changes, see `linux/Documentation/sysctl/vm.txt`). For a single-purpose machine that had to run many processes, other options could be modified, making the buffer cache claim a major chunk of the total memory and then restricting the pruning of this cache until nearly all of this memory was consumed:

```
echo "60 80 80" >/proc/sys/vm/buffermem
```

Keep in mind that these changes may improve file or process performance for one purpose, but they might upset this machine terribly for many other purposes. Be certain you know what you are doing before you install any optimization.

Other tunable vm parameters include setting the number of pages that can be read in one transaction and removing the page-table caching for single-CPU machines with limited memory such as embedded systems and older machines.

Filesystem Tuning

Filesystem performance tuning is a common use of `sysctl`. The `/proc/sys/fs` directory contains diagnostic and control pseudo-files for reading the number of file handles, inodes, and superblock and quota entries, with corresponding files for setting maximum values for these items. For example, systems that require many open files (such as very busy Web servers) may see a flurry of file-handle messages in the logs. You can query the current number of files with `cat file-nr`, and then set a new limit by echoing a higher number to the `sysctl file-max`.

Support for Misc Binaries

Long before other operating systems supported Java from the command line, this feature was added to the Linux kernel. Later, this was generalized to all binary and interpreter types. Using the `sysctl` pseudo-files, Linux can integrate Java, MS-DOS, Windows, tk/tcl, Perl, or any other strange executable as seamlessly as an ELF binary or a shell script.

To use the misc binaries support, you must register the "magic cookie" of the file type and the corresponding interpreter through the `sysctl` pseudo-files in `/proc/sys/fs/binfmt_misc`. The magic cookie can be derived from the first few bytes of the file or from the filename (such as `.com` or `.exe`), and can be registered by `echo`ing a control string to `/proc/sys/fs/binfmt_misc/register`. The format of the command string is

`:name:type:offset:magic:mask:interpreter:`

where

- `name` is an arbitrary identifier for this executable type.
- `type` specifies `M` or `E` denoting whether the cookie is by mask or by extension.
- `offset` is the count in bytes from the front of the file where the cookie occurs. If omitted, the default is zero.
- `magic` is the sequence of bytes to match. Hex codes may be specified as `\x0A` or `\xFF` (be careful to escape the slash character if you set this through a shell statement!). For Extension matching, the magic pattern is the extension string that follows the last dot in the filename.
- `mask` is also optional and, if included, must be the same length as the magic sequence. The bits in the mask are applied against the file contents before comparison to the magic cookie sequence.
- `interpreter` is the program invoked to run the executable.

To use misc binary support, you could create a boot script in `/etc/rc.d/init.d` to echo the control strings to `/proc/sys/fs/binfmt_misc`, or add these statements to your `/etc/rc.d/rc.local`. For example, to emulate the original Java support, you might add the following line to the end of `/etc/rc.d/rc.local`:

```
echo ':Java:M::\xca\xfe\xba\xbe::/opt/jdk/bin/javawrapper:' > \
    /proc/sys/fs/binfmt_misc/register
```

This creates `/proc/sys/fs/binfmt_misc/Java` in the `sysctl` directories, and lets you run any Java application by simply using the full filename on the command line. Support for running applets through `appletviewer` might be added by the following:

```
echo ':Applet:E::html::/usr/local/jdk/bin/appletviewer:' > \
    /proc/sys/fs/binfmt_misc/register
```

Before this will work, you need a special wrapper script to run the Java interpreter. Brian Lantz provides a sample script in `linux/Documentation/java.txt` (see Listing 27.2). Once installed and registered, Java applications and applets can be run from the command line. Use `chmod +x` to set the `.class` or `.html` file as executable and then simply call it from the command line:

```
./HelloWorld.class
```

or

```
./HelloApplet.html
```

Adding similar support for JDK 1.2 `jar` files is left as an exercise for the reader.

LISTING 27.2   Lantz's Wrapper Script for `binfmt_misc` Java Support

```bash
#!/bin/bash
# /opt/jdk/bin/javawrapper for binfmt_misc/java

CLASS=$1
# if classname is a link, we follow it

if [ -L "$1" ] ; then
    CLASS=\
    `ls --color=no -l $1 |tr -s '\t ' ' '|cut -d ' ' -f 11`
fi

CLASSN=`basename $CLASS .class`
CLASSP=`dirname $CLASS`

FOO=$PATH
PATH=$CLASSPATH

if [ -z "`type -p -a $CLASSN.class`" ] ; then
# class is not in CLASSPATH
   if [ -e "$CLASSP/$CLASSN.class" ] ; then

# append dir of class to CLASSPATH

      if [ -z "${CLASSPATH}" ] ; then
         export CLASSPATH=$CLASSP
      else
         export CLASSPATH=$CLASSP:$CLASSPATH
      fi
   else

# uh! now we would have to create a symbolic link - really
# ugly, i.e. print a message that one has to change the setup

   echo "Hey! This is not a good setup to run $1 !"
   exit 1
   fi
fi

PATH=$FOO
shift
/usr/local/jdk/bin/java $CLASSN "$@"
```

To run Windows applications via the WINE emulator, you could add the following line:

```
echo ':DOSWin:M::MZ::/usr/local/bin/wine:' >
    /proc/sys/fs/binfmt_misc/register
```

You can read the status of a `binfmt_misc` file by using `cat` on the filename. For example, `cat /proc/sys/fs/binfmt_misc/Java` might produce the following:

```
enabled
interpreter /usr/local/jdk/bin/javawrapper
offset 0
magic cafebabe
```

String Limits in `binfmt_misc`

The `binfmt_misc` register control string may not exceed 255 characters; the magic cookie must be within the first 128 bytes of the file; offset + size (*magic*) must be less than 128; and the interpreter string may not exceed 127 characters.

For more tips on using `binfmt_misc` and creating magic cookie patterns, see Richard Günther's `binfmt_misc` home page (`http://www.anatom. uni-tuebingen.de/~richi/linux/binfmt_misc.html`).

Power Management

New to 2.4, Linux includes support for the more complete Advanced Configuration and Power Interface. ACPI is an open and extensible power-saving specification co-developed by Compaq, Intel, Microsoft, Phoenix, and Toshiba and is intended to supercede the older APM standard. ACPI features support for "smart batteries," general-purpose event trapping, and Super I/O (SIO) devices.

Like APM, ACPI requires hardware support on the motherboard. The complete protocol is described on the ACPI home page (`http://www.teleport.com/~acpi/`). For the very adventurous, Linux includes an ACPI Interpreter, which can be added to the kernel to allow experimenting with the power-saving modes.

The older Advanced Power Management (APM) is more widely supported and has been included on most motherboards since about 1996. Note that Linux APM does not power down hard drives and the use of APM is almost exclusively restricted to battery-powered computers such as laptops. Although APM is a very good idea in principle, there are many different interpretations of the standard among laptop manufacturers.

Using GMT

The APM section includes the option to set your real-time clock (RTC) to use Greenwich Mean Time or local time. Unless you are using the same computer to run another operating system with broken GMT support, you will want to select GMT as the reference time because this will allow Linux to automatically adjust for your local daylight savings time rules.

APM support is a prime suspect when debugging laptop kernel problems, so when in doubt, turn off all APM options and only enable each one as you verify that it is either useful or benign.

Possible APM Conflicts

Since you may not be in the habit of reading every option description in the kernel configuration, it is worth repeating here the list of fixes to "weird problems" that are reported with APM conflicts. Symptoms such as spontaneous lockups of the kernel or sporadic kernel oops may be avoided by working down the following checklist:

- If you are using the "sleep" mode, make sure that you have enough swap space and that it is enabled.
- Pass the `no-hlt` bootparam option to the kernel.
- Enable floating-point emulation (see the section "Processor Type and Features") and use the `no387` bootparam.
- Use the `floppy=nodma` bootparam.
- Use the `mem=4M` bootparam (see the section "High Memory Support").
- Make sure that the CPU is not over clocked.
- Read the sig11 FAQ (`http://www.bitwizard.nl/sig11/`).
- Disable the cache from your BIOS settings.
- Install a fan for the video card or exchange video RAM.
- Install a better fan for the CPU.
- Exchange RAM chips.
- Exchange the motherboard.

Another caution with APM/ACPI support is to remember that your machine may be running many processes as automatically scheduled `cron` jobs. Placing your machine into a sleep state or awaking it out of a sleep or suspend state may have strange consequences if the background tasks were depending on time-of-day measurements. For similar reasons, it is often a bad idea to correct your RTC *backwards* (turning the clock back) by more than a few minutes; it is much safer to adjust the time using the boot CMOS editor before restarting Linux.

In addition to the traditional battery-control support, Linux 2.4 now provides limited energy-savings support for "green" monitors. Similar support at the application level is also now appearing in GNOME and KDE.

Memory Technology Devices (Flash Memory)

Memory Technology Devices are the "flash" memory cards (typically found in digital cameras and other portable devices) and "disk on a chip" components used in embedded applications. The MTD support is also responsible for RAM disks and can be used to access otherwise inaccessible memory regions (see the section "High Memory Support").

Watchdog Support

Detailed support for hardware-based watchdog systems comes later in the configuration, but this general option also allows for a software-based watchdog. The watchdog option enables a periodic update of `/dev/watchdog`; userspace software can then force a reboot if these updates fail to occur. This is useful where the machine is unattended and must be rebooted if any sort of lockup occurs. If you are using the software watchdog, you may also want to append `panic=60` as a boot parameter in `/etc/lilo.conf`.

`linux/Documentation/watchdog.txt` includes information on watchdog hardware manufacturers and source code for creating a software watchdog update program.

Parallel Ports (parport)

Parports are an abstract representation of the parallel ports separating architecture-dependent code from the parallel interface. Parports allow developers to create parallel port device drivers for multiple hardware architectures, and the separation also allows sharing the same physical parallel port between many devices. For example, you can use the same port for both a printer and a ZIP drive or Qcam video camera.

Parallel ports can be dangerous beasts to probe, especially when many onboard ports may be fixed at IRQ numbers that conflict with sound and network cards. It is best to avoid probing and to specify the port addresses and IRQ settings of the parallel port hardware by setting the IRQ values in your computer CMOS and then appending the parameters to the bootparams, or by loading parport as a module and specifying the parameters on the `insmod` command line or in `/etc/modules.conf`. By default, the parport module does not probe for IRQs and will initialize all parallel ports in "polling" mode.

Parport splits parallel port control into two modules: the basic parport to manage port sharing and an architecture-dependent layer, for example, `parport_pc`. Either may be compiled into the kernel, or built as a module and loaded as needed. Port configurations can be set with bootparams, or, when built as modules, with `insmod` command line or `/etc/modules.conf`. For example, to manually load `parport` and the `parport_pc` as modules:

```
# insmod parport.o
# insmod parport_pc.o io=0x3bc,0x378,0x278 irq=none,7,auto
```

This would install three parallel ports, where the first is in polling mode, the second on IRQ7, and the third is probed for the current values. A more common method is to specify the `parport_pc` options in `/etc/modules.conf` and to load the port with `modprobe` or to let the `kmod` load it automatically.

Once these modules are installed, `parport_probe` can be inserted to query for IEEE1284-compliant devices—this will output a status report to the system messages and to `/proc/parport/x/autoprobe`. Other files in `/proc/parport/x` include the devices file where `parport` will record the attached devices and flag those currently using the port, as well as the `irq` file. `irq` can be used to query the IRQ number of the port and also to set this value by echoing either the number or `none` to that file.

Modules that require the parallel port can be given bootparam options to direct them to a particular port. For example:

```
# insmod lp.o parport=0,2
```

This will install printer support only on ports 0 and 2, rather than the default action of installing the module on all available ports. As with all bootparams, you can also do this by adding `lp=parport0 lp=parport2` to the boot prompt or in `/etc/lilo.conf`.

27

CONFIGURING AND
BUILDING KERNELS

Sharing Parallel Ports

A common use of parports is to share a parallel port between several devices by dynamically inserting device support and then removing that device before inserting the module for an alternate device. For example, you can share a single parallel port between a printer and a scanner, a ZIP drive, or PLIP (parallel port network connection) by scripting load-wrappers (by shell scripts or `modules.conf` directives) to remove one module before installing another.

Plug-and-Play Support

These options enable kernel support of generic plug-and-play devices, and enable probing of devices attached to the parallel ports for mapping peripherals to parport modules. In general, probing parallel ports for IRQ numbers can cause problems. A better course is to explicitly specify your parport options through bootparams (see the preceding section).

Block Devices

The Block Devices dialog contains options for out-of-the-ordinary disks such as Parallel-Port IDE, Logical Volumes, and RAID systems. With the 2.4 kernel, options for the low-cost IDE/ATA disks have been factored out into the section "ATA/IDE Support."

Floppy Disk Driver

Because of its use for other devices (such as tape backup units) and its capability to run multiple disk controllers, the floppy disk driver is worth some attention. It also serves as a typical example of the fine control achieved through the bootparam interface.

The following is a partial list of floppy driver options:

- `floppy=daring`—With well-behaved (modern Pentium) controllers, this option enables optimizations that can improve throughput, but may fail on incompatible systems.

- `floppy=one_fdc, floppy=two_fdc, floppy=address,two_fdc`—These options set the number of controllers. The default is a single FDC. The dual controller option can specify the address, use a default of `0x370`, or query CMOS memory if the `cmos` option is selected.

- `floppy=drive,type,cmos`—Sets the CMOS type of the specified drive to the given type and is a required option on systems with more than two floppy drives. Codes for the CMOS types can be found in `drivers/block/README.fd`.

- `floppy=thinkpad`—Alerts the driver to the inverted convention for the disk change line used in some IBM ThinkPad laptops.

- `floppy=L40SX`—Prevents the printing of messages when unexpected interrupts are received, and it is required on IBM L40SX laptops to prevent a conflict between the video and floppy disk controllers.

- `floppy=omnibook, floppy=nodma`—Prevents using DMA for data transfers. You will need this option if you get frequent "Unable to allocate DMA memory" messages or if you are using an HP Omnibook. DMA is also not available on 386 computers or if your FDC does not have a FIFO buffer (for example, 8272A and 82072). When using `nodma`, the FIFO threshold should also be set to 10 or lower to limit the number of data transfer interrupts.

- `floppy=yesdma`—Forces DMA mode. When using a FIFO-enabled controller, the driver will fall back to `nodma` mode if it cannot find the contiguous memory it needs. The `yesdma` option will prevent this. This option is the default setting.

- `floppy=nofifo`—Required if you receive "Bus master arbitration" errors from the ethernet card (or any other devices) while using your floppy controller. The default is the fifo option.

- `floppy=threshold,fifo_depth`—Sets the FIFO depth for DMA mode. A higher setting will tolerate more latency, but will trigger more interrupts and impose more load on the system; a lower setting will generate fewer interrupts but will require a faster processor.

- `floppy=nr,irq`, `floppy=nr,dma`—Sets the IRQ and DMA for the given device. The defaults are 6 and 2, respectively.

- `Floppy=slow`—Required on some PS/2 machines that have a dramatically slower step rate.

Optimizing Floppy Controllers

If the driver is compiled as a module, you can experiment with `floppy=threshold,fifo_depth` to find optimum settings. To do this, use the `floppycontrol` utility with the `--messages` flag to log controller diagnostics. After inserting the `floppy.o` module and running `floppycontrol --messages`, access the floppy disk; a rush of "Over/Underrun-retrying" messages indicates your FIFO threshold is too low. You can then find an optimum value by unloading the module and trying higher values until these messages are very infrequent.

The full list of FDC module options can be found in `drivers/block/README.fd` and the `fdutils` package. A set of floppy driver utility programs, including an enhanced mtools kit, can be downloaded from the misc directory on MetaLab (`ftp://metalab.unc.edu/pub/Linux/system/Misc/`).

Configuring the Linux Floppy Driver

Floppy driver options are specified using the `floppy=` syntax, but unlike some kernel drivers, this device accepts only one such declaration. For example, to set both `daring` and `two_fdc`, both options must be separated by a space in a single command:

```
insmod floppy 'floppy="daring two_fdc"'
```

PARIDE and parports

Parallel-IDE support (PARIDE) can safely combine both parports and paride devices on the same physical parallel port; if `parport` is included as a loadable module, `paride` must also be included as a module. Also, if `paride` is included directly into the kernel, individual protocols for disks, tapes, and CD drives may still be included as modules and loaded dynamically as needed.

> **Note**
>
> In most instances, you can assign many modules to a parport simultaneously without needing to first remove the prior module. When conflicts occur, however, modules can be removed and inserted as needed.

Loopback Disk Devices

Loopback disks are somewhat cool: `loopback` allows you to treat a normal file as a separate filesystem. For example, you can mount and test a CD-ROM or floppy disk image before committing the image to the physical disk. This also allows you to use cryptographic methods to secure a filesystem. Before using the loopback disk devices, you will need to ensure that your util-linux package is up to date with the requirements of `linux/Documentation/Changes`.

Network Block Devices

Using Network Block devices allows the client to transparently use a remote block device over TCP/IP—this is very different from NFS or CODA. For example, a thin client could use an NBD disk for any filesystem type, including as a swap disk.

Logical Volume Manager (LVM)

LVM puts an additional layer between the physical filesystems and the OS and allows binding two or more partitions or disks into a single virtual disk. These storage units are then accessed through special device files of the form `/dev/groupname/volumename`. LVM also allows changing the logical groups at runtime, effectively altering the size of the storage unit as required.

Multiple Devices and Software-RAID

For those needing reliable and reasonably efficient redundant filesystems on a tight budget, Linux includes a Software-RAID package that binds several disks as one RAID unit. Multiple Devices support can be used to append, stripe, or mirror partitions together to form one logical partition.

More information on Software-RAID can be found on in the Software-RAID HOWTO (`ftp://metalab.unc.edu/pub/Linux/docs/HOWTO/mini`).

Networking Options

UNIX was designed from the start to be a networking operating system, and Linux follows this tradition. In UNIX, computers are not isolated personal possessions, but nodes, mere portals, points of entry into a much larger network. Building a workstation without network services is like building an office with no windows or doors. Yes, it's is very secure, but…

Most small-network installations will only need `TCP/IP` and perhaps `IPX` to coexist with Windows machines or to run the DOSEMU MS-DOS emulator. You can also add `CODA` or `NFS` network filesystems to share disks between machines. A popular option is to configure a Linux machine as a firewall and dialup-gateway for a home office or small enterprise. Small Novell-based shops will also require IPX support en route to using Linux as a high-powered NetWare fileserver.

For the enterprise network administrator, however, this dialog box is a playground of protocols, with options, system diagnostics, and controls that position Linux as the glue holding the enterprise together. Linux can be optimized for routing or forwarding between interfaces, and set as a secure WAN router for a virtual private network over the Internet. Linux speaks IPX, Appletalk, Acorn Econet, and Ipv6. It can log attacks, perform multicast (MBONE) routing, encapsulate IP over IP, do IP masquerading (to give machines inside the firewall access to services without using a proxy server), provide ARP services over huge networks, and boot a diskless client. It's pretty darn amazing, and it keeps getting better.

Kernel Netlink Socket

Netlink is a communication channel between kernel services and user programs through a special character device in the `/dev` directory. This interface can be used by the `Routing Messages` package to log network behavior, or by the `IP Firewall Netlink` device to log information about possible attacks. Netlink is also required when you're using the `arpd` daemon to map IP numbers to local network hardware addresses outside of kernel space, or when using ethertap (user programs using raw ethernet frames).

Network Firewall

The only firewall impervious to attack is implemented with scissors. We all do what we can to be as secure as we need to be, balancing cost, necessity, and practical realities. If you need almost-scissors, Linux will take you there, too, but for more modest security requirements, the stock kernel firewall provides decent protection with a minimum of fuss.

The Network Firewall is a packet-based protection that will accept or deny incoming or outbound packets based on the port, the protocol, and the originating and/or destination network IP addresses. Proxy-based firewalls can expand this protection and use knowledge about the protocols to provide additional security, but this most often requires modified software, and more work to install. Even if you plan to use a proxy-based system, most often these systems also require including the packet-based firewall. For most situations of a gateway firewall for a small or medium-sized enterprise or a home office, packet-based protection is simple, easy to install, and offers pretty good security.

To set up a TCP/IP firewall, you must include `Network Firewall` and `IP:Firewalling`. Adding `IP:masquerading` will give inside machines access to services outside the firewall; the remote computer will perceive these connections as originating from the firewall machine, removing the need to register IP addresses for all local network hosts that require outside connections.

For example, Let's say your office LAN includes a workstation that needs HTTP and ICQ access. Using `IP:masquerading`, this workstation can run Netscape or ICQ without any proxy and can connect directly to the Web site or ICQ servers. An extra level of security can be added to this scheme by enabling `IP:Transparent Proxy`, which silently redirects traffic from local machines to a predesignated proxy server address.

> **Note**
>
> Network Firewall support is not compatible with the Fast Switching ultra-fast network option.

Basic IP:Masquerading will only redirect UDP and TCP traffic. This blocks some Windows applications that depend on ICMP packets, such as `ping` and `tracert`. Support for these applications can be enabled through the IP:ICMP Masquerading option.

Inside hosts cannot receive connections unless port forwarding is enabled using the `Special Modules` options. Through the external port administration utilities `ipautofw` and `ipportfw`, the Linux firewall can provide a gateway for outside machines to reach services on inside machines by forwarding packets for predefined ports. For example, if the gateway machine is not using X11, port 6001 can be forwarded to another machine to run remote X11 applications.

Optimize as Router

This option prevents checksum operations on incoming packets that are not required when using the machine exclusively as a router. In the future, this option may contain other router-only optimizations.

IP Tunnelling

IP Tunnelling connects two LANs across another network while staying under the same network address. For example, machines at a trade show could use services only available inside the corporate firewall, or a roaming user in a hotel room could be granted access to his office files. The basic support for IP Tunnelling wraps plain IPv4 inside IPv4. The GRE tunnel support is more useful if you are connecting through Cisco routers, and can also encode IPv6 inside IPv4.

GRE/IP can create what appears to be a normal ethernet network, but which can be distributed all over the Internet. For example, this would allow all branch offices of a global enterprise to use the same LAN IP numbers and to appear to be within a single firewall. This feature requires GRE Tunnelling with the GRE Broadcast and IP:multicast.

Kernel Options for Web Hosting

The IP Aliasing option provides multihoming of IP addresses. This is typically used to serve different documents or services to outside hosts depending on the IP address they've called. IP Aliasing will let you create virtual network interfaces attached to distinct IP addresses that are registered with ifconfig as eth0:1, eth0:2, and so on. Newer editions of Apache can provide much the same service by only using the hostnames, which removes some of the need for this feature, but there are other applications such as the RealMedia PNM server where the virtual network interface must be provided at the kernel level. More information on configuring virtual hosts and IP aliasing can be found in Documentation/networking/alias.txt.

Another Web-host and Internet server option is the TCP SYN-Cookie trap. SYN Cookies are an easy but effective means to mount a denial-of-service attack on a public site. Although enabling this protection may not accurately report the source of the attack, it will ensure that legitimate users can get access to your machine. To use SYN-Cookie, you must also select the /proc filesystem and sysctl, and enable this support in your boot scripts with

```
echo 1 >/proc/sys/net/ipv4/tcp_syncookies
```

Tuning Linux for Apache for Performance

Although most Web sites will perform quite adequately for their traffic loads, there will always be a need for more speed. Before delving into kernel tuning, Webmasters seeking high performance should first look at their CGI and

27

CONFIGURING AND
BUILDING KERNELS

dataservers as possible bottlenecks. Also, Apache users should check the Apache performance-tuning FAQ (`http://www.apache.org/docs/misc/perf-tuning.html`).

Performance tuning of the kernel depends on the specific release, but there are still a few things that can be done at the kernel level to prep your machine for Apache. If you have RAM available, you can modify the virtual memory manager to limit swapping and avoid expensive disk activity, or increase the number of tasks and file descriptors (through the `/proc/sys` files `file-max` and `inode-max`).

Web sites serving substantial static content (for example, images) can now use the kernel-level `httpd` server to vastly improve server performance by responding to these static requests through the kernel daemon while passing all server parsed and DHTML requests through to the normal userspace Web server software. This server is a very basic implementation of HTTP 1.1 with no options and no extensions, but, being close to the heart of the machine, it can deliver static content at blazing speeds.

If performance is crucial, you can always switch Web server software. Apache is not the only server software in the world (only just over half of them!), and its process forking method is not exactly the most efficient design server for Linux. Apache is designed more for robustness and portability than for raw performance, and while the Apache approach of pre-forking child processes is good enough for most applications, a better approach would be to use native kernel threads (pthreads). An intelligent use of thread-pools would produce performance orders of magnitude higher than current levels. Although the core of Apache 1.3 is multithread aware, and there are projects afoot to adapt it to a multithread model for version 2, the excellent (and also Open Source) Roxen server can offer this performance today (see `http://www.roxen.com/`).

IPX and Appletalk Support

IPX adds Novell NetWare services and enables your Linux machine to communicate with NetWare file and print servers through the `ncpfs` client program, available from the MetaLab Archives (`ftp://metalab.unc.edu/pub/Linux/system/filesystems/`). IPX also allows DOSEMU programs to access the network.

AppleTalk provides similar support for Apple services using the `netatalk` program. Details can be found in the Netatalk FAQ (`http://www.umich.edu/~rsug/netatalk/faq.html`). Linux supports both AppleTalk and LocalTalk Mac protocols. According to the recent kernel help files, the GNU boycott of Apple is now over, and so even politically correct people may now set this option.

Linux may be configured as a fully functional NetWare server, and even provides support for the SPX protocol. For more information on IPX services, see the IPX-HOWTO, which can be found at the Linux Documentation Project (http://www.linuxdoc.org).

Installing Linux as the Grand Unified Network Field is content enough for its own book, but general information on configuring Linux to glue together a heterogeneous network of Novell, Macintosh, and TCP/IP workstations can be found at Linux/Mac/Win Web page (http://www.eats.com/linux_mac_win.html).

Enterprise Networks and X.25 Support

Enterprise administrators will be most interested in the Linux support for X.25 protocol. This is a method for putting many virtual circuits through one high-speed line. This support is presently labeled experimental and does not yet include support for dedicated X.25 network cards. Linux does provide X.25 services over ordinary modems and Ethernet networks using the 802.2 LLC or LAPB protocols.

The WAN option is also of interest to enterprise admins looking for an inexpensive alternative to a dedicated WAN router. Using commercially available WAN interface cards and the WAN-tools package from Sangoma (ftp://ftp.sangoma.com), a low-cost Linux machine will make a perfectly serviceable WAN router. This router can also still be used for other purposes, such as providing a firewall, a Web server, or an FTP site. For the serious enterprise, the FreeS/WAN project in Toronto has a free encryption layer for the Linux WAN, using 1,024-bit keys and 168-bit Triple-DES technology, and incorporating the Internet Protocol Security (IPSEC).

Related to X.25 and WAN, Linux also provides support for frame-relay. Look under the DLCI options in Network Devices for more information.

Ethernet Bridging

Ethernet Bridging will bind together the network segments on multiple Ethernet cards to create one seamless network. Several such nodes can be used to link multiple composite networks. For more information, consult the Ethernet Bridge Mailing List home page (http://openrock.net/mailman/listinfo/bridge).

Forwarding on High-Speed Interfaces and Slow CPUs

One popular use of Linux is to breathe new life into aging hardware. This can, however, lead to networking problems because even a 120MHz machine can be overrun by a 10Mb/sec ethernet connection. If you experience trouble with network overruns, these options will modify the network support to accommodate the slower machines.

27

CONFIGURING AND
BUILDING KERNELS

Telephony Support

Telephony support is the product of work done by Quicknet Technologies
(http://www.quicknet.net) to support their Internet PhoneJACK and Internet
LineJACK telephone, key system, and PBX connectors for Voice over IP (VoIP) applications. These drivers are *highly* experimental and are only intended as development tools
for Quicknet card owners.

ATA/IDE Support

Linux will support up to eight low-cost ATA/IDE drives. With Linux 2.1/2.2, support was
also added for IDE ATAPI floppy drives, tape drives, and CD-ROM drives (with auto-detection of interfaces), IRQs, and disk geometries. The new driver now adds support for
PIO modes on OPTi chipsets, SCSI host adapter emulation, and PCI Bus-master DMA,
as well as support for many PCI chipsets, and detection of buggy PCI IDE systems, such
as the prefect feature of the RZ1000 or "IRQ unmasking" on the CMD640. Full details
of the IDE driver and supported systems can be found in
linux/Documentation/ide.txt.

While the driver automatically probes for disk drives, geometries, and IRQs, these interfaces may be specified using kernel bootparam. For example, to set the port addresses
and the IRQ for the fourth controller set ide3=0x168,0x36e,10.

The driver will probe for the IRQ if it is omitted. Any number of interfaces may also
share an IRQ, although this will degrade performance. The driver will detect and
account for this situation, but your controller cards may suffer damage in the process
(theoretically).

Disk geometry can also be specified on the command line as three numbers for sectors,
cylinders, and head, as in hdc=768,16,32. If your CD-ROM is not being detected, you
can give the kernel an extra nudge by using the hdd=cdrom option.

IDE interfaces on sound cards may require initialization before they can be used. The
program to initialize the driver is most often among the software that comes with the
card and is usually part of the MS-DOS driver—the only alternative for using these
devices is to boot your computer under MS-DOS, to allow the drivers to initialize the
device, and then to use loadlin to switch to Linux.

Older hard drives may not be compatible with the newer IDE driver. In this situation, you
can include both interfaces in the kernel. The older driver will command the primary IDE
interface while still allowing newer hardware to be used on the other interfaces.

> **Caution**
>
> When passing IDE options to loadable modules using bootparams, substitute semicolons (;) for any commas in the command line, for example:
>
> ```
> insmod ide.o options="ide0=serialize ide2=0x1e8;0x3ee;11"
> ```

SCSI Support

SCSI drives are more expensive than IDE, but give much higher performance and are the method of choice for large enterprise servers. Linux SCSI support is also required for certain parallel-port disk devices, such as the Omega ZIP drive. Linux also supports SCSI CD-writers, scanners, and synthesizers via the SCSI Generic option, and provides options for logging errors and activity on these devices.

To enable SCSI support, you need to know your hardware. The Low-Level Drivers dialog presents a long list of supported adapters, with some options for setting device parameters.

IEEE 1394 FireWire Support

FireWire is a high-performance serial bus, also known as i.Link and described by the IEEE 1394 standard. This hardware is most often used with digital video cameras and other high-speed peripherals, and I/O cards with this support are available from Texas Instruments, Adaptec, and on the Miro DV boards. With the exception of the RAW option to enable direct manipulation of FireWire by userspace programs, the remaining options in this section select among specific vendor implementations.

I^2O Support

Intelligent Input/Output uses a coprocessor for interface adapters and is designed to separate the logical device from the physical implementation. Drivers for I^2O devices can be written to an abstract Operating System Module (OSM) definition that is portable across many hardware implementations of the standard. These devices include block devices (disks), network interfaces, and SCSI devices.

I^2O also includes a `sysctl` option to allow probing the driver through the `/proc/i2o` files.

Network Device Support

If you have a network card, you must specify the network hardware. If you have a network card but don't know what it is, if it is a cheap one, it is more than likely an NE2000-compatible.

The main network device option links in the basic network subsystem. You must enable this support even if you only connect to networks via local SLIP, PPP, or PLIP, or if your machine will dial an ISP to connect to the Internet.

Dummy Network Device

The Dummy device is just that: It holds a place for a device and discards any traffic sent to it. This is most often used to make SLIP or PPP interfaces appear to be active even while offline. For example, if you are using a demand-dialing program such as `diald`, the Dummy device will enable network programs to function, but the packets sent to this interface will be re-routed through to the Internet after the dialer has established the connection.

EQL and Ethernet Bonding

EQL is rarely used, but extremely useful. In these days of wave modems and cheap xDSL lines, we often forget that many do not have the luxury of cheap, high-speed dialup lines. Using EQL, Linux can bind together several modems as the same IP interface and effectively multiply the bandwidth. For example, a rural school could install a Linux gateway server with demand-dialing sensitive to the bandwidth requirements. When one phone line became saturated (old-copper rural lines are often 31.2KB), a second line could be opened to the same ISP, and then a third, and so on, giving the school symmetric, ISDN-like bandwidth for the cost of a few extra phone lines. EQL does require support at both ends of the connection. It works very well with the Livingstone Portmaster 2e, which is fortunately a popular choice among smaller ISPs.

> **Note**
>
> Unfortunately, EQL requires support at the remote end and this often prevents its use in remote areas. Eqlplus (`http://www.cwareco.com/eqlplus.html`) is a Linux modem combining strategy based upon IP masquerading and eql. This package includes kernel patches to the EQL support to allow multiple connections to *any* external networks.

Ethernet Bonding provides the same service for ethernet cards, tying together multiple network interfaces as a single virtual interface.

PLIP, PPP, and SLIP Dialup Networking Support

PLIP is a means to network two machines over a null-printer ("Turbo Laplink") cable to provide four or eight parallel data channels. This is often used to NFS-install to a laptop where there is no CD-ROM. Wiring for this cable is described in `Documentation/networking/PLIP.txt`. Russell Nelson has also created MS-DOS drivers for PLIP to connect DOS-based machines (such as that old PS/1 space heater I keep in the workshop).

SLIP is the ancestor of PPP, and although 99.9% of all ISPs will only offer PPP connections, SLIP still has some viable uses. SLIP is an essential ingredient as an intermediary device in the diald demand dialer or to gain a network connection over a telnet session (using SliRP).

Amateur Radio and Wireless Support

Another low-cost Internet solution for impossible remote locations is the Amateur Radio Support. By encoding packets over short-wave radio, Linux systems have been used to provide as much as 64KB of symmetric bandwidth over long distances. For examples of packet radio in action, see the Wireless Papers (`http://www.ictp.trieste.it/~radionet/papers`) or visit the Packet Radio home page (`http://www.tapr.org/tapr/html/pkthome.html`).

A related feature of interest to campus and rural development projects is the kernel support for Wireless LAN, AT&T WaveLAN, and DEC RoamAbout DS (see `Documentation/networking/wavelan.txt`). There is also support for the MosquitoNet (`http://mosquitonet.stanford.edu/`) StarMode RadioIP systems used by many laptop owners.

IrDA: Infrared Port Device Drivers

Infrared Data Associations protocols provide wireless infrared communications between laptops and PDAs at speeds up to 4Mbps, and the Linux driver makes supported devices transparent to the networking system. More information on this support, and on the utility programs for IrDA, can be found at the Linux Documentation Project (`http://www.linuxdocs.org`) or the Linux IrDA home page (`http://www.cs.uit.no/linux-irda/`).

ISDN Subsystem

To use ISDN, you must obtain the isdn4k-utils utility programs (`ftp://ftp.franken.de/pub/isdn4linux/`). When the module is loaded, `isdn.o` can support up to 64 channels (you can add more by changing the `isdn.h` file directly). Each channel will be given read/write access to the D-Channel messages and `ioctl` functions, with non-synchronized read/write to B-Channel and 128 tty-devices. Modem emulation provides a standard AT-style command set compatible with most dialup tools, such as `minicom`, `pppd`, and `mgetty`.

The second step in configuring for ISDN is to select your specific ISDN modem card. Some ISDN cards will require initialization before the vendor-independent setup. Details can be found in the appropriate `README` file under `linux/Documentation/isdn`.

Old CD-ROM Drivers (Not SCSI or IDE)

Old CD-ROM drivers include the early SoundBlaster Matsushita and Panasonic CD-ROMs included on many 16-bit sound cards. If you have a clone card with a socket for a CD-ROM drive, and it was made before 1994, it is likely one of these interfaces; if it is newer, it could still be an IDE-type CD-ROM.

Character Devices

Character devices communicate with the kernel via a stream of characters. These include terminals, serial ports, printers, cameras, voice synthesizers, and also some virtual devices such as the CMOS memory and the watchdog. If you're working with most desktop installations, this section option will be simply a matter of adding or removing printer support. On the other hand, you'll find this option very interesting if you're working with data acquisition projects.

Terminals and Consoles

Most applications will configure the kernel for at least one console. There are some embedded applications where this code will not be needed, but for most people, having multiple virtual consoles mapped to the Alt+F*n* keys is very useful.

Another useful feature is to have console messages sent to a terminal attached to a serial device. This can be used to keep a printed log of system messages or have an emergency terminal port available on an otherwise head-less embedded application. Keep in mind that the serial console will not be enabled by default if you have a VGA card installed, and it must be explicitly enabled using the `console=ttyN` bootparam.

Serial Ports

In addition to plain old serial ports, Linux also permits IRQ sharing (where supported by the hardware) and systems with more than four serial ports. Many data-acquisition systems and smaller ISPs also use the multiport serial boards that can be included with these options.

Unix98 PTY

Linux now supports the Unix98 standard for the `/dev/pts` ports. This option requires glib-2.1 and also requires the `/dev/pts` filesystem, but it is highly recommended. Although it will take you some time to shift habits to the new naming convention, Linux has a clear resolve to move toward this system and obsolesce the old `/dev/tty` conventions. Under the new rules, pseudo-terminals are created on-the-fly under `/dev/pts/N`. The old convention of `/dev/ttyp2` will become `/dev/pts/2` under the Unix98 system.

Parallel Printer

You need this option to add a parallel-port printer, but keep in mind that this module supports the printer, not the port. You will also need to install and configure the parallel port (parport) module. Also, by default, the `lp.o` module will install itself on *all* available parports unless specified by bootparams.

I²C Support

This option adds support for the alternate devices on Matrox graphics cards; this is a feature that lets you add multiple independent monitors to the same console.

Mice

These options are for bus mice and PS/2-style mouse connectors, as found in some laptop computers. Note that although some laptops do support PS/2-style mice (such as the ThinkPad 560), the internal pointer may still be a plain COM1-based serial mouse.

Watchdog, NVRAM, and RTC Devices

The watchdog timer enables a character device (`mknod c /dev/watchdog c 10 130`) used to reboot a locked machine. This feature is most often used with a watchdog daemon that will write to this device within the time limit. Linux includes support for a software watchdog and also for watchdog boards, which are not only more reliable, but several of them can also monitor the temperature inside your machine and force a shutdown/reboot when this rises above the allowed range.

The `/dev/nvram` option enables a new character device (`mknod c /dev/nvram 10 144`) for read/write access to the 50-byte CMOS memory.

All computers have a real-time clock; Linux lets you use it. This option will support a new character device (`mknod c /dev/rtc 10 135`) to generate reliable signals from 2Hz to 8kHz. The clock can also be programmed as a 24-hour alarm to raise IRQ8 when the alarm goes off. The rtc module is controlled by synchronized `ioctl` calls and is most often used for high-frequency data acquisition where you don't want to burn up CPU cycles polling through the time-of-day calls. Example code for using the rtc module can be found in `Documentation/rtc.txt`.

DoubleTalk Speech Synthesizer

No surprises here, however users of speech synthesizers may also be interested in the Blinux (distribution for the blind) and Emacspeak. Linux stands alone as the one OS that grants blind users total access to all functions of their computers and full access to all services on the Internet.

Video for Linux (V4L)

Video4Linux (V4L) is a common programming API for audio/video capture or overlay cards, radio tuning sources, teletext, and other TV-related VBI data. V4L support is needed if you plan to use any of the current TV/FM cards, and V4L can be used for videoconferencing cameras such as the Connectix Qcam. To use these services, you will also need v4L-aware applications. A few applications are currently archived at the V4L Archives (ftp://ftp.uk.linux.org/pub/linux/video4linux), and a few more, including capture and Webcam applications, are listed at the Room Three Web site (http://roadrunner.swansea.linux.org.uk/v4l.shtml).

Joystick Support

Linux will now support digital, serial, and some USB joystick controllers. The developers also hope to include support for force-feedback joysticks. A current list of supported devices and applications can be found at the Linux Joystick Web page (http://atrey.karlin.mff.cuni.cz/~vojtech/joystick/).

Ftape, the Floppy Tape Device Driver

This option is for tape drives that are connected to your existing floppy drive controller or that include their own high-performance FDC. With the widespread availability of cheap CD-writers, tape backup systems are becoming rare beasts, but still have a niche use.

Filesystems

Linux is the only operating system to offer a common ground for heterogeneous computer networks. During your first Linux install, one of your tasks was to select from a long list of supported filesystems for your Linux partition. This tradition continues with the kernel filesystem and network filesystem support. When all of this is combined with the capability to launch arbitrary executables transparently through an emulator (see the section "Support for Misc Binaries"), the degree of inter-OS integration in Linux becomes very clear.

The Filesystems dialog itself has few surprises. If you need floppy disks, CD-ROMs, ZIP drives, or hard drive partitions in any of the supported filesystems, you can include it in the core kernel, or, preferably, build it as a module. The /proc and /dev/pts filesystems are highly recommended unless the kernel is being built for a specialized embedded application; without these features, many standard utilities will not work.

MS-DOS and VFAT (Windows) Filesystems

The MS-DOS and VFAT filesystems are worth some special consideration, if only because they are so ubiquitous. The current kernel support for the MS-DOS/VFAT disks used by DOS, Windows, Windows 95, and Windows NT will only read and write to uncompressed disks and cannot be used on DoubleSpaced disks or partitions. To access DoubleSpaced drives, you will need to use the DOSEMU emulator, or try the dmsdosfs tools (`ftp://metalab.unc.edu/pub/Linux/system/filesystems/dosfs`).

MS-DOS support is not needed if you only plan to access MS-DOS disks through the mtools programs (`mdir`, `mcopy`, and so on). MS-DOS support is needed only if you plan to run Linux on a second partition or hard drive and need access to files on the MS-DOS side, or if you want to mount ZIP drives or other shared media to move files between Linux and MS-DOS.

VFAT adds the additional support for long filenames and also provides several options for the DOS codepage and National Language Support for the default behavior in coping with the DOS 11-character filename limit. Details of these translation options can be found in `Documentation/filesystems/vfat.txt`.

ISO 9660, UDF, and DVD Support

UDF is the new standard CD-ROM format and is intended to replace ISO9660. At this point in time, UDF support means Digital Video Disk (DVD) support. Although the kernel supports the conventional ISO 9660-format CD-ROMs and will also support the Microsoft Joliet extensions for Unicode filesystems, it does not yet offer UDF. A driver for DVD and other UDF peripherals is available through the TryLinux UDF project (`http://www.trylinux.com/projects/udf/`).

Native Language Support

This section is a bit of a misnomer. These options do support different cultural languages, but they only support reading and displaying these character sets on Microsoft filesystems.

The first section option lists Microsoft codepages and is only an issue if your system needs to read filenames from an MS-DOS or Windows filesystem. Note that codepage support applies to filenames only, and not to the contents of the file. Similarly, to display characters from Microsoft VFAT or Joliet CD-ROM filesystems, you will also need to include at least one of the NLS options. You may select any number of languages for both systems, and any of these can be built as a module to be loaded only when needed.

Network Filesystems

Network filesystems allow you to share disk resources. Although there are obvious applications for this on a large network, even those in a small office/home office setting may want to distribute their resources. For example, our office uses an old salvaged 486/33 machine as a multiuser X-terminal for the smoking lounge. This machine runs Linux 2.2.7 from a 60MB hard drive. 60MB is enough to get the system up and running, and from there, NFS is used to supply software directories and user disk resources from upstairs in the lab.

As with the filesystems and partitions support, Linux provides a common glue for almost any heterogeneous network. Network filesystems are no exception. The 2.4 kernel can create a hub where old and new UNIX filesystems, Windows 95/NT, OS/2, and Novell can all be bound together in one workstation or one server.

CODA Distributed Filesystem

CODA is a new distributed filesystem technology, somewhat like NFS, only more flexible, more secure, and more efficient. CODA includes authentication and encryption features, disk replication, caching, and support for discontinuous connections such as laptops and teleworkers. Current Linux kernel support will allow you to use CODA client programs. Client programs and other information about this filesystem are available from the Coda home page (`http://www.coda.cs.cmu.edu`). The Venus client support is also described in great detail in `Documentation/filesystems/coda.txt`.

NFS

NFS, the old workhorse of distributed filesystems, takes a lot of criticism, but it is still the standard. CODA may take over from NFS as time goes on, but for the foreseeable future, NFS is all we have. NFS will also require running `portmap` with the `nfsd` and `mountd` daemons. If you are configuring a kernel for a diskless workstation, NFS cannot be loaded as a module (obviously) and you will need the `IP:Kernel Level Autoconfiguration` and `NFS Root Partition` options.

For NFS servers, you have the option of running the `nfsd` daemon or enabling the kernel-level NFS server. The latter choice has the advantage of being much faster (since it's in kernel space), but is still somewhat experimental.

SMB (Windows Shares) and NCP

If your LAN includes Windows for Workgroups, Windows 95/97, OS/2-LanManager, or NT machines using TCP/IP, this option will enable mounting shared directories from those machines. Note that SMB support is for the client side; exporting directories to Windows machines is done through the Samba daemon.

NCP (NetWare Core Protocol) provides similar facilities for the NetWare (IPX) file sharing used by Novell networks. As with the SMB support, this is used for mounting remote NCP drives on this machine. You do not need this option to be an NCP server.

Partition Types

Linux is unique as the only O/S to offer filesystem compatibility right down to the partition formats. This section option adds support for BSD, SunOS, Solaris, and Macintosh partitions and allows you to directly read and write disks in those proprietary formats.

For example, by including foreign partition support, you can access all partitions in a multi-boot machine (such as MacOS versus Linux or BSD versus Linux), or exchange optical disks or ZIP drives with one or more of the other systems.

Console Drivers

The first two options under `Console Drivers` are very straightforward. The first enables support for the standard VGA graphics card (text mode), and the second adds support for the vga option in `/etc/lilo.conf`, which sets the VGA text mode during the boot sequence.

The remaining options are more obscure.

Option 3 adds support for using old monochrome display adapters (MDA) as a "second head" to display a text console while the main system runs X on the VGA monitor. The MDA option is only for this configuration and is not for systems using the MDA as the primary display.

Frame Buffer Support

Historically, Linux had no need for a graphical console, at least not until the Motorola 68K port, where there was no concept of a text console. As of the 2.1 kernels, all ports now have the same console code, with a hardware-specific frame buffer supporting a graphical console device (`fbcon`).

Frame buffers are also an alternative means to control the graphic system via a dedicated device (`/dev/fb0`). This is mostly an issue when compiling for platforms other than the Intel x86 or when using a Matrox Millenium or similar PC graphics card. To use frame buffers, your X-server must be aware of the feature. Although you can include FB support on an Intel platform (see `Documentation/fb/vesafb.txt`), be aware that mixing software that talks directly to the hardware with the `fbdev` method may cause a system crash. For more information, look up the `FB-HOWTO` (`http://www.linuxdoc.org/HOWTO/framebuffer-HOWTO.html`) or read `Documentation/fb/framebuffer.txt`.

Sound

The Linux sound driver was derived from the OSS/Free driver by Hannu Savolainen. The current kernel driver is maintained by Alan Cox and is funded by Red Hat, and this should be taken into consideration when reporting problems. For very new and/or obscure sound card support, you may need to obtain the commercial edition of the OSS drivers from 4Front Technologies (`http://www.opensound.com/`).

The first option in the sound configuration section is a master switch for enabling sound support. If this option is switched off in a kernel previously configured for sound, all options are preserved in the `.config` file, but the sound module will not be included in the resulting kernel. This is useful when you're experimenting with sound system options, or when you suspect an IRQ conflict between the sound system and some other device, such as a printer port (IRQ 7) or a network card (often on IRQ 10 or 11).

Most of this section option is what you might expect. You will need the IRQ numbers, DMA channels, and port addresses of your audio hardware. When in doubt, the HELP option will offer some advice on the compatibility of various options. There are a few items that provoke misunderstandings, for example enabling MIDI support versus enabling MIDI emulation in a SoundBlaster card, but all of these issues are explained in the HELP pages.

Linux includes support for a wide array of sound cards, from the legacy 8-bit AdLib cards to the latest high-performance wave-table systems. Since Linux 2.2, OSS/Free now also provides a software wave-table engine to bring realistic MIDI patches to even old 8-bit sound cards. This wave-table support allows for samples between 8kHz and 44kHz and up to 32 simultaneous voices; obviously, the sampling rate and the number of voices your system can handle will depend on RAM and CPU speed, but 22kHz in eight voices runs quite comfortably on a 486/33.

Frequent causes of mishaps in configuring sound cards arise from IRQ or DMA and port conflicts, from configuring a clone card as a "Sound Blaster-compatible" (most mean "SBPro-compatible" although they may run better in MSS mode), or due to plug-and-play problems. Detailed information on compatibility issues and tips on troubleshooting sound support can be found in `Documentation/sound/README.OSS`.

Plug-and-Play Sound Cards

Most modern plug-and-play (PnP) sound cards have very little trouble with Linux, but in some situations you may need to experiment with using `pnpdump` and `isapnp` to generate and then load acceptable settings into the card before you can use the sound system. To do this, the sound card must be compiled as a module to allow using `isapnp` to set the device before the module is loaded.

To configure PnP devices, you first need to obtain the possible settings using the `pnpdump` utility:

```
pnpdump > /etc/isapnp.conf
```

This will create a long text file of configuration options for all PnP devices on your system. You then must edit this file to uncomment the settings for your specific configuration.

> Once you have set this configuration file to be compatible with your system, you can then add the lines to your boot scripts to first load the configuration and then load the driver:
>
> ```
> isapnp -c /etc/isapnp.conf
> insmod sound.o
> ```
>
> In rare circumstances, the card needs to be initialized by Windows before it can accept any service requests and this technique will not work. The only way around this, outside of lobbying the manufacturer to be more friendly, is to boot your system under Windows and then use the DOS-based `loadlin.exe` boot loader to switch to Linux.
>
> Also, most modern BIOS will allow setting or restricting the PnP assignments of IRQ numbers to certain devices. This is a handy thing for Linux as well as NT 4.0 because you can restrict all PCI devices from using an IRQ required by an old ISA card.

27

CONFIGURING AND
BUILDING KERNELS

USB Support

The Universal Serial Bus (USB) standard was initiated in 1994 by Compaq, Intel, Microsoft, and NEC, originally as a means to connect the PC to telephones and to allow easily adding many new devices. Today, USB is commonly used for pointers, printers, cameras, and other peripherals that can function in the effective 2Mbit/s transfer rate of USB. USB support was originally developed by Linus Torvalds; this feature is new to the 2.4 kernel but can be grafted on to 2.2.16+ kernels.

Linux USB supports Compaq's Open Host Controller Interface (OHCI) and the Intel Universal Host Controller Interface (UHCI). Both methods have the same capabilities and all USB devices will work with both host controller types. UHCI hardware is simpler and cheaper, but requires a more complex device driver and thus causes slightly more CPU load.

More information on USB can be found at the Linux-USB Project (`http://www.linux-usb.org`).

Kernel Hacking

As of Linux 2.2, Kernel Hacking contains only one option: to toggle `SysRQ` support. `SysRQ` adds several very useful commands binding recovery and diagnostic operations to Ctrl+Alt+SysRq key sequences. For example, if the console or X-server becomes locked because some renegade process is blocking all I/O, you could telnet to the machine, open a superuser shell, and then kill that process or reboot the machine, but a simpler and more convenient path is to use `SysRQ` commands to kill the errant process, or even `sync` and `umount` the filesystems, and to force a reboot. See Table 27.2.

Security and SysRQ

Kiosks, workstations, and production machines should disable SysRQ; you may want to also disable the Ctrl+Alt+Backspace command to exit the X Window System. This prevents novice (or knowledgeable) users from bringing down the machine without authorization. In /etc/inittab, you can also customize the Ctrl+Alt+Del reboot interrupt to give a longer grace period or to disable the command entirely.

TABLE 27.2   Kernel SysRQ Commands

Command	Description
r	Turns off keyboard Raw mode and sets it to XLATE. This is useful when the console or the X-server is hung.
k	Kills all programs on the current virtual console. Use this to shut down a locked X-server.
b	Immediately reboots the system without syncing or unmounting filesystems. This command may corrupt your filesystem if you have not already synced and unmounted your disks.
o	Shuts off system power via APM (if configured and supported).
s	Syncs all mounted filesystems to minimize the filesystem corruption that may occur from an ungraceful shutdown.
u	Unmounts and remounts all filesystems as read-only, much like the shutdown command. This allows your system to read the binaries required for an orderly shutdown.
p	Dumps the current registers and flags to your console (that is, generates a kernel panic).
t	Dumps a list of current tasks and their information to your console, giving you the diagnostic details for isolating the cause of the hang.
m	Dumps current memory info to your console.
0-9	Sets the console log level that filters kernel messages. For example, a level of 0 would filter out everything except panics and oops messages.
e/i	Sends tErm or kIll signals to all processes except init, effectively throwing you into single-user mode.
l	Sends SIGKILL to all processes, including init, which effectively halts your system.

Alternate Configurations

The `Load/Save` options are a convenience for those who need to maintain several alternate configurations, for example on a machine used to compile kernels for other machines, or where you need alternate kernels for different purposes. As you would expect, this option pops up a dialog asking for the filename and then saves `.config` to the named location.

Saving Your Configuration

Once the kernel is configured, `save and exit` creates `.config`, and, if the kernel has been configured for sound, generates `linux/include/linux/autoconf.h`. The kernel is now primed and ready for building.

CML2: The Next-Generation Configuration Tool

While the configuration scripts that drive the makefile do the job with a fair degree of assurance, this system was never intended to manage a project with close to two million lines of code and hundreds of interdependent options. To ease this situation, Eric Raymond has devoted his air travel and hotel time to creating a next-generation solution, the Configuration Management Language, or CML2.

Although CML2 was not ready for the 2.4 kernel, it will be included in 2.5 as an alternative configuration method and will either become the standard by 2.6 or will be superceded by some other CML. As much pain as this causes in maintaining parallel versions, the payoff for Linux 2.6 and on will be considerable.

The current CML2 will handle all kernel configuration options, and will report and prevent incompatible or inconsistent configurations. The design of this new scripting language may also allow for someday configuring the kernel in reverse, by specifying the hardware on a form and having the CML2 interpreter deduce the correct kernel options, a large step toward someday having kernel configuration proceed automatically from the hardware detection stage.

Using CML2

In most cases, migrating configuration specs to CML2 only involves patching the main rules file `kernel-rules.cml`, adding the symbol declarations to `kernel-symbols.cml`, and ensuring the correct entry in `kernel-menus.cml`. Once your rules have been entered into these files, configuration specs can be tested and debugged using the `cmlcompile.py` utility to display the menu tree or to run the compiler in interactive mode.

`kernel-rules.cml` specifies all options with their suboptions and required components. For example, the menu rule for `Network File Systems` states

```
unless INET suppress CODA_FS NFS_FS SMB_FS NFSD
unless (IPX!=n or INET!=n) suppress NCP_FS
...
menu nfs # Network file systems
        CODA_FS? NFS_FS? {NFS_V3 ROOT_NFS} NFSD? {NFSD_V3}
        SMB_FS?
        NCP_FS? {ncpfs}
...
menu ncpfs # NCP filesystem configuration
        NCPFS_PACKET_SIGNING NCPFS_IOCTL_LOCKING
        NCPFS_STRONG NCPFS_NFS_NS NCPFS_OS2_NS NCPFS_SMALLDOS
        NCPFS_MOUNT_SUBDIR NCPFS_NDS_DOMAINS NCPFS_NLS NCPFS_EXTRAS
...
unless NCP_FS!=n suppress ncpfs
...
derive NLS from JOLIET==y or FAT_FS!=n or NTFS_FS!=n or NCPFS_NLS==y
```

This provides all five different network filesystems when `INET` is enabled, but only offers the `NCP_FS` if `IPX` is set but `INET` is not. Where `NCP_FS` is enabled, the configuration will include the related `NCPFS_*` options. Also, `NCP_FS` will imply including the `NLS` code page support.

`kernel-symbols.cml` defines the pretty-print strings for the kernel symbols and is factored out of the rules file to allow for translations. This file holds no surprises:

```
NCP_FS              'NCP file system support (to mount NetWare volumes)'
#
# NCP Filesystem configuration
#
NCPFS_PACKET_SIGNING    'Packet signatures'
NCPFS_IOCTL_LOCKING     'Proprietary file locking'
NCPFS_STRONG            'Clear remove/delete inhibit when needed'
NCPFS_NFS_NS            'Use NFS namespace if available'
NCPFS_OS2_NS            'Use LONG (OS/2) namespace if available'
NCPFS_SMALLDOS          'Lowercase DOS filenames'
NCPFS_MOUNT_SUBDIR      'Allow mounting of volume subdirectories'
NCPFS_NDS_DOMAINS       'NDS authentication support'
NCPFS_NLS               'Use Native Language Support'
NCPFS_EXTRAS            'Enable symbolic links and execute flags'
```

Similarly, `kernel-menus.cml` simply defines the top-level menus for the kernel configuration process.

Kernel configurations are generated in two stages, first to compile the menu source file with the `cmlcompile.py` program, and then to run `cmlconfigure.py` to set kernel options. Like the `Makefile` rules it replaces, CML2 (shown in Figure 27.3) offers X, curses, and line-oriented interfaces selected by the default mode or with the `-c` and `-t` options:

```
cmlcompile.py kernel-rules.cml
cmlconfigure.py
```

Figure 27.3

CML2 v.0.7.1

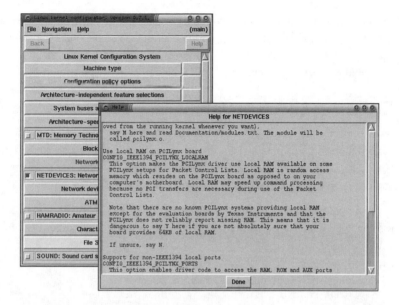

CML2 is coded in the Python 1.5.2 to ensure portability and to allow direct compilation to a native binary. A complete guide to CML2 and the current source files can be downloaded from Eric Raymond's KBuild Web page (`http://www.tuxedo.org/~esr/kbuild/`).

Building and Installing the Kernel

Configuration creates one precious file, `/usr/src/linux/.config`. This file contains the list of #defines for selected options; once you have a working configuration, you will want to keep a backup copy in a safe place.

You can now apply your updated configuration to build the new kernel, create the modules, and install the works. It's also now time to give your wrists a break and return to the command line to put it all together.

Scheduling a Kernel Rebuild Using at

If you are reasonably certain a kernel build will not fail, schedule your build using the at command. This lets you shift the system load to off-peak hours and sends the build output to you as email.

Before building the new kernel, you must regenerate all dependency files to account for any changes in include or module options. Until CML2 becomes the standard, this step is needed whenever the kernel configuration is changed. The `make dep clean` command will rebuild these dependency files and remove any stray generated files.

Building the Kernel

As with everything else about Linux, building the kernel offers many choices. All the build options are outlined in `linux/Documentation/kbuild/commands.txt`; the most common cases are building just the kernel file, building only the modules, building both, and doing an install of the kernel and/or the modules after the build.

For example, you may need to build a kernel file for some other computer (such as a laptop) or to be installed by hand under some very logical new name. Building this image could be done with

```
make bzImage && \
    cp /usr/src/linux/arch/i386/boot/bzImage \
       /boot/vmlinuz-scsi
```

The first command compiles and compresses the kernel (for a "large kernel" image, leaving the result in `arch/$(ARCH)/boot`; the image is then copied manually to the `/boot` directory. This new image will not be installed until it is registered with a boot loader such as `lilo` (see "Manually Installing a New Kernel"). To automatically install a kernel image, use the command

```
make bzlilo
```

This will create the same compressed image and copy the file to `$INSTALL_PATH/vmlinuz`, then run the `lilo` command; `make bzlilo` assumes your `/etc/lilo.conf` expects this filename in this location.

Big Kernels on Intel Machines

Each of the kernel build commands has a "big-kernel" counterpart that is needed if the kernel grows to be over 1MB in size when uncompressed. Installing these large kernel images with older versions of `lilo` will overwrite part of the boot loader and the system will not boot. Since most configurations result in a big kernel and building small kernels with the big-kernel commands seems benign, unless you are building a very simple kernel for an old machine or an embedded device, router, and so on, use `bzlilo` and `bzImage make` targets just to be sure.

All z* targets are specific to the ix386 platform, and these will be removed during the 2.5 development and replaced by the bz* equivalents. For this reason, this chapter will use the normal z* commands.

The most common and convenient command for creating a new kernel is

```
make dep clean zlilo modules modules_install
```

This one command line will do the following:

- Perform the dependency file generation.
- Clean the sources.
- Create a compressed kernel image.
- Move `$(INSTALL_PATH)/vmlinuz` to `$(INSTALL_PATH)/vmlinuz.old`, copy the new `zImage` kernel file to `$(INSTALL_PATH)vmlinuz`, and run `lilo` to install the new images.
- Build all modules and install these under `$(INSTALL_MOD_PATH)/lib/modules/2.2.5`.

Putting all these commands on one line will ensure that if any stage of this build fails, subsequent stages will not be started. The whole process can also be scheduled to run in an xterm window or alt-console, can be run during off-peak hours as an at job, or can be used as an excuse to play some serious `Nethack` or `XPilot`.

Manually Installing a New Kernel

The new kernel file is always found in `/usr/src/linux/arch/$(ARCH)/boot/zImage` and must be installed using the `lilo` boot loader or some other Linux loader before it can be used.

For example, to emulate the Red Hat `/boot` path scheme, you would need to copy the new `zImage` to `/boot/vmlinuz` (save the old one first!) and modify `/etc/lilo.conf` to include the backup version. Alternatively, to accommodate stubborn plug-and-play devices, you may need to copy this new kernel to your Windows 95 partition for use by the Linux `loadlin.exe` boot loader.

One frequent requirement is to create boot floppies. A boot floppy is nothing more than a kernel copied directly to a floppy disk and set to mount the `root` filesystem from the hard drive.

While it is far more mnemonic to create a boot floppy using the command

```
make zdisk
```

this is equivalent to using `dd` to copy the file directly to the raw sectors of the floppy disk device:

```
dd if=arch/i386/zImage of=/dev/fd0
```

Compiling for a Remote Machine

When you're creating a kernel for some other machine (such as a laptop), you can put the compressed kernel file and all modules into an alternate directory tree by giving alternate values for the INSTALL_* path variables on the make command line, for example:

```
INSTALL_PATH=/psitta \
    INSTALL_MOD_PATH=/psitta ROOT_DEV=/dev/hda1 \
        make bzlilo modules_install
```

This will move the generated kernel, map, and module files to /psitta/vmlinuz, /psitta/System.map, and /psitta/lib/modules, where you can conveniently tar the whole directory for shipment to the remote machine with the following:

```
cd /psitta && \
  tar cf - vmlinuz System.map lib | \
      rsh psitta tar xCf / -
```

There is one side effect: The command will also run lilo, but since the /etc/lilo.conf file does not reference these new /psitta files, there is no adverse effect.

The only potential hazard of this trick is a possible change to files in /usr/include/linux, which may affect programs subsequently compiled on the build host. Some care must be taken to ensure that the alternate kernel build does not leave unwanted changes in this directory on the build machine. Also, if the remote machine will be used to build software, after compiling the new kernel, you should copy the /usr/include/linux directory onto the remote machine after compiling the new kernel.

Troubleshooting the New Kernel

/proc is your friend. The pseudo-files in the /proc directory hold a wealth of diagnostic information and a simple means to set runtime parameters.

System Information Files

The most frequently useful /proc diagnostic files are as follows:

- /proc/cpuinfo lists the processor type, number of ports, and other essential information about the computer hardware:

  ```
  $cat /proc/cpuinfo

  processor : 0
  vendor_id : AuthenticAMD
  ```

```
cpu family : 5
model : 8
model name : AMD-K6(tm) 3D processor
stepping : 12
cpu MHz : 350.804507
fdiv_bug : no
hlt_bug : no
sep_bug : no
f00f_bug : no
fpu : yes
fpu_exception : yes
cpuid level : 1
wp : yes
flags : fpu vme de pse tsc msr mce cx8 sep pge mmx 3dnow
bogomips : 699.60
```

27

CONFIGURING AND
BUILDING KERNELS

- /proc/interrupts maps IRQ lines to devices:

```
$ cat /proc/interrupts

CPU0
0: 30200579 XT-PIC timer
1: 251230 XT-PIC keyboard
2: 0 XT-PIC cascade
4: 996021 XT-PIC serial
5: 1 XT-PIC soundblaster
7: 2 XT-PIC parport1
8: 1 XT-PIC rtc
11: 3984 XT-PIC MSS audio codec
12: 973494 XT-PIC eth0
13: 1 XT-PIC fpu
14: 4253923 XT-PIC ide0
15: 4713361 XT-PIC ide1
NMI: 0
```

- /proc/sound reports the current sound system configuration and the installed services:

```
$ cat /proc/sound

OSS/Free:3.8s2++-971130

Load type: Driver compiled into kernel
Kernel: Linux maya.dyndns.org 2.2.5 #2 Thu Apr 15 18:34:07 EDT 1999 i586
Config options: 0

Installed drivers:

Type 10: MS Sound System
Type 27: Compaq Deskpro XL
```

```
Type 1: OPL-2/OPL-3 FM
Type 26: MPU-401 (UART)
Type 2: Sound Blaster
Type 29: Sound Blaster PnP
Type 7: SB MPU-401
Type 36: SoftOSS Virtual Wave Table

Card config:
SoftOSS Virtual Wave Table
Compaq Deskpro XL at 0x530 irq 11 drq 0,0
Sound Blaster at 0x220 irq 5 drq 1,5
(SB MPU-401 at 0x330 irq 5 drq 0)
OPL-2/OPL-3 FM at 0x388 drq 0

Audio devices:

0: MSS audio codec (SoundPro CMI 8330)
1: Sound Blaster 16 (4.13) (DUPLEX)

Synth devices:

0: SoftOSS
1: Yamaha OPL3

Midi devices:

Timers:

0: System clock
1: SoftOSS

Mixers:

0: MSS audio codec (SoundPro CMI 8330)
1: Sound Blaster
```

- `/proc/parport` contains directories for each parallel port and reports on the devices attached to each port:

```
$ cat /proc/parport/0/hardware

base: 0x378
irq: none
dma: none
modes: SPP,ECP,ECPEPP,ECPPS2
```

Setting Kernel Parameters and Options

Kernel and other low-level runtime parameters can be set through the `/proc/sys` pseudo-files. For example, to set the maximum number of file handles to a higher value, you can include a line in the boot scripts that echoes the new number directly into `/proc/fs/file-max`.

/proc Interfaces Changes

There are a number of differences between the 2.0, 2.2, and 2.4 kernels regarding the organization and format of /proc files. For example, the `file-max` pseudo-file was located in the kernel subdirectory for 2.0, but has now moved to the `fs` subdirectory. Changes in formats can also cause utility programs such as `top` and `xosview` to fail. When in doubt, check the `linux/Documentation/Changes` file for compatibility reports.

Recovering from Faulty Kernels

It happens. You execute an orderly shutdown and reboot, the monitor flashes (or your connection goes dead), and you wait for the boot, only to be greeted with a partial LILO prompt...or worse.

Disaster Recovery in Kernel Compiles

The worst that can happen with a modified kernel is boot failure. It happens to the best of us, and usually happens because of incompatible settings or forgetting to run `lilo` after changing a kernel. There are few things as frightening as the dread LI- boot prompt.

Before you reboot a new kernel, you should take a few precautions to ensure a backup boot method. If your hardware has a floppy drive, keep your install/rescue disks handy. Production machines should always keep a boot floppy with their current stable kernel and your /etc/lilo.conf should define at least one backup kernel image.

There is a South African proverb, "If you hear hoof-beats in the street, it is probably not a zebra." With a Linux system, your darkest hour still probably does not require reinstalling the entire distribution. Even in seemingly hopeless situations, it is far more likely that your system can be safely rescued and repaired.

When the worst happens, use your rescue disks to boot your system, manually `fsck` and `mount` the hard drive, restore order, rerun `lilo`, and breathe easier. You can also find a number of rescue disks and tools in the Metalab archive (ftp://metalab.unc.edu/pub/Linux).

> **Note**
>
> The meaning of the preceding proverb is "When something odd happens, it is usually the most common thing, not the most exceptional" and in this context, having to reinstall Red Hat is a very exceptional situation (in 6 years, I have had to do this only once, when the Windows partition scrambled my Linux partition). In the Linux support and IRC channels, those just starting to experment with Linux most often ask (or state) "Should I reinstall" and although the answer can be yes, it is overwhelmingly more often no.

Typically, a faulty kernel will exhibit one of the following behaviors:

- The machine cycles through repeated rebooting.
- You see some substring of the LILO prompt, such as LIL- followed by a halt.
- Linux begins to load but halts at some point during the kernel messages.
- Linux loads but ends in a kernel panic message.
- Linux loads, runs, lets you log in, and then dies when it is least convenient.

If you are prepared, your prognosis for a full recovery is very good. If you can get up to the LILO: prompt, the most convenient recovery is to load your backup kernel by specifying its label to the boot loader:

```
LILO: backup
```

This will boot from your previous kernel and allow you in so you can fix the problem and try your luck again. If you cannot get to the LILO: prompt, your only alternative is to use your boot disk or to use a rescue disk. The boot disk makes life much easier because the running system will be identical to your normal system. If you use a rescue disk, you must manually mount your system partitions and enable any extra modules.

Where alternate kernels and boot disks are not practical, for instance on thin clients with limited diskspace, and if you can reach the LILO: prompt, you can try to start your system in single-user mode to prevent the probing and loading of many modules, such as your network card (a frequent culprit). The default configuration for single-user (a.k.a. *runlevel 1*) mode is specified by the files in /etc/rc.d/rc1.d, and it is a good idea to double-check the symlinks in that directory after each system upgrade to ensure that the choices are intelligent for the purpose. Single-user mode will put you directly into a system shell; once the problem has been corrected, you can either reboot the system or exit the shell to return to multiuser mode.

Repeated Rebooting

Nine times out of ten, repeated rebooting is caused by changing the kernel file and forgetting to run lilo to register the new image with the boot loader. lilo needs the raw sector location of the kernel; copying a kernel image will move it to a new disk sector and leave the previous pointer stored by lilo dangling over an abyss.

This problem can be corrected by booting from the boot floppy and running lilo, or by using a rescue disk, mounting the boot partition under /mnt, and running lilo with the options to use a relative path:

```
lilo -r /mnt
```

Partial LILO Prompt

A partial LILO prompt is the most terrifying of all kernel boot errors. Each letter of the L-I-L-O signifies a stage in the boot process:

- L- or LIL: Usually a media error or failure to include the boot partition or filesystem support (or including it as a module).
- LI or LIL?: /boot/boot.b is missing, moved, or corrupt. The solution is the same for all: re-run lilo.

More information on using lilo and the diagnosis of lilo error codes can be found in /usr/doc/lilo-0.x/TechnicalGuide.ps .

Kernel Halts While Loading

Device probing is risky business and a frequent cause of kernel halts while loading. For example, if you are configuring for a gateway/firewall machine with two network interfaces, the second probe may cause the kernel to halt. Other causes of kernel halts are IRQ conflicts, memory conflicts, and mismatched devices selecting similar but not-quite-identical drivers.

You can avoid probing, memory, and IRQ conflicts for most kernel modules and devices by supplying configuration parameters in the /etc/lilo.conf append line or at the LILO: prompt. The exact parameters to use depend on your device, but you can find advice in the README files, either in linux/Documentation or in the subdirectories of the driver source code.

27

CONFIGURING AND BUILDING KERNELS

Kernel Panic

A kernel panic message has a certain cryptic poetry to it, like a robotic haiku, a snapshot testament to the last moments of a Linux kernel. A kernel panic usually has the following form:

```
unable to handle kernel paging request at address C0000010
Oops: 0002
EIP: 0010:XXXXXXXX
eax: xxxxxxxx ebx: xxxxxxxx ecx: xxxxxxxx edx: xxxxxxxx
esi: xxxxxxxx edi: xxxxxxxx ebp: xxxxxxxx
ds: xxxx es: xxxx fs: xxxx gs: xxxx
Pid: xx, process nr: xx

xx xx xx xx xx xx xx xx xx xx
```

For most practical purposes, knowing where the panic occurs is more useful than interpreting the message itself. The leading text tells what triggered the event, and this is followed by the addresses held in various registers. Intrepid readers can find detailed instructions on decoding this message in the `linux/Documentation/oops-tracing.txt` file.

In production kernels, panic messages are rare and are usually due to a misconfiguration problem, missing modules, failure to load a module before using some essential feature, or using hardware not supported by the current kernel. With development kernels, kernel panics can become a way of life.

Kernel Oops and Bug Reporting

Linux is highly stable and resilient to application failures, but when you start experimenting with odd kernel combinations or experimental editions, hardware, and configurations, stuff happens. In the parlance of the kernel developers, an "oops" is a kernel panic message that occurs spontaneously, often mercilessly, and for no apparent reason. The message reported is similar to the kernel panic that can occur during the boot, but it may not be visible if you are running X Windows. The cause of both the boot halting and a spontaneous oops are is the same: the kernel has reached an impasse.

When an oops occurs during a user session, the kernel panic message may be displayed on one of the Linux Alt consoles (seen by pressing Ctrl+Alt and a function key) or by checking the system log file in /var/log/messages (another good reason to echo all system messages to /dev/tty12). If you can see the panic report, the activity just prior to this in the log may give some clues to the cause of the panic.

Linux is maintained and developed by volunteers, so the first advice for reporting problems and bugs is to be polite. Chances are good someone will take personal interest in this bug, and you will have a fix or a workaround in record time. You are far less likely to get a timely response if you take your frustrations out on the developers. Unlike other proprietary systems, when dealing with the Linux community, you are not dealing with underpaid droogs. You are dealing with the masters themselves, the people who take personal ownership and pride in their work. Show some respect and they will repay your thoughtfulness.

Before you report any bug, you should always check to see if this bug is known. If you have access to a Web browser, look into the linux-kernel archive (http://www.tux.org/lkml/). If you have IRC access, you can ask directly on one of the #linux, #linuxOS, or #kernelnewbie channels.

If you still think you have found a new bug in the kernel, the kernel development community will be more than interested...providing you can supply enough information to lead to a fix. If you can isolate the module where the oops occurred, you can locate the author of that module either in the linux/MAINTAINERS file or in the source code of the module itself. You can also post your report to the linux-kernel mailing list.

When reporting a suspected bug, you should specify which kernel you are using, outline your hardware setup (RAM, CPU, and so on), and describe the situation where the problem occurred. If there is a kernel panic message, copy the message exactly as displayed on your screen.

Summary

Linux is the kernel, and the kernel is Linux. Linus Torvalds once wrote that he never expected Linux would to become the size of EMACS, but he is quick to point out that "at least Linux has the excuse that it needs to be." The development of this beast over the past decade has been meteoric and has probably left some broken hearts along the way, but the result of this experiment in community cooperation now stands as a major contender in the operating systems marketplace.

As with any technical software installation, configuring an optimal kernel does require planning, preparation, and some knowledge of the target machine to ensure an exact fit. It is not unreasonable to expect that someday the Linux kernel will be self-configuring (IRIX has done this for years). While kernel configuration is nowhere near as frightening as it once was, for the foreseeable future configuration still demands a certain amount of attention and a small measure of sysadmin savvy.

Building the Linux kernel is not a rite of passage or a task to be feared; kernel building just takes some common sense, care, and attention, and is yet another of the reasons you chose to run Linux in the first place.

CHAPTER 28

Emulators, Tools, and Window Clients

One of the many wonderful things about Linux is the wealth of software extending the operating system's capabilities. When you use Red Hat Linux, you'll find a wealth of software tools at your fingertips. This chapter introduces several software packages you can use to

- Easily transfer files between different media (such as floppies)
- Run a DOS session under the Linux console or X11
- Run applications from Windows on your Linux desktop
- Install, configure, and run different operating systems under Linux
- Run legacy MacOS applications under Linux and X11
- Install, configure, and run Linux under different operating systems
- Create and run virtual networks, enabling you to operate your Linux desktop from Windows, or work in Windows from your Linux desktop.

Emulators

Emulators have been used since the early days of computing. An *emulator* is a software program designed to mimic a Central Processing Unit (CPU), computer language, or entire operating system on a foreign computer platform. Emulators are used to test CPUs, hardware devices, programs, and operating systems. They are also used to enable the porting or building of applications on one computer when the programs are destined for other, usually quite dissimilar, computing platforms.

Many of the early emulators under UNIX were assembler language macros that translated the low-level code for foreign CPUs into native code on the computer. In this way, programs could be transferred from one computer system to the next. This chapter does not detail how modern-day emulators work or cover all the emulators available for Linux (such as those used to run read-only memory programs from arcade machines under X11), but you'll find that Linux supports some useful and ingenious emulators.

Emulating DOS with DOSEMU

DOSEMU, based on the early work of Matthias Lautner and currently maintained by Hans Lermen, is not (according to its author) an emulator. Instead, Lautner claims it is a virtual machine for DOS. This means that the program creates a virtual computer in your system's memory. A copy of Pat Vallani's FreeDOS kernel (actually a 16MB DOS filesystem named under the `/var/lib/dosemu` directory) is included with the Red Hat Linux Powertools CD-ROM (and is available for download from Red Hat's site). After installation, you'll find most of DOSEMU's documentation under the `/usr/share/doc/dosemu` directory.

To download and install the latest copy of DOSEMU, go to `ftp.dosemu.org`, log in, and then navigate to the `dosemu` directory. You can download DOSEMU in a compressed tarball (`.tgz` format), or as an `.rpm` file. You'll find `.rpm` files similar to Red Hat's DOSEMU `.rpm` files (except for the FreeDOS `.rpm`) under the `/pub/dosemu` directory, which can then be downloaded and installed easily with the rpm command like this:

```
# rpm -ivh dosemu-1.0.1.2.i386.rpm
dosemu                  #############################################
# rpm -ivh xdosemu-1.0.1.2.i386.rpm
xdosemu                 #############################################
# rpm -ivh dosemu-freedos-1.0.1.2.i386.rpm
dosemu-freedos          #############################################
```

> **Note**
>
> You'll always find the latest copies of Red Hat Linux `.rpm` files at `ftp://ftp.redhat.com`. However, traffic at this (and associated) server(s) is always high, so you're better off exploring other servers available through `http://www.redhat.com/download/mirror.html`. To get the `dosemu-freedos .rpm` file, navigate to the latest Red Hat `powertools` directory on one of the mirrors.

The Red Hat DOSEMU distribution consists of 151 files found under the `/etc`, `/usr/bin`, `/usr/share/doc`, `/usr/man/man1`, and `/var/lib/dosemu` directories. DOSEMU may be used from the command line of a Linux console or launched in its own window during an X session. The main configuration file, `global.conf`, is located under the `/var/lib/dosemu` directory. However, to configure most system-wide settings, you should only edit the file `/etc/dosemu.conf`. This file has nearly 80 different settings through which you can configure how DOSEMU works.

After a fresh install, you may have to set up DOSEMU (as `root`) by editing the `/etc/dosemu.conf` and changing the entry for the name of the hard drive used for booting. Check to make sure the default entry will look like this:

```
$_hdimage = "hdimage.first" # list of hdimages under /var/lib/dosemu
```

If the entry does not look like the above, change the name of the `hdimage` entry, then save your changes. You can then launch DOSEMU from the console by using the `dos` command. Type the command and press Enter:

```
# dos

    The Linux DOSEMU, Copyright (C) 2000 the 'DOSEMU-Development-Team'.
    This program is  distributed  in  the  hope that it will be useful,
    but  WITHOUT  ANY  WARRANTY;   without even the implied warranty of
```

```
MERCHANTABILITY  or  FITNESS FOR A PARTICULAR PURPOSE. See the file
COPYING for more details.  Use  this  program  at  your  own risk!

By continuing execution of this program,  you are stating that you
have read the file  COPYING  and the above liability disclaimer and
that you accept these conditions.

Enter 'yes' to confirm/continue:
```

Type **yes** and press Enter. You'll then see:

```
Loading device driver c:\ems.sys at segment 1513
[dosemu EMS 4.0 driver installed]
KERNEL: Boot drive = C

DOS-C compatibility 3.31
(C) Copyright 1995, 1996, 1997, 1998
Pasquale J. Villani
All Rights Reserved

DOS-C version 1.0 Beta 2 [FreeDOS Release] (Build 1937).

DOS-C is free software; you can redistribute it and/or modify it under the
terms of the GNU General Public License as published by the Free Software
Foundation; either version 2, or (at your option) any later version.

For technical information and description of the DOS-C operating system
consult "FreeDOS Kernel" by Pat Villani, published by Miller
Freeman Publishing, Lawrence KS, USA (ISBN 0-87930-436-7).

Running dosemu-1.0.1.0 compatibility, DosC patch 1
Process 0 starting: command.com

"Welcome to FreeDOS (http://www.freedos.org)!"
C:\>
```

If you first try launching the program and see this:

 # dos
```
Sorry bball. You are not allowed to use DOSEMU. Contact System Admin.
```

You may need to edit the file /etc/dosemu.users to allow other users to launch and use
DOSEMU. Create an entry in /etc/dosemu.users:

```
root c_all
all c_all
```

Save the file. Your users can then start a DOS session. You can also start a DOS session
in an X11 window with the xdos command. Type the command's name:

 # xdos

You'll then see a DOS session start, as shown in Figure 28.1.

FIGURE 28.1
Use DOSEMU to run a DOS session from the console or during an X11 session.

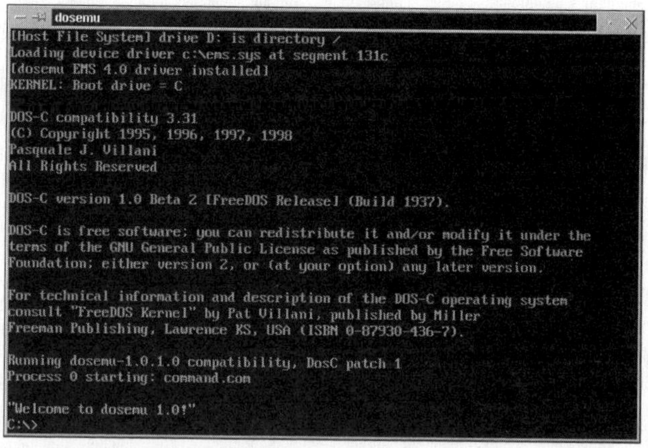

To get the latest version of DOSEMU, browse to http://www.dosemu.org. You'll find links to the very latest documentation and updates. For updates to FreeDOS, browse to http://www.freedos.org. You'll also find hundreds of utilities, commands, and additional software packages you can add to your DOSEMU system.

28

EMULATORS,
TOOLS, AND
WINDOW CLIENTS

Running Windows Clients with Wine

The Wine emulator, supported by programmers contributing the Wine project, allows you to run many DOS, Windows 3.1, or Win32 programs. This emulator may be downloaded from http://www.winehq.com in binary or source archives.

Note

Corel Corporation, the same kind folks who made a free, for-personal-use-only version of WordPerfect 8 available for Linux in 1998, announced at the March 1999 Linuxworld Conference that it would make versions of its WordPerfect Office 2000, CorelDRAW, and Corel PHOTO PAINT available for Linux. One year later, Corel released its WordPerfect Office 2000 Deluxe for Linux suite. The suite, composed of WordPerfect 9, Quattro Pro 9, Paradox 9, and Corel Presentations 9 (along with fonts, clipart, a copy of Corel Linux, and a commercial game), depends heavily on the Wine Project's software libraries. Corel PHOTO-PAINT, WordPerfect 8 for Linux, and the latest version of Corel Linux are also available for free download at http://linux.corel.com/download/.

As part of this effort, Corel also pledged active support and development of Wine "to speed the process of moving our office suite applications to Linux." Corel also said that the results of development work on Wine would be returned to the Wine project.

The easiest way to install Wine is to download a prebuilt `.rpm` file (such as from the Red Hat PowerTools CD-ROM) and to then install the program with this code:

```
# rpm -ivh wine-20000725-1.i386.rpm
```

After installation, edit the file `wine.conf` under the `/etc/wine` directory as `root` to tell `wine` the location of your Windows directory and settings for your floppy drive and CD-ROM. First look for the floppy drive entry:

```
[Drive A]
Path=/mnt/fd0
...
Device=/dev/fd0
```

If your floppies are mounted under the `/mnt/floppy` directory, you should then change the `Path=` entry to reflect this:

```
Path=/mnt/floppy
```

Next, look for the entry for Drive C:

```
[Drive C]
Path=/c
```

Change the drive entry to reflect the path to your Windows filesystem. Under Red Hat Linux, the corresponding entry to Windows's drive C: (in your system's filesystem table, `/etc/fstab`) will probably point to `/mnt/dos`. If so, change the `wine.conf` entry to

```
[Drive C]
Path=/mnt/dos
```

Continue through the `wine.conf` file, editing entries to match your system's filesystems, devices, and mount points. Another important entry will point to your system's CD-ROM drive:

```
[Drive D]
Path=/cdrom
...
Device=/dev/cdrom
```

In this example, your computer's CD-ROM drive is assigned as Drive D. You may need to change this entry to reflect the proper mount point and device like this:

```
[Drive D]
Path=/mnt/cdrom
...
Device=/dev/hdc
```

Wine without Windows?

Earlier versions of Wine required a copy of Windows installed on your system. However, work on Wine has progressed to the point that Wine may be able to run without an installed copy. However, you do need to create the following empty directories:

```
C:\windows

C:\windows\system

C:\windows\Start Menu

C:\windows\Start Menu\Programs
```

For additional details on setting up Wine with Windows, see the file `no-windows` under the `/usr/doc/wine*/documentation` directory. You'll also find extra tips on getting troublesome programs to run.

If you have your Windows partition mounted, you can then try to run the Windows WordPad client by typing this:

```
# wine /mnt/dos/Prog*/Accessories/wordpad.exe
```

The editor's window appears, as shown in Figure 28.2.

FIGURE 28.2

The Wine emulator allows you to run some Windows programs during your Linux X11 sessions.

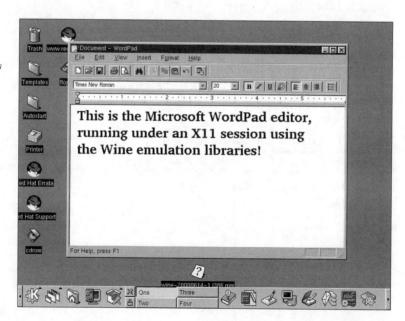

If you'd like to learn more about Wine or exchange tips and hints with other users or developers, read the Usenet newsgroup `comp.emulators.ms-windows.wine`. You'll also find nearly 30 newsgroups focused on discussions about emulators if you search at `http://www.deja.com`.

Emulating the Apple Macintosh with Executor

Executor, by ARDI, is a commercial software emulator you can use to run MacOS applications under Linux. According to ARDI, Executor on a 90MHz Pentium can run most applications almost as fast as a 50 MHz 68040. The Executor software is distributed in a series of `.rpm` archives, and a demo version is available through `http://www.ardi.com`.

This software may help you run one of nearly 340 legacy Macintosh applications, but the software emulation of the Apple Macintosh is not perfect and does have some limitations. The default emulated MacOS is System 6.0.7, although some System 7.0 applications may work. More importantly, though, other exclusions include

- Access to serial ports
- AppleTalk (LocalTalk)
- CDEVs
- INITs
- Internationalization
- Modem usage

There is limited sound support, and the software can read and write 1.44MB Macintosh-formatted floppy disks. According to ARDI, "Desk Accessory support is very weak; most will not run." On the other hand, you'll find excellent support for some major Macintosh clients, as listed in Table 28.1.

TABLE 28.1 Executor-compatible Macintosh Clients

Name	Version(s) Supported
Adobe Dimensions	2.0
Adobe Illustrator	1.9.5, 5.5
Adobe Photoshop	4.0
Aldus Freehand	2.2
Aldus Persuasion	2.1, 3.0
Claris Draw	1.0v1
Claris Works	2.01, 2.1, 3.0
File Maker Pro	2.0, 2.1, 3.0, 4.0

TABLE 28.1   continued

Name	Version(s) Supported
HyperCard	2.1, 2.2, 2.3
Microsoft Excel	3.0a, 4.0
Microsoft Word	5.1
Microsoft Works	2.00a
QuarkXPress	3.32
Quicken	4.0, 5.0, 6.0
WordPerfect	3.1
WriteNow	4.0

Installing Executor

Install the software (as root) with the rpm command. After installation, the main executable is found under /opt/executor/bin, but symbolic links will be created under the /usr/local/bin directory. Although an SVGA version is included, the easiest way to run the executor command is during an X11 session. Start X, then type the following at the command line of a terminal to start the program:

 # executor &

A splash screen will appear, and then the main window will appear, as shown in Figure 28.3.

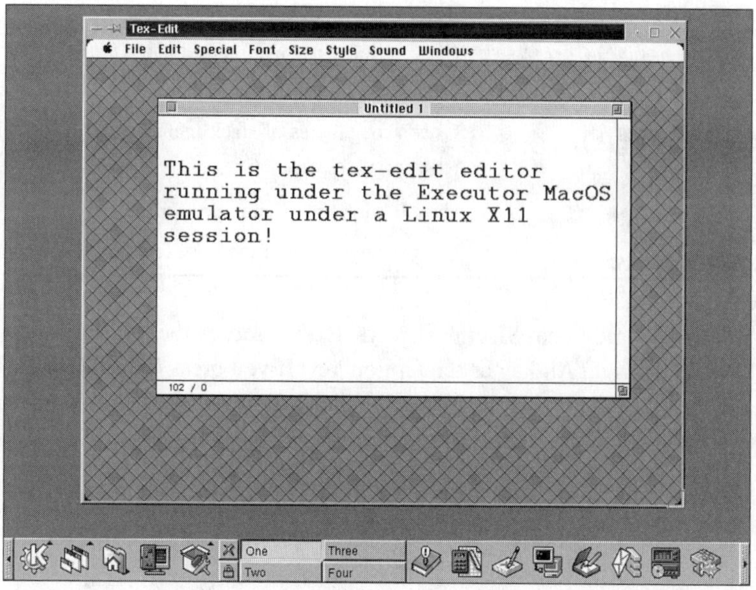

FIGURE 28.3

ARDI's Executor emulates a legacy Apple Macintosh and runs more than 300 different Macintosh applications.

The default screen size of the emulation window is 640×480, but you can alter this by using one of Executor's command-line switches, as shown in Table 28.2.

TABLE 28.2   Executor Command-Line Switches

Option	Action
applzone *n*[k]	Uses *n* kilobytes of memory for an application
applzone *n*[MB]	Uses *n* megabytes of memory for an application
bpp *n*	Uses *n* bits per pixel (1 or 8)
desparate	Minimalist mode (only for DOS)
geometry *heightxwidth*	Standard X geometry settings
grayscale	Uses grayscale when running
help	Prints help message on options and quits
info	Prints system information
keyboard *keyboard*	Uses specified *keyboard*
keyboards	Prints available keyboard maps
memory *n*	Creates *n* megabytes of use for system memory
nobrowser	Disables file browser when starting
nodiskcache	Disables internal disk cache
nodotfiles	Doesn't list filenames beginning with a period
nosound	Disables sound
privatecmap	Uses a private colormap for X
refresh *n*	Refreshes screen every *n*th of a second
size *heightxwidth*	Uses initial window of *height* and *width* pixels
stack *n*[k]	Uses *n* kilobytes of stack memory for the system
stack *n*[MB]	Uses *n* megabytes of stack memory for the system
sticky	Uses sticky menus
syszone *n*[k]	Uses *n* kilobytes of memory for the system
syszone *n*[MB]	Uses *n* megabytes of memory for the system

To emulate traditional Macintosh keys, Executor uses the left Alt key as the Command key and the right Alt key as the Option key. If you press Cmd+Shift+5 (left Alt+Shift+5), a preferences dialog box appears. The dialog box, which is shown in Figure 28.4, is used to set compatibility options.

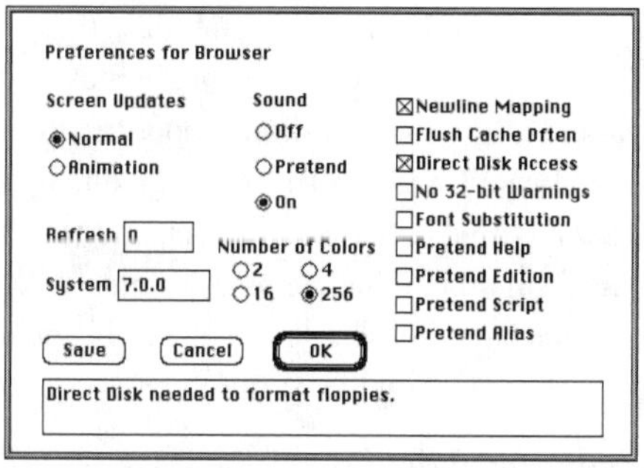

FIGURE 28.4

You can set System 7 compatibility options by using the left Alt+Shift+5 key combination.

```
Preferences for Browser

Screen Updates      Sound      ☒ Newline Mapping
 ⦿ Normal            ○ Off       ☐ Flush Cache Often
 ○ Animation         ○ Pretend   ☒ Direct Disk Access
                     ⦿ On        ☐ No 32-bit Warnings
 Refresh [0]                     ☐ Font Substitution
                     Number of Colors  ☐ Pretend Help
 System [7.0.0]      ○ 2    ○ 4          ☐ Pretend Edition
                     ○ 16   ⦿ 256        ☐ Pretend Script
  ( Save )  ( Cancel )  ( OK )           ☐ Pretend Alias

Direct Disk needed to format floppies.
```

Printing under Linux is supported through configuration of the `printers.ini` file found under the `/opt/executor` directory. The default output is PostScript, which will print through the `apsfilter` system using the `lpr` command.

VMware for Linux and Windows

VMware from VMware, Inc. is a software package for Linux, Win32 operating systems, and others that you can use to install and run an operating system using a virtual filesystem on your computer. This approach, similar to the hard drive image used by DOSEMU, can be used to install and run Linux under a Win32 operating system without partitioning the hard drive. It can also be used to install and run a Win32 operating system under Linux.

VMware for Linux is available for download on a limited trial basis. Unlike the free AT&T Laboratories Cambridge virtual network software (discussed in this chapter's "Windowing Network Clients" section), VMware is a commercial software package. This section discusses installing and running VMware under Linux, although VMware is available for other platforms. For details, browse to `http://www.vmware.com`.

The VMware software for Linux is distributed as a 6MB compressed archive, and requires at least a 266MHz processor and the X Window System.

Installing VMware for Linux

To install VMware under Linux, download the package and then decompress the archive with the **tar** command:

```
# tar xvzf vmware*gz
```

Navigate to the resulting `vmware-distrib` directory and run the file `vmware-install.pl` as root:

```
# ./vmware-install.pl
Creating a new installer database using the tar2 format.
Installing the content of the package

In which directory do you want to install the binary files?
[/usr/bin]
```

The installation script starts and you are asked where to install the binary files. By default, this location is the `/usr/bin` directory, but you can specify an alternate location, such as `/usr/local/bin`. You'll then be asked a series of questions about file locations, and will be asked to type **yes** to agree to the VMware End User License Agreement (EULA). The script then checks your system, builds any required software modules, and asks whether you'd like a closed or working networking configuration. (This helps determine whether to allow the installed operating system to communicate with other computers.) If you need networking support for your intended operating system, allow the script to enable networking support.

After you choose your configuration, the script installs the VMware software under the designated directories and exits. In order to run VMware, you must have a license file from VMware, Inc. This license can be obtained by registering at the VMware home page, and it will be emailed to you. When you receive the license, save the email message as a text file named `license`.

Next, use the **mkdir** command to create a directory in your home directory named `.vmware`. Copy the license into the `.vmware` directory:

```
# mkdir .vmware ; cp license .vmware
```

Starting and Configuring VMware

To start VMware, type **vmware** at the command line of your terminal window. (You do not need to be logged in as the `root` operator, but you will need read and write permission for the device `/dev/zero`.) The VMware configuration window and configuration dialog box appear, as shown in Figure 28.5.

FIGURE 28.5

Before you can install another operating system, you must first run VMware's Configuration Wizard.

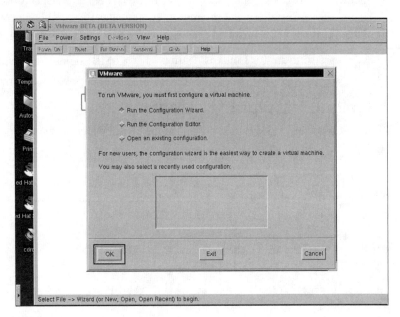

Click OK to continue. You'll see the Configuration Wizard screen. Click Next to continue, and you'll see a list of supported operating systems, as shown in Figure 28.6.

FIGURE 28.6

Use VMware's Configuration Wizard to select an operating system to install.

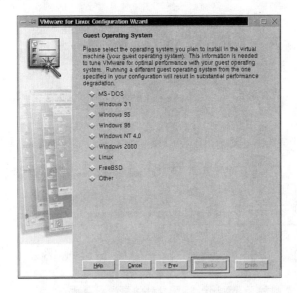

Note that you can even install another Linux distribution, or if you click Other, another UNIX variant, such as FreeBSD. To start your configuration, click the button next to an operating system, and then click Next. Throughout the configuration process, you can step forward or backward to change settings. After selecting your operating system, click Next.

> **Note**
>
> You can also use VMware to install and run several different operating systems simultaneously on your computer. In fact, it is even possible to install and run multiple operating systems at the same time on a single computer and then network the different operating systems. I guess this would be called a "LAN-in-a-box."

You are then asked to select the location of the virtual filesystem, a type of virtual disk, a file size for the new operating system's virtual disk, the CD-ROM and floppy device, and the type of networking, as shown in Figure 28.7.

FIGURE 28.7

Select a type of networking to restrict or allow your new operating system to communicate over a network.

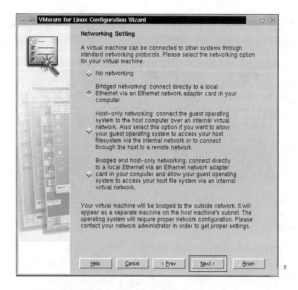

You are then asked to confirm your settings, as shown in Figure 28.8.

FIGURE 28.8

Confirm your configuration settings before using VMware.

After you click Done, you're ready to install an operating system.

Installing Your Operating System

To start the installation process, insert a floppy disk or CD-ROM into your computer and then click the Power On button in the VMware window. The software boots, as shown in Figure 28.9.

FIGURE 28.9

Power on VMware with an inserted floppy or CD-ROM operating system installation disk to install your new operating system.

Note that VMware comes with an industry-standard PC BIOS. Continue through and finish your operating system installation. The next time you start VMware, you'll be asked to select a desired configuration, usually found under the directory you designated when you configured your virtual machine. The configuration file will have a name ending in .cfg in the directory (usually under the vmware directory in your home directory or other volume). To start your session, select the file and then click the Power On button. Your operating system will boot, as shown in Figure 28.10.

When you click in the VMware window, your mouse will become "attached" to the operating system's window. To release your mouse, press Ctrl+Alt+Esc. When you're finished working with VMware, make sure to properly shut down the running operating system and then click the Power Off button in the VMware window.

For tips and hints on troubleshooting problems, or to learn more about VMware for other operating systems, browse to http://www.vmware.com.

28

EMULATORS, TOOLS, AND WINDOW CLIENTS

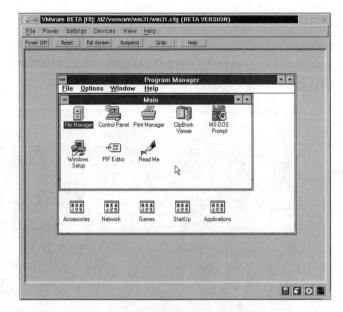

FIGURE 28.10
The VMware software supports many different types of operating systems, including legacy software such as the now-defunct Windows for Workgroups.

The mtools Package

The mtools package, originally by Emmet P. Gray and now maintained by Alain Knaff and David Niemi, is a public-domain set of programs you can use in just about any operation on MS-DOS floppies. The mtools package can help you when working with the DOS or Windows operating system while running Linux, and facilitate the transfer of information and manipulation of removable media for those operating systems.

These commands are useful because you don't need to reboot to DOS or Windows, run an emulator, or mount the floppy in order to read, write, or make changes to the floppy's contents. Table 28.3 lists the tools included in the package.

TABLE 28.3 mtools Package Contents

Program Name	Function
mattrib	Changes file attributes
mbadblocks	Floppy testing program
mcd	Changes directory command
mcheck	Checks a floppy
mcopy	Copies files to and from floppy disk
mdel	Deletes files on disk

TABLE 28.3   continued

Program Name	Function
mdeltree	Recursively deletes files and directories
mdir	Lists contents of a floppy
mformat	Formats a floppy
minfo	Categorizes, prints floppy characteristics
mkmanifest	Restores Linux filenames from floppy
mlabel	Labels a floppy
mmd	Creates subdirectory
mmount	Mounts a floppy
mmove	mv command for floppy files and directories
mpartition	Makes a DOS filesystem as a partition
mrd	Deletes directories
mren	Renames a file
mtoolstest	Tests mtools package installation
mtype	Types (lists) a file
mzip	ZIP/JAZ drive utility

The most often used will be the mformat, mdir, mcopy, and mdel commands. The mformat command formats nearly any type of floppy device. One of this software package's nice features is that you don't have to remember the specific names of floppy devices, such as /dev/fd0, and can use the (possibly) familiar A or B drive designators. This is possible because of mtool's use of the configuration file, /etc/mtools.conf.

Entries for different disk devices are listed in the file. You can edit the file (as root) to configure mtools for your system without having to rebuild the software. (If you need the source, however, you can readily find a copy on your favorite Linux site, or at ftp://ftp.tux.org/pub/knaff/mtools, along with numerous add-ons and utilities.) If you examine the /etc/mtools.conf file, you'll see entries for different devices and configurations for other operating systems. For example, the floppy device entries look like this:

```
# Linux floppy drives
drive a: file="/dev/fd0" exclusive 1.44m mformat_only
drive b: file="/dev/fd1" exclusive 1.44m mformat only
```

These entries allow you to easily format a floppy in drive A without mounting the disk:

```
# mformat a:
```

Note

In most Linux distributions, such as Red Hat's, strict read and write permissions are enforced on your system's devices. Some default mtools configurations can force you to use mtools as `root`. Although this is the safest and most secure approach, you can use the `chmod` command with 666 permissions to enable anyone to manipulate floppies, like this:

```
# chmod 666 /dev/fd0
```

Tip

The mtools distribution may also be broken! If you receive the error `mformat: Non-removable media is not supported (You must tell the complete geometry of the disk, either in /etc/mtools or on the command line)`, you'll need to fix the entry for your floppy drive in `/etc/mtools.conf`.

Log in as the `root` operator and then use your favorite text editor to change your floppy's `/etc/mtools.conf` entry from this

```
drive a: file="/dev/fd0" exclusive
```

to this

```
drive a: file="/dev/fd0" fat_bits=12 tracks=80 heads=2 sectors=18
```

Save the `/etc/mtools.conf` file. Details about creating custom device entries can be found in the mtools man page in section 5 of your Linux manual. Read the man page like this:

```
# man 5 mtools
```

After the `mformat` command has finished, you can copy files to and from the disk with the `mcopy` command. Here is an example:

```
# mcopy *.txt a:
```

This copies all files ending in `.txt` to your disk. To copy files from your disk, reverse the arguments (in DOS form) to the `mcopy` command:

```
# mcopy a:*.txt
```

This copies all files ending in `.txt` to the current directory, or to whatever directory you specify. To see what is on the disk, use the `mdir` command. Here is an example:

```
# mdir a

Volume in drive A has no label
Volume Serial Number is 4917-9EDD
```

```
Directory for A:/
launch   gif     62835 04-09-1999  13:43  launch.gif
vmware   gif     10703 04-09-1999  13:44  vmware.gif
vnc      gif     21487 04-09-1999  13:44  vnc.gif
         3 files             95 025 bytes
                          1 362 432 bytes free
```

You can use the `mlabel` command to label the disk:

```
# mlabel a:
 Volume has no label
Enter the new volume label : LINUX
```

You can also use special shell command-line quoting to label the disk from the command line:

```
# mlabel a:'DOS DISK'
```

This is a handy way to use spaces in a disk's label. If you want to delete files on your disk, use the `mdel` command:

```
# mdel a:*.txt
```

This deletes all files ending in `.txt` on the disk in the A drive. You can also mount your disk. For details, see the `mmount` command manual page, along with the `mount` command manual page.

Windowing Network Clients

While software and hardware emulators can ease many computing tasks, the demands on system resources such as memory or storage can be tremendous. If you have extra computers or work in a networked environment, an easier approach is to use the X Window system and networking protocols to communicate with other systems and run other clients.

Thanks to AT&T Laboratories Cambridge and Red Hat, Red Hat Linux users can now enjoy working on the desktops of foreign operating systems with relative ease through virtual networking computing. Even better news is that the software, called `vnc`, is available under the GNU General Public License with source code for Linux, comes with the latest version of Red Hat Linux, and if downloaded in source code form, readily builds and installs under Red Hat Linux.

The `vnc` Linux software consists of several major components: an X server named `Xvnc`, a server named `vncserver`, a password utility named `vncpasswd`, and a network communication viewer named `vncviewer`. The `vnc` software is also available for other computers and operating systems, such as these:

- DEC Alpha OSF1 3.2
- Macintosh OS (68K and PPC)

28

EMULATORS,
TOOLS, AND
WINDOW CLIENTS

- Solaris 2.5 (SPARC)
- Win32 (such as Windows 9x/2000/NT)
- Windows CE2 (for the SH3 and MIPS processors)

The latest version of this software is available at `http://www.uk.research.att.com/vnc`. A compressed archive of binaries for Linux is available, and you can download the 2.5MB UNIX source code tarball.

Building and Installing the vnc Software

This section details how to download and install the vnc software. If you download the binaries, decompress the file with the `tar` command:

```
# tar xvzf vnc-3.3.3r1_x86_linux_2.0.tgz
```

This creates a `vnc_x86_linux_2.0` directory. Read the included README file in the directory, and copy the files `Xvnc`, `vncserver`, `vncviewer`, and `vncpasswd` to the `/usr/local/bin` directory. If you install the vnc software from your Red Hat Linux CD-ROMs, you'll find the command under the `/usr/bin` directory. If you download the vnc source, decompress the archive with the `tar` command:

```
# tar xvzf vnc-3.3.3r1_unixsrc.tgz
```

This creates the `vnc_unixsrc` directory. Navigate into the directory and then start the build with the `xmkmf` command:

> **Note**
>
> The `xmkmf` command (actually a shell script) is installed from your CD-ROM when you install development software for the X Window System. You'll find `xmkmf`, along with other software tools such as `imake`, in the XFree86 RPM development archive. For more information about `xmkmf`, see Chapter 24, "Linux C/C++ Programming Tools."

```
# xmkmf
# make World
```

Navigate into the Xvnc directory and build the vnc X server like this:

```
# cd Xvnc
# make World
```

Finally, install the vnc software (as root) with the included installation script, specifying an installation directory:

```
# ./vncinstall /usr/local/bin
```

This completes your Linux software installation. However, if you want to work on the desktops of other computers, you need to download and install the vnc software for the desired platform. For example, if you want to work with a Windows 95 or Windows 98 desktop, download the Win32 vnc software onto the desired computer.

Enabling Virtual Network Service

The vnc server software must be started on a remote computer in order to work on the remote computer's desktop. Under Linux, this may be done through a Telnet session or by sitting at the console and starting the software.

To start the server for Linux, use the vncserver script from the command line:

```
# vncserver
You will require a password to access your desktops.
```

```
Password:
```

Enter a password used to allow remote access and press Enter. The script then loads and starts the Xvnc X11 server (a customized X11R6.3 server based on XFree86 3.3.2).

In order to start the vnc server software on a remote Windows computer, the vnc software for Win32 must be downloaded and copied onto the remote Windows computer. The Win32 software must then be extracted with an archive utility such as WinZip.

Decompress the Win32 vnc software and install the software using the vnc Setup. You can run Win32 vnc software as a server or as a program. To start the server, click the Install Default Registry Settings menu item from the vnc folder on your desktop's Start menu, then click the Install WinVNC Service menu item.

If you run WinVNC as a program, click the Run WinVNC (App Mode) menu item. You'll see a dialog, as shown in Figure 28.11.

Enter a password in the dialog, and click OK. If you need to customize your settings or change the password for access to the Win32 desktop, click the WinVNC settings menu item. That's all there is to do! From another computer on the network, use the vncviewer command, along with the server Display Number (default of 0 for Win32) and password to log in to your computer.

FIGURE 28.11

The Win32 vnc software provides easy-to-use dialogs and menus you can use to offer remote operation via your network.

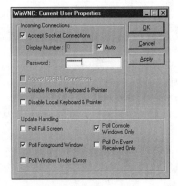

Viewing Remote Desktops

To view the remote Win32 desktop from Linux, use the vncviewer command, followed by the hostname or IP address of the Win32 computer. Type the command in an X11 terminal window like this:

```
# vncviewer thinkpad.home.org:0
```

You are prompted for the password of the remote vnc server:

```
vncviewer: VNC server supports protocol version 3.3 (viewer 3.3)
Password:
```

After you type in the password and press Enter, an X11 window appears with the remote desktop (as shown in Figure 28.12). You can then launch remote applications and work on the computer as if it were your own!

> **Note**
>
> The vncviewer client and vncserver script also recognize several X11 Toolkit options, such as geometry settings. For example, if you start the vncserver on a remote Linux computer (such as through a Telnet session), you can specify the size of remotely viewed desktops with the geometry option, followed by the size of the desktop in horizontal and vertical pixels. To start an 800×600-pixel server desktop, use vncserver like this:
>
> ```
> # vncserver -geometry 800x600 hostname:displaynumber
> ```
>
> When this desktop is viewed remotely from another computer, the desktop will use an 800×600 display. (The default size of a vnc desktop is 1,024×768 pixels.) For more information about X11 Toolkit options, see the X man page.

FIGURE 28.12

The Linux vncviewer *client launches and displays a remote Windows desktop session.*

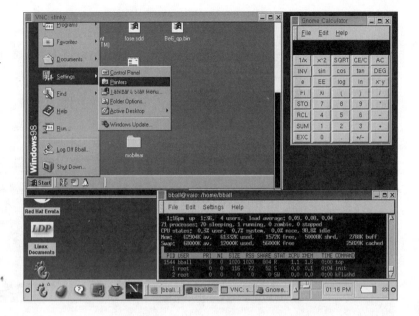

You can also use the vncviewer client on remote computers to view the Linux desktop. The settings and X resource files for the Linux vnc desktop may be quite different from your normal X session! Look in the .vnc directory for the file xstartup, which will look like this:

```
#!/bin/sh

xrdb $HOME/.Xresources
xsetroot -solid grey
xterm -geometry 80x24+10+10 -ls -title "$VNCDESKTOP Desktop" &
twm &
```

Note that only a single X terminal and the twm window manager are used! Edit this file to suit your needs. Of course, with all this flexibility, remote sessions can get a little confusing. For example, Figure 28.13 shows a remote computer using KDE for its X11 session; this session is being viewed by a Windows 98 desktop, which in turn is being remotely viewed through a Red Hat Linux GNOME Enlightenment X session!

FIGURE 28.13

A chain of three remote virtual network sessions can get a bit confusing, but works quite well thanks to the vnc software.

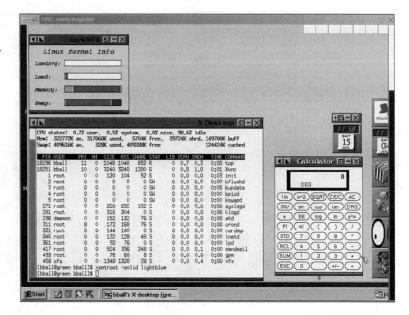

Summary

This chapter introduced you to a number of useful software tools that can be used to extend the Linux computing experience. Emulators or virtual networks can be used to add flexibility to your computing environment or to breathe new life into legacy operating systems and applications. As you can see, there are quite a few programs and suites of software available for Linux that interact and work with Apple Computer's MacOS and Microsoft's Windows operating systems. You'll also find a host of software tools that make life a lot easier when dealing with removable media (such as floppies) for other operating systems. It is up to you to explore the networking limits of these applications or to find new uses for older software through emulators.

Appendixes

PART V

The Linux
Documentation
Project

APPENDIX A

> **Note**
>
> According to Matt Welsh, the original maintainer of the LDP Web pages, LDP authors "wishing to send new or updated HOWTOs" (and other documentation) should send them to:
>
> `ldp-submit@lists.linuxdoc.org`
>
> There are also, according to Welsh, several mailing lists of interest about LDP. For general discussion concerning the LDP:
>
> `ldp-discuss@lists.linuxdoc.org`
>
> An announcement list concerning new LDP documents:
>
> `ldp-announce@lists.linuxdoc.org`
>
> An LDP author discussion list concerning the DocBook (SGML) format:
>
> `ldp-docbook@lists.linuxdoc.org`
>
> Authors or interested parties can subscribe to the lists by sending mail with the Subject: "subscribe" to:
>
> `list-name-REQUEST@lists.linuxdoc.org`
>
> For the latest information regarding the LDP, browse to:
>
> `http://www.linuxdoc.org`

Revised by: David S. Lawyer (`dave@lafn.org`)

Last Revision: 18 July 2000

Describes the goals, status, documentation conventions, and license requirements of the Linux Documentation Project.

1. Overview of The Linux Documentation Project

The Linux Documentation Project is working on developing free, high quality documentation for the GNU/Linux operating system. The overall goal of the LDP is to collaborate in all of the issues of Linux documentation. This includes the creation of "HOWTOs" and "Guides". We hope to establish a system of documentation for Linux that will be easy to use and search. This includes the integration of the manual pages, info docs, HOWTOs, and other documents.

LDP's goal is to create the canonical set of free Linux documentation. While online (and downloadable) documentation can be frequently updated in order to stay on top of the many changes in the Linux world, we also like to see the same docs included on CDs and printed in books. If you are interested in publishing any of the LDP works, see the section "Publishing LDP Documents", below.

The LDP is essentially a loose team of volunteers with minimal central organization. Anyone who would like to help is welcome to join in this effort. We feel that working together informally and discussing projects on our mailing lists is the best way to go. When we disagree on things, we try to reason with each other until we reach an informed consensus.

2. Current Projects and Getting Involved

Currently, the major effort of the LDP is the writing of HOWTOs. If you think you would like to write a certain HOWTO first check to see if one already exists on your topic. If so, you may contact the maintainer and offer to help. If there is no HOWTO about it, you may want to create a new HOWTO. See the LDP Author Guide (formerly the HOWTO-HOWTO) and/or the HOWTO-INDEX for more details.

The "Guides" are large book-size LDP documents covering broad topics such as system administration. We also maintain the man-pages for C-programming and devices.

Other tasks include checking the HOWTOs for clarity and errors, improving our website, and developing an integrated system of documentation for Linux. If you are interested in any such project (other than writing HOWTOs), contact the current LDP coordinator Guylhem Aznar at `guylhem@metalab.unc.edu` or email the LDP discussion list at `ldp-discuss@lists.linuxdoc.org`.

3. LDP Websites

The LDP has over 250 mirror sites worldwide where one may inspect and/or download LDP documents. The main site is `http://www.linuxdoc.org`. Go here to find the list of mirror sites and then use the nearest mirror site.

4. Documentation Conventions

Here are the conventions that are currently used for LDP documents. If you are interested in writing another document using different conventions, please let us know of your plans first.

A

THE LINUX DOCUMENTATION PROJECT

All HOWTO documents must be in one of the two SGML formats: LinuxDoc or DocBook. LinuxDoc is the simplest while DocBook is more complex with more features.

The guides - full books produced by the LDP - have historically been done in LaTeX, as their primary goal has been to be printed documentation. However, guide authors have been moving towards SGML with the DocBook DTD, because it allows them to create more different kinds of output, both printed and on-line. If you use LaTeX, we have a style file you can use to keep your printed look consistent with other LDP documents.

The man pages - the Unix standard for online manuals - are created with the Unix standard `nroff` man (or BSD `mdoc`) macros.

5. LICENSE REQUIREMENTS

Anyone may copy and distribute (sell or give away) LDP documents (or other LDP works) in any media and/or format. No fees are required to be paid to the authors. It is not required that the documents be modifiable, but it is encouraged.

You can come up with your own license terms that satisfy these conditions, or you can use a previously prepared license. The LDP has a boilerplate license that you can use if you wish. Some people like to use the GPL, while others write their own. There is a project underway to create a special GPL license just for documents and this may turn out to be a good choice.

The copyright for each document should be in the name of the principal authors. "The Linux Documentation Project" isn't a formal entity and thus can't be used as a copyright owner.

6. Boilerplate License

Here is a sample copyright notice and "boilerplate" license you may want to use for your work:

Copyright (c) 2000 by John Doe (change to your name)

Please freely copy and distribute (sell or give away) this document in any format. It's requested that corrections and/or comments be fowarded to the document maintainer. You may create a derivative work and distribute it provided that you:

1. Send your derivative work (in the most suitable format such as sgml) to the LDP (Linux Documentation Project) or the like for posting on the Internet. If not the LDP, then let the LDP know where it is available.

2. License the derivative work with this same license or use GPL. Include a copyright notice and at least a pointer to the license used.

3. Give due credit to previous authors and major contributors. If you're considering making a derived work other than a translation, it's requested that you discuss your plans with the current maintainer.

7. Publishing LDP Documents

If you're a publishing company interested in distributing any of the LDP documents, read on. By the license requirements given previously, anyone is allowed to publish and distribute verbatim copies of the Linux Documentation Project documents. You don't need our explicit permission for this. However, if you would like to distribute a translation or derivative work based on any of the LDP documents, you may need to obtain permission from the author, in writing, before doing so, if the license requires that.

You may, of course, sell the LDP documents for profit. We encourage you to do so. Keep in mind, however, that because the LDP documents are freely distributable, anyone may make copies and distribute them. Thus the parts of a book which may be freely copied should be separated (and identified) in such a manner as to facilitate copying them without infringing on the copyright of other material.

We do not require you to pay royalties from any profit earned by selling LDP documents. However, we would like to suggest that if you do sell LDP documents for profit, that you either offer the author royalties, or donate a portion of your earnings to the author, the LDP as a whole, or to the Linux development community. You may also wish to send one or more free copies of the LDP documents that you are distributing to the authors. Your show of support for the LDP and the Linux community will be very much appreciated.

We would like to be informed of any plans to publish or distribute LDP documents, just so we know how they're becoming available. If you are publishing or planning to publish any LDP documents, please send mail to ldp-discuss@lists.linuxdoc.org. It's nice to know who's doing what.

We encourage Linux software distributors to distribute the LDP documents on CDs with their software. The LDP documents are intended to be used as "official" Linux documentation, and we are glad to see distributors bundling the LDP documents with the software.

A

THE LINUX DOCUMENTATION PROJECT

Top Linux Commands and Utilities

In This Appendix

This appendix is not meant to replace the man pages and does not detail all of the options for each command. You will find most of the information you need in the man pages for these programs or, in the case of a shell operator such as > or <, in the man pages for the shell commands. This appendix is designed to give you a feel for the commands and a brief description as to what they do. In most cases, more parameters are available than are shown here.

Many descriptions also have examples. If these examples are not self-evident, an explanation is provided. This is not an exhaustive list—Red Hat Linux comes with many more commands—but these are the most common, and you will find yourself using them over and over again.

To keep things simple, the commands are listed in alphabetical order; however, the list starts with what are usually the 10 most common commands—they are also listed alphabetically. This list of essential commands could be compared to a list of the top 10 words spoken by the cavemen when searching for food and a mate:

- cat
- cd
- cp
- find
- grep

- ls
- more
- rm
- vi
- who

General Guidelines

Many of the programs distributed with Red Hat Linux descended from counterparts in the UNIX world and have inherited the terse, sometimes cryptic naming style. In general, if you want to change something that already exists, the command with which to do that usually begins with ch. If you want to do something for the first time, the command usually begins with mk. If you want to undo something completely, the command usually begins with rm. For example, you use the mkdir command to make a new directory, and you use the rmdir command to remove a directory.

The List

The commands listed in this appendix are some of the most common commands used in Red Hat Linux. An example is provided in cases where the command seems ambiguous. With each of these commands, the man pages can provide additional information, as well as more examples.

Remember that the GUI environments (like GNOME and KDE) provide tools that supplement or replace many of the commands listed. GUI tools are easier to learn but command-line environments tend to be more flexible and faster once you learn them.

If your focus is general UNIX, you will want to learn the regular commands since the wonderful tools in the GUI environments are not available in most versions of UNIX.

It is very important that you remember that Linux installation is configurable. That means that you get to select (configure or pick) the tools and utilities that are loaded during the install. If you find a command in this section that does not work on your machine, it is most likely that you have not loaded it.

.

The . shell command tells the shell to execute all of the commands in the file that are passed an argument to the command. This works in `bash` or `pdksh`. The equivalent in `tcsh` is the `source` command. The following example executes the command `adobe`:

```
. adobe
```

&

The & shell operator that is inserted after any other command tells the computer to run the command in the background. By placing a job in the background, the user can continue using that shell to process other commands. If the command is run in the foreground, the user cannot continue using that shell until the process finishes.

|

The | (pipe) shell operator is used between separate programs on the command line to "pipe" the output of one command to another. This type of operation is one of the principal strengths of Linux and the shell and can be used to construct complex commands from a series of simple programs. For example, you can pipe the output of the `cat` command through the `sort` command to sort the contents of a file:

```
# cat long_list.txt | sort
```

>

The > (standard output) shell operator sends the output of a program to a file or other device. Use this operator with caution: It will overwrite an existing file! To save a listing of the current directory to a text file, use the > operator like this:

```
# ls > dir.txt
```

Note that if the file `dir.txt` exists, it will be erased and overwritten with the new contents! Also, because Linux works much like other versions of UNIX, you can send the contents of programs directly to a device:

```
# cat welcome.au >/dev/audio
```

This plays a sound file by sending it directly to a Linux audio device.

<

The < (standard input) shell operator is used to feed a program the contents of a file or input from another device or source. For example, you can use this operator like the `cat` command to sort a file and save the results:

```
# sort < unsorted.txt > sorted.txt
```

>>

The >> (append) shell operator will not replace a designated file, but appends the output of a program onto the end of a specified file. This can be used, for example, to build log files:

```
# cat newfile.txt >> oldfile.txt
```

The contents of `newfile.txt` will not overwrite `oldfile.txt`, but will append to the end of it.

<<

The << (known as "here document") shell operator is used to tell a program when end-of-input is reached. For example, to use the shell as a text editor, tell the shell to stop accepting input when the word `end` is used like this:

```
# > document.txt << end
This is a line of text.
end
```

After you type the word end, the shell saves your text into the file `document.txt` because you told the shell that the word end terminates input.

adduser

The `adduser` command used by `root` (or someone else who has the authority) creates a new user. The `adduser` command is followed by the account name to be created:

```
# adduser dpitts
```

alias

The `alias` command is used to make aliases or alternative names for commands. Typically, these aliases are abbreviations of the actual commands. In the following example, the user (probably a DOS user) is adding an alias of `dir` for a directory listing:

```
alias dir=ls
```

Typing `alias` by itself gives you a list of all of your current aliases. Such a list might look like this:

```
svr01:/home/dpitts$ alias
alias d='dir'
alias dir='/bin/ls $LS_OPTIONS --format=vertical'
alias ls='/bin/ls $LS_OPTIONS'
alias v='vdir'
alias vdir='/bin/ls $LS_OPTIONS --format=long'
```

apropos *parameter*

apropos literally means appropriate or regarding (others). When followed by a parameter, apropos searches the man pages for entries that include the parameter, performing a keyword search on all of the man pages. This is the equivalent of the `man -k parameter` command.

ash

ash is a simple shell with features much like the `sh`, or Bourne shell. The `ash` shell is run by the symbolic link `bsh`, which is found under the `/bin` directory.

at

at runs a program at a specified time. You can use the `at` command to schedule a task or job to run at a time you specify on the command line or in a file.

atq

Use atq to list the queue of waiting jobs. The `atq` command prints a list of waiting jobs or events for the at command (usually found under the `/var/spool/at` directory).

atrm

Use atrm to remove a specified job. The `atrm` command removes one or several jobs waiting in the at queue. The `atrm` command can be used by users or the `root` operator to delete pending events (stop at commands from running).

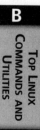

banner

banner prints a large, high-quality banner to the standard output. If the message is omitted, banner prompts for and reads one line from the standard input. For example, enter $ banner hi to create the following banner:

```
   ##                                                              ###
   ##                                                              ###
   ########################################################
   ########################################################
   ########################################################
   ########################################################
   ########################################################
   ##                               ###
                                    ###
                                    ###
                                    ####
                                    ####
                                    ####
   ##                        ######
   ##############################
   ##############################
   ##############################
   #########################
   #######################
   ##
   ##                              ##
   ##                              ##            ####
   ##############################          ########
   ##############################          ########
   ##############################          ########
   ##############################           ######
   ##############################            ####
   ##
```

bash

bash is the GNU Bourne Again Shell. The default shell for Red Hat Linux, bash has many features, such as command-line editing, built-in help, and command history. The bash shell is run by the symbolic link sh, which is found under the /bin directory.

batch

The batch command runs jobs according to load average. This program is used to run events when the computer reaches a certain load average, as determined by real-time values found in the loadavg file in the /proc directory. batch also has other options; read the at command manual pages for details.

bc

A calculator language, bc is an interpreter and language for building calculator programs and tools. You can use this interpreter and language to program custom calculators.

bg

The bg command is used to force a suspended process to run in the background. Assume you have started a command in the foreground (without using the & after the command) and realize it is going to take a while, but you still need your shell. You can use Ctrl+Z to place the current process on hold. Then you can either leave it on hold—just as if you called your telephone company—or you can type **bg** to place that process in the background and free your shell to allow you to execute other commands.

bind

Used in pdksh, the bind command enables the user to change the behavior of key combinations for the purpose of command-line editing. Many times people bind the up, down, left, and right arrow keys so they work the way they would in the Bourne Again Shell (bsh). The syntax used for the command is as follows:

```
bind key sequence command
```

The following examples are the bind commands to create bindings for scrolling up and down the history list and for moving left and right along the command line:

```
bind `^[[`=prefix-2
bind `^XA`=up-history
bind `^XB`=down-history
bind `^XC`=forward-char
bind `^XD`=backward-char
```

cat

cat concatenates text files and sends them to stdout. If the file contains binary data instead of text, cat acts like it has a hairball and shows the data in the file to you on the screen (even though it is not something that you can really read). You can also redirect the output of cat to a file. As you might have surmised, the cat command requires something to display and has the following format:

```
cat <filename
```

cd

cd stands for *change directory*. You will find this command extremely useful. The three typical ways of using this command are

`cd ..`	Moves one directory up the directory tree.
`cd ~`	Moves to your home directory from wherever you currently are. This is the same as issuing `cd` by itself.
`cd directory name`	Changes to a specific directory. This can be a directory relative to your current location or can be based on the `root` directory by placing a forward slash (`/`) before the directory name.

These examples can be combined. For example, suppose you are in the directory `/home/dsp1234` and want to go to `tng4321`'s home account. You can perform the following command to move back up the directory one level and then down into the `tng4321` directory:

```
cd ../tng4321
```

chfn

The `chfn` command changes finger information. You can use this command to enter or update information used by the finger networking tool from the `/etc/passwd` entry for your Linux system. You can enter full names, offices, and office and home phone numbers. Follow `chfn` by a user's name:

```
# chfn willie
```

chgrp

The `chgrp` command is used to change the group associated with the permissions of the file or directory. The file's owner (and, of course, `root`) has the authority to change the group associated with the file. The format for the command is simply this:

```
chgrp <new group> <file>
```

chmod

The `chmod` command is used to change the permissions associated with the object (typically a file or directory). What you are really doing is changing the file mode. You can specify the permissions of the object in two ways: by the numeric coding system or by the letter coding system. If you recall, three sets of users are associated with every object: the owner of the object, the group for the object, and everybody else. Using the letter coding system, they are referred to as u for user, g for group, o for other, and a for all. The three basic types of permissions you can change are r for read, w for write, and x for execute. These three permissions can be changed by using the plus (+) and minus (-) signs. For example, you would issue the following command to add read and execute to owner and group of the file test1:

```
chmod ug+rx test1
```

To remove the read and execute permissions from the user and group of the test1 file, you would change the plus (+) sign to a minus (-) sign:

```
chmod ug-rx test1
```

This is referred to as making *relative changes* to the mode of the file.

When using the numeric coding system, you always have to give the absolute value of the permissions, regardless of their previous permissions. The numeric system is based on three sets of base 2 numbers—one set for each category of user, group, and other. The values are 4, 2, and 1, where 4 equals *read*, 2 equals *write*, and 1 equals *execute*. These values are added together to give the set of permissions for that category. With numeric coding, you always specify all three categories. Therefore, to give read, write, and execute permissions to the owner of the file test1, and no permissions to anyone else, you would use the value 700, like this:

```
chmod 700 test1
```

To make the same file readable and writable by the user, and readable by both the group and others, you would use the following mathematical logic. For the first set of permissions—the user—the value for readable is 4 and the value for writable is 2. The sum of these two is 6. The next set of permissions—the group—only gets readable, so that is 4. The setting for others, as for the group, is 4. Therefore, the command would be as follows:

```
chmod 644 test1
```

The format for the command, using either method, is the same. You issue the chmod command followed by the permissions, either absolute or relative, followed by the objects for which you want the mode changed:

```
chmod <permissions> <file>
```

chown

This command is used to change the user ID (owner) associated with the permissions of the file or directory. The owner of the file (and, of course, root) has the authority to change the user associated with the file. The format for the command is simply this:

```
chown new user id file
```

chroot

The `chroot` command makes the / directory (called the `root` directory) be something other than / on the filesystem. For example, when working with an Internet server, you can set the `root` directory to equal `/usr/ftp`. Then, anyone who logs on using FTP (which goes to the `root` directory by default) will actually go to the directory `/usr/ftp`. This protects the rest of your directory structure from being seen or even changed by this anonymous guest to your machine. If someone were to enter `cd /etc`, the ftp program would try to put her in the `root` directory and then in the `etc` directory off of that. Because the `root` directory is `/usr/ftp`, the ftp program will actually put the user in the `/usr/ftp/etc` directory (assuming there is one).

The syntax for the command is this:

```
chroot original filesystem location new filesystem location
```

chsh

You can use this program to change the type of shell you use when you log into your Linux system. The shell must be available on the system and must be allowed by the `root` operator by having its name listed in the `/etc/shells` file. Type the name of a shell, following the `chsh` command:

```
# chsh zsh
```

control-panel

The `control-panel` command is one of several Red Hat Linux system administration tools. This command is an X11 client (actually a Python language script) used to display several system administration tools, such as timetool, netcfg, or modemtool.

cp

The `cp` command is an abbreviation for copy; therefore, this command enables you to copy objects. For example, to copy the file `file1` to `file2`, issue the following command:

```
cp file1 file2
```

As the example shows, the syntax is very simple:

```
cp original object name new object name
```

cpio

The `cpio` command copies files in and out of file archives. `cpio` works much like the `tar` (tape archive) command, but with a slightly different syntax. Many Red Hat Linux users are more familiar with the `tar` command.

crond

This is the `cron` daemon. This program, started when you first boot Linux, scans the `/etc/crontab` file and the `/var/spool/cron` directory, looking for regularly scheduled jobs entered by the `root` operator or other system users. It is started when you first boot Linux.

crontab

The `crontab` command, not to be confused with the `/etc/crontab` file, is used by your system's users to schedule personal cron events. The cron files are stored under the `/var/spool/cron` directory. System administrators can control whether this facility exists on the system through the `/etc/cron.allow` and `/etc/cron.deny` files. All current jobs are listed when the `crontab` command is used with the `-l` option. Use the `-e` option to create or edit a job, and the `-r` option to delete a job.

cu

`cu` is a communications program used to call up other computers. This program is text-based and is not as user-friendly as the `minicom` or `seyon` communications programs for Linux.

cut

This program cuts specified columns or fields from input text. The `cut` command, a text filter, can be used to manipulate the output of other text utilities or contents of your files by selectively displaying fields of text.

dc

`dc` is a command-line desk calculator. This calculator, which does not have a graphical interface, uses reverse-polish notation to perform calculations entered from the command line or a file.

dd

The `dd` command converts file formats. For example, to copy a boot image to a disk (assuming the device name for the disk is `/dev/fd0`), you issue this command:

```
dd if=filename of=/dev/fd0 obs=18k
```

`filename` might be `BOOT0001.img`, `of` is the object format (what you are copying to), and `obs` is the output block size.

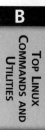

df

Use the df command to show the amount of free disk space on any currently mounted filesystem. This information is useful in determining whether you have available storage for programs or data.

dir

dir lists the contents of directories. This command has many of the same command-line options as the ls command.

display

This program requires X11 and is part of the ImageMagick package. This is a menu-driven application you can use to create, edit, change, print, and save graphics during your X11 session. ImageMagick is typically started in the background from the command line of a terminal window like this:

```
# display &
```

dmesg

The dmesg command prints a system boot log, dmesg, found in the /var/log directory. This program is handy to diagnose system problems, listing software services and hardware devices found while your system is starting.

du

The du command shows how much disk space is used by various files or directories, and can show where the most or least disk space is used on your system.

dump

The dump command, usually used by the root operator, creates a backup of either the whole filesystem or selected directories. The companion program to the dump command is the restore command, which extracts files and directories from a dump backup.

echo

echo echoes a string to the display. The echo command is generally used to print lines of text to your display console or—through redirection—to files, devices, programs, or the standard output of your shell. The -e option lets you use certain control characters in your output string.

ed

ed is a bare-bones line editor.

edquota

The edquota program, meant to be used by the root operator, is used to change the amount of disk space a user can use. It is used in conjunction with the quota, quotaon, or quotaoff commands.

efax

This is a communications program for sending and receiving faxes under Linux. This command is part of the efax software package and does the actual sending and receiving when called by the shell script fax.

efix

efix is used to convert files between text and fax graphics formats. The efix program is called by the shell script fax to convert sent or received fax documents.

elm

elm is a mail-handling program you can use to create, compose, edit, and send mail. You can organize your mail into different folders and also organize how your want your incoming mail to be filed. This program is similar to the pine mail program.

emacs

emacs is the GNU text (edit macros) editor. It can be used not only to edit text files but also as a calendar, diary, and appointment scheduler (and much more). emacs is also a complete environment to support programming and electronic mail.

emacs-nox

emacs-nox is the non-X11 version of the emacs editor.

env

The env command is used to see the exported environment variables. The result of the command is a two-column list in which the variable's name is on the left and the value

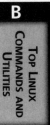

associated with that variable is on the right. The command is issued without any parameters. Hence, typing **env** might get you a list similar to this one:

```
svr01:/home/dpitts$ env
HOSTNAME=svr01.mk.net
LOGNAME=dpitts
MAIL=/var/spool/mail/dpitts
TERM=vt100
HOSTTYPE=i386
PATH=/usr/local/bin:/usr/bin:/bin:.:/usr/local/java/bin
HOME=/home2/dpitts
SHELL=/bin/bash
LS_OPTIONS=--8bit --color=tty -F -b -T 0
PS1=\h:\w\$
PS2=>
MANPATH=/usr/local/man:/usr/man/preformat:/usr/man:/usr/lib/perl5/man
LESS=-MM
OSTYPE=Linux
SHLVL=1
```

ex

ex is a symbolic link to the vim editor. In this mode, the vim editor emulate the ex line editor.

fax

Use fax to create, transmit, receive, display, or print a fax. This complex shell script is the driver program for the efax software package and provides an easy-to-use way to send or receive fax documents under Linux.

faxq

Use faxq to list faxes in the fax-sending queue. This program is part of the mgetty+send-fax software package for allowing Linux logins and fax transmission and reception.

faxrm

Use faxrm to delete faxes in the sending queue. You can use this program, part of mgetty+sendfax, to delete faxes waiting to be sent.

faxrunq

faxrunq sends spooled faxes from the fax queue. This program, run by the root operator or process, sends faxes waiting in the fax queue, usually the /var/spool/fax directory.

faxspool

`faxspool` prepares and sends fax documents to the fax queue. This shell script is a driver program for the mgetty+sendfax program and recognizes nine different file formats when converting and sending documents.

fc

The `fc` command is used to edit the history file. The parameters passed to it, if there are any, can be used to select a range of commands from the history file. This list is then placed in an editing shell. Which editor `fc` uses is based on the value of the variable `FCEDIT`. If no value is present for this variable, the command looks at the `EDITOR` variable. If it is not there, the default (`vi`) is used.

fdformat

This command only performs a low-level format of a floppy disk. You must then use the `mkfs` command to place a specified filesystem on the disk.

fetchmail

This program gets your mail from your Internet service provider and can handle a number of electronic mail protocols besides the Post Office Protocol, or POP. You use this program by itself or in a shell script to get your mail after you establish a Point-to-Point, or PPP, connection.

fg

Processes can be run in either the background or the foreground. The `fg` command enables you to take a suspended process and run it in the foreground. This is typically used when you have a process running in the foreground and need to suspend it for some reason (thus allowing you to run other commands). The process will continue until you either place it in the background or bring it to the foreground.

file

The `file` command tests each argument passed to it for one of three things: the filesystem test, the magic number test, or the language test. The first test to succeed causes the file type to be printed. If the file is text (an ASCII file), it guesses which language. A *magic number file* is a file that has data in particular, fixed formats. Here is an example for checking the file nquota to see what kind of file it is:

```
file nquota
```

Which identifies the file `nquota` as a text file that contains Perl commands:

```
nquota: perl commands text
```

find

Did you ever say to yourself, "Self, where did I put that file?" Now, instead of talking to yourself and causing those nearby to wonder, you can ask the computer. The `find` command looks in whatever directory you specify, as well as all subdirectories under that directory, for the file you specify. After it finds this list, it follows your instructions about what to do with the list. Typically, you just want to know where it is, so you ask it, nicely, to print out the list. The syntax of the command is the command itself, followed by the directory you want to start searching in, followed by the filename (metacharacters are acceptable), and then what you want done with the list. In the following example, the `find` command searches for files ending with `.pl` in the current directory (and all subdirectories). It then prints the results to standard output.

```
find . -name *.pl -print
./public_html/scripts/gant.pl
./public_html/scripts/edit_gant.pl
./public_html/scripts/httools.pl
./public_html/scripts/chart.no.comments.pl
```

finger

Use the `finger` command to look up user information (usually found in the `/etc/passwd` file) on your computer or other computer systems.

fmt

`fmt` formats input text into page and line sizes you specify on the command line.

free

The `free` command shows how memory is being used on your system.

ftp

This is the File Transfer Protocol program. You can use the `ftp` command to send and receive files interactively from your computer's hard drive or other remote computer systems. The `ftp` command features built-in help. To see the latest offerings from Macmillan Publishing, try this:

```
# ftp ftp.mcp.com
```

glint

This X11 client can be called from the command line or the Control Panel and uses the rpm command, or Red Hat Package Manager, to control the software installed on your system. glint presents a graphical interface for software installation, maintenance, or removal. It is usually started in the background:

```
# glint &
```

gnuplot

gnuplot, which can generate graphic displays of mathematical formulas or other data under the X Window System, supports a variety of displays and printers. You can use this program to visualize equations and other data.

grep

The grep (global regular expression parse) command searches the object you specify for the text you specify. The syntax of the command is grep *text file*. In the following example, I am searching for instances of the text httools in all files in the current directory:

```
grep httools *
edit_gant.cgi:require 'httools.pl';
edit_gant.pl:require 'httools.pl';
gant.cgi:    require 'httools.pl';  # Library containing reusable code
gant.cgi:        &date;     # Calls the todays date subroutine from httools.pl
gant.cgi:        &date;    #  Calls the todays date subroutine from httools.pl
gant.cgi:    &header;  # from httools.pl
```

Although this is valuable, the grep command can also be used in conjunction with the results of other commands. For example, the following command calls for the grep command to take the output of the ps command and take out all instances of the word root (the -v means everything but the text that follows):

```
ps -ef |grep -v root
```

The same command without the -v (ps -ef |grep root) returns all instances that contain the word root from the process listing.

groff

groff is the front end to the groff document-formatting program. This program, by default, calls the troff program.

gs

This is the Ghostscript interpreter. This program can interpret and prepare PostScript documents and print on more than three dozen displays and printers.

gunzip

Use this program to decompress files compressed with the gzip command back to their original form.

gv

A PostScript and PDF document previewer, this X11 client previews and prints PostScript and portable document files and is handy for reading documentation or pre-viewing graphics or documents before printing. Start the gv client by itself in the background, or specify a file on the command line like this:

```
# gv myPostScriptdoc.ps &
```

gvim

This program is a graphical version of the vim editor and is used under the X Window System.

gzip

gzip is GNU's version of the zip compression software. The syntax can be as simple as this:

```
gzip filename
```

It also many times contains some parameters between the command and the filename to be compressed.

halt

The halt command tells the kernel to shut down. This is a superuser-only command. (You must be root.)

head

The head command is a text filter, similar to the tail command, but prints only the number of lines you specify from the beginnings of files.

hostname

hostname is used to either display the current host or domain name of the system or to set the hostname of the system. Here is an example:

```
svr01:/home/dpitts$ hostname
svr01
```

ical

This is an X11 calendar program. The ical client can be used to create and maintain personal or group calendars and to schedule alarms or reminders of important dates or appointments. The calendar files can be printed, along with custom versions of multiday calendars.

ifconfig

This is one of several programs you can use to configure network interfaces. Although usually used by the root operator, the ifconfig command can be handy to use as a check on currently used network interfaces and lists a snapshot of the interfaces and traffic on the interface at the time the program is run.

irc

The Internet Relay Chat program. You can use irc to communicate interactively with other persons on the Internet. The irc program has built-in help and features a split-window display so you can read ongoing discussions and type your own messages to other people.

ispell

This flexible, interactive spelling checker is used by emacs and other text editors under Linux to check the spelling of text documents. You can also use ispell like the traditional UNIX spell command by using the -l command-line option:

```
# ispell -l < document.txt
```

jed

This editor can emulate the emacs, Wordstar, and Brief editors. The X11 version is called xjed.

jmacs

This version of the joe editor emulates the emacs editor and uses its keyboard commands.

joe

joe is a recursive acronym, in the GNU tradition, for *Joe's own editor*. It is a very small (160k) and very fast full-screen editor; joe is a popular alternative to vi.

This editor features online help, multiple document editing in split screen, fast search and replace, keystroke macros, bookmarks, and hooks to allow running external filters— for compiling projects or for running ispell, as examples.

jpico

This version of the joe editor emulates the pico editor included in the pine mail program distribution.

jstar

A Wordstar-compatible version of the joe editor. This editor uses keyboard commands, such as the famous Control-key diamond (e,s,d,x) for cursor movement, and emulates most other keyboard commands.

kill

kill sends the specified signal to the specified process. If no signal is specified, the TERM (15) signal is sent. The TERM signal kills processes that do not process the TERM signal. For processes that do process the TERM signal, you might need to use the KILL (9) signal because it cannot be caught. The syntax for the kill command is kill *option pid*, and an example follows:

```
svr01:/home/dpitts$kill -9 1438
```

kwrite

kwrite (also known on the KDE menu as "Advanced Editor") is a language-sensitive editor that highlights your program code to make it easier to distinguish various language components. It also will auto-indent your code for you. This editor behaves a lot like some of the IDE (Integrated Development Environment) tools on other platforms. The languages KDE recognizes include C, C++, Java, HTML, Bash, Perl, Latex, and others.

less

less is a program similar to more, but allows backward as well as forward movement in the file. less does not have to read the entire input file before starting, so with large input files it starts up faster than text editors such as vi.

ln

The ln command is used to make a copy of a file that is either a shortcut (symbolic link) or a duplicate file (hard link) to a file. Use the ls command's -1 option to see which files in a directory are symbolic links.

locate

The locate program prints locations of files. You can use this command to quickly find files on your system because it uses a single database of file locations in the locatedb database under the /var/lib directory.

login

login is used when signing on to a system. It can also be used to switch from one user to another at any time.

logout

logout is used to sign off a system as the current user. If it is the only user you are logged in as, you are logged off the system.

look

The look command is used to search text files for matching lines for a given string. You can also use this command to quickly look up the spelling of a word. The default file it searches is the system dictionary, found under the /usr/dict directory.

lpc

lpc is used by the system administrator to control the operation of the line printer system. lpc can be used to disable or enable a printer or a printer's spooling queue, to rearrange the order of jobs in a spooling queue, as well as to determine the status of printers, of the spooling queues, and of the printer daemons. The lpc command can be used for any of the printers configured in /etc/printcap.

lpd

lpd is the line printer daemon and is normally invoked at boot time from the rc file. lpd makes a single pass through the /etc/printcap file to find out about the existing printers and prints any files left after a crash. It then uses the system calls listen and accept to receive requests to print files in the queue, transfer files to the spooling area, display the queue, or remove jobs from the queue.

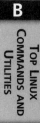

lpq

lpq examines the spooling area used by lpd for printing files on the line printer and reports the status of the specified jobs or all jobs associated with a user. If invoked without any arguments, lpq reports on any jobs currently in the print queue.

lpr

The line printer command uses a spooling daemon to print the named files when facilities become available. The standard input is assumed if no names appear. The following is an example of the lpr command:

```
lpr /etc/hosts
```

lprm

The lprm command removes a print job from the document queue. This program is used to stop a print job by specifying its job number on the command line. The following example stops print job 28 (which was shown by the lpq command):

```
# lprm 28
```

ls

The ls command lists the contents of a directory. The output's format is manipulated with options. The ls command with no options lists all visible files (a file that begins with a dot is a hidden file) in alphabetical order, filling as many columns as fit in the window. Probably the most common set of options used with this command is the -la option. The a means list all (including hidden) files, and the l means make the output a long listing. Here is an example of this command:

```
svr01:~$ ls -la
total 35
drwxr-xr-x   7 dpitts    users        1024 Jul 21 00:19 ./
drwxr-xr-x 140 root      root         3072 Jul 23 14:38 ../
-rw-r--r--   1 dpitts    users        4541 Jul 23 23:33 .bash_history
-rw-r--r--   1 dpitts    users          18 Sep 16  1996 .forward
-rw-r--r--   2 dpitts    users         136 May 10 01:46 .htaccess
-rw-r--r--   1 dpitts    users         164 Dec 30  1995 .kermrc
-rw-r--r--   1 dpitts    users          34 Jun  6  1993 .less
-rw-r--r--   1 dpitts    users         114 Nov 23  1993 .lessrc
-rw-r--r--   1 dpitts    users          10 Jul 20 22:32 .profile
drwxr-xr-x   2 dpitts    users        1024 Dec 20  1995 .term/
drwx------   2 dpitts    users        1024 Jul 16 02:04 Mail/
drwxr-xr-x   2 dpitts    users        1024 Feb  1  1996 cgi-src/
-rw-r--r--   1 dpitts    users        1643 Jul 21 00:23 hi
-rwxr-xr-x   1 dpitts    users         496 Jan  3  1997 nquota*
drwxr-xr-x   2 dpitts    users        1024 Jan  3  1997 passwd/
drwxrwxrwx   5 dpitts    users        1024 May 14 20:29 public_html/
```

lynx

The `lynx` browser is a fast, compact, and efficient text-only Web browser with nearly all the capabilities of other Web browsers. Start `lynx` from the command line of your console or an X11 terminal window, specifying a Web address:

```
# lynx http://www.mcp.com
```

mail

This program provides a bare-bones interface to sending, handling, or reading mail, but can be very handy when sending one-line mail messages from the command line. You may prefer using the Pine mail program instead.

make

The `make` utility automatically determines which pieces of a large program need to be recompiled and to then issue the commands necessary to recompile them.

makewhatis

The `makewhatis` command builds the `whatis` command database, which is located in the `/usr/man` directory. Look at the `whatis` command database for more information on the `whatis` command database.

man

The `man` command is used to format and display the online manual pages. In the following example, I have called the man page that describes the man pages:

```
svr01:~$ man man
man(1)                                                      man(1)


NAME
       man - format and display the on-line manual pages
       manpath - determine user's search path for man pages
SYNOPSIS
       man  [-adfhktwW]  [-m system] [-p string] [-C config_file]
       [-M path] [-P pager] [-S section_list] [section] name  ...

DESCRIPTION
       man  formats  and displays the on-line manual pages.  This
       version knows about the MANPATH and PAGER  environment
       variables, so you can have your own set(s) of personal man
       pages and choose whatever program you like to display  the
       formatted  pages.  If section is specified, man only looks
       in that section of the manual.  You may also  specify  the
```

```
order to search the sections for entries and which prepro-
cessors to run on the source files via command line
options or environment variables. If name contains a /
then it is first tried as a filename, so that you can do...
```

mcopy

The mcopy command is part of the mtools software package and copies files to and from DOS-formatted disks without having to mount the disk drive first.

mdel

This command, part of the mtools package, deletes files from a DOS disk without mounting the disk drive.

mdir

The mdir command lists files on a DOS disk and is part of the mtools disk drive support package.

mesg

The mesg utility is run by a user to control the write access others have to the terminal device associated with the standard error output. If write access is allowed, programs such as talk and write have permission to display messages on the terminal. Write access is allowed by default.

mformat

The mformat command performs a low-level format of a floppy disk with a DOS filesystem. This command is part of the mtools software package.

mgetty

Use the mgetty program to monitor incoming logins to set terminal speed, type, and other parameters. This command is part of the mgetty+sendfax package.

minicom

minicom is a serial communications program. The minicom program provides an easy-to-use interface with menus and Custom colors and is a capable, flexible communications program used to dial out and connect with other computers.

mkdir

The mkdir command is used to make a new directory.

mke2fs

The mke2fs command is used to make a second extended Linux filesystem on a specified hard drive or other device, such as a floppy disk. This command does not format the new filesystem, but makes it available for use. mke2fs can also be used to label a partition and to specify a mount point or directory where the partition can be accessed after it is mounted.

mkfs

mkfs is used to build a Linux filesystem on a device, usually a hard disk partition. The syntax for the command is mkfs *filesystem*, where *filesystem* is either the device name (such as /dev/hda1) or the mount point (for example, /, /usr, /home) for the filesystem.

mkswap

mkswap sets up a Linux swap area on a device (usually a disk partition).

The device is usually of the following form:

```
/dev/hda[1-8]
/dev/hdb[1-8]
/dev/sda[1-8]
/dev/sdb[1-8]
```

mlabel

The mlabel command, part of the mtools package, is used to label (name) a DOS floppy disk.

more

more is a filter for paging through text one screen at a time. This command can only page down through the text, as opposed to less, which can page both up and down though the text.

mount

mount attaches the filesystem specified by *specialfile* (which is often a device name) to the directory specified as the parameter. Only the superuser can mount files. If the mount command is run without parameters, it lists all currently mounted filesystems. The following is an example of the mount command:

```
svr01:/home/dpitts$ mount
/dev/hda1 on / type ext2 (rw)
/dev/hda2 on /var/spool/mail type ext2 (rw,usrquota)
/dev/hda3 on /logs type ext2 (rw,usrquota)
/dev/hdc1 on /home type ext2 (rw,usrquota)
none on /proc type proc (rw)
```

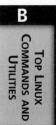

mpage

The `mpage` command formats multiple pages on a single sheet, saving money and a number of trees your printer would otherwise eat. After you install your printer, try printing a document with two sheets per page, like this:

```
# mpage -2 myfile.txt | lpr
```

mt

`mt` is a magnetic tape command. You can use this command to erase, rewind, or re-tension tapes in your tape drive. You can perform nearly 40 different actions with this command.

mv

The `mv` command is used to move an object from one location to another. If the last argument names an existing directory, the command moves the rest of the list into that directory. If two files are given, the command moves the first into the second; it renames the file. It is an error to have more than two arguments with this command unless the last argument is a directory.

netcfg

This is a Red Hat Linux network configuration tool. The `netcfg` command is an X11 client used to configure Linux networking hardware, interfaces, and services.

netstat

`netstat` displays the status of network connections on either TCP, UDP, RAW, or UNIX sockets to the system. The `-r` option is used to obtain information about the routing table. The following is an example of the `netstat` command:

```
svr01:/home/dpitts$ netstat
Active Internet connections
Proto Recv-Q Send-Q Local Address           Foreign Address         (State)
User
tcp        0  16501 www.mk.net:www          sdlb12119.sannet.:3148  FIN_WAIT1
root
tcp        0  16501 auth02.mk.net:www       sdlb12119.sannet.:3188  FIN_WAIT1
root
tcp        0      1 www.anglernet.com:www   ts88.cctrap.com:1070    SYN_RECV
root
tcp        0      1 www.anglernet.com:www   ts88.cctrap.com:1071    SYN_RECV
```

```
root
udp        0        0 localhost:domain      *:*
udp        0        0 svr01.mk.net:domain   *:*
udp        0        0 poto.mk.net:domain    *:*
udp        0        0 stats.mk.net:domain   *:*
udp        0        0 home.mk.net:domain    *:*
udp        0        0 www.cmf.net:domain    *:*
Active UNIX domain sockets
Proto RefCnt Flags     Type          State         Path
unix  2      [ ]       SOCK_STREAM   UNCONNECTED   1605182
unix  2      [ ]       SOCK_STREAM   UNCONNECTED   1627039
unix  2      [ ]       SOCK_STREAM   CONNECTED     1652605
```

newgrp

newgrp is used to enter a new group. You can use this command to temporarily become a member of a different group so you can access or work on different files or directories.

passwd

For the normal user (non-superuser), no arguments are used with the passwd command. The command asks the user for the old password. Following this, the command asks for the new password twice, to make sure it was typed correctly. The new password must be at least six characters long and must contain at least one character that is either upper-case or not a letter. Also, the new password cannot be the same password as the one being replaced, nor can it match the user's ID (account name).

If the command is run by the superuser, it can be followed by either one or two arguments. If the command is followed by a single user's ID, the superuser can change that user's password. The superuser is not bound by any of the restrictions imposed on the user. If there is an argument after the single user's ID, that argument becomes that user's new password.

pdksh

This public domain Korn shell is a workalike shell with features nearly compatible to the commercial Korn shell, and is found on your Linux system with the name ksh.

pico

The pico command is a handy, virtually crash-proof text editor that is part of the pine mail program's software distribution. One handy command-line option is -w, which disables line wrapping. (This is useful when you are manually configuring system files.) pico performs spell-checking of text files, but does not print.

pine

pine is the program for Internet news and email. The pine program, though normally thought of as a mail-handling program, can also be used to read Usenet news. This mail program also comes with a handy editor, called pico. You can organize your incoming mail and file messages into different folders.

ping

This command requests packet echoes from network hosts. The ping command sends out a request for an echo of an information packet from a specific computer on a network. It can be used to check communication links or to determine whether the specific host exists and is running. ping is used from the command line, followed by an Internet Protocol number or domain name:

```
# ping staffnet.com
```

ping continues to send requests until you stop the program with Ctrl+C.

pppd

The Point-to-Point Protocol, or PPP, daemon. This program runs in the background in your Linux system while you have a PPP connection with your ISP and handles the transmission and format of data into and out of your computer.

pppstats

pppstats prints Point-to-Point Protocol network statistics. This program prints a variety of information about a current PPP network connection. It can be useful for determining if the PPP connection is active and how much information is being transferred.

pr

The pr command performs basic formatting of text documents for printing and can also be used to convert input text into different formats through 19 command-line options. One is the -h, or header option, which puts specified text at the top of each page. Try this:

```
# ls | pr -h "TOP SECRET DOCUMENT" | lpr
```

printtool

printtool is the Red Hat Linux printer configuration tool. This X11 client can be run from the command line of a terminal window or through the Control Panel, and is used to install, set up, and configure printers for Linux.

procmail

The `procmail` command processes incoming mail by searching messages for specified strings and either discards, files, or replies to messages according to filters or recipes you specify. This is a handy way to handle unwanted incoming mail or organize vast amounts of incoming mail

ps

ps gives a snapshot of the current processes. An example follows:

```
svr01:/home/dpitts$ ps -ef

PID TTY STAT  TIME COMMAND
10916  p3 S    0:00 -bash TERM=vt100 HOME=/home2/dpitts PATH=/usr/local/bin:/us
10973  p3 R    0:00 \_ ps -ef LESSOPEN=|lesspipe.sh %s ignoreeof=10 HOSTNAME=s
10974  p3 S    0:00 \_ more LESSOPEN=|lesspipe.sh %s ignoreeof=10 HOSTNAME=svr
```

pwd

pwd prints the current working directory. It tells you what directory you are in currently.

quota

The `quota` command reports on disk quota settings. This command, usually used by the root operator, shows how much disk space users can use by user or group.

quotacheck

Gives a report on disk quota usage. This command, usually used by the root operator, scans a specified or current filesystem, reporting on disk usage if disk quotas for users are turned on.

quotaoff

Turns off disk quotas. This command is used by the root operator to disable disk quota checking for users.

quotaon

Turns on disk quotas. This command is used by the root operator to enable or enforce disk quotas for users and can be helpful in limiting how much disk space a user can take up with programs or data.

rclock

An X11 clock client and appointment reminder. The rclock program, besides displaying a variety of clock faces in different colors, can also be used as an appointment or reminder system and features pop-up notes.

red

The restricted ed editor. With this version of the ed command, you can only edit files in the current directory. red does not have a shell escape command.

repquota

Gives a report on disk usage. This command scans different filesystems and reports on usage and quotas if disk quotas are enabled.

restore

Restores a dump backup. The restore command features built-in help and an interactive mode to restore files and directories of a backup created by the dump command.

rjoe

rjoe is a restricted joe editor. With this version of the joe editor, you can only edit files specified on the command line.

rm

rm is used to delete specified files. With the -r option—be aware, this can be dangerous!—rm recursively removes files. Therefore if you type the command rm -r / as root, you had better have a good backup—all of your files are now gone. This is a good command to use in conjunction with the find command to find files owned by a certain user or in a certain group and delete them. By default, the rm command does not remove directories.

rmdir

rmdir removes a given empty directory; the word *empty* is the key word. The syntax is simply rmdir *directory name*.

route

Use route to show or configure the IP routing table. This is another network utility you can use to monitor communication through interfaces on your computer. Although normally used by system administrators, you can use this command to monitor your PPP connection while you are online.

rxvt

rxvt is a color-capable, memory-efficient terminal emulator for X11 with nearly all of the features of the xterm client. This client is usually started in the background:

```
# rxvt &
```

sed

This is the stream editor, a noninteractive text editor designed to change or manipulate streams of text. The sed command can be used to quickly perform global search-and-replace operations on streams of text (for example, through pipes).

```
# cat employees.txt | sed 's/Bill/William/g' >newemployees.txt
```

This example changes all instances of Bill to William in the original file and creates a new file.

sendfax

Use this to send fax documents. The sendfax program, part of the mgetty+sendfax software package, dials out and sends prepared fax-format graphics documents. This program is usually run by the faxspool shell script.

set

The set command is used to temporarily change an environment variable. In some shells, the set -o vi command allows you to bring back previous commands you have in your history file. It is common to place the set command in your .profile. Some environment variables require an equals sign, and some, as in the example set -o vi, do not.

setfdprm

Set floppy drive parameters with this command. This command, usually run by the root operator, is used to set the current floppy device, usually in preparation for a low-level format.

setserial

The `setserial` command is used to configure or fine-tune specific serial ports in your computer. This command can also be used to report on a serial port's status or identity.

shutdown

Once during *Star Trek: The Next Generation*, Data commanded the computer to "Shut down the holodeck!" Unfortunately, most systems do not have voice controls, but systems can still be shut down. This command happens to be the one to do just that. Technically, the following `shutdown` call causes all or part of a full-duplex connection on a socket associated with s to be shut down:

```
int shutdown(int s, int how));
```

The `shutdown` command can also be used to issue a "Vulcan Nerve Pinch" (Ctrl+Alt+Del) and restart the system.

slrn

A news reading program, the `slrn` newsreader provides an easy-to-use interface for reading Usenet news. It has some advantages over the `tin` newsreader by providing custom colors for different parts of messages and support for mouse clicks and function keys.

sort

The `sort` command comes in handy whenever you need to generate alphabetical lists of the information from your files. Information can also be listed in reverse order. See the `sort` command manual page for more information.

stat

Use `stat` to print file information. The `stat` command prints a variety of information about a specified file and can also be used to check for the validity of symbolic links.

statserial

Use the `statserial` command to print serial port statistics. This command, run only by the `root` operator, shows the current condition of a specified serial port and can be helpful in diagnosing serial port problems.

strings

The `strings` command outputs all text strings found inside binary programs. This can be useful to view the contents of files when you do not have a viewer program for a file's format or for looking at the contents of a binary program (such as to search for help text). For example, try this to look at all strings inside the `pico` editor:

```
# strings /usr/bin/pico | less
```

su

su enables a user to temporarily become another user. If a user ID is not given, the computer thinks you want to be either the `superuser` or `root`. In either case, a shell is spawned that makes you the new user, complete with that user ID, group ID, and any supplemental groups of that new user. If you are not `root` and the user has a password (and the user should!), su prompts for a password. `root` can become any user at any time without knowing passwords. Technically, the user just needs to have a user ID of `0` (which makes a user a `superuser`) to log on as anyone else without a password.

swapoff

`swapoff` is the command that stops swapping to a file or block device.

swapon

`swapon` sets the swap area to the file or block device by path. `swapoff` stops swapping to the file and is normally done during system boot.

tail

`tail` prints to standard output the last 10 lines of a given file. If no file is given, it reads from standard input. If more than one file is given, it prints a header consisting of the file's name enclosed in left and right arrows (==> <==) before the output of each file. The default value of 10 lines can be changed by placing a `-###` in the command. The syntax for the command follows:

```
tail [-# of lines to see] [filename(s)]
```

talk

The `talk` command is used to have a "visual" discussion with someone else over a terminal. The basic idea behind this visual discussion is that your input is copied to the other person's terminal, and the other person's input is copied to your terminal. Thus, both people involved in the discussion see the input from both themselves and the other person.

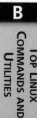

taper

A tape archiving and backup program, the `taper` command features a friendly interface to the `tar` and `gzip` programs to provide archive backups and compression.

tar

`tar` is an archiving program designed to store and extract files from an archive file. A tarred file (called a *tar file*) can be archived to any medium, including a tape drive or a hard drive. The syntax of a `tar` command is this:

```
tar action optional functions file(s)/directory(ies)
```

If the last parameter is a directory, all subdirectories under the directory are also tarred.

tcsh

This enhanced `csh` shell has all of the features of the `csh` shell, with many improvements, such as command-line editing, job control, and command history. This shell is run by the symbolic link, `csh`, found under the `/bin` directory.

telnet

Start and run a Telnet session. You can use the `telnet` command to log into remote computer systems and run programs or retrieve data.

tin

This is a Usenet news reading program. The `tin` newsreader, like the `slrn` newsreader, provides a menu system for reading Usenet news, allowing you to quickly browse, save, post, or reply to messages found in a specific Usenet newsgroup. The `tin` reader looks for a list of desired newsgroups in the file `.newsrc` in your home directory and can be started like this from the command line of your console or terminal window:

```
# tin -nqr
```

top

You can display CPU processes with the `top` command. This command can be used to print the most active or system resource-intensive processes or programs.

touch

You can use the `touch` command to quickly create a file or update its timestamp.

tput

Change or reset terminal settings. The tput command, found under the /usr/bin directory, uses terminal capabilities found in the terminfo database under the /usr/lib directory. This database contains character sequences recognized by different terminals. You can use tput in a variety of ways. One handy feature is the reset option, which can help you clear up a terminal window if your display becomes munged because of spurious control codes echoed to the screen.

tr

Transliterates characters. The tr command, a text filter, translates sets of characters you specify on the command line. The classic example is to translate a text file from all uppercase to lowercase:

```
# cat uppercase.txt | tr A-Z a-z > lowercase.txt
```

tree

Use tree to print a visual directory. If you would like to see how your directories are organized, you can use this command to print a graphic tree.

twm

This is the Tab window manager for X11, from which the fvwm window manager, and others, are descended. Although this window manager does not support virtual desktops, you can customize its menus and windows. The twm window manager is usually started from the contents of your .xinitrc in your home directory.

ulimit

Show resource limit settings with ulimit. This is a built-in command for the bash or ksh shell and can be used to set limits on a number of system resources. This command is similar to the limit command of the tcsh or csh shells.

umount

Just as cavalry soldiers unmount from their horses, filesystems unmount from their locations. The umount command is used to perform this action. The syntax of the command follows:

```
umount <filesystem>
```

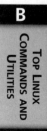

unalias

unalias is the command to undo an alias. In the alias command section earlier in this appendix, I aliased dir to be the ls command. To unalias this command, you would simply type **unalias dir**.

uname

uname is the command to show hostname and additional information (like operating system, version, Kernel date, and so on).

unzip

The unzip command lists, tests, or extracts files from a zipped archive. The default is to extract files from the archive. The basic syntax is unzip *filename*.

updatedb

This command builds the locate command's database, called locatedb, in the /var/lib directory.

uptime

You can show how long your system has been running (in case you want to brag to your NT friends) with uptime. The uptime command shows how long your Linux system has been running, who is currently logged on, and what the average system load has been for the last 5, 10, and 15 minutes. Linux system uptimes are generally measured in years (and almost always end due to hardware failure)!

uugetty

Sets login parameters, such as terminal type, speed, and protocol. You can use uugetty to monitor incoming connections to your Linux system. This program can display login messages or run programs when you log in.

vdir

List the contents of directories with vdir. This command is the same as using the ls command with the -l option to get a detailed directory listing.

vi

Normally known as the vi (visual) editor under Red Hat Linux, vi is a symbolic link to the vim editor. In this mode, the vim editor closely emulates the classic vi editor, originally distributed with the Berkeley Software Distribution.

view

This is a symbolic link to the vim editor.

vim

vim stands for *VIsual editor iMproved*. This editor is an improvement of the vi editor and can also emulate the ex line-oriented editor. The X11 version of this editor is called gvim.

vimx

This is a symbolic link to the gvim X11 editor.

vmstat

vmstat prints virtual memory statistics. This command shows how much disk space has been used by your system, usually on the swap file partition.

w

Show who is logged on to your system by using the w command, which also shows the same information as the uptime command.

wall

wall displays the contents of standard input on all terminals of all currently logged-in users. Basically, the command writes to all terminals; hence, its name. The contents of files can also be displayed. Either the superuser or root can write to the terminals of those who have chosen to deny messages or are using a program that automatically denies messages.

wc

This is a word-count program. The wc command counts the number of characters, words, and lines in your file and prints a small report to your display. The default is to show all three, but you can limit the report by using the -c, -w, or -l options.

whatis

This command searches the whatis database (located under the /usr/man directory) for command names and prints a one-line synopsis of what each command does. Use the whatis command, followed by the name of another command:

```
# whatis emacs
```

whereis

Use whereis to find commands, command sources, and manual pages. This program searches a built-in list of directories to find and then prints matches of the command name you specify.

which

Use which to find commands. This program searches your path to find and then prints matches of the command name you specify.

who

The who command prints the login name, terminal type, login time, and remote hostname of each user currently logged on. The following is an example of the who command:

```
$ who
root       ttyp0    Jul 27 11:44 (www01.mk.net)
dpitts     ttyp2    Jul 27 19:32 (d12.dialup.seane)
ehooban    ttyp3    Jul 27 11:47 (205.177.146.78)
dpitts     ttyp4    Jul 27 19:34 (d12.dialup.seane)
```

The -u option is nice if you want to see how long it has been since that session has been used, such as in the following:

```
$ who -u
root       ttyp0    Jul 27 11:44 08:07 (www01.mk.net)
dpitts     ttyp2    Jul 27 19:32   .   (d12.dialup.seane)
ehooban    ttyp3    Jul 27 11:47 00:09 (205.177.146.78)
dpitts     ttyp4    Jul 27 19:34 00:06 (d12.dialup.seane)
```

whoami

To show your current user identity, the whoami command prints the username of who you currently are. It is useful for checking who you are if you are running as the root operator.

xclock

This is an X11 clock client that can be run with a standard clock face or as a digital clock.

xcutsel

This is an X11 client that provides a buffer for copy and paste operations. This program is handy for copying and pasting information between programs that may not support direct copying and pasting.

xdm

This X11 Display Manager provides a log-in interface, called the chooser, which—when properly configured on your system—can manage several X displays.

xfig

This is an X11 drawing program. The xfig client is an interactive drawing program that uses objects rather than pixel images to display figures. You can use this program to develop blueprints or other technical drawings.

xhost +

The xhost + command allows xterms to be displayed on a system. Probably the most common reason a remote terminal cannot be opened is that the xhost + command has not been run. Use the xhost - command to turn off the capability to allow xterms.

xjed

The X11 version of the jed editor. This version of the jed editor runs under the X Window System and offers keyboard menus.

xload

The X11 system load reporting client shows a graphic of the system load average, a combination of memory, CPU, and swap-file space usage. This program, like may X11 clients, is started in the background:

```
# xload &
```

xloadimage

An X11 client that can load, translate, and display graphic images or window dumps created by the xwd client on your display or desktop. You can also use the xloadimage command to provide slide shows of graphics.

xlock

xlock is an X11 terminal-locking program that provides password protection and more than 50 screensavers.

xlsfonts

This X11 client displays and searches for fonts recognized by the current X11 server and is useful for finding a specific font or for getting detailed font reports.

xmessage

This is an X11 client that displays messages on your display. You can also program your own custom messages with labels, buttons, and other information. Although this client is often used with other programs to provide appointment reminders, an xmessage can also be used as a sticky-note reminder.

xminicom

Runs the minicom program in an X11 terminal window. This is the preferred way to run the minicom communications program under the X Window System.

xmkmf

The xmkmf command (a shell script) is used to create the Imakefiles for X sources. It actually runs the imake command with a set of arguments.

xmodmap

A utility for modifying keyboards or mouse buttons during an X session. You can use xmodmap to remap your keyboard or rearrange your mouse buttons.

xscreensaver

A screensaver for X11, this client is usually run in the background to blank your screen and run a screensaver program after a preselected time. The xscreensaver client is usually controlled with the xscreensaver-command client.

xscreensaver-command

This X11 client is used to control the xscreensaver program to turn screensaving on or off and to cycle through various screensaving displays.

xset

The xset command sets some of the options in an X Window session. You can use this option to set your bell (xset b *volume frequency duration in milliseconds*), your mouse speed (xset m *acceleration threshold*), and many other options.

xsetroot

An X11 client to change how the root window or background of your display appears, as well as how the cursor looks. You can use this client to add background patterns, colors, or pictures, or to change your root window cursor. Want a blue background for your X11 desktop? Try this:

```
# xsetroot -solid blue
```

xv

You can display images in X11 with xv. This X11 client provides many controls for capturing, changing, saving, and printing images and comes with extensive documentation.

xwd

An X11 window-dumping client. You can use this client to take pictures of windows or the entire display. Do not forget to specify an output file like this:

```
# xwd >myscreendump.xwd
```

xwininfo

This X11 information client gathers available information about a window and prints a short report. You can use the xwininfo utility to determine a window's size and placement.

xwud

An X11 graphics utility client that displays window dumps created by the xwd X11 client.

zip

The zip command lists, tests, or adds files to a zipped archive. The default is to add files to an archive.

zsh

The z shell is the largest shell for Linux, with many features and lots of documentation. This shell has features derived from the csh and tcsh shells and can emulate the ksh (Korn) and sh (Bourne) shells.

Summary

You noticed two things if you read this entire appendix: First, it contains more than 200 commands. Second, you have way too much time on your hands—go out and program some new Linux drivers or something!

There are many more commands than those listed. You may have noticed that scripting languages like awk, perl, tcl/tk, and others were not listed, and all the compiled language commands (like gcc, g++, g77, gjc, and so on) are also missing. It would be possible to write an entire book that did nothing but list the commands and a short description. That book comes with every Linux system; it is called the manual and can be accessed with the man command!

Most of the commands have arguments that can be passed to them and, although this appendix attempts to point out a few of them, an entire book would be needed to hold the detail provided in the man pages.

APPENDIX C

The GNU General Public License

IN THIS APPENDIX

Note

Without a doubt, GNU/Linux (and every other distribution, including Red Hat) owes much of its success to Richard Stallman, the Free Software Foundation, and the GNU General Public License. Without the freedom to freely distribute software in source code form, and the ability to make and share changes, Linux may not have spread and improved as quickly as it did over the Internet.

You can find out more about GNU's Not Unix and the GNU Project by browsing to:

`http://www.gnu.org`

To find out more about the Free Software Foundation, point your browser to:

`http://www.fsf.org/fsf/fsf/hmtl`

This appendix contains a copy of the GNU General Public License. However, you should know there are many different types of software licenses used by software available for Linux. These licenses cover a broad range, such as the BSD-style license, a public domain license, an Artistic License, and restrictive proprietary licensing.

The GNU General Public License

Version 2, June 1991

Copyright (C) 1989, 1991 Free Software Foundation, Inc.

59 Temple Place, Suite 330, Boston, MA 02111-1307 USA

Everyone is permitted to copy and distribute verbatim copies of this license document, but changing it is not allowed.

Preamble

The licenses for most software are designed to take away your freedom to share and change it. By contrast, the GNU General Public License is intended to guarantee your freedom to share and change free software—to make sure the software is free for all its users. This General Public License applies to most of the Free Software Foundation's software and to any other program whose authors commit to using it. (Some other Free Software Foundation software is covered by the GNU Library General Public License instead.) You can apply it to your programs, too.

When we speak of free software, we are referring to freedom, not price. Our General Public Licenses are designed to make sure that you have the freedom to distribute copies of free software (and charge for this service if you wish), that you receive source code or can get it if you want it, that you can change the software or use pieces of it in new free programs; and that you know you can do these things.

To protect your rights, we need to make restrictions that forbid anyone to deny you these rights or to ask you to surrender the rights. These restrictions translate to certain responsibilities for you if you distribute copies of the software, or if you modify it.

For example, if you distribute copies of such a program, whether gratis or for a fee, you must give the recipients all the rights that you have. You must make sure that they, too, receive or can get the source code. And you must show them these terms so they know their rights.

We protect your rights with two steps: (1) copyright the software, and (2) offer you this license which gives you legal permission to copy, distribute and/or modify the software.

Also, for each author's protection and ours, we want to make certain that everyone understands that there is no warranty for this free software. If the software is modified by someone else and passed on, we want its recipients to know that what they have is not the original, so that any problems introduced by others will not reflect on the original authors' reputations.

Finally, any free program is threatened constantly by software patents. We wish to avoid the danger that redistributors of a free program will individually obtain patent licenses, in effect making the program proprietary. To prevent this, we have made it clear that any patent must be licensed for everyone's free use or not licensed at all.

The precise terms and conditions for copying, distribution and modification follow.

GNU GENERAL PUBLIC LICENSE

TERMS AND CONDITIONS FOR COPYING, DISTRIBUTION AND MODIFICATION

0. This License applies to any program or other work which contains a notice placed by the copyright holder saying it may be distributed under the terms of this General Public License. The "Program", below, refers to any such program or work, and a "work based on the Program" means either the Program or any derivative work under copyright law: that is to say, a work containing the Program or a portion of it, either verbatim or with modifications and/or translated into another language. (Hereinafter, translation is included without limitation in the term "modification".) Each licensee is addressed as "you".

Activities other than copying, distribution and modification are not covered by this License; they are outside its scope. The act of running the Program is not restricted, and the output from the Program is covered only if its contents constitute a work based on the Program (independent of having been made by running the Program). Whether that is true depends on what the Program does.

1. You may copy and distribute verbatim copies of the Program's source code as you receive it, in any medium, provided that you conspicuously and appropriately publish on each copy an appropriate copyright notice and disclaimer of warranty; keep intact all the notices that refer to this License and to the absence of any warranty; and give any other recipients of the Program a copy of this License along with the Program.

You may charge a fee for the physical act of transferring a copy, and you may at your option offer warranty protection in exchange for a fee.

2. You may modify your copy or copies of the Program or any portion of it, thus forming a work based on the Program, and copy and distribute such modifications or work under the terms of Section 1 above, provided that you also meet all of these conditions:

a) You must cause the modified files to carry prominent notices stating that you changed the files and the date of any change.

b) You must cause any work that you distribute or publish, that in whole or in part contains or is derived from the Program or any part thereof, to be licensed as a whole at no charge to all third parties under the terms of this License.

c) If the modified program normally reads commands interactively when run, you must cause it, when started running for such interactive use in the most ordinary way, to print or display an announcement including an appropriate copyright notice and a notice that there is no warranty (or else, saying that you provide a warranty) and that users may redistribute the program under these conditions, and telling the user how to view a copy of this License. (Exception: if the Program itself is interactive but does not normally print such an announcement, your work based on the Program is not required to print an announcement.)

These requirements apply to the modified work as a whole. If identifiable sections of that work are not derived from the Program, and can be reasonably considered independent and separate works in themselves, then this License, and its terms, do not apply to those sections when you distribute them as separate works. But when you distribute the same sections as part of a whole which is a work based on the Program, the distribution of the whole must be on the terms of this License, whose permissions for other licensees extend to the entire whole, and thus to each and every part regardless of who wrote it.

Thus, it is not the intent of this section to claim rights or contest your rights to work written entirely by you; rather, the intent is to exercise the right to control the distribution of derivative or collective works based on the Program.

In addition, mere aggregation of another work not based on the Program with the Program (or with a work based on the Program) on a volume of a storage or distribution medium does not bring the other work under the scope of this License.

3. You may copy and distribute the Program (or a work based on it, under Section 2) in object code or executable form under the terms of Sections 1 and 2 above provided that you also do one of the following:

a) Accompany it with the complete corresponding machine-readable source code, which must be distributed under the terms of Sections 1 and 2 above on a medium customarily used for software interchange; or,

b) Accompany it with a written offer, valid for at least three years, to give any third party, for a charge no more than your cost of physically performing source distribution, a complete machine-readable copy of the corresponding source code, to be distributed under the terms of Sections 1 and 2 above on a medium customarily used for software interchange; or,

c) Accompany it with the information you received as to the offer to distribute corresponding source code. (This alternative is allowed only for noncommercial distribution and only if you received the program in object code or executable form with such an offer, in accord with Subsection b above.)

The source code for a work means the preferred form of the work for making modifications to it. For an executable work, complete source code means all the source code for all modules it contains, plus any associated interface definition files, plus the scripts used to control compilation and installation of the executable. However, as a special exception, the source code distributed need not include anything that is normally distributed (in either source or binary form) with the major components (compiler, kernel, and so on) of the operating system on which the executable runs, unless that component itself accompanies the executable.

If distribution of executable or object code is made by offering access to copy from a designated place, then offering equivalent access to copy the source code from the same place counts as distribution of the source code, even though third parties are not compelled to copy the source along with the object code.

4. You may not copy, modify, sublicense, or distribute the Program except as expressly provided under this License. Any attempt otherwise to copy, modify, sublicense or distribute the Program is void, and will automatically terminate your rights under this License.

However, parties who have received copies, or rights, from you under this License will not have their licenses terminated so long as such parties remain in full compliance.

5. You are not required to accept this License, since you have not signed it. However, nothing else grants you permission to modify or distribute the Program or its derivative works. These actions are prohibited by law if you do not accept this License. Therefore, by modifying or distributing the Program (or any work based on the Program), you indicate your acceptance of this License to do so, and all its terms and conditions for copying, distributing or modifying the Program or works based on it.

6. Each time you redistribute the Program (or any work based on the Program), the recipient automatically receives a license from the original licensor to copy, distribute or modify the Program subject to these terms and conditions. You may not impose any further restrictions on the recipients' exercise of the rights granted herein. You are not responsible for enforcing compliance by third parties to this License.

7. If, as a consequence of a court judgment or allegation of patent infringement or for any other reason (not limited to patent issues), conditions are imposed on you (whether by court order, agreement or otherwise) that contradict the conditions of this License, they do not excuse you from the conditions of this License. If you cannot distribute so as to satisfy simultaneously your obligations under this License and any other pertinent obligations, then as a consequence you may not distribute the Program at all. For example, if a patent license would not permit royalty-free redistribution of the Program by all those who receive copies directly or indirectly through you, then the only way you could satisfy both it and this License would be to refrain entirely from distribution of the Program.

If any portion of this section is held invalid or unenforceable under any particular circumstance, the balance of the section is intended to apply and the section as a whole is intended to apply in other circumstances.

It is not the purpose of this section to induce you to infringe any patents or other property right claims or to contest validity of any such claims; this section has the sole purpose of protecting the integrity of the free software distribution system, which is implemented by public license practices. Many people have made generous contributions to the wide range of software distributed through that system in reliance on consistent application of that system; it is up to the author/donor to decide if he or she is willing to distribute software through any other system and a licensee cannot impose that choice.

This section is intended to make thoroughly clear what is believed to be a consequence of the rest of this License.

8. If the distribution and/or use of the Program is restricted in certain countries either by patents or by copyrighted interfaces, the original copyright holder who places the Program under this License may add an explicit geographical distribution limitation excluding those countries, so that distribution is permitted only in or among countries not thus excluded. In such case, this License incorporates the limitation as if written in the body of this License.

9. The Free Software Foundation may publish revised and/or new versions of the General Public License from time to time. Such new versions will be similar in spirit to the present version, but may differ in detail to address new problems or concerns.

Each version is given a distinguishing version number. If the Program specifies a version number of this License which applies to it and "any later version", you have the option of following the terms and conditions either of that version or of any later version published by the Free Software Foundation. If the Program does not specify a version number of this License, you may choose any version ever published by the Free Software Foundation.

10. If you wish to incorporate parts of the Program into other free programs whose distribution conditions are different, write to the author to ask for permission. For software which is copyrighted by the Free Software Foundation, write to the Free Software Foundation; we sometimes make exceptions for this. Our decision will be guided by the two goals of preserving the free status of all derivatives of our free software and of promoting the sharing and reuse of software generally.

NO WARRANTY

11. BECAUSE THE PROGRAM IS LICENSED FREE OF CHARGE, THERE IS NO WARRANTY FOR THE PROGRAM, TO THE EXTENT PERMITTED BY APPLICABLE LAW. EXCEPT WHEN OTHERWISE STATED IN WRITING THE COPYRIGHT HOLDERS AND/OR OTHER PARTIES PROVIDE THE PROGRAM "AS IS" WITHOUT WARRANTY OF ANY KIND, EITHER EXPRESSED OR IMPLIED, INCLUDING, BUT NOT LIMITED TO, THE IMPLIED WARRANTIES OF MERCHANTABILITY AND FITNESS FOR A PARTICULAR PURPOSE. THE ENTIRE RISK AS TO THE QUALITY AND PERFORMANCE OF THE PROGRAM IS WITH YOU. SHOULD THE PROGRAM PROVE DEFECTIVE, YOU ASSUME THE COST OF ALL NECESSARY SERVICING, REPAIR OR CORRECTION.

12. IN NO EVENT UNLESS REQUIRED BY APPLICABLE LAW OR AGREED TO IN WRITING WILL ANY COPYRIGHT HOLDER, OR ANY OTHER PARTY WHO MAY MODIFY AND/OR REDISTRIBUTE THE PROGRAM AS PERMITTED ABOVE, BE LIABLE TO YOU FOR DAMAGES, INCLUDING ANY GENERAL,

SPECIAL, INCIDENTAL OR CONSEQUENTIAL DAMAGES ARISING OUT OF THE USE OR INABILITY TO USE THE PROGRAM (INCLUDING BUT NOT LIMITED TO LOSS OF DATA OR DATA BEING RENDERED INACCURATE OR LOSSES SUSTAINED BY YOU OR THIRD PARTIES OR A FAILURE OF THE PROGRAM TO OPERATE WITH ANY OTHER PROGRAMS), EVEN IF SUCH HOLDER OR OTHER PARTY HAS BEEN ADVISED OF THE POSSIBILITY OF SUCH DAMAGES.

END OF TERMS AND CONDITIONS

How to Apply These Terms to Your New Programs

If you develop a new program, and you want it to be of the greatest possible use to the public, the best way to achieve this is to make it free software which everyone can redistribute and change under these terms.

To do so, attach the following notices to the program. It is safest to attach them to the start of each source file to most effectively convey the exclusion of warranty; and each file should have at least the "copyright" line and a pointer to where the full notice is found.

> <one line to give the program's name and a brief idea of what it does.>
>
> Copyright (C) 19yy <name of author>
>
> This program is free software; you can redistribute it and/or modify it under the terms of the GNU General Public License as published by the Free Software Foundation; either version 2 of the License, or (at your option) any later version.
>
> This program is distributed in the hope that it will be useful, but WITHOUT ANY WARRANTY; without even the implied warranty of MERCHANTABILITY or FITNESS FOR A PARTICULAR PURPOSE. See the GNU General Public License for more details.
>
> You should have received a copy of the GNU General Public License along with this program; if not, write to the Free Software Foundation, Inc., 59 Temple Place, Suite 330, Boston, MA 02111-1307 USA

Also add information on how to contact you by electronic and paper mail.

If the program is interactive, make it output a short notice like this when it starts in an interactive mode:

Gnomovision version 69, Copyright (C) 19yy name of author

Gnomovision comes with ABSOLUTELY NO WARRANTY; for details type `show w '. This is free software, and you are welcome to redistribute it under certain conditions; type `show c ' for details.

The hypothetical commands `show w ' and `show c ' should show the appropriate parts of the General Public License. Of course, the commands you use may be called something other than `show w ' and `show c '; they could even be mouse-clicks or menu items—whatever suits your program.

You should also get your employer (if you work as a programmer) or your school, if any, to sign a "copyright disclaimer" for the program, if necessary. Here is a sample; alter the names:

Yoyodyne, Inc., hereby disclaims all copyright interest in the program `Gnomovision ' (which makes passes at compilers) written by James Hacker.

<signature of Ty Coon>, 1 April 1989

Ty Coon, President of Vice

This General Public License does not permit incorporating your program into proprietary programs. If your program is a subroutine library, you may consider it more useful to permit linking proprietary applications with the library. If this is what you want to do, use the GNU Library General Public License instead of this License.

APPENDIX D

Red Hat Linux RPM Package Listings

This appendix (containing Tables D.1 and D.2) is a cross-reference of the Red Hat Linux software included on this book's CD-ROM. Table D.1 lists the individual package name, its size, and a short description. Table D.2 lists the individual package groups used by Red Hat to organize its distribution. These tables can help you choose packages in order to build and install custom configurations for your workstation, server, or portable system.

If you have resource constraints, such as limited hard drive space or RAM, Table D.2 can help you build a minimal system (by installing only those packages in the System Environment/Base group). It's also handy to see exactly how many editors, database managers, or games are included with Red Hat Linux! If you're unsure whether a package is installed on your system, you can run a quick check by using the rpm command with its query or -q option, like this:

```
# rpm -q abiword
abiword-0.7.10-3
```

This shows that the package, abiword-0.7.10-3, is installed on your system. However, if you use the rpm command and you get output like this:

```
# rpm -q abiword
package abiword is not installed
```

You'll see from the output that the package is not installed.

This appendix was created with the rpm command using various --queryformat options. Your system's RPM databases (found under the /var/lib/rpm directory) contain indexes to installed packages, and you can perform queries on the installed packages or packages still on the Red Hat Linux CD-ROM. The tables in this appendix were built using the rpm command like this:

```
# rpm -qa --queryformat '%{NAME}\t%{SIZE}\t%{SUMMARY}\n' | sort >table.txt
```

TABLE D.1 Red Hat Linux Package Listing

Package Name	Size (bytes)	Description
abiword	8840772	A word processor.
adjtimex	48535	Utility for adjusting kernel time variables.
amanda	457009	Network-capable tape backup solution.
amanda-client	306525	Client component of the AMANDA tape backup system.
amanda-server	562912	The server side of the AMANDA tape backup system.
am-utils	1492186	Automount utilities.

TABLE D.1 continued

Package Name	Size (bytes)	Description
anaconda	6516899	The Red Hat Linux installer.
anaconda-runtime	5997770	Red Hat Linux installer portions needed only for fresh installs.
anacron	56411	A cron-like program that can run jobs lost during downtime.
anonftp	1772916	A fast, read-only, anonymous FTP server.
apache	1179253	The most widely used Web server on the Internet.
apache-devel	403592	Development tools for the Apache Web server.
apache-manual	1492008	Documentation for the Apache Web server.
apmd	92957	Advanced Power Management (APM) BIOS utilities for laptops.
arpwatch	140762	Network monitoring tools for tracking IP addresses on a network.
ash	462099	A smaller version of the Bourne shell (sh).
asp2php	105178	A VBScript/Active Server Pages (ASP) to PHP converter.
asp2php-gtk	17972	A GUI frontend for the asp2php converter.
aspell	7972944	A spelling checker.
aspell-ca	7734941	Catalan files for aspell.
aspell-cs	64434227	Czech files for aspell.
aspell-da	13396490	Danish files for aspell.
aspell-de	10277107	German files for aspell.
aspell-devel	2711586	Static libraries and header files for aspell development.
aspell-en-ca	139452	Canadian dictionary for aspell.
aspell-en-gb	139448	British dictionary for aspell.
aspell-eo	23179323	Esperanto files for aspell.
aspell-es	15876306	Spanish files for aspell.
aspell-fr	7005038	French files for aspell.
aspell-it	1597499	Italian files for aspell.
aspell-nl	7110712	Dutch files for aspell.

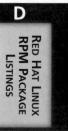

D

RED HAT LINUX RPM PACKAGE LISTINGS

TABLE D.1 continued

Package Name	Size (bytes)	Description
aspell-no	11497743	Norwegian files for `aspell`.
aspell-pl	35622968	Polish files for `aspell`.
aspell-sv	4381827	Swedish files for `aspell`.
at	76032	Job spooling tools.
audiofile	334641	A library for accessing various audio file formats.
audiofile-devel	646171	Libraries, includes, and other files to develop audiofile applications.
aumix	120433	An ncurses-based audio mixer.
aumix-X11	45728	GTK+ GUI interface for the `aumix` sound mixer.
authconfig	151177	Text-mode tool for setting up NIS and shadow passwords.
auth_ldap	93355	An Apache module for authenticating HTTP clients using LDAP.
autoconf	597534	GNU tool for automatically configuring source code.
autofs	661056	A tool for automatically mounting and unmounting filesystems.
automake	905153	GNU tool for automatically creating Makefiles.
autorun	63762	A CD-ROM mounting utility.
awesfx	314567	Utility programs for the AWE32 sound driver.
basesystem	0	The skeleton package that defines a Red Hat Linux system.
bash	1216755	The GNU Bourne Again shell (`bash`) version 1.14.
bash-doc	2520970	Documentation for the GNU Bourne Again shell (`bash`) version 2.04.
bc	104008	GNU's `bc` (a numeric processing language) and `dc` (a calculator).
bdflush	9141	The daemon that starts the flushing of dirty buffers back to disk.

TABLE D.1 continued

Package Name	Size (bytes)	Description
bind	5285346	A DNS (Domain Name System) server.
bind-devel	1572427	Include files and libraries needed for bind DNS development.
bind-utils	1813123	Utilities for querying DNS name servers.
binutils	3256936	GNU collection of binary utilities.
bison	158146	GNU general-purpose parser generator.
blt	5829766	A Tk toolkit extension.
bootparamd	18062	A server process that provides boot information to diskless clients.
bug-buddy	724703	A GUI bug reporting tool for the GNOME GUI desktop.
byacc	59513	A public-domain yacc parser generator.
bzip2	151702	A file compression utility.
bzip2-devel	84138	Files needed to develop applications that will use bzip2.
caching-nameserver	8557	The configuration files for setting up a caching name server.
cdda2wav	243450	Utility for sampling/copying .wav files from digital audio CDs.
cdecl	68551	Encoding/decoding utilities for C/C++ function declarations.
cdp	37509	An interactive text-mode program for playing audio CD-ROMs.
cdparanoia	198634	A Compact Disc Digital Audio (CDDA) extraction tool.
cdparanoia-devel	138483	Development tools for libcdda_paranoia (Paranoia III).
cdrecord	672463	A command-line CD/DVD recording program.
cdrecord-devel	293953	The libschily SCSI user-level transport library.
chkconfig	128905	System tool for maintaining the /etc/rc.d hierarchy.
chkfontpath	11069	Utility for editing X font server font path.

D

RED HAT LINUX
RPM PACKAGE
LISTINGS

TABLE D.1 continued

Package Name	Size (bytes)	Description
cipe	100713	Kernel Module and Daemon for VPN.
cleanfeed	76856	Spam filter for Usenet news servers.
compat-egcs	126752	A C compiler for Red Hat Linux 5.2 backward compatibility.
compat-egcs-c++	4864671	C++ support for the Red Hat Linux 5.2 backward-compatible C compiler.
compat-egcs-g77	4468108	Fortran 77 support for the Red Hat Linux 5.2 compatible C compiler.
compat-egcs-objc	2015471	Ojective C support for Red Hat Linux 5.2 compatible C compiler.
compat-glibc	6909510	GNU libc for Red Hat Linux 5.2 backward compatibility.
compat-libstdc++	3468701	Standard C++ libraries for Red Hat 6.2 backward-compatibility C++ compiler
comsat	15576	A mail checker client and the comsat mail checking server.
console-tools	2698298	Tools for configuring the console.
control-center	2483111	The GNOME Control Center.
control-center-devel	43364	The GNOME Control Center development environment.
control-panel	184859	A Red Hat sysadmin utility program launcher for X.
cpio	68153	GNU archiving program.
cpp	270465	The GNU C-Compatible Compiler Preprocessor.
cproto	86966	Generates function prototypes and variable declarations from C code.
cracklib	91786	A password-checking library.
cracklib-dicts	875815	The standard CrackLib dictionaries.
crontabs	17351	Root crontab files used to schedule the execution of programs.
ctags	170918	A C programming language indexing and/or cross-reference tool.
cvs	2540907	A version control system.

TABLE D.1   continued

Package Name	Size (bytes)	Description
cxhextris	43769	An X Window System color version of xhextris.
cyrus-sasl	538298	The SASL library API for the Cyrus mail system.
db1	76370	The BSD database library for C (version 1).
db1-devel	953495	Development libs/header files for Berkeley DB (version 1) library.
db2	293071	The BSD database library for C (version 2).
db2-devel	3302591	Development libs/header files for Berkeley DB (version 2) library.
db3	1605861	The Berkeley DB database library for C.
db3-devel	11231721	Development libraries/header files for the Berkeley DB library.
db3-utils	2289578	Command-line tools for managing Berkeley DB databases.
desktop-backgrounds	10474182	Desktop background images.
dev	155947	The most commonly-used entries in the /dev directory.
dev86	822227	A real mode 80x86 assembler and linker.
dhcp	237676	A DHCP (Dynamic Host Configuration Protocol) server and relay agent.
dhcpcd	393790	A DHCP (Dynamic Host Configuration Protocol) client.
dia	1606755	Program for drawing diagrams.
dialog	204888	Utility for creating TTY dialog boxes.
diffstat	11942	Utility that provides statistics based on the output of diff.
diffutils	164342	GNU collection of diff utilities.
dip	81331	Handles the connections needed for dialup IP links.
docbook	493501	An SGML DTD for technical documentation.
dosfstools	130775	Utilities for making and checking MS-DOS FAT filesystems on Linux.

TABLE D.1   continued

Package Name	Size (bytes)	Description
doxygen	3461244	A documentation system for C and C++.
dump	171377	Programs for backing up and restoring filesystems.
dump-static	1018345	Statically linked versions of dump and restore.
e2fsprogs	1246735	Utilities for managing the second extended (ext2) filesystem.
e2fsprogs-devel	289433	Ext2 filesystem-specific static libraries and headers.
ed	99563	The GNU line editor.
ee	633901	The Electric Eyes image viewer application.
efax	208634	Program for faxing using a Class 1, 2, or 2.0 fax modem.
eject	47234	Program that ejects removable media using software control.
ElectricFence	56282	A debugger that detects memory allocation violations.
elm	608950	The `elm` mail user agent.
emacs	20390136	The libraries needed to run the GNU Emacs text editor.
emacs-el	22249392	The sources for elisp programs included with Emacs.
emacs-leim	4383466	Emacs Lisp code for input methods for international characters.
emacs-nox	3306580	The Emacs text editor without support for the X Window System.
emacs-X11	7021739	The Emacs text editor for the X Window System.
enlightenment	15671643	The Enlightenment window manager.
enscript	1507927	ASCII to PostScript converter.
esound	396909	GNOME sound daemon.
esound-devel	55819	Development files for EsounD applications.
exmh	2404282	The `exmh` mail handling system.
expect	770412	A `tcl` extension for simplifying program-script interaction.

TABLE D.1 continued

Package Name	Size (bytes)	Description
ext2ed	301487	An ext2 filesystem editor.
extace	275998	GNOME sound displayer.
fbset	57226	Tools for managing a frame buffer's video mode properties.
fetchmail	654481	A remote mail retrieval and forwarding utility.
fetchmailconf	71376	A GUI utility for configuring your fetchmail preferences.
file	257032	Utility for determining file types.
filesystem	368688	The basic directory layout for a Linux system.
fileutils	1905548	The GNU versions of common file management utilities.
findutils	131585	The GNU versions of find utilities (`find` and `xargs`).
finger	19851	The `finger` client.
finger-server	10174	The `finger` daemon.
firewall-config	232964	A configuration tool for IP firewalls and masquerading.
flex	245903	A tool for creating scanners (text pattern recognizers).
fnlib	381203	A color font rendering library for X11R6.
fnlib-devel	40816	Headers, static libraries, and documentation for Fnlib.
fortune-mod	2393924	Program that will display a fortune.
freeciv	6525100	The Freeciv multiplayer strategy game.
freetype	900158	A free and portable TrueType font rendering engine.
freetype-devel	380677	Header files and static library for development with FreeType.
freetype-utils	169696	Several utilities to manipulate and examine TrueType fonts.
fribidi-gtkbeta	86602	Library implementing the Unicode BiDi algorithm.

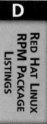

D

RED HAT LINUX
RPM PACKAGE
LISTINGS

TABLE D.1 continued

Package Name	Size (bytes)	Description
fribidi-gtkbeta-devel	53473	Development library for implementing the Unicode BiDi algorithm.
ftp	75693	FTP client.
ftpcopy	120419	A mirroring tool.
fvwm2	1626309	An improved version of the FVWM window manager for X.
fvwm2-icons	421699	Graphics used by the FVWM2 window manager.
gated	2328921	The public release version of the GateD routing daemon.
gawk	2413564	GNU awk.
gcc	8245787	Various compilers.
gcc-c++	4624258	C++ support for the GNU gcc compiler.
gcc-chill	3307789	CHILL support for the GNU gcc compiler.
gcc-g77	4046240	Fortran 77 support for gcc.
gcc-java	3252004	Java support for gcc.
gcc-objc	2919163	Objective C support for gcc.
gd	446058	A graphics library for quick creation of PNG or JPEG images.
gdb	2071995	GNU source-level debugger for C, C++, and other languages.
gdbm	29066	GNU set of database routines that use extensible hashing.
gdbm-devel	76698	Development libraries and header files for the gdbm library.
gd-devel	214903	Development libraries and header files for gd.
gdk-pixbuf	555051	An image loading library used with GNOME.
gdk-pixbuf-devel	418686	Files needed for developing apps to work with the GdkPixBuf library.
gdm	312215	The GNOME Display Manager.
gd-progs	238738	Utility programs that use libgd.
gedit	1145739	A text editor for GNOME.

TABLE D.1   continued

Package Name	Size (bytes)	Description
genromfs	11490	Utility for creating romfs filesystems.
gettext	995408	GNU libraries and utilities for producing multilingual messages.
getty_ps	124282	The `getty` and `uugetty` programs.
gftp	1001973	A multithreaded FTP client for X.
ghostscript	4420856	A PostScript interpreter and renderer.
ghostscript-fonts	1506042	Fonts for the Ghostscript PostScript interpreter.
giftrans	19702	Program for making transparent GIFs from nontransparent GIFs.
gimp	17889232	The GNU Image Manipulation Program.
gimp-data-extras	8021917	Extra files for the GNU Image Manipulation Program (GIMP).
gimp-devel	722853	The GIMP plug-in and extension development kit.
gimp-perl	658192	Perl extensions and plug-ins for the GIMP.
gkermit	109989	Utility for transferring files using the Kermit protocol.
glade	2050395	A GTK+ GUI builder.
glib10	59339	A library of handy utility functions.
glib	355265	A library of handy utility functions.
glibc	40413517	The GNU libc libraries.
glibc-devel	32897732	Files needed for development using standard C libraries.
glibc-profile	30190826	The GNU libc libraries, including support for gprof profiling.
glib-devel	340735	A library that supports GDK and GTK+.
glib-gtkbeta	524632	A library of handy utility functions.
glib-gtkbeta-devel	757490	The GIMP ToolKit (GTK+) and GIMP Drawing Kit (GDK) support library, beta version.
glms	78043	A GNOME interface for `lm_sensors`.
gmc	1728500	GNOME version of the Midnight Commander file manager.

TABLE D.1   continued

Package Name	Size (bytes)	Description
gmp	458058	GNU arbitrary precision library.
gmp-devel	1592424	Development tools for the GNU MP arbitrary precision library.
gnome-applets	6460214	Small clients for the GNOME panel.
gnome-audio	857873	Sounds for GNOME events.
gnome-audio-extra	2723528	Files needed for customizing GNOME event sounds.
gnome-core	6587412	The core programs for the GNOME GUI desktop environment.
gnome-core-devel	299462	The core libraries and include files for GNOME panel development.
gnome-games	5521482	GNOME games.
gnome-games-devel	26097	GNOME games development libraries.
gnome-kerberos	125769	Kerberos 5 tools for GNOME.
gnome-libs	2882873	The libraries needed to run the GNOME GUI desktop environment.
gnome-libs-devel	5481042	Libraries and include files for developing GNOME clients.
gnome-linuxconf	75117	GNOME front end for `linuxconf`.
gnome-lokkit	169309	Firewall configuration application for an average end user.
gnome-media	792598	GNOME media programs.
gnome-objc	689654	Objective C libraries for the GNOME desktop environment.
gnome-objc-devel	932327	Files needed to develop Objective C GNOME clients.
gnome-pim	1461902	GNOME personal productivity clients.
gnome-pim-devel	9306	Files needed for developing apps that interact with GNOME PIM.
gnome-print	1905456	Printing libraries for GNOME.
gnome-print-devel	4288766	Libraries and include files for developing GNOME clients.
gnome-users-guide	7536063	GNOME Users' Guide in HTML format.
gnome-utils	2862201	GNOME utility programs.

TABLE D.1 continued

Package Name	Size (bytes)	Description
gnorpm	445933	A graphical front end to RPM for GNOME.
gnotepad+	655213	A simple GUI text editor
gnuchess	1373871	The GNU chess program.
gnumeric	8748468	A spreadsheet program for GNOME.
gnupg	1722839	GNU utility for secure communication and data storage.
gnuplot	1964779	Program for plotting mathematical expressions and data.
gperf	123291	A perfect hash function generator.
gphoto	2169453	Digital camera software.
gpm	208900	A mouse server for the Linux console.
gpm-devel	29135	Libraries and header files for developing mouse-driven programs.
gqview	289833	An image viewer.
grep	368145	GNU pattern matching utilities.
groff	3388034	Document formatting system.
groff-gxditview	70763	X `groff` output previewer.
groff-perl	18089	Parts of the `groff` formatting system that require Perl.
gsl	4569792	The GNU Scientific Library for numerical analysis.
gtk+10	1247834	Compatibility libraries for apps linked against GTK+ and GLib 1.0.
gtk+	2338238	The GIMP ToolKit (GTK+), a library for creating GUIs for X.
gtk+-devel	3675170	Development tools for GTK+ clients.
gtk-engines	1708757	Theme engines for GTK+.
gtk+-gtkbeta	2905316	GTK+, a beta library for creating GUIs for X.
gtk+-gtkbeta-devel	3973360	Development tools for beta GTK+ clients.
gtop	957846	The GNOME system monitor.
guile	1360488	GNU implementation of Scheme for application extensibility.

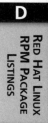

D

RED HAT LINUX
RPM PACKAGE
LISTINGS

TABLE D.1 continued

Package Name	Size (bytes)	Description
guile-devel	1132080	Libraries and header files for the GUILE extensibility library.
gv	419497	An X front end for the Ghostscript PostScript interpreter.
gzip	261125	The GNU data compression program.
hdparm	42773	Utility for displaying and/or setting hard disk parameters.
ical	795039	An X Window System–based calendar program.
im	677098	Internet message and news package.
ImageMagick	4998912	X image display and manipulation client.
ImageMagick-devel	8151574	Static libraries and header files for ImageMagick app development.
imap	1991186	Server daemons for IMAP and POP network mail protocols.
imap-devel	3169442	Development tools for programs that will use the IMAP library.
imlib	456966	An image loading and rendering library for X11R6.
imlib-cfgeditor	343036	A configuration editor for the Imlib library.
imlib-devel	581125	Development tools for Imlib applications.
indent	85062	GNU program for formatting C code.
indexhtml	24569	Default Netscape Web page.
inews	59230	Sends Usenet articles to a local news server for distribution.
info	241771	GNU `texinfo` page.
initscripts	397361	The `inittab` file and the `/etc/rc.d` scripts.
inn	6964581	The InterNetNews (INN) system.
inn-devel	1815884	The INN library.
Inti	1528438	Inti Libraries.
Inti-devel	2914982	Inti foundation libraries.
ipchains	514071	Tools for managing Linux kernel packet filtering capabilities.

TABLE D.1   continued

Package Name	Size (bytes)	Description
iproute	877488	Enhanced configuration tools for IP routing and network devices.
iptables	220057	Tools for managing Linux kernel packet filtering capabilities.
iputils	129964	The ping program for checking to see if network hosts are alive.
ipxutils	68737	Tools for configuring and debugging IPX interfaces and networks.
ircii	1135309	An Internet Relay Chat (IRC) client.
irda-utils	99062	Utilities for infrared communication between devices.
isapnptools	417378	Utilities for configuring ISA Plug-and-Play (PnP) devices.
isdn4k-utils	7790542	ISDN configuration utilities.
isdn-config	360797	A tool for configuring ISDN dialup connections.
isicom	30620	Tools to support Multi-Tech ISI multiport serial cards.
itcl	3824554	Object-oriented mega-widgets for Tcl.
jadetex	3062572	LaTeX macros for converting Jade TeX output into DVI/PS/PDF.
jed	147452	A fast, compact editor based on the S-Lang screen library.
jed-common	1474211	Files needed by any Jed text editor.
jed-xjed	174508	X version of the Jed text editor.
jikes	2681897	A Java source file to bytecode compiler.
joe	278121	An easy-to-use, modeless text editor.
joystick	127188	Utilities for configuring most popular joysticks.
kaffe	2731967	A free virtual machine for running Java(TM) code.
kapm	176631	APM details and battery monitor for KDE environment.
kbdconfig	85998	Text-based interface for setting and loading a keyboard map.

TABLE D.1   continued

Package Name	Size (bytes)	Description
kdeadmin	1878092	System administration tools for KDE.
kdebase	17294077	Core files for KDE.
kdebase-3d-screensavers	223688	3D (OpenGL) screensavers for KDE.
kdebase-lowcolor-icons	280862	Low color icons for KDE.
kdegames	5667135	Games for KDE.
kdegraphics	3415710	Graphics clients for KDE.
kdelibs	4416531	Libraries for KDE.
kdelibs-devel	4283590	Header files and documentation for compiling KDE clients.
kdemultimedia	2921272	Multimedia clients for KDE.
kdenetwork	8381316	Network clients for KDE.
kdesupport	811126	Support libraries for KDE.
kdesupport-devel	383650	Header files and documentation for the KDE support libraries.
kdetoys	551618	Toys for KDE.
kdeutils	4186987	Utilities for KDE GUI desktop.
kdevelop	17081457	A C/C++ Integrated Development Environment (IDE).
kdoc	225468	Documentation for KDE 2.0.
kdpms	154431	KDE Utility for power saving functionality of a DPMS-conpatible monitor.
kernel	15211490	The Linux kernel.
kernelcfg	63644	A Red Hat utility for configuring the kernel daemon.
kernel-doc	3111179	Various pieces of documentation found in the kernel source.
kernel-enterprise	14974012	Kernal for typical large enterprise servers.
kernel-headers	3145486	Header files for the Linux kernel.
kernel-ibcs	70905	Files that allow iBCS2 programs to run.
kernel-pcmcia-cs	635722	The daemon and device drivers for using PCMCIA adapters.
kernel-source	74135677	The source code for the Linux kernel.

TABLE D.1   continued

Package Name	Size (bytes)	Description
kernel-utils	379365	The `ksymoops` utility.
kgcc	2650442	The GNU C Compiler for kernel compilation.
Korganizer	1557528	Calendar and scheduling for KDE.
Kpackage	802529	KDE package manager.
Kpilot	1491380	Palm sync with your KDE desktop.
kpppload	120142	A PPP connection load monitor for KDE.
krb5-devel	2952382	Development files needed for compiling Kerberos 5 programs.
krb5-libs	1203948	Shared libraries used by Kerberos 5.
krb5-server	1063530	Server programs for Kerberos 5.
krb5-workstation	1218407	Kerberos 5 programs for use on workstations.
krbafs	659097	A Kerberos to AFS bridging library, built against Kerberos 5.
krbafs-utils	17480	Kerberos/AFS utility binaries.
kterm	150991	Terminal emulator for Kanji Japanese character set.
kudzu	625647	The Red Hat Linux hardware probing tool.
kudzu-devel	139855	The development library for hardware probing.
lam	4430423	The LAM (Local Area Multicomputer) programming environment.
less	119726	A text file browser similar to more, but better.
libelf	81010	An ELF object file access library.
libgcj	8620329	The Java runtime library.
libgcj-devel	12262526	Libraries for Java development using `gcc`.
libghttp	95807	GNOME HTTP client library.
libghttp-devel	45686	GNOME HTTP client development files.
libglade	272584	Library for loading a UI from an XML description at runtime.
libglade-devel	385515	The files needed for libglade application development.

TABLE D.1 continued

Package Name	Size (bytes)	Description
libgtop	583734	A library that retrieves system information.
libgtop-devel	336070	Files needed for development of LibGTop apps.
libgtop-examples	583056	Development examples for the LibGTop library.
libjpeg	258877	A library for manipulating JPEG image format files.
libjpeg6a	138281	A backward-compatible JPEG image manipulation library.
libjpeg-devel	409239	Development tools for programs that will use the libjpeg library.
libodbc++	3681105	An ODBC class library that emulates the JDBC interface.
libodbc++-devel	843065	Development files for programs that use the odbc++ library.
libodbc++-qt	2462052	qt libodbc++ libraries.
libpcap	144193	A system-independent interface for user-level packct capture.
libpng	340314	A library of functions for manipulating PNG image format files.
libpng-devel	358842	Development tools for programs that manipulate PNG images.
libPropList	117985	Utility library for storing application configuration information.
librep	1247983	A shared library that implements a Lisp dialect.
librep-devel	606640	Include files and link libraries for librep development.
libstdc++	416569	GNU C++ library.
libstdc++-devel	1736604	The header files and libraries needed for C++ development.
libtermcap	12088	A basic system library for accessing the termcap database.
libtermcap-devel	58003	Development tools for programs that will access the termcap database.

TABLE D.1   continued

Package Name	Size (bytes)	Description
libtiff	531562	A library of functions for manipulating TIFF format image files.
libtiff-devel	1057497	Development tools for programs that will use the libtiff library.
libtool	961139	The GNU libtool, which simplifies the use of shared libraries.
libtool-libs	17662	Runtime libraries for GNU libtool.
libungif	88300	A library for manipulating GIF format image files.
libungif-devel	284108	Development tools for programs that will use the libungif library.
libungif-progs	366036	Programs for manipulating GIF format image files.
libunicode	241917	A unicode manipulation library.
libunicode-devel	286707	A unicode manipulation library.
libxml10	166465	A backward-compatibility XML library.
libxml	1379126	An XML library.
libxml-devel	1480747	Files needed for developing libxml applications.
licq	5177074	An ICQ clone for online messaging.
lilo	1160300	The boot loader for Linux and other operating systems.
links	482951	Text mode WWW browser with support for frames.
linuxconf	18249949	A system configuration tool.
linuxconf-devel	3993875	The tools needed for developing linuxconf modules.
lm_sensors	563806	Hardware monitoring tools.
lm_sensors-devel	119201	Development files for programs that will use sensors.
locale_config	15459	Locale configuration tool.
lockdev	48959	A library for locking devices.
lockdev-devel	39276	The header files and a static library for the lockdev library.

D

RED HAT LINUX
RPM PACKAGE
LISTINGS

TABLE D.1   continued

Package Name	Size (bytes)	Description
logrotate	40438	Rotates, compresses, removes, and mails system log files.
losetup	10560	Programs for setting up and configuring loopback devices.
lout	4847751	The Lout document formatting language.
lout-doc	2294098	The documentation for the Lout document formatting language.
LPRng	4648329	An enhanced version of the Berkeley LPR print spooler.
lrzsz	367409	A modem communications package.
lslk	28630	A lock file lister.
lsof	548533	Utility that lists open files on a Linux/UNIX system.
ltrace	115381	Tracks runtime library calls from dynamically linked executables.
lynx	2409265	A text-based Web browser.
m4	135369	The GNU macro processor.
macutils	211107	Utilities for manipulating Macintosh file formats.
magicdev	64956	A GNOME daemon for automatically mounting/playing CDs.
mailcap	21040	Associates helper applications with particular file types.
mailx	78868	The `/bin/mail` program for sending email messages.
make	554132	GNU tool that simplifies the build process.
MAKEDEV	400200	A script for creating the device files in `/dev`.
man	240957	A set of documentation tools: `man`, `apropos`, and `whatis`.
man-pages	1058115	Man (manual) pages from the Linux Documentation Project.
man-pages-cs	269163	Czech man pages from the Linux Documentation Project (LDP).
man-pages-da	23462	Danish man pages from the LDP.

TABLE D.1 continued

Package Name	Size (bytes)	Description
man-pages-de	683207	German man pages from the LDP.
man-pages-es	1266410	Spanish man pages from the LDP.
man-pages-fr	1391152	French man pages from the LDP.
man-pages-it	605488	Italian man pages from the LDP.
man-pages-ja	1903919	Japanese man pages from the LDP.
man-pages-pl	1373648	Polish man pages from the LDP.
man-pages-ru	227861	Russian man pages from the LDP.
mars-nwe	729383	NetWare file and print servers that run on Linux systems.
mawk	123325	An interpreter for the awk programming language.
mc	3557022	A user-friendly file manager and visual shell.
mcserv	19630	Server for the Midnight Commander network file management system.
memprof	444262	A tool for memory profiling and leak detection.
Mesa	2176650	A 3D graphics library with an API very similar to OpenGL's.
Mesa-devel	2756672	The development environment for the Mesa 3D graphics library.
metamail	309655	Program for handling multimedia mail using the mailcap file.
mgetty	432885	A getty replacement for use with data and fax modems.
mgetty-sendfax	247858	Provides support for sending faxes over a modem.
mgetty-viewfax	98967	An X fax viewer.
mgetty-voice	912312	Program for using your modem and mgetty as an answering machine.
mikmod	834271	A MOD music file player.
mingetty	35300	A compact getty program for virtual consoles only.
minicom	312191	A text-based modem control and terminal emulation program.

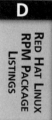

TABLE D.1   continued

Package Name	Size (bytes)	Description
mkbootdisk	5392	Creates an initial ramdisk image for preloading modules.
mkinitrd	9742	Creates an initial ramdisk image for preloading modules.
mkisofs	483539	Creates an image of an ISO9660 filesystem.
mkkickstart	8266	Writes a `kickstart` description of the current machine.
mktemp	6538	A small utility for safely making `/tmp` files.
mkxauth	12576	Utility for managing `.Xauthority` files.
mod_dav	277643	Distributed Authoring and Versioning protocol for Apache.
modemtool	16480	A tool for selecting the serial port your modem is connected to.
mod_perl	2219030	A Perl interpreter for the Apache Web server.
mod_php	1129376	The PHP HTML-embedded scripting language for use with Apache.
modutils	661757	Kernel module management utilities.
mount	109350	Programs for mounting and unmounting filesystems.
mouseconfig	303724	The Red Hat Linux mouse configuration tool.
mpage	92534	A tool for printing multiple pages of text on each printed page.
mpg123	189002	An MPEG audio player.
mtools	291187	Programs for accessing MS-DOS disks without mounting the disks.
mtr	78763	A network diagnostic tool.
mtr-gtk	108610	The GTK+ GUI interface for the `mtr` network diagnostic utility.
mt-st	61827	Install mt-st if you need a tool to control tape drives.
mtx	69584	A SCSI media changer control program.
multimedia	337756	Several X utilities mainly for use with multimedia files.

TABLE D.1   continued

Package Name	Size (bytes)	Description
mutt	2295794	A text mode mail user agent.
mysql	3934584	The daemon and core programs for the MySQL database system.
mysql-devel	1104208	Files need for MySQL database system development.
mysql-server	1557605	MySQL server.
nasm	518007	A portable x86 assembler that uses Intel-like syntax.
nasm-doc	864548	Documentation for the Netwide Assembler (NASM).
nasm-rdoff	87147	Tools for the RDOFF binary format, sometimes used with NASM.
nc	117390	Reads and writes data across network connections using TCP or UDP.
ncftp	934020	An improved FTP client.
ncompress	31374	Fast compression and decompression utilities.
ncpfs	1077622	Utilities for the ncpfs filesystem, a NetWare client for Linux.
ncurses	2961599	A CRT screen handling and optimization package.
ncurses4	374980	A CRT screen handling and optimization package.
ncurses-devel	1482195	The development files for apps that use ncurses.
netcfg	176736	A network configuration tool.
netpbm	206819	A library for handling different graphics file formats.
netpbm-devel	103162	Development tools for programs that will use the netpbm libraries.
netpbm-progs	1875448	Tools for manipulating graphics files in netpbm supported formats.
netscape-common	15188564	Files shared by Netscape Navigator and Communicator.
netscape-communicator	14128484	The Netscape Communicator suite of tools.

D

RED HAT LINUX
RPM PACKAGE
LISTINGS

TABLE D.1 continued

Package Name	Size (bytes)	Description
netscape-navigator	7679037	The Netscape Navigator Web browser.
net-tools	581572	The basic tools for setting up networking.
newt	132717	A development library for text-mode user interfaces.
newt-devel	146774	Newt windowing toolkit development files.
nfs-utils	537641	NFS utilities and supporting daemons for the kernel NFS server.
njamd	121650	An advanced debugger that detects memory allocation violations.
nmh	5131438	A mail handling system with a command-line interface.
nscd	35004	A Name Service Caching Daemon (nscd).
nss_ldap	371786	NSS library and PAM module for LDAP.
ntp	1877840	Synchronizes system time using the Network Time Protocol (NTP).
ntsysv	17055	A tool to set the stop/start of system services in a runlevel.
nut	316850	Network UPS Tools.
nut-cgi	79688	CGI utilities for the Network UPS Tools.
nut-client	88172	Network UPS Tools client monitoring utilities.
octave	14499306	A high-level language for numerical computations.
open	12259	A tool that will start a program on a virtual console.
openjade	14482477	A DSSSL implementation.
openldap	210490	LDAP servers, libraries, utilities, tools and sample clients.
openldap-devel	1192294	OpenLDAP development libraries and header files.
openldap-servers	2024269	OpenLDAP server.
openssh	212286	Secure Shell.
openssh-askpass	48199	Contains the X11 passphrase dialog.
openssh-askpass-gnome	7696	Contains the GNOME passphrase dialog.

TABLE D.1 continued

Package Name	Size (bytes)	Description
openssh-clients	247026	Clients necessary to make encrypted connections.
openssh-server	198813	The secure shell daemon for OpenSSH
openssl	2636141	OpenSSL certificate management tool.
openssl-devel	2410826	OpenSSL development libraries and header files.
openssl-perl	11450	Perl scripts for use with OpenSSL.
openssl-python	447709	Python scripts for use with OpenSSL
ORBit	938792	A high-performance CORBA Object Request Broker.
ORBit-devel	1511166	Development libraries, header files, and utilities for ORBit.
p2c	712493	A Pascal to C translator.
p2c-devel	30523	Files for p2c Pascal to C translator development.
pam	1992770	A security tool that provides authentication for applications.
pam_krb5	245059	A Pluggable Authentication Module (PAM) for Kerberos 5.
pango-gtkbeta	536695	System for layout and rendering of internationalized text.
pango-gtkbeta-devel	319515	System for layout and rendering of internationalized text.
parted	425976	The GNU disk partition manipulation program.
parted-devel	232335	The GNU disk partition manipulation program development files.
passwd	17004	The passwd utility for setting/changing passwords using PAM.
patch	121820	The GNU patch command, for modifying/upgrading files.
pax	91025	The POSIX file system archiver.
pciutils	232457	Linux PCI utilities.
pciutils-devel	52159	Linux PCI development library.

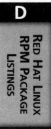

D

RED HAT LINUX
RPM PACKAGE
LISTINGS

TABLE D.1   continued

Package Name	Size (bytes)	Description
pdksh	341930	A public domain clone of the Korn shell (`ksh`).
perl	19842391	The Perl programming language.
php	1205008	The PHP HTML-embedded scripting language.
php-imap	781420	An Apache module for PHP applications that use IMAP.
php-ldap	29862	An Apache Web server module for PHP3 applications that use LDAP.
php-manual	4161797	The PHP manual, in HTML format.
php-mysql	37742	A module for PHP4 applications that use MySQL databases.
php-pgsql	37989	A PostgreSQL database module for PHP.
pidentd	96248	An implementation of the RFC1413 identification server.
pilot-link	596516	File transfer utilities for Linux to PalmPilots and vice versa.
pilot-link-devel	257241	PalmPilot development header files.
pine	4206185	A commonly used, MIME-compliant mail and news reader.
pinfo	188705	An info file viewer.
playmidi	100153	A MIDI sound file player.
playmidi-X11	40313	X-based MIDI sound file player.
plugger	51604	A multimedia plug-in for Netscape 3.0 or later.
pmake	1039546	The BSD 4.4 version of `make`.
pmake-customs	1005288	A remote execution facility for `pmake`.
pnm2ppa	680994	Drivers for printing to HP PPA printers.
popt	72529	A C library for parsing command-line parameters.
portmap	52441	Program that manages RPC connections.
postgresql	7156111	PostgreSQL client programs and libraries.
postgresql-devel	1791581	PostgreSQL development header files and libraries.

TABLE D.1 continued

Package Name	Size (bytes)	Description
postgresql-jdbc	699239	Files needed for Java programs to access a PostgreSQL database.
postgresql-odbc	162548	The ODBC driver needed for accessing a PostgreSQL DB using ODBC.
postgresql-perl	156329	Development module needed for Perl code to access a PostgreSQL DB.
postgresql-python	129707	Development module for Python code to access a PostgreSQL DB.
postgresql-server	1753508	The programs needed to create and run a PostgreSQL server.
postgresql-tcl	64964	A Tcl shell client for PostgreSQL.
postgresql-tk	994016	The Tk shell and Tk-based GUI for PostgreSQL clients.
ppp	360415	The PPP (Point-to-Point Protocol) daemon.
printtool	125827	A printer configuration tool with a graphical user interface.
procinfo	55506	A tool for gathering and displaying system information.
procmail	233075	The procmail mail processing program.
procps	333524	System and process monitoring utilities.
procps-X11	213	X-based system message monitoring utility.
psacct	84291	Utilities for monitoring process activities.
psgml	596990	GNU Emacs major mode for editing SGML documents.
psmisc	43668	Utilities for managing processes on your system.
pspell	664653	Provides a generic interface to spell checker libraries.
pspell-devel	212977	Static libraries and header files for the Pspell library.
pump	86679	A BOOTP and DHCP client for automatic IP configuration.
pump-devel	80587	Development tools for sending DHCP and BOOTP requests.
pvm	6808811	Libraries for distributed computing.

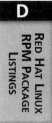

D

RED HAT LINUX
RPM PACKAGE
LISTINGS

TABLE D.1   continued

Package Name	Size (bytes)	Description
pvm-gui	2597301	Tcl/Tk graphical interface monitoring and managing a PVM cluster.
pwdb	440294	The password database library.
pxe	247716	A Linux PXE (Preboot eXecution Environment) server.
pygnome	987204	Python bindings for GNOME libraries.
pygnome-applet	32392	Python bindings for GNOME Panel applets.
pygnome-capplet	14364	Python bindings for GNOME Panel applets.
pygnome-libglade	7610	GNOME support for the libglade Python wrapper.
pygtk	1831323	Python bindings for the GTK+ widget set.
pygtk-libglade	24374	A wrapper for the libglade library for use with PyGTK.
python	6791771	An interpreted, interactive object-oriented programming language.
python-devel	3993215	The libraries and header files needed for Python development.
python-docs	2723823	Documentation for the Python programming language.
pythonlib	273427	A library of Python code used by various Red Hat Linux programs.
python-tools	376098	A collection of development tools included with Python.
python-xmlrpc	58557	Python implementation for Userland's XML-RPC protocol.
qt1x	2179867	A backward-2180036 library for apps linked to Qt 1.x.
qt1x-devel	5756286	Qt 1.x development files for legacy clients.
qt1x-GL	42405	An OpenGL (3D graphics) add-on for the Qt GUI toolkit version1.
qt	14877298	The shared library for the Qt GUI toolkit.
qt-devel	23387507	Development files and docs for the Qt GUI toolkit.
qt-Xt	27512	An Xt (X Toolkit) compatibility add-on for the Qt GUI toolkit.

TABLE D.1 continued

Package Name	Size (bytes)	Description
quota	118214	System admin tools for monitoring users' disk usage.
raidtools	107290	Tools for creating and maintaining software RAID devices.
rarpd	19649	The RARP daemon.
rcs	500214	Revision Control System (RCS) file version management tools.
rdate	5839	Tool for retrieving the date/time from another machine on your network.
rdist	144266	Maintains identical copies of files on multiple machines.
readline2.2.1	195060	A library for reading and returning lines from a terminal.
readline	270507	A library for editing typed in command lines.
readline-devel	296003	Files needed to develop programs that use the readline library.
redhat-logos	644872	Red Hat-related icons and pictures.
redhat-release	37	The Red Hat Linux release file.
rep-gtk	585293	GTK+ bindings for the librep LISP environment.
rep-gtk-gnome	399099	GNOME bindings for the librep Lisp interpreter.
rep-gtk-libglade	33209	A librep binding of libglade, for loading user interfaces.
rgrep	15790	A grep utility that can recursively descend through directories.
rhcfile	26741	Library for accessing config files.
rhcfile-devel	25945	Header files and libraries for rhcfile development.
rhclib	25664	A library for parsing and editing configuration files.
rhclib-devel	384230	Header files and libraries for rhclib development.

TABLE D.1 continued

Package Name	Size (bytes)	Description
rhmask	8065	Generates and restores mask files based on original and update files.
rhn_register	140966	Allows register with Red Hat Network Services.
rhn_register-gnome	151255	GNOME interface for RHN registration program.
rhs-printfilters	122797	Red Hat print filters, for use with the print-tool.
rmt	8971	Provides certain programs with access to remote tape devices.
rootfiles	1998	The basic required files for the root user's directory.
routed	34969	The routing daemon that maintains routing tables.
rp3	557559	The Red Hat graphical PPP management tool.
rpm2html	245472	Translates an RPM database and dependency information into HTML.
rpm	2853571	The Red Hat package management system.
rpm-build	183838	Scripts and executable programs used to build packages.
rpmdb-redhat	20870144	The entire RPM database for the packages in Red Hat Linux.
rpm-devel	632393	Development files for apps that will manipulate RPM packages.
rpmfind	137566	Finds and transfers RPM files for a specified program.
rpmlint	148303	A development tool for checking the correctness of RPM packages.
rpm-python	47442	Python bindings for apps that will manipulate RPM packages.
rp-pppoe	132370	A client for connecting via ADSL and PPPoE to an ISP.
rsh	49900	Clients for remote access commands (rsh, rlogin, rcp).

TABLE D.1 continued

Package Name	Size (bytes)	Description
rsh-server	45703	Servers for remote access commands (rsh, rlogin, rcp).
rsync	208083	Program for synchronizing files over a network.
rusers	23252	Displays the users logged into machines on the local network.
rusers-server	29119	Server for the rusers protocol.
rwall	7505	Client for sending messages to a host's logged in users.
rwall-server	9367	Server for sending messages to a host's logged in users.
rwho	32658	Displays who is logged in to local network machines.
rxvt	524087	A color VT102 terminal emulator for X.
samba	7704190	The Samba SMB server.
samba-client	1688108	Samba (SMB) client programs.
samba-common	3342271	Files used by both Samba servers and clients.
sane	2700890	Scanner access software.
sane-devel	2383917	The SANE (a universal scanner interface) development toolkit.
sash	444918	A statically linked shell, including some built-in basic commands.
sawfish	2839606	An extensible window manager for X.
sawfish-themer	88166	A GUI for creating sawfish window manager themes.
screen	387777	A screen mgr that supports multiple logins on one terminal.
SDL	413363	The Simple DirectMedia Layer multimedia library.
SDL-devel	793250	Libraries, includes and more for developing SDL applications.
SDL_image	61041	A sample image loading library for SDL.
SDL_image-devel	34077	Development files for the SDL image loading library.

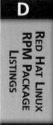

D

RED HAT LINUX
RPM PACKAGE
LISTINGS

TABLE D.1   continued

Package Name	Size (bytes)	Description
sed	69413	GNU stream text editor.
sendmail	618757	A widely used Mail Transport Agent (MTA).
sendmail-cf	737233	The files needed to reconfigure Sendmail.
sendmail-doc	1264302	Documentation about the Sendmail Mail Transport Agent program.
setserial	31193	Utility for configuring serial ports.
setup	21233	A set of system configuration and setup files.
setuptool	6748	A text mode system configuration tool.
sgml-common	71469	Common SGML catalog and DTD files.
sgml-tools	905766	A text formatting package based on SGML.
shadow-utils	783277	Utilities for managing shadow password files and user/group accounts.
shapecfg	29863	A configuration tool for setting traffic bandwidth parameters.
sharutils	212795	GNU shar utilities for packaging and unpackaging shell archives.
sh-utils	364366	A set of GNU utilities commonly used in shell scripts.
slang	397647	The shared library for the S-Lang extension language.
slang-devel	1711001	The static library and header files for development using S-Lang.
sliplogin	52488	A login program for SLIP connections.
slocate	61600	Finds files on a system via a central database.
slrn	441871	A threaded Internet news reader.
slrn-pull	82860	Offline news reading support for the SLRN news reader.
smpeg	443827	SDL MPEG Library.
smpeg-devel	327833	Libraries, includes, and more to develop SMPEG applications.
sndconfig	449212	The Red Hat Linux sound config tool.

TABLE D.1   continued

Package Name	Size (bytes)	Description
sox	218360	A general-purpose sound file conversion tool.
sox-devel	258904	The SoX sound file format converter libraries.
specspo	9601028	Red Hat package descriptions, summaries, and groups.
squid	2441002	The Squid proxy caching server.
stat	8985	A tool for finding out information about a specified file.
statserial	406001	A tool that displays the status of serial port modem lines.
strace	119479	Tracks and displays system calls associated with a running process.
stylesheets	5076834	The stylesheets used at Cygnus for SGML conversion.
sudo	298776	Allows restricted root access for specified users.
SVGATextMode	810393	Utility for improving the appearance of text consoles.
switchdesk	160821	A desktop environment switcher for GNOME, KDE, and AnotherLevel.
switchdesk-gnome	12968	A GNOME interface for the Desktop Switcher.
switchdesk-kde	34616	A KDE interface for the Desktop Switcher.
symlinks	9177	Utility that maintains a system's symbolic links.
sysctlconfig	75081	A configuration tool for operating system tunable parameters.
sysklogd	90657	System logging and kernel message trapping daemons.
syslinux	65042	Simple kernel loader that boots from a FAT filesystem.
sysreport	19572	Gathers system hardware and configuration information.

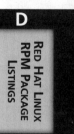

Table D.1   continued

Package Name	Size (bytes)	Description
sysstat	206212	The sar and iostat system monitoring commands.
SysVinit	157593	Programs that control basic system processes.
talk	19382	Talk client for one-on-one Internet chatting.
talk-server	17309	The talk server for one-on-one Internet chatting.
taper	929176	A menu-driven file backup system.
tar	642651	GNU file archiving program.
tcl	5045632	An embeddable scripting language.
tcllib	328990	A library of utility modules for Tcl.
tclx	1988207	Extensions for Tcl.
tcpdump	269383	A network traffic monitoring tool.
tcp_wrappers	185960	A security tool that acts as a wrapper for TCP daemons.
tcsh	656821	An enhanced version of csh, the C shell.
telnet	88786	The client program for the telnet remote login protocol.
telnet-server	43575	The telnet server.
termcap	700845	The terminal feature database used by certain applications.
tetex	30915458	The TeX text formatting system.
tetex-afm	3308842	A converter for PostScript font metric files, for use with TeX.
tetex-doc	40099309	Documentation files for the TeX text formatting system.
tetex-dvilj	344662	A DVI to HP PCL (Printer Control Language) converter.
tetex-dvips	788976	A DVI to PostScript converter for the TeX text formatting system.
tetex-fonts	19477829	The font files for the TeX text formatting system.
tetex-latex	9693003	The LaTeX front end for the TeX text formatting system.

TABLE D.1 continued

Package Name	Size (bytes)	Description
tetex-xdvi	1267677	An X viewer for DVI files.
texinfo	917438	Tools needed to create Texinfo format documentation files.
textutils	1776429	A set of GNU text file modifying utilities.
tftp	17998	The client for the Trivial File Transfer Protocol (TFTP).
tftp-server	15182	The server for the Trivial File Transfer Protocol (TFTP).
time	21619	GNU utility for monitoring a program's use of system resources.
timeconfig	680319	Text mode tools for setting system time parameters.
timed	57292	Programs for maintaining networked machines' time synchronization.
timetool	23484	Utility for setting the system's date and time.
tin	1347613	A basic Internet news reader.
tix	1416387	A set of capable widgets for Tk.
tk	3648804	The Tk GUI toolkit for Tcl, with shared libraries.
tkinter	741333	A graphical user interface for the Python scripting language.
tksysv	42351	An X editor for editing runlevel services.
tmpwatch	10796	Utility for removing files based on when they were last accessed.
traceroute	21877	Traces the route taken by packets over a TCP/IP network.
transfig	361877	Utilities for creating TeX docs with portable graphics.
tree	20043	Displays a tree view of the contents of directories.
trn	369873	A news reader that displays postings in threaded format.
trojka	15856	A non-X game of falling blocks.

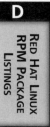

TABLE D.1 continued

Package Name	Size (bytes)	Description
ucd-snmp	2222893	A collection of SNMP protocol tools from UC-Davis.
ucd-snmp-devel	815616	The development environment for the UCD-SNMP project.
ucd-snmp-utils	378166	Network management utilities using SNMP, from the UCD-SNMP project.
umb-scheme	2100877	An implementation of the Scheme programming language.
unarj	29878	An uncompressor for .arj format archive files.
units	182247	Utility for converting amounts from one unit to another.
unixODBC	1585840	A complete ODBC Driver Manager for Linux.
unixODBC-devel	1859239	Development files for programs that will use the unixODBC library.
unzip	345286	Utility for unpacking .zip files.
up2date	156741	Utility for updating installed packages on your machine.
up2date-gnome	157694	GNOME interface to the Update Agent.
urlview	46510	A URL extractor/viewer for use with Mutt.
urw-fonts	2750588	Free versions of the 35 standard PostScript fonts.
usbview	53172	USB topology and device viewer.
usermode	177301	Graphical tools for certain user account management tasks.
utempter	43468	A privileged helper for utmp/wtmp updates.
util-linux	2079735	A collection of basic system utilities.
uucp	2132563	The uucp utility for copying files between systems.
vim-common	7078030	The common files needed by any version of the VIM editor.
vim-enhanced	1802487	A version of the VIM editor that includes recent enhancements.
vim-minimal	361860	A minimal version of the VIM editor.
vim-X11	1942741	The VIM version of the vi editor for X.

TABLE D.1 continued

Package Name	Size (bytes)	Description
vixie-cron	59289	The Vixie `cron` daemon for executing specified programs at set times.
vlock	8857	Program that locks one or all virtual consoles.
vnc	89635	A remote display system.
vnc-doc	1481964	Complete documentation for VNC.
vnc-server	1312583	Virtual Network Computing Server
w3c-libwww	2267103	A general-purpose Web API written in C.
w3c-libwww-apps	53268	A robot and command-line tool built using the libwww Web API.
w3c-libwww-devel	1721934	Libraries and header files for programs that use libwww.
wget	329955	Utility for retrieving files using the HTTP or FTP protocols.
which	26542	Displays where a particular program in your path is located.
whois	37411	Internet `whois`/nicname client.
WindowMaker	3869467	A window manager for X.
WindowMaker-libs	5729386	WindowMaker libraries.
wireless-tools	56646	Wireless ethernet configuration tools.
wmakerconf	885352	A configuration tool for the Window Maker window manager.
wmconfig	58408	A helper application for configuring X window managers.
words	424642	A dictionary of English words for the `/usr/dict` directory.
wu-ftpd	461030	An FTP daemon provided by Washington University.
wvdial	247994	A heuristic autodialer for PPP connections.
x3270	573552	X-based IBM 3278/3279 terminal emulator.
Xaw3d	598744	A version of the MIT Athena widget set for X.
Xaw3d-devel	674793	Header files and static libraries for development using Xaw3d.
xbill	197354	Stop Bill from loading his OS into all the computers.

D

RED HAT LINUX
RPM PACKAGE
LISTINGS

TABLE D.1 continued

Package Name	Size (bytes)	Description
xbl	129095	A three-dimensional game of falling blocks for X.
xboard	495610	An X graphical chessboard.
xboing	1069896	A Breakout style X-based game.
xcdroast	1215139	X-based tool for creating CDs.
xchat	1788486	A GTK+ IRC (chat) client.
Xconfigurator	964752	The Red Hat Linux configuration tool for X.
xcpustate	29944	X-based CPU state monitor.
xdaliclock	79843	A clock for X.
xemacs	43435983	X-based version of GNU Emacs.
xemacs-el	25475863	The .el source files for XEmacs.
xemacs-info	1497165	Info files for XEmacs.
xfig	2965224	An X tool for drawing basic vector graphics.
XFree86-100dpi-fonts	1262325	X 100-dpi fonts.
XFree86	31871061	The basic fonts, programs, and docs for X.
XFree86-75dpi-fonts	1090616	A set of 75-dpi resolution fonts for X.
XFree86-cyrillic-fonts	380836	Cyrillic fonts for X.
XFree86-devel	8917829	X11R6 static libraries, headers, and programming man pages.
XFree86-doc	11337189	Documentation on various X11 programming interfaces.
XFree86-FBDev	3483164	The X server for the generic frame buffer device on some machines.
XFree86-ISO8859-2-100dpi-fonts	1030916	ISO 8859-2 fonts in 100-dpi resolution for X.
XFree86-ISO8859-2-75dpi-fonts	789939	A set of 75-dpi Central European language fonts for X.
XFree86-ISO8859-2	88914	Central European language fonts for X.
XFree86-ISO8859-2-Type1-fonts	1960851	Type 1 scalable Central European language (ISO8859-2) fonts for X.
XFree86-ISO8859-7-100dpi-fonts	322958	ISO 8859-7 fonts in 100-dpi resolution for X.
XFree86-ISO8859-7	305451	Greek language fonts for X.
XFree86-ISO8859-7-75dpi-fonts	641297	ISO 8859-7 fonts in 75-dpi resolution for X.

TABLE D.1   continued

Package Name	Size (bytes)	Description
XFree86-ISO8859-7-Type1-fonts	1154338	Type 1 scalable Greek (ISO 8859-7) fonts
XFree86-ISO8859 9-100dpi-fonts	1171192	100-dpi Turkish (ISO8859-9) fonts for X.
XFree86-ISO8859-9-75dpi-fonts	1058962	75-dpi Turkish (ISO8859-9) fonts for X.
XFree86-ISO8859-9	92722	Turkish language fonts and modmaps for X.
XFree86-KOI8-R-100dpi-fonts	299406	KOI8-R fonts in 100-dpi resolution for the X Window System.
Xfree86-KOI8-R	220085	Russian and Ukrainian language fonts for the X Window System.
Xfree86-KOI8-R-75dpi-fonts	684211	A set of 75-dpi Russian and Ukrainian language fonts for X.
XFree86-libs	3242045	Shared libraries needed by X programs.
Xfree86-3DLabs	3675034	An XFree86 server for 3Dlabs video cards.
Xfree86-8514	3204178	An XFree86 server for older 8514 or compatible video cards.
Xfree86-AGX	3387057	An XFree86 server for AGX-based video cards.
Xfree86-I128	3638866	An XFree86 server for Number Nine Imagine 128 video cards.
Xfree86-Mach32	3342045	An XFree86 server for Mach32 video cards.
Xfree86-Mach64	3481748	An XFree86 server for Mach64 video cards.
Xfree86-Mach8	3215443	An XFree86 server for Mach8 video cards.
Xfree86-Mono	3503450	An XFree86 server for Monochrome.
Xfree86-P9000	3407123	An XFree86 server for P9000 cards.
Xfree86-S3	3900464	An XFree86 server for S3-based chips.
Xfree86-S3V	3621936	An XFree86 server for S3 Virge chips.
Xfree86-SVGA	4766499	An XFree86 server for most simple frame-buffer SVGA devices.
Xfree86-VGA16	3442524	An Xfree86 server for generic VGA16 boards
Xfree86-W32	3267985	An Xfree86 server for ET4000/W32 chips.
XFree86-tools	975383	Various tools for XFree86.
XFree86-twm	140965	A simple, lightweight window manager for X.

D

RED HAT LINUX
RPM PACKAGE
LISTINGS

TABLE D.1 continued

Package Name	Size (bytes)	Description
XFree86-V4L	14951	Video for Linux (V4L) support for XFree86 4.X.
XFree86-xdm	245175	The X display manager.
XFree86-xf86cfg	268396	A configuration tool for XFree86.
XFree86-xfs	1047081	A font server for the X Window System.
XFree86-Xnest	874345	A nested XFree86 server.
XFree86-Xvfb	3750713	A virtual framebuffer X Window System server for XFree86.
xgammon	3357707	An X Window System-based backgammon game.
xinetd	198478	A secure replacement for inetd.
xinitrc	20632	The default startup script for X.
xisdnload	51985	An ISDN connection load average display for the X.
xjewel	49674	X11 falling blocks game.
xlispstat	2994104	An implementation of the Lisp language with statistics extensions.
xloadimage	241191	An X Window System-based image viewer.
xlockmore	1711610	An X terminal locking program.
xmailbox	31378	An X Window System utility that notifies you of new mail.
xmms	1918426	An MP3 player for X that resembles Winamp.
xmms-devel	77443	Static libraries and header files for Xmms plug-in development.
xmms-gnome	39389	A GNOME panel applet for the Xmms multimedia player.
xmorph	151565	An X Window System tool for creating morphed images.
xosview	91714	An X Window System utility for monitoring system resources.
xpaint	464813	An X Window System image editing or paint program.
xpat2	995694	X11 Solitaire game.

TABLE D.1   continued

Package Name	Size (bytes)	Description
xpdf	3093974	A PDF file viewer for the X Window System.
xpilot	2150441	An X Window System-based multiplayer aerial combat game.
xpuzzles	425134	Geometric puzzles and toys for X.
xrn	294526	An X Window System-based news reader.
xsane	2257260	An X Window System front end for the SANE scanner interface.
xsane-gimp	289052	A GIMP plugin that provides a scanner interface.
xscreensaver	5432030	A set of X Window System screensavers.
xsri	7884	Program for displaying images on the background for X.
xsysinfo	26560	An X11 kernel parameter monitoring client.
xtoolwait	8493	Utility that aims to decrease X session startup time.
xtrojka	218996	An X Window System falling blocks game.
xxgdb	96983	An X Window System graphical interface for the GNU gdb debugger.
ypbind	43179	The NIS daemon that binds NIS clients to an NIS domain.
ypserv	277008	The NIS (Network Information Service) server.
yp-tools	149844	NIS (or YP) client programs.
ytalk	69246	A chat program for multiple users.
zip	271467	A file compression and packaging utility compatible with PKZIP.
zlib	70155	The zlib compression and decompression library.
zlib-devel	156331	Header files and libraries for developing apps that use zlib.
zsh	1338154	A shell similar to ksh, but with improvements.

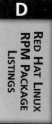

D

RED HAT LINUX
RPM PACKAGE
LISTINGS

Group and Package Listing

Table D.2 provides a listing of Red Hat Linux RPM packages cross-referenced by Group. You'll quickly recognize these Groups when you use either GNOME's gnorpm or KDE's kpackage to manage your system's software. RPM Groups are organized according to Amusements, Applications, Development, Documentation, Networking, System Environment, and User Interface. You may also find subgroups under a group, such as Games and Graphics under Amusements.

You can use Table D.2 as a reference if you're looking for packages to install or remove from a particular group, or to check the completeness of an install of a specific group of software. This organization can also help desktop users remove redundant software. For example, how many falling block games or text editors do you really need installed on your system? (System administrators of multiuser systems may want to keep a full installation to make everyone happy!)

TABLE D.2   Red Hat Linux Group and Package Listing

Group	Packages
Amusements/Games	cxhextris, fortune-mod, freeciv, gnome-games, gnuchess, kdegames, trojka, xbill, xbl, xboard, xboing, xgammon, xjewel, xpat2, xpilot, xpuzzles, xtrojka
Amusements/Graphics	kdetoys, xdaliclock, xloadimage, xlockmore, xmorph, xscreensaver, xsri
Applications/Archiving	cdrecord, cpio, dump, dump-static, pax, rmt, sharutils, taper, tar, unarj, unzip, zip
Applications/Communications	dip, efax, getty_ps, gkermit, licq, lrzsz, mgetty, mgetty-sendfax, mgetty-viewfax, mgetty-voice, minicom, pilot-link, sliplogin, uucp
Applications/Databases	db3-utils, mysql, mysql-server, mysql-dev, postgresql, postgresql-jdbc, postgresql-odbc, postgresql-perl, postgresql-python, postgresql-server, postgresql-tcl, postgresql-test, postgresql-tk
Applications/Editors	abiword, emacs, emacs-el, emacs-leim, emacs-nox, emacs-X11, gedit, gnotepad+, jed, jed-common, jed-xjed, joe, psgml, vim-common, vim-enhanced, vim-minimal, vim-X11, xemacs, xemacs-el, xemacs-info
Applications/Engineering	bc, gnuplot, octave, units, xlispstat
Applications/File	bzip2, file, fileutils, findutils, gzip, ncompress, slocate, stat, tree

TABLE D.2   continued

Group	Packages
Applications/Internet	elm, exmh, fetchmail, fetchmailconf, finger, ftp, ftpcopy, gftp, gnome-lokkit, im, ircii, kdenetwork, kpppload, links, lynx, mailx, metamail, mtr, mtr-gtk, mutt, nc, ncftp, netscape-common, netscape-communicator, netscape-navigator, nmh, openldap-clients, openssh, openssh-askpass, openssh-askpass-gnome, openssh-clients, openssl-perl, openssl-python, pine, plugger, rsh, rsync, slrn, slrn-pull, stunnel, talk, tcpdump, telnet, tftp, tin, traceroute, trn, urlview, w3c-libwww-apps, wget, whois, xchat, xmailbox, xrn, ytalk
Applications/Multimedia	aumix, aumix-X11, awesfx, cdda2wav, cdp, cdparanoia, desktop-backgrounds, dia, ee, extace, gd-progs, giftrans, gimp, gimp-data-extras, gimp-devel, gnome-audio, gnome-media, ImageMagick, kdegraphics, kdemultimedia, libungif-progs, mikmod, mpg123, multimedia, netpbm-progs, playmidi, playmidi-X11, sndconfig, sox, transfig, xcdroast, xfig, xmms, xmms-gnome, xpaint, xsane, xsane-gimp
Applications/Productivity	gnome-pim, gnumeric, ical, korganizer
Applications/Publishing	enscript, freetype-utils, ghostscript, ghostscript-fonts, gphoto, groff, groff-gxditview, groff-perl, gv, jadetex, lout, lout-doc, mpage, pnm2ppa, printtool, rhs-printfilters, sgml-tools, tetex, tetex-afm, tetex-doc, tetex-dvilj, tetex-dvips, tetex-fonts, tetex-latex, tetex-xdvi, texinfo, xpdf
Applications/System	amanda, amanda-client, amanda-server, anaconda, anaconda-runtime, arpwatch, auth_ldap, autorun, bind-utils, bug-buddy, console-tools, control-panel, dialog, dosfstools, ext2ed, fbset, firewall-config, gnome-linuxconf, gnome-utils, gnorpm, gtop, hdparm, iproute, ipxutils, irda-utils, isdn4k-utils, isdn-config, isi-com, kapm, kdeadmin, kdeutils, kdpms, kpackage, krbafs-utils, kudzu, linuxconf, lm_sensors, locale_config, macutils, magicdev, mkisofs, mkxauth, modemtool, mtools, mt-st, mtx, ncpfs, netcfg, nut, nut-cgi, nut-client, open, parted, pciutils, procinfo, procps, procps-X11, psacct, psmisc, pvm-gui, rdate, rdist, rhmask, rp3, rpm2html, rpmfind, samba-client, samba-common, sane, screen, setserial, setuptool, statserial, sudo, SVGATextMode, symlinks, sysctlconfig, syslinux, sysstat, time, timeconfig, timetool, tksysv, tripwire, ucd-snmp-utils, usbview, usermode, vlock, which, xcpus-tate, xisdnload, xosview, xsysinfo, xtoolwait

TABLE D.2 continued

Group	Packages
Applications/Text	aspell, aspell-ca, aspell-cs, aspell-da, aspell-de, aspell-en-ca, aspell-en-gb, aspell-eo, aspell-es, aspell-fr, aspell-it, aspell-nl, aspell-no, aspell-pl, aspell-sv, diffutils, docbook, ed, gawk, grep, indent, less, m4, mawk, openjade, pspell, rgrep, sed, sgml-common, stylesheets, textutils,
Development/Debuggers	gdb, lslk, lsof, ltrace, memprof, strace, sysreport, xxgdb
Development/Languages	compat-egcs-c++, compat-egcs, compat-egcs-g77, compat-egcs-objc, cpp, dev86, expect, gcc, gcc-c++, gcc-chill, gcc-g77, gcc-java, gcc-objc, gnome-objc, guile, itcl, jikes, kaffe, kgcc, libgcj-devel, librep, librep-devel, nasm, nasm-doc, p2c, p2c-devel, perl, php, php-imap, php-ldap, php-pgsql, pygnome, pygnome-applet, pygnome-capplet, pygnome-libglade, pygtk, pygtk-libglade, python, rep-gtk, rep-gtk-gnome, rep-gtk-libglade, tcl, tclx, tix, tk, tkinter, umb-scheme
Development/Libraries	apache-devel, aspell-devel, audiofile-devel, bind-devel, bzip2-devel, cdparanoia-devel, cdrecord-devel, control-center-devel, db1-devel, db2-devel, e2fsprogs-devel, esound-devel, fnlib-devel, freetype-devel, fribidi-gtkbeta-devel, gdbm-devel, gd-devel, gdk-pixbuf-devel, glibc-devel, glibc-profile, glib-devel, glib-gtkbeta-devel, gmp-devel, gnome-core-devel, gnome-games-devel, gnome-libs-devel, gnome-objc-devel, gnome-pim-devel, gnome-print-devel, gpm-devel, gtk+-devel, gtk+-gtkbeta-devel, guile-devel, ImageMagick-devel, imap-devel, imlib-devel, inn-devel, Inti, Inti-devel, kdelibs-devel, kdesupport-devel, krb5-devel, kudzu-devel, lam, libghttp-devel, libglade-devel, libgtop-devel, libjpeg-devel, libodbc++, libodbc++-devel, libpcap, libpng-devel, libstdc++-devel, libtermcap-devel, libtiff-devel, libungif-devel, libunicode-devel, libxml-devel, linuxconf-devel, Mesa-devel, ncurses-devel, netpbm-devel, newt-devel, openldap-devel, openssl-devel, ORBit-devel, pango-gtkbeta-devel, parted-devel, pciutils-devel, pilot-link-devel, popt, postgresql-devel, pspell-devel, pump-devel, pvm, python-devel, python-xmlrpc, qt1x-devel, qt-devel, readline-devel, rhcfile, rhcfile-devel, rhclib, rhclib-devel, rpm-devel, rpm-python, sane-devel, SDL-devel, SDL_image-devel, slang-devel, smpeg-devel, sox-devel, tcllib, ucd-snmp-devel, unixODBC-devel, w3c-libwww-devel, WindowMaker-libs, Xaw3d-devel, XFree86-devel, xmms-devel, zlib-devel

TABLE D.2   continued

Group	Packages
Development/System	kernel-headers, kernel-source, lm_sensors-devel, rpmdb-redhat, rpmlint
Development/Tools	asp2php, asp2php-gtk, autoconf, automake, binutils, bison, blt, byacc, cdecl, cproto, ctags, cvs, diffstat, doxygen, ElectricFence, flex, gettext, glade, gperf, kdevelop, libtool, make, nasm-rdoff, njamd, patch, pmake, pmake-customs, python-tools, rcs, rpm-build
Documentation	apache-manual, bash-doc, gnome-users-guide, indexhtml, kdoc, kernel-doc, man-pages, man-pages-cs, man-pages-da, man-pages-de, man-pages-es, man-pages-fr, man-pages-it, man-pages-ja, man-pages-pl, man-pages-ru, php-manual, python-docs, sendmail-doc, specspo, Xfree86-doc
System Environment/Base	adjtimex, anacron, authconfig, basesystem, chkconfig, chkfont-path, crontabs, dev, dhcpcd, e2fsprogs, eject, filesystem, gen-romfs, gnome-print, info, initscripts, ipchains, iptables, isapnptools, joystick, kbdconfig, kernelcfg, krb5-workstation, lilo, logrotate, losetup, mailcap, MAKEDEV, man, mingetty, mkbootdisk, mkinitrd, mkkickstart, mktemp, mount, mouseconfig, net-tools, nss_ldap, ntsysv, pam, pam_krb5, passwd, pwdb, quota, raidtools, redhat-logos, redhat-release, rhn_register, rhn_register-gnome, rootfiles, rpm, setup, shadow-utils, shapecfg, SysVinit, termcap, tmpwatch, up2date, up2date-gnome, utempter, util-linux, vixie-cron, wireless-tools, yp-tools
System Environment/ Daemons	am-utils, anonftp, apache, apmd, at, autofs, autofs-ldap, bdflush, bind, bootparamd, caching-nameserver, cipe, cleanfeed, comsat, dhcp, esound, finger-server, gated, gpm, imap, inews, inn, iputils, krb5-server, LPRng, mars-nwe, mcserv, mod_dav, mod_perl, mod_php, mod_ssl, nfs-utils, nscd, ntp, openldap, openldap-servers, openssh-server, ORBit, pidentd, portmap, ppp, procmail, pump, pxe, rarpd, routed, rp-pppoe, rsh-server, rusers, rusers-server, rwall, rwall-server, rwho, samba, sendmail, sendmail-cf, squid, sysklogd, talk-server, tcp_wrappers, telnet-server, tftp-server, timed, ucd-snmp, wu-ftpd, wvdial, XFree86-xfs, xinetd, ypbind, ypserv
System Environment/ Kernel	kernel, kernel-enterprise, kernel-ibcs, kernel-pcmcia-cs, kernel-utils, modutils

D

RED HAT LINUX
RPM PACKAGE
LISTINGS

TABLE D.2   continued

Group	Packages
System Environment/ Libraries	audiofile, compat-libstdc++, cracklib, cracklib-dicts, cyrus-sasl, db1, db2, db3, db3-devel, fnlib, freetype, fribidi-gtkbeta, gd, gdbm, gdk-pixbuf, glib10, glib, glibc, glib-gtkbeta, gmp, gnome-audio-extra, gnome-core, gnome-libs, gsl, gtk+10, gtk+, gtk-engines, gtk+-gtkbeta, imlib, imlib-cfgeditor, kdelibs, krb5-libs, krbafs, libconf, libelf, libgcj, libghttp, libglade, libgtop, libgtop-examples, libjpeg, libjpeg6a, libodbc++-qt, libpng, libPropList, libstdc++, libtermcap, libtiff, libtool-libs, libungif, libunicode, libxml10, libxml, lockdev, lockdev-devel, Mesa, ncurses, ncurses4, netpbm, newt, openssl, pango-gtkbeta, pythonlib, qt1x, qt1x-GL, qt, qt-Xt, readline2.2.1, readline, SDL, SDL_image, slang, smpeg, unixODBC, w3c-libwwwwords, Xaw3d, XFree86-libs, zlib
System Environment/ Shells	ash, bash, mc, pdksh, sash, sh-utils, tcsh, zsh
User Interface/Desktops	control-center, enlightenment, fvwm2, fvwm2-icons, gmc, gnome-applets, kdebase, kdebase-3d-screensavers, kdebase-lowcolor-icons, kdesupport, sawfish, sawfish-themer, switchdesk, switchdesk-gnome, switchdesk-kde, vnc, vnc-doc, WindowMaker, wmakerconf, wmconfig
User Interface/X	gdm, glms, gnome-kerberos, gqview, kterm, rxvt, urw-fonts, vnc-server, x3270, XFree86-100dpi-fonts, XFree86, XFree86-75dpi-fonts, XFree86-cyrillic-fonts, XFree86-ISO8859-2-100dpi-fonts, XFree86-ISO8859-2-75dpi-fonts, XFree86-ISO8859-2, XFree86-ISO8859-2-Type1-fonts, XFree86-ISO8859-7-100dpi-fonts, XFree86-ISO8859-7, XFree86-ISO8859-7-75dpi-fonts, XFree86-ISO8859-7-Type1-fonts, XFree86-ISO8859-9-100dpi-fonts, XFree86-ISO8859-9-75dpi-fonts, XFree86-ISO8859-9, XFree86-K018-R, XFree86-K018-R-100dpi-fonts, XFree86-K018-R-75dpi-fonts, XFree86-tools, XFree86-twm, XFree86-xdm, XFree86-xf86cfg, xinitrc
User Interface/X Hardware	XconfiguratorSupport Xfree86-3Dlabs, Xfree86-8514, Xfree86-AGX, Xfree86-FBDev, Xfree86-I128, Xfree86-Mach32, Xfree86-Mach64, Xfree86-Mach8, Xfree86-Mono, Xfree86-P9000, Xfree86-S3, Xfree86-S3V, XFree86-SVGA, XFree86-V4L, XFree86-VGA16, Xfree86-W32, XFree86-Xnest, XFree86-Xvfb

INDEX

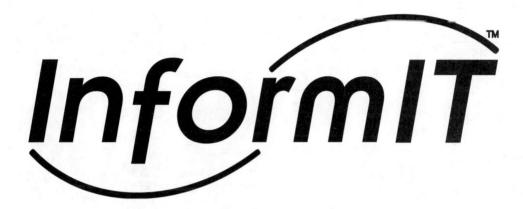

Other Related Titles

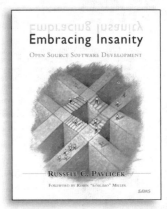

Embracing Insanity: Open Source Software Development
Russell C. Pavlicek
ISBN: 0-672-31989-6
$29.99 US

What's on the Discs

The companion CD-ROMs contain Red Hat Linux 7, Publisher's Edition, and the source code for the examples in the book.

Installing Red Hat Linux from the CD-ROM

1. Insert the installation disc (Disc 1) in the CD drive.
2. Restart your computer.
3. You may need to change your BIOS settings to boot from the CD-ROM. Typically, you enter your BIOS setup program with the F2 or Delete keys during the boot sequence.
4. Make your changes (if any) and exit the BIOS setup utility.
5. If your CD drive is capable of booting from CD-ROMs, you will boot into the Red Hat Linux setup program.
6. Follow the onscreen prompts to complete the installation.

Installing Red Hat Linux from Boot Floppies

1. Using DOS or Windows, format one 1.44MB floppy disk.
2. Navigate to the DOSUTILS directory on the installation disc (Disc 1).
3. Double-click on RAWRITE.EXE or type RAWRITE from a DOS prompt.
4. When prompted to do so, type in the name ..\IMAGES\BOOT.IMG and press Enter.
5. When prompted to do so, type in the drive letter of the disk(s) you are going to prepare and press Enter. Since you are going to be booting from this disk, it's typically A:.
6. If you don't already have the boot floppy in your disk drive, insert it now.
7. Restart your computer.
8. You may need to change your BIOS settings to boot from the floppy drive. Typically, you enter your BIOS setup program with the F2 or Delete keys during the boot sequence.
9. Make your changes (if any) and exit the BIOS setup utility.
10. If your computer is set up properly, you will boot into the Red Hat Linux setup program.
11. Follow the onscreen prompts to complete the installation.